THE ROUGH GUIDE TO

Scottish Highlands & Islands

This seventh edition updated by

Rob Humphreys, Norm Longley, Helena Smith,
James Stewart and Steve Vickers

ROUGH GUIDES

roughguides.com

Contents

Introduction to
Scottish Highlands & Islands

Wild and weather-beaten, the Scottish Highlands and Islands feel another world compared to the pastoral character of much of Great Britain. Closer to the Arctic Circle than London in places, this is a land where the elements govern much of everyday life and the shipping forecast is more than just an aural sleeping pill. The scenery is raw and magnificent, shaped over thousands of years by geological forces, glaciers and the weather systems of the North Atlantic. Yet, experience a glorious sunset that turns the sea lochs gold or find yet another empty white-powder beach, and you'll discover the romance of the place, too. Sure, the roads can be tortuous and the weather can be grim. And let's not even start on the midges in high summer. But when the mood takes it, the Highlands and Islands has a unique glory to make the soul sing.

Although escapism accounts for much of the area's appeal, it's impossible to travel in the Highlands and Islands without being touched by the fragility of life here. The Jacobite defeat at Culloden in 1746 was a blow to Scottish pride generally, but it was an unmitigated disaster for the Highlands and Islands, signalling the destruction of the Highland clan system and ultimately the entire Highland way of life. The Clearances that followed in the nineteenth century more than halved the population, and even today the Highland landscape is littered with the shells of pre-Clearance crofting communities. The economy struggles, too, despite government and European Union subsidies, and while recent census figures in 2013 reveal a rise in population, some of the larger islands such as Bute, Arran and Islay have suffered depopulation as the traditional Highland industries of farming, crofting and fishing no longer provide enough jobs for the younger generation. Forestry, fish-farming and the oil industry

ABOVE EILEAN DONAN CASTLE; GOAT FELL **OPPOSITE** BEACH ON TIREE are now the bigger employers, alongside the region's other main industry – tourism. Since the former depends on development, and the latter conservation, it's a fine balancing act between tapping new opportunities and maintaining traditional values: a dilemma that has been voiced repeatedly in debates before the vote over Scottish independence in September 2014.

For all that, the region is no time warp. Although tradition remains part of the weft and weave of Highlands life, you don't have to travel far to see a renewal of Highlands culture. Nowadays, shortbread and twee tearooms are out, superb super-fresh local ingredients are in, showcased at outstanding gastropubs and gourmet restaurants in some of the most remote locations. Similarly, artists have reinvigorated traditional crafts as more people seek a life in the slow lane and set up shop in former crofts. Even the visitor profile is changing: the visitors still come to clamber over castles and wrap themselves in tartan nostalgia, but just as many people now visit specifically to see whales and dolphins, to summit a Munro or wild camp their way along the West Highland Way. Nor is walking the only activity on the agenda. In recent years, the potential of the wilderness in Britain's backyard has been realized too, as adventure-junkies explore the frontiers of Scotland's mountains and coastline; the opportunities for mountain biking, scuba diving, surfing, kite surfing and sea-kayaking here are truly world-class, and there's also the best ice-climbing and skiing in Britain.

Of course, activities here can be a mite colder than elsewhere, but what could be more Scottish than shrugging off a wee bit of weather?

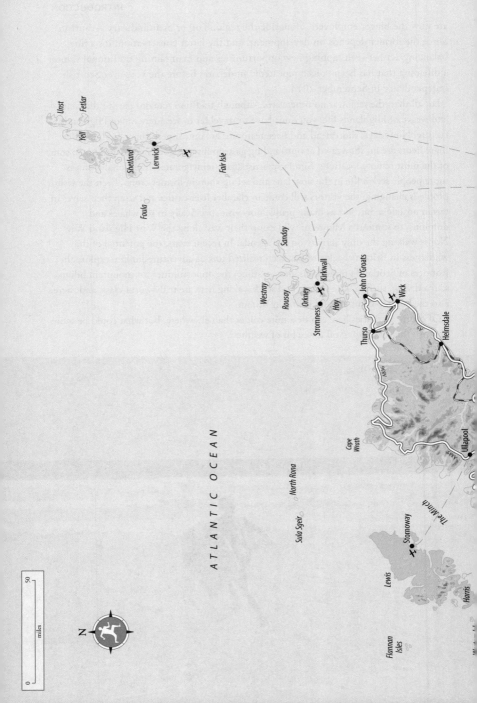

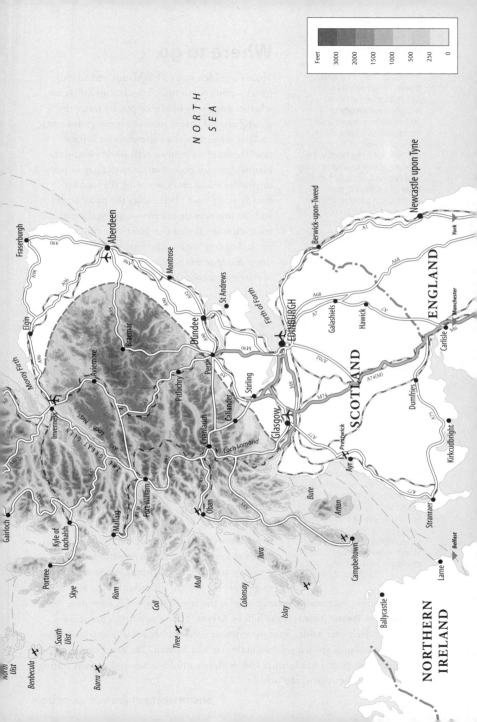

Where to go

There's a golden rule to Highlands and Islands travel – don't try to rush. It makes no difference whether you go by public or private transport, getting around here is time-consuming: distances on land are greater than elsewhere in Britain (and there are no motorways), while visiting the islands demands coordination with ferry or plane timetables – and that's assuming the weather doesn't affect your plans. Relax the pace, however, and the journeys themselves – the spectacular train trips, the flights that scud over tiny islands, the sailings on inter-island ferries or the winding drives along scenic roads – are often as memorable as the destinations themselves. This is slow travel at its best.

The most accessible parts of the region are not far from **Glasgow** and **Edinburgh**: you can be by the banks of Loch Lomond in half an hour, or Highland Perthshire in a little over an hour. As a result, **Loch Lomond,** and the hills and wooded glens of the **Trossachs** tend to be busier than other parts of the Highlands, and while the tourist infrastructure here is hardly theme-park standard, to escape the day-trippers you need to head further north into **Perthshire** and the **Grampian hills** of Angus and Deeside where the Highland scenery is at its richest. South of Inverness the mighty **Cairngorm** massif hints at the raw wilderness Scotland still provides. To reach the lonely north and western Highlands, you'll have to cross the **Great Glen**, an ancient geological fissure that cuts across the country from **Ben Nevis** to **Loch Ness**, a moody stretch of water where tourists still hope to glimpse its resident monster. Yet the area with arguably the most memorable scenery of all is the jagged west coast, stretching from **Argyll** north to **Wester Ross** and the hills of **Assynt**. Here you'll find a beautiful coastline that feels ever wilder, ever more remote, the further north you go, not least around spectacular dome-shaped mountains such as Suilven. The north coast of Sutherland is less visited but lonelier still, with beautiful beaches and an exhilarating sense of being at the edge of the world.

OPPOSITE FROM TOP PIPERS IN TRADITIONAL DRESS; SKYE

The Highlands are splendid, but the islands scattered off the west and north coasts are an essential part of the region's identity. As varied in size and character as accessibility, the rocky Hebrides, which necklace Scotland's Atlantic shoreline, include **Mull** and the nearby pilgrimage centre of **Iona**; **Islay** and **Jura**, famous for their wildlife and whisky; **Skye**, the most visited of the lot because of its sophisticated hotels and restaurants as much as the superb walking in the Cuillin mountains; and the **Western Isles**, an elongated archipelago that is still a bastion of Gaelic culture. With their rich Norse heritage, **Orkney** and **Shetland** differ not only from each other, but from the dialect and culture of mainland Scotland too. These are the most far-flung islands, buffeted by wind and sea and offering some of the country's wildest scenery, finest birdwatching and best archeological sites.

A WEE DRAM

No Highland village would be complete without its pub and no pub would be complete without a line of amber whisky bottles glinting behind the bar. Single malts have grown in popularity as a new audience discovers a drink nurtured by a well-marketed mix of soft Scottish rain, Highland streams, rich peaty soil, smoke and craftsmanship.

Not only is whisky the national drink, enjoying it is often regarded as the national pastime too, lubricating any social gathering from a Highland ceilidh to a Saturday night session. While it can be drunk neat, the truth is that a splash of water releases the whisky's flavours. It's no surprise, then, that the Scots also turn a healthy profit by bottling the country's abundant spring water and selling it around the world.

Author picks

The Highlands has its poster places: Loch Lomond or Eilean Donan castle for example. But the most treasured memories of a country are usually more personal discoveries. Here are those of Rough Guides' authors as they travelled down every lane and supped in every pub in the cause of researching the Guide.

Skye crafts The mountains are marvellous, but who knew that Skye (p.270) also had such a vibrant modern-crafts scene? Pick up a galleries brochure in Portree tourist office or visit ⓦ art-skye.co.uk.

Island-hopping in the Small Isles If there's an easier free-wheelin' mini-adventure than a few days' bouncing between the Small Isles (p.285), they're keeping it quiet.

Pitch perfect Only in Scotland can adventurous campers head out into Great Britain's wilds then legally pitch a tent (p.285) in the grandest scenery.

Foula The most isolated island community in the UK, Foula (p.391) sits 14 miles off the coast of Shetland, with forty inhabitants, no shop, and some of the largest cliffs in the country.

Flying visit The trip in an eight-seater plane to North Ronaldsay (p.366) alone is worth it, even without a night at the ecofriendly bird observatory and the chance to visit a lighthouse or meet weavers and seaweed-eating sheep.

St Kilda The trip out by RIB is not cheap and it can be bouncy, but fifty miles off the Western Isles, St Kilda (p.310) has the UK's biggest bird colony on its highest cliffs.

Beaver Trial, Knapdale Beavers are back after 400 years' absence and this reintroduction project at Knapdale (p.96) offers a rare opportunity to see the creatures in the wild – if the lodges are startling, the 60ft-long dam is a feat of engineering.

Our author recommendations don't end here. We've flagged up our favourite places – a perfectly sited hotel, an atmospheric café, a special restaurant – throughout the Guide, highlighted with the ★ symbol.

FROM TOP WILD CAMPING NEAR ULLAPOOL; PLANE TO NORTH RONALDSAY; FOULA

When to go

Predictably unpredictable is probably the best way to sum up Highlands weather, and for many people that's the greatest deterrent to a visit. It's not so much that the weather's always bad, it's just changeable: four seasons in a day, as the old Islands' cliché goes, as weather systems barrel across from the Atlantic Ocean. Even if the weather's not necessarily good, it's generally interesting: often exhilarating, frequently dramatic and certainly photogenic. Well suited, in fact, to the landscapes over which it plays such an important role.

The **summer** months of June, July and August are the high season, with local school holidays making July and early August the busiest period. Days are generally warm, but the weather is often variable. Daylight hours are long, however, and, in the far north, darkness hardly falls at all in midsummer. The warmer weather does have its drawbacks, though, in the form of clouds of **midges**, the tiny biting insects that appear around dusk, dawn and in dank conditions, and can drive even the most committed adventurer scurrying indoors.

Commonly, **May** and **September** provide weather as good as, if not better than, high summer. You're less likely to encounter crowds, and the mild temperatures combined with the changing **colours** of nature mean both are great for outdoor activities, particularly hiking. May is also a good month for watching nesting **seabirds**; September, however, is stalking season for deer, which can disrupt **access** to the countryside.

AVERAGE DAILY TEMPERATURES AND MONTHLY RAINFALL

	Jan	Feb	Mar	Apr	May	Jun	Jul	Aug	Sep	Oct	Nov	Dec
OBAN												
Max/min (°C)	7/2	7/2	9/3	11/4	14/7	16/9	18/11	18/11	15/9	13/7	9/4	8/3
Max/min (°F)	45/36	45/36	48/37	52/40	58/44	61/48	64/52	64/52	60/49	55/45	49/40	46/37
mm	146	109	83	90	72	87	120	116	141	169	146	172
inches	5.8	4.3	3.3	3.5	2.8	3.4	4.7	4.6	5.6	6.7	5.8	6.8
BRAEMAR												
Max/min (°C)	4/-2	5/-1	7/0	10/1	13/4	16/7	18/9	18/9	15/6	11/4	7/1	5/-2
Max/min (°F)	40/29	40/30	44/32	50/34	56/39	61/44	64/48	64/48	58/43	51/39	45/34	40/29
mm	93	59	59	51	65	55	58	76	73	87	87	96
inches	3.7	2.3	2.3	2	2.6	2.2	2.3	3	2.9	3.4	3.4	3.8
FORT WILLIAM												
Max/min (°C)	5/-1	5/-1	8/1	10/3	14/7	17/10	18/11	18/11	15/8	11/5	8/2	6/1
Max/min (°F)	41/30	41/30	46/34	50/37	57/45	63/50	64/52	64/52	59/46	52/41	46/36	52/34
mm	200	132	152	111	103	124	137	150	199	215	220	238
inches	7.8	5.1	5.9	4.3	4	4.8	5.3	5.9	7.8	8.4	8.6	9.3
SHETLAND												
Max/min (°C)	5/1	5/1	6/2	8/3	11/5	13/7	14/10	14/10	13/8	10/6	8/4	6/3
Max/min (°F)	41/34	41/34	43/36	46/37	52/41	55/45	57/50	57/50	55/46	50/43	46/39	43/37
mm	127	93	93	72	64	64	67	78	113	119	140	147
inches	5	3.7	3.7	2.8	2.5	2.5	2.6	3	4.5	4.7	5.5	5.8

OPPOSITE DEER IN HIGHLANDS FOREST

CEILIDHS

Highlanders know how to throw a good party, so if you hear rumours of a ceilidh (pronounced "kay-lee") nearby, change your plans to be there. From the Gaelic for "a visit", a ceilidh has its roots in an informal, homespun gathering of music, song, poetry and dance. These days, often helped along by a dram or two of whisky, they're lively events in the local pub or village hall. The main activity is dancing to set patterns, with music traditionally provided by a fiddler and an accordionist, though modern drums, guitar and electric bass are now common too. While the whirling reels or jigs appear fiendishly complex, the popular ones aren't hard to pick up and to help novices a dance "caller" teaches the steps beforehand. You'll find a whisky or two helps you get into the swing of things as well. Either way, the fun is infectious.

The months of **April** and **October** bracket the season for many parts of rural Scotland. Many attractions, tourist offices and guesthouses open for business at Easter and close after the school half-term in October. If places do stay open through the winter, it's normally with reduced opening hours; the October-to-March period is also the best time to pick up **special offers** for accommodation. Note, too, that public transport will often operate on a reduced winter timetable.

Winter days, from November to March, can be crisp and bright, but are more often cold, overcast and all too short. Nevertheless, **Hogmanay** and **New Year** has traditionally been a good time to visit Scotland for partying and warm hospitality. On a clear night in winter, visitors in the far north might see displays of the **aurora borealis**, while a fall of snow in the Highlands will prompt plenty of activity in the **ski resorts**.

28

things not to miss

It's not possible to see everything that the Highlands and Islands have to offer in one trip – and we don't suggest you try. What follows is a selective taste of the highlights: natural wonders and outstanding sights, plus the best activities and experiences. All highlights have a page reference to take you straight into the Guide, where you can find out more. Coloured numbers refer to chapters in the Guide section.

1

1 GLEN COE
Page 193

Scotland's most spectacular glen puts Munro summits, glacial valleys and clear waterfalls within day-trip distance of Fort William.

2 TOBERMORY
Page 74

A riot of colour, Mull's chief town is the quintessential Scottish fishing port.

3 WHISKY ON ISLAY
Page 115

There's definitely something in the water that makes this Hebridean island home to eight distilleries.

4 EIGG
Page 288

Perfect example of a tiny Hebridean island, with a golden beach to stroll on, a hill to climb and gorgeous views across to its neighbour, Rùm.

5 ASSYNT
Page 242

Golden eagles, more deer than cows and strange mountains with poetic names like Suilven – nowhere in the Highlands is more spectacular nor more exhilaratingly remote.

6 WHALE WATCHING, MULL
Page 76

Close encounters with a very different type of Highland wildlife.

7 GOLF
Page 103

Regardless of your ability, no visit to Scotland is complete without a round, and few courses are more beautiful (or more challenging) than Machrihanish Dunes in Kintyre.

8 UP HELLY-AA
Page 376

Pack your thermals and head to Shetland in January for this spectacular Viking fire festival.

9 PUBS
Page 34

What better end to a day in the hills than a good meal, a dram and perhaps a singalong?

10 WEST HIGHLAND RAILWAY
Page 133

From Glasgow to Mallaig, this is one of the great railway journeys of the world – 264 miles of ever more spectacular scenery with steam trains in summer to boot.

9

10

14

15

16 SOUTH HARRIS BEACHES
Page 314

Take your pick of deserted golden beaches in South Harris.

17 THE CUILLIN, SKYE
Page 276

The most spectacular mountain range on the west coast, for viewing or climbing.

18 ST MAGNUS CATHEDRAL
Page 343

A medieval cathedral in miniature, built out of red and yellow sandstone by the Vikings.

19 SHETLAND FOLK FESTIVAL
Page 378

Shetland excels at traditional folk music, not least when the annual folk festival takes over the islands.

20 MOUSA, SHETLAND
Page 382

The mother of all Iron Age brochs offers a wonderful wildlife experience too when thousands of storm petrels return to their roosts at dusk.

21 WEST HIGHLAND WAY
Page 133

Ninety-six miles, five days, one utterly spectacular walk from Glasgow to Fort William.

22 KINLOCH CASTLE, RÙM
Page 287

The interiors are not just expressions of Edwardian decadence, they are, quite frankly, barmy.

16

17

18

19

20

21

22

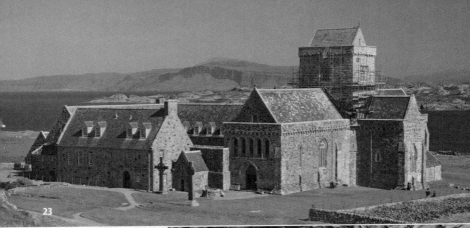

23

23 IONA
Page 82

There's an ancient abbey and glorious beaches at the north of this beautiful island.

24 STAFFA AND THE TRESHNISH ISLES
Page 79

The basalt columns of Staffa's Fingal's Cave and puffins on the Isle of Lunga combine to make this a superb trip.

25 ARRAN
Page 106

The most accessible of the islands, Arran offers fascinating geology, and superb walking and cycling.

26 MAES HOWE, ORKNEY
Page 337

Amazingly preserved, this five-thousand-year-old burial chamber also contains smutty Viking graffiti.

27 HIGHLAND GAMES
Page 37

Part summer sports day, part traditional gathering, these entertaining get-togethers are well worth a diversion wherever you find one in the Highlands.

28 SEA-KAYAKING
Page 43

Clean seas and empty beaches plus a wild-camping spot or B&B and that fresh mackerel you caught en route equal a magical mini-expedition.

24

Itineraries

The following itineraries will help you to explore the drama and variety of the Highlands and Islands. Whether you're after a fortnight of island-hopping and empty beaches off the western coast, a cultural break spanning thousands of years of history, or want to discover whales and ospreys, our themed suggestions offer an insight into Scotland's stunning natural and historic wonders.

TWO WEEKS ON THE ISLANDS

While Orkney and Shetland deserve a dedicated trip, the west coast islands seem tailor-made to explore by ferry. Who needs Greece?

❶ **Mull** Embark from one of the Highlands' loveliest fishing ports, Tobermory (p.74), for one of its best wildlife adventures – whale-watching trips (p.76). **See p.71**

❷ **Iona** A tiny island just off Mull (p.71) but almost another world, its atmosphere steeped in millennia as a pilgrimage destination. **See p.81**

❸ **Barra** A pipsqueak among the Western Isles (p.294) whose azure seas, white beaches, mountains and sense of utter escapism deliver a concentrated dose of Hebridean magic. **See p.324**

❹ **The Uists** Trout-fishing doesn't get much more fun than in the half-drowned lochs of North Uist. **See p.316**

❺ **Lewis and Harris** The conjoined twins of the Hebrides have astonishing beaches like Luskentyre (p.314), mysterious standing stones at Callanish and a time warp back a century in the restored village of Garenin (p.307). **See p.297**

❻ **Skye** Skip back to Skye to tackle the Cuillin ridge (p.276) or discover Loch Coruisk by boat. Either way, your reward is fine hotels and food. **See p.270**

❼ **Small Isles** So, what do you feel like doing today: sampling genuine island life on Eigg (p.288); discovering a barmy baronial manor on Rùm (p.287); or spotting wildlife on a stroll around tiny Muck (p.290)? **See p.286**

WILDLIFE WONDERS

There's more here than the world's second-largest seal population and abundant red deer. Here's our pick of the best Scottish animal encounters to tick off on a two-week adventure.

❶ **Beavers at Knapdale** Take the Beaver Detective Trail to see the lodges and dams of a population reintroduced in 2009. Best seasons: late spring, early summer. **See p.99**

❷ **Whales and puffins off Mull** One island, two of the Highlands' finest wildlife encounters: whales on trips from Tobermory and Scotland's favourite seabird on cruises to the Treshnish Isles. Best seasons: spring, summer. **See p.76**

❸ **Storm petrels on Mousa, Shetland** There are Arctic terns, black guillemots, skuas, shags, ringed plovers and seals on Mousa. But no sight is more spectacular than 12,000 storm petrels returning at dusk to a 2000-year-old broch. Best season: summer. **See p.382**

❹ **Dolphins in Moray Firth** The world's most northerly pod of bottlenose dolphins – around 190 strong – and groups of porpoises can be seen from a viewing point or boat on the Moray Firth. Best seasons: spring, summer. **See p.208**

ABOVE MOUNT STUART

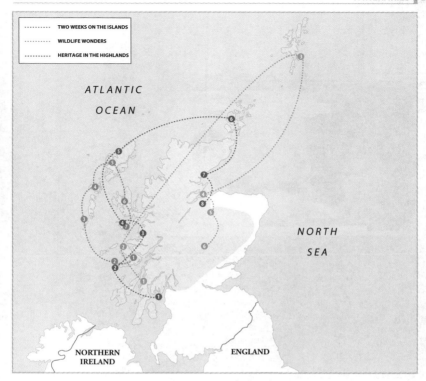

········· TWO WEEKS ON THE ISLANDS
········· WILDLIFE WONDERS
········· HERITAGE IN THE HIGHLANDS

ATLANTIC OCEAN

NORTH SEA

NORTHERN IRELAND

ENGLAND

❺ Ospreys and reindeer in the Cairngorms
The must-see on any twitchers' checklist
migrates from West Africa to breed on Loch
Garten, and Britain's only herd of reindeer lives
on the surrounding hills. Best seasons: spring,
summer. **See p.164**

❻ Salmon at Pitlochry Not as spectacular as
the salmon that leap up the Falls of Shin (p.261),
but more fish climb the famous fish ladder
at Pitlochry. Best seasons: summer, autumn.
See p.135

HERITAGE IN THE HIGHLANDS

Running the gamut from Stone Age villages to a
Highlands chateau, mysterious standing stones
to the trail of Bonnie Prince Charlie, this route
showcases the region's varied history on a
two-week tour through astonishing scenery.

❶ Mount Stuart A no-expense-spared slice of
neo-Gothic baronial splendour on the Isle of
Bute. **See p.61**

❷ Iona This tiny island has the finest Celtic
crosses in Scotland, plus an atmosphere steeped
in centuries of pilgrimage. **See p.81**

❸ The Road to the Isles Follow in the footsteps
of Bonnie Prince Charlie from Glenfinnan or let
the Jacobite steam train take the strain from
Fort William to Mallaig. **See p.221**

❹ Kinloch Castle, Rùm A pile contemporary to
Mount Stuart yet fabulously over-the-top, its
eccentric interiors capturing the decadence of
Edwardian shooting estates. **See p.287**

❺ Callanish Standing Stones, Lewis
Prehistoric sights don't come more mysterious
than this lochside circle erected around five
thousand years ago. **See p.307**

❻ Skara Brae and Maes Howe, Orkney Two
of Britain's finest prehistoric sights – an intact
village and a Stone Age tomb (graffitied by
smutty Vikings) – lie ten miles apart. **See p.337**

❼ Dunrobin Castle, Golspie The extravagant
scale of the Highlands' largest house testifies to
the brutality of the Clearances as much as the
Sutherland family's wealth. **See p.263**

❽ Culloden Battlefield A top-notch visitor
centre tells the tale of the last battle fought on
British soil. **See p.208**

JACOBITE STEAM TRAIN

Basics

Getting there

There are numerous ways of getting to the Scottish Highlands and Islands. For most, the quickest and easiest way is by plane. Inverness is an obvious gateway for much of the region, but you'll get a wider selection of flights to Scotland's three main international airports – Glasgow, Edinburgh and Aberdeen – each of which is only a short hop from most areas of interest.

With most airlines nowadays, how much you pay depends on how far in advance you book and how much demand there is during that period – generally speaking, the earlier you book, the cheaper the prices. That said, it's worth looking out for sales, which often start 10–12 weeks before the departure date.

If you're coming from elsewhere in Britain, from Ireland or even northwest Europe, you can reach Scotland easily enough by **train**, **bus** or **ferry** – it probably won't work out cheaper or faster than flying, but it's undoubtedly better for the environment.

From England and Wales

If you're heading out to the Highlands and Islands from **England** or **Wales**, flying is the quickest way to travel. If your ultimate destination is Argyll, Loch Lomond or the Hebrides, Glasgow is the natural gateway; for Perthshire and the Cairngorms, Edinburgh or Glasgow are good; for anywhere further north, Inverness is the best hub. **Airfares** are most competitive on popular routes such as London or Birmingham to Edinburgh and Glasgow, which can cost as little as £50 return (journey time around 1hr). Once you add on the cost of transport to the airport and flying with luggage (many budget airlines charge for all but the smallest cabin bags), the savings on the same journey overland are often minimal – and then, of course, there's the environmental impact to consider.

Flying with airlines such as British Airways (Wba .com), Ryanair (Wryanair.com) and easyJet (Weasyjet .com) may be quick, but coach and train fares can be pretty competitive. If you book far enough in advance, **train** fares can cost as little as £70 for a London to Inverness return (journey time from 8hr). A more flexible or last-minute fare will obviously cost two or three times that amount. Another option is the overnight **Caledonian Sleeper** run by ScotRail from London Euston (daily; journey time to Inverness

around 11hr 30min); again, if you book in advance, single overnight fares cost around £35, though most return fares are more like £150.

The **coach** can be slower than the train but costs less, with a London or Birmingham to Inverness overnight return starting for as little as £36 return (journey time 11hr 30min–13hr).

From Ireland

Travel from Ireland is quickest by plane, with **airfares** from either Belfast or Dublin to Glasgow from as little as €45 return. Try Aer Lingus (Waerlingus.com) and Ryanair (Wryanair.com), both based in Ireland. There are also good **ferry** links with Northern Ireland and the combined coach and ferry fares are very competitive: Belfast to Glasgow (via Cairnryan) is just £56 return (journey time 6hr). P&O Ferries runs several sea crossings daily from Larne to Cairnryan (1hr) and Troon (2hr 15min) and Stena Line operates several services daily from Belfast to Stranraer (2hr 10min; single passenger without car £28).

From the US and Canada

If you fly nonstop to Scotland from **North America**, you'll arrive in either Glasgow or Edinburgh. The majority of cheap fares, however, route through Amsterdam, London, Manchester, Dublin or Paris. To reach any other Scottish airport, you'll definitely need to go via London, Glasgow or Edinburgh.

Figure on six to seven hours' flight time nonstop from the east coast to Glasgow, or seven hours to London plus an extra hour and a quarter from London to Glasgow or Edinburgh (not including stopover time). Add three or four hours more for travel from the west coast.

United (Wunited.com) flies direct from Newark Liberty International Airport in New York to Glasgow, with return fares (including taxes) from around $850. Air Canada (Waircanada.com) has direct flights to Edinburgh from Toronto. Return fares for nonstop flights (including taxes) cost around $1000.

From Australia and New Zealand

Flight time from **Australia** and **New Zealand** to Scotland is at least 22 hours. There's a wide variety of routes, with those touching down in Southeast Asia the quickest and cheapest on average. To reach Scotland, you usually have to change planes either in London – the most popular choice – or in another European gateway such as Paris or Amsterdam. Given the length of the journey involved, you might be better off including a night's **stopover** in your itinerary.

The cheapest direct scheduled flights to London are usually to be found on one of the Asian airlines, such as Malaysia Airlines (ⓦ malaysiaairlines.com) or Thai Airways (ⓦ thaiair.com). Average **return fares** (including taxes) from eastern cities to London are Aus$1500–2000 in low season, Aus$2000–2500 in high season. Fares from Perth or Darwin cost around Aus$200 less. Return fares from Auckland to London range between NZ$2000 and NZ$3000 depending on the season, route and carrier.

From South Africa

There are no direct flights from **South Africa** to Scotland, so you must change planes en route. The quickest and cheapest route to take is via London, with flight time around eleven hours, usually overnight. **Return fares** from Cape Town to London are around ZAR10,000; try British Airways (ⓦ ba.com), South African Airways (ⓦ flysaa.com) or Virgin Atlantic (ⓦ virgin-atlantic.com). You'll save money if you buy the next leg of your journey to Scotland separately, through one of the budget airlines.

From mainland Europe

Ferries run by DFDS Seaways go overnight from Ijmuiden, near Amsterdam, to Newcastle (daily; 16–17hr), less than an hour's drive south of the Scottish border. High-season return fares start at around €500, for a passenger with a car and an overnight berth. The very useful Direct Ferries website (ⓦ directferries.co.uk) gives you the latest information on crossings and allows you to compare all the options. A much quicker (and usually cheaper) alternative is to fly with one of Europe's big budget carriers, such as easyJet (ⓦ easyjet.com), Ryanair (ⓦ ryanair.com), Norwegian (ⓦ norwegian.com) or Jet2 (ⓦ jet2.com).

AGENTS AND OPERATORS

ebookers ⓦ ebookers.com, ☎ 02033 203320. Low fares on an extensive selection of scheduled flights and package deals.
North South Travel ⓦ northsouthtravel.co.uk, ☎ 01245 608291. Friendly, competitive travel agency, offering discounted fares worldwide. Profits are used to support projects in the developing world, especially the promotion of sustainable tourism.
STA Travel ⓦ statravel.com, ☎ 0333 321 0099. Worldwide specialists in independent travel; also student IDs, travel insurance, car rental, rail passes and more. Good discounts for students and under-26s.
Trailfinders ⓦ trailfinders.com ☎ 02073 681200. One of the best-informed and most efficient agents for independent travellers.

Travel CUTS ⓦ travelcuts.com ☎ 1800 667 2887. Canadian youth and student travel firm.
USIT ⓦ usit.ie ☎ 016 021906. Ireland's main student and youth travel specialists.

TRAIN AND COACH INFORMATION

East Coast ⓦ eastcoast.co.uk ☎ 08457 225333. Trains to Edinburgh, Glasgow, Aberdeen and Inverness.
Man in Seat 61 ⓦ seat61.com. The best train information website on the internet.
National Express ⓦ nationalexpress.com ☎ 0871 781 8178. Coaches to Scotland.
National Rail ⓦ nationalrail.co.uk ☎ 0845 748 4950. Information and fares for all train services and companies.
ScotRail ⓦ scotrail.co.uk ☎ 0845 601 5929. Caledonian Sleeper train to Glasgow, Edinburgh, Aberdeen, Inverness and Fort William.
Traveline Scotland ⓦ travelinescotland.com ☎ 0871 200 2233. Excellent Scotland-wide journey planner, connected to the latest bus and train timetables.
Virgin ⓦ virgintrains.co.uk ☎ 0871 977 4222. Trains to Edinburgh and Glasgow.

FERRY COMPANIES

DFDS Seaways ⓦ dfdsseaways.com ☎ 0871 522 9955. Ferries from Europe.
P&O Ferries ⓦ poferries.com ☎ 0871 664 2121. Ferries from Ireland.
Stena Line ⓦ stenaline.co.uk ☎ 0844 770 7070. Ferries from Ireland.

Getting around

There's no getting away from the fact that getting around the Highlands and Islands is a time-consuming business: off the main routes, public transport services are few and far between, particularly in more remote parts of Argyll, the Highland region and the Islands. With careful planning, however, practically everywhere is accessible and you'll have no trouble getting to the main tourist destinations. And in most parts of Scotland, especially if you take the scenic backroads, the low level of traffic makes driving wonderfully stress free.

By train

Scotland has a modest **rail network**, at its densest in the central belt, skeletal in the Highlands, and nonexistent in the Islands. ScotRail runs the majority of train services, reaching all the major towns, sometimes on lines rated among the great scenic routes of the world.

You can buy train **tickets** at most stations, but if the ticket office at the station is closed, or the automatic machine isn't working, you may buy your ticket on board from the inspector using cash or a credit card. Those eligible for a **national rail pass** (£30) can obtain discounted tickets, with up to a third off most fares. These include the **16–25 Railcard**, for full-time students and those aged between 16 and 25, and the **Senior Railcard** for people over 60. Alternatively, a **Family & Friends Railcard** entitles up to four adults and up to four children to a reduction.

In addition, ScotRail offers several regional passes. The most flexible is the **Freedom of Scotland Travelpass**, which gives unlimited train travel within Scotland. It's also valid on all CalMac ferries and on various buses in the remoter regions. The pass costs £134 for four days' travel in an eight-day period, or £179.70 for eight days' travel in a fifteen-day period. The **Highland Rover** allows unlimited train travel within the Highlands; it costs £81.50 for four out of eight consecutive days.

BritRail passes (Wbritrail.com) are only available to visitors not resident in the UK and must be purchased before you leave your home country. The pass is available in a wide variety of types; for example the Adult pass allows unlimited train travel for eight days and costs €249. If you've been resident in a European country other than the UK for at least six months, an **InterRail** pass, allowing unlimited train travel within Britain, might be worth it if Scotland is part of a longer European trip. For more details, visit Winterrail.eu. Note that **Eurail** passes are not valid in the UK.

On most ScotRail routes **bicycles** are carried free, but since there are only between two and six bike spaces available, it's a good idea to reserve ahead and a requirement on longer journeys.

By coach and bus

The main centres of the Highlands are served by a few long-distance bus services, known across Britain as **coaches**. Scotland's national operator is **Scottish Citylink** (T08712 663333, Wcitylink.co.uk). On the whole, coaches are cheaper than trains and, as a result, are very popular, so for longer journeys it's advisable to book ahead.

There are various **discounts** on offer for those with children, those under 26 or over 60, and full-time students (contact Scottish Citylink for more details), as well as an **Explorer Pass**, which gives unlimited travel throughout Scotland; the £93 pass gives you eight days' travel over a sixteen-day period. Overseas passport holders can buy a **Brit Xplorer pass** (in 7-, 14- or 28-day versions) in the UK, from National Express (Wnationalexpress.com), or at major ports and airports; the seven-day pass costs £79, though you'd have to do a lot of bus travelling to make it worthwhile.

Local bus services are run by a bewildering array of companies, many of which change routes and timetables frequently. Local tourist offices can provide free timetables or you can contact **Traveline Scotland** (T0871 200 2233, Wtraveline scotland.com), which provides a reliable service both online and by phone. There is also a free app available for download.

Some remote areas of the Highlands and Islands are only served by **postbuses**, which are vehicles carrying mail and a handful of fare-paying passengers. They set off early in the morning, usually around 8am and, though sociable, can be excruciatingly slow. You can view routes and timetables on the **Royal Mail website** (T08457 740740, Wroyal mail.com/postbus).

MINIBUS TOURS

Minibus tours that operate out of Edinburgh (and Glasgow) and head off into the Highlands are popular with backpackers who want a quick taste of Scotland. Aimed at the youth market, they adopt an upbeat and irreverent approach to sightseeing, as well as offering a good opportunity to get to know fellow travellers.

The current leading operator, **Haggis** (T01315 579393, Whaggisadventures.com), has bright yellow minibuses setting off daily on whistle-stop tours lasting between one and ten days, in the company of a live-wire guide. A three-day trip from Edinburgh to Skye via Loch Ness costs £119 (food and accommodation not included).

Several other companies offer similar packages, including **Macbackpackers** (T01315 589900, Wmacbackpackers.com), which runs tours linking up their own hostels round the country. The popular **Rabbie's** tours (T01312 263133, Wrabbies.com) don't aim squarely at the backpacker market and have a mellower outlook.

By car

In order to **drive** in Scotland you need a current full driving licence. If you're bringing your own vehicle into the country you should also carry your vehicle registration, ownership and insurance documents at all times. In Scotland, as in the rest of the UK, you **drive on the left**. Speed limits are 20–40mph in built-up areas, 70mph on motorways and dual carriageways (freeways) and 60mph on most other roads. As a rule, assume that in any area with street lighting the limit is 30mph.

In the Highlands and Islands, there are still plenty of **single-track roads** with passing places (see box, p.12); in addition to allowing oncoming traffic to pass at these points, you should also let cars behind you overtake. These roads can be frustrating but take care and stay alert for vehicles coming in the opposite direction, which may have been hidden by bends or dips in the road. In remoter regions, the roads are dotted with sheep, which are entirely oblivious to cars, so slow down and edge your way past; should you kill or injure one, it is your duty to inform the local farmer.

The AA (☎0800 887766, ⊛theaa.com), RAC (☎0844 8913111, ⊛rac.co.uk) and Green Flag (☎0845 2462766, ⊛greenflag.com) all operate 24-hour **emergency breakdown** services. You may be entitled to free assistance through a reciprocal arrangement with a motoring organization in your home country. If not, you can make use of these emergency services by joining at the roadside, but you will incur a hefty surcharge. In remote areas, you may have a long wait for assistance.

Renting a car

Car rental in Scotland is expensive. Most firms charge £25–50 per day, or around £130–200 a week. The major chains are confined mostly to the big cities, so it may be cheaper to use small **local agencies** – we've highlighted some in the Guide. The best deals are usually found in advance, through sites such as Auto Europe (⊛auto-europe .co.uk). With all rentals it's worth checking the terms and conditions carefully; some rentals only allow you to drive a limited number of miles before paying extra.

Remember, too, that **fuel** in Scotland is expensive – petrol (gasoline) and diesel cost well over £1.35 per litre. **Automatics** are rare at the lower end of the price scale – if you want one, you should book well ahead. **Camper vans** are another option; rates start at around £400 a week in the high season, but you'll save on accommodation (see p.31).

By ferry

Scotland has more than sixty inhabited islands, and nearly fifty of them have scheduled **ferry** links. Most ferries carry cars and vans, and the vast majority can – and should – be booked as far in advance as possible.

CalMac has a virtual monopoly on services on the River Clyde and to the Hebrides, sailing to 22 islands and 4 peninsulas. They aren't quick – no catamarans or fast ferries – or cheap, but they do have two types of reduced-fare pass. If you're taking more than one ferry, ask for one of the discounted **Island Hopscotch** tickets (there are more than 20 different variations to choose between). If you're going to be taking a lot of ferries, you might be better off with an **Island Rover**, which entitles you to eight or fifteen consecutive days' unlimited ferry travel. It does not, however, guarantee you a place on any ferry, so you still need to book ahead. Prices for the eight-day/fifteen-day pass are around £57/£82 for passengers and around £270/£400 for cars.

Car ferries to **Orkney and Shetland** are run by Northlink Ferries. Pentland Ferries also run a car ferry to Orkney, and John O'Groats Ferries run a summer-only passenger service to Orkney. The various Orkney islands are linked to each other by Orkney Ferries; Shetland's inter-island ferries are mostly council-run so the local tourist board (⊛shetland.gov.uk) is your best bet for information. There are also numerous **small operators** round the Scottish coast that run fast RIB taxi services, day-excursion trips and even the odd scheduled service; their contact details are given in the relevant chapters of the Guide.

FERRY COMPANIES

CalMac ☎ 0800 066 5000, ⊛ calmac.co.uk
John O'Groats Ferries ☎ 01955 611353, ⊛ jogferry.co.uk
NorthLink Ferries ☎ 0845 600 0449, ⊛ northlinkferries.co.uk
Orkney Ferries ☎ 01856 872044, ⊛ orkneyferries.co.uk
Pentland Ferries ☎ 01856 831226, ⊛ pentlandferries.co.uk

By plane

Aside from the international airport at Inverness, there are numerous minor **airports** around the Scottish Highlands and Islands, some of which are little more than gravel airstrips. Airfares fluctuate enormously depending on demand – if you book early enough you can fly from Glasgow to Islay for £45 one way, but leave it to the last minute and it could cost you more than twice that. Most flights within Scotland are operated by **flybe** (⊛flybe .com), or its franchise partner **Loganair** (⊛loganair .co.uk). For inter-island flights in Shetland, you need to book direct through **Directflight** (☎01595 840246, ✆directflight.co.uk). Competition emerges from time to time, with **Eastern Airways** (✆eastern airways.com) currently offering flights from Aberdeen to Stornoway and Wick.

Accommodation

In common with the rest of Britain, accommodation in the Highlands and Islands is fairly expensive. Budget travellers are well catered for, however, with numerous hostels, and those with money to spend will relish the more expensive country-house hotels. In the middle ground, however, the standard of many B&Bs, guesthouses and hotels can be disappointing. Welcoming, comfortable, well-run places do, of course, exist in all parts of the country – and you'll find the best ones listed in this Guide.

Star ratings

VisitScotland, the country's tourist board, operates a system for grading accommodation, which is updated annually. However, not every establishment participates, and you shouldn't assume that a particular B&B is no good simply because it's not on VisitScotland's lists. The tourist board uses star awards, from one to five, which are supposed to reflect the quality of welcome, service and hospitality – though it's pretty clear that places without en-suite toilets, a TV in every room, matching fabrics or packets of shortbread on the sideboard are likely to be marked down.

Booking accommodation

If you decide not to book online, most **tourist offices** will help you find accommodation and **book a room** directly, for which they normally

---

ACCOMMODATION PRICES

Throughout the Guide, accommodation prices are quoted according to the least expensive **double room** in high season. Individual prices for **dorm beds** and (if available) double or twin rooms are given for hostels. For campsites the figure given is for a **pitch** including a vehicle and two people, or else per person.

---

charge a flat fee of £4. If you take advantage of this service, it's worth being clear as to what kind of place you'd prefer, as the tourist office quite often selects something quite randomly across the whole range of their membership. Bear in mind, too, that outside the main towns and cities many places are only open for the **tourist season** (Easter to Oct): you'll always find somewhere to stay outside this period, but the choice may be limited.

Hotels

Hotels come in all shapes and sizes. At the upper end of the market, they can be huge country houses and converted castles offering a very exclusive and opulent experience. Most will have a licensed bar and offer both breakfast and dinner, and often lunch as well. In the cities the increasing prevalence of modern budget hotels run by national (and international) chains may not win any prizes for aesthetics or variety, but they are competitively priced and for the most part meet criteria for clean, smart, serviceable accommodation. Also making a bit of a comeback are inns (in other words, pubs), or their modern equivalent, "restaurants with rooms". These will often have only a handful of rooms, but their emphasis on creating an all-round convivial atmosphere as well as serving top-quality food often make them worth seeking out.

Guesthouses and B&Bs

Guesthouses and B&Bs offer the widest and most diverse range of accommodation. VisitScotland uses the term "guesthouse" for a commercial venture that has four or more rooms, at least some of which are en suite, reserving "B&B" for a predominantly private family home that has only a few rooms to let. In reality, however, most places offer en-suite facilities, and the different names often reflect the pretensions of the owners and the cost of the rooms more than differences in service: in general, guesthouses cost more than B&Bs.

A surprising number of guesthouses and B&Bs still have decor that consists of heavy chintz and floral designs, but the location, and the chance to get an insight into the local way of life, can be some compensation. Many B&Bs, even the pricier ones, have only a few rooms, so **advance booking** is recommended, especially in the Islands.

Hostels

There's an ever-increasing number of **hostels** in the Highlands and Islands to cater for travellers –

youthful or otherwise – who are unable or unwilling to pay the rates charged by hotels, guesthouses and B&Bs. Most hostels are clean and comfortable, sometimes offering doubles and even singles as well as dormitory accommodation. Others concentrate more on keeping the price as low as possible, simply providing a roof over your head and a few basic facilities. Whatever type of hostel you stay in, expect to pay £10–22 per night.

The **Scottish Youth Hostels Association** (Ⓦ syha .org.uk), referred to throughout the Guide as "SYHA hostels", run the longest-established hostels in the Highlands and Islands. While these places sometimes occupy handsome buildings, many retain an institutionalized air. Bunk-bed accommodation in single-sex dormitories, lights out before midnight and no smoking/no alcohol policies are the norm outside the big cities. Breakfast is not normally included in the price, though most hostels have self-catering facilities.

If you're not a **member** of one of the hostelling organizations affiliated to **Hostelling International** (HI), you can pay your £10 joining fee at most hostels. **Advance booking** is recommended, and essential at Easter, Christmas and from May to August. You can book online, in person or by phone.

The **Gatliff Hebridean Hostels Trust** or GHHT (Ⓦ gatliff.org.uk) is allied to the SYHA and rents out very simple croft accommodation in the Western Isles. Accommodation is basic, and you can't book ahead, but it's unlikely you'll be turned away. Elsewhere in the Highlands and Islands, these places tend to be known as **bothies** or bunkhouses, and are usually independently run. In Shetland, **camping böds**, operated by the Shetland Amenity Trust (Ⓦ camping-bods.co.uk), offer similarly plain accommodation: you need all your usual camping equipment to stay at one (except, of course, a tent). For more details about Gatliff hostels and camping böds, see the relevant chapters in the Guide.

There are also loads of **independent hostels** across the Highlands and Islands. These are usually laidback places with no membership, fewer rules, mixed dorms and no curfew. You can find most of them in the annually updated *Independent Hostel Guide* (Ⓦ independenthostelguide.co.uk). Many of them are also affiliated to Scottish Independent Hostels (Ⓦ hostel-scotland.co.uk), which has a programme of inspection and lists members in the *SIH Hostel Guide*, available free online.

Camping

There are hundreds of **caravan and camping parks** around Scotland, most of which are open from April to October. The most expensive sites charge about £10–15 for two people with a car to pitch a tent, and are usually well equipped, with shops, a restaurant, a bar and, occasionally, sports facilities. Most of these, however, are aimed principally at caravans, trailers and motorhomes, and generally don't offer the tranquil atmosphere and independence that those travelling with just a tent are seeking.

That said, peaceful and **informal sites** do exist, and are described throughout this guide, though they are few and far between. Many **hostels** allow camping, and farmers will usually let folk camp on their land for free or for a nominal sum. In this guide, we've listed the price for a pitch (ie one tent for two people, plus a car) wherever possible; where campsites charge per person, we've listed prices in that format instead.

Scotland's relaxed land access laws allow **wild camping** in open country. The basic rule is "leave no trace", but for a guide to good practice, visit Ⓦ outdooraccess-scotland.com.

The great majority of **caravans** are permanently moored nose to tail in the vicinity of some of Scotland's finest scenery; others are positioned singly in back gardens or amid farmland. Some can be booked for self-catering, and with prices starting at around £100 a week, this can work out as one of the cheapest options if you're travelling with kids in tow.

If you're planning to do a lot of camping at official camping and caravanning sites, it might be worthwhile joining the **Camping and Caravanning Club** (Ⓦ campingandcaravanningclub.co.uk). Membership costs £51 (£41 if paying by direct debit) and entitles you to pay only a per-person fee, not a pitch fee, at CCC sites. Those coming from abroad can get the same benefits by buying an international camping carnet, available from home motoring organizations or a CCC equivalent.

Another good option, if you want to roll your accommodation and travel costs into one, is to rent a camper van – visit Ⓦ walkhighlands.co.uk for a range of options. Few companies will rent to drivers with less than one year's experience and most will only rent to people over 21 or 25 and under 70 or 75 years of age.

Self-catering

A huge proportion of visitors to the Highlands and Islands opt for **self-catering**, booking a cottage or apartment for a week and often saving themselves a considerable amount of money by doing so. In most cases, the minimum period of rental is a week, and therefore this isn't a valid option if you're aiming to tour round the country. The least you can

Food and drink

The remoteness of parts of the Highlands and Islands will inevitably restrict your eating and drinking choices. It's often a good idea to plan meal locations ahead as you might find serving times restrictive or popular restaurants booked out, particularly in summer. Stocking up on picnic food from a good deli is also worthwhile.

5 CAMPSITES NOT TO MISS

Long beach Knoydart. See p.226.
Camusdarach Campsite Camusdarach. See p.223.
Red Squirrel Glen Coe. See p.194.
Rubha Phoil Armadale, Skye. See p.274.
Glenbrittle Campsite Glenbrittle. See p.277.

expect to pay in the high season is around £250 per week for a place sleeping four, but something special, or somewhere in a popular tourist area, might cost £500 or more. Such is the number and variety of self-catering places on offer that we've mentioned very few in the Guide. A good source of information is **VisitScotland**'s self-catering website (𝕎 visitscotland.com/accommodation/self -catering), updated frequently and listing more than 2700 properties. Alternatively, you could try one of the websites listed below.

SELF-CATERING AGENCIES

Cottages and Castles 𝕎 cottages-and-castles.co.uk ☎ 01738 451610. A range of self-catering properties, mostly in mainland Scotland.
Cottages4you 𝕎 cottages4you.co.uk ☎ 08452 680760. Hundreds of reasonably priced properties all over Scotland.
Ecosse Unique 𝕎 uniquescotland.com 𝕎 01835 822277. Carefully selected cottages across mainland Scotland, plus a few in the Hebrides and Orkney.
Landmark Trust 𝕎 landmarktrust.org.uk ☎ 01628 825925. A very select number of historical properties, often in prime locations.
LHH 𝕎 lhhscotland.com ☎ 01381 610496. Attractive homes across Scotland, including mansions, castles and villas.
Mackay's Agency 𝕎 mackays-self-catering.co.uk ☎ 01315 501180. A whole range of properties in every corner of mainland Scotland (plus Skye and Orkney), from chalets and town apartments to remote stone-built cottages.
National Trust for Scotland 𝕎 nts.org.uk ☎ 01312 439331. The NTS lets around forty of its converted historic cottages and houses.
Scottish Country Cottages 𝕎 scottish-country-cottages.co.uk ☎ 08452 680801. Superior cottages with lots of character, scattered across the Scottish mainland plus some of the Inner Hebrides.

Breakfast

In most hotels and B&Bs you'll be offered a **Scottish breakfast**, similar to its English counterpart of sausage, bacon and egg, but typically with the addition of black pudding (blood sausage) and potato scones. Porridge is another likely option, as is fish in the form of kippers, smoked haddock or even kedgeree. Scotland's staple drink, like England's, is **tea**, drunk strong and with milk, though **coffee** is just as readily available everywhere. However, while smart coffee shops are now a familiar feature in the cities, execrable versions of espresso and cappuccino, as well as instant coffee, are still all too familiar.

Lunches and snacks

The most common lunchtime fare in Scotland remains the **sandwich**. A bowl or cup of hearty **soup** is a typical accompaniment, particularly in winter. A **pub lunch** is often an attractive alternative. Bar menus generally have standard, filling but unambitious options including soup, sandwiches, scampi and chips, or steak pie and chips, with vegetarians suffering from a paucity of choice. That said, some bar food is freshly prepared and filling, equalling the à la carte dishes served in the adjacent hotel restaurant. Pubs or hotel bars are among the cheapest options when it comes to eating out – in the smallest villages, these might be your only option.

CLASSIC SCOTTISH DISHES

Arbroath smokies Powerful smoked haddock (see p.98).
Cullen skink Rich soup made from smoked haddock, potatoes and cream.
Haggis Flavoursome sausage meat (spiced liver, offal, oatmeal and onion) cooked inside a bag made from a sheep's stomach. Tasty and satisfying, particularly when eaten with its traditional accompaniments "bashed neeps" (mashed turnips) and "chappit tatties" (mashed potatoes).
Porridge A breakfast staple, this is properly made with oatmeal and water, and cooked with a pinch of salt. Some prefer to add milk and honey, fruit or sugar to sweeten.
Scots broth Hearty soup made with stock (usually mutton), vegetables and barley.

Restaurants are often, though not always, open at lunchtimes, when they tend to be less busy and generally offer a shorter menu compared with their evening service: this can make for a more pleasant and less expensive experience. For morning or afternoon snacks, as well as light lunches, **tearooms** are a common feature where you will often find decent home-baking.

As for **fast food**, chip shops, or chippies, abound – the best are often found in coastal towns within sight of the fishing boats. Deep-fried battered fish is the standard choice – when served with chips it's known as a "fish supper", even if eaten at lunchtime – though everything from hamburgers to haggis suppers is normally on offer, all deep-fried, of course. Scotland is even credited with inventing the **deep-fried Mars bar**, the definitive badge of a nation with the worst heart disease statistics in Western Europe. For alternative fast food, major towns feature all the usual pizza, burger and baked potato outlets, as well as Chinese, Mexican and Indian takeaways.

Evening meals

There's no doubt that, as with the rest of the UK, eating out in the Highlands and Islands is expensive. Our restaurant listings include a mix of high-quality and budget establishments. Wine in restaurants is marked up strongly, so you'll often pay £15 for a bottle selling for £5 in the shops; house wines generally start around the £10 mark.

If you're travelling in remoter parts of the Highlands and Islands, or staying at a B&B or guesthouse in the countryside, ask advice about nearby options for your **evening meal**. Many B&Bs and guesthouses will cook you dinner, but you must book ahead and indicate any dietary requirements.

As for **restaurants**, standards vary enormously, but independent restaurants using good-quality local produce are now found all over Scotland. Less predictable are hotel restaurants, many of which

MEAL TIMES

In many parts of Scotland outside the cities, inflexible **meal times** mean that you'll have to keep an eye on your watch if you don't want to miss out on eating. B&Bs and hotels frequently serve breakfast only until 9am, lunch is usually over by 2pm, and, despite the long summer evenings, pub and hotel kitchens often stop serving dinner as early as 8pm.

serve non-residents. Some can be very ordinary despite the descriptions on the à la carte menu. You could easily end up paying £30–40 a head for a meal with wine.

In Inverness and some of the larger towns on the mainland, you'll find a wide range of **international** cuisines including Japanese, Thai, Caribbean and Turkish, as well as the more common Indian, Chinese and Italian establishments.

Among traditional **desserts**, "clootie dumpling" is a sweet, stodgy fruit pudding bound in a cloth and cooked for hours, while Cranachan, made with toasted oatmeal steeped in whisky and folded into whipped cream flavoured with fresh raspberries, or the similar Atholl Brose, are considered more refined.

Food shopping

Most Scots get their supplies from supermarkets, but you're increasingly likely to come across good delis, farm shops and specialist **food shops**. Many stock local produce alongside imported delicacies, as well as organic fruit and veg, specialist drinks such as locally brewed beer, freshly baked bread, and sandwiches and other snacks for takeaway. Look out too for **farmers' markets** (ⓦ scottishfarmersmarkets .co.uk), which generally take place on Saturday and Sunday mornings; local farmers and small producers from pig farmers to cheese-makers and small smokeries set up stalls to sell their specialist lines.

Scotland is notorious for its sweet tooth, and **cakes and puddings** are taken very seriously. Bakeries with extensive displays of iced buns, cakes and cream-filled pastries are a typical feature of any Scottish high street, while home-made shortbread, scones or tablet (a hard, crystalline form of fudge) are considered great treats. In the summer, Scottish berries, in particular raspberries and strawberries, are particularly tasty.

Drinking

As in the rest of Britain, Scottish **pubs**, which originated as travellers' hostelries and coaching inns, are the main social focal points of any community. Pubs in Scotland vary hugely, from old-fashioned inns with open fires and a convivial atmosphere to raucous theme-pubs with jukeboxes and satellite TV. Out in the islands, pubs are few and far between, with most drinking taking place in the local hotel bar. In some larger towns, traditional pubs are being supplemented by modern café-bars.

Scotland has very relaxed licensing laws. Pub **opening hours** are generally 11am to 11pm, but some places stay open later. Whatever time the pub

MAKING MALT WHISKY

Malt whisky is made by soaking barley in **steeps** (water cisterns) for two or three days until it swells, after which it is left to germinate for around seven days, during which the starch in the barley seed is converted into soluble sugars – this process is known as **malting**. The malted barley or "green malt" is then dried in a **kiln** over a furnace, which can be oil-fired, peat-fired or, more often than not, a combination of the two.

Only a few distilleries still do their own malting and kilning in the traditional pagoda-style kilns; the rest simply have their malted barley delivered from an industrial maltings. The first process in most distilleries is therefore **milling**, which grinds the malted barley into "grist". Next comes the **mashing**, during which the grist is infused in hot water in mashtuns, producing a sugary concoction called "wort". After cooling, the wort passes into the washbacks, traditionally made of wood, where it is fermented with yeast for two to three days. During **fermentation**, the sugar is converted into alcohol, producing a brown foaming liquid known as "wash".

Distillation now takes place, not once but twice: the wash is steam-heated, and the vapours siphoned off and condensed as a spirit. This is the point at which the whisky is poured into oak casks – usually ones which have already been used to store bourbon or sherry – and left to age for a minimum of three years.

The average **maturation** period for a single malt whisky, however, is ten years; and the longer it matures, the more expensive it is, because two percent evaporates each year. Unlike wine, as soon as the whisky is bottled, maturation ceases.

---

closes, "last orders" will be called by the bar staff about fifteen minutes before closing time to allow "drinking-up time". In general, you have to be 16 to enter a pub unaccompanied, though some places are easy about having folk with children in, or have special family rooms and beer gardens where the kids can run free. The legal drinking age is 18.

Whisky

Whisky – *uisge beatha*, or the "water of life" in Gaelic – has been produced in Scotland since the fifteenth century, but only really took off in popularity after the 1780 tax on claret made wine too expensive for most people. The taxman soon caught up with whisky, however, and drove the stills underground. Today, many distilleries operate on the site of simple cottages that once distilled the stuff illegally.

Despite the dominance of the blended whiskies such as Johnnie Walker, Bell's, Teacher's and The Famous Grouse, **single malt whisky** is infinitely superior and, as a result, a great deal more expensive. Single malts vary in character enormously depending on the amount of peat used for drying the barley, the water used for mashing and the type of oak cask used in the maturing process. Malt whisky is best drunk with a splash of water to release its distinctive flavours.

Beer

Traditional Scottish beer is a thick, dark ale known as **heavy**, served at room temperature in pints or half-pints, with a full head. Quite different in taste from English "bitter", heavy is a more robust, sweeter beer with less of an edge. All of the big-name breweries – McEwan's, Tennents, Bellhaven and Caledonian – produce a reasonable selection of heavies. However, if you really want to discover Scottish beer, look out for the products of small **local breweries** such as Cairngorm, the Black Isle, Arran, Fyne Ales, Isle of Skye, Orkney or Valhalla. Look out, too, for Froach, available mostly in bottles, a very refreshing, lighter-coloured ale made from heather according to an ancient recipe.

Water and soft drinks

Scotland produces a prodigious amount of **mineral water**, much of which is exported – tap water is chill, clean and perfectly palatable in most parts of the country, including the areas of the Highlands and Islands where it's tinged the colour of weak tea by peat in the ground. Locally produced **Irn-Bru**, a fizzy orange, sickly sweet concoction, has been known to outsell Coke and Pepsi in Scotland.

The media

When you're up in the Highlands and Islands, the UK's national media may seem London-based and London-biased. Most locals prefer to listen to Scottish radio programmes, read local newspapers, and – albeit to a much lesser extent – watch Scottish TV.

The press

Provincial dailies are more widely read in the Highlands and Islands than anywhere else in Britain. The biggest-selling regional title is Aberdeen's famously parochial *Press and Journal*, which has special editions for each area of the Highlands and Islands. For an insight into local life, there's the staid **weekly** *Oban Times*. More entertaining and radical is the campaigning weekly *West Highland Free Press*, printed on Skye. All carry articles in Gaelic as well as English. Further north, the lively *Shetland Times* and Orkney's sedate *Orcadian* are essential weekly reads for anyone living in or just visiting those islands.

Given the distances in the Highlands and Islands, you shouldn't always expect to find a daily newspaper arriving with your early morning cup of tea, though unless you're in a particularly remote spot or bad weather is affecting transport links, the papers are normally around by mid-morning. Most easily obtained are **Scottish newspapers**. Principal among these are the two serious dailies – *The Scotsman*, based in Edinburgh, and *The Herald*, published in Glasgow, both offering reasonable coverage of the current issues affecting Scotland, along with British and foreign news, sport, arts and lifestyle pages. You should also be able to find a selection of popular tabloids, including Scotland's biggest-selling daily, the downmarket *Daily Record*, along with various national titles – from the reactionary *Sun* to the vaguely left-leaning *Daily Mirror* – which appear in specific Scottish editions.

Many **Sunday newspapers** published in London have a Scottish edition, although again Scotland has its own offerings – *Scotland on Sunday*, from the *Scotsman* stable, and the *Sunday Herald*, complementing its eponymous daily. Far more fun and widely read is the anachronistic *Sunday Post*, published by Dundee's mighty D.C. Thomson publishing group. It's a wholesome paper, uniquely Scottish, and has changed little since the 1950s, since which time its two long-running cartoon strips, *Oor Wullie* and *The Broons*, have acquired cult status.

Scottish **monthlies** include the *Scottish Field*, a lowbrow version of England's *Tatler*, and the widely read *Scots Magazine*, an old-fashioned middle-of-the-road publication which promotes family values and lots of good fresh air.

TV and radio

In Scotland there are five main (sometimes called "terrestrial") **TV channels**: state-owned BBC1 and BBC2, and three commercial channels: ITV1, Channel 4 and Channel 5. **BBC Scotland** produces news programmes and a regular crop of local-interest lifestyle, current affairs, drama and comedy shows which slot into the schedules of both BBC channels. The commercial channel ITV1 (branded in Scotland as STV), shows the same mix of talent shows, soaps and celebrity-driven programmes as the same channel south of the border, but with regional news broadcasts and some locally made shows slotted into the schedules. Channel 4 blends hard-hitting documentaries with comedy series and trashy fly-on-the-wall stuff, while downmarket Channel 5 focuses on reality shows and celebrity profiles. The vast majority of homes receive dozens of additional TV channels and radio stations through digital services like Freeview and Sky.

The **BBC radio** network broadcasts six main FM stations in Scotland, five of which are national stations originating largely from London. Only the award-winning BBC Radio Scotland offers a Scottish perspective on news, politics, arts, music, travel and sport. Gaelic-language BBC Radio nan Gàidheal, meanwhile, broadcasts news, chat, sport and music. Note that in large areas of the Highlands and Islands, some or all of these stations are impossible to receive.

A web of local **commercial radio** stations helps to fill in the gaps, mostly mixing rock and pop music with news bulletins, but a few tiny community-based stations such as Lochbroom FM in Ullapool – a place famed for its daily midge count – transmit documentaries and discussions on local issues. The most populated areas of Scotland also receive UK-wide commercial stations such as Classic FM, Virgin Radio and TalkSport. With a DAB **digital radio**, you can get all the main stations crackle-free along with special interest and smaller-scale stations.

SOME SCOTTISH RADIO STATIONS

BBC Radio Scotland 92–95FM, 810MW ⓦ bbc.co.uk/radio scotland. Nationwide news, sport, music, current affairs and arts.

BBC Radio nan Gàidheal 103.4FM ⓦ bbc.co.uk/scotland/alba. An opt-out from Radio Scotland, with Gaelic-language news and phone-ins, and great traditional-music shows.

Lochbroom FM 102.2 & 96.8FM ⓦ lochbroomfm.co.uk. A small local radio station broadcasting to the northwest coast from Ullapool.

Moray Firth 97.4FM, 1107MW ⓦ mfr.co.uk. Mainstream rock and pop for the Inverness area.

Nevis Radio 96.6 & 102.3FM ⓦ nevisradio.co.uk. All that's happening in Fort William and its surrounds, from the slopes of Ben Nevis.

SIBC 96.2FM ⓦ sibc.co.uk. Shetland's own independent station.

Events and spectator sports

There's a huge range of organized annual events on offer in the Highlands and Islands, reflecting both vibrant contemporary culture and well-marketed heritage. Many tourists will home straight in on the Highland Games and other tartan-draped theatricals, but there's more to Scotland than this: numerous regional celebrations perpetuate ancient customs. A few of the smaller, more obscure events, particularly those with a pagan bent, do not always welcome the casual visitor. The tourist board publishes a weighty list of all Scottish events on its website (Ⓦ visitscotland.com).

Events calendar

DECEMBER–JANUARY

Dec 31 and Jan 1 Hogmanay and Ne'er Day. Traditionally more important to the Scots than Christmas, and known for the custom of "first-footing", when groups of revellers troop into neighbours' houses at midnight bearing gifts. More popular these days are huge and highly organized street parties in the larger towns.

Jan 1 Kirkwall Boys' and Men's Ba' Games, Orkney. Mass, drunken football game through the streets of the town, with the castle and the harbour the respective goals. As a grand finale the players jump into the harbour.

Last Tues in Jan Up-Helly-Aa, Lerwick, Shetland Ⓦ visitshetland .com. Norse fire festival culminating in the burning of a specially built Viking longship. Visitors will need an invite from one of the locals, or you can buy a ticket for the Town Hall celebrations.

Jan 25 Burns Night. Scots worldwide get stuck into haggis, whisky and vowel-grinding poetry to commemorate Scotland's greatest poet, Robert Burns.

FEBRUARY

Feb Fort William Mountain Festival Ⓦ mountainfestival.co.uk. Films, lectures, guided walks and music sessions in celebration of mountain culture.

MAY

Early May Spirit of Speyside Scotch Whisky Festival Ⓦ spiritof speyside.com. Four-day binge with pipe bands, gigs and dancing as well as distillery crawls. **Shetland Folk Festival** (Ⓦ shetlandfolkfestival .com). One of the liveliest and most entertaining of Scotland's round of folk festivals.

Late May Atholl Highlanders Parade at Blair Castle, Perthshire Ⓦ blair-castle.co.uk. The annual parade and inspection of Britain's last private army by their colonel-in-chief, the Duke of Atholl, on the eve of their Highland Games.

JUNE–JULY

June Beginning of the Highland Games season across the Highlands and Argyll; St Magnus Festival, Orkney Ⓦ stmagnus festival.com. A classical and folk music, drama, dance and literature festival celebrating the islands. **Rock Ness** Ⓦ rockness.co.uk. A big outdoor electronic, rock and dance festival on the shores of Loch Ness.

July Mendelssohn on Mull Ⓦ mullfest.org.uk. Music festival celebrating classical music. **Hebridean Celtic Festival, Stornoway** Ⓦ hebceltfest.com. International Celtic music festival that takes place over four days in Stornoway in the Outer Hebrides.

Tarbert Seafood Festival Ⓦ tarbertfestivals.co.uk. This weekend of gorging on seafood also sees live music and dance events around Tarbert's sheltered harbour.

Late July West Highland Yachting Week Ⓦ whyw.co.uk. A week of yacht racing and shore-based partying which moves en masse between Oban, Craobh and Tobermory.

SEPTEMBER

Early Sept The Ben Nevis Race (for amateurs) Involves running to the top of Scotland's highest mountain and back again. **Shinty's Camanachd Cup final** Ⓦ shinty.com. The climax of the season for Scotland's own stick-and-ball game, normally held in one of the main Highland towns.

Blas Ⓦ blas-festival.com The premier Gaelic and traditional-music festival, at venues across the Highlands.

Late Sept Annual World Stone Skimming Championships, Easdale Island, near Oban Ⓦ stoneskimming.com. No previous experience is required; if you can make a stone bounce three times before sinking, you're in.

OCTOBER–NOVEMBER

Oct The National Mod Ⓦ the-mod.co.uk. Held over nine days at a different venue each year. It's a competitive festival and features all aspects of Gaelic performing arts. **The Golden Spurtle World Porridge Making Championships, Carrbridge, Speyside** Ⓦ goldenspurtle .com. Celebrity chefs preside over this competition, designed to find the best traditionally made porridge.

Tiree Wave Classic Ⓦ tireewaveclassic.co.uk. Annual event attracting windsurfers from around the world to the breezy Hebridean island.

Late Oct Glenfiddich Piping and Fiddle Championships Ⓦ blairatholl .org.uk. Held at Blair Atholl for the world's top ten solo pipers.

Nov 30 St Andrew's Day. Celebrating Scotland's patron saint.

Highland Games

Despite their name, **Highland Games** are held all over Scotland between May and mid-September, varying in size and in the range of events they offer. The Games probably originated in the fourteenth century as a means of recruiting the best fighting men for the clan chiefs, and were popularized by **Queen Victoria** to encourage the traditional dress, music, games and dance of the Highlands; indeed, various royals still attend the Games at Braemar.

Apart from **Braemar**, the most famous games take place at **Oban** and **Cowal**, but the smaller events are often more fun – like a sort of Highland version of a school sports day. There's money to be won, too, so the Games are usually pretty competitive. The most distinctive events are known as the "heavies" – tossing the caber (pronounced "kabber"), putting the stone, and tossing the weight over the bar – all of which require prodigious strength and skill, and the wearing of a kilt. Tossing the caber is the most spectacular, when the athlete must lift an entire tree trunk up, cupping it in his hands, before running with it and attempting to heave it end over end. Just as important as the sporting events are the **piping** competitions – for individuals and bands – and **dancing** competitions, where you'll see girls as young as 3 tripping the quick, intricate steps of dances such as the Highland Fling.

Football

While **football** (soccer) is far and away Scotland's most popular spectator sport, its popularity in the Highlands and Islands is a little muted in comparison to the game's following in the Central Belt of the country. The strength of the Highland League (Ⓦ highlandfootballleague.com) was, however, recognized in the mid-1990s with the inclusion of Inverness Caledonian Thistle and Ross County in the Scottish Leagues. Inverness Caledonian Thistle have subsequently risen to Scotland's top division, the Scottish Premiership, and as a result the Caledonian Stadium on the shores of the Moray Firth regularly hosts the multinational stars of Glasgow's and Edinburgh's top teams. The **season** begins in early August and ends in mid-May, with most matches taking place on Saturday afternoons at 3pm, and also often on Sunday afternoons and Wednesday evenings. Tickets for Scottish League games cost around £25, but less for Highland League fixtures.

Shinty

Played throughout Scotland but with particular strongholds in the West Highlands and Strathspey, the game of **shinty** (the Gaelic *sinteag* means "leap") arrived from Ireland around 1500 years ago. Until the latter part of the nineteenth century, it was played on an informal basis and teams from neighbouring villages had to come to an agreement about rules before matches could begin.

However, in 1893, the **Camanachd Association** – the Gaelic word for shinty is *camanachd* – was set up to formalize the rules, and the first Camanachd Cup Final was held in Inverness in 1896. Today, shinty is still fairly close to its Gaelic roots, like the Irish game of hurling, with each team having twelve players including a goalkeeper and each goal counting for a point. The game, which bears similarities to an undisciplined version of hockey, isn't for the faint-hearted; it's played at a furious pace, with sticks – called camans or cammocks – flying alarmingly in all directions. Support is enthusiastic and vocal, and if you're in the Highlands during the season, which runs from March to October, it's well worth trying to catch a match: check with tourist offices or the local paper, or go to Ⓦ shinty.com.

Curling

The one winter sport which enjoys a strong Scottish identity is **curling** (Ⓦ royalcaledoniancurlingclub .org), occasionally still played on a frozen outdoor rink, or "pond", though most commonly these days seen at indoor ice rinks. The game, which involves gently sliding smooth-bottomed 18kg discs of granite called "stones" across the ice towards a target circle, is said to have been invented in Scotland, although its earliest representation is in a sixteenth-century Flemish painting. Played by two teams of four, it's a highly tactical and skilful sport, enlivened by team members using brushes to sweep the ice furiously in front of a moving stone to help it travel further and straighter. If you're interested in seeing curling being played, go along to the ice rink in places such as Perth, Pitlochry or Inverness on a winter evening.

Outdoor activities

Scotland boasts a landscape that, weather conditions apart, is extremely attractive for outdoor pursuits at all levels of fitness and ambition, and legislation enacted by the Scottish Parliament has ensured a right of access to hills, mountains, lochs and rivers. Within striking distance of its cities are two national parks, remote wilderness areas and vast stretches of glens and moorland, while sea-kayakers, sailors and surfers can enjoy excellent conditions along the rugged but beautiful coastline.

Walking and climbing

The whole of Scotland offers superb opportunities for **walking**, with some of the finest areas in the ownership of bodies such as the National Trust for Scotland and the John Muir Trust (Ⓦjmt.org); both permit year-round access. Bear in mind, though, that restrictions may be in place during lambing and deerstalking seasons. See Ⓦ outdooraccess-scotland .com for information about **hiking safely** during the stalking season. In addition, the green signposts of the Scottish Rights of Way Society point to established paths and routes all over the country.

There are several **long-distance footpaths**, such as the well-known West Highland Way (see box, p.133), which take between three and seven days to walk, though you can, of course, just do a section of them. Paths are generally well signposted and well supported, with a range of services from bunkhouses to baggage-carrying services.

Numerous short walks (from accessible towns and villages) and several major walks are touched on in this Guide. However, you should only use our notes as general outlines, and always in conjunction with a good map. Where possible, we have given details of the best maps to use – in most cases one of the excellent and reliable **Ordnance Survey** (OS) series (see p.45), usually available from local tourist offices, which, along with outdoor shops, can also supply other local maps, safety advice and guidebooks/leaflets.

For relatively gentle walking in the company of knowledgeable locals, look out for guided walks offered by rangers at many National Trust for Scotland, Forestry Commission and Scottish Natural Heritage sites. These often focus on local **wildlife**, and the best can lead to some special sightings, such as a badger's sett or a golden eagle's eyrie.

WALKING INFORMATION

Ⓦ **outdooraccess-scotland.com** All you need to know about the Scottish Outdoor Access Code, plus daily information for hillwalkers about deerstalking activities (July–Oct).

Ⓦ **walking.visitscotland.com** Official site from VisitScotland, with good lists of operators, information on long-distance footpaths, and details of deerstalking restrictions and contact phone numbers.

Ⓦ **wildlife.visitscotland.com** Highlights the fauna and flora you may spot on a walk.

WALKING CLUBS AND ASSOCIATIONS

Mountain Bothies Association Ⓦ mountainbothies.org.uk. Charity dedicated to maintaining huts and shelters in the Scottish Highlands.

Mountaineering Council of Scotland Ⓦ mountaineering -scotland.org.uk. The representative body for all mountain activities, with detailed information on access and conservation issues.

Ramblers Association Scotland Ⓦ ramblers.org.uk/scotland. Campaigning organization with network of local groups, and news on events and issues.

Scottish Mountaineering Club Ⓦ smc.org.uk. The largest mountaineering club in the country. A well-respected organization which publishes a popular series of mountain guidebooks.

WALKING TOUR OPERATORS

Adventure Scotland ☎ 01479 811411, Ⓦ adventure-scotland .com. Highly experienced operator providing a wide range of courses and one-day adventures, from telemark skiing to climbing, kayaking and biking.

C-N-Do Scotland ☎ 01786 445703, Ⓦ cndoscotland.com. Prides itself on offering the "best walking holidays in Scotland". Munro-bagging for novices and experts with qualified leaders.

G2 Outdoor ☎ 01479 811008, Ⓦ g2outdoor.co.uk. Personable, highly qualified adventure specialists offering gorge scrambling, hillwalking, rock climbing, canoeing and telemark skiing in the Cairngorms.

Glenmore Lodge ☎ 01479 861256, Ⓦ glenmorelodge.org.uk. Based within the Cairngorm National Park, and internationally recognized as a leader in outdoor skills and leadership training.

Hebridean Pursuits ☎ 01631 720002, Ⓦ hebrideanpursuits.com. Offers hillwalking and rock climbing in the Hebrides and West Highlands, as well as surf-kayaking and sailing trips.

Nae Limits ☎ 08450 178177, Ⓦ naelimits.co.uk. This excellent Perthshire-based operator offers everything from wet 'n' wild rafting to bug canyoning and cliff jumping.

North-West Frontiers ☎ 01997 421474, Ⓦ nwfrontiers.com. Based in Ullapool, offering guided mountain trips with small groups in the northwest Highlands, Hebrides and even the Shetland Islands.

Rua Reidh Lighthouse Holidays ☎ 01445 771263, Ⓦ ruareidh .co.uk. From its spectacular northwest location, this company offers guided walks highlighting wildlife, rock-climbing courses and week-long treks into the Torridon hills.

Vertical Descents ☎ 01855 821593, Ⓦ verticaldescents.com. Ideally located for the Glencoe and Fort William area, activities and courses include canyoning, "funyakking" (a type of rafting) and climbing.

Walkabout Scotland ☎ 0845 686 1344, Ⓦ walkaboutscotland .com. A great way to get a taste of hiking in Scotland, from exploring Ben Lomond to the Isle of Arran. Guided day and weekend walking trips from Edinburgh with all transport included.

Wilderness Scotland ☎ 01479 420020, Ⓦ wildernessscotland .com. Guided, self-guided and customized adventure holidays, and trips that focus on exploring the remote and unspoiled parts of Scotland by foot, bike, sea-kayak, yacht and even on skis.

Winter sports

Skiing and **snowboarding** take place at five different locations in Scotland – Glen Coe, the Nevis Range beside Fort William, Glen Shee, the Lecht and the Cairngorms near Aviemore. The resorts can go for months on end through the winter with insufficient snow, then see the approach roads suddenly

MUNRO-BAGGING

In recent years hillwalking in Scotland has become synonymous with "**Munro-bagging**". Munros are the hills in Scotland over 3000ft in height, defined by a list first drawn up by Sir Hugh Munro in 1891. You "bag" a Munro by walking to the top of it, and once you've bagged all 284 you can call yourself a Munroist and let your chiropodist retire in peace.

Sir Hugh's challenge is an enticing one: **3000ft** is high enough to be an impressive ascent but not so high that it's for expert mountaineers only. Nor do you need to aim to do them all – at heart, Munro-bagging is simply about appreciating the great Scottish outdoors. Munros are found across the Highlands and on two of the islands (Mull and Skye), and include many of the more famous and attractive mountains in Scotland.

However, while the Munros by definition include all the highest hills in Scotland, there isn't any quality control, and one of the loudest arguments of critics of the game (known by some as "de-baggers") is that Munro-seekers will plod up a boring pudding of a mountain because it's 3000ft high and ignore one nearby that's much more pleasing but a few feet short of the requisite mark.

Judgement is also required in a few other ways. You do have to be properly equipped, and be aware what you're tackling before you set off – the hills are hazardous in all seasons. But for many the trickiest part of Munro-bagging is getting to grips with the Gaelic pronunciation of some of the hill names. However, as it's bad form not to be able to tell the folk in the pub at the end of the day which hills you've just ticked off, beginners are encouraged to stick to peaks such as Ben Vane or Ben More, and resign themselves to the fact that Beinn Fhionnlaidh (pronounced "Byn Yoonly") and Beinn an Dothaidh (pronounced "Byn an Daw-ee") are for the really experienced.

If you want some training, you can set about the **Corbetts** (hills between 2500 and 2999ft) or even the **Donalds** (lowland hills above 2000ft).

made impassable by a glut of the stuff. When the conditions are good, Scotland's **ski resorts** have piste and off-piste areas that will challenge even the most accomplished alpine or cross-country skier.

Expect to pay up to £35 for a standard day-pass at one of the resorts, or around £110 for a four-day pass; rental of skis or snowboard comes in at around £30 per day, with reductions for multi-day rentals. At weekends, in good weather with decent snow, expect the slopes to be packed with trippers from the central belt, although midweek usually sees queues dissolving. For a comprehensive rundown of all the resorts, including ticket prices and conditions, visit Ⓦ ski.visitscotland.com.

Cross-country skiing (along with the related telemark or Nordic skiing) is becoming increasingly popular in the hills around Braemar near Glenshee and the Cairngorms. The best way to get started or to find out about good routes is to contact an outdoor pursuits company that offers telemark or Nordic rental and instruction; in the Aviemore area try Adventure Scotland or G2 Outdoor (see p.168). Also check out the Huntly Nordic and Outdoor Centre in Huntly, Aberdeenshire (Ⓣ01466 794428, Ⓦnordicski.co.uk/hnoc). For equipment hire, sales or advice for Nordic and ski mountaineering equipment, contact Mountain Spirit (Ⓣ01479 811788, Ⓦmountainspirit.co.uk), located at the southern entrance to Aviemore village.

Pony trekking and horseriding

There are approximately sixty pony-trekking or riding centres across the country, most approved by either the Trekking and Riding Society of Scotland (TRSS; Ⓦridinginscotland.com) or the British Horse Society (BHS; Ⓦbhs.org.uk). As a rule, any centre will offer the option of **pony trekking** (leisurely ambles on sure-footed Highland ponies), **hacking** (for experienced riders who want to go for a short ride at a fast-ish pace) and **trail riding** (over longer distances, for riders who feel secure at a canter). In addition, a network of special horse-and-rider B&Bs means you can ride independently on your own horse.

Cycling and mountain biking

Cycle touring is a great way to see some of the remoter parts of Scotland and navigate city streets. You'll find cycle shops in towns but few dedicated cycle lanes. In the countryside it can be tricky finding spare parts unless you are near one of Scotland's purpose-built mountain-bike trail centres.

Scotland is now regarded as one of the world's top destinations for **off-road mountain biking**. The Forestry Commission has established more than 1150 miles of excellent off-road routes. These are detailed in numerous "Cycling in the Forest" leaflets, available from Forest Enterprise offices. Alternatively, get hold of the *Scottish Mountain Biking Guide* from tourist information centres. Some of the tougher routes are best attempted on full-suspension mountain bikes although the easier (blue/green) trails can be ridden on a standard mountain or road bike. Pocket Mountains also publish a series of compact cycling guides to the country (ⓦpocketmountains.com).

For up-to-date information on long-distance routes, including **The Great Glen Cycle Way**, along with a list of publications detailing specific routes, contact the cyclists campaigning group Sustrans (ⓦsustrans.co.uk), as well as the other organizations listed here (see opposite).

Another option is to shell out on a cycling holiday package. Britain's biggest cycling organization, the **Cycle Touring Club**, or CTC (ⓦctc.org.uk), provides lists of tour operators and rental outlets in Scotland, and supplies members with touring and technical advice, as well as insurance. Visit Scotland's *Cycling in Scotland* brochure is worth getting hold of, with practical advice and suggestions for itineraries around the country. The tourist board's "Cyclists Welcome" scheme gives guesthouses and B&Bs around the country a chance to advertise that they're cyclist-friendly, and able to provide an overnight laundry service, a late meal or a packed lunch.

Travelling with bikes

Transporting your bike **by train** is a good way of getting to the interesting parts of Scotland without a lot of hard pedalling. Bikes are allowed free on mainline East Coast and ScotRail trains, but you need to book the space as far in advance as possible. Bus and coach companies, including National Express and Scottish Citylink, rarely accept cycles unless they are dismantled and boxed. Large towns and tourist centres offer **bike rental**. Expect to pay around £20 per day; more for top-notch mountain bikes. Most outlets also give good discounts for multi-day rents.

CYCLING INFORMATION

Cycle Scotland ☎ 01315 565560, ⓦ cyclescotland.co.uk. Fully organized cycle tours at all levels, with accommodation ranging from campsites to country-house hotels, and a good range of bikes available for rent, from tandems to children's bikes.

Cyclists' Touring Club ☎ 01483 238337, ⓦ ctc.org.uk. Britain's largest cycling organization, and a good source of general advice; their handbook has lists of cyclist-friendly B&Bs and cafés in Scotland. Annual membership £41.

MIDGES AND TICKS

Despite being only just over a millimetre long, and enjoying a life span on the wing of just a few weeks, the **midge** (genus: *culicoides*) – a tiny biting fly prevalent in the Highlands (mainly the west coast) and Islands – is considered to be second only to the weather as the major deterrent to tourism in Scotland. There are more than thirty varieties of midge, though only half of these bite humans. Ninety percent of all midge bites are down to the female *Culicoides impunctatus* or **Highland midge** (the male does not bite), which has two sets of jaws sporting twenty teeth each; she needs a good meal of blood in order to produce eggs.

These persistent creatures can be a nuisance, but some people also have a violent allergic reaction to midge bites. The easiest way to avoid midges is to visit in the winter, since they only appear between April and October. Midges also favour still, damp, overcast or shady conditions and are at their meanest around sunrise and sunset, when clouds of them can descend on an otherwise idyllic spot. Direct sunlight, heavy rain, noise and smoke discourage them to some degree, though wind is the most effective means of dispersing them. If they appear, cover up exposed skin and get your hands on some kind of repellent. Recommendations include Autan, Eureka!, Jungle Formula (widely available from pharmacists) and the herbal remedy citronella. An alternative to repellents for protecting your face, especially if you're walking or camping, is a **midge net**, a little like a beekeeper's hat; though they appear ridiculous at first, you're unlikely to care as long as they work. The latest deployment in the battle against the midge is a gas-powered machine called a "midge magnet" which sucks up the wee beasties and is supposed to be able to clear up to an acre; each unit costs £520 and upwards, but there's been a healthy take-up by pubs with beer gardens and by campsite owners.

If you're walking through long grass or bracken, there's a possibility that you may receive attention from **ticks**, tiny parasites no bigger than a pin head, which bury themselves into your skin. Removing ticks by dabbing them with alcohol, butter or oil is now discouraged; the medically favoured way of extracting them is to pull them out carefully with small tweezers. There is a very slight risk of catching some nasty diseases, such as encephalitis, from ticks. If flu-like symptoms persist after a tick bite, you should see a doctor immediately.

STAYING SAFE IN THE HILLS

Due to rapid weather changes, the **mountains** are potentially extremely **dangerous** and should be treated with respect. Every year, in every season, climbers and walkers lose their lives in the Scottish hills.

- Wear sturdy, ankle-supporting **footwear** and wear or carry with you warm, brightly coloured and **waterproof** layered clothing, even for what appears to be an easy expedition in apparently settled weather.
- Always carry adequate **maps**, a **compass** (which you should know how to use), food, water and a whistle. If it's sunny, make sure you use **sun protection**.
- Check the **weather forecast** before you go. If the weather looks as if it's closing in, get down from the mountain fast.
- Always **leave word** with someone of your route and what time you expect to return, and remember to contact the person again to let them know that you are back.
- In an emergency, call **mountain rescue** on ☎ 999.

Forestry Commission ☎ 0845 367 3787, ⓦ forestry.gov.uk/mtbscotland. The best source of information on Scotland's extensive network of forest trails – ideal for mountain biking at all levels of ability.

Full On Adventure ☎ 01479 420123, ⓦ fullonadventure.co.uk. Among its many offerings, provides fully guided mountain-bike tours of Highland trails.

Highland Wildcat Trails ⓦ highlandwildcat.com. Scotland's most northerly dedicated mountain-bike centre, complete with one of the country's longest downhill tracks.

Nevis Range ⓦ ridefortwilliam.co.uk. For information on all the trails around Fort William, including the home of Scotland's World Cup downhill and cross-country tracks at Nevis Range.

North Sea Cycle Route ⓦ www.northsea-cycle.com. Signposted 3725-mile (6000km) route round seven countries fringing the North Sea, including 772 miles (1242km) in Scotland along the east coast, and in Orkney and Shetland.

Spokes ☎ 01313 132114, ⓦ spokes.org.uk. Active Edinburgh cycle campaign group with plenty of good links, and news on events and cycle-friendly developments.

WolfTrax Mountain Bike Centre ☎ 01528 544786, ⓦ www.forestry.gov.uk/wolftrax. This Central Highland bike centre near Newtonmore has almost 22 miles of routes for every standard of rider.

Golf

There are over four hundred golf courses in Scotland, where the game is less elitist and more accessible than anywhere else in the world. **Golf** took shape in the fifteenth century on the dunes of Scotland's east coast, and today you'll find some of the oldest courses in the world on these early coastal sites, known as "links". It's often possible just to turn up and play, though it's sensible to phone ahead; booking is essential for the championship courses.

Public courses are owned by the local council, while **private courses** belong to a club. You can play on both – occasionally the private courses require that you are a **member** of another club, and the odd one asks for introductions from a member, but these rules are often waived for overseas visitors and all you need to do is pay a one-off fee. The cost of a round will set you back around £15 on a small nine-hole course, and more than £50 on many good-quality eighteen-hole courses. In remote areas the courses are sometimes unstaffed; just put the admission fee into the honesty box.

Scotland's championship courses, which often host the British Open, are renowned for their immaculately kept greens and challenging holes and, though they're favoured by serious players, anybody with a valid handicap certificate can enjoy them. The most famous course in the Highland region is at **Royal Dornoch** in Sutherland (ⓦ royaldornoch.com; £100). Otherwise, see ⓦ scotlands-golf-courses.com.

Fishing

Scotland's serrated **coastline** – with the deep sea lochs of the west, the firths of the east and the myriad offshore islands – ranks among the cleanest coasts in Europe. Combine this with an abundance of salmon, sea trout, brown trout and pike, acres of open space and easy access, and you have a wonderful location for game-, coarse- or sea-fishing.

No licence is needed to fish in Scotland, although nearly all land is privately owned and its fishing therefore controlled by a landlord/lady or his/her agent. Permission, however, is usually easy to obtain: permits can be bought at local tackle shops, rural post offices or through fishing clubs in the area – if in doubt, ask at the nearest tourist office. Salmon and sea trout have strict **seasons**, which usually stretch from late August to late February. Individual tourist offices will know the precise dates, or see Visit Scotland's excellent *Fish Scotland* brochure (W fishpal.com/VisitScotland). For more information and contacts see W fishscotland.co.uk.

Watersports

Opportunities for **sailing** are outstanding and tainted only by the unreliability of the weather. Even in summer, the full force of the North Atlantic can be felt, and changeable conditions combined with tricky tides and rocky shores demand good sailing and navigational skills. Yacht charters are available from various ports, either bareboat or in yachts run by a skipper and crew; contact Sail Scotland (W sailscotland.co.uk) or the Association of Scottish Yacht Charterers (W asyc.co.uk).

An alternative way to enjoy Scotland under sail is to spend a week at one of the sailing schools. Many schools, as well as small boat-rental operations dotted along the coast, rent sailing dinghies by the hour or day, as well as **windsurfing gear**, though the chilly water means you'll always need a wetsuit. The Hebridean island of Tiree is internationally renowned for its beaches and waves and has an excellent surf, windsurfing and kitesurfing school, Wild Diamond Watersports (W surfschoolscotland.co.uk).

In recent years **sea-kayaking** has witnessed an explosion in popularity, with a host of operators offering sea-kayaking lessons and expeditions across the country. Canoe Scotland (W canoe scotland.org) offers useful advice, while Glenmore Lodge (W glenmorelodge.org.uk), Uist Outdoor Centre (W seakayakouterhebrides.co.uk) and Skyak Adventures (W skyakadventures.com) are highly reputable for either training or tours.

Surfing

In addition to sea-kayaking, Scotland is fast gaining a reputation as a **surfing** destination. However, the northern coastline lies on the same latitude as Alaska and Iceland, so the water temperature is very low: even in midsummer it rarely exceeds 15°C, and in winter can drop to as low as 7°C. The one vital accessory, therefore, is a good wet suit (ideally a 5/3mm steamer), wet-suit boots and, outside summer, gloves and a hood, too.

Many of the best spots are surrounded by stunning scenery, and you'd be unlucky to share the waves with other surfers. However, this isolation – combined with the cold water and big, powerful waves – means that many of the best locations can only be enjoyed by experienced surfers. If you're a beginner, consider a lesson with a qualified coach such as Craig "Suds" Sutherland at Wild Diamond

Watersports in Tiree (T 07793 063849, W surfschool scotland.co.uk).

Surf shops rent or sell equipment and provide good information about local breaks and events on the surfing scene. Two further sources of information are *Surfing Britain and Ireland* by Nelson/Taylor (Footprint; £14.99), which details breaks around Scotland, and the Surfing Great Britain website (W surfinggb.com).

SURF SHOPS AND SCHOOLS

Tempest Surf Riverside Road, Thurso T 01847 892500. At the harbourside, you'll find lessons, a shop and a café that may tempt you to remain snug indoors.

Wild Diamond Watersports Isle of Tiree T 07793 063849, W surfschoolscotland.co.uk. Professional instruction and hire for surfing, windsurfing, kitesurfing and kayaking.

Travel essentials

Costs

Scotland is a relatively **expensive** place to visit, with travel, food and accommodation costs higher than the EU average. The minimum expenditure for a couple travelling on public transport, self-catering and camping, is in the region of £30 each a day, rising to around £50 per person a day if you're staying at hostels and eating the odd meal out. Staying at budget B&Bs, eating at unpretentious restaurants and visiting the odd tourist attraction, means spending at least £75 each per day. If you're renting a car, staying in comfortable B&Bs or hotels and eating well, you should reckon on at least £100 a day per person.

Crime and personal safety

The **crime rate** in the Scottish Highlands and Islands is very low indeed. Even the largest urban centre, Inverness, sees very few offences committed. Out on the islands, the situation is often even more tranquil: until a fight at a wedding in 2010, the Isle of Muck (population 27) managed 50 years without a single reported crime.

Discounts

Most attractions in Scotland offer **concessions** for senior citizens, the unemployed, full-time students and children under 16, with under-5s being admitted free almost everywhere – proof of eligibility will be required in most cases. Family tickets are often available for those travelling with kids.

HISTORIC SCOTLAND AND NATIONAL TRUST FOR SCOTLAND

Many of Scotland's most treasured sights – from castles and country houses to islands, gardens and tracts of protected landscape – come under the control of the privately run **National Trust for Scotland** (ⓦnts.org.uk) or the state-run **Historic Scotland** (ⓦhistoric -scotland.gov.uk); we've quoted "**NTS**" or "**HS**" respectively for each site reviewed in this guide. Both organizations charge an admission fee for most places, and these can be quite high, especially for the more grandiose NTS estates.

If you think you'll be visiting more than half a dozen NTS properties, or more than a dozen HS ones, it's worth taking **annual membership**, which costs around £48 (HS) or £50 (NTS), and allows free admission to their properties. In addition, both the NTS and HS offer short-term passes: the NTS has the **Discovery Ticket**, which costs between £25 for an adult ticket lasting three days to £70 for a family ticket lasting fourteen days; and HS's **Explorer Pass**, ranging from £29 for three days (out of five) to £76 for seven days (out of fourteen) for a family.

Once obtained, **youth/student ID cards** soon pay for themselves in savings. Full-time students are eligible for the International Student Identity Card or **ISIC** (ⓦisiccard.com), which costs around £12 and entitles the bearer to special air, rail and bus fares, and discounts at museums, theatres and other attractions. If you're not a student, but you're 25 or younger, you can get an International Youth Travel Card or **IYTC**, which costs the same as the ISIC and carries the same benefits.

Electricity

The current in Scotland is the **EU standard** of approximately 230v AC. All sockets are designed for British three-pin plugs, which are totally different from the rest of the EU. Adapters are widely available at airports and electronics stores.

Emergencies

For **police**, **fire** and **ambulance** services phone ☎999.

Entry requirements

Citizens of all European countries – except Albania, Bosnia and Herzegovina, Macedonia, Montenegro, Serbia and all the former Soviet republics (other than the Baltic states) – can enter Britain with just a **passport**, for up to three months (and indefinitely if you're from the EU). Americans, Canadians, Australians and New Zealanders can stay for up to six months, providing they have a return ticket and adequate funds to cover their stay. Citizens of most other countries require a **visa**, obtainable from the British consulate or mission office in the country of application.

Note that visa regulations are subject to frequent changes, so it's always wise to contact the nearest British embassy or high commission before you travel. If you visit ⓦukvisas.gov.uk, you can download the full range of **application forms** and information leaflets and find out the contact details of your nearest embassy or consulate. In addition, an independent charity, the Immigration Advisory Service or IAS (ⓦiasuk.org), offers free and confidential advice to anyone applying for entry clearance into the UK.

If you want to **extend your visa**, you should contact the UK Border Agency (ⓦukba.homeoffice .gov.uk), before the expiry date given in your passport.

Gay and lesbian travellers

While there's **no gay scene** as such out in the Highlands and Islands, nearly three-quarters of Scots have a positive opinion of gay and lesbian people. In more remote areas, and in particular in those areas where religious observance is high, attitudes tend to be more conservative, and gay and lesbian locals are extremely discreet about their sexuality.

Health

Pharmacists (known as chemists in Scotland) can dispense only a limited range of drugs without a doctor's prescription. Most pharmacies are open standard shop hours, though there are also late-night branches in large cities and at 24-hour supermarkets.

If your condition is serious enough, you can turn up at the Accident and Emergency (A&E) department of local **hospitals** for complaints that require immediate attention. Obviously, if it's an absolute emergency, you should ring for an ambulance

(☎999). Air ambulances also operate in remote areas. These services are free to all.

You can get free medical advice from NHS Direct, the health service's 24-hour helpline (☎111, ⓦnhs direct.nhs.uk).

Insurance

Even though EU health-care privileges apply in the UK, it's a good idea to take out **travel insurance** before travelling to cover against theft, loss and illness or injury. For non-EU citizens, it's worth checking whether you are already covered before you buy a new policy. If you need to take out insurance, you might want to consider the travel insurance deal we offer.

Internet

Internet cafés are still found occasionally in the Highlands and Islands, but wi-fi is now the best way to get online, with free networks available at most B&Bs and hostels. If you don't have your own smart-phone, laptop or tablet, the tourist office should be able to help – sometimes they will have an access point – and public libraries often provide cheap or free access.

Laundry

Coin-operated **laundries** are still found in a few Scottish cities and towns, but are becoming less and less common. A wash followed by a spin or tumble dry costs about £3.50; a "service wash" (having your laundry done for you in a few hours) costs about £2 extra. In the more remote regions of Scotland, you'll have to rely on hostel and campsite laundry facilities.

Mail

A stamp for a **first-class letter** to anywhere in the British Isles currently costs 60p and should arrive the next day; second-class letters cost 50p, taking three days. Note that there are now size restrictions: letters over 240 x 165 x 5mm are designated as "Large letters" and are correspondingly more expensive to send. Prices to Europe and the rest of the world vary depending on the size of the item and how quickly you would like it delivered. To get an idea of how much you'll need to spend, check the Royal Mail website (ⓦroyalmail.com/price-finder).

Note, that in many parts of the Highlands and Islands there will only be one or two mail collections each day, often at lunchtime or even earlier. **Stamps** can be bought at post office counters or from newsagents, supermarkets and local shops, although they usually only sell books of four or ten stamps.

For general postal enquiries phone ☎0845 774 0740 (Mon–Fri 8am–6pm, Sat 8am–1pm), or visit the website ⓦroyalmail.com. Most **post offices** are open Monday to Friday 9am–5.30pm and Saturday 9am–12.30pm. In small communities you'll find post office counters operating out of a shop, shed or even a private house and these will often keep extremely **restricted hours**.

Maps

The most comprehensive maps of Scotland are produced by the **Ordnance Survey** or OS (ⓦordnancesurvey.co.uk), renowned for their accuracy and clarity. Scotland is covered by 85 maps in the 1:50,000 (pink) **Landranger** series which show enough detail to be useful for most walkers and cyclists. There's more detail still in the full-colour 1:25,000 (orange) **Explorer** series, which covers Scotland in around 170 maps. The full Ordnance Survey range is only available at a few big-city stores or online, although in any walking district of Scotland you'll find the relevant maps in local shops or tourist offices. If you're planning a walk of more than a couple of hours in duration, or intend to walk in the Scottish hills at all, it is strongly recommended that you carry the relevant OS

ROUGH GUIDES TRAVEL INSURANCE

Rough Guides has teamed up with **WorldNomads.com** to offer great travel insurance deals. Policies are available to residents of over 150 countries, with cover for a wide range of adventure sports, 24hr emergency assistance, high levels of medical and evacuation cover, and a stream of travel safety information. **Roughguides.com** users can take advantage of their policies online 24/7, from anywhere in the world – even if you're already travelling. And since plans often change when you're on the road, you can extend your policy and even claim online. Roughguides.com users who buy travel insurance with WorldNomads.com can also leave a positive footprint and donate to a community development project. For more information, go to ⓦroughguides.com/travel-insurance/.

map and familiarize yourself with how to navigate using it.

Virtually every service station in Scotland stocks at least one large-format **road atlas**, covering all of Britain at around three miles to one inch, and generally including larger-scale plans of major towns. For getting between major towns and cities a sat nav or GPS-enabled smartphone is hard to beat, but you'll have less luck in rural areas, where landmarks and even entire roads can be positioned incorrectly, leading to long and sometimes expensive detours.

Money

The basic unit of **currency** in the UK is the pound sterling (£), divided into 100 pence (p). Coins come in denominations of 1p, 2p, 5p, 10p, 20p, 50p, £1 and £2. Bank of England £5, £10, £20 and £50 banknotes are legal tender in Scotland; in addition the **Bank of Scotland** (HBOS), the **Royal Bank of Scotland** (RBS) and the **Clydesdale Bank** issue their own banknotes in all the same denominations, plus a £100 note. All Scottish notes are legal tender throughout the UK, no matter what shopkeepers south of the border might say. In general, few people use £50 or £100 notes, and shopkeepers are likely to treat them with suspicion; fear of forgeries is widespread. At the time of going to press, £1 was worth around $1.50, €1.20, Can$1.60, Aus$1.70 and NZ$1.90. For the most up-to-date exchange rates, check the useful website Ⓦ xe.com.

Credit/debit cards are by far the most convenient way to carry your money, and most hotels, shops and restaurants in Scotland accept the major brand cards. In every sizeable town in Scotland, and in some surprisingly small places too, you'll find a branch of at least one of the big Scottish high-street **banks**, usually with an **ATM** attached. However, on some islands, and in remoter parts, you may find there is only a **mobile bank** that runs to a timetable (usually available from the local post office). General **banking hours** are Monday to Friday from 9 or 9.30am to 4 or 5pm, though some branches are open until slightly later on Thursdays. Post offices charge **no commission**, have longer opening hours, and are therefore often a good place to change money and cheques. Lost or stolen credit/debit cards should be reported to the police and the following numbers: MasterCard ☏ 0800 964767; Visa ☏ 0800 891725.

Opening hours and public holidays

Traditional **shop hours** in Scotland are Monday to Saturday 9am to 5.30 or 6pm. In the bigger towns,

many places now stay open on Sundays and late at night on Thursdays or Fridays. Large supermarkets typically stay open till 8pm or 10pm and a few manage 24-hour opening (excluding Sunday). However, there are also plenty of towns and villages where you'll find very little open on a Sunday, and in the Outer Hebrides in particular, the Sabbath is strictly observed. Many small towns across the Highlands and Islands also retain an **"early closing day"** – often Wednesday – when shops close at 1pm. In the Highlands and Islands you'll find precious few attractions open outside the tourist season (Easter to Oct), though ruins, parks and gardens are normally accessible year-round. Note that last entrance can be an hour (or more) before the published closing time.

Phones

Public **payphones** are still occasionally found in the Highlands and Islands, though with the ubiquity of mobile phones, they're seldom used.

If you're taking your **mobile phone** with you to Scotland, check with your service provider whether your phone will work abroad and what the call charges will be. The cost of calls within the EU has decreased significantly within recent years, but calls to destinations further afield are still unregulated and can be prohibitively expensive. Unless you have a tri-band phone, it's unlikely that a mobile bought for use in the US will work outside the States and vice versa. Mobiles in Australia and New Zealand generally use the same system as the UK so should work fine. All the main UK networks cover the Highlands and Islands, though you'll still find many places in among the hills or out on the islands where there's **no signal** at all. If you're in a rural area and having trouble with reception, simply ask a local where the strongest signals are found nearby.

PUBLIC HOLIDAYS

Official **bank holidays** in Scotland operate on: January 1 and 2; Good Friday; the first and last Monday in May; the last Monday in August; St Andrew's Day (Nov 30); Christmas Day (Dec 25); and Boxing Day (Dec 26). In addition, all Scottish towns have one-day holidays in spring, summer and autumn – dates vary from place to place but normally fall on a Monday. While many local shops and businesses close on these days, few tourist-related businesses observe the holidays, particularly in the summer months.

Beware of premium-rate numbers, which are common for pre-recorded information services – and usually have the prefix ☎09.

Time

Greenwich Mean Time (GMT) – equivalent to Co-ordinated Universal Time (UTC) – is used from the end of October to the end of March; for the rest of the year the country switches to **British Summer Time** (BST), one hour ahead of GMT.

Tipping

There are no fixed rules for **tipping**. If you think you've received good service, particularly in restaurants or cafés, you may want to leave a tip of ten percent of the total bill (unless service has already been included). It's not normal, however, to leave tips in pubs, although bar staff are sometimes offered drinks, which they may accept in the form of money. The only other occasions when you'll be expected to tip are in hairdressers, taxis and smart hotels, where porters, bellboys and table waiters rely on being tipped to bump up their often dismal wages.

Tourist information

The official tourist board is known as **VisitScotland** (🌐visitscotland.com) and they run **tourist offices** (often called Visitor Information Centres, or even "VICs") in virtually every Scottish town. Opening hours are often fiendishly complex and often change at short notice.

As well as being stacked full of souvenirs and other gifts, most TICs have a decent selection of leaflets, displays, maps and books relating to the local area. The staff are usually helpful and will do their best to help with enquiries about accommodation, local transport, attractions and restaurants, although it's worth being aware that they're sometimes reluctant to divulge information about local attractions or accommodation options that are not paid-up members of the Tourist Board, and a number of perfectly decent guesthouses and the like choose not to pay the fees.

Travellers with disabilities

Scottish attitudes towards travellers with **disabilities** still lag behind advances towards independence

---

> ## PHONING HOME
> **To Australia** ☎0061 + area code without the zero + number
> **To Ireland** ☎00353 + area code without the zero + number
> **To New Zealand** ☎0064 + area code without the zero + number
> **To South Africa** ☎0027 + area code without the zero + number
> **To US and Canada** ☎001 + area code + number

---

made in North America and Australia. Access to many public buildings has improved, with legislation ensuring that all new buildings have appropriate facilities. Some hotels and a handful of B&Bs have one or two adapted rooms, usually on the ground floor and with step-free showers, grab rails and wider doorways. It's worth keeping in mind, however, that installing ramps, lifts, wide doorways and disabled toilets is impossible in many of Scotland's older and historic buildings.

Most **trains** in Scotland have wheelchair lifts and assistance is, in theory, available at all manned stations – for more, go to 🌐scotrail.co.uk and click on "Facilities". Wheelchair-users and blind or partially sighted people are automatically given thirty to forty percent reductions on train fares, and people with other disabilities are eligible for the **Disabled Persons Railcard** (£20/year; 🌐disabledpersons-railcard.co.uk), which gives a third off most tickets. There are no bus discounts for disabled tourists. **Car rental** firm Avis will fit their cars with Lynx Hand Controls for free as long as you give them a few days' notice.

For more information and advice, contact the disability charity Capability Scotland (☎0131 313 5510, 🌐capability-scotland.org.uk).

Working in Scotland

All Swiss nationals and EEA citizens can work in Scotland without a permit, though Bulgarian, Croatian and Romanian nationals may need to apply for permission. Other nationals need a **work permit** in order to work legally in the UK, with eligibility worked out on a points-based system. There are exceptions to the above rules, and these are constantly changing, so for the latest regulations visit 🌐ukvisas.gov.

Argyll

SUNBATHER ON GOAT FELL

1

Argyll

Cut off for centuries from the rest of Scotland by the mountains and sea lochs that characterize the region, Argyll remains remote, its scatter of offshore islands forming part of the Inner Hebridean archipelago (the remaining Hebrides are dealt with in chapters 5 and 6). Geographically as well as culturally, this is a transitional area between Highland and Lowland, boasting a rich variety of scenery, from lush, subtropical gardens warmed by the Gulf Stream to flat and treeless islands on the edge of the Atlantic. And it's these islands that are the real magnet, from magnificent sea-bound wildlife to endless walking possibilities and some of the world's finest whiskies. It's in the folds and twists of the countryside, the interplay of land and water and the views out to the islands that the strengths and beauties of mainland Argyll lie.

Much of mainland Argyll comprises remote peninsulas separated by a series of long sea lochs. The first peninsula you come to from Glasgow is **Cowal**, cut off from the rest of Argyll by a series of mountains including the Arrochar Alps. Nestling in one of Cowal's sea lochs is the **Isle of Bute**, whose capital, Rothesay, is probably the most appealing of the old Clyde steamer resorts. **Kintyre**, the long finger of land that stretches south towards Ireland, is less visually dramatic than Cowal, though it does provide a stepping stone for several islands, including Arran.

Arran, Scotland's most southerly big island – now strictly speaking part of North Ayrshire – is justifiably popular, with spectacular scenery ranging from the granite peaks of the north to the Lowland pasture of the south. Of Argyll's Hebridean islands, mountainous **Mull** is the most visited, though it's large enough to absorb the crowds, many of whom are only passing through en route to the tiny isle of **Iona**, a centre of Christian culture since the sixth century, or to **Tobermory**, the island's impossibly picturesque port (aka "Balamory"). Beautiful **Islay** draws the crowds primarily because of its fantastic whisky distilleries, while neighbouring **Jura** offers excellent walking opportunities. And, for those seeking further solitude, there's the island of **Colonsay**, with its beautiful golden sands, and the windswept islands of **Tiree** and **Coll**, which also boast great beaches and enjoy more sunny days than anywhere else in Scotland.

If you can, avoid **July** and **August**, when the crowds on Mull, Iona and Arran are at their densest – there's no guarantee the weather will be any better than during the rest

Highlights

❶ Loch Fyne Oyster Bar, Cairndow Dine in or take away at Scotland's finest smokehouse and seafood outlet. **See p.56**

❷ Mount Stuart, Bute Architecturally overblown mansion set in the most beautiful grounds in the region. **See p.61**

❸ Tobermory, Mull The archetypal fishing village ranged around a sheltered harbour and backed by steep hills. **See p.74**

❹ Boat trip to Staffa and the Treshnish Isles Visit the "basalt cathedral" of Fingal's Cave, and then picnic amid puffins on the Isle of Lunga. **See p.79**

❺ Golden beaches Kiloran Bay on Colonsay is one of the most perfect sandy beaches in Argyll, but there are plenty more on Islay, Coll and Tiree. **See p.90**

❻ Isle of Gigha The ideal island-scape: sandy beaches, friendly folk and the azaleas of Achamore Gardens – you can even stay at the laird's house. **See p.102**

❼ Goat Fell, Arran An easy climb rewarded by spectacular views over craggy peaks to the Firth of Clyde. **See p.110**

❽ Whisky distilleries, Islay With eight, often beautifully situated, distilleries to choose from, Islay is the ultimate whisky-lover's destination. **See p.115**

HIGHLIGHTS ARE MARKED ON THE MAP ON PP.52–53

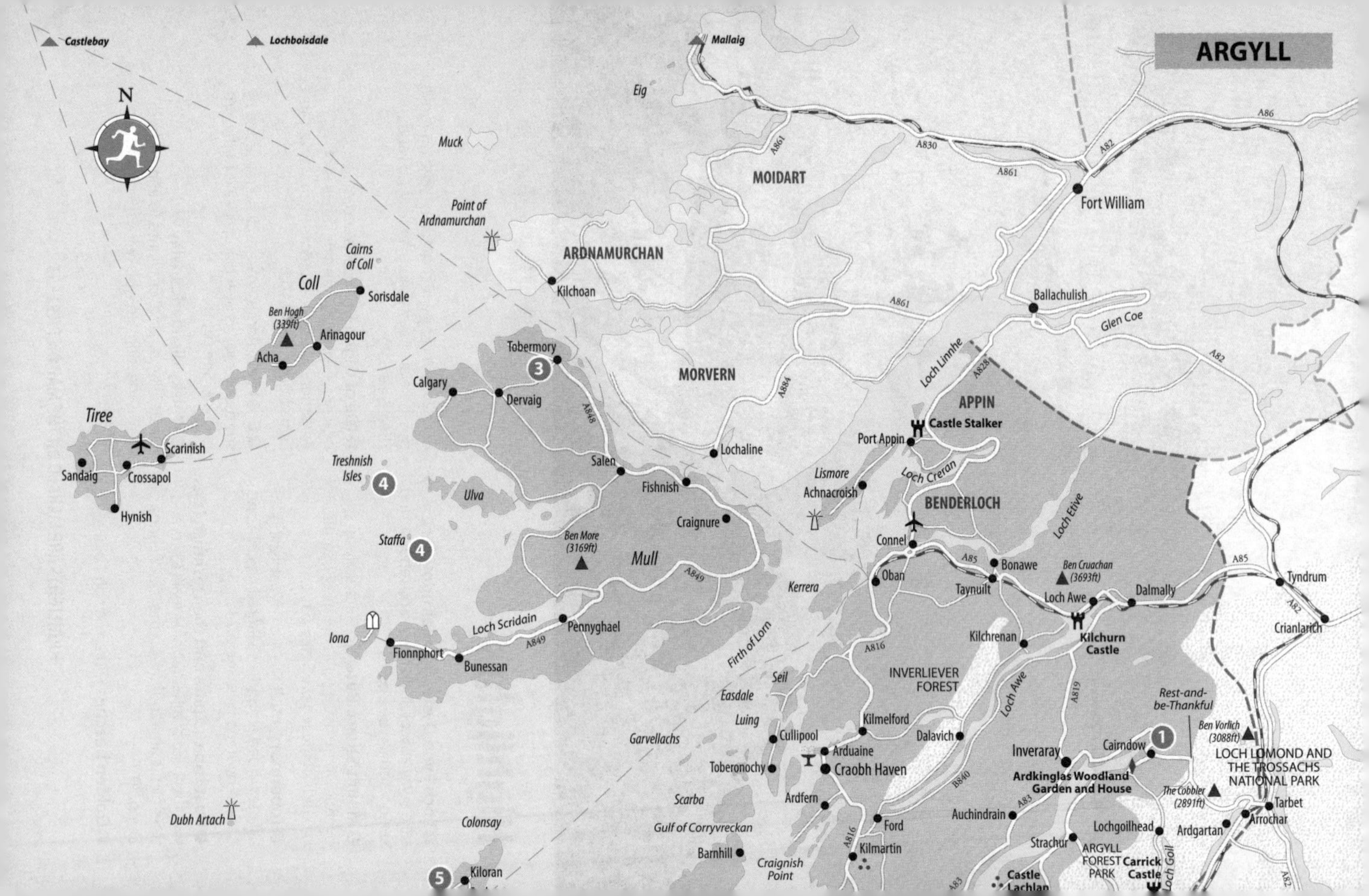
ARGYLL
Castlebay
Lochboisdale
Mallaig
N
Eig
Muck
MOIDART
Point of Ardnamurchan
ARDNAMURCHAN
Kilchoan
Fort William
Ballachulish
Glen Coe
Cairns of Coll
Coll
Sorisdale
Ben Hogh (339ft)
Arinagour
Acha
Tobermory
3
MORVERN
Calgary
Dervaig
Tiree
Scarinish
Sandaig
Crossapol
Hynish
Treshnish Isles
4
Ulva
Salen
Fishnish
Lochaline
Loch Linnhe
APPIN
Castle Stalker
Port Appin
Lismore
Achnacroish
Loch Creran
BENDERLOCH
Loch Etive
Craignure
Ben More (3169ft)
Mull
Staffa
Connel
Oban
Bonawe
Taynuilt
Ben Cruachan (3693ft)
Loch Awe
Dalmally
Tyndrum
Crianlarich
Kilchurn Castle
Kerrera
Kilchrenan
Iona
Fionnphort
Bunessan
Loch Scridain
Pennyghael
Firth of Lorn
Seil
Easdale
Luing
INVERLIEVER FOREST
Rest-and-be-Thankful
Ben Vorlich (3088ft)
LOCH LOMOND AND THE TROSSACHS NATIONAL PARK
Garvellachs
Cullipool
Kilmelford
Dalavich
Inveraray
Cairndow
1
Arduaine
Craobh Haven
Toberonochy
Ardkinglas Woodland Garden and House
The Cobbler (2891ft)
Tarbet
Arrochar
Scarba
Ardfern
Auchindrain
Lochgoilhead
Ardgartan
Dubh Artach
Colonsay
Gulf of Corryvreckan
Ford
Strachur
ARGYLL FOREST PARK
Carrick Castle
Loch Goil
Barnhill
Kilmartin
Craignish Point
Castle Lachlan
Kiloran
5
A86
A82
A830
A861
A828
A884
A848
A849
A85
A816
A819
B840
A83

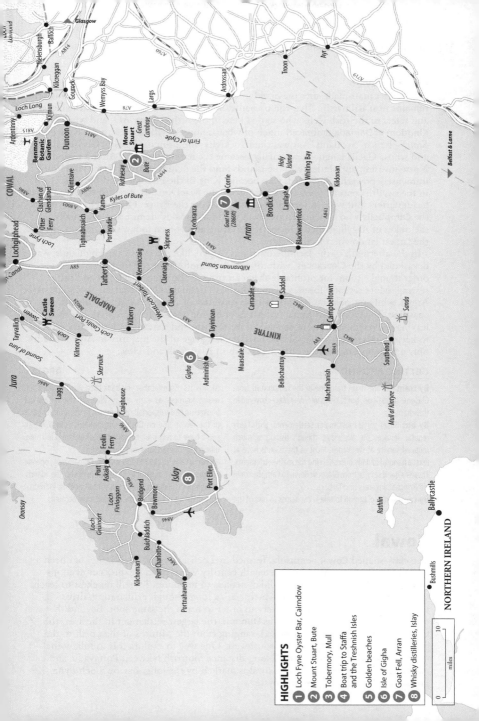

HIGHLIGHTS

1. Loch Fyne Oyster Bar, Cairndow
2. Mount Stuart, Bute
3. Tobermory, Mull
4. Boat trip to Staffa and the Treshnish Isles
5. Golden beaches
6. Isle of Gigha
7. Goat Fell, Arran
8. Whisky distilleries, Islay

NORTHERN IRELAND

1

of the year, and you might have more chance of avoiding the persistent **Scottish midge** (see p.41).

Brief history

The earliest man-made sites preserved in Argyll are the cluster of **Celtic** and **prehistoric remains** near Kilmartin. The region's name, however, means "Boundary of the Gaels", and refers to the Irish Celts who settled here in the fifth century AD, and whose **Kingdom of Dalriada** embraced much of what is now Argyll. Known to the Romans as *Scotti* – hence "Scotland" – it was the Irish Celts who promoted Celtic Christianity, and whose Gaelic language eventually became the national tongue. After a period of Norse invasion and settlement, the islands (and the peninsula of Kintyre) fell to the immensely powerful Somerled, who became King of the Hebrides and Lord of Argyll in the twelfth century. Somerled's successors, the MacDonalds, established Islay as their headquarters, but were in turn dislodged by Robert the Bruce. Of Bruce's allies, it was the **Campbells** who benefited most from the MacDonalds' demise and eventually, as the dukes of Argyll, gained control of the entire area – even today, they remain one of the largest landowners in the region.

In the aftermath of the Jacobite uprisings, Argyll, like the rest of the Highlands, was devastated by the **Clearances**, with thousands of crofters evicted from their homes in order to make room for profitable sheep farming – "the white plague" – and cattle rearing. More recently forestry plantations have dramatically altered the landscape of Argyll, while purpose-built marinas have sprouted all around the heavily indented coastline. Today the traditional industries of fishing and farming are in deep crisis, leaving the region ever more dependent on tourism and a steady influx of new settlers to keep things going, while Gaelic, once the language of the majority in Argyll, retains only a tenuous hold on the outlying islands of Islay, Coll and Tiree.

GETTING AROUND — ARGYLL

By train The one main train-line in the region runs from Glasgow up to Oban, but takes in very few places covered in this chapter.

By bus Buses serve most major settlements, with fairly regular services on weekdays, though usually a much reduced service at weekends. Most of the islands have at least a handful of daily buses serving the main settlements. There's a good service from Glasgow down to Campbeltown via Arrochar, Inverary and Tarbert.

By car If you're planning to take a car across to one of the islands, it's essential that you book both your outward and return journeys as early as possible, as the ferries get booked up early, especially in summer. In the remoter parts of the region and on the islands, without your own car, you'll have to rely on a combination of walking, hitching, bike rental, shared taxis and the postbus.

By ferry CalMac (☎ 0800 066 5000, ⍈ calmac.co.uk) operate a comprehensive timetable of ferries between the islands, though this is reduced during the winter months. Individual ferry crossings are given in the relevant town accounts.

Cowal

The claw-shaped **Cowal** peninsula, formed by Loch Fyne and Loch Long, has been a popular destination since the nineteenth century when rapid steamer connections brought hordes of Glaswegian holiday-makers to its shores. It's still quickest to reach Cowal by ferry across the Clyde – by car, it's a long, though exhilarating, drive through some rich Highland scenery in order to reach the same spot. Beyond the old-fashioned coastal towns such as **Dunoon**, the largest settlement in the area, the Cowal landscape is extremely varied, ranging from the Munros of the north to the gentle, low-lying coastline of the southwest. One way to explore it is to follow the 47-mile **Cowal Way**, a waymarked long-distance footpath between Portavadie and Ardgartan. The western edge of Cowal is marked by the long, narrow Loch Fyne, famous for both its kippers and oysters.

1

CLIMBING THE COBBLER

The jagged, triple-peaked ridge of Ben Arthur (2891ft) – better known as **The Cobbler** because of its resemblance to a cobbler bent over his work – is the most enticing of the peaks within the Argyll Forest Park. It's surprisingly accessible, with the most popular route starting from the car park at Succoth, on the road to Ardgartan. Skirting the woods, you join the Allt a'Bhalachain, which climbs steeply up to the col between the northern peak (known as The Cobbler's Wife) and The Cobbler itself. Traversing the ridge in order to ascend one or all of the three peaks is a tricky business, and the final scramble should only be attempted by experienced hikers. The total distance of the climb is only five miles, but the return trip will probably take you between five and six hours.

Arrochar and around

Approaching by road from Glasgow, the entry point to Cowal is **Arrochar**, at the head of Loch Long. The village itself is ordinary enough, but the area has the peninsula's most grandiose scenery, including the ambitiously named **Arrochar Alps**, whose peaks offer some of the best climbing in Argyll: Ben Ime (3318ft) is the tallest of the range, while Ben Arthur or "The Cobbler" (2891ft), named after the anvil-like rock formation at its summit, is the most distinctive (see box, p.55).

Heading west from Arrochar, you climb **Glen Croe**, a strategic hill-pass whose saddle is called – for obvious reasons – **Rest-and-be-Thankful**. Here the road forks, with the single-track B828 heading down to **Lochgoilhead**, an isolated village overlooking Loch Goil. A road tracks the west side of the loch, petering out after five miles at the picturesque ruins of **Carrick Castle**, a classic tower-house castle built around 1400 and used as a hunting lodge by James IV. Facing this across the water is a hilly peninsula known as **Argyll's Bowling Green** – no ironic nickname, but an English corruption of the Gaelic *Baile na Greine* (Sunny Hamlet).

Ardkinglas Woodland Garden and House

Just off the A83, behind the village of Cairndow • Daily dawn–dusk; Ardkinglas House visits by guided tour only, April–Oct Fri at 2pm • £4.50; Ardkinglas House £7 • ☎ 01499 600261, ⊕ ardkinglas.com

The wonderful **Ardkinglas Woodland Garden** contains exotic rhododendrons, azaleas, hydrangeas and a superb collection of conifers, including five so-called Champion Trees – those deemed to be the tallest or broadest examples of their kind within Britain. Indeed, the garden is home to what is still the tallest tree in the British Isles, a Grand Fir introduced by David Douglas in 1830 and now standing at a mighty 210ft. Look out, too, for the magnificent Silver Fir (159ft), typically found in Central Europe. Pick up a *Woodland Garden Map* at the entrance to guide you around. In the southern part of the gardens stands **Ardkinglas House**, a particularly handsome Scottish Baronial mansion, built in 1907 by Robert Lorimer for the Noble family.

ARRIVAL AND DEPARTURE | ARROCHAR AND AROUND

By train Arrochar & Tarbet train station is a mile or so east of Arrochar, just off the A83 to Tarbet.
Destinations Glasgow (Mon–Sat 4–5 daily, Sun 3 daily; 1hr 15min).

By bus Buses stop just on the A814 near Church Rd in Arrochar.
Destinations Glasgow (6 daily; 1hr 10min); Inveraray (6 daily; 35min).

ACCOMMODATION AND EATING

Ben Bheula Succoth ☎ 01301 702184, ⊕ benbheula .co.uk. Set back from the head of the loch, in nearby Succoth, this clean, three-bedroom B&B is run by a very friendly couple. **£55**

Fascadail Church Rd, Arrochar ☎ 01301 702344, ⊕ fascadail.com. A Victorian guesthouse set within its own grounds in the quieter southern part of the village, with five colourfully furnished and superbly equipped rooms. Enjoy breakfast in the dining room with glorious views across the garden. **£75**

1

LOCH FYNE OYSTER BAR

Loch Fyne Oyster Bar On the A83 two miles north of Cairndow and eight miles east of Inveraray ☎ 01499 600236, ⓦ loch-fyne.com. On the shores of Loch Fyne sits the *Loch Fyne Oyster Bar*, which spawned the Loch Fyne chain of restaurants. The food is utterly delicious and beautifully thought out, from the chilled crab gazpacho and salmon ceviche (£9.50), to grilled halibut (£21) and hand-dived Islay scallops (£16.50). The restaurant itself oozes class, though it's anything but stuffy, and there's also a superb marble-topped oyster bar where you can tuck into prawns, clams, cockles and heaps of other tasty wet stuff. The gorgeous on-site shop/deli is a great place to assemble a gourmet picnic. Daily 9am–10pm; reservations advised.

Village Inn In the southern part of Arrochar ☎ 01301 702279. If you need a bite to eat, head for the *Village Inn*, which has tables outside overlooking the loch as well as a cosy real-ale bar. Daily 10am–midnight.

Dunoon

The principal entry point into Cowal by sea is **Dunoon**. In the nineteenth century it grew from a village to a major Clyde seaside resort and favourite holiday spot for Glaswegians, but nowadays there's little to tempt you to stay, particularly with attractive countryside beckoning just beyond. That said, it is worth visiting on the last weekend in August, when the famous **Cowal Highland Gathering** (ⓦ cowalgathering.com) takes place here. The largest event of its kind in the world, it culminates in the awesome spectacle of the massed pipes and drums of more than 150 bands marching through the streets.

Castle House Museum

Castle Gardens • Easter–Oct Mon–Sat 10.30am–4.30pm, Sun 2–4.30pm • £2 • ☎ 01369 701422, ⓦ castlehousemuseum.org.uk

The centre of town is dominated by a grassy lump of rock known as **Castle Hill**, crowned by Castle House, built in the 1820s by a wealthy Glaswegian and the subject of a bitter dispute with the local populace over closure of the common land around his house. The people eventually won, and the grounds remain open to the public to this day, as does the house, which is home to the **Castle House Museum**. There's some good hands-on nature stuff for kids, and an excellent section on the Clyde steamers, as well as information about "Highland Mary", betrothed to Rabbie Burns (despite the fact that he already had a pregnant wife), who died of typhus before the pair could see through their plan to elope to the West Indies. A statue of her is in the grounds.

ARRIVAL AND INFORMATION   DUNOON

By ferry There are two 20-minute ferry crossings across the Clyde from Gourock to Dunoon. The more frequent service is on Western Ferries (☎ 01369 704452, ⓦ western-ferries.co.uk) to Hunter's Quay, a mile north of the town centre. CalMac's ferries (☎ 0800 066 5000, ⓦ calmac.co.uk) arrive at the main pier, and have better transport connections if you're on foot.
Destinations Gourock–Dunoon (hourly; 20min); McInroy's Point–Hunter's Quay (every 30min; 20min).

By bus Buses stop on Alexandra Parade, not far from the main pier.
Destinations Colintraive (Mon–Sat 2–3 daily; 1hr); Inveraray (Mon–Sat 3 daily; 1hr 10min).
Tourist office On Alexandra Parade, a five-minute walk from the CalMac terminal (Easter–Oct daily 9am–5pm; Nov–Easter Mon–Sat 10am–4pm; ☎ 01369 703785, ⓦ visitcowal.co.uk).

ACCOMMODATION AND EATING

Abbot's Brae West Bay ☎ 01369 705021, ⓦ abbots brae.co.uk. The welcoming *Abbot's Brae* is a beautiful family-run Victorian villa set in woods above West Bay with lovely views over the Clyde. The eight spacious rooms hold photographs depicting local history. **£75**
Chatters 58 John St ☎ 01369 706402, ⓦ chatters dunoon.co.uk. Despite its unappealing location next to a supermarket, this is Dunoon's one real restaurant of merit, offering delicious meat dishes like pan-fried wood pigeon on couscous (£9) and roast saddle of lamb (£19.50). Tues noon–3pm, Wed–Sat noon–3pm & 6–11pm.

Benmore Botanic Garden

On the A815, seven miles north of Dunoon • Daily: March & Oct 10am–5pm; April–Sept 10am–6pm • £5.50 • ☎ 01369 706261,
ⓦ rbge.org.uk

Serenely pitched amid lush mountain scenery at the foot of Loch Eck, **Benmore Botanic Garden** is an offshoot of Edinburgh's Royal Botanic Garden. It's a beautifully laid-out garden occupying 120 acres of lush hillside, the mild, moist climate allowing a vast range of unusual plants to grow, with different sections devoted to rainforest species native to places as exotic as China, Chile and Bhutan. The garden boasts three hundred species of rhododendron and a memorably striking avenue of great redwoods, planted in 1863 and now over 150ft high. You can also wander through a Victorian fernery, as impressive for its architectural features – notably a fine vaulted entrance, grotto and pool – as for the plants housed within. Look out, too, for "Puck's Hut", designed by the prolific Scottish architect Sir Robert Lorimer. Clad in various timbers and tiled with red cedar, it originally stood in Puck's Glen in the Eachaig Valley, hence the name.

Kyles of Bute

The mellower landscape of southwest Cowal, which stands in complete contrast to the bustle of Dunoon or the Highland grandeur of the Argyll Forest Park, becomes immediate as soon as you head into the area. And there are few more beautiful sights in Argyll than the **Kyles of Bute**, two slivers of water that separate Cowal from the bleak bulk of the Isle of Bute and constitute some of the best sailing territory in Scotland.

Colintraive and Tighnabruaich

Separated from the Isle of Bute by barely more than a couple of hundred yards, **Colintraive**, on the eastern Kyles, is not especially noteworthy, but you may well wind up here as it's where the CalMac car ferry departs to Bute. The most popular spot from which to appreciate the Kyles, however, is along the A8003 as it rises dramatically above the sea lochs before descending to the peaceful, lochside village of **Tighnabruaich**. Peaceful that is, until the local shinty team, Kyles Athletic, takes to the field; founded in 1896, they remain one of the sport's most illustrious names, though success has been hard to come by in recent years. However, their reputation was well and truly restored in 2012 following victory in the Camanachd Cup, Scotland's most prestigious national shinty competition.

ARRIVAL AND ACTIVITIES

BY FERRY

Colintraive Ferries to Bute depart from the ferry slip in the centre of the village.

Portavadie If you're driving to Kintyre, Islay or Jura, you can avoid the long haul around Loch Fyne – some seventy miles or so – by using the ferry to Tarbert from Portavadie, three miles southwest of Kames.

Destinations Portavadie–Tarbert (hourly; 25min);

KYLES OF BUTE

Colintraive–Rhubodach, Bute (every 20–30min; 5min).

BY BUS

Colintraive Buses drop off and pick up by the ferry slipway.

Tighnabruaich Buses stop near the post office.

Destinations Colintraive–Dunoon (Mon–Sat 2–3 daily; 1hr); Colintraive–Tighnabruaich (Mon–Sat 2 daily; 35min); Tighnabruaich–Portavadie (Mon–Sat 3–4 daily; 25min).

WALKING UP PUCK'S GLEN

It's possible to combine a visit to Benmore Botanic Garden with one of the local **forest walks**, the most popular being a leisurely stroll up the rocky ravine of **Puck's Glen**, which begins from the car park a mile south of the gardens. Roughly two miles long, and with a total ascent of some 170 metres, it's a beautiful little walk up a narrow defile enclosed by rocky walls and dense trees, and replete with rushing burns, waterfalls and footbridges.

1

ACTIVITIES

Sailing school The Tighnabruaich Sailing School (☎01700 811717, ⓦtssargyll.co.uk) is located two miles south of the village at Carry Farm; dinghy sailing courses usually last a week, but day-sails are also possible.

ACCOMMODATION AND EATING

Colintraive Hotel South of the ferry slipway, Colintraive ☎01700 841207, ⓦcolintraivehotel.com. A favourite with yachties, the *Colintraive Hotel* is worth seeking out for its four crisply decorated rooms (two with views of the Kyles), as well as its delicious fresh dishes. **£90**

Royal An Lochan Tighnabruaich ☎01700 811239, ⓦtheroyalanlochan.co.uk. There's impressive waterside accommodation at the classy *An Lochan*, which also serves exceptionally good seafood bar meals and has wonderful views over the Kyles. **£125**

Isle of Bute

The island of **Bute** is in many ways simply an extension of the Cowal peninsula, from which it is separated by the narrow Kyles of Bute. Thanks to its mild climate and its ferry link with Wemyss Bay, Bute has been a popular holiday and convalescence spot for Clydesiders for over a century. Its chief town, **Rothesay**, rivals Dunoon as the major seaside resort on the Clyde, easily surpassing it thanks to some splendid Victorian architecture, decent accommodation and eating options and the chance to visit **Mount Stuart**, one of Scotland's most singular aristocratic piles. The Highland–Lowland dividing line passes through Bute, which is all but sliced in two by the freshwater Loch Fad. As a result, the northern half of the island is hilly and uninhabited, while the southern half is made up of Lowland-style farmland. Bute's inhabitants live around the two wide bays on the island's east coast, which resembles one long seaside promenade. To escape the crowds head for the sparsely populated west coast, which, in any case, has the sandiest beaches.

Bute stages a couple of terrific annual events, namely its own **Highland Games Festival** on the third weekend of August, and the **Bute Jazz Festival** over the May Bank Holiday, usually featuring renowned international artists.

ARRIVAL AND DEPARTURE **ISLE OF BUTE**

By ferry Two CalMac ferry services operate from the mainland to Bute; the main one is from Wemyss Bay to Rothesay, and the other is the very short crossing at the northern tip of the island from Colintraive in Cowal to Rhubodach.

Destinations Colintraive–Rhubodach (every 20–30min; 5min); Wemyss Bay–Rothesay (every 45min; 30min).

Rothesay

Bute's only town, **ROTHESAY** is a handsome Victorian resort, set in a wide sweeping bay, backed by green hills, with a classic palm-tree promenade and 1920s pagoda-style pavilion originally built to house the **Winter Gardens**. Though often busy with day-trippers from Glasgow, and in need of a lick of paint here and there, there's plenty that's attractive about the place, with some handsome buildings, a prominent Art Deco pavilion and occasional flourishes of wrought-ironwork.

Pavilion toilets

The Pier • Daily: Easter–Sept 8am–7.45pm; Oct–Easter 9am–4.45pm • 20p

Rothesay's **Victorian toilets**, built in 1899 by Twyfords, are a feast of marble, ceramics and brass so ornate that they're now one of the town's most celebrated sights. The Victorians didn't make provision for ladies' conveniences, so the women's half is a modern add-on, but if the coast is clear the attendant – attired in a neat burgundy waistcoat – will allow ladies a tour of the gents, clad in colourfully painted ceramic tiles and mosaics, and starring an impressive central stand with six urinals; never has the call of nature seemed so attractive.

Rothesay Castle

Castle Hill St • April–Sept daily 9.30am–5.30pm; Oct–March Mon–Wed, Sat & Sun 9.30am–4.30pm • £4.50; HS • ☎ 01700 502691

Rothesay boasts the militarily useless, but architecturally impressive, moated ruins of **Rothesay Castle**, hidden amid the town's backstreets. Built around the twelfth century, it was twice captured by the Norwegians, firstly in 1230, then in 1263; such vulnerability was the reasoning behind the unusual, almost circular, curtain wall, with its four big drum towers, only one of which remains fully intact. Look upwards inside the tower and you'll see a superbly preserved dovecot (with nesting boxes), which was a seventeenth-century addition. The wall was actually heightened in the early sixteenth century – the line of which is clearly identifiable in the

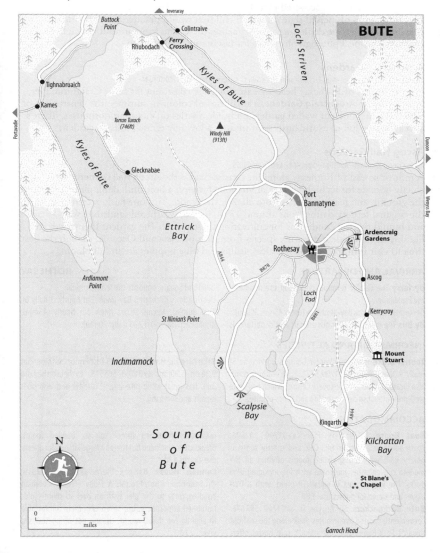

1

stonework: the earlier, lower half comprising light ashlar, the upper half darker and of rougher hew.

Bute Museum

Stuart St • April–Sept Mon–Sat 10.30am–3.30pm, Sun 1.30–3.30pm; Feb, March, Oct & Nov Tues–Thurs & Sat 1.30–3.30pm • £3 • Ⓦ butemuseum.org

At first glance, **Bute Museum**, just up behind the castle, looks like your average, rather dull local-history museum, but it's well worth popping into. Inchmarnock, a tiny island to the west of Bute, provides the greatest source of treasures, not least a stunning beaded necklace made of jet, which belonged to the so-called "Queen of the Inch", whose remains were discovered in a Bronze Age cist in 1961. Look out, too, for some exquisite pieces of incised slate on which children would practice their writing or drawing, such as one depicting horses grazing; these date from around the eighth century. The local photographs make for fascinating viewing too.

Ardencraig Gardens

Ardencraig Lane • May–Sept Mon–Fri 9am–4pm, Sat & Sun 1–4.30pm • Free • ☎ 01700 504644

On the fringes of Rothesay heading east along the coast, not far from Craigmore Pier, you'll come to **Ardencraig Gardens**, a small riot of colour in summer, the centrepiece of which is a magnificent walled garden alongside a series of Victorian hothouses. There's also an aviary full of exotic birds surrounding a lovingly tended hillside garden.

Ascog Hall Gardens

Ascog • Easter–Oct Wed–Sun 10am–5pm • £4 • ☎ 01700 504555

A mile or so east of Rothesay along the coastal road is the **Ascog Hall Gardens**, which is chiefly notable for its highly unusual **Victorian fernery**, a beautiful, dank place, sunk into the ground, and featuring ferns from all over the world. This one fairly recently replaced the original fernery dating from around 1870, its red, weathered sandstone walls, shade and humidity ideal conditions for cultivating these plants. The gardens themselves are likeably dishevelled, and feature species from Europe, Asia and Oceania, though the best time to visit is in spring, when azaleas, tulips and blue poppies are in full bloom.

ARRIVAL AND DEPARTURE

ROTHESAY

By ferry The CalMac terminal is right in the middle of the Esplanade.

Destinations Wemyss Bay–Rothesay (every 45min; 30min).

By bus The main point for bus arrivals and departures is Guildford Square, opposite the ferry terminal.

Destinations Kilchattan Bay (Mon–Sat hourly, 3 daily on Sun; 30min); Mount Stuart (Mon–Sat hourly; 15min); Rhubodach (Mon–Fri 2–3 daily; 20min).

INFORMATION AND ACTIVITIES

Tourist office Inside the Winter Gardens on Victoria St (daily 9.30am–5pm; ☎ 01700 502151, Ⓦ visitbute.com); also located here is the "Discovery Centre", which has some well-presented displays on the life and times of Bute.

Bike hire The Bike Shed, 23–25 East Princes St (Mon–Sat 9.30am–5.30pm; ☎ 01700 505515, Ⓦ thebikeshed.org .uk), has great-value bike hire (£10/day) and also does repairs and servicing.

ACCOMMODATION

Boat House 15 Battery Place ☎ 01700 502696, Ⓦ theboathouse-bute.co.uk. Chic and utterly contemporary B&B with ten sparkling rooms offering all the modern conveniences you could wish for, including iPod docks. The lounge area is equally inviting, with a DVD player and stereo for guests' use. __£80__

Bute Backpackers 36 Argyle St ☎ 01700 501876. Conveniently located five minutes' walk along the seafront towards Port Bannatyne, the island's sole hostel offers reasonably furnished three- to- six bedded rooms. Breakfast not included but there's a large kitchen for guests' use. Dorms __£20__

Cannon House Battery Place ☎ 01700 502819, Ⓦ cannonhousehotel.co.uk. A really elegant Georgian building close to the pier with an ever-so-slightly old-fashioned atmosphere, but seven extremely comfortable (if slightly too floral) rooms, though not all possess sea views. __£70__

EATING AND DRINKING

Musicker 11 High St ☎ 01700 502287. Funky café-cum-music-retailer just across from the castle, with delicious coffee, decent snacks and even better music, courtesy of the rather ace jukebox and occasional live performances. Friday jam sessions at 3pm. Mon–Sat 10am–5pm.

No. 29 29 Gallowgate ☎ 01700 500685, ⓦ no29bute .com. Seared loin of tuna with tomato compote, samphire grass and citrus foam (£17.95) gives you some idea of what to expect from Rothesay's most refined restaurant,

complete with a smart, all-grey interior and impeccably mannered staff. Mon–Sat 6–10pm, Sun 1–10pm.

Squat Lobster The Harbour ☎ 07748 552761. Housed in a mid-nineteenth-century hut that used to be a refuge for horse cabbies, this super chippie next to the putting green doles out freshly caught fish of the day as well as mussels, whelks, langoustines, and the eponymous squat lobster, served with garlic butter (£5.95). Daily noon–8pm.

Mount Stuart

Mount Stuart, 4 miles south of Rothesay • **House** April–Oct; phone for times • £11 **Grounds** Daily 10am–6pm • £6.50 • ☎ 01700 503877, ⓦ mountstuart.com

Bute's most compelling sight is **Mount Stuart**, a huge, fantasy Gothic mansion set amid acres of lush woodland gardens overlooking the Firth of Clyde, and ancestral home of the seventh marquess of Bute, John Crichton-Stuart (or, as he was known in his Formula 1 racing days, Johnny Dumfries). The building was created by the marvellously eccentric, and architecturally brilliant, third marquess Robert Rowand Anderson after a fire in 1877 destroyed the family seat. With little regard for expense, the marquess shipped in tonnes of Italian marble, built a railway line to transport it down the coast and employed craftsmen who had worked with William Burges on the marquess's other medieval concoction, Cardiff Castle. With 127 rooms spread out over five floors, it's on quite some scale.

The *pièce de résistance* is the columned **Marble Hall**, its vaulted ceiling and stained-glass windows decorated with the signs of the zodiac, reflecting the marquess's taste for mysticism. He was equally fond of animal and plant imagery; hence you'll find birds feeding on berries in the dining-room frieze, and monkeys reading (and tearing up) books and scrolls in the library. Look out also for the unusual heraldic ceiling in the drawing room, which is otherwise notable for its astonishing collection of art; casually dotted along the walls, you'll find paintings by Tintoretto, Titian and Veronese, among others. After all the heavy furnishings, seek aesthetic relief in the vast **Marble Chapel**, built entirely out of dazzling white Carrara marble, with a magnificent Cosmati floor pattern. Upstairs, along with three impressive bathrooms, check out the **Horoscope Room**, where you can see a fine astrological ceiling and adjacent observatory/conservatory.

The grounds

There are a number of fine **walks** to be had within the vast **grounds**, ranging from a 45-minute stroll down through the woods to the seashore, to a more vigorous, two-hour walk taking in the **Wee Garden** and **Calvary Pond**, the latter located at the head of a small burn. Before you leave Mount Stuart, take a look at the planned village of **Kerrycroy**, just beyond the main exit. It was built by the second Marquess in the early nineteenth century, allegedly for his wife, Lady Maria North, who was missing

---

JOHNNY DUMFRIES

As unlikely as it seems, the current Marquess of Bute was once a hugely successful **motor racing driver**. Racing as one **Johnny Dumfries** (he was, at that time, the Earl of Dumfries), the marquess began racing in the 1980s, starting out in Formula 3 before graduating to Formula 1 in 1986, racing for the JPS Lotus team as second driver to the legendary Ayrton Senna – he raced fifteen times, compiling three points. Dumfries' greatest achievement, however, came in 1988, when he won the Le Mans 24 Hours as part of the Jaguar team.

1

her home town of Guildford so much that he ordered elements of it to be replicated, hence the semidetached houses – alternately mock-Tudor and whitewashed stone – that form a crescent overlooking a pristine village green and, beyond, the sea.

ACCOMMODATION AND EATING

Mount Stuart ☎ 01700 503877, ⓦ mountstuart.com. Scattered around the estate are four stunning self-catering properties, each one sleeping between four and six. Furnished to impeccably high standards, they've got more than ample space, with bright bedrooms and bathrooms, superb kitchens and cosy open-plan living spaces complete with attractive wood burners. One week **£350**
Mount Stuart restaurant ☎ 01700 505276,

ⓦ mountstuart.com. Located on the second floor of the sleek glass-and-timber visitor centre, Mount Stuart's on-site restaurant is certainly worth making a trek to even if you're not visiting the estate. The majority of ingredients are sourced from the estate's kitchen garden, resulting in scrumptious dishes like seared west-coast scallops with salad leaves in a chilli and coriander dressing (£9.95). Daily: May–Aug 10am–6pm; Sept & Oct 11am–4pm.

Kilchattan Bay and around

Six miles south of Rothesay, east-facing **Kilchattan Bay** has a lovely arc of sand overlooked by a row of grand Victorian houses. The bay is also the starting point for the wonderful **West Island Way Walk**, which runs the complete length of the island for about thirty miles, taking in coastline, farmland, moors and forests.

St Blane's Chapel

Just after the road turns off left to Kilchattan Bay, another road (next to the *Kingarth Hotel*) runs south to the chapel

St Blane's Chapel is a twelfth-century ruin beautifully situated in open countryside amid the foundations of an earlier Christian settlement established in the sixth century by St Catan, uncle to the local-born St Blane. From the car park, it's a short uphill walk through farmland; over the brow of a hill you come upon a well-built churchyard wall surrounded by mature trees. The ruined chapel sits amid a rather peculiar two-tier graveyard, the upper area reserved for the men of the parish while the women were consigned to the lower one.

Scalpsie Bay and around

Four miles up the coast from St Blane's is the sandy strand of **Scalpsie Bay**, which is by far the best spot on the island for **seal watching**. From the small car park on the main road, a footpath runs down to the beach, from where you walk west along the increasingly rocky shore to a couple of excellent viewing points. The many sunken timber posts dotted along the beach are the remains of World War II anti-glider defences, as the area was particularly susceptible to German invasion. Indeed, Scalpsie's military role continued right up until the end of the Cold War; the cottage near the car park was used as a listening post for enemy submarines patrolling the Firth of Clyde.

Further on, beyond the village of Straad, lies **St Ninian's Point**, where the ruins of a sixth-century chapel overlook another fine sandy strand and the uninhabited island of **Inchmarnock** – to which, according to tradition, alcoholics were banished in the nineteenth century. Here, too, a number of superb relics have been uncovered, many of which are now on display in Bute Museum in Rothesay.

> ### BUTE'S HIGHEST PEAKS
> The two highest peaks on the island are **Windy Hill** (913ft) and **Torran Turach** (746ft), both in the north; from the latter, there are fine views of the Kyles, but for a gentler overview of the island you can simply walk up to the **viewpoint**, in the midst of the golf course, on **Canada Hill** just east of Rothesay.

Inveraray

The traditional county town of Argyll, and a classic example of an eighteenth-century planned town, **INVERARAY** was built in the 1770s by the Duke of Argyll, in order to distance his newly rebuilt castle from the hoi polloi in the town and to establish a commercial and legal centre for the region. Inveraray has changed very little since and remains an absolute set-piece of Scottish Georgian architecture, with a truly memorable setting, the brilliant white arches of Front Street reflected in the still waters of Loch Fyne.

Main Street

Despite its picture-book location, there's not much more to Inveraray than its distinctive **Main Street** (perpendicular to Front St), flanked by whitewashed terraces, characterized by black window casements. At the top of the street, the road divides to circumnavigate the town's Neoclassical church: originally the southern half served the Gaelic-speaking community, while the northern half served those who spoke English.

Inveraray Jail

Church Square • Daily: April–Oct 9.30am–6pm; Nov–March 10am–5pm • £8.95 • ☎ 01499 302381, ⓦ inverarayjail.co.uk

The town's most enjoyable attraction is **Inveraray Jail**, comprising an attractive Georgian courthouse and two grim prison blocks that, in their day, were the principal ones in Argyll. The latter both ceased to function in 1889, though the courthouse continued in one form or another until 1954. The jail is now a thoroughly enjoyable **museum**, which graphically recounts prison conditions from medieval times to the twentieth century.

Following a trawl through some of the region's most notorious crimes, you get to listen to a re-enactment of a trial of the period, staged in the original semicircular courthouse of some 170 years ago. More fascinating, though, are the prisons themselves; built in 1820, the Old Prison housed all convicts – men, women, children, the insane – until 1849 when the New Prison was built and whose twelve cells held male prisoners only. In the courtyard stands the minute "Airing Yards", two caged cells where the prisoners got to exercise for an hour a day, though they were forbidden to talk to each other.

Bell Tower

The Avenue • July to mid-Sept Mon–Fri 10.30am–4.30pm • £4 • ⓦ inveraraybelltower.co.uk

The one sight that often gets overlooked in Inveraray is the **Bell Tower**, a magnificent 126ft-high, free-standing structure adjacent to the All Saints Church. The tower was originally built as a war memorial, in honour of members of the Campbell clan (it was commissioned by Niall Campbell, the tenth Duke of Argyll), and not long after its completion, the bells – allegedly the second heaviest peal of ten bells in the world after those in Wells Cathedral – were cast. The bells remain the standout feature of the tower, and you can view these close up as you make your way up the dizzying spiral staircase. Having climbed the last of the 176 steps, you are rewarded with superlative views of Loch Fyne and the forested hills beyond.

Inveraray Castle

A ten-minute walk north of Main St • April–Oct daily 10am–5.45pm • £10 • ☎ 01499 302203, ⓦ inveraray-castle.com

Inveraray Castle remains the family home of the Duke of Argyll, the present (thirteenth) incumbent being Duke Torquhil Ian Campbell. Built in 1745, it was

1

given a touch of the Loire in the nineteenth century with the addition of dormer windows and conical corner spires. In truth, the interior is fairly dull, save for a pair of Beauvais tapestries in the Drawing Room, and the armoury hall, whose displays of weaponry – supplied to the Campbells by the British government to put down the Jacobites – rise through several storeys. Otherwise, look out for the small exhibition on Rob Roy, complete with his belt, sporran and dirk handle. The castle's more recent claim to fame is that it was chosen as the location for the shooting of an episode of *Downton Abbey*.

Gracing the extensive **castle grounds** is an attractive Celtic cross from Tiree, and one of three elegant bridges built during the relandscaping of Inveraray (the other two are on the road from Cairndow). Of the walks marked out in the grounds, the most strenuous takes you to the tower atop **Dùn na Cuaiche** (813ft), from where there's a spectacular view over the castle, town and loch.

ARRIVAL AND INFORMATION INVERARAY

By bus Buses stop on Front St, opposite the tourist office. Destinations Dalmally (Mon–Sat 3 daily, Sun 2 daily; 25min); Dunoon (3 daily; 1hr 10min); Glasgow (4–6 daily; 2hr); Lochgilphead (2–3 daily; 40min); Oban (Mon–Sat 3 daily, Sun 2 daily; 1hr 5min); Tarbert (2–3 daily; 1hr 30min).

Tourist office Front St (daily: April, May, Sept & Oct 10am–5pm; June–Aug 9am–5.30pm; Nov–March 10am–4pm; ☎01499 302063); it has stacks of information and can also arrange local accommodation.

ACCOMMODATION

Creag Dhubh Shore Rd ☎01499 302430, ⓦcreag dhubh.com. Set in a large, lush garden overlooking Loch Fyne down the A83 to Lochgilphead, this lovely mid-nineteenth-century sandstone building accommodates five warmly decorated, and very reasonably priced, rooms, two of which overlook the loch. March–Oct. **£70**

Loch Fyne Hotel Shore Rd ☎01499 302980, ⓦcrerar hotels.com. Refined spa hotel out on the road to Lochgilphead offering the full complement of spa facilities (pool, hot tub, steam room and jacuzzi), in addition to a supremely comfortable range of rooms, many with a tartan theme. **£110**

★ **Newton Hall** Shore Rd ☎01499 302484, ⓦnewtonhallguesthouse.co.uk. This former church now

accommodates an outstanding ensemble of seven rooms, each one named after an Argyll island. Each has been conceived in a completely different style, though they're all possessed of strikingly bold colours and cool, modern furnishings; a couple of rooms have even retained the Gothic-style church windows, through which there are splendid views across the loch. Particularly welcoming to families. **£90**

SYHA hostel A short walk up the A819 to Oban, just beyond the petrol station ☎0870 004 1125, ⓦsyha .org.uk. Small, low-key hostel in a low, wood-and-stone chalet-type building. Twin and quad rooms, all with shared shower facilities, as well as a lounge and kitchen for use. Breakfast £3.75. Easter to Oct. Dorms **£18.50**

EATING AND DRINKING

Brambles Main St West ☎01499 302252. Fabulous bistro/bakery that's invariably packed to the gunnels with punters to natter over a cup of freshly roasted coffee and home-made cake. Daily 8.30am–6pm.

George Hotel Main St East ☎01499 302111. The rambling, and very convivial, restaurant/bar of the *George*

feels like a truly proper pub, with its flagstone flooring, log fires, and dimly-lit nooks and crannies in which to linger in over a pint. Decent food too: haggis, neeps and tatties (£7.95), and steak pie with mash and buttered carrots (£9) are typical of the menu. Daily 11am–11pm.

Oban and around

The solidly Victorian resort of **OBAN** enjoys a superb setting – the island of Kerrera to the southwest providing its bay with a natural shelter – distinguished by a bizarre granite amphitheatre, dramatically lit at night, on the hilltop above the town. Despite a population of just eight thousand, it's by far the largest port in northwest Scotland, the second-largest town in Argyll, and the main departure point for ferries to the Hebrides.

Although Oban is not blessed with a particularly stunning array of sights, there's more than enough to keep you entertained for a day or so, and it's one of the best places in Scotland to eat fresh seafood.

Oban lies at the centre of the coastal region known as Lorn, named after the Irish Celt Loarn, who, along with his brothers Fergus and Oengus, settled here around 500 AD. The mainland is very picturesque, although its beauty is no secret – to escape the crowds, head off and explore the nearby islands, like **Lismore** or **Kerrera**, just offshore, or to the peninsula of Appin or quiet, freshwater Loch Awe.

OBAN

▲ Dunollie Castle

▲ A85, Connel & Dunstaffnage Castle

Saint Columba's Cathedral

Corran Halls

Atlantis Leisure Centre

War & Peace Exhibition

Oban Distillery

McCaig's Tower

North Pier

Waterfront Centre

Railway Pier

Train Station

STATION SQUARE

Bus Station

CalMac Ferry Terminal

South Pier

●TAKEAWAYS, CAFÉS & RESTAURANTS	
Coast	2
Ee-usk	4
Fishouse Restaurant	7
Julie's Coffee House	3
Kitchen Garden	5
Oban Fish and Chips	1
Original Green Shack	6

■ ACCOMMODATION	
Dungallan House Hotel	7
Hawthornbank Guest House	3
Jeremy Inglis	6
Kilchrenan House	1
Oban Backpackers	5
Oban Caravan & Camping Park	8
The Old Manse Guest House	4
SYHA hostel	2

0   150
yards

N

Kerrera Ferry & 7

▼ 8

▼ Lochgilphead & A816

1

McCaig's Tower

Apart from the setting and views, the only truly remarkable sight in Oban is the town's landmark, **McCaig's Tower**, a stiff ten-minute climb from the quayside. Built in imitation of Rome's Colosseum, it was the brainchild of a local businessman a century ago, who had the twin aims of alleviating off-season unemployment among the local stonemasons and creating a museum, art gallery and chapel. Originally, the plan was to add a 95-foot central tower, but work never progressed further than the exterior granite walls before McCaig died. In his will, McCaig gave instructions for the lancet windows to be filled with bronze statues of the family, though no such work was ever undertaken. Instead, the folly has been turned into a sort of walled garden which is a popular rendezvous for Oban's youth after dark, but for the rest of the time simply provides a wonderful seaward panorama, particularly at sunset.

Oban Distillery

Stafford St • Jan, Feb & Dec Mon–Fri 12.30–4pm; March & Nov Mon–Fri 10am–5pm; April Mon–Sat 9.30am–5pm; May, June & Oct daily 9.30am–5pm; July–Sept Mon–Fri 9.30am–7.30pm, Sat & Sun 9.30am–5pm • £7.50 • ☎ 01631 572004, ⓦ discovering-distilleries.com

Oban Distillery is one of Scotland's oldest, founded in 1794 by the Stevenson brothers, and today it produces in excess of a million bottles a year of its lightly peaty malt, which is acknowledged to be a touch easier on the palette than many other whiskies produced hereabouts. The excellent forty-five-minute-long guided **tours** take in the Mash House, holding four massive Scandinavian larch washbacks, and the Still House, with its beautifully proportioned copper stills. The tour ends, as is the custom, with a generous dram.

War and Peace Exhibition

Corran Esplanade • May–Oct Mon–Sat 10am–6pm, Sun 10am–4pm; March, April & Nov daily 10am–4pm • Free • ☎ 01631 570007, ⓦ obanmuseum.org.uk

Housed in the old *Oban Times* building beside the Art Deco *Regent Hotel* on the Esplanade, the charming **War and Peace Exhibition** is stuffed full of local (and not so local) memorabilia – bizarrely, a chunk of the Berlin Wall has ended up here. Overall though, the emphasis is on the wartime role of the area around Oban, when it operated as a flying-boat base, mustering point for Atlantic convoys and training centre for the D-Day landings. Also on display are bits of cargo (including a ladder) washed ashore from the Dutch cargo steamer, the *Breda*, which was attacked in nearby Ardmucknish Bay in 1940. It's now a popular dive wreck.

ARRIVAL AND INFORMATION   OBAN

By plane Six miles north of town, tiny Oban Airport in North Connel (☎ 0845 805 7465, ⓦ hebrideanair.co.uk) has flights to Coll, Tiree, Islay and Colonsay; the nearest train station to the airport is Connel Ferry, or take bus #405 from Oban to Barcaldine.

Destinations Coll (Mon & Wed 2–3 daily; Sat & Sun 1 daily; 30min); Colonsay (Tues & Thurs 2 daily, Sat & Sun 1 daily; 30min); Islay (Tues & Thurs 2 daily; 40min); Tiree (Mon & Wed 2 daily; 1hr).

By train The station is on Railway Pier.

Destinations Glasgow, Queen St (3 daily; 3hr 10min).

By bus The bus station is on Station Rd, adjacent to the train station.

Destinations Appin (Mon–Sat 2–3 daily; 30min); Connel (Mon–Sat hourly; 10–15min); Fort William (Mon–Sat 4 daily; 1hr 30min); Glasgow (4 daily; 3hr); Inveraray (4 daily; 1hr 10min); Kilmartin (Mon–Fri 4 daily, Sat 2 daily; 1hr 15min).

By ferry The CalMac terminal (☎ 01631 566688, ⓦ calmac.co.uk) is on Railway Pier, close to both the train and bus stations.

Destinations Oban–Coll (daily except Wed & Fri; 2hr 40min); Oban–Colonsay (daily except Tues & Sat; 2hr 15min); Oban–Craignure on Mull (daily every 2hr; 45min); Oban–Achnacroish on Lismore (Mon–Sat 4–5 daily, Sun 2 daily; 50min); Oban–Tiree (1 daily; 3hr 40min).

By car Arriving in Oban by car can be a bit of a nightmare in the summer, when traffic chokes the main drag. If you're heading straight for the ferry, make sure you leave an extra hour to allow for sitting in the tailbacks.

Tourist office 3 North Pier (April–June, Sept & Oct Mon–Sat 9am–6pm, Sun 10am–5pm; July & Aug Mon–Sat 9am–7pm, Sun 10am–5pm; Nov–March Mon–Sat 10am–5pm, Sun 11am–3pm; ☎01631 563122, ⓦoban .org.uk). There's stacks of info here, and the office can book accommodation.

ACTIVITIES AND TOURS

Bike rental Bike Fix, George St (Mon–Fri 10am–5pm, Sat 10am–4pm; ☎01631 566033, ⓦobanbikehire.co.uk), rents bikes (£20/day) and also does repairs and servicing.
Diving If you fancy something a little more vigorous, head to the Puffin Dive Centre, based a mile south of Oban at Port Gallanach (☎01631 566088, ⓦpuffin.org .uk), where you can take the plunge with a fully qualified instructor (£58/90 minutes).
Wildlife-watching tours The best of the wildlife-watching companies hereabouts is Coastal Connection, based on Oban Pier (☎01631 565833, ⓦcoastal -connection.co.uk), who offer two- to five-hour-long trips (£30–40) spotting bird- and sealife.

ACCOMMODATION

Oban is positively heaving with **hotels** and **B&Bs**, most of them reasonably priced and many within easy walking distance of the quayside. Unlikely as it is, if you're struggling to find a place, there are stacks more guesthouses in Connel, five miles north. The town is flush with **hostels** too, and there's a decent campsite in the vicinity.

Dungallan House Hotel Gallanach Rd ☎01631 563799, ⓦdungallanhotel-oban.co.uk. Tucked away to the south of town, this solid Victorian villa hotel offers a dozen classy, but expensive, rooms set in its own woodland grounds, with great views across the Sound of Kerrera. No under-12s. March–Oct. **£145**
Hawthornbank Guest House Dalriach Rd ☎01631 562041, ⓦsmoothound.co.uk/hotels/hawthorn. Decent, traditional guesthouse in the lower backstreets of Oban, just across the road from the leisure centre. The rooms, one of which has a four-poster bed, are immaculately kept. March–Oct. **£65**
Jeremy Inglis 21 Airds Crescent ☎01631 565065. A somewhat eccentrically-run hostel near the train station, with a maze of shared, double and family rooms (no bunks throughout), plus kitchen facilities; it's the cheapest bed in town, with breakfast included. Dorms **£17**
Kilchrenan House Corran Esplanade ☎01631 562663, ⓦkilchrenanhouse.co.uk. A bright and hospitable home located near the cathedral, with ten rooms, most of which have antique furnishings to go alongside the tremendous sea views. **£70**
Oban Backpackers Breadalbane St ☎01631 562107, ⓦobanbackpackers.com. Large, friendly and colourful hostel with a range of differently sized dorms (largest has twelve beds) as well as doubles, both here and in two buildings nearby. The big, open lounge-dining area has mismatched sofas, pool table and a real fire. Breakfast included. Dorms **£17**; doubles **£50**
★ **The Old Manse Guest House** Dalraich Rd ☎01631 564886, ⓦobanguesthouse.co.uk. There are few more welcoming places in town than this spotlessly clean Victorian villa whose rooms have unobstructed sea views. There are thoughtful touches all round, including CD players, complimentary sherry and a great selection of toiletries. The breakfast is top-notch too. **£84**
SYHA hostel Corran Esplanade ☎01631 562025, ⓦsyha.org.uk. Occupying a super seafront position in a converted Victorian house, this hostel might be a bit too clinical for some, but the two- to six-bed en-suite rooms are kept to a very high standard. The only downside is that it's a fair trek with a backpack from the ferry terminal. Breakfast £4.50. Dorms **£19.75**; doubles **£46**

CAMPSITE
Oban Caravan & Camping Park Gallanach Rd ☎01631 562425, ⓦobancaravanpark.com. Two miles southwest of Oban up a pretty glen, this is a huge, well-equipped site with lots of camping space and great views across to Kerrera, with a good chance of a breeze to blow the midges away. Facilities include a self-catering kitchen, TV/games lounge, BBQs and on-site shop. Open April to mid-Oct. **£15**/pitch

EATING AND DRINKING

Oban now rates as one of the finest places in Scotland to eat fresh **seafood**, with more than half a dozen highly commendable restaurants to choose from. If you're on the go, or just need a quick bite while waiting for the ferry, there are a cluster of excellent seafood stalls down by the harbour.

TAKEAWAYS
★ **Oban Fish and Chips** 116 George St ☎01631 567000. A cut above your average chippie (and the best one in Oban), with some surprisingly sophisticated food like Oban Bay chowder, and spicy crab and avocado salad (£8.80) to go alongside the stock fish and chips; good ice cream too. Seating available. Daily 11.30am–10.30pm.

1

Original Green Shack Railway Pier. Long-standing and hugely popular seafood shack that also goes by the name of *John Ogden's*, serving langoustine sandwiches, scallops in hot garlic butter (£6.95), mussels in white wine (£3.95), oysters, prawns, cockles and much, much more. Wooden benches available for seating. Mon–Fri & Sun 10am–6pm, Sat 10am–8pm.

CAFÉS AND RESTAURANTS

★ **Coast** 104 George St ☎01631 569900, ⓦcoast oban.com. A slick place with a metropolitan atmosphere, serving acclaimed and original fish dishes like seared scallops with ham-hock potato croquettes and pea purée (£17.50). As you'd expect from one of the town's classiest outfits, the atmosphere and service is first rate. Mon–Sat noon–2.30pm & 5.30–10pm, Sun 5.30–10pm.

Ee-usk North Pier ☎01631 565666, ⓦeeusk.com. Salmon mousse, sea bass with creamed leeks and savoury mash, and glistening seafood platters (£19.95 for two) are typical offerings here in this lively waterfront restaurant that makes the most of the uninterrupted harbour views. Daily noon–3pm & 5.45–10pm.

Fishouse Restaurant 1 Railway Pier ☎01631 563110, ⓦwaterfrontoban.co.uk. Despite the unprepossessing exterior, this is a great place with an open kitchen rustling up impressive dishes primarily using scallops (Isle of Mull scallop salad), langoustine (crispy tails) and the best of the daily catch; for example, lobster ravioli (£13.99). Mon–Fri & Sun noon–2.15pm & 5.30–10pm, Sat noon–10pm.

Julie's Coffee House 33 Stafford St ☎01631 565952. The pick of the many cafés hereabouts, this is a warm, friendly local with super home-baked treats and tasty coffee. Tues–Sat 10am–5pm, also Mon in July & Aug.

Kitchen Garden 14 George St ☎01631 566332, ⓦkitchengardenoban.co.uk. Impressive, central deli with a licensed café up on the mezzanine offering breakfast rolls, filled toasted croissants, and sweet and savoury scones, among other delicious options. Mon–Sat 9am–5.30pm, Sun 10am–4.30pm.

Isle of Kerrera

One of the best places to escape from the crowds in Oban is the low-lying island of **Kerrera**, which shelters Oban Bay from the worst of the westerly winds. Measuring just five miles by two, the island is easily explored on foot. The most prominent landmark is the **Hutcheson's Monument**, best viewed, appropriately enough, from the ferries heading out of Oban, as it commemorates David Hutcheson, one of the Victorian founders of what is now Caledonian MacBrayne. The most appealing vistas, however, are from Kerrera's highest point, **Càrn Breugach** (620ft), over to Mull, the Slate Islands, Lismore, Jura and beyond.

The ferry lands roughly halfway down the east coast, at the north end of **Horseshoe Bay**, where King Alexander II died in 1249. If the weather's good and you feel like lazing by the sea, head for the island's finest sandy beach, **Slatrach Bay**, on the west coast, one mile northwest of the ferry jetty. Otherwise, there's a very rewarding trail down to **Gylen Castle**, a clifftop ruin enjoying a majestic setting on the south coast, built in 1582 by the MacDougalls and burnt to the ground by the Covenanter General Leslie in 1647. You can head back to the ferry via the Drove Road, where cattle from Mull and other islands were once herded to be swum across the sound to the market in Oban.

ARRIVAL AND DEPARTURE   ISLE OF KERRERA

By ferry The passenger and bicycle ferry (summer at 8am & 8.40am, then every 30min until the last ferry at 7pm; winter every 1–2hr; 10min; £5 return; ☎01631 563665) crosses regularly through the day from the mainland two miles down the Gallanach road from Oban. In summer, bus #431 from Oban train station connects with the ferry once a day.

ACCOMMODATION AND EATING

Kerrera Bunkhouse ☎01631 566637, ⓦkerrera bunkhouse.co.uk. Located in a lovely spot at Lower Gylen, a 45-minute walk from the ferry, this converted eighteenth-century stable building, with seven rooms, also has a byre living space for hire by the evening. They also rent a room in the farmhouse for B&B. Bed **£15**/person

Kerrera Teagarden Lower Gylen, next to the bunkhouse. Given that Kerrera has no shop, you may well find yourself at this delightful café where you can eat home-made veggie snacks, cakes and coffee. Easter–Sept daily 10am–4.30pm.

Appin

Seventeen miles north of Oban is **Appin**, best known as the setting for Robert Louis Stevenson's *Kidnapped*, a fictionalized account of the "Appin Murder" of 1752, when Colin Campbell was shot in the back, allegedly by one of the disenfranchised Stewart clan. The name Appin derives from the Gaelic *abthaine*, meaning "lands belonging to the abbey", in this case the one on the island of Lismore, which is linked to the peninsula by passenger ferry from Port Appin.

Port Appin

A pretty little fishing village at the peninsula's westernmost tip, **Port Appin** overlooks a host of tiny islands dotted around Loch Linnhe, with Lismore and the mountains of Morvern and Mull in the background. Without doubt, it is one of Argyll's most picturesque spots.

Castle Stalker

A828, between Connel and Ballachulish • Visits by tour only, roughly mid-July to early Sept • £10 • ☎ 01631 740315 or ☎ 01631 730354, ⓦ castlestalker.com

Framed magnificently as you wind along the single-track road to Port Appin is one of Argyll's most romantic ruined castles, the much-photographed sixteenth-century ruins of **Castle Stalker**. The castle, which is privately owned, can only be visited on one of the pre-booked **tours**, which are limited to five weeks of the year over the summer. Otherwise, there is a footpath from the Stalker View café which winds down to a point some 200 metres from the castle affording some cracking photo opportunities.

ARRIVAL AND ACTIVITIES   PORT APPIN

By ferry Ferries to Lismore (hourly; 5min) depart from a small jetty at the southernmost point of the village, by the *Pierhouse Hotel*.

Bike rental Port Appin Bikes (☎ 01631 730391; £10/day) are useful if you're popping across to Lismore; you can take a bike for free on the ferry.

Watersports The Linnhe Marine Water Sports Centre (May–Sept; ☎ 07721 503981), in Lettershuna (just north of Castle Stalker), rents out boats of all shapes and sizes and offers sailing and windsurfing lessons, as well as water-skiing, clay-pigeon shooting and even pony trekking.

ACCOMMODATION AND EATING

Castle Stalker View Overlooking Castle Stalker ☎ 01631 730444. In a tip-top position overlooking the castle, this large, light-filled café makes for a super little pit stop, serving up fluffy jacket spuds with unusual fillings like crayfish tails or haggis (£7.95), and a mouthwatering selection of baked goodies. Daily: March–Oct 9.30am–5pm; Nov–Feb 10am–4pm.

Pierhouse Hotel A few paces from the jetty ☎ 01631 730302, ⓦ pierhousehotel.co.uk. Ideally situated just along from the jetty, the whitewashed *Pierhouse* has twelve sumptuously furnished rooms decorated in cool beige and mocha tones, most with unrivalled loch views – it's pricey, mind. The hotel's sparkling seafood restaurant is highly rated in these parts too. __£130__

Isle of Lismore

Lying in the middle of Loch Linnhe, to the north of Oban, and barely rising above a hillock, the narrow island of **Lismore** (around ten miles long and a mile wide) offers wonderful gentle walking and cycling opportunities, with unrivalled views, in fine weather, across to the mountains of Morvern, Lochaber and Mull. Legend has it that saints Columba and Moluag both fancied the skinny island as a missionary base, but as they raced towards it Moluag cut off his finger and threw it ashore ahead of Columba, claiming the land for himself. Of Moluag's sixth-century foundation nothing remains, but from 1236 until 1507 the island served as the seat of the bishop of Argyll. Lismore is one of the most fertile of the Inner Hebrides – its name, coined by Moluag himself, derives from the Gaelic *lios mór*, meaning "great garden" – and before the Clearances (see p.415) it supported nearly 1400 inhabitants; the population today is only 180,

1

half of them over 60. The ferry from Oban lands at **Achnacroish**, roughly halfway along the eastern coastline.

Ionad Naomh Moluag

500 metres west of Achnacroish • Daily: mid-April to Sept 11am–4pm; March to mid-April & Oct noon–3pm • £3.50 • ☎ 01631 760030

To get to grips with the history of the island and its Gaelic culture, follow the signs to the Heritage Centre, **Ionad Naomh Moluag**, a turf-roofed, timber-clad building with a permanent exhibition on Lismore, a reference library, a gift shop and a **café** with an outdoor terrace. Your ticket also covers entry to the nearby restored nineteenth-century cottar's (landless tenant's) cottage, **Tigh Iseabal Dhaibh**, with its traditionally built stone walls, birch roof timbers and thatched roof.

Cathedral of St Moluag and around

In **Clachan**, two and a half miles north of Achnacroish, you'll find the diminutive, whitewashed fourteenth-century **Cathedral of St Moluag**, whose choir was reduced in height and converted into the parish church in 1749; inside you can see a few of the original seats for the upper clergy, a stone basin in the south wall and several medieval doorways. Due east of the church – head north up the road and take the turning signposted on the right – the circular **Tirefour Broch**, over two thousand years old, occupies a commanding position and boasts walls almost 10ft thick in places.

ARRIVAL AND DEPARTURE ISLE OF LISMORE

By ferry Two ferries serve Lismore: a small CalMac car ferry from Oban to Achnacroish (Mon–Sat 4 daily, Sun 2 daily; 50min), and a shorter passenger- and bicycle-only crossing from Port Appin to Point, the island's northerly point (hourly; 5min).

GETTING AROUND AND INFORMATION

Bike rental Bike rental is available from Lismore Bike Hire (☎ 01631 760213), who will deliver to the ferry upon request.

Tourist information In the absence of a tourist office, ⊕ isleoflismore.com has some useful information.

ACCOMMODATION AND EATING

The Old Schoolhouse ☎ 01631 760262. Accommodation on the island is extremely limited, but this budget B&B, with three rooms, all sharing bathroom facilities, is perfectly acceptable. They also serve evening meals for a very reasonable £10/person. **£60**

Taynuilt

Taynuilt, eleven miles east of Oban, at the point where the River Awe flows into the sea at **Loch Etive**, is a small but sprawling village, best known for its iron-smelting works, though it's a great little spot from which to explore the loch itself. From the pier beyond the iron furnace, **boat cruises** run by Loch Etive Cruises (Easter to Christmas daily except Sat at 10am, noon & 2pm; 2–3hr; £10/£15; ☎ 07721 732703) check out the local seals and explore the otherwise inaccessible reaches of the loch.

Bonawe Iron Furnace

B845, two miles from Taynuilt, just off the A85 • April–Sept daily 9.30am–5.30pm • £4.50; HS • ☎ 01866 822432

The **Bonawe Iron Furnace** was originally founded by Cumbrian ironworkers in 1753, employing six hundred people at its height. Its decline and eventual closure, in 1876, was largely as a result of the introduction of more efficient coke-fired methods of production. During its heyday, though, the surrounding hills of birch and oak made for first-class charcoal, which was the principal fuel used to smelt iron in these early blast furnaces. The site remains hugely evocative, from the cavernous charcoal sheds with their sunken roofs, to the far smaller iron-ore sheds, one of which now has an enlightening exhibition charting the development of iron making. The furnace house itself also remains largely intact, though sadly the water wheel is no more, having been sold for scrap during World War II.

Inverawe Fisheries and Smokery

A85, one mile east of Taynuilt • Easter–Oct & Dec daily 8.30am–5pm; Nov Fri–Sun 8.30am–5pm • Smokery free; exhibition £1.50 • ⊕ 0844 847 5490, ⓦ smokedsalmon.co.uk

A mile or so east up the A85 from Taynuilt, a sign invites you down a minor road to visit the tucked-away **Inverawe Fisheries and Smokery**, where you can buy lots of lovely local food including traditionally smoked fish and mussels, eat the same in their casual little café, check out the exhibition on traditional smoking techniques, learn how to fly-fish, or go for a stroll down to nearby Loch Etive with your picnic.

Loch Awe

Legend has it that **Loch Awe**, twenty miles east of Oban, was created by a witch and inhabited by a monster even more gruesome than the one at Loch Ness. At more than 25 miles in length, Loch Awe is actually the longest stretch of fresh water in the country, but most travellers only encounter the loch's north end as they speed along its shores by car or train on the way to or from Oban.

Kilchurn Castle

Several tiny islands on the loch sport picturesque ruins, including the fifteenth-century ruins of **Kilchurn Castle**, strategically situated on a rocky spit (once an island) at the head of the loch; to visit the castle, you can approach by foot from the A85 to the east. The castle is essentially a shell, but its watery setting and imposing outlines make it well worth a detour.

Cruachan Power Station

A85, 19 miles east of Oban • Easter–Oct daily 9.30am–4.45pm; Nov–March Mon–Fri 10am–3.45pm; tours every 30min • Tours £6.50 • ⊕ 01866 822618, ⓦ visitcruachan.co.uk

The main attraction on the shores of Loch Awe is none too picturesque. **Cruachan Power Station** is actually constructed inside mighty Ben Cruachan (3693ft), which looms over the head of Loch Awe; it was built in 1965 as part of the hydroelectric network, which generates around ten percent of Scotland's electricity. Thirty-minute guided tours set off from the **visitor centre** by the loch, taking you to a viewing platform above the generating room deep inside the "hollow mountain", a 91-metre-long cavern big enough to contain the Tower of London. The whole experience of visiting an industrial complex hidden within a mountain is very James Bond, and it certainly pulls in the tour coaches. Even if you don't partake in a tour, the visitor centre offers some thoroughgoing and interesting explanations of the workings of the power station and renewable energy projects, while the adjoining café has marvellous loch views.

Isle of Mull and around

The second largest of the Inner Hebrides, **Mull** is by far the most accessible: just forty minutes from Oban by ferry. As so often, first impressions largely depend on the weather – it is the wettest of the Hebrides (and that's saying something) – for without the sun the large tracts of moorland, particularly around the island's highest peak, Ben More (3169ft), can appear bleak and unwelcoming. There are, however, areas of more gentle pastoral scenery around **Dervaig** in the north and **Salen** on the east coast, and the indented west coast varies from the sandy beaches around **Calgary** to the cliffs

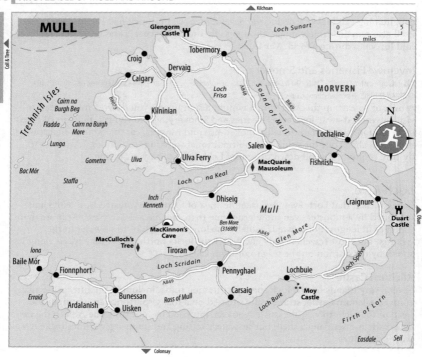

of Loch na Keal. The most common mistake is to try and "do" the island in a day or two: slogging up the main road to the picturesque capital of **Tobermory**, then covering the fifty-odd miles between there and Fionnphort, in order to visit **Iona**. Mull is a place that will grow on you only if you have the time and patience to explore.

Historically, crofting, whisky distilling and fishing supported the islanders (*Muileachs*), but the population – which peaked at ten thousand – decreased dramatically in the late nineteenth century due to the Clearances and the 1846 potato famine. On Mull, it is a trend that has been reversed, mostly owing to the large influx of settlers from elsewhere in the country, which has brought the current population up to over 2500. One of the main reasons for this resurgence is, of course, tourism – more than half a million visitors come here each year. As good a reason as any to visit Mull, and one of the main reasons why many do so, is to view the abundant **wildlife**, with whale watching the highlight for most visitors, though there's fantastic birdlife here too.

Mull also makes particular efforts to draw visitors to **special events** through the year, including the Mendelssohn on Mull Festival in July, which commemorates the composer's visit here in 1829; the Mull Highland Games, also in July; and a rally car event around the island's winding roads in October.

ARRIVAL AND GETTING AROUND   ISLE OF MULL AND AROUND

By ferry Craignure is the main ferry terminal, with a frequent daily car-ferry link to Oban, though booking ahead on this route is strongly advised. A smaller and less-expensive car ferry crosses daily from Lochaline on the Morvern peninsula (see p.218) to Fishnish, six miles

northwest of Craignure. Another even smaller car ferry connects Kilchoan on the Ardnamurchan peninsula (see p.219) with Tobermory, the island capital.

By bus Public transport on Mull is not too bad on the main A849, with a steady stream of buses plying the route

between Craignure and Tobermory, but there's more or less no service along the west coast.
By car If driving, note that the roads are still predominantly single-track, with passing places, which can slow journeys down considerably.

Craignure and around

Craignure is little more than a scattering of cottages, though there is a small shop, a bar, some toilets and a CalMac ticket and tourist office situated opposite the pier. However, there is plenty of accommodation here, as well as a few places to eat and drink, so it's a useful place to base yourself if you have a car.

Duart Castle

A848, three miles south of Craignure • May to mid-Oct daily 10.30am–5.30pm • £5.75 • ☎ 01680 812309, ⓦ duartcastle.com

Perched on a rocky promontory sticking out into the Sound of Mull, and buffeted by winds and weather, **Duart Castle** makes for a striking landmark from the Oban–Craignure ferry. Duart was headquarters of the once-powerful MacLean clan from the thirteenth century, but was burnt down by the Campbells and confiscated after the 1745 rebellion. In 1911, the 26th clan chief, Fitzroy MacLean – not to be confused with the Scottish writer of the same name – managed to buy it back and restore it, and he remained here until his death, in 1936, at the ripe old age of 101 – look out for the wonderful black-and-white photos of MacLean on his 100th birthday, still looking remarkably fit even then. The top-floor room showcases some superb exhibits, particularly items belonging to Fitzroy from his time serving in the 13th Light Dragoons and 13th Hussars, while you can also learn about the world scout movement; in 1959, Charles MacLean (the 27th clan chief) became Chief Scout, a role he performed with some distinction until 1971. From the exhibition room, climb up to the **ramparts** for superlative views of the island and beyond, while on a clear day, you can just make out the summit of Ben Nevis. After your visit, head to the castle's pretty, barnlike tearoom, where there's an impressive array of home-made cakes on offer.

ARRIVAL AND INFORMATION

CRAIGNURE AND AROUND

By ferry The ferry terminal dominates the centre of the village, with the CalMac office located directly opposite, in the same building as the tourist office.
Destinations Oban (daily every 2hr; 45min).
By bus Buses pick up and drop off by the main road by the ferry terminal.
Destinations Fionnphort (Mon–Sat 3 daily, Sun 1 daily;

1hr 10min); Fishnish (1–4 daily; 10min); Salen (4–6 daily; 20min); Tobermory (4–6 daily; 45min).
Tourist office Opposite the ferry terminal in shared premises with CalMac (April–Oct daily 9am–5pm, till 7pm in July & Aug; Nov–March Mon–Sat 9am–5pm, Sun 10am–noon & 2–5pm; ☎ 01680 812377), the tourist office has an accommodation booking service.

ACCOMMODATION AND EATING

Craignure Inn 400 metres up the road towards Fionnphort ☎ 01680 812305, ⓦ craignure-inn.co.uk. A two-minute stroll up the road towards Fionnphort, this eighteenth-century whitewashed inn, frequented by locals and tourists alike, is a snug little place to hole up in. Quiz nights and live music are regular weekly fixtures. Daily 11.30am–11pm.
Isle of Mull Hotel About half a mile from the ferry terminal along the road to Tobermory ☎ 01680 812544, ⓦ crerarhotels.com. The hotel exterior is somewhat unprepossessing, but its super waterfront setting, polished rooms and friendly staff more than compensate. **£95**
Old Mill Cottage Lochdon ☎ 01680 812442, ⓦ oldmill mull.com. A sensitively converted mill three miles south

on the A849, accommodating three pretty rooms with wood furnishings and cool little touches like roll-top baths; they also provide attractive self-catering accommodation in the old smiddy. **£75**
★ **Shieling Holidays** Above a shingle beach half a mile or so from the ferry terminal on the road to Fionnphort ☎ 01680 812496, ⓦ shielingholidays.co.uk. This tidy campsite also offers cool accommodation in the form of "shielings" (large, sometimes furnished, hard-top tents – think downmarket glamping), sleeping between two and six. Some are en suite and some self-catering. Boats, canoes and bikes for rent. April–Oct. **£16.50**/pitch; shielings **£32**

1

Tobermory

Mull's chief town, **TOBERMORY**, at the northern tip of the island, is easily the most attractive fishing port on the west coast of Scotland, its clusters of brightly coloured houses and boats sheltering in a bay backed by a steep bluff. Founded in 1788 by the British Society for Encouraging Fisheries, it never really took off as a fishing port and only survived due to the steady influx of crofters evicted from other parts of the island during the Clearances (see p.415). It is now the most important, and by far the most vibrant, settlement on Mull, and if you've got young kids, you'll instantly recognize it as the place where *Balamory* was filmed.

The harbour – known as **Main Street** – is one long parade of multicoloured hotels, guesthouses, restaurants and shops, and you could happily spend an hour or so meandering around. The rest of the upper town, laid out on a classic grid-plan, merits a stroll, if only for the great views over the bay.

Mull Museum

Main St • Easter to mid-Oct Mon–Fri 10am–4pm, Sat 10am–1pm • Free • ☎ 01688 301100

A good wet-weather retreat is the **Mull Museum**, essentially a tiny room packed with fascinating local information and artefacts. Among these are a handful of objects salvaged from the *San Juan de Sicilia*, a ship from the Spanish Armada which sank in 1588 and now lies at the bottom of Tobermory harbour; even today, it remains subject to repeated salvage attempts by locals still, somewhat optimistically, seeking gold. During World War II, Tobermory was an important naval base, in particular as a centre for the training of Escort vessels, whose job it was to protect convoy ships from being attacked by U-boats. Leading the training was one Vice Admiral Gilbert Stephenson, whose prolific and strict regime (he trained up over nine hundred ships in just four years) earned him the moniker "The Terror of Tobermory". Such was the Admiral's notoriety that he even had a beer named after him.

Tobermory Distillery

Ledaig car park • Easter–Oct Mon–Fri 10am–5pm; tours hourly between 11am and 4pm • £6 • ☎ 01688 302645,
🌐 tobermorymalt.com

Founded in 1798, the miniscule **Tobermory Distillery** has had a chequered history, closing down three times since then, though today it's back in business and thriving thanks to its signature 15-year-old Tobermory and 10-year-old Ledaig malts. Although its tour is rather drab compared to most distilleries, you do get to see the four magnificent copper stills, as well as try a dram or two at the end.

Glengorm Castle

Five miles north of Tobermory • Easter to mid-Oct daily 10am–5pm • £6 • ☎ 01688 302932, 🌐 glengormcastle.co.uk

Lying along a dead-end single-track road, **Glengorm Castle** is a Scots Baronial pile overlooking the sea. Here too is an attractively converted steading, housing a delightful café, well-stocked farm shop, craft shop and art gallery. You can walk around the walled garden or make for the longer forest, archeological and coastal trails; they also offer free guided walks, though you need to book in advance. There's luxury accommodation available here too (see p.76).

ARRIVAL AND DEPARTURE   TOBERMORY

By ferry The CalMac terminal is at the far end of Main St, in the northernmost part of the bay.
Destinations Kilchoan (May–Aug daily; Sept–April Mon–Sat; every 1hr 30min; 35min).
By bus The bus station is in the town's main Ledaig

car park, by the distillery.
Destinations Calgary (Mon–Sat 2–3 daily; 45min); Craignure (4–6 daily; 45min); Dervaig (Mon–Sat 2–3 daily; 25min); Fishnish (2–4 daily; 40min).

1

WILDLIFE-WATCHING TRIPS FROM TOBERMORY

Although boat trips leave from several different places around Mull, Tobermory is as good a place as any from which to begin a tour. Prices with most companies range from around £10 for a half-hour seal cruise to £80 for a full day's whale-watching. Easily the best of these is **Sea Life Surveys** situated in the main car park (Easter–Oct; ☎01688 302916, ⓦsealifesurveys.com). Linked to the Hebridean Whale and Dolphin Trust, they focus on seeking out the whales (minke and even killer whales are the most common), porpoises, dolphins and basking sharks that spend time in the waters around the Hebrides; their seven-hour whale-watching trips are not recommended for under-14s, though their two-hour Ecocruz (adult £30, child £20) is much more family oriented. Rather more sedate are the six-hour wildlife cruises with **Hebridean Adventure**, based in Ulva House (April–Sept; £60; ☎01688 302044, ⓦhebrideanadventure.co.uk), who also organize a dinner cruise.

INFORMATION AND ACTIVITIES

Tourist office The Pier, in the same building as the CalMac ticket office at the far end of Main St; it's not manned, but there's plenty of literature to take away and the CalMac staff can help with any queries (Mon–Fri 9am–5pm).
Tourist information Privately-run Explore Mull, located in a cabin in the Ledaig car park (April–Oct daily 9am–7pm; ☎01688 302875, ⓦexploremull.co.uk) has more information than the tourist office, and they also arrange accommodation and wildlife tours.
Bike rental Archibald Brown, the endearingly old-fashioned ironmongers at 21 Main St (Mon–Sat 8.30am–5pm; ☎01688 302020, ⓦbrownstobermory.co.uk), charges £15/day.

ACCOMMODATION

Glengorm Castle Five miles northwest of Tobermory ☎01688 302321, ⓦglengormcastle.co.uk. Fairy-tale, rambling Baronial mansion in a superb, secluded setting, with incredible coastal views, lovely gardens and local walks. Guests enjoy use of the castle's wood-panelled library and lounge; the five large bedrooms are full of splendid features and there are self-catering cottages available too. **£130**
★ **Highland Cottage** Breadalbane St ☎01688 302030, ⓦhighlandcottage.co.uk. Super-luxurious B&B run by a very welcoming couple in a quiet street high above the harbour; the six stunningly furnished rooms, each one named after an Argyll island, are fashioned with home comforts firmly in mind. **£150**
★ **Strongarbh House** Upper Tobermory ☎01688 302319, ⓦstrongarbh.com. Erstwhile bank, doctors surgery and officers mess, but now a fantastic and engagingly run B&B with four rooms that brilliantly combine elements of Victorian and modern; each room has an iPad for starters. There's also a library with books, newspapers and games, while complimentary tea and coffee is served between 4pm and 6pm every day for guests. Not cheap but worth every penny. Mid-March to mid-Oct. **£130**
SYHA hostel Main Street ☎0870 004 1151, ⓦsyha
.org.uk. Small, friendly and superbly located on the harbour front, with two- to six-bed rooms, all with shared shower facilities, kitchen, TV lounge and laundry. Breakfast £3.75. Mid-March to mid-Oct. Dorms **£18**; doubles **£45**
Tobermory Hotel 53 Main St ☎01688 302091, ⓦthetobermoryhotel.com. Smallish, fairly smart hotel converted from fishermens' cottages, hence the maze-like warren of variously sized rooms, some with coved ceilings, others with window seats, though all are extremely cosy. Open April–Oct. **£98**
Western Isles Hotel Above the harbour ☎01688 302012, ⓦwesternisleshotel.com. The decor – moth-eaten stag heads and floral drapes – isn't for everyone, but the *Western Isles* continues to undergo gradual renovation. The setting above town is impressive, and the hotel has a glamorous pedigree as a location for the Powell and Pressburger classic *I Know Where I'm Going!* **£95**

CAMPSITE

Newdale Camping One and a half miles uphill from Tobermory on the B8073 to Dervaig ☎01688 302624, ⓦtobermory-campsite.co.uk. Small, spruce and cheap campsite serenely situated in woodland. Limited facilities include a sink and a couple of showers. April–Oct. **£14**/pitch

EATING AND DRINKING

TAKEAWAY

Fisherman's Pier Fish & Chip Van Fisherman's Pier ☎01688 301109. The friendly proprietors of this venerable takeaway van serve up all the traditional fish suppers, though most people venture here for their scrumptious scallops and chips (£8.50). Mon–Sat 12.30–9pm, also Sun in July & Aug.

CAFÉS AND RESTAURANTS

An Tobar Argyll Terrace ☎01688 302211, ⊛antobar
.co.uk. Housed in a converted Victorian schoolhouse at
the top of Back Brae, this small but attractive café doubles
up as the town's principal arts centre, with a strong and
imaginative programme of visual art and live music. Mon–
Sat 10am–5pm.

Café Fish The Pier ☎01688 301253, ⊛thecafefish
.com. Stylish restaurant above the tourist office, sporting
an all-glass frontage with superb harbour views. Fresh
from their own boat, the day's catch is prominently
displayed in a large glass cabinet. The menu could feature
anything from *linguine vongole* with surf clams (£16) to
halibut with roasted red pepper and chorizo. Easter–Oct
daily 11.30am–10pm.

★ **Highland Cottage** Breadalbane St ☎01688
302030, ⊛highlandcottage.co.uk. If you're going to
treat yourself, then look no further than this sublime
guesthouse restaurant, which offers an evening four-
course menu for £39. Once you've had a glass of fizz and
some canapés, dishes might include the likes of diver
scallops with cauliflower tempura and spring onion mash,
or leek, blue cheese and walnut strudel. No set opening
hours; reservations only.

Island Diner 53 Main St ☎01688 302091, ⊛the
tobermoryhotel.com. Highly creditable restaurant in the
Tobermory Hotel, which conjures up tempting seasonal
dishes like gin-cured Isle of Ghiga halibut and salmon.
Committed whisky fanatics, meanwhile, might care to try
the honey and malt whisky panacotta. Two courses £25.
Tues–Sun 6–10pm.

PUBS

MacGochan's Ledaig car park ☎01688 302350. Heaving,
hugely popular harbourside pub just a few paces from the
distillery, with a terrific beer garden (albeit one facing a car
park), well-frequented restaurant-bar and occasional live
music to liven things up further. Daily 11am–1am.

Mishnish Main St ☎01688 302009. Inside the hotel of
the same name (it's the garishly yellow building), this has
been the most popular local watering hole for many years,
with a couple of superb snugs rammed with maritime and
musical paraphernalia, and regular evenings of live music.
Daily 11am–1am.

Dervaig

The gently undulating countryside west of Tobermory, beyond the freshwater Mishnish
lochs, provides some of the most beguiling scenery on the island. Added to this, the
road out west, the B8073, is exceptionally dramatic. The only village of any size on this
side of the island is **Dervaig**, which nestles beside narrow Loch Chumhainn, just eight
miles southwest of Tobermory, distinguished by its unusual pencil-shaped church spire
and single street of dinky whitewashed cottages and old corrugated-iron shacks.
Dervaig has a shop, a bookshop/café and a wide choice of accommodation.

ACCOMMODATION AND EATING   DERVAIG

Am Birlinn Penmore ☎01688 400619, ⊛ambirlinn
.com. The cross-country road from Dervaig takes you
through Penmore where you'll find this striking wood-and-
glass-clad building serving up steaks and seafood of the
highest order: slow roasted lamb shank with apricots and
tomatoes in a chardonnay and herb sauce (£16.95) being
one of the restaurant's typically flamboyant dishes. April–
Oct Wed–Sun noon–2.30pm & 5–11pm.

The Bellachroy In the heart of Dervaig ☎01688 400314,
⊛thebellachroy.co.uk. Rugged, early seventeenth-century
inn, with an attractive whitewashed interior serving good
seafood (mussels and frites for £11.50) and local real ales.
Daily 8.30am–11pm.

Bunkhouse Dervaig village hall ☎01688 400491 or
☎07919 870664, ⊛mull-hostel-dervaig.co.uk. Somewhat peculiarly located inside the village hall, though
certainly none the worse for it, this clean and welcoming
bunkhouse offers two bunkrooms, one sleeping six,
the other four, each with its own wetroom. Bedding is
provided. There's also a self-catering kitchen, sitting room
and washing machine. Breakfast not included. Dorms **£15**

Druimnacroish Hotel Two miles out of Dervaig on the
Salen road ☎01688 400274, ⊛druimnacroish.co.uk. A
lovely country house pleasantly secreted away with six amply-
sized but very reasonably priced rooms. Breakfast is taken in
the conservatory overlooking the gardens. Easter–Oct. **£64**

Calgary

Some five miles beyond Dervaig is **Calgary**, once a thriving crofting community, now a
quiet glen which opens out onto Mull's finest sandy bay, backed by low-lying dunes
and machair, with wonderful views over to Coll and Tiree. Aside from the beach,
there's a super little **sculpture trail** which begins at the *Calgary Farmhouse* and winds

gently down through the woodland to the beach. It encompasses some twenty cleverly constructed pieces of artwork hewn from various materials – bronze, copper, steel, willow and so on; a little map (£1) outlining the trail is available from the farmhouse. For the record, the city of Calgary in Canada does indeed take its name from this little village, though it was not so named by Mull emigrants, but instead by one Colonel McLeod of the North West Mounted Police, who once holidayed here.

ACCOMMODATION AND EATING   CALGARY

Calgary Farmhouse ☎01688 400256, ⓦcalgary .co.uk. A few hundred yards back up the road from the beach is this delightful farmhouse providing glamorous self-catering accommodation in studio lofts, sleeping between two and four people. The daytime café and art gallery are both worth venturing to. Café: daily 7.30am– 5pm. Three-day minimum stay **£450**

Camping Down by the beach itself, there's a spectacular and very popular spot for camping rough; the only facilities are the basic public toilets.

Isle of Ulva

A chieftain to the Highlands bound/Cries "Boatman, do not tarry!/And I'll give thee a silver pound/To row us o'er the ferry!"/"Now who be ye, would cross Lochgyle/This dark and stormy water?"/"O I'm the chief of Ulva's isle,/And this, Lord Ullin's daughter."

Lord Ullin's Daughter by Thomas Campbell (1777–1844)

Around the time Poet Laureate Campbell penned this tragic poem, the population of **Ulva** (from the Norse *ulv øy*, or "wolf island") was a staggering 850, sustained by the huge quantities of kelp that were exported for glass and soap production. That was before the market for kelp collapsed and the 1846 potato famine hit, after which the remaining population was brutally evicted. Nowadays around fifteen people live here, and the island is littered with ruined crofts, not to mention a church, designed by Thomas Telford, which would once have seated over three hundred parishioners. It's great **walking** country, however, with several clearly marked paths crisscrossing the native woodland and the rocky heather moorland interior – and you're almost guaranteed to spot some of the abundant **wildlife**: at the very least deer, if not buzzards, golden eagles and even sea eagles, with seals and divers offshore. If you like to have a focus for your wanderings, head for the ruined crofting villages and basalt columns similar to those on Staffa along the island's southern coastline; for the island's highest point, Beinn Chreagach (1027ft); or along the north coast to Ulva's tidal neighbour, Gometra, off the west coast.

Heritage Centre and Sheila's Cottage

You can learn more about the history of the island from the exhibition inside the **Heritage Centre** (just up from the pier on the Ulva side) and, nearby, the newly restored thatched smiddy housing **Sheila's Cottage**, which has been restored to the period when islander Sheila MacFadyen lived there in the first half of the last century. Originally a milkmaid, Sheila later made her living by gathering and selling winkles to locals and visitors to the island.

ARRIVAL AND INFORMATION   ISLE OF ULVA

By bus/ferry To get to Ulva, which lies just a hundred yards or so off the west coast of Mull, follow the signs for "Ulva Ferry" west from Salen or south from Calgary – if you've no transport, a postbus can get you there, but you'll have to make your own way back. From Ulva Ferry, a small bicycle/passenger-only ferry (£6 return) is available on demand (Mon–Fri 9am–5pm; June–Aug also Sun; at other times by arrangement on ☎01688 500226).

Tourist information ⓦisleofulva.com is a very useful website detailing all you need to know about visiting the island.

ACCOMMODATION AND EATING

The Boathouse Near the ferry slip on the Ulva side ☎01688 500241, ⓦtheboathouseulva.co.uk. Cheery tearoom serving a mouthwatering selection of seafood tempters like mackerel pâté (£7.50), potted crab (£9.50) and

Ulva oysters, alongside cakes and coffee. There's no accommodation, but with permission from the present owners of the café, you might be able to camp rough overnight for free. Easter–Sept Mon–Fri 9am–5pm, June–Aug also Sun.

Isle of Staffa and around

Five miles southwest of Ulva, **Staffa** is one of the most romantic and dramatic of Scotland's many uninhabited islands. On its south side, the perpendicular rockface features an imposing series of black basalt columns, known as the Colonnade, which have been cut by the sea into cathedralesque caverns, most notably **Fingal's Cave**. The Vikings knew about the island – the name derives from their word for "Island of Pillars" – but it wasn't until 1772 that it was "discovered" by the world. Turner painted it, Wordsworth explored it, but Mendelssohn's *Die Fingalshöhle* (the lovely "Hebrides Overture"), inspired by the sounds of the sea-wracked caves he heard on a visit here in 1829, did most to popularize the place – after which Queen Victoria gave her blessing, too. The polygonal basalt organ-pipes were created some sixty million years ago when a huge mass of molten basalt burst forth onto land and, as it cooled, solidified into hexaganol crystals. The same phenomenon produced the Giant's Causeway in Northern Ireland, and Celtic folk tales often link the two with rival giants Fionn mac Cumhail (Irish) and Fingal (Scottish) throwing rocks at each other across the Irish Sea.

Treshnish Isles

Northwest of Staffa lie the **Treshnish Isles**, an archipelago of uninhabited volcanic islets, none more than a mile or two across. The most distinctive is **Bac Mór**, shaped like a Puritan's hat and popularly dubbed the Dutchman's Cap. **Lunga**, the largest island, is a summer nesting-place for hundreds of seabirds, in particular guillemots, razorbills and puffins, as well as a breeding ground for seals. The two most northerly islands, **Cairn na Burgh More** and **Cairn na Burgh Beag**, have the remains of ruined castles, the first of which served as a lookout post for the Lords of the Isles and was last garrisoned in the Civil War; Cairn na Burgh Beag hasn't been occupied since the 1715 Jacobite uprising.

TOURS   **ISLE OF STAFFA AND AROUND**

Boat tours From April to October several operators offer boat trips to Staffa and the Treshnish Isles.

Long-established Turus Mara, based in Penmore (☎01688 400242, ⌨turusmara.com), sets out from Ulva Ferry and is

---

WHALES AND DOLPHINS

Watching whales, dolphins and porpoises – collectively known as cetaceans – is a growing tourist industry in Scotland. The Moray Firth (see p.208) is one of the best places in the UK to watch **bottlenose dolphins**, but the waters around the Inner Hebrides have, if anything, a wider variety of cetaceans on offer. Although there are several operators who offer whale-watching boat trips from Oban and Tobermory (see p.76), it is quite possible to catch sight of marine mammals from the shore, or from a ferry. The chief problem is trying to identify what you've seen.

The most common sightings are of **harbour porpoises**, the smallest of the marine mammals, which are about the size of an adult human and have a fairly small dorsal fin. Porpoises are easily confused with dolphins; however, if you see it leap out of the water, then you can be sure it's a dolphin, as porpoises only break the surface with their backs and fins. If you spot a whale, the likelihood is that it's a **minke whale**, which grows to about 30ft in length, making it a mere tiddler in the whale world, but a good four or five times bigger than a porpoise. Minkes are baleen whales, which is to say they have no teeth; instead, they gulp huge quantities of water and sift their food through plates of whalebone. Whales do several things dolphins and porpoises can't do, such as blowing water high into the air, and breaching, which is when they launch themselves out of the water and belly-flop down. The two other whale species regularly seen in Hebridean waters are the **killer whale** or orca, distinguished by its very tall, pointed, dorsal fin, and the **pilot whale**, which is even smaller than the minke, has no white on it, and no throat grooves.

1

a classy outfit, charging around £50 for a five-hour round trip, as does Gordon Grant Marine (☎01681 700338, ⓦstaffatours.com), who depart from Fionnphort. If you just want to go to Staffa, try Iolaire (☎01681 700358, ⓦstaffatrips.co.uk), who charge around £30 for passage from Fionnphort.

Ben More

From the southern shores of Loch na Keal, which almost splits Mull in two, rise the terraced slopes of **Ben More** (3169ft) – literally "big mountain" – a mighty extinct volcano, and the only Munro in the Hebrides outside of Skye. It's most easily climbed from Dhiseig, halfway along the loch's southern shores, though an alternative route is to climb up to the col between Beinn Fhada and A'Chioch, and approach via the mountain's eastern ridge. Further west along the shore the road carves through spectacular overhanging cliffs before heading south past the Gribun rocks which face the tiny island of **Inch Kenneth**, where Unity Mitford lived until her death in 1948. There are great views out to Staffa and the Treshnish Isles as the road leaves the coast behind, climbing over the pass to Loch Scridain, where it eventually joins the equally dramatic Glen More road (A849) from Craignure.

Mull Eagle Watch

Glen Seilisdeir, just off the B8035 · April–Sept · £6 · ☎01680 812556, ⓦwhite-tailed-sea-eagle.co.uk

Located a short way north of Loch Scridain, you'll find Britain's only hide dedicated to spotting the magnificent **White-tailed eagle**, which nests here between April and September. The largest and heaviest bird of prey, White-tailed (or sea) eagles became an extinct species in the British Isles in 1916, but since a successful reintroduction programme in the late 1970s, the population has thrived, and today there are currently nineteen pairs of breeding eagles on Mull. Guided access to the hide is available through the RSPB, with the rendezvous point arranged at the time of booking and tours lasting around two hours.

Ardmeanach peninsula

If you're properly equipped for walking, you can explore the NTS-owned **Ardmeanach peninsula**, a rugged landscape of spectacular volcanic geology located just west of the B8035. The best access point is the car park just beyond *Tiroran House*. Otherwise, you'll need a good map and sturdy boots, and you'll need to time your arrival with a falling tide.

Mackinnon's Cave

On the north coast, a mile or so from the road, is **Mackinnon's Cave** – at 100ft high, one of the largest caves in the Hebrides, and accessible only at low tide. As so often, there's a legend attached to the cave, which tells of an entire party, led by a lone piper, who were devoured by evil spirits here.

MacCulloch's Tree

On the south coast of the peninsula, it's a longer, rougher six-mile hike from the road to **MacCulloch's Tree**, a forty-foot-high conifer that was engulfed by a lava flow some fifty million years ago and is now embedded in the cliffs at Rubha na h-Uambha.

The Ross of Mull

Stretching for twenty miles west as far as Iona is Mull's rocky southernmost peninsula, the **Ross of Mull**, which, like much of Scotland, appears blissfully tranquil in good weather, and desolate and bleak in bad climes. Most visitors simply drive through the Ross en route to Iona, but if you have the time it's definitely worth considering exploring, or even staying, in this little-visited part of Mull.

The most scenic spots on the Ross are hidden away on the south coast. If you're approaching the Ross from Craignure, the first of these (to Lochbuie) is signposted even before you've negotiated the splendid Highland pass of **Glen More**, which brings you to the Ross itself.

Lochbuie

The road to **Lochbuie** skirts Loch Spelve, a sheltered sea loch, followed by freshwater Loch Uisg, which is fringed by woodland, before emerging, after eight miles, on a fertile plain beside the sea. The bay here is rugged and wide, and overlooked by the handsome peak of Ben Buie (2352ft), to the northwest. Hidden behind a patch of Scots pine are the ivy-strewn ruins of **Moy Castle**, an old MacLean stronghold; in the fields to the north is one of the few **stone circles** in the west of Scotland, dating from the second century BC, the tallest of its stones about 6ft high. A popular and fairly easy walk is the five-mile hike west from Lochbuie along the coastal path to Carsaig (see below).

Carsaig

A rickety single-track road heads south four miles from Lochbuie to **Carsaig**, which enjoys an idyllic setting, looking south out to Colonsay, Islay and Jura. Most folk come here either to walk east to Lochbuie, or west under the cliffs, to the **Nuns' Cave**, where nuns from Iona are alleged to have hidden during the Reformation, and then, after four miles or so, at Malcolm's Point, the spectacular **Carsaig Arches**, formed by eroded sea-caves, which are linked to basalt cliffs.

Bunessan

From Carsaig, the main road continues for another twelve miles to **Bunessan**, the largest village on the peninsula, roughly two-thirds of the way along the Ross. Just beyond the *Argyll Arms Hotel*, drop in at **Ardalanish Weavers** (daily 10am–5pm; free; ☎01681 700265, ⦾ardalanish.com), where beautiful, durable organic tweed is produced on Victorian looms originally from Torosay Castle. The tweed is snapped up by high-end high-street stores, and is used for the elegant couture collection displayed in the small shop; you can also buy smaller items such as scarves and balls of wool. A couple of miles out of Bunessan is the wide expanse of **Ardalanish Bay**.

Fionnphort and around

The road ends at **Fionnphort**, from where ferries ply the short route across to Iona; there's also some handy accommodation here and a superb restaurant. Around a mile and a half south of Fionnphort are the golden sands of **Fidden beach**, which looks out to the **Isle of Erraid**, where Robert Louis Stevenson is believed to have written *Kidnapped* while staying in one of the island's cottages; *Kidnapped*'s hero, David Balfour, is shipwrecked on the **Torran Rocks**, out to sea to the south of Erraid, beyond which lies the remarkable, stripy **Dubh Artach lighthouse**, built by Stevenson's father in 1862. In the book, Balfour spends a miserable time convinced that he's stranded on Erraid, which can, in fact, be reached across the sands on its eastern side at low tide. The island is now in Dutch ownership, and cared for by the Findhorn Community.

ARRIVAL AND DEPARTURE   THE ROSS OF MULL

By ferry The CalMac passenger ferry from Fionnphort to Iona is very frequent (every 30min in summer; £4.95 return, cycles free), and takes just ten minutes.

ACCOMMODATION AND EATING

Fidden Farm Campsite Knockvologan Road, Fidden, Fionnphort ☎01681 700427. This simple, getting-away-from-it-all campsite has a wonderful location, with direct access to Fidden beach. There's a Portakabin with toilets and showers, and best of all, campfires are allowed. Easter–Oct. **£12**/pitch

1

★**Ninth Wave** Bruach Mhor ☎01681 700757, ⓦninthwaverestaurant.co.uk. For something a little special, head to this upmarket restaurant – in a renovated 200-year-old bothy – secreted away in wonderful rural isolation about a mile north of Fionnphort (it's well signposted). The owner catches and then serves up crab, lobster and other treats, while the veg is supplied from their own kitchen garden, resulting in fantastic dishes like pan-seared fillet of Mull Highland beef with baby beetroot and horseradish mousse. Three-course meal £42. Reservations required. Tues–Sun 7–11pm.

Seaview About 200m up from Fionnphort ferry terminal, on the main road ☎01681 700235, ⓦiona -bed-breakfast-mull.com. This conscientiously-run sand-stone Victorian villa has five somewhat boxy, but pretty and well-equipped, rooms adorned with splashes of artwork. They've also got bikes for hire. March to mid-Nov. **£80**

Staffa House 100m back along the road from Seaview ☎01681 700677, ⓦstaffahouse.co.uk. Handsome whitewashed building with four light and immaculately presented rooms, and a lovely glass conservatory for breakfast. March–Oct. **£70**

Uisken beach Two miles south of Bunessan. Uisken beach is a wonderful spot for wild camping, but ask permission first at *Uisken Croft* (☎01681 700307), just up the hill.

Isle of Iona

Less than a mile off the southwest tip of Mull, **IONA** – just three miles long and not much more than a mile wide – has been a place of pilgrimage for several centuries, and a place of Christian worship for more than 1400 years. For it was to this flat Hebridean island that St Columba fled from Ireland in 563 and established a monastery which was responsible for the conversion of more or less all of pagan Scotland as well as much of northern England. This history and the island's splendid isolation have lent it a peculiar religiosity; in the much-quoted words of Dr Johnson, who visited in 1773, "That man is little to be envied… whose piety would not grow warmer among the ruins of Iona." Today, however, the island can barely cope with the constant flood of day-trippers, so to appreciate the special atmosphere and to have time to see the whole island, including the often overlooked west coast, you should plan on staying at least one night.

Brief history

Whatever the truth about Columba's life, in the sixth and seventh centuries Iona enjoyed a great deal of autonomy from Rome, establishing a specifically **Celtic Christian** tradition. Missionaries were sent out to the rest of Scotland and parts of England, and Iona quickly became a respected seat of learning and artistry; the monks compiled a vast library of intricately **illuminated manuscripts** – most famously the *Book of Kells* (now on display in Trinity College, Dublin) – while the masons excelled in carving peculiarly intricate crosses. Two factors were instrumental in the demise of the Celtic tradition: a series of Viking raids, the worst of which was the massacre of 68 monks on the sands of Martyrs' Bay in 806; and relentless pressure from the established Church,

---

WALKING IONA

Not many day-visitors get further than the village and abbey, but it's perfectly possible to walk to the stunning sandy beaches and turquoise seas at the **north end** of the island, or up to the highest point, **Dún I**, a mere 328ft above sea level but with views on a clear day to Skye, Tiree and Jura. Alternatively, it takes about half an hour to walk over to the **machair**, or common grazing land, on the west side of Iona (also used as a rough golf course). On the edge of this is a series of pretty sandy beaches, the largest of which is the evocatively named **Camus Cúl an t-Saimh** ("Bay at the Back of the Ocean"), a crescent of pebble and shell-strewn sand with a spouting cave to the south. Those with more time (2–3hr) might hike over to the **south** of the island, where Port a'Churaich ("Bay of the Coracle", also known as St Columba's Bay), the saint's traditional landing place on Iona, is filled with smooth round rocks and multicoloured pebbles and stones. A short distance to the east is the **disused marble quarry** at Rubha na Carraig Geire on the southeasternmost point of Iona, finally closed down in 1914.

ST COLUMBA

Legend has it that **St Columba** (Colum Cille), born in Donegal some time around 521, was a direct descendant of the semi-legendary Irish king, Niall of the Nine Hostages. A scholar and soldier priest, who founded numerous monasteries in Ireland, he is thought to have become involved in a bloody dispute with the king when he refused to hand over a copy of *St Jerome's Psalter*, copied illegally from the original owned by St Finian of Moville. This, in turn, provoked the Battle of Cúl Drebene (Cooldrumman) – also known as the **Battle of the Book** – at which Columba's forces won, though with the loss of over 3000 lives. The story goes that, repenting this bloodshed, Columba went into exile with twelve other monks, eventually settling on Iona in 563, allegedly because it was the first island he encountered from which he couldn't see his homeland. The bottom line, however, is that we know very little about Columba, though he undoubtedly became something of a cult figure after his death in 597. He was posthumously credited with miraculous feats such as defeating the Loch Ness monster – it only had to hear his voice and it recoiled in terror – and casting out snakes (and, some say, frogs) from the island. He is also famously alleged to have banned women and cows from Iona, exiling them to Eilean nam Ban (Woman's Island), just north of Fionnphort, for, as he believed, "Where there is a cow there is a woman, and where there is a woman there is mischief."

---

beginning with the Synod of Whitby in 664, which chose Rome over the Celtic Church, and culminated in its suppression by King David I in 1144.

In 1203, Iona became part of the mainstream Church with the establishment of an **Augustinian nunnery** and a **Benedictine monastery** by Reginald, son of Somerled, Lord of the Isles. During the Reformation, the entire complex was ransacked, the contents of the library burnt and all but three of the island's 360 crosses destroyed. Although plans were drawn up at various times to turn the abbey into a Cathedral of the Isles, nothing came of them until 1899, when the (then) owner, the eighth Duke of Argyll, donated the abbey buildings to the **Church of Scotland**, who restored the abbey church for worship over the course of the next decade. Iona's modern resurgence began in 1938, when **George MacLeod**, a minister from Glasgow, established a group of ministers, students and artisans to begin rebuilding the remainder of the monastic buildings. What began as a mostly male, Gaelic-speaking, strictly Presbyterian community is today a lay, mixed and ecumenical retreat. The entire abbey complex has been successfully restored, and is now looked after by Historic Scotland, while the island, apart from the church land and a few crofts, is in the care of the NTS.

Baile Mór

The passenger ferry from Fionnphort drops you off at the island's main village, **BAILE MÓR** (literally "Large Village"), which is in fact little more than a single terrace of cottages facing the sea. You will, though, find most things of a practical nature located here, including the island's main hotel, restaurant and a well-stocked shop.

Augustinian nunnery

Just inland lie the extensive pink-granite ruins of the **Augustinian nunnery**, disused since the Reformation. A beautifully maintained garden now occupies the cloisters, and if nothing else the complex gives you an idea of the state of the present-day abbey before it was restored.

Iona Heritage Centre

Across the road to the north from the Augustinian nunnery • Easter–Oct Mon–Sat 10.30am–4.15pm • £3

In the former manse, the **Iona Heritage Centre** has displays on the social history of the island over the last 200 years, including the Clearances, which nearly halved the island's population of 500 in the mid-nineteenth century. One of the more intriguing exhibits is

1

part of the stern belonging to *Guy Mannering*, a sailing packet on the New York to Liverpool route which sank in machair in 1865 – indeed, it was just one of twenty or so vessels believed to have been lost in waters hereabouts around that time. At a bend in the road, just south of the manse, stands the slender, fifteenth-century **MacLean's Cross**, a fine, late medieval example of the distinctive, flowing, three-leaved foliage of the Iona school.

Iona Abbey

North of the Augustinian nunnery • Daily: April–Sept 9.30am–5.30pm; Oct–March 9.30am–4.30pm; there are free daily guided tours of the abbey (the times are posted up at the ticket office) • £7.10; HS • ☎ 01681 700512

A five-minute walk up the road from the heritage centre stands **Iona Abbey**. Although no buildings remain from Columba's time, the present abbey dates from the arrival of the Benedictines in around 1200, though it was extensively rebuilt in the fifteenth and sixteenth centuries, and restored virtually wholesale last century.

St Oran's Chapel

Iona's oldest building, the plain-looking eleventh-century **St Oran's Chapel**, lies south of the abbey, to your right. Legend has it that the original chapel could only be completed

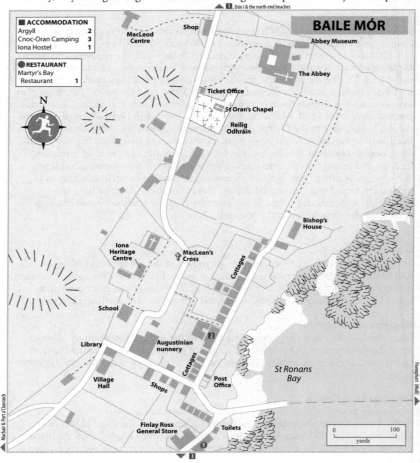

1

through human sacrifice. Oran apparently volunteered to be buried alive, and was found to have survived the ordeal when the grave was opened a few days later. Declaring that he had seen hell and it wasn't all bad, he was promptly reinterred for blasphemy. Oran's Chapel stands at the centre of Iona's sacred burial ground, **Reilig Odhráin** (Oran's Cemetery), which is said to contain the graves of sixty kings of Norway, Ireland, France and Scotland, including Duncan and Macbeth.

Street of the Dead

Approaching the abbey itself, from the ticket office, you cross an exposed section of the evocative medieval **Street of the Dead**, whose giant pink-granite cobbles once stretched from the abbey, past St Oran's Chapel, to the village. Beside the road stands the most impressive of Iona's Celtic high crosses, the eighth-century **St Martin's Cross**, smothered with figural scenes – the Virgin and Child at the centre, Daniel in the lion's den, Abraham sacrificing Isaac, and David with musicians in the shaft below. The reverse side features Pictish serpent-and-boss decoration. Standing directly in front of the abbey are the base of St Matthew's Cross (the rest of which is in the Infirmary Museum) and, to the left, a concrete cast of the eighth-century **St John's Cross**, decorated with serpent-and-boss and Celtic spiral ornamental panels. Before you enter the abbey, take a look inside **St Columba's Shrine**, a small steep-roofed chamber to the left of the main entrance. Columba is believed to have been buried either here or under the rocky mound to the west of the abbey, known as Tórr an Aba.

The abbey

The **abbey** itself has been simply and sensitively restored to incorporate the original elements. You can spot many of the medieval capitals in the south aisle of the choir and in the south transept, where the white-marble effigies of the eighth Duke of Argyll and his wife, Ina, lie in a side-chapel – an incongruous piece of Victorian pomp in an otherwise modest and tranquil place. The finest pre-Reformation effigy is that of John MacKinnon, the last abbot of Iona, who died around 1500, and now lies on the south side of the choir steps. For reasons of sanitation, the **cloisters** were placed, contrary to the norm, on the north side of the church (where running water was available); entirely reconstructed in the late 1950s, they now shelter lots of medieval grave-slabs.

ARRIVAL AND GETTING AROUND

ISLE OF IONA

By ferry The CalMac passenger ferry from Fionnphort is very frequent (every 30min in summer, less frequent in winter; £4.95 return, cycles free), and takes just ten minutes.

By taxi Believe it or not, there is a taxi on the island (☎07810 325990).

Bike rental Visitors are not allowed to bring cars onto the island, but bikes can be rented from the Finlay Ross general store, just up from the jetty (£8/day) and the *Seaview* guesthouse in Fionnphort (see p.82).

INFORMATION AND TOURS

Tourist information There's no tourist office on Iona, but there is a useful information board just up from the jetty, as well as the website ⓦisle-of-iona.com.

Boat tours Mark Jardine's Alternative Boat Hire (☎01681 700537, ⓦboattripsiona.com), based on Iona, takes the lovely wooden gaff-rigged sailing boat *Birthe Marie* on

short trips to some of the less-visited spots around the Sound of Iona and Erraid (Easter–Oct; £25 for a three-hour trip; booking advised).

Wildlife tours Whale-watching and wildlife outings are organized by Volante (☎01681 700362, ⓦvolanteiona .com; £40/3hr 30min).

ACCOMMODATION AND EATING

Argyll On Baile Mór's main street ☎01681 700334, ⓦargyllhoteliona.co.uk. Inviting, stone-built hotel in the village's terrace of cottages overlooking the Sound of Iona, with sixteen sweet, though somewhat boxy, rooms spread throughout a maze of corridors. It is very overpriced, but it

can afford to be. Feb–Nov. **£140**

Cnoc-Oran Camping ☎01681 700112, ⓦiona campsite.co.uk. Turn left at the jetty and it's a twenty-minute walk to this super little campsite, which has a couple of showers and toilets, firepits and BBQs. You can

1

also hire tents and sleeping bags. **£6.50**/person
Iona Hostel Lagandorain ☎01681 700781, ⓦiona
hostel.co.uk. Terrific hostel located to the north of the
island, with impeccable green credentials, rooms with
bunks sleeping two to six people, and a main living space
filled with lovely wooden furniture, a wood-burning stove
and with views out to the Treshnish Isles. To reach it, follow

the road past the abbey for half a mile. Dorms **£19.50**
Martyr's Bay Restaurant ☎01681 700382. A self-
service canteen by day, a fully fledged restaurant come
evening; either way, the tourist hordes invariably pack
this place out for steaks and seafood. Lunch dishes like
haddock and chips (£9.95) and baked potato with haggis
are worth a punt. Daily 11am–11pm.

Isle of Coll

Roughly thirteen miles long and three miles wide, the fish-shaped rocky island of **COLL**,
with a population of around a hundred, lies less than seven miles off the coast of Mull.
For the most part, this remote island is low lying, treeless and exceptionally windy, with
white sandy beaches and the highest sunshine records in Scotland.

Like most of the Hebrides, Coll was once ruled by Vikings, and didn't pass into
Scottish hands until the thirteenth century. In the 1830s, the island's population
peaked at 1440, but was badly affected by the Clearances, which virtually halved its
population in a generation. Coll was fortunate to be in the hands of the enlightened
MacLeans, but they were forced to sell in 1856 to the Stewart family, who raised the
rents, forcing the island's population to move wholesale from the more fertile southeast
to the northwest coast. However, overcrowding led to widespread emigration; a few of
the old crofts in Bousd and Sorisdale, at Coll's northernmost tip, have more recently
been restored. From here, there's an impressive view over to the headland, the Small
Isles and the Skye Cuillin beyond. The majority of visitors to Coll stay for a week in
self-catering accommodation, though there are hotels and B&Bs on the islands, which
should be booked in advance – as should the ferries.

Arinagour

The ferry docks at Coll's only real village, **Arinagour**, whose whitewashed cottages line
the western shore of Loch Eatharna, a popular safe anchorage for boats. Half the
island's population lives in the village, and it's here you'll find the island's hotel and
pub, post office, churches and a couple of shops; two miles northwest along the
Arnabost road, there's even a golf course. The island's petrol pump is also in Arinagour,
and is run on a volunteer basis – it's basically open when the ferry arrives.

The Breachacha castles

On the southwest coast there are two edifices, both confusingly known as **Breachacha
Castle**, and both built by the MacLeans. The older, at the head of Loch Breachacha,
is a fifteenth-century tower house with an additional curtain wall, now used by
Project Trust overseas-aid volunteers. The less attractive "new castle", to the
northwest, is made up of a central block built around 1750 and two side-pavilions
added a century later, now converted into holiday cottages. It was here that
Dr Johnson and Boswell stayed in 1773 after a storm forced them to take refuge en
route to Mull. Much of the surrounding area is now owned by the RSPB, in the hope
of protecting the island's corncrakes.

Ben Hogh

For an overview of the whole island, and a fantastic Hebridean panorama, you can
follow in Johnson's and Boswell's footsteps and take a wander up **Ben Hogh** – at 339ft,
Coll's highest point – two miles west of Arinagour, close to the shore. On the summit
is a giant boulder known as an "erratic", perilously perched on three small boulders.

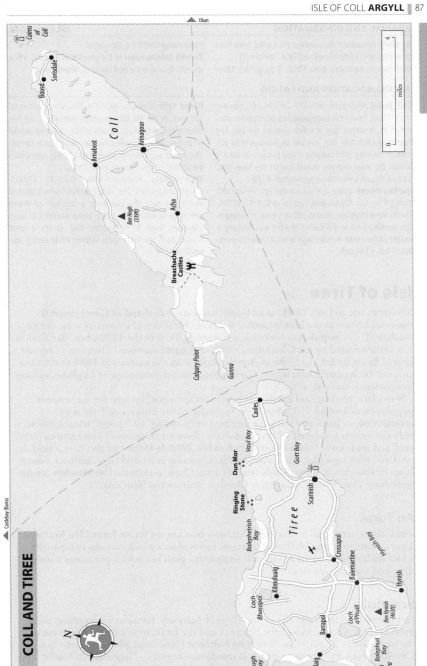

COLL AND TIREE

Oban

Castlebay (Barra)

miles

0   4

Cairns
of Coll

Sorisdale

Bousd

Arnabost

C o l l

Cliad

Arinagour

Acha

Ben Hogh
(339ft)

Breachacha
Castles

Calgary Point

Gunna

Caoles

Vaul Bay

Dun Mor

Ringing
Stone

Gott Bay

Scarinish

Rhu na Faod

T i r e e

Balephetrish
Bay

Crossapol

Balemartine

Hynish

Kilmoluaig

Loch
Bhasapol

Barrapol

Loch
a'Phuill

Ben Hynish
(463ft)

Hough
Bay

Sandaig

Balephuil
Bay

Ceann
a'Mhara

N

1

ARRIVAL AND INFORMATION

By ferry Throughout the summer, the CalMac ferry from Oban calls at Coll (2hr 40min) and Tiree (3hr 40min). Destinations Castlebay, Barra (Thurs 1 daily; 4hr); Oban (daily except Wed & Fri; 2hr 40min).

Tourist information In the absence of a tourist office, ⓦ visitcoll.co.uk is the best source of information.

ACCOMMODATION AND EATING

Coll Hotel Arinagour ☎01879 230334, ⓦcollhotel .com. Small, family-run hotel providing decent accommodation in six rooms, four of which overlook the bay. The hotel also offers bike hire, and can do pick-ups/drop-offs from/to the ferry. Wild camping is also possible on the hill behind the hotel, but you should contact the hotel first; it's free, though a donation is appreciated. **£100**

Garden House Down a track on the left before the turn-off for the Breachacha castles ☎01879 230374. There's more complete, though still very basic, camping at this working farm in the shelter of what was formerly a walled garden, with showers, toilets and a camper's room. April–Oct. **£14**/pitch

Island Café Arinagour ☎01879 230262, ⓦfirstportof coll.com. In the old harbour stores overlooking the bay, offering hot meals all day, though Sundays are most popular when they rustle up a superb two-course late lunch, comprising a roast and a dessert (until 6pm; £12.50); reservations are advised for this. Daily 11am–7.30pm.

Tigh-na-Mara Arinagour Bay ☎01879 230354, ⓦtighnamara.info. The "House by the Sea" is a modern guesthouse near the pier, with a selection of shared and en-suite rooms, the latter being around £10 more expensive. Such is its location that there's a good chance you'll see some great wildlife while eating your breakfast. **£70**

Isle of Tiree

Similar in size to Coll, **TIREE**, as its Gaelic name *tir-iodh* (Land of Corn) suggests, was once known as the breadbasket of the Inner Hebrides, thanks to its acres of rich machair. Tiree's population peaked at a staggering 4450 in the 1830s, but, like Coll, it was badly affected by the Clearances, which decimated numbers. Tiree was ruthlessly cleared by its owner, the Duke of Argyll, who sent in the marines in 1885 to evict the crofters. Both islands have strong Gaelic roots, but the percentage of English-speaking newcomers is rising steadily.

Nowadays, crofting and tourism are the main sources of income for the resident population of around 750. One of the most distinctive features of Tiree is its **architecture**, in particular the large numbers of "pudding" or "spotty" houses, where only the mortar is painted white. In addition, there are numerous "white houses" (*tigh geal*) and traditional "black houses" (*tigh dubh*). **Wildlife**-lovers can also have a field day on Tiree, with lapwings, wheatears, redshank, greylag geese and large, laidback brown hares in abundance. Tiree's sandy beaches attract large numbers of **windsurfers** for the week-long Tiree Wave Classic every October (ⓦtireewaveclassic.co.uk).

An Turas

The CalMac ferry calls at Gott Bay Pier, now best known for **An Turas** (The Journey), Tiree's award-winning "shelter", an artistic extravaganza which features two parallel white walls connected via a black felt section to a glass box which punctures a stone dyke and frames a sea view.

Scarinish

Just up the road from the pier is the village of **Scarinish**, home to a post office, some public toilets, a supermarket, the butcher's and the bank, with a petrol pump back at the pier. Also in Scarinish you'll find **An Iodhlann** (June–Sept Mon–Fri 9am–5pm; Oct–May Tues–Fri 11am–5pm; £3; ⓦaniodhlann.org.uk) – "haystack" in Gaelic – the island's two-roomed archive, which puts on exhibitions in the summer. To the east of Scarinish, **Gott Bay** is backed by a two-mile stretch of sand.

Dun Mor and around

A mile to the north of Scarinish is Vaul Bay, on the north coast, where the well-preserved remains of a dry-stone broch, **Dun Mor** – dating from the first century BC – lie hidden in the rocks to the west of the bay. From Dun Mor it's another two miles west along the coast to the *Clach a'Choire* or **Ringing Stone**, a huge glacial boulder decorated with mysterious prehistoric markings, which when struck with a stone gives out a metallic sound, thus giving rise to the legend that inside is a crock of gold. The story goes that, should the Ringing Stone ever be broken in two, Tiree will sink beneath the waves.

A mile further west you come to lovely **Balephetrish Bay**, where you can watch waders feeding in the breakers, and look out to sea to Skye and the Western Isles.

Ben Hynish

The most intriguing sights lie in the bulging western half of the island, where Tiree's two landmark hills rise up. The higher of the two, **Ben Hynish** (463ft), is unfortunately occupied by a "golf-ball" radar station, which tracks incoming transatlantic flights; the views from the top, though, are great.

Hynish

Below Ben Hynish, to the east, is **Hynish**, with its recently restored **harbour**, designed by Alan Stevenson in the 1830s to transport building materials for the magnificent 140-foot-tall **Skerryvore Lighthouse**, which lies on a sea-swept reef some twelve miles southwest of Tiree. The harbour features an ingenious reservoir to prevent silting and, up on the hill behind, beside the row of lightkeepers' houses, a stumpy granite signal-tower. The tower, whose signals used to be the only contact the lighthouse keepers had with civilization, now houses a **museum** (Easter to mid-Oct daily 9am–5pm; £3; ⓣ 01879 220726), telling the history of the herculean effort required to erect the lighthouse.

Ceann a'Mhara and around

A mile or so across the golden sands of Balephuil Bay, is the spectacular headland of **Ceann a'Mhara** (pronounced "kenavara"). The cliffs here are home to thousands of seabirds, including fulmar, kittiwake, guillemot, razorbill, shag and cormorant, with gannet and tern feeding offshore; the islands of Barra and South Uist are also visible on the northern horizon.

Taigh Iain Mhoir

June–Sept Mon–Fri 2–4pm • Free

In the scattered west-coast settlement of **Sandaig**, to the north of Ceann a'Mhara, three thatched white houses in a row have been turned into the **Taigh Iain Mhoir**, which gives an insight into how the majority of islanders lived in the nineteenth century.

ARRIVAL AND DEPARTURE — ISLE OF TIREE

By plane Tiree Airport (ⓣ 01879 220456, ⓦ hial.co.uk) is around three miles west of Scarinish, with flights to and from Glasgow (Mon–Sat 1 daily; 45min). You should ask your hosts to collect you; most of them will.

By ferry Throughout the summer, the CalMac ferry from Oban calls daily at Coll (2hr 40min) and Tiree (3hr 40min). On Thursdays – though the day may change – the ferry continues to Barra in the Western Isles, and calls in at Tiree on the way back, making a day-trip from Oban possible; a minibus tour of the island is thrown in as part of the package.

Destinations Castlebay, Barra (Thurs 1 daily; 2hr 45min); Oban (1 daily; 3hr 40min).

GETTING AROUND AND INFORMATION

By minibus Tiree has a Ring'n'Ride minibus service (Mon & Wed–Sat 7am–6pm, Tues 7am–10pm; ☎01879 220419), which will take you anywhere on the island, though you should book in advance.

Bike/car rental Based at Scarinish Pier, MacLennan Motors (☎01879 220555, ⊛maclennanmotors.com)

offers both car (£45/day) and bike (£10/day) rental. They can also drop cars at the airport.

Tourist information For a map of the island and the daily papers, you need to go to the supermarket at Crossapol. The website ⊛isleoftiree.com is also a useful resource.

ACCOMMODATION AND EATING

Balinoe Camping Balinoe ☎01879 220399, ⊛wild diamond.co.uk. Located in the southwest of the island, six miles from Scarinish, the island's only formal campsite is operated by Wild Diamond Watersports, and is well-equipped with showers, toilets, a self-catering kitchen and washing/drying facilities. **£24**/pitch

Elephant's End Kirkapol ☎01879 220694. Homely, wonderfully named restaurant serving local goodies such as crab, lobster and langoustine, alongside lamb and beef from the island. Mon–Sat 10am–4pm & 7–11pm, Sun 12.30–2.30pm.

Millhouse Hostel near Loch Bhasapol, in the northwest of the island ☎01879 220435,

⊛tireemillhouse.co.uk. This superbly converted, early twentieth-century barn now accommodates a colourful hostel, with two dorms each sleeping six and a couple of doubles. The excellent open-plan kitchen/lounge opens up onto a patio where you can kick back with a beer and watch the sunset. Dorms **£17**; doubles **£40**

Scarinish Hotel Scarinish ☎01879 220308, ⊛tiree scarinishhotel.com. Super location overlooking the old harbour offering six pristine rooms (a couple with shared bathroom facilities), furnished in solid, if not spectacular, fashion. The Upper Deck lounge is a lovely spot to while away an hour or so watching the comings and goings around the harbour. **£80**

Isle of Colonsay and around

Isolated between Mull and Islay, **Colonsay** — measuring just eight miles by three – is nothing like as bleak and windswept as Coll or Tiree. Its craggy, heather-backed hills even support the occasional patch of woodland, plus a bewildering array of plant and birdlife, wild goats and rabbits, and a very fine quasi-tropical garden. The population of around a hundred is down from a pre-Clearance peak of nearly a thousand, and with only one hotel and infrequent ferry links with the mainland, there's no fear of mass tourism taking over. Colonsay organizes its own annual, small (but very popular), four-day **folk festival**, Ceòl Cholasa (⊛ceolcholasa.co.uk), in mid-September. The ferry terminal is at **Scalasaig**, on the east coast, where there's a post office/shop, a petrol pump, a brewery, a café and the island's hotel.

Colonsay House

Two miles north of Scalasaig • Gardens April–Sept Wed & Fri noon–5pm • £3 • ☎01951 200316, ⊛colonsayestate.co.uk

Colonsay House was built in 1722 by Malcolm MacNeil, and in 1904, the island and house were bought by Lord Strathcona, who made his fortune building the Canadian Pacific Railway (and whose descendants still own the island). He was also responsible for the house's romantically dilapidated woodland **gardens**, which shelter the strange eighth-century **Riasg Buidhe Cross**, decorated with an unusually lifelike mug shot (possibly of a monk) – ask for directions from the tearoom.

Kiloran Bay and around

To the north of Colonsay House is the island's finest sandy beach, the breathtaking **Kiloran Bay**, where spectacular breakers roll in from the Atlantic. There's another unspoilt sandy beach backed by dunes at Balnahard, two miles northeast along a rough track; en route, you might spot wild goats, choughs and even a golden eagle.

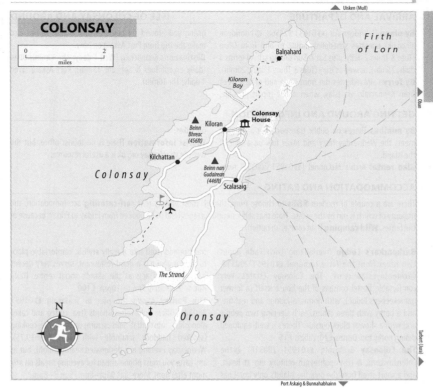

Beinn Bhreac

The island's west coast forms a sharp escarpment, quite at odds with the gentle undulating landscape that characterizes the rest of the island. Due west of Colonsay House around **Beinn Bhreac** (456ft), the cliffs are at their most spectacular, and in their lower reaches provide a home to hundreds of seabirds, among them kittiwake, cormorant and guillemot in spring and early summer.

Isle of Oronsay

While on Colonsay, it's worth taking a day out to visit the **Isle of Oronsay**, half a mile to the south, with its ruined Augustinian priory. The two islands are separated by "The Strand", a stretch of tidal mudflats, which act as a causeway for two hours either side of low tide (check locally for timings); you can drive over to the island at low tide, though most people park their cars and walk across. Legends (and etymology) link saints Columba and Oran with Colonsay and Oronsay, although the ruins only date back to the fourteenth century. You can, nevertheless, still make out the original church and tiny cloisters, abandoned since the Reformation and now roofless. The highlight, though, is the **Oronsay Cross**, a superb example of late medieval artistry from Iona which, along with thirty or so beautifully carved grave-slabs, can be found in the restored side-chapel. It takes about an hour to walk from the tip of Colonsay across The Strand to the priory (Wellington boots are a good option).

1

ARRIVAL AND DEPARTURE

By plane Hebridean Air (☎01631 524568, ⓦhebridean air.co.uk) operates scheduled flights to and from Oban (Tues & Thurs 2 daily, plus Sat & Sun during school terms 1 daily; 25min), as well as Islay (Tues & Thurs 1 daily; 20min).
By ferry CalMac ferries run from Oban and once a week from Kennacraig via Islay, when a day-trip is possible,

ISLE OF COLONSAY AND AROUND

giving you around six hours on the island. Ferries also make the trip from Port Askaig on Islay.
Destinations Kennacraig (Wed 1 daily; 3hr 40min); Oban (daily except Tues & Sat; 2hr 15min); Port Askaig (Wed 1 daily; 1hr 10min).

GETTING AROUND AND INFORMATION

By minibus There's no public transport, but a minibus meets the Wednesday ferry and takes folk on a tour of the island.
Bike rental Archie McConnel (☎01951 200355) rents

out bikes.
Tourist information There is no tourist office, but the website ⓦcolonsay.org.uk is a useful resource.

ACCOMMODATION AND EATING

There are a couple of modern **B&Bs** to choose from, though most visitors rent **self-catering** accommodation, the majority of which is run by the estate. Note that self-catering cottages tend to be booked from Friday to Friday, because of the ferries. **Wild camping** is, of course, an option.

Backpacker's Lodge Overlooking Loch Fada about two miles from the ferry terminal ☎01951 200312, ⓦcolonsayestate.co.uk. The Colonsay Estate's very comfortable hostel consists of the house itself (a former gamekeeper's lodge), with dorms, a lounge and real fire, and a bothy with three cabins, each sleeping two people and with a shower block outside. There's a well-equipped dining bothy too. Dorms £20; cabins £15
The Colonsay Scalasaig ☎01951 200316, ⓦthe colonsay.com. A cosy eighteenth-century inn at heart, and a short stroll from the pier, the island's only hotel has

transformed itself into a really stylish, comfortable place to stay; it also has a good restaurant, serves very decent bar snacks and acts as the island's social centre. Daily noon–2.30pm & Sun 6–10pm. £100
The Pantry Above the pier in Scalasaig ☎01951 200325. Offers light refreshments (tea, coffee and cake) alongside substantial and scrumptious home-cooking (smoked haddock scramble with chips for £9.75). Wednesday evening is a designated seafood night, but in any case, you must phone ahead for evening meals on any night after 8pm. Mon–Sat 9am–8pm, Sun 3–8pm.

Mid-Argyll

Mid-Argyll loosely describes the central wedge of land south of Oban and north of Kintyre. **Lochgilphead**, on Loch Fyne, is the chief town in the area, but has little to offer beyond its practical uses. The highlights of this gently undulating scenery lie along the sharply indented and remote western coastline. Closest to Oban are the melancholy former slate-mining settlements known collectively as the **Slate Islands**. Further south, **Arduaine Garden** is among Argyll's most celebrated horticultural sights, while the rich Bronze Age and Neolithic remains in the **Kilmartin** valley comprise one of the most important prehistoric sites in Scotland. Separating Kilmartin Glen from the **Knapdale** peninsula is the **Crinan Canal**, a short cut for boats disinclined to round the Mull of Kintyre, ending in the picturesque, pint-sized port of **Crinan**.

The Slate Islands

Eight miles south of Oban, a road heads off the A816 west to the miniscule **Slate Islands**, which at their peak in the mid-nineteenth century quarried over nine million slates annually. Today the old slate villages are sparsely populated, and an inevitable air of melancholy hangs over them, but their dramatic setting amid crashing waves makes for a rewarding day-trip.

1

Isle of Seil

The most northerly of the Slate Islands is **Seil**, a lush island, now something of an exclusive enclave. It's separated from the mainland only by the thinnest of sea channels and spanned by the elegant humpback **Clachan Bridge**, built in 1793 and popularly known as the "Bridge over the Atlantic". The **pub** next door to the bridge is the *Tigh na Truish* (House of the Trousers), where kilt-wearing islanders would change into trousers to conform to the post-1745 ban on Highland dress.

Ellenabeich

The main village on Seil is **Ellenabeich**, its neat white terraces of workers' cottages – featured in the film *Ring of Bright Water* – crouching below black cliffs on the westernmost tip of the island. This was once the tiny island of Eilean a'Beithich (hence "Ellenabeich"), separated from the mainland by a slim sea channel until the intensive slate quarrying succeeded in silting it up. Confusingly, the village is often referred to by the same name as the nearby island of Easdale, since they formed an interdependent community based exclusively around the slate industry. The **Slate Islands Heritage Centre** (April–Oct daily 10.30am–1pm & 2–5pm; free; ☉slateislands .org.uk), in one of the little white cottages, has a model of the slate quarry as it would have been in its heyday.

Isle of Easdale

☉ easdale.org

Easdale remains an island, though the few hundred yards that separate it from Ellanabeich have to be dredged to keep the channel open. On the eve of a great storm in 1881, Easdale, less than a mile across at any one point, supported an incredible 452 inhabitants. That night, waves engulfed the island and flooded the quarries. The island never really recovered, slate quarrying stopped in 1914, and by the 1960s the population had dwindled to single figures.

With lots of wonderfully flat stones freely available, Easdale makes the perfect venue for the annual **World Stone Skimming Championships**, held on the last Sunday of September.

Easdale Folk Museum

Near the main square • Daily: April–June, Sept & Oct 11am–4.30pm; July & Aug 11am–5pm • £2.50 • ☉ easdalemuseum.org

Many of the old workers' cottages have been restored recently: some as holiday homes, others sold to new residents. One of the cottages houses the interesting **Easdale Folk Museum**, which has surprisingly expansive collections covering not just the local slate industry, but the island's social and military associations. It also sells a useful historical map of the island and you can buy some interesting slate souvenirs in the shop.

Isle of Luing

☉ isleofluing.co.uk

South of Seil, across the narrow, treacherous Cuan Sound, lies **Luing** – pronounced "Ling" – a long, thin, fertile island which once supported more than six hundred people, but now has a third of that. During the Clearances, the population was drastically reduced to make way for cattle; Luing is still renowned for its beef and for the chocolate-brown crossbreed named after it.

Cullipool, a mile or so southwest of the ferry slipway, is the main village, its whitewashed cottages (mostly built by the slate company) dotted along the shore facing Scarba and Mull. Luing's only other village, **Toberonochy**, lies on the more sheltered east coast, three miles southeast, and boasts the same distinctive white cottages.

GETTING AROUND AND TOURS   **THE SLATE ISLANDS**

By ferry The Cuan Ferry (Seil) to Luing runs every 30min (5min). The ferry from Ellenabeich on Seil to the Isle of

Easdale runs more or less on demand (press the buttons in the ferry shed or phone ☎ 01852 300559).

1

ISLANDS GALORE

Scarba is the largest of the islands around Luing, a brooding 1500-foot hulk of slate, a couple of miles wide, inhospitable and wild – most of the fifty or so inhabitants who once lived here had left by the mid-nineteenth century. The string of uninhabited islands visible west of Luing are known collectively as the **Garvellachs**, after the largest, **Garbh Eileach** (Rough Rock), which was inhabited as recently as sixty years ago. The most northerly, **Dún Chonnuill**, contains the remains of an old fort thought to have belonged to Conal of Dalriada, and **Eileach an Naoimh** (Holy Isle), the most southerly, is where the Celtic missionary Brendan the Navigator founded a community in 542, twenty years before Columba landed on Iona. Nothing survives from Brendan's day, but there are a few ninth-century remains, among them a double-beehive cell and a grave enclosure. One school of thought has it that the island is Hinba, Columba's legendary secret retreat, where he founded a monastery before settling on Iona. If you're interested in taking a boat trip to Scarba or the nearby Garvellach Islands contact Sea.fari (☎ 01852 300003, ⓦ seafari.co.uk) based at Easedale, or Craignish Cruises, in Ardfern (☎ 07747 023038, ⓦ craignishcruises.co.uk).

Boat tours High-adrenaline boat trips are offered by Sea.fari (☎ 01852 300003, ⓦ seafari.co.uk), who are based at the Ellenabeich jetty; the boats are rigid inflatables (RIBs) and travel at some speed round the offshore islands and through the Corryvreckan Whirlpool (see p.122).

EATING AND DRINKING

Oyster Brewery Ellenabeich, Isle of Seil ☎ 01852 300121, ⓦ seilislandpub.co.uk. For home-made pasties, seafood and real ale, pop inside the snug wood-panelled bar of the *Oyster*, on the way to the ferry. Daily 11am–1pm.

Puffer Bar Isle of Easdale ☎ 01852 300022, ⓦ pufferbar.com. Should you wish to hang about, then you could do worse than visit the terrific *Puffer* restaurant and bar; the former serves the best of the day's fresh catch, while the latter is a convivial spot for a drink. Mon–Sat 11am–1am, Sun 12.30–11pm.

Arduaine Garden

A816, 10 miles north of Kilmartin • Daily 9.30am–dusk • £6; NTS • ☎ 0844 493 2216

A great spot at which to stop and have a picnic on the A816 from Oban to Lochgilphead is **Arduaine Garden**, overlooking Asknish Bay and the islands of Shuna, Luing, Scarba and Jura. The garden, whose original foundations were laid in 1898, is stupendous, particularly in May and June, and has the feel of an intimate private garden, with immaculately mown lawns, lily-strewn ponds, mature woods and spectacular rhododendrons and azaleas. You can follow several pathways through the garden, one of which is the woodland walk, which leads down to the lakeshore where there's a good chance of spotting otters, sea eagles and hen harriers.

ACCOMMODATION AND EATING   ARDUAINE GARDEN

Chartroom Bistro Next to Arduaine Garden ☎ 01852 200233. The sparky little bistro in the *Loch Melfort Hotel* offers similarly outstanding views, and the food isn't half bad either; their west-coast langoustines and mussels (£11.99) rate highly in these parts, though there's plenty more on the menu, including home-made burgers and scrummy pizzas. Daily 11am–10pm.

★ **Loch Melfort Hotel** Next to Arduaine Garden ☎ 01852 200233, ⓦ lochmelfort.co.uk. This fine, privately-run country-house hotel overlooking Asknish Bay offers a selection of beautifully appointed rooms, each with its own private patio or balcony; best of all, though, are the views, which are unquestionably some of the finest in Scotland. **£160**

Kilmartin Glen

Kilmartin Glen – on the road from Oban to Lochgilphead – is the most important prehistoric site on the Scottish mainland. The most remarkable relic is the **linear cemetery**, where several cairns are aligned for more than two miles, to the south of

1

Kilmartin village. These are thought to represent the successive burials of a ruling family or chieftains, but nobody can be sure. The best view of the cemetery's configuration is from the Bronze Age **Mid-Cairn**, but the Neolithic **South Cairn**, dating from around 3000 BC, is by far the oldest and the most impressive, with its large chambered tomb roofed by giant slabs.

Close to the Mid-Cairn, the two **Temple Wood stone circles** appear to have been the architectural focus of burials in the area from Neolithic times to the Bronze Age. Visible to the south are the impressively cup-marked **Nether Largie standing stones**, the largest of which looms over 10ft high. **Cup- and ring-marked rocks** are a recurrent feature of prehistoric sites in the Kilmartin Glen and elsewhere in Argyll. There are many theories as to their origin: some see them as Pictish symbols, others as primitive solar calendars. The most extensive markings in the entire country are at Achnabreck, off the A816 towards Lochgilphead.

Kilmartin House Museum

In the old manse adjacent to the village church, Kilmartin • Daily: March–Oct 10am–5.30pm; Nov to Christmas 11am–4pm • £5 •
☎ 01546 510278, ⓦ kilmartin.org

Situated on high ground to the north of the cairns is the tiny village of **Kilmartin**, an unremarkable place but home to the superb **Kilmartin House Museum**. Not only can you learn about the various theories concerning prehistoric crannogs, henges and cairns, but you can practise polishing an axe, examine different types of wood, and listen to a variety of weird and wonderful sounds (check out the Gaelic bird

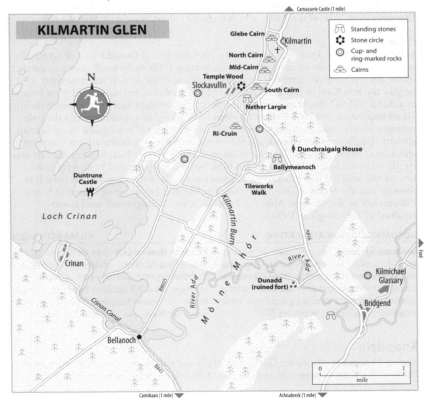

KILMARTIN GLEN

Carnasserie Castle (1 mile)

Glebe Cairn — Kilmartin
North Cairn
Mid-Cairn
Temple Wood
Slockavullin — South Cairn
Nether Largie
Ri-Cruin
Dunchraigaig House
Ballymeanoch
Duntrune Castle
Tileworks Walk
Loch Crinan
Kilmartin Burn
Crinan
Dunadd (ruined fort)
Kilmichael Glassary
Bridgend
River Add
Moine Mhór
Crinan Canal
Bellanoch

Standing stones
Stone circle
Cup- and ring-marked rocks
Cairns

0   1
mile

Cairnbaan (1 mile) ▼   Achnabreck (1 mile) ▼

1

imitations). One of the most remarkable exhibits is a large carved stone head, found in a garden in Port Appin just a few years ago and which is thought to be around two thousand years old. It's worth noting that the museum staff offer superb, free two-hour **guided walks** of the cairns, usually on Wednesdays and Saturdays, though it's best to check in advance.

Kilmartin church

Kilmartin church shelters several richly sculptured graves and crosses, while a separate enclosure in the graveyard houses a large collection of medieval grave slabs of the Malcolms of Poltalloch. These are believed to have been crafted by a group of sculptors working around Loch Awe in the late fourteenth and fifteenth centuries.

Carnasserie Castle

Kilmartin's own castle is ruined beyond recognition; head instead for the much less ruined **Carnasserie Castle**, built in the 1560s on a high ridge a mile up the road towards Oban. Architecturally, the castle is interesting, too, as it represents the transition between fully fortified castles and later mansion houses, and has several original, finely carved stone fireplaces and doorways, as well as numerous gun-loops and shot holes.

Mòine Mhór

To the south of Kilmartin, beyond the linear cemetery, lies the raised peat-bog of **Mòine Mhór** (Great Moss), now a nature reserve and home to remarkable plant, insect and birdlife. To get a close look at the sphagnum moss and wetlands, head for the **Tileworks Walk**, just off the A816, which includes a short boardwalk over the bog.

Dunadd

Mòine Mhór is best known as home to the Iron Age fort of **Dunadd**, one of Scotland's most important Celtic sites, occupying a distinctive 176ft rocky knoll once surrounded by the sea but currently stranded beside the winding River Add. It was here that Fergus, the first King of Dalriada, established his royal seat, having arrived from Ireland in around 500 AD. Its strategic position, the craggy defences and the view from the top are all impressive, but it's the **stone carvings** (now fibreglass copies) between the twin summits which make Dunadd so remarkable: several lines of inscription in ogham (an ancient alphabet of Irish origin), the faint outline of a boar, a hollowed-out footprint and a small basin. The boar and the inscriptions are probably Pictish, since the fort was clearly occupied long before Fergus got here, but the footprint and basin have been interpreted as being part of the royal coronation rituals of the kings of Dalriada. It is thought that the Stone of Destiny was used at Dunadd before being moved to Scone Palace, then to Westminster Abbey in London, where it languished until it was returned to Edinburgh in 1996.

ACCOMMODATION AND EATING	KILMARTIN GLEN
Dunchraigaig House One Mile south of Kilmartin ☎01546 510396, ⌨dunchraigaig.co.uk. This large detached Victorian house situated opposite the Ballymeanoch standing stones offers five spotless en-suite rooms with either woodland or Jura Island views, and you can enjoy terrific home-made clootie dumpling for breakfast. **£80**	**Kilmartin Museum Café** Kilmartin Museum ☎01546 510278. Smoked salmon fishcakes and hot steak and mushroom baguette make this a great pit-stop for lunch, and there's lots of delicious home-baked fare to feast on too, not least a divine selection of cakes and buns. Daily: March–Oct 10am–5pm; Nov & Dec 11am–4pm.

Knapdale

Forested **Knapdale** – from the Gaelic *cnap* (hill) and *dall* (field) – forms a buffer zone between the Kintyre peninsula and the rest of Argyll, bounded to the north by the

MOUNT STUART (P.61) >

1

Crinan Canal and to the south by West Loch Tarbert and consisting of three fingers of land, separated by Loch Sween and Loch Caolisport. Knapdale is a little visited area, which is surprising, as the ancient wooded landscape is among some of the most beautiful, and unique, in the country. Not only that, but there is some spectacular wildlife to observe, not least thanks to the recent reintroduction of beavers to the area (see box, p.99).

Crinan Canal

In 1801 the nine-mile-long **Crinan Canal** opened, linking Loch Fyne, at Ardrishaig south of Lochgilphead, with the Sound of Jura, thus cutting out the long and treacherous journey around the Mull of Kintyre. John Rennie's original design, although an impressive engineering feat, had numerous faults, and by 1816 Thomas Telford was called in to take charge of the renovations. The canal runs parallel to the sea for quite some way before cutting across the bottom of Mòine Mhór and hitting a flight of locks either side of **Cairnbaan** (there are fifteen in total). The walk along the towpath is utterly delightful, both picturesque and pleasantly unstrenuous, though you could, of course, cycle too.

Crinan

There are usually one or two yachts passing through the locks, but the most relaxing place from which to view the canal in action is **Crinan**, the pretty little fishing port at the western end of the canal. Crinan's tiny harbour is, for the moment at least, still home to a small fishing fleet; a quick burst up through Crinan Wood to the hill above the village will give you a bird's-eye view of the sea lock and its setting.

ACCOMMODATION AND EATING   **CRINAN CANAL**

CAIRNBAAN

Cairnbaan Hotel By lock number five ☎01546 603668, ⓦcairnbaan.com. This eighteenth-century coaching inn built at the same time as the canal, which it overlooks, accommodates twelve very well-designed rooms; it's charmingly staffed too. The hotel's lively restaurant-cum-bar makes for a useful pit stop, with lots of passing trade from the canal. Although local seafood is the main staple, there's much more besides, such as tempura of haggis and a wickedly tasty Argyll game pie (£14). Daily 11am–10pm. **£85**

CRINAN

Coffee Shop By the lockside ☎01546 830261. If you only fancy a quick refresher, head down to the cheery lockside café for a homemade sausage roll or a mug of tea

with an enormous scone with jam and butter (£3.85). Easter–Oct: daily 10am–5pm.

Crinan Hotel Overlooking the harbour ☎01546 830261, ⓦcrinanhotel.com. Occupying an enviable position, this long-standing family-run hotel has twenty artistically decorated rooms (indeed the hotel has its own gallery), many with a private balcony from which to take in the loch views. They do, though, come at a price. **£180**

Seafood Bar Crinan Hotel, overlooking the harbour ☎01546 830261. Reward yourself after the long canalside walk with some steamed mussels or an Arbroath smokie (£13) washed down with a pint. This place enjoys one of the most beautiful views in Scotland, especially at sunset, when the myriad islets and the distinctive Paps of Jura are reflected in the waters of the loch. Easter–Oct: daily noon–12.30pm & 6–8.30pm.

Knapdale Forest

South of the Crinan Canal, **Knapdale Forest** stretches virtually uninterrupted from coast to coast, across hills sprinkled with tiny lochs. There are several waymarked walks in the area to choose from: a circular, mile-long path will take you deep into the forest just past **Achnamara**, a three-mile route around **Loch Coille-Bharr**, and a two-and-a-half-mile path which runs along the canal and ascends **Dunardry** (702ft).

Tayvallich and the Chapel of Keills

Continuing down the western finger of Knapdale you come to **Tayvallich**, with its attractive horseshoe bay, after which the peninsula splits again. The western arm leads to the medieval **Chapel of Keills**, housing a display of late medieval carved stones, and

THE BEAVER TRIAL

In 2009, a colony of beavers from Norway were introduced into Knapdale Forest as part of a five-year project by the **Scottish Beaver Trial** (W scottishbeavertrial.org.uk). The first beavers to be released into the wilds of Scotland for over four hundred years, their reintroduction met with a rather mixed reaction, though their effect on the environment (and to a lesser degree the local economy) has been, and continues to be, closely monitored by an independent project team.

From the **interpretation centre** at Barnluasgan (four miles west of Cairnbaan), it's a twenty-minute walk to Dubh Loch, where most of the beaver activity takes place. Here, there's a **viewing platform** and another rough path that cuts through to Loch Coille Bharr, the two lochs separated by an 18-metre-long **dam** that took the beavers around four to five months to build – a quite remarkable feat of engineering. Either side of these two lochs, you'll also see their lodges, large and impressive tangles of severed branches, wood and mud. The best time to see these fascinating creatures is either at dawn or dusk, and although sightings are by no means guaranteed, there is a strong possibility that you will witness some beaver activity. Take along some binoculars, midge repellent and refreshments (you could be waiting a while), and don't bring dogs. You can follow the trail yourself or, alternatively, join one of the free **guided tours** that take place on Tuesday and Saturday evenings between June and September.

the remains of a small port where cattle used to be landed from Ireland. There's also a fine view of the **MacCormaig Islands**, the largest of which, Eilean Mór (owned by the Scottish National Party), was once a retreat of the seventh-century St Cormac.

Loch Sween

Six miles south of Achnamara on the eastern shores of **Loch Sween** is the "Key of Knapdale", the eleventh-century **Castle Sween**, the earliest stone castle in Scotland but in ruins since 1647. The tranquility and beauty of the setting is spoilt by the nearby caravan park, an eyesore which makes a visit pretty depressing. You're better off continuing south to the thirteenth-century **Kilmory Chapel**, also in ruins but with a new roof protecting the medieval grave-slabs and the well-preserved MacMillan's Cross, an eight-foot fifteenth-century Celtic cross showing the Crucifixion on one side and a hunting scene on the other.

Kilberry

The bulk of Knapdale is isolated and fairly impenetrable, but it's worth persevering the fourteen miles of single-track road in order to reach **Kilberry**, where you can camp at *Port Bàn* (see below), and enjoy the fantastic sunsets and views over Jura. There's also a church worth viewing in Kilberry and a small collection of carved medieval grave-slabs.

ACCOMMODATION AND EATING   KILBERRY

Kilberry Inn T 01880 770223, W kilberryinn.com. You'll find some of the finest food for miles around at the *Kilberry*, which punters flock to for its fantastically creative seafood dishes like potted crab with fennel and pink grapefruit, and Sound of Jura scallops seared with puy lentils, pancetta and salsa verde (£19). April–Oct Tues–Sun noon–2pm & 6.30–10pm.

Port Bàn T 01880 770224, W portban.com. With fantastic views and sunsets over Jura, this secluded caravan and camping site is a wonderful place to hide away for a few nights. Brilliant facilities include a shop, café, playpark and games field (with putting and crazy golf), while the nearby beach is great for mucking about on. April–Oct. **£16**/pitch

ENTERTAINMENT

Crear A mile from Kilberry T 01880 770369, W crear .co.uk. Look out for the concerts put on at Crear, a barn that's been transformed into an artists' retreat, studio and concert hall; it attracts an impressive roster of top classical musicians.

1

Kintyre

But for the mile-long isthmus between West Loch Tarbert and the much smaller East Loch Tarbert, the little-visited, sparsely populated peninsula of **KINTYRE** – from the Gaelic *ceann tire*, "land's end" – would be an island. Indeed, in the eleventh century, when the Scottish king, Malcolm Canmore, allowed Magnus Barefoot, King of Norway, to lay claim to any island he could circumnavigate by boat, Magnus dragged his boat across the Tarbert isthmus and added the peninsula to his Hebridean kingdom. During the Wars of the Covenant, the majority of the population and property was wiped out by a combination of the 1646 potato blight and the destructive attentions of the Earl of Argyll. Kintyre remained a virtual desert until the earl began his policy of transplanting Gaelic-speaking Lowlanders to the region. They probably felt quite at home here, as the southern third of the peninsula lies on the Lowland side of the Highland Boundary Fault. Despite its relative proximity to Scotland's Central Belt, Kintyre remains quiet and unfashionable; its main towns of **Tarbert** and **Campbeltown** have few obvious attractions, but that's part of their appeal.

Kintyre's bleak but often beautiful **west coast** ranks among the most exposed stretches of coastline in Argyll. Atlantic breakers pound the rocky shoreline, while the persistent westerly wind forces the trees against the hillside. However, when the weather's fine and the wind not too fierce, there are numerous deserted sandy beaches to enjoy, with great views over to Gigha, Islay, Jura and even Ireland. By way of contrast, the **east coast** of Kintyre is gentler than the west, sheltered from the Atlantic winds and in parts strikingly beautiful, with stunning views across to Arran.

ARRIVAL AND GETTING AROUND   KINTYRE

By plane Campbeltown has an airport, with flights to and from Glasgow, which is only 40 miles away by air, compared to over 120 miles by road.

By bus There are regular daily buses from Glasgow to Campbeltown, via Tarbert and the west coast. On the east coast, buses from Campbeltown only go as far as the fishing village of Carradale, some thirteen miles distant.

By ferry Kintyre is well served with ferries: the main port is at Kennacraig, five miles south of Tarbert on the west coast, with ferries serving Port Askaig and Port Ellen on Islay. There are also ferries from Tarbert to Portavadie on the Cowal peninsula, from Claonaig to Lochranza on Arran, and a summer-only one from Campbeltown to Ardrossan.

Tarbert

A distinctive rocket-like church steeple heralds the fishing village of **TARBERT** (in Gaelic *an tairbeart*, meaning "isthmus"), sheltering an attractive little bay backed by rugged hills. Tarbert's herring industry was mentioned in the *Annals of Ulster* as far back as 836 AD, though now the local fishing industry is down to its lowest level ever. Ironically, it was local Tarbert fishermen, who, in the 1830s, pioneered the method of herring-fishing known as trawling, seining or ring-netting, which eventually wiped out the Loch Fyne herring stocks.

Tourism is now an increasingly important source of income, and though there's little of substance to see in Tarbert itself, it's a good hub, with excellent transport links, a decent stock of accommodation, and some even better seafood restaurants. Moreover, it stages two prestigious annual events: the Scottish Series **yacht races** in late May, and the **Tarbert Seafood Festival** in early July, when traditional boats also hit town. Tarbert is also the starting point of the **Kintyre Way**, an 89-mile walk that zigzags its way down the peninsula to Southend.

Tarbert Castle

South of town, steps lead up from Tarbert's pretty harbourfront to Robert the Bruce's fourteenth-century **castle**. The oldest part of the ivy-strewn ruins date from around the seventh century, though the most substantial remains (albeit now with some rather ugly modern accretions) belong to the fifteenth-century Tower House, with its intact arrow slits and gun loops. The best reason to make the short stroll up here, however, is to take in the **views**, glorious across Loch Fyne and all the way across to the Cowal peninsula.

ARRIVAL AND INFORMATION — TARBERT

By bus Buses stop in the centre of town on Campbeltown Rd and Barmore Rd.
Destinations Campbeltown (5 daily; 1hr 15min); Claonaig (Mon–Sat 3 daily; 30min); Glasgow (5 daily; 3hr 15min); Kennacraig (3–6 daily; 15min); Kilberry (2 daily on schooldays; 40min); Skipness (Mon–Sat 3 daily; 35min); Tayinloan (3–6 daily; 30min).

By ferry The ferry terminal is on Pier Rd, a ten-minute walk along Harbour St.
Destinations Portavadie (hourly; 25min).
Tourist office On Harbour St (April–June, Sept & Oct Mon–Sat 10am–5pm, Sun 11am–5pm; July & Aug Mon–Sat 9am–6pm, Sun 10am–5pm; ☎01880 820429, ⓦ kintyreway.com).

ACCOMMODATION AND EATING

Ca'Dora Harbour St ☎01880 820258. The pick of several cafés ranged along the seafront which, despite looking rather dull from the outside, pulls in the punters for its pizza and pasta, though it's renowned, above all, for its ice cream. Daily 10am–7pm.
★**Knap Guest House** Campbeltown Rd ☎01880 820015, ⓦ knapguesthouse.co.uk. Handsome Victorian townhouse with four pristine rooms leading off a beautifully appointed lounge; each room manifests a curious mixture of traditional Scottish and Asian furnishings, which somehow works. A little tricky to find as there's no sign; it's next to the Woods Financial Services shop. **£70**
Scott's Harbour St ☎01880 820190, ⓦ struan.biz. Classy, contemporary bistro inside *Struan House* with just half a dozen tables. The food is fabulous, notably

the seafood dishes like crab and chilli bruschetta, and scallops and chorizo with linguini (£11.95). Tues–Sat 6–10pm.
★**Starfish** Castle St ☎01880 820733, ⓦ starfish tarbert.com. Sparkling, informally run seafood restaurant where scallops are king. A plate of these will set you back £17, as will the Starfish stew, comprising mussels, queen scallops and the catch of the day. Complete your meal with the crumble of the day. Mon–Thurs & Sun 6–10pm, Fri & Sat noon–2pm & 6–10pm.
Struan House Harbour St ☎01880 820190, ⓦ struan .biz. Built in 1846 as a small hotel, it's now a charming six-room guesthouse with bespoke furnishings, grand wooden bedsteads, and some sweet little touches like bedside lamps, books and pictures on the walls. **£75**

Carradale and around

The only place of any size on the east coast is the fishing village of **Carradale** which, according to one 1930s guide, was "popular with those who like unsophisticated resorts". The village itself is rather drab, but the tiny, very pretty harbour with its small fishing fleet, and the wide, sandy beach to the south, make up for it. On the east side of the beach is **Carradale Point**, a wildlife reserve with feral goats and a good example of a vitrified fort built more than two thousand years ago on a small tidal island off the headland (best approached from the beach). There are several pleasant **walks** with good views across to Arran laid out in the woods around Carradale, for which the best starting-point is the car park at Port na Storm on the road into the village. The B842 ends fourteen miles north of Carradale at **Claonaig**, little more than a slipway for the small summer car ferry to Arran.

Network Carradale Heritage Centre

On the road into Carradale • April–Sept Mon–Wed & Fri–Sun 10am–5pm; Oct–March Mon, Tues & Fri–Sun 11am–4pm • Free • ☎ 01583 431296

The small but informative **Network Carradale Heritage Centre** has exhibits pertaining to the local fishing and farming industries. It also offers a wide selection of bikes to rent, and there's good home-baking to be had in the tearoom.

ARRIVAL AND GETTING AROUND — CARRADALE AND AROUND

By ferry The ferry terminal is at Claonaig, fourteen miles north of Carradale.
Destinations Claonaig–Lochranza, Arran (8–9 daily; 30min).

Bike rental You can rent bikes at the Network Carradale Heritage Centre (see above; £14/5hr, £20/day).

1

ACCOMMODATION AND EATING

Ashbank Hotel Centre of Carradale, by the shops ☎01583 431650, ⓦashbankhotel.com. A dinky little place in the heart of the village, run by two very welcoming sisters. It's nothing flashy, but the five en-suite rooms are homely enough and the Egyptian-cotton bedding is something to savour. **£75**

Carradale Bay Caravan Park Carradale Bay ☎01583 431665, ⓦcarradalebay.com. The nearest campsite to town is the superbly equipped and well-sheltered *Carradale Bay Caravan Park*, right by, and with great access to, the sandy beach. Although it's predominantly a caravan site, there is a separate area to pitch tents. Easter–Oct. **£21**/pitch

Dunvalanree Port Righ Bay ☎01583 431226, ⓦdunvalanree.com. Imposing house overlooking the sheltered little bay of Port Righ, towards Carradale Point; the five rooms are of the highest order, with beautiful, bespoke beds, though for those on a tighter budget, there are a couple of budget rooms available. Dinner costs just £20 extra, which is great value. **£80**

★**The Green Room** Above Carradale harbour ☎07972 683984, ⓦgreenroomteas.co.uk. Utterly delightful tearoom perched high above the harbour and with glorious views across Kilbrannan Sound to Arran. Apart from the main café area (serving sausage rolls, rock cake, flapjacks and the like), there's a glass conservatory overlooking the croquet lawn (where you are free to play) and, better still, a lounge-cum-observatory with a swallow-cam and binoculars for wildlife spotting. Mon, Tues & Thurs–Sun 10am–4pm.

Skipness

Heading north of the Claonaig ferry terminal, a dead-end road winds its way along the shore a few miles further north to the tiny village of **Skipness**, where the considerable ruins of the enormous thirteenth-century **Skipness Castle** and a chapel look out across the Kilbrannan Sound to Arran. There are also several gentle **walks** laid out in the nearby mixed woodland, up the glen. The main reason people make the effort to visit Skipness, however, is the wonderful *Skipness Seafood Cabin* (see below).

ARRIVAL AND EATING SKIPNESS

By bus Buses run between Skipness and Kennacraig via the ferry terminal at Claonaig (Mon–Sat 3 daily; 20min).

Skipness Seafood Cabin Below Skipness Castle ☎01880 760207. Little more than a hut just below the castle, the *Cabin* has been doling out fresh local seafood for years; hot smoked salmon or crab rolls (£4), fresh oysters, queenies (queen scallops), langoustines, mussels and home-baked cakes are just some of the treats. There are wooden tables and bench seating from which to admire the splendid views across to Arran. Whit Sunday to Sept Mon–Fri & Sun 11am–7pm.

Isle of Gigha

Gigha – pronounced "Geeya", with a hard "g" – is a low-lying, fertile island, with a population of around 150, just three miles off the west coast of Kintyre. The island's Ayrshire cattle produce over a quarter of a million gallons of milk a year, though the island's distinctive (occasionally fruit-shaped) cheese is actually produced on the mainland. Like many of the smaller Hebrides, Gigha was bought and sold numerous times after its original lairds, the MacNeils, sold up, before being bought by the islanders themselves in 2002. The most visible sign of the island's regeneration are the three community-owned wind turbines – the "Dancing Ladies" of Faith, Hope and Charity – at the southern tip of the island, which supply Gigha's electricity needs and feed the surplus into the national grid. The real draw of Gigha, apart from the peace and quiet, are the white sandy **beaches** – including one at Ardminish itself – that dot the coastline.

Ardminish

The ferry from Tayinloan, 23 miles south of Tarbert, deposits you at the island's only village, **Ardminish**, where you'll find the post office and shop and the all-denominations island church with some interesting stained-glass windows, including one to Kenneth MacLeod, composer of the well-known ditty *Road to the Isles*.

1

Achamore Gardens

A mile and a half south of Ardminish • Daily 9am–dusk • £4

The main attraction on the island is the **Achamore Gardens**. Established by the first postwar owner, Sir James Horlick of hot-drink fame, their spectacularly colourful display of azaleas are best seen in early summer. Elsewhere, the rhododendrons merit seeking out, as does the walled garden, with its hugely diverse collection of plants, a bamboo maze, and a superb panorama across the island's west coast and beyond to Islay and Jura.

To the southwest of the gardens, the ruins of the thirteenth-century **St Catan's Chapel** are floored with weathered medieval gravestones; the ogham stone nearby is the only one of its kind in the west of Scotland.

ARRIVAL AND INFORMATION   ISLE OF GIGHA

By ferry CalMac ferries depart more or less hourly from Tayinloan, 23 miles south of Tarbert, for the twenty-minute crossing to Ardminish.

Tourist information There's no tourist office, but ⓦ gigha.org.uk is a useful resource.

ACCOMMODATION AND EATING

Achamore House Achamore Gardens ☎ 01583 505400, ⓦ achamorehouse.com. If you want to stay in the style of a laird, book into one of the grand rooms at the beautiful house in the midst of Achamore Gardens; bay windows and antique wardrobes and chests are standard features, though some rooms do have shared bathroom facilities. **£90**

The Boathouse By the pier in Ardminish ☎ 01583 505123, ⓦ boathousegigha.co.uk. The place to go for delicious food, good company, and occasionally, live music and quiz nights. April–Oct: daily 11.30am–10pm.

Boathouse Camping By the pier in Ardminish ☎ 01583 505123, ⓦ boathousegigha.co.uk. There's a designated camping area on the grass adjacent to the *Boathouse*, with fantastic beach views. Facilities are limited to showers (£1) and toilets, though they sell some basic foodstuffs too. Only twenty pitches, so booking ahead is advisable. **£9**/pitch

Gigha Hotel 200m from the ferry terminal in Ardminish ☎ 01583 505254, ⓦ gigha.org.uk. This is the social centre of the island and a very welcoming place to stay; the rooms are inviting and spotlessly clean without being particularly spectacular. **£80**

Machrihanish and around

The only major development along the entire west coast is **MACHRIHANISH**, at the southern end of Machrihanish Bay, the longest continuous stretch of sand in Argyll. There are two approaches to the **beach**: from Machrihanish itself, or from Westport, at the north end of the bay, where the A83 swings east towards Campbeltown; either way, the sea here is too dangerous for swimming. Machrihanish itself was once a thriving salt-producing and coal-mining centre – you can still see the miners' cottages at neighbouring Drumlemble – with a light railway link to Campbeltown, but now survives almost exclusively on **golf**.

Machrihanish Golf Club

Between the beach and Campbeltown Airport • April–Oct £65, Nov–March £30 • ☎ 01586 810213, ⓦ machgolf.com

Dominating the village of Machrihanish, and the main draw in these parts, is the exposed 18-hole championship **Machrihanish golf course** between the beach and Campbeltown Airport on the nearby flat and fertile swath of land known as the Laggan. One of Scotland's finest links courses (established in 1876), it plays out on a quite spectacular landscape, and is particularly notable for its first hole, which cuts across the Atlantic in dramatic fashion.

Machrihanish Dunes Golf Club

East of Campbeltown Airport • April–Oct £70, Nov–March £30 • ☎ 01586 810000, ⓦ machrihanishdunes.com

Established as recently as 2009, the sister course of Machrihanish golf course, **Machrihanish Dunes**, on the other side of the airport, is perhaps even more impressive.

1

The course layout, including the tee and green positions, is dictated solely by the lay of the land.

Seabird observatory

Uisead Point • April–Oct daily • Free • ☎ 07919 660292, ⓦ machrihanishbirdobservatory.org.uk

Fifteen minutes' walk west of Machrihanish, at Uisaed Point, is a tiny **seabird observatory**, which is best visited in the migration periods, when it provides a welcome shelter for ornithologists trying to spot a rare bird blown off-course. Over two hundred species have been recorded here, including some very rare birds, like Sabine's Gull and Balearic Shearwater. There's a very good chance of seeing lots of ocean-going wildlife too, such as otters, grey seals and basking sharks.

ACCOMMODATION AND EATING	MACHRIHANISH AND AROUND

Machrihanish Holiday Park Machrihanish Village ☎ 01586 810366, ⓦ campkintyre.co.uk. Superbly located next to the fairways and with direct sea views, this large, fully equipped family-run campsite has a terrific mix of caravan and tent sites, as well as heated wooden wigwams and fully fitted bell tents. March–Oct. **£14**/pitch; wigwams **£32.50**; bell tents **£50**

Old Clubhouse Pub Machrihanish Village ☎ 01586 810000. Overlooking the first tee, the erstwhile clubhouse is now the very agreeable village pub, frequented by golfers and locals alike, which means it's not nearly as pretentious as it might be. Good bar food and decent ales.

Daily 11am–11pm.

The Putechan Bellochantuy ☎ 01586 421323, ⓦ theputechan.co.uk. Located in a roadside hamlet some nine miles from Campbeltown on the A83, this former hunting lodge is now a tip-top restaurant with a cool interior of charcoal-grey painted walls and carpets, and gorgeous, bespoke wooden tables. The food is similarly impressive, from the likes of smoked haddock Mornay, to monkfish wrapped in Parma ham (£17.95). You're best off making a reservation, and when you do, request a window table as the sea views are fantastic. Daily noon–10pm.

Campbeltown

CAMPBELTOWN's best feature is its setting, in a deep bay sheltered by Davaar Island and the surrounding hills. With a population of around five thousand, it is also one of the largest towns in Argyll and, if you're staying in the southern half of Kintyre, you may need to come here to stock up on supplies. Originally known as Kinlochkilkerran (*Ceann Loch Cill Chiaran*), the town was renamed in the seventeenth century by the Earl of Argyll – a Campbell – when it became one of the main points for immigration from the Lowlands. As is evident from the architecture, Campbeltown's heyday was the Victorian era, when **shipbuilding** was going strong, **coal** was shipped by canal from Drumlemble, there was a light-railway connection with Machrihanish, the **fishing** fleet was vast and Campbeltown Loch was said to be made of whisky. Nineteenth-century visitors to Campbeltown frequently found the place engulfed in a thick fog of pungent peat smoke from the town's 34 **distilleries** – today, only a handful are left to maintain this regional subgroup of single malt whiskies.

If you're here in the middle of August, be prepared for the **Mull of Kintyre Music & Arts Festival** (ⓦ mokfest.com), which pulls in a few old rock bands, plus some good traditional Irish and Scottish performers.

Springbank distillery

55 Longrow; sign up at Cadenhead's whisky shop at 30–32 Union St • Mon–Sat 10am & 2pm • £6.50 • ☎ 01586 551710, ⓦ springbankwhisky.com

If you're at all interested in whisky, pop into **Cadenhead's** whisky shop, where you can sign up for a guided tour of the nearby **Springbank distillery**, a deeply traditional, family-owned business that does absolutely everything – from malting to bottling – on its own premises, and produces three different single malts.

Burnet Building

St John St • Mon–Fri 9am–5pm • Free

Built as the town library in 1897, the **Burnet Building** is crowned by a distinctive lantern and decorated with four relief panels depicting the town's main industries at the time. The building harbours a very old-fashioned one-room local museum, and also includes the **Linda McCartney Memorial Garden**, which you should approach from Shore Street. Here, you'll find a slightly ludicrous bronze statue of Linda holding a lamb, a piece commissioned by Paul McCartney, who spent many happy times with Linda and the kids on the farm he owns near Campbeltown.

Campbeltown Heritage Centre

Lorne St • April–Sept Mon–Sat 9am–5pm • £2 • ☎ 07733 485387, ⓦ campbeltownheritagecentre.co.uk

The former Lorne Street Church, with its stripy bell-cote and pinnacles, has been cleverly converted into the intermittently interesting **Campbeltown Heritage Centre**. Due prominence is given to the town's once-glittering industrial heritage, in particular the local fishing and whisky industries; going hand in hand with the local malt production was a significant coopering industry, and at one stage there were more than sixty coopers in Campbeltown. By far the most prominent exhibit here, however, and occupying the spot where the main altar once stood, is a beautiful wooden skiff, *Yerda*, dating from 1906. Look out, too, for the model of the Victorian harbour-front with the light railway running along Hall Street.

ARRIVAL AND INFORMATION   CAMPBELTOWN

By plane Campbeltown Airport (☎ 01586 553797, ⓦ hial .co.uk) lies three miles west of town towards Machrihanish. Destinations Glasgow (Mon–Fri 2 daily; 40min).

By bus The main bus terminal is in front of the swimming pool on the Esplanade.
Destinations Carradale (Mon–Fri 5 daily, 4 on Sat; 45min); Glasgow (5 daily; 4hr 15min); Machrihanish (Mon–Sat 9 daily; 20min); Southend (Mon–Sat 6 daily; 25min); Tarbert (5 daily; 1hr 10min).

By ferry The ferry terminal is on the south side of the harbour, from where it's a five-minute walk into the centre. Destinations Ardrossan (June–Sept Fri & Sun 1 daily; 2hr 40min).

Tourist office Old Quay (April–June & Sept Mon–Sat 10am–5pm, Sun noon–4pm; July & Aug Mon–Sat 9am–6pm, Sun 11am–5pm; Oct–March Mon–Fri 10am–4pm; ☎ 01586 552056). They have lots of useful information and can book local accommodation.

ACCOMMODATION

Ardshiel Hotel Kilkerran Rd ☎ 01586 552133, ⓦ ardshiel.co.uk. A former whisky distiller's Victorian mansion situated on a lovely leafy square, just a block or so back from the harbour front. The rooms are functional more than anything, but there's adequate comfort and they are reasonably priced. More impressive is the hotel's glamorous, grown-up whisky bar, stocking in excess of 500 malts. **£70**

Campbeltown Backpackers Big Kiln ☎ 01586 551188, ⓦ campbeltownbackpackers.co.uk. Occupying the old school house in the courtyard across from the heritage centre, this new, community trust-run bunkhouse has sixteen firm, pine beds in two dormitories, a self-catering kitchen and small lounge. There's no reception as such: if there's no one here, pop into the heritage centre, but if

that's closed just call the number on the door. Dorms **£18**

Oatfield House Three miles down the B842 ☎ 01586 551551, ⓦ oatfield.org. A beautifully renovated white-washed laird's house set in its own grounds on the road to Southend, retaining three rooms of some character and distinction. Guests are also free to avail themselves of the panelled dining room and parlour. **£80**

Royal Hotel Main St ☎ 0800 151 3701, ⓦ machrihanishdunes.com. New, high-end hotel that sits well with the recent redevelopment of the harbour-front area, and injects a big dollop of colour to this otherwise dull street. The supremely comfortable rooms are mostly furnished in bold tartan colour schemes, with deep armchairs, big beds with thick duvets and fluffy pillows, and a host of other neat touches. **£130**

EATING AND DRINKING

Black Sheep Pub Main St ☎ 0800 151 3701. The *Royal Hotel*'s pub is by far the most enjoyable watering hole in town, with seating arranged around a shiny, semicircular

bar, in addition to some outdoor tables overlooking the harbour. The eponymous Black Sheep cask ale trumps all other ales here. Daily noon–1am.

1

Café Bluebell 6 Hall St ☎01586 552800. Simple-looking but warm and welcoming café near the tourist office offering a terrific selection of light snacks (soups, sandwiches, sausage rolls), as well as a gut-busting all-day breakfast (£7.50). Tues–Sat 9am–4.30pm, Sun 11am–4pm.

Southend and around

Southend itself, a bleak, blustery spot, comes as something of a disappointment, though it does have a golden sandy beach. Below the cliffs to the west of the beach, a ruined thirteenth-century chapel marks the alleged arrival-point of St Columba prior to his trip to Iona, and on a rocky knoll nearby a pair of footprints carved into the rock are known as **Columba's footprints**, though only one is actually of ancient origin. Jutting out into the sea at the east end of the bay is **Dunaverty Rock**, where a force of three hundred Royalists was massacred by the Covenanting army of the Earl of Argyll in 1647, despite having surrendered voluntarily. Southend also marks the end (or start) of the 89-mile-long Kintyre Way.

A couple of miles out to sea lies **Sanda**, a privately owned island containing the remains of St Ninian's chapel, plus two ancient crosses, a holy well, an unusual lighthouse comprised of three sandstone towers, and lots of seabirds.

Mull of Kintyre

Most people venture south of Campbeltown to make a pilgrimage to the **Mull of Kintyre**, made famous by the mawkish number-one hit by sometime local resident Paul McCartney, with the help of the Campbeltown Pipe Band. It's also infamous as the site of the **RAF's worst peacetime accident** when, on June 2, 1994, a Chinook helicopter on its way from Belfast to Inverness crashed, killing all 29 on board. The Ministry of Defence blamed the pilots and, despite the findings of a Scottish enquiry and the opinions of a cross-party select committee, still maintains there were no technical problems with the helicopter. A small **memorial** can be found on the hillside, not far from the **Gap** (1150ft) – after which no vehicles are allowed.

The Mull is the nearest Britain gets to Ireland, just twelve miles away, and the Irish coastline appears remarkably close on fine days. There's nothing specifically to see, but the trek down to the **lighthouse**, itself 300ft above the ocean waves, is challengingly tortuous. It's about a mile from the "Gap" to the lighthouse (and a long haul back up), though there's a strategic viewpoint just ten-minutes' walk from the car park.

Saddell Abbey

Ten miles up the coast from Campbeltown

The ruins of **Saddell Abbey**, a Cistercian foundation thought to have been founded by Somerled in 1148, are set at the lush, wooded entrance to Saddell Glen. The abbey fell into disrepair in the sixteenth century and, though the remains are not exactly impressive, there's a good collection of medieval grave-slabs decorated with full-scale relief figures of knights housed in a new shelter in the grounds. Standing by the privately owned shoreline there's a splendid memorial to the last Campbell laird to live at Saddell Castle, which he built in 1774.

Isle of Arran

Shaped like a kidney bean and occupying centre stage in the Firth of Clyde, **Arran** is the most southerly (and therefore the most accessible) of all the Scottish islands. The Highland–Lowland dividing line passes right through its centre – hence the cliché about it being like "Scotland in miniature" – leaving the northern half sparsely populated, spectacularly mountainous and forbidding, while the lush southern half enjoys a much milder climate. The population of around 5000 – many of whom are incomers – tend to stick to the southeastern quarter of the island, leaving the west and the north relatively undisturbed.

There are two big crowd-pullers on Arran: **geology** and **golf**. The former has fascinated rock-obsessed students since Sir James Hutton came here in the late

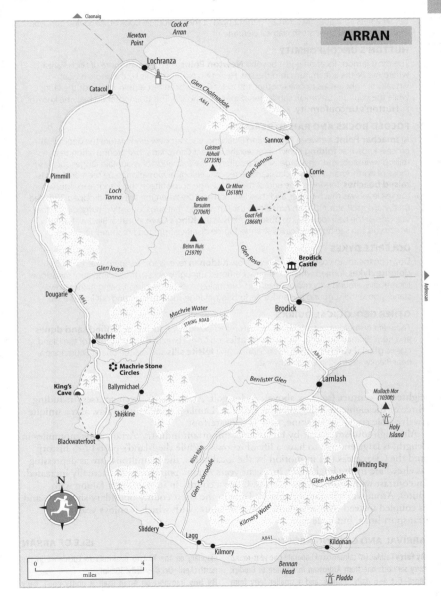

1

ARRAN ROCKS

Arran is a top destination for the country's **geology** students. First, this small island is split in two by the **Highland Boundary Fault**, and therefore contains a superb variety of rock formations, typical of both the Highlands and the Lowlands. And, second, it is the place where **Sir James Hutton** (1726–97), the "father of modern geology" came in 1787, in order to lay down research for his epic work, *A Theory of the Earth*. Even if you know very little about geology, it is possible to appreciate some of the island's more obvious features. If any of the below whets your appetite, start by getting hold of the geological booklet, *Arran and the Clyde Islands*, produced by Scottish Natural Heritage.

HUTTON'S UNCONFORMITY

The most famous location is just beyond **Newton Point**, on the north shore of Loch Ranza, where Allt Beithe stream runs into the sea. Here, two types of rocks by the shore are set virtually at right angles to one another, the older Cambrian schist dipping towards the land, while the younger Devonian sandstone slopes into the sea. This phenomenon became known as **Hutton's Unconformity**.

FOLDED ROCKS AND RAISED BEACHES

At **Imachar Point**, between Pirnmill and Dougarie, you can view in miniature the geological process known as **folding**, which affected the ancient Cambrian schist around a hundred million years ago, and, on a larger scale, resulted in the formation of mountain ranges such as those of north Arran. Another classic, more recent geological formation to be seen on Arran is **raised beaches**, formed at the end of the last Ice Age, some fifteen thousand years ago, when the sea level was much higher, and then left high and dry when the sea level dropped. The road that wraps itself around Arran runs along the flat ground that subsequently emerged from the sea. One of the best locations to observe this is at the **King's Cave**, north of Blackwaterfoot, where you can see huge sea caves stranded some distance from today's shoreline.

DOLERITE DYKES

Down on the south coast, the shoreline below **Kildonan** reveals some superb examples of **dolerite dykes**, formed when molten rock erupted through cracks in the sedimentary sandstone rocks above, around sixty million years ago. The molten rock solidified and, being harder, now stands above the surrounding sandstone, forming strange, rocky piers jutting out into the sea.

OTHER GEOLOGICAL QUIRKS

There are numerous other interesting features to look out for, such as **solidified sand dunes** and huge granite boulders, known as **erratics**, on Corrie beach in the northeast of the island, classic **glacial valleys** such as Glen Sannox, and **felsite sills** such as the one at Drumadoon, near Blackwaterfoot, in the southwest.

---

eighteenth century (see box above). As for golf, Arran boasts seven courses, including three of the eighteen-hole variety at Brodick, Lamlash and Whiting Bay, and a unique twelve-hole course at Shiskine, near Blackwaterfoot.

Although **tourism** is now by far its most important industry, Arran, at twenty miles in length, is large enough to have a life of its own. While the island's post-1745 history and the Clearances (set in motion by the local lairds, the Hamiltons) are as depressing as elsewhere in the Highlands, in recent years Arran's population has actually increased, in contrast with more remote islands. Once a county in its own right (along with Bute), Arran was left out of Argyll & Bute in the latest county boundary shake-up, and is coupled instead with mainland North Ayrshire, with which it enjoys year-round transport links, but little else.

ARRIVAL AND GETTING AROUND   ISLE OF ARRAN

By ferry CalMac (ⓦcalmac.co.uk) operate two year-round ferry services: one from Ardrossan in Ayrshire to Brodick (April–Oct 4–6 daily; 55min), and a smaller ferry from Claonaig on the Kintyre peninsula to Lochranza in the north (April–Oct 8–9 daily; 30min).

By bus Transport on Arran itself is pretty good: daily

buses circle the island (Brodick tourist office has time-tables) while the Arran Day Rider (£5.40) allows you to hop on and off as you please. Buses also link in with the two ferry services.

Brodick and around

Although the resort of **BRODICK** (from the Norse *breidr vik*, "broad bay") is a place of only moderate charm, it does at least have a grand setting in a wide, sandy bay set against a backdrop of granite mountains. Its development as a tourist resort was held back for a long time by its elitist owners, the dukes of Hamilton, though nowadays, as the island's capital and main communication hub, Brodick is by far the busiest town on Arran.

Brodick's shops and guesthouses are spread out along the south side of the bay, along with the tourist office and the CalMac pier. Its tourist sights, meanwhile, are clustered on the west and north side of the bay, a couple of miles from the ferry terminal.

Arran Heritage Museum

Rosaburn • April–Oct daily 10.30am–4.30pm • £3 • ☎ 01770 302636, ⓦ arranmuseum.co.uk

Up along the road to the castle, the intermittently interesting **Arran Heritage Museum** is housed in a whitewashed eighteenth-century crofter's farm, and contains an old smiddy and a cutesy Victorian cottage with box bed and range. In the old stables, the main exhibition considers the island's intriguing geological and archeological heritage – the most notable exhibit is an incredibly well preserved, early Bronze Age cist grave, complete with intact food vessel, while another section recalls the island's prominent wartime role, as testified by the dozen or so air crashes here during the course of World War II.

Arran Visitor Centre

Home Farm • **Arran Aromatics** Daily 9.30am–6pm; factory tours June–Sept Thurs at 6pm • Free • ☎ 01770 303003, ⓦ arranaromatics.com **Island Cheese Company** Daily 9.30am–6pm • ☎ 01770 302788, ⓦ arranscheeseshop.co.uk

The **Arran Visitor Centre**, half a mile or so up the road from the heritage museum, incorporates a couple of superb outlets, foremost of which is **Arran Aromatics**, producers of luxury toiletries and fragrances. As well as the opportunity to participate in natural soapmaking, the outlet offers factory tours in the summer months. At the **Island Cheese Company**, you can see the soft, creamy Crofter's Crowdie or the piquant Arran Blue cheese being made. Here too is *Creelers* smokehouse, the island's finest restaurant (see p.110).

Brodick Castle

Two miles north of Brodick • **Castle** Daily April–Sept 11am–4pm; Oct 11am–3pm • £12; NTS **Gardens** Daily 9.30am–dusk • £6.50; NTS • ☎ 0844 493 2152

Former seat of the dukes of Hamilton, **Brodick Castle** is set on a steep bank on the north side of Brodick Bay. The bulk of the castle was built in the nineteenth century, giving it a domestic rather than military look, and although the interior is decidedly dour in tone, there are a few gems to look out for. Don't miss the portrait of the eleventh duke's faithful piper, who injured his throat on a grouse bone, was warned never to pipe again, but did so and died, while there are also a handful of sketches by **Gainsborough** in the boudoir. Probably the most atmospheric room is the copper-filled Victorian **kitchen**, which conjures up a vision of the sweating labour required to feed the folk upstairs.

ARRAN GOLF PASS

The **Arran Golf Pass** (ⓦ golfonarran.com) currently costs £99, which is remarkable value given that it entitles you to a round on each of the island's seven courses: three 18-hole and three 9-hole courses, as well as the superb 12-hole course at Shiskine. You can buy the pass online or at any of the seven clubs.

1

GOAT FELL

Arran's most accessible peak is also the island's highest, **Goat Fell** (2866ft) – take your pick from the Gaelic, *goath*, meaning "windy", or the Norse, *geit-fjall*, "goat mountain" – which can be ascended in just three hours from Brodick or from Corrie (return journey 5hr), though it's a strenuous hike.

Much more attractive, however, are the walled **gardens** and extensive grounds, a treasury of exotic plants and trees enjoying the favourable climate (including one of Europe's finest collections of rhododendrons), and commanding a superb view across the bay. There is an adventure playground for kids, but the whole area is a natural playground, with waterfalls, a giant pitcher-plant that swallows thousands of midges daily, and a maze of paths. Buried in the grounds there is a bizarre Bavarian-style **summerhouse** lined entirely with pine cones, one of three built by the eleventh duke to make his wife, Princess Marie of Baden, feel at home. For the energetic there's also a **country park** with scenic walks and mountain-bike trails, starting from a small, informative, hands-on nature centre. In summer there are **guided walks** with the rangers, but at any time you can be surprised by red squirrels, nightjars and an abundance of fungi.

ARRIVAL AND INFORMATION
BRODICK

By bus The main bus station is by the ferry terminal. Destinations Blackwaterfoot (Mon–Sat 8–10 daily, Sun 4 daily; 30min); Kildonan (4–6 daily; 40min); Lamlash (Mon–Sat hourly, Sun 4 daily; 10–15min); Lochranza (3–5 daily; 45min); Whiting Bay (Mon–Sat hourly, Sun 4 daily;

25min).
Tourist office By the CalMac pier (Mon–Sat 9am–5pm, also June–Sept Sun 10am–5pm; ☎01770 303776, ⊛ visitarran.net).

ACCCOMMODATION AND EATING

Brodick Bar and Brasserie Alma Rd ☎01770 302169, ⊛ brodickbar.co.uk. There's decent fare on offer at this big, family-oriented restaurant opposite the post office. Chalked up on a huge board, the diverse menu features lots of meaty treats (pan-fried calves liver with Arran mustard; honey-glazed belly of pork), while the home-made thin-crust pizzas are worth a punt. Mon–Sat noon–2.30pm & 5.30–10pm.

Creelers Home Farm, in the Aran Visitor Centre complex along the road to the castle ☎01770 302810, ⊛ creelers.co.uk. *Creelers* is the island's standout restaurant; fillet of halibut with chive mash and squat lobster (£16.95) is typical of the dinner menu, while the cheaper lunch menu features the likes of salt-and-pepper fried squid with chips (£7.95). You can bring your own bottle too (£3 corkage). Easter–Oct Tues–Sat noon–2.30pm & 6–10pm.

Dunvegan Guest House Shore Rd ☎01770 302811, ⊛ dunveganhouse.co.uk. Within striking distance of

the ferry terminal, this prominently positioned sandstone guesthouse has a selection of bright, modern and comfortable rooms, most with direct sea views. £80

★ **Glen Rosa** Two miles from town off the B880 to Blackwaterfoot ☎01770 302380, ⊛ arrancamping .co.uk. This very basic, almost wild, campsite (no showers and cold water only) enjoys a wonderful setting beside a burn, with superb views across the glen. Campfires are allowed too. There's no reception; the owner will pitch up at some point and collect your money. £4/person

★ **Glenartney Guest House** Mayish Rd ☎01770 302220, ⊛ glenartney-arran.co.uk. Tucked away just uphill from the post office, this is the pick of the town's guesthouses, with a dozen or so immaculately presented, albeit not overly spacious, rooms. Two homely lounges and an evening bar enhance the *Glenartney*'s charms, while you can expect a spectacular breakfast to see you on your way. £80

Lamlash and around

With its distinctive Edwardian architecture and mild climate, **Lamlash**, four miles south of Brodick, epitomizes the sedate charm of southeast Arran. Lamlash Bay has in its time sheltered King Håkon's fleet in 1263 before the Battle of Largs and, more recently, served as a naval base in both world wars. The major drawback for the visitor, however, is that its beach is made not of sand but of boulder-strewn mud flats.

Holy Island

The Holy Island boat runs May–Sept daily and more or less hourly, though it's subject to cancellations in windy weather • £11 return • ☎ 01770 600998, ⓦ holyisland.org

The best reason for coming to Lamlash is to visit the slug-shaped hump of **Holy Island**, which shelters the bay. The island is owned by a group of Tibetan Buddhists who have established a long-term retreat at the lighthouse on the island's southern tip and built a Peace Centre at the north end of the island. Providing you don't dawdle, it's possible to scramble up to the top of Mullach Mór (1030ft), the island's highest point, and still catch the last ferry back. En route, you might well bump into the island's most numerous residents: feral goats, Eriskay ponies, Soay sheep and rabbits.

ACCOMMODATION AND EATING

LAMLASH AND AROUND

Drift Inn In the centre of Lamlash Bay ☎ 01770 600608. Despite its undistinguished exterior, the food at this seafront pub – including smoked haddock Scotch egg (£9.95) – and its convivial beer garden, make the *Drift Inn* a fun place to hang out, plus there's live music at weekends. Daily noon–midnight.

Glenisle Hotel In the centre of Lamlash Bay ☎ 01770 600559, ⓦ glenislehotel.com. High-end and by no means cheap option with thirteen gorgeous rooms, each

of which has been painted and furnished in colours that reflect those of the island itself. Only the Superior rooms have a sea view. **£120**

Lilybank In the centre of Lamlash Bay ☎ 01770 600230, ⓦ lilybank-arran.co.uk. Just a few paces along from the *Glenisle*, this sunny B&B is a typically welcoming island guesthouse, offering six floral, pastel-coloured rooms, four of which overlook the bay. **£70**

Whiting Bay

An established Clydeside resort for over a century now, **Whiting Bay**, four miles south of Lamlash, is spread out along a very pleasant bay, though it doesn't have quite the distinctive architecture of Lamlash. It is, however, a good base for walking, with the gentle hike up to the **Glenashdale Falls** probably the most popular excursion; this two-hour walk sets off from Ashdale Bridge at the southern end of the bay, for the most part passing through pretty woodland. With more time, you can branch off this path up to the **Giant's Graves**, a group of Neolithic chambered cairns. The walk is well signposted from the bridge.

EATING

WHITING BAY

The Coffee Pot Shore Rd ☎ 01770 700382. This unassuming white building on the corner of a residential street is deservedly popular for its freshly baked baguettes

and home-made cakes, not to mention great coffee. Daily 10am–5pm.

Kildonan

Access to the sea is tricky along the south coast, but worth the effort, as the sandy **beaches** here are among the island's finest. One place you can get down to the sea is at **Kildonan**, an attractive small village south of Lamlash, set slightly off the main road, with a good sandy beach, which you share with the local wildlife, and views out to the tiny flat island of Pladda, with its distinctive lighthouse and, in the distance, the great hump of Ailsa Craig.

ACCOMMODATION AND EATING

KILDONAN

Kildonan Hotel On the beachfront ☎ 01770 820207, ⓦ kildonanhotel.co.uk. Smart, sixteen-room country hotel enjoying a prominent position right on the beachfront; the restaurant is of a high standard too, with unbeatable views from its patio terrace. **£99**

Sealshore Camping ☎ 01770 820320, ⓦ campingarran

.com. Lovely, laidback family-owned campsite next to the *Kildonan* with its own private beach. Facilities include modern shower blocks, self-catering kitchen, lounge and undercover BBQ area, plus there's an onsite shop. March– Oct. **£14**/pitch

1

King's Cave

A gentle two-mile walk north along the coast will bring you to the **King's Cave**, one of several where Robert the Bruce is said to have encountered the famously patient arachnid, while hiding during his final bid to free Scotland in 1306. Inside the cave you'll find various carved symbols, typically early Christian crosses and Pictish animals.

Machrie Moor

North of Blackwaterfoot, the wide expanse of **Machrie Moor** boasts a wealth of Bronze Age sites, many of which were excavated as recently as the 1980s. Entrance to the site is via the car park just off the main road; from here, it's a good thirty-minute walk (you can cycle too) across windswept, peaty moorland to a scattered group of **stone circles**, which vary from chunky boulders to slim pillars, the tallest surviving monolith being over 18ft high. The most striking configuration is at Fingal's Cauldron Seat, with two concentric circles of granite boulders; legend has it that Fingal tied his dog to one of them while cooking at his cauldron.

EATING AND DRINKING	MACHRIE MOOR

Machrie Bay Machrie Bay ☎ 01770 840392. After a bracing walk to the stones on Machrie Moor, make a beeline for this busy and colourful roadside tearoom that also functions as the social centre for the adjoining golf course; toasties, sandwiches and a scrumptious selection of cakes are just some of the goodies on offer. Daily 9am–5pm.

Lochranza

On fair Lochranza streamed the early day/Thin wreaths of cottage smoke are upward curl'd/From the lone hamlet, which her inland bay/And circling mountains sever from the world.

The Lord of the Isles by Sir Walter Scott

The ruined castle which occupies the mud flats of the bay, and the brooding north-facing slopes of the mountains which frame it, make for one of the most

---

WALKING IN NORTH ARRAN

Ordnance Survey Explorer map 361

The ferociously jagged and barren outline of the mountains of **north Arran** is on a par with that of the Cuillin of Skye. None of the peaks is a Munro, but they are spectacular, nevertheless, partly because they rise up so rapidly from sea level and, in fine weather, offer such wonderful views over sea and land.

One of the most popular walks is the circuit of peaks that surround Glen Rosa. The walk begins with the relatively straightforward ascent of **Goat Fell** (2866ft), which is normally approached from the grounds of Brodick Castle, to the south. From Goat Fell, you can follow a series of rocky ridges that spread out in the shape of an "H". In order to keep to the crest of the ridge, head north to the next peak of **North Goat Fell** (2657ft), and then make the sharp descent to the Saddle, a perfect spot for a rest, before making the ascent of **Cir Mhòr** (2618ft), by far the most exhilarating peak in the whole range, and the finest viewpoint of all. The next section of the walk, southwest across the knife's-edge ridge of **A'Chir**, is quite tricky due to the Bad Step, a lethal gap in the ridge, which you can avoid by dropping down slightly on the east side. Beyond A'Chir, the ascent of **Beinn Tarsuinn** (2706ft) and **Beinn Nuis** (2597ft) is relatively simple. A path leads down from the southeast face of Beinn Nuis to Glen Rosa and back to Brodick. If you don't fancy attempting A'Chir, or if the weather closes in, you can simply descend from the Saddle, or from the southwest side of Cir Mhor, to Glen Rosa.

The walk described above covers a total distance of eleven miles, with over 4600ft of climbing, and should take between eight and ten hours to complete. All walks should be approached with care, and the usual **safety precautions** should be observed (see p.42).

1

spectacular settings on the island – yet **Lochranza**, despite being the only place of any size in this sparsely populated area, attracts far fewer visitors than Arran's southern resorts.

Lochranza distillery

South end of the village • Daily: March–Oct 10am–6pm, Nov–Feb 10am–5pm; first tour 10.15am, then every 1hr 30min • £6 • ☎ 01770 830264, ⓦ arranwhisky.com

Lochranza's main tourist attraction is the island's modern **distillery**, distinguished by its pagoda-style roofs at the south end of the village. Established as recently as 1995 – the first on the island since 1837 – the distillery produces the relatively little known, fourteen-year-old single Arran malt. The **tour** is an entertaining and slick affair, beginning with an audiovisual presentation in a mock-up crofter's cottage, before you are led through the distillery. There are thorough explanations of the various processes, and the tour concludes, naturally, with a dram.

ACCOMMODATION AND EATING   LOCHRANZA

Apple Lodge The old village manse ☎ 01770 830229, ⓦ applelodgearran.co.uk. The old village manse accommodates several beautifully conceived rooms decked out with colourful embroidery and paintings, and an abundance of antique furnishings; one contains a superb four-poster bed. **£80**

Lochranza Camping By the golf course ☎ 01770 830273, ⓦ arran-campsite.com. Relaxed and scenically placed campsite, where red deer come to graze in the early evening. There are also a couple of cool two-man pods. Reception is basically the golf clubhouse (a hut). March–Oct. **£16**/pitch; pods **£60**

Sandwich Station Opposite the CalMac slipway ☎ 07810 796248. If you're just passing through, or need a packed lunch, pop into this super little sandwich bar and deli; hot breakfast rolls, grilled panini and home-made

soup are sample offerings. April–Oct Mon 5.30–10pm, Tues–Sun 9am–5pm; Nov–March Tues–Fri 9am–2pm.

Stags Pavilion At the entrance to Lochranza Camping ☎ 01770 830600, ⓦ stagspavilion.com. Accomplished restaurant located in an attractive pavilion at the entrance to the campsite, with yummy Italian dishes like *pollo cacciatore* (hunter's chicken in a tomato, mushroom and olive sauce). It's not licensed but you can bring your own bottle. Reservations advised. Mon 5.30–10pm, Tues–Sun 10am–4pm & 5.30–10pm.

SYHA hostel Not far from the castle, en route to the ferry terminal ☎ 01770 830631, ⓦ syha.org.uk. Friendly and well-equipped SYHA hostel with views over the bay. Breakfast £4.50, packed lunch £5.50. Mid-Feb to Oct. Dorms **£17**; doubles **£38**

Isle of Islay

The fertile, largely treeless island of **ISLAY** (pronounced "eye-la") is famous for one thing – single malt **whisky**. The smoky, peaty, pungent quality of Islay whisky is unique, recognizable even to the untutored palate, and all eight of the island's distilleries will happily take visitors on a guided tour, ending with the customary complimentary tipple. Yet, despite the fame of its whiskies, Islay still remains relatively undiscovered, especially when compared with Arran, Mull or Skye. Part of the reason may be the expense of the two-hour ferry journey from Kennacraig on Kintyre. If you do make the effort, however, you'll be rewarded with a genuinely friendly welcome from islanders proud of their history, landscape and Gaelic culture.

In medieval times, Islay was the political centre of the Hebrides, with **Finlaggan**, near Port Askaig, the seat of the MacDonalds, Lords of the Isles. The picturesque, whitewashed villages you see on Islay today, however, date from the planned settlements founded by the Campbells in the late eighteenth and early nineteenth centuries. Apart from whisky and solitude, the other great draw is the **birdlife** – there's a real possibility of spotting a golden eagle, or the rare crow-like chough, and no possibility at all of missing the white-fronted and barnacle geese that winter here in their thousands. In late May, the **Fèis Ìle**, or Islay Festival of Music and Malt

1

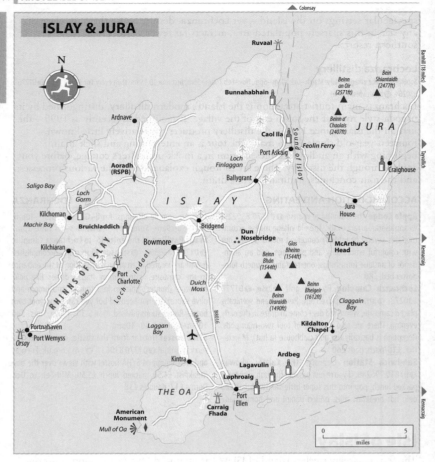

ISLAY & JURA

(ⓦtheislayfestival.co.uk), takes place, with whisky tasting, piping recitals, folk dancing and other events celebrating the island's Gaelic roots.

ARRIVAL AND GETTING AROUND   ISLE OF ISLAY

By plane Islay's airport (ⓣ01496 302361, ⓦhial.co.uk) is five miles north of Port Ellen on the A846.
Destinations Colonsay (Tues & Thurs 1 daily; 20min); Glasgow (Mon–Fri 2 daily, Sat & Sun 1 daily; 40min); Oban (Tues & Thurs 2 daily; 35min).
By ferry CalMac ferries from Kennacraig on Kintyre connect with both Port Ellen and Port Askaig. There's also a ferry that makes the short trip across to Jura (see p.121).

By bus The island's main bus route links Port Askaig with Bridgend, from where buses continue down to Port Ellen, via Bowmore, and Portnahaven, via Port Charlotte.
By car If you're thinking of driving, it's worth considering car rental on the island itself and saving on ferry fares – Islay Car Hire (ⓣ01496 810544, ⓦislaycarhire.co.uk) will deliver to both ferry terminals.

Port Ellen and around

Laid out as a planned village in 1821 by Walter Frederick Campbell, and named after his wife, **PORT ELLEN** is the chief port on Islay, with the island's largest fishing

1

ISLAY WHISKY DISTILLERIES

It goes without saying that Islay's **whisky distilleries** are now a major tourist attraction. Nowadays, every distillery offers guided **tours**, which usually last an hour and traditionally end with a generous dram, and occasionally a free glass. Most also offer more comprehensive tours with more tastings, and some even do warehouse tours. Phone ahead to make sure there's a tour running, as times do change frequently.

Ardbeg Port Ellen ☎01496 302244, ⓦardbeg.com. Ardbeg is traditionally considered the saltiest, peatiest malt on Islay (and that's saying something). Bought by Glenmorangie in 1997, the distillery has been thoroughly overhauled and restored, yet it still has bags of character inside. Its café, the *Old Kiln*, is excellent; tours £5. Guided tours 10.30am, noon & 3.30pm; Old Kiln Café June–Aug daily 10am–5pm; Sept–May Mon–Fri 10am–4.30pm.

Bowmore School St, Bowmore ☎01496 810671, ⓦbowmore.com. Bowmore is the most touristy of the Islay distilleries – too much so for some. However, it is by far the most central (with unrivalled disabled access), and also one of the few still doing its own malting and kilning; tours £6. Guided tours Easter–June Mon–Sat 10am, 11am, 2pm & 3pm; July–Sept Mon–Sat 10am, 11am, 2pm & 3pm, Sun 1pm & 2pm; Oct–Easter Mon–Fri 10.30am & 3pm, Sat 10am.

Bruichladdich Bruichladdich ☎01496 850190, ⓦbruichladdich.com. In the centre of the village of the same name, this independent distillery was rescued in 2001 by a group of whisky fanatics, but was bought out by the French drinks giants, Remy-Cointreau, in 2012; tours £5. Guided tours Easter–Oct Mon–Fri 10.30am, 11.30am, 1pm, 2pm, 3pm & 4pm, Sat 10.30am, 1pm & 2pm, Sun 1pm & 2pm; Nov–Easter Mon–Fri 11.30am & 2.30pm, Sat 11.30am.

Bunnahabhain Four miles north of Port Askaig ☎01496 840646, ⓦbunnahabhain.com. A visit to Bunnahabhain (pronounced "Bunna-have-in") is really only for whisky obsessives. The road from Port Askaig is windy, the whisky the least characteristically Islay and the distillery itself only in production for a few months each year; tours £6. Guided tours April–Oct Mon–Fri 10.30am, 1.30pm & 3.30pm; Nov–March by appointment.

Caol Ila Port Askaig ☎01496 302760, ⓦdiscovering-distilleries.com. Caol Ila (pronounced "Cull-eela"), just north of Port Askaig, is a modern distillery, the majority of whose lightly peaty malt goes into blended whiskies; tours £6. Guided tours April–Aug daily 9.30am, 11.30am, 12.30pm, 2.30pm & 3.30pm; Sept & Oct same times but closed Sun; Nov–March daily 10.30am & 1.30pm.

Kilchoman Rockside Farm, Bruichladdich ☎01496 850011, ⓦkilchomandistillery.com. Established in 2005 as the first new distillery on Islay for over a century, Kilchoman is a very welcoming, tiny, farm-based enterprise that grows its own barley, as well as distilling, maturing and bottling its whisky on site. The café serves good coffee, plus home-made soup and baked items; tours £4.50. Guided tours April–Oct Mon–Sat 11am & 3pm; Nov–March Mon–Fri 11am & 3pm; café Mon–Sat 10am–5pm.

Lagavulin Port Ellen ☎01496 302749, ⓦdiscovering-distilleries.com. Lagavulin probably is the classic, all-round Islay malt, with lots of smoke and peat. The distillery enjoys a fabulous setting and is extremely busy all year round; tours £6. Guided tours May–Sept Mon–Fri 9.30am, 11.30am, 12.30pm, 2.30pm, 3.30pm, 4.30pm & 5.30pm, Sat & Sun 9.30am, 11.30am, 12.30pm, 2.30pm & 3.30pm; Oct–April daily 9.30am, 11.30am, 12.30pm, 2.30pm & 3.30pm.

Laphroaig Port Ellen ☎01496 302418, ⓦlaphroaig.com. Another classic smoky, peaty Islay malt, and another great setting. One bonus at Laphroaig is that you get to see the malting, and see and smell the peat kilns; tours £5. Guided tours March–Oct Mon–Fri 10am, 11.30am, 2pm & 3.30pm; Nov–Feb 11.30am & 2pm.

fleet and main CalMac ferry terminal. The neat, whitewashed terraces which overlook the town's bay of golden sand are pretty enough, but the strand to the north, up Charlotte Street, is dominated by the modern maltings, whose powerful odours waft across the town. Arriving at Port Ellen by boat, it's impossible to miss the unusual, square-shaped **Carraig Fhada lighthouse**, at the western entrance to the bay, erected in 1832 in memory of Walter Frederick Campbell's aforementioned wife. Just beyond the lighthouse is the prettiest bay on the island's south coast, Traigh Bhàn, or the **Singing Sands**, a perfect sandy beach peppered with jagged rocky extrusions.

1

The distilleries

Heading east out of Port Ellen, a dead-end road passes three **distilleries** in as many miles. First up is **Laphroaig**, which, as every bottle tells you, is Gaelic for "the beautiful hollow by the bay", and, true enough, the whitewashed distillery is indeed in a gorgeous setting by the sea. Laphroaig also has the stamp of approval from Prince Charles, who famously paid a flying visit to the island in 1994, crashing an airplane of the Queen's Flight in the process.

A mile down the road lies **Lagavulin** distillery, beyond which stands **Dunyvaig Castle**, a romantic ruin on a promontory looking out to the tiny isle of Texa. Another mile further on, **Ardbeg** distillery sports the traditional pagoda-style kiln roofs. In common with all Islay's distilleries, the above three offer guided tours (see box, p.115).

Kildaton Chapel

Two miles down the track from Ardbeg, you eventually come to the simple thirteenth-century **Kildalton Chapel**, which has a wonderful eighth-century Celtic ringed cross made from the local "bluestone". The quality of the scenes matches any to be found on the crosses carved by the monks in Iona: the Virgin and Child are on the east face, with Cain murdering Abel to the left, David fighting the lion on the top, and Abraham sacrificing Isaac on the right; on the west side amid the serpent-and-boss work are four elephant-like beasts.

ARRIVAL AND DEPARTURE	PORT ELLEN AND AROUND
By ferry The ferry terminal is a two-minute walk from the village's main through roads. Destinations Kennacraig (3–4 daily; 2hr 20min).	**By bus** Buses pick up and drop off on Charlotte St. Destinations Bowmore (Mon–Sat 10 daily, Sun 4 daily; 20–30min).

ACCOMMODATION AND EATING

Caladh Sona 53 Frederick Crescent ☎ 01496 302694, ✉ hamish.scott@lineone.net. Simple, unassuming detached house in the heart of the village with three en-suite ground-floor rooms (all twins) at a very reasonable price. **£72**

Islay Hotel 18 Charlotte St ☎ 01496 300109, ⊛ islay hotel.com. One of the finest hotels on the island, rebuilt from scratch a few years ago, hence the thoroughly modern, sharp-looking rooms and superbly-equipped and very large bathrooms (some with whirlpool bathtub). The *Islay* is also Port Ellen's social hub, with a fine restaurant and a buzzy, more informal whisky bar. The former rustles

up sublime dishes like pan-fried turbot with herbed mash and hollandaise sauce (£20), while at the latter you can grab a steak sandwich (£9.50) washed down with a microbrew beer. Restaurant daily noon–2.30pm & 6–10pm; bar daily 11am–11pm. **£120**

★ **Kintra Farm campsite** Three miles northwest of Port Ellen ☎ 01496 302051, ⊛ kintrafarm.co.uk. Enjoying a stunning situation at the southern tip of sandy Laggan Bay among the grassy dunes, this is not far off wild camping at its best. Facilities are basic, but there are showers and running water as well as laundry facilities. April–Sept. **£14**/pitch

The Oa

The most dramatic landscape on Islay is to be found in the nub of land to the southwest of Port Ellen known as **The Oa** (pronounced "O"), a windswept and inhospitable spot, much loved by illicit whisky distillers and smugglers over the centuries. Halfway along the road, a ruined church is visible to the south, testament to the area's once large population dispersed during the Clearances – several abandoned villages lie in the north of the peninsula, near **Kintra**.

American Monument

The chief target for most visitors to The Oa is the gargantuan **American Monument**, built in the shape of a lighthouse on the clifftop above the Mull of Oa. It was erected by the American National Red Cross in memory of those who died in two naval disasters that took place in 1918. The first occurred when the troop transporter

1

SS *Tuscania*, carrying over two thousand American army personnel, was torpedoed by a German U-boat seven miles offshore in February 1918. As the lifeboats were being lowered, several ropes broke and threw the occupants into the sea, drowning 266 of those on board. The monument also commemorates those who drowned when the HMS *Otranto* was shipwrecked off Kilchoman (see p.118) in October of the same year. The memorial is inscribed with the unusual sustained metaphor: "On Fame's eternal camping ground, their silent tents are spread, while glory keeps with solemn round, the bivouac of the dead."

If you're driving, you can park in a car park, just before Upper Killeyan farm, and follow the duckboards across the soggy peat. En route, look out for choughs, golden eagles and other birds of prey, not to mention feral goats and, down on the shore, basking seals; for a longer walk, follow the coast five miles round to or from Kintra.

Bowmore

On the other side of the monotonous peat bog of Duich Moss, on the southern shores of the tidal Loch Indaal, lies **Bowmore**, Islay's administrative capital, with a population of around eight hundred. It was founded in 1768 to replace the village of Kilarrow, which was deemed by the local laird to be too close to his own residence. It's a striking place, laid out in a grid plan rather like Inveraray, with the whitewashed terraces of Main Street climbing up the hill in a straight line from the pier on Loch Indaal.

The Round Church

High St · Daily 9am–6pm · ⓦ theroundchurch.org.uk

Built in 1767 by Daniel Campbell, then owner of the island, the town's crowning landmark is the **Round Church**, whose central tower looks uncannily like a lighthouse. Built in the round, so that the devil would have no corners in which to hide, it's well worth a look for its wood-panelled interior, lovely tiered balcony and big, central, mushroom pillar.

ARRIVAL AND DEPARTURE
BOWMORE

By bus Buses stop on the main square, which, strangely enough, is called The Square.

Destinations Port Askaig (Mon–Sat 6–8 daily, Sun 4 daily; 25min); Port Charlotte (Mon–Sat 5–6 daily, Sun 3 daily; 25min); Port Ellen (Mon–Sat 10 daily, Sun 4 daily; 20–30min); Portnahaven (Mon–Sat 6 daily, Sun 3 daily; 50min).

GETTING AROUND AND INFORMATION

Bike rental Bike rental is available from the post office at the top of Main St (Mon–Fri 9am–5.30pm, Sat 9am–12.30pm; £10/day; ☏ 01496 850232).

Tourist office The Square, Main St (April–Oct Mon–Sat 9.30am–5.30pm, Sun noon–3pm; Nov–March Mon–Fri 10am–3pm; ☏ 01496 810254). The staff here can help you find accommodation anywhere on the island and also on Jura.

ISLAY GEESE

Between mid-September and the third week of April, it's impossible to miss the island's staggeringly large wintering population of **Greenland Barnacle** and **Greater White-fronted geese**. During this period, the geese dominate the landscape, feeding incessantly off the rich pasture, strolling by the shores, and flying in formation across the winter skies. In the spring, the geese hang around just long enough to snap up the first shoots of new grass, in order to give themselves enough energy to make the 2000-mile journey to Greenland, where they breed in the summer. Understandably, many local farmers are not exactly happy about the geese feeding off their land, and some receive compensation for the inconvenience.

ACCOMMODATION AND EATING

★ **Bowmore House** Shore St ☎ 01496 810324, �🌐 the bowmorehouse.co.uk. Run by an amiable couple, this grand-looking house, positioned on the main road entering the village, accommodates five fabulous rooms exquisitely furnished in different styles, but all with plush carpets and plump beds, as well as sparkling bathrooms replete with luxury toiletries. There's a complimentary laundry service too. **£130**

Harbour Inn The Square ☎ 01496 810330, �🌐 harbour -inn.com. Smartly appointed and fairly expensive maritime-themed restaurant serving sumptuous dishes like halibut, salmon and cod poached in a fish bouillon with saffron potatoes (£21.50). Alternatively, you can warm yourself by a peat fire in the adjoining pub, where they also do lunchtime bar snacks. Daily noon–2pm & 6–10pm.

Lambeth Guesthouse Jamieson St ☎ 01496 810597, ✉ lambethguesthouse@tiscali.co.uk. Just off Main Street, this is a jovially run guesthouse with six modestly sized but impeccably prepared en-suite rooms. A little tricky to find as there's no sign, but it's next to the tiny filling station, the door being around to the side. **£94**

Loch Gruinart

Aoradh visitor centre: Seven miles north of Bridgend on the B8017 • Daily 10am–5pm • Free • ☎ 01496 850505, �🌐 rspb.org.uk /lochgruinart

You can see Islay geese just about anywhere on the island (see box, p.117) – there are an estimated 15,000 white-fronted and 40,000 barnacles here (and rising) – though they are usually at their most concentrated in the fields between Bridgend and Ballygrant. In the evening, they tend to congregate in the tidal mud flats and fields around **Loch Gruinart**, which is an **RSPB nature reserve**. The nearby farm of **Aoradh** (pronounced "oorig") is run by the RSPB, and one of its outbuildings contains a **visitor centre**, housing an observation point with telescopes and a CCTV link with the mud flats; there's also a hide across the road looking north over the salt flats at the head of the loch. From the hide, you're more likely to see reed bunting, redshank, lapwing, pintail, wigeon, teal and other waterfowl rather than geese.

The road along the western shores of Loch Gruinart to Ardnave is a good place to spot **choughs**, members of the crow family, distinguished by their curved red beaks and matching legs. Halfway along the road, there's a path off to the ruins of **Kilnave Chapel**, whose working graveyard contains a very weathered, eighth-century Celtic cross. The road ends at Ardnave Loch, beyond which lie numerous sand dunes, where seals often sun themselves, and otters sometimes fish offshore. Anyone interested in **birding** or **bushcraft** should get in touch with the Islay Natural History Trust in Port Charlotte (see opposite), who organize all sorts of adventures and activities.

Machir Bay

Without doubt the best **sandy beaches** on Islay are to be found on the isolated northwest coast, in particular, the lovely golden beach of **Machir Bay**, which is backed by great white-sand dunes. The sea here has dangerous undercurrents, however, and is not safe to swim in (the same goes for the much smaller **Saligo Bay**, to the north).

Kilchoman

At the settlement of **Kilchoman**, set back from Machir Bay, beneath low rocky cliffs, where fulmars nest inland, the church is in a sorry state of disrepair. Its churchyard, however, contains a beautiful fifteenth-century cross, decorated with interlacing on one side and the Crucifixion on the other; at its base there's a wishing stone that should be turned sunwise when wishing. Across a nearby field towards the bay lies the **sailors' cemetery**, containing just 75 graves of the 400 or so who were drowned when the armed merchant cruiser SS *Otranto* collided with another ship in its convoy in a storm in October 1918. The ship was carrying 1000 army personnel (including 665 Americans), the majority of whom made it safely to a ship that came to their aid; of the 400 who had to try and swim ashore, only 16 survived. The sailors' graves lie in three neat rows, from the cook to the captain, who has his own, much larger gravestone.

Sanaigmore

Another poignant memorial stands at **Sanaigmore**, at the end of a road three miles due west of Loch Gruinart, commemorating 241 Irish emigrants, fleeing the potato famine, drowned when the *Exmouth of Newcastle* was wrecked off the coast in April 1847 – another beautiful sandy beach lies a short walk north of the settlement.

Port Charlotte

Port Charlotte, founded in 1828 by Walter Frederick Campbell and named after his mother, is generally agreed to be Islay's prettiest village. Known as the "Queen of the Rhinns" (derived from the Gaelic word for a promontory), its immaculate whitewashed cottages cluster around a sandy cove overlooking Loch Indaal.

Museum of Islay Life

Daal Terrace • April–Sept Mon–Fri 10.30am–4.30pm • £3 • ☎ 01496 850358, ⓦ islaymuseum.org

On the northern fringe of the village, in a whitewashed former chapel, the imaginative **Museum of Islay Life** is crammed to bursting with local memorabilia. As well as tantalizing snippets about eighteenth-century illegal whisky distillers, there are some terrific photos and a good library of books about the island. Best of all, though, are the displays on the SS *Tuscania* and HMS *Otranto*, both of which were sunk in the waters hereabouts during World War I. Among the exhibits is the bell from the *Tuscania* and the notebook belonging to Sergeant Malcolm McNeill, in which he records the names and conditions of those who perished, including one, he writes rather grimly, "whose body is so much decayed that it is crumbling to pieces".

Islay Natural History Trust Visitor Centre

Main St • May–Sept Mon–Fri 10am–4pm • £3; nature rambles £2.50 • ☎ 01496 850288, ⓦ islaynaturalhistory.org

The **Islay Natural History Trust Visitor Centre**, housed in the former distillery warehouse, is well worth a visit for anyone interested in the island's fauna and flora. As well as an extensive library to browse, there's lots of hands-on stuff for kids: microscopes, a touch table full of natural goodies, a sea-water aquarium, a bug world and owl pellets to examine. Tickets are valid for a week, allowing you to go back and identify things you've seen on your travels. They also organize weekly nature rambles in July and August, which could include anything from rockpooling to beachcombing.

ARRIVAL AND DEPARTURE

PORT CHARLOTTE

By bus Buses stop just outside the *Port Charlotte Hotel*. Destinations Bowmore (Mon–Sat 5–6 daily, Sun 3 daily; 25min).

ACCOMMODATION AND EATING

Croft Kitchen Opposite the museum ☎ 01496 850230. Somewhere between a café and a restaurant, this sparsely furnished place nevertheless knocks up some decent food, as well as tea, coffee and cakes. March–Oct Mon, Tues & Thurs–Sun 11am–9pm.

Port Charlotte Hotel In the heart of the village overlooking the beach ☎ 01496 850360, ⓦ port charlottehotel.co.uk. A handful of the ten rooms at this smart, though terrifically expensive, hotel have retained their original exposed-stone walls, but they're all thoughtfully designed and decorated in bold but beautiful colours. The hotel restaurant is a cut above anything else in Port Charlotte, though it's much more fun to tuck into one of their seafood lunches out on the grassy terrace; try the

1

cracked Islay crab claws (£14.95). Live music usually takes place on Wed and Sun evenings in the bar. Daily noon–2pm & 6–11pm. **£190**

Port Mòr Campsite Just outside the village out on the road to Portnahave ☎ 01496 850441, ⓦ islandofislay .co.uk. A community-run campsite with glorious sea views and tip-top facilities: modern shower block, games room, laundry, café and a brilliant playpark for the kids. **£16**/pitch

SYHA hostel Next door to the Natural History Trust Visitor Centre ☎ 0870 004 1128, ⓦ syha.org.uk. Islay's only hostel is housed in an old bonded warehouse by the sea. It possesses a handy mix of doubles and triples all the way up to six-bed dorms, and all with shared bathroom facilities; there's also a large kitchen and common room open to all. Breakfast £3.75. Mid-March to mid-Oct. Dorms **£17**; doubles **£42**

Portnahaven and Port Wemyss

The main coastal road culminates seven miles south of Port Charlotte at **Portnahaven**, a fishing and crofting community since the early nineteenth century. The familiar whitewashed cottages wrap themselves prettily around the steep banks of a deep bay, where seals bask on the rocks in considerable numbers; in the distance, you can see Portnahaven's twin settlement, **Port Wemyss**, a mile south. The communities share a little whitewashed church, located above the bay in Portnahaven, with separate doors for each village.

A short way out to sea are two islands, the largest of which, Orsay, sports the **Rhinns of Islay Lighthouse**, built by Robert Louis Stevenson's father in 1825; ask around locally if you're keen to visit the island.

ARRIVAL AND DEPARTURE   PORTNAHAVEN AND PORT WEMYSS

By bus Buses make their way into the centre of both villages, dropping off first at Portnahaven.

Destinations Bowmore (Mon–Sat 6 daily; Sun 3 daily; 50min).

ACCOMMODATION AND EATING

Burnside B&B Shore St, Port Wemyss ☎ 01496 860296, ⓦ burnsidelodge.co.uk. Located just off the coastal path, this sweet little place offers three rooms (one en suite) of modest proportions, but they're absolutely up to the mark. The friendly owner here also rustles up delectable home-baked goodies, in particular cupcakes

and muffins; you can enjoy these, with a mug of tea, in the cosy residents' lounge or outside on one of the barrel seats looking across to Rhinns Point, below which seals bask on the shore. Snacks and drinks served April–Sept Fri–Mon 10.30am–4.30pm. **£90**

Loch Finlaggan

Just beyond Ballygrant, on the road to Port Askaig, a narrow road leads off north to **Loch Finlaggan**, site of a number of prehistoric crannogs (artificial islands) and, for four hundred years from the twelfth century, headquarters of the Lords of the Isles, semi-autonomous rulers over the Hebrides and Kintyre. The site is evocative enough, but there are, in truth, very few remains beyond the foundations. Remarkably, the palace that stood here appears to have been unfortified, a testament perhaps to the prosperity and stability of the islands in those days.

To the northeast of the loch, the **information centre** (Easter–Oct Mon–Sat 10.30am–4.30pm, Sun 1.30–4.30pm; £2) exhibits a number of superb finds uncovered on the site, notably the head of the commemorative medieval cross. From the centre a path leads down to the site itself (access at any time), which is dotted with interpretive panels. Duckboards allow you to walk out across the reed beds of the loch and explore the main crannog, **Eilean Mor**, where several carved gravestones are displayed under cover in the chapel, all of which seem to support the theory that the Lords of the Isles buried their wives and children, while having themselves interred on Iona. Further out into the loch is another, smaller crannog, **Eilean na Comhairle**, originally connected to Eilean Mor by a causeway, where the Lords of the Isles are thought to have held meetings of the Council of the Isles.

Port Askaig

Islay's other ferry connection with the mainland, and its sole link with Colonsay and Jura, is from **Port Askaig**, a scattering of buildings which tumbles down a little cove by the narrowest section of the Sound of Islay or Caol Ila. There's next to nothing here, save for a hotel, shop and post office.

ARRIVAL AND TOURS
PORT ASKAIG

By ferry To all intents and purposes, Port Askaig is the second of the island's main ferry terminals.
Destinations Colonsay (Wed 1 daily; 1hr 10min); Feolin ferry to Jura (Mon–Sat hourly, Sun 7 daily; 5min); Kennacraig (3–4 daily; 2hr 5min).
By bus Buses depart from a spot just up from the ferry terminal.

Destinations Bowmore (Mon–Sat 6–8 daily, Sun 4 daily; 25min).
Boat tours For high-adrenalin boat trips, contact Islay Sea Safari (☎ 01496 40510), which is based in Port Askaig and best known for whizzing round the distilleries in a rigid inflatable.

ACCOMMODATION AND EATING

★ **Kilmeny Farmhouse** Ballygrant ☎ 01496 840668, ⓦ kilmeny.co.uk. Three miles south of Port Askaig, this whitewashed farmhouse is a place that richly deserves all the superlatives it regularly receives. Antique furnishings, locally made fabrics and slipper baths feature in some or all of the four colour-coordinated rooms. You can expect to be well pampered for the duration of your stay, and the gourmet breakfast is a real treat, comprising, among other things, fresh fruit salad, poached plums, and smoked salmon and scrambled eggs. March–Nov. **£125**
Port Askaig Hotel Opposite the ferry terminal ☎ 01496

840245, ⓦ portaskaig.co.uk. Brilliantly convenient for the ferry and with wonderful views over to the Paps of Jura, though there's no doubt that this warm and welcoming hotel could do with a lick of paint here and there. Both the restaurant and bar of the *Port Askaig Hotel* are busy, convivial places any night of the week, popular with local fishermen and tourists alike. The restaurant serves a quality menu of seafood, while the snug, low-ceilinged *Port Bar* (allegedly dating back to the sixteenth century) is about as relaxing a place as you could wish for. Restaurant daily noon–2.30pm & 6.30–10.30pm; bar daily 11am–11pm. **£125**

Isle of Jura

Twenty-eight miles long and eight miles wide, the long whale-shaped island of **JURA** is one of the wildest and most mountainous of the Inner Hebrides, its entire west coast uninhabited and inaccessible except to the dedicated walker. The distinctive **Paps of Jura** – so called because of their smooth breast-like shape, though there are, in fact, three of them – seem to dominate every view off the west coast of Argyll, their glacial rounded tops covered in a light dusting of quartzite scree. The island's name is commonly thought to derive from the Norse *dyr-oe* (deer island) and, appropriately enough, the current deer population of 6000 outnumbers the 180 humans 33 to 1; other wildlife to look out for include mountain hares and eagles. With just one road, which sticks to the more sheltered eastern coast of the island, and only one hotel, a couple of B&Bs and some self-catering cottages, Jura is an ideal place to go for peace and quiet and some great walking.

Jura House

Five miles south of the ferry terminal • Daily 9am–5pm; tea tent June–Aug Mon–Fri • £2.50

Five miles south of the ferry terminal are the lovely wooded grounds of **Jura House**, originally built by the Campbells in the early nineteenth century. Pick up a booklet at the entrance to the grounds, and follow the path that takes you down to the sandy shore, a perfect picnic spot in fine weather. Closer to the house itself, there's an idyllic **walled garden**, divided in two by a natural rushing burn that tumbles down in steps. The garden specializes in antipodean plants, which flourish in the frost-free climate; in season, you can buy some of the garden's organic produce or take tea in the tea tent.

1

WALKING THE PAPS OF JURA
Ordnance Survey Explorer map 355

Perhaps the most popular of all the hillwalks on Jura is an ascent of any of the island's famous **Paps of Jura** – Beinn an Oir (2571ft), Beinn a'Chaolais (2407ft) and Beinn Shiantaidh (2477ft) – which cluster together in the south half of the island. It's possible to do a round trip from Craighouse itself, or from the Feolin ferry, but the easiest approach is from the three-arched bridge on the island's main road, three miles north of Craighouse. From the bridge, keeping to the north side of the Corran River, you eventually reach Loch an t'Siob. If you only want to climb **one Pap**, then simply climb up to the saddle between Beinn an Oir and Beinn Shiantaidh and choose which one (Beinn an Oir is probably the most interesting), returning to the bridge the same way. The trip to and from the bridge should take between five and six hours; it's hard going and care needs to be taken, as the scree is unstable.

If you want to try and bag **all three Paps**, you need to attack Beinn Shiantaidh via its southeast spur, leaving the loch at its easternmost point. This makes for a more difficult ascent, as the scree and large lumps of quartzite are tough going. Descending to the aforementioned saddle, and climbing Beinn an Oir is straightforward enough, but make sure you come off Beinn an Oir via the south spur, before climbing Beinn a'Chaolais, as the western side of Beinn an Oir is dangerously steep. Again, you can return via the loch to the three-arched bridge.

Every year, in the last bank-holiday weekend in May, hundreds of masochists take part in a **fell race** up the Paps, which the winner usually completes in three hours. Given the number of deer on Jura, it's as well to be aware of the **stalking season** (July–Feb), during which you should check with the *Jura Hotel* (see opposite) before heading out. At all times of year, you should take all the usual **safety precautions** (see p.42); beware, too, of adders; which are quite numerous on Jura.

Craighouse

Anything that happens on Jura happens in the island's only real village, **Craighouse**, eight miles up the road from the Feolin ferry. The village enjoys a sheltered setting, overlooking Knapdale on the mainland – so sheltered, in fact, that there are even a few palm trees thriving on the seafront. There's a shop/post office, the island hotel and a tearoom.

Jura distillery

Opposite the *Jura Hotel* • Guided tours Mon–Fri 11am & 2pm • Free • ☎ 01496 820601, ⓦ jurawhisky.com

Established in 1810 by the Campbells, the **Isle of Jura distillery** has endured a somewhat chequered history. It went out of business in the early 1900s, before reopening in 1963 on the premises of the then-derelict distillery. It now produces five distinctive single malts, with two notable success stories, the ten-year-old "Origin", and the sixteen-year-old "Diurachs" – you'll get to sample one or both of these on one of the free guided tours.

Corryvreckan Whirlpool

ⓦ whirlpool-scotland.co.uk

Between the islands of Scarba and Jura is the raging **Corryvreckan Whirlpool**, one of the world's most spectacular whirlpools, thought to be caused by a rocky pinnacle some 100ft below the sea. Exactly how the whirlpool appears depends on the tide and wind, but there's a potential tidal flow of over eight knots, which, when accompanied by gale force winds, can create standing waves up to 15ft high. Inevitably there are numerous legends about the place – known as *coire bhreacain* (speckled cauldron) in Gaelic – concerning *Cailleach* (Hag), the Celtic storm goddess. From the land, the best place from which to view it is Carraig Mhór on the northern tip of Jura.

GEORGE ORWELL ON JURA

In April 1946, Eric Blair (better known by his pen name of **George Orwell**), intending to give himself "six months' quiet" in which to complete his latest novel, moved to a remote farmhouse called **Barnhill**, at the northern end of Jura, which he had visited for the first time the previous year. He appears to have relished the challenge of living in Barnhill, fishing almost every night, shooting rabbits, laying lobster pots, and even attempting a little farming. Along with his adopted 3-year-old son Richard, and later his sister Avril, he clearly enjoyed his spartan existence. The book Orwell was writing, under the working title *The Last Man in Europe*, was to become *1984* (the title was arrived at by simply reversing the last two digits of the year in which it was finished – 1948). During his time on Jura, however, Orwell was suffering badly from tuberculosis, and eventually he was forced to return to London, where he died in January 1950.

Barnhill, 23 miles north of Craighouse, is as remote today as it was in Orwell's day. The road deteriorates rapidly beyond Lealt, where vehicles must be left, leaving pilgrims a four-mile walk to the house itself. Alternatively, the Richardsons of Kinauachdrachd (☎07899 912116) can organize a taxi and guided walk, and also run a bunkhouse. Orwell wrote most of the book in the bedroom (top left window as you look at the house); the place is now a self-catering cottage (☎01786 850274). If you're keen on making the journey out to Barnhill, you might as well combine it with a trip to the nearby **Corryvreckan Whirlpool** (see opposite), which lies between Jura and Scarba, to the north. Orwell nearly drowned in the whirlpool during a fishing trip in August 1947, along with his three companions (including Richard): the outboard motor was washed away, and they had to row to a nearby island and wait for several hours before being rescued by a passing fisherman.

ARRIVAL AND TOURS
ISLE OF JURA

By ferry The Feolin ferry from Port Askaig will not run if there's a strong northerly or southerly wind, so bring your toothbrush if you're coming for a day-trip. Very occasionally the Jura minibus (☎01496 820314) meets the car ferry from Port Askaig – phone ahead to check times. Between April and September, there's also a passenger ferry service (☎07768 450000, ⓦ jurapassengerferry.com) from Tayvallich, on the Argyll mainland, to Craighouse.

Destinations Port Askaig (Mon–Sat hourly, Sun 7 daily; 5min).

Boat tours If you're interested in taking a boat trip to Scarba, Corryvreckan or the nearby Garvellach islands, contact Sea.fari, (☎01852 300003, ⓦ seafari.co.uk), based at Easdale, or Craignish Cruises (☎07747 023038, ⓦ craignishcruises.co.uk), in Ardfern.

ACCOMMODATION AND EATING

The Antlers 100m north of Jura Distillery ☎01496 820123. Unlicensed bistro restaurant that serves up burgers, sandwiches and salads for lunch, and beautifully presented Jura lamb (£14.95), pork and salmon in the evening. Tues–Sun noon–2.30pm & 7–10pm.

Jura Hotel Craighouse ☎01496 820243, ⓦ jurahotel .co.uk. The island's one and only hotel is not much to look at from the outside, but it's warm and friendly within, and centre of the island's social scene. The hotel does the

usual bar meals, and has a shower block and laundry facilities round the back for those who wish to camp in the hotel gardens. Camping free, showers £1. Bar daily 11am–11pm. __£95__

Sealladh na Mara Four miles north of Craighouse ☎01496 820349, ⓦ isleofjura.net. A modern croft house with just two rooms, both of which have stunning views; guests are also free to avail themselves of the adjoining lounge/dining room. __£76__

The Central Highlands

DRUM CASTLE IN THE SNOW

The Central Highlands

The Central Highlands lie right in the heart of Scotland, bounded by the country's two major geological fissures: the Highland Fault, which runs along a line drawn approximately from Arran to Aberdeen and marks the southern extent of Scotland's Highlands, and the Great Glen, the string of lochs that runs on a similar southwest–northeast axis between Fort William and Inverness. The appeal of the region is undoubtedly its landscape, a concentrated mix of mountain, glen, loch and moorland that responds to each season with a dramatic blend of colour and mood, combined with the outdoor activities the landscape inspires. It's also an area with a rich history, stemming in large part from the fact that along the geological divide of north and south is a significant cultural and social shift, and it is no surprise that the region is littered with castles, battlefields and monuments from the centuries of power struggle between the Highlanders and the Sassenachs, whether from lowland Scotland or south of the border.

Northwest of Glasgow, the elongated teardrop of **Loch Lomond** is at the heart of Scotland's first national park. The magnificent scenery around the loch continues east into the fabled mountains and lochs of the **Trossachs**, where hikers and mountain-bikers are drawn to explore the forested glens and fugitive Highlanders such as **Rob Roy** once roamed. North of the Trossachs, the massive county of **Perthshire** lies right at the heart of the Central Highlands, with **lochs Tay** and **Rannoch** stacked up across the middle of the region, each surrounded by impressive hills and progressively more remote countryside.

Further to the east are the **Grampian Mountains**. Within this range the **Angus glens**, immediately north of Perth and Dundee, are renowned for their prettiness and easy accessibility, while closer to Aberdeen the river valleys of **Deeside** and **Donside** combine the drama of peaks such as **Lochnagar** with the richly wooded glens and dramatic castles which so enchanted Queen Victoria. The northern side of the Grampians are dominated by the dramatic **Cairngorm** massif, the largest area of land over 2500ft in Britain and centre of Scotland's second national park. These hills, with their deserved reputation for superb outdoor sports in both summer and winter, are complemented by the atmospheric ancient woodlands of **Strathspey**. A little way downstream is the whisky-producing region of **Speyside**, where various trails lead you to the distilleries, home of some of the world's most famous single malts.

With no sizeable towns in the region other than useful service centres such as Callander, Pitlochry and Aviemore, **orientation** is best done by means of the traditional transport routes – many of which follow historic trading or military roads between the

RED GROUSE IN THE CAIRNGORMS

Highlights

❶ Mountain biking in the Trossachs Pocket Highlands with shining lochs, wooded glens and noble peaks, and some superb forest trails. **See p.139**

❷ Folk music Join in a session at the bar of the *Taybank Hotel* in the dignified town of Dunkeld. **See p.141**

❸ Blair Castle Observe the grand life of the Highland nobility, along with extensive parkland and the country's only private army. **See p.147**

❹ Schiehallion Scale Perthshire's "fairy mountain" for the views over lochs, hills, glens and moors. **See p.148**

❺ Rannoch Moor One of the most inaccessible places in Scotland, where hikers can discover a true sense of remote emptiness. **See p.150**

❻ The castles of Deeside and the Don Valley A trail of some of Scotland's finest castles, from stately piles to moody ruins. **See p.162**

❼ The Cairngorms Scotland's grandest mountain massif, a place of wild animals, ancient forests, inspiring vistas – and terrific outdoor activities. **See p.164**

❽ Speyside Way Walking route taking in Glenfiddich, Glenlivet and Glen Grant, with the chance to drop in and taste their whiskies too. **See p.176**

HIGHLIGHTS ARE MARKED ON THE MAP ON PP.128–129

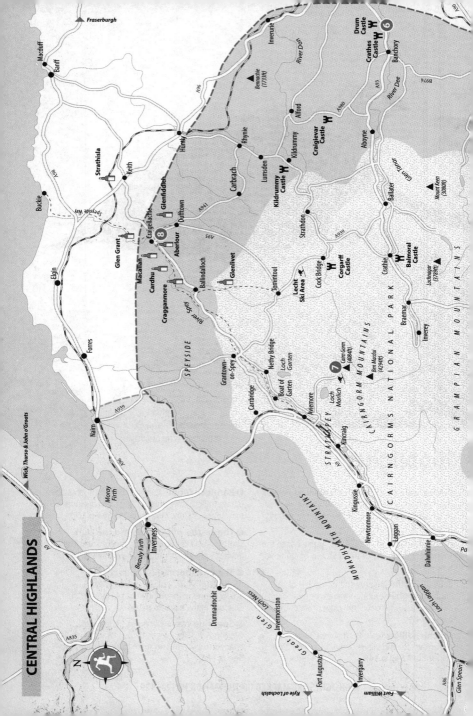

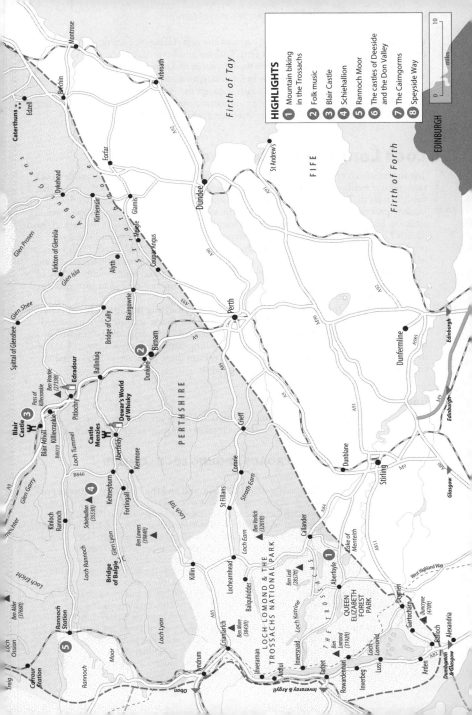

important population centres on the edges of the area: Glasgow, Stirling and Perth to the south, Aberdeen to the east, and Fort William and Inverness to the north. The main route on the **western** side is along the western shore of Loch Lomond, where both the A82 and the railway line wind north to Crianlarich en route to Oban and Fort William. In the **centre** of the country, the A84 cuts through the heart of the Trossachs between Stirling and Crianlarich, while the most important route to the **eastern** side is the busy A9 trunk road and the nearby railway between Perth and Inverness.

Loch Lomond and around

The largest stretch of fresh water in Britain (23 miles long and up to five miles wide), **Loch Lomond** is the epitome of Scottish scenic splendour, thanks in large part to the ballad that fondly recalls its "bonnie, bonnie banks". The song was said to have been written by a Jacobite prisoner captured by the English, who, sure of his fate, wrote that his spirit would return to Scotland on the low road much faster than his living compatriots on the high road.

Loch Lomond is undoubtedly the centrepiece of the national park, and the most popular gateway into the park is **Balloch**, the town on the southern tip of Loch Lomond; with Glasgow city centre just nineteen miles away, both Balloch and the southwest side of the loch around **Luss** are often packed with day-trippers and tour coaches. Many of these continue up the western side of the loch, though the fast A82 road isn't ideal for a leisurely lochside drive.

Very different in tone, the eastern side of the loch, abutting the Trossachs, operates at a different pace with wooden ferryboats puttering out to a scattering of tree-covered islands off the village of **Balmaha**. Much of the eastern shore can only be reached by boat or foot, although the West Highland Way long-distance footpath (see p.133) and the distinctive peak of **Ben Lomond** ensure that even these parts are well travelled in comparison to many other areas of the Highlands.

Balloch

The main settlement by Loch Lomond is **BALLOCH** at its southwestern corner, where the water channels into the River Leven for its short journey south to the sea in the

---

HIGH ROADS AND LOW ROADS AROUND LOCH LOMOND

Ordnance Survey Explorer Maps 347 & 364

The popularity of hiking and biking within **Loch Lomond and the Trossachs National Park** (w lochlomond-trossachs.org) has been recognized in an initiative entitled "4Bs" which aims to improve the links between boats, boots (ie walking), bikes and buses around the park. Signposting and information are increasingly good, with new cycle paths and trails being set out all the time, in addition to enhanced provision for walking and nature trails. Indeed, with a seaplane and wooden mail boats operating on Loch Lomond as well as a 100-year-old steamship on Loch Katrine, getting around the park is very much part of the experience.

For those keen to take to the high road there are three obvious targets offering different levels of challenge. Most prominent, **Ben Lomond** (3192ft) is the most southerly of the "Munros" (see p.40) and one of the most popular hills in Scotland, its commanding position above Loch Lomond affording amazing views of the Highlands and Lowlands. The well-signposted route to the summit and back from Rowardennan takes five to six hours. If you're looking for an easier climb, but an equally impressive view over Loch Lomond, start at Balmaha for the ascent of **Conic Hill** (1175ft), a two- to three-hour walk through forest and hillside.

Finally, you need less than an hour to complete the ascent of **Duncryne** (470ft), a small conical hill beside Gartocharn to the east of Balloch on the south side of the loch. The route up is undemanding and the view wonderfully rewarding.

Firth of Clyde. Surrounded by housing estates and overstuffed with undistinguished guesthouses, Balloch has few redeeming features and is little more than a suburb of the factory town of Alexandria. You might want to arrange a loch trip from here though, or shop at the Loch Lomond stores complex. Across the river in the extensive mature grounds of **Balloch Castle Country Park**, there are shoreside and sylvan walks.

The Maid of the Loch

The Pier, Pier Rd • May–Sept daily 11am–4pm; Oct–April Sat & Sun 11am–4pm • Free • ☎ 01389 711865, Ⓦ maidoftheloch.com

Restored 1950s **paddle steamer** *The Maid of the Loch* is permanently moored at Balloch pier; aboard you can find out about her glory days sailing the loch and have a cup of tea in the onboard café.

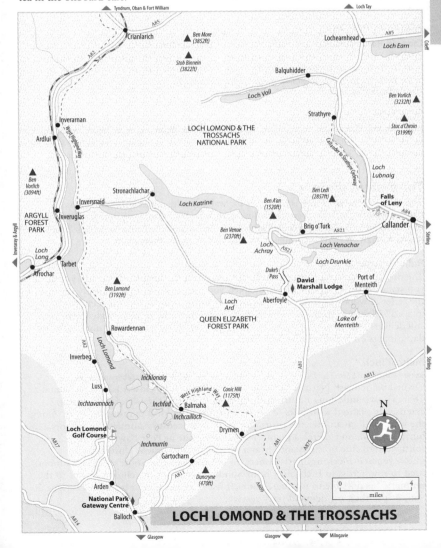

By train Balloch has a direct train connection with Glasgow Queen St (every 30min; 50min).
By bus Regular buses connect Balloch with nearby towns. Destinations Balmaha (every 2hr; 25min); Luss (hourly; 15min).

Tourist office The Old Station Building opposite the train station is a small tourist office (daily: June–Aug 9.30am–6pm; Sept–May 10am–5pm; ☎ 08707 200607).

ACTIVITIES

Can You Experience ☎ 01389 602576, ⓦ canyouexperience.com. Based right beside Drumkinnon Tower, Can You Experience rents out canoes, bikes and even pedalos. They also organize "aquasphering" in summer, allowing kids to literally walk on water, in large plastic balls.
Sweeney's Cruises ☎ 01389 752376, ⓦ www.sweeneyscruises.com. In the centre of town near the bridge, Sweeney's Cruises make loch trips, including a two-hour sailing to Luss.

ACCOMMODATION

Cameron House Alexendria, just north of Balloch ☎ 0871 222 4681, ⓦ devere-hotels.co.uk. This exclusive resort has its own spa and championship golf course as well as the area's best restaurant, an offshoot of Edinburgh's *Martin Wishart*. **£180**
Dumbain Farm Balloch ☎ 01389 752263, ⓦ dumbainfarm.co.uk. Rambling whitewashed farm with bright and elegant rooms. Traditional Scottish breakfast, cooked on an Aga. **£70**

SHOPPING

Loch Lomond Shores Ben Lomond Way, Balloch ☎ 01389 751031, ⓦ lochlomondshores.com. A "retail crescent" of shops including branches of Edinburgh's venerable department store, Jenners, and of the city's best deli, *Valvona & Crolla*. The centre can be accessed from town on a miniature train, or by the lakeside path.

The eastern shore

The tranquil **eastern shore** is far better for walking and appreciating the loch's natural beauty than the overcrowded western side. It's the access point for climbing **Ben Lomond** and visiting **Inchcailloch** island, and where the minor road peters out at **Rowardennan** you can continue on foot to the village of **Inversnaid**.

Balmaha and around

The tiny lochside settlement of **BALMAHA** stands on the Highland Boundary Fault: if you stand on the viewpoint above the pier, you can see the fault line clearly marked by the series of woody islands that form giant stepping stones across the loch. Many of the loch's 37 **islands** are privately owned, and, rather quaintly, an old wooden mail boat still delivers post to four of them. Balmaha gets very busy in summer, not least with day-trippers on the West Highland Way.

Inchcailloch

Boat rental MacFarlane & Son • From £10/hr or £40/day, ferry service £5 return • ☎ 01360 870214, ⓣ balmahaboatyard.co.uk
Owned by Scottish Natural Heritage, **Inchcailloch** is the closest island to Balmaha. There's a two-mile-long nature trail signposted around the island, which was extensively planted with oaks to provide bark for the local tanning industry. Along the way you'll encounter the ruins of a fourteenth-century nunnery and associated burial ground, and there's a picnic and camping site at Port Bawn on the southwestern side of the island, near a pleasant sandy beach. Until the mid-seventeenth century parishioners on the far (western) shore of Loch Lomond used to row across to Inchcailloch for Sunday services at the church linked to the nunnery. It's possible to row here yourself using a boat rented from MacFarlane & Son, or use their on-demand ferry service.

2

THE WEST HIGHLAND WAY

Ordnance Survey Explorer maps 392, 384, 377, 364, 385, 342, 347 & 348

Opened in 1980, the spectacular **West Highland Way** was Scotland's first long-distance footpath, stretching some 96 miles from Milngavie (pronounced "mill-guy"), six miles north of central Glasgow, to Fort William, where it reaches the foot of Ben Nevis, Britain's highest mountain. Today, it is by far the most popular such footpath in Scotland, and while for many the range of scenery, relative ease of walking and nearby facilities make it a classic route, others find it a little too busy in high season, particularly in comparison with the isolation of many other parts of the Highlands.

THE ROUTE

The route follows a combination of ancient **drove roads**, along which Highlanders herded their cattle and sheep to market in the Lowlands, military roads, built by troops to control the Jacobite insurgency in the eighteenth century, old coaching roads and disused railway lines. In addition to the stunning scenery, which is increasingly dramatic as the path heads north, walkers may see some of Scotland's rarer **wildlife**, including red deer, feral goats and, soaring over the highest peaks, golden eagles.

Passing through the lowlands north of Glasgow, the route runs along the eastern shores of Loch Lomond, over the Highland Boundary Fault Line, then round Crianlarich, crossing open heather moorland across the **Rannoch Moor** wilderness area. It passes close to **Glen Coe** (see p.193) before reaching **Fort William** (see p.184). Apart from a stretch between Loch Lomond and Bridge of Orchy, when the path is within earshot of the main road, this is wild, remote country: north of Rowardennan on Loch Lomond, the landscape is increasingly exposed, and you should be well prepared for changeable weather.

TACKLING THE ROUTE

Though this is emphatically not the most strenuous of Britain's long-distance walks – it passes between lofty mountain peaks, rather than over them – a moderate degree of fitness is required as there are some steep ascents. If you're looking for an added challenge, you could work a climb of Ben Lomond or Ben Nevis into your schedule. You might choose to walk individual sections of the Way (the eight-mile climb from Glen Coe up the Devil's Staircase is particularly spectacular), but to tackle the whole thing you need to set aside at least seven days; avoid a Saturday start from Milngavie and you'll be less likely to be walking with hordes of people, and there'll be less pressure on accommodation. Most walkers tackle the route from south to north, and manage between ten and fourteen miles a day, staying at hotels, B&Bs and bunkhouses en route. Camping is permitted at recognized sites.

INFORMATION

The West Highland Way Official Guide (£16.99). Includes a foldout map as well as descriptions of the route, with detailed cultural, historical, archeological and wildlife information.
The official website ⓦ west-highland-way.co.uk.

Further details about the Way, including a comprehensive accommodation list. The site also has links to tour companies and transport providers, who can take your luggage from one stopping point to the next.

Rowardennan

Public transport ends at Balmaha, but another seven miles north through the woods brings you to the end of the road at **ROWARDENNAN**, a scattered settlement that sits below Ben Lomond (see below).

Ben Lomond

Ben Lomond (3192ft) is the most southerly of the "Munros" (see p.40) and one of the most popular mountains in Scotland, its commanding position above Loch Lomond affording amazing views of both the Highlands and Lowlands. The well-signposted route to the summit and back from Rowardennan takes five to six hours.

Inversnaid

Only walkers can continue up the lochside beyond Rowardennan, where the only settlement is seven miles north at **INVERSNAID**, made famous by a poem of the same name by Gerard Manley Hopkins about a frothing waterfall nearby ("This darksome burn, horseback brown/His rollrock highroad roaring down…").

ARRIVAL AND DEPARTURE   THE EASTERN SHORE

By car/bus The dead-end B837 from Drymen will take you halfway up the east bank to Rowardennan, as far as you can get by car or bus (#309 from Balloch and Drymen runs to Balmaha every 2hr), while the West Highland Way sticks close to the shores for the entire length of the loch.
Ferry to Rowardennan Passenger ferries (Easter–Sept

2 daily; ☎01301 702356, ⓦcruiselochlomond.co.uk) cross from Tarbert, on the west shore.
Ferry to Inversnaid It's possible to get to or from Inversnaid by ferry (£4 one way/£5 return), which crosses from Inveruglas, directly opposite on the western shore. You'll have to phone the *Inversnaid Hotel* to make arrangements.

INFORMATION AND TOURS

National Park Centre Balmaha (April–Sept daily 9.30am–4pm). Beside the large car park and offering information about local forest walks and occasional wildlife workshops.
Boat tours It's possible to join the mail boat cruise, which is run by MacFarlane & Son, from the jetty at Balmaha. The timetable allows a one-hour stop on Inchmurrin Island,

which has just ten permanent residents; it has the ruins of a monastery and castle, and food is served in the bar of the *Inchmurrin Hotel* (May–Oct Mon, Thurs & Sat 11.30am returns 2pm; July & Aug daily 11.30am returns 2pm; Oct–April Mon & Thurs 10.50am returns noon; £9; ☎01360 870214, ⓦbalmahaboatyard.co.uk.

ACCOMMODATION AND EATING

BALMAHA

Balmaha B&B and Bunkhouse Balmaha House ☎01360 870218, ⓦbalmahahouse.co.uk. Warmly welcoming West Highland Way accommodation on the loch shore. The bunkhouse is brand new. **£70**, bunkhouse bed **£15**
Oak Tree Inn Balmaha ☎01360 870357, ⓦoak-tree -inn.co.uk. This well-run inn is set back from the boatyard, and offers en-suite doubles and bunk-bed quads. There's also a convivial pub, and food is served all day. **£85**
Passfoot Cottage B&B Balmaha ☎01360 870324, ⓦpassfoot.com. This friendly and appealing little option is housed in a whitewashed toll cottage, enjoying an idyllic location and lochside garden. Great for walks along the shore. **£75**

ROWARDENNAN

Cashel Rowardennan, 2 miles north of Balmaha ☎01360 870234. A lovely, secluded Forestry Commission campsite on the loch shore with a decent loo block. Campers can launch craft from here onto the loch, and Ben Lomond is just 4 miles away. April–Oct. Pitch from **£16.10**
Clansman Bar Rowardennan Hotel ☎01360 870273, ⓦrowardennanhotel.co.uk. Nightlife in the area centres on the hotel's *Clansman Bar*, which features open fires, a beer garden and weekend live music. Closes weekdays out of season.
Rowardennan Lodge Youth Hostel Rowardennan ☎01360 870259, ⓦsyha.org.uk. A wonderfully situated SYHA hostel in a classic turreted Scots Baronial lodge with lawns running down to the shore. March–Oct. **£16.10**

The western shore

Despite the roar of traffic hurtling along the upgraded A82, the **west bank** of Loch Lomond is an undeniably beautiful stretch of water.

Luss

LUSS is the prettiest village in the region, with its prim, identical sandstone and slate cottages garlanded in rambling roses, and its narrow sand-and-pebble strand. However, its charms are no secret, and its streets and beach can become crowded in summer. If you want to escape the hordes, pop into the parish **church**, which is a haven of peace and has a lovely ceiling made from Scots-pine rafters and some fine Victorian stained-glass windows.

Tarbet and Inverarnan

Ten miles north of attractive Luss is the small settlement of **TARBET**, where the West Highland **train** reaches the shoreline. North of Tarbet, the A82 turns back into the narrow, winding road of old, making for slower but much more interesting driving. There's one more **train station** on Loch Lomond at Ardlui, at the mountain-framed head of the loch, but most travellers continue a couple of miles further north to **INVERARNAN**, where the *Drovers Inn* is arguably the most idiosyncratic **hotel** in Scotland.

ARRIVAL, INFORMATION AND TOURS
THE WESTERN SHORE

LUSS

By bus Buses run from Tarbet to Luss (hourly; 10min).
Tourist office Pick up local information at the Luss Visitor Centre (daily 9am–5pm; ☎01436 860229).

TARBERT

Tourist office Tarbet has a small tourist office (April–Oct

daily; ☎01301 702260).
Boat tours At the pier over the road from the prominent *Tarbet Hotel* you can hop on an hour-long loch cruise run by Cruise Loch Lomond (☎01301 702356, ⓦcruiseloch lomond.co.uk). The same operator also offers trips to Inversnaid and Rowardennan on the eastern side.

ACCOMMODATION AND EATING

LUSS

Coach House Loch Lomond Trading Company Limited ☎01436 860341. A spruce and lively little tearoom serving a range of teas, cakes, ciabattas, Orkney ice cream and its own take on haggis. Daily 10am–5pm.

Lodge on Loch Lomond ☎01436 860201, ⓦloch -lomond.co.uk. This modern lodge, just north of town, has a string of rooms with balconies and views over the loch, and serves decent meals in its restaurant, *Colquhoun's*. **£179**

INVERARNAN

Drover's Inn By Ardlui, North Loch Lomond ☎01301 704234, ⓦthedroversinn.co.uk. The bar features a roaring fire, barmen dressed in kilts, weary hillwalkers sipping pints and bearded musicians banging out folk songs. Down the creaking corridors, past moth-eaten stuffed animals, are a number of supposedly haunted and resolutely old-fashioned rooms. **£65**

Crianlarich and Tyndrum

CRIANLARICH, some eight miles north of the head of Loch Lomond, is an important staging post on various transport routes, including the West Highland Railway which divides here, one branch heading due west towards Oban, the other continuing north over Rannoch Moor to Fort William. The West Highland Way long-distance footpath (see box, p.133) also trogs past. Otherwise, there's little reason to stop here, unless you're keen on tackling some of the steep-sided hills that rise up from the glen.

Five miles further north from here on the A82/A85, the village of **TYNDRUM** owes its existence to a minor (and very short-lived) nineteenth-century gold rush, but today supports little more than a busy service station and several characterless hotels.

ARRIVAL AND DEPARTURE
CRIANLARICH AND TYNDRUM

By train Crianlarich is well served by regular trains. Destinations Fort William (3–4 daily Mon–Sat, 1–3 on Sun; 1hr 50min); Glasgow Queen Street (6–8 daily Mon–Sat, 1–3 on Sun; 1hr 50min); Oban (3–4 daily Mon–Sat,

1–3 on Sun; 1hr 15min).
By car At Tyndrum the road divides, with the A85 heading west to Oban, and the A82 heading for Fort William via Glen Coe.

ACCOMMODATION AND EATING

By The Way Hostel and Campsite Lower Station Road ☎01838 400333, ⓦtyndrumbytheway.com. Right beside Tyndrum Lower railway station is a good campsite and small purpose-built bunkhouse; the cute wooden "hobbit houses" in the grounds sleep four and are self-catering. Camping **£8pp**; hostel **£16pp**; hobbit house from **£40**

Real Food Café Tyndrum ☎01838 400235, ⓦthereal foodcafe.com. For a refreshingly different roadside dining experience, it's well worth trying the airy café on the main road serving fresh, fast food that's locally sourced and cooked to order. Mon–Thurs & Sun 9am–10pm, Fri 11am–10pm, Sat 7.30am–9pm.

The Trossachs

Often described as the Highlands in miniature, the **Trossachs** area boasts a magnificent diversity of scenery, with distinctive peaks, silvery lochs and mysterious, forest-covered

2

ROB ROY

A member of the outlawed Macgregor clan, **Rob Roy** (meaning "Red Robert" in Gaelic) was born in 1671 in Glengyle, just north of Loch Katrine, and lived for some time as a respectable cattle farmer and trader, supported by the powerful duke of Montrose. In 1712, finding himself in a tight spot when a cattle deal fell through, Rob Roy absconded with £1000, some of it belonging to the duke. He took to the hills to live as a brigand, his feud with Montrose escalating after the duke repossessed Rob Roy's land and drove his wife from their house. He was present at the Battle of Sheriffmuir during the Jacobite uprising of 1715, ostensibly supporting the Jacobites but probably as an opportunist: the chaos would have made cattle-raiding easier. Eventually captured and sentenced to transportation, Rob Roy was pardoned and returned to **Balquhidder** (see p.139), northeast of Glengyle, where he remained until his death in 1734.

Rob Roy's status as a local hero in the mould of Robin Hood should be tempered with the fact that he was without doubt a bandit and blackmailer. His life has been much romanticized, from Sir Walter Scott's 1818 novel *Rob Roy* to the 1995 film starring Liam Neeson, although the tale does serve well to dramatize the clash between the doomed clan culture of the Gaelic-speaking Highlanders and the organized feudal culture of lowland Scots, which effectively ended with the defeat of the Jacobites at Culloden in 1746. His **grave** in Balquhidder, a simple affair behind the ruined church, is mercifully free of the tartan trappings that plague parts of the Trossachs, predictably dubbed "Rob Roy Country" by the tourist board.

slopes. It is country ripe for stirring tales of brave kilted clansmen, a role fulfilled by Rob Roy Macgregor, the seventeenth-century outlaw whose name seems to attach to every second waterfall, cave and barely discernible path. Strictly speaking, the name "Trossachs", normally translated as either "bristly country" or "crossing place", originally referred only to the wooded glen between **Loch Katrine** and Loch Achray, but today it is usually taken as being the whole area from **Callander** right up to the eastern banks of Loch Lomond, with which it has been grouped as one of Scotland's national parks.

The Trossachs' high tourist profile was largely attributable in the early days to Sir Walter Scott, whose novels *Lady of the Lake* and *Rob Roy* were set in and around the area. According to one contemporaneous account, after Scott's *Lady of the Lake* was published in 1810, the number of carriages passing Loch Katrine rose from fifty the previous year to 270. Since then, neither the popularity nor beauty of the region has waned, and in high season the place is jam-packed with coaches full of tourists as well as walkers and mountain-bikers taking advantage of the easily accessed scenery. Autumn is a better time to come, when the hills are blanketed in rich, rusty colours and the crowds are thinner. In terms of where to stay, **Aberfoyle** has a rather dowdy air while **Callander** feels somewhat overrun, and you're often better off seeking out one of the guesthouses or B&Bs tucked away in secluded corners of the region.

Aberfoyle

Each summer the sleepy little town of **ABERFOYLE**, twenty miles west of Stirling, dusts itself down for its annual influx of tourists. Though of little appeal itself, Aberfoyle's position in the heart of the Trossachs is ideal, with **Loch Ard Forest** and **Queen Elizabeth Forest Park** stretching across to Ben Lomond and Loch Lomond to the west, the long curve of Loch Katrine and Ben Venue to the northwest, and Ben Ledi to the northeast. Don't come here for lively nightlife or entertainment, but for a good, healthy blast of the outdoors.

Fairy Knowe

From Aberfoyle you might like to wander north of the village to **Doon Hill**: cross the bridge over the Forth, continue past the cemetery and then follow signs to the **Fairy Knowe** (knoll). A toadstool marker points you through oak and holly trees to the summit of the Knowe where there is a pine tree said to contain the unquiet spirit of the

Reverend Robert Kirk, who studied local fairy lore and published his enquiries in *The Secret Commonwealth* (1691). Legend has it that, as punishment for disclosing supernatural secrets, he was forcibly removed to fairyland where he has languished ever since, although his mortal remains can be found in the nearby graveyard. This short walk should preferably be made at dusk, when it is at its most atmospheric.

Scottish Wool Centre
Off Main St, Aberfoyle • Daily: May–Sept 9.30am–5.30pm; Oct–April 10am–5pm • Free

The **Scottish Wool Centre** – a popular stop-off point with tour buses – is a glorified country knitwear shop selling all the usual jumpers and woolly toys as well as featuring daily seasonal displays of sheep-gathering and -shearing.

2

ARRIVAL AND INFORMATION
ABERFOYLE

By bus Regular buses from Stirling pull into the car park on Aberfoyle's Main Street.
Destinations Late June to mid-Oct Thurs–Tues 4 daily to: Callander (25min); Port of Menteith (10min).

Tourist office Trossachs Discovery Centre, Main St (April–Oct daily 10am–5pm; Nov–March Sat & Sun only; ☎ 08707 200604). It has full details of local accommodation, sights and outdoor activities.

ACCOMMODATION
Creag-Ard House Loch Ard ☎ 01877 382297, ⓦ creag -ard.co.uk. Accommodation options in Aberfoyle itself aren't all that inspiring. Head a mile west out of the town to this beautifully sited B&B which serves lovely breakfasts in a Victorian house overlooking Loch Ard. Easter–Oct. **£70**

Trossachs Holiday Park ☎ 01877 382614, ⓦ trossachs holidays.co.uk. This excellent family-run 40-acre park is fringed by oak and bluebell woods. Bikes for rent. March–Oct. Pitches from **£17**

The Lake of Menteith

About four miles east of Aberfoyle towards Doune, the **Lake of Menteith** is a superb fly-fishing centre and Scotland's only lake (as opposed to loch), so named due to a historic mix-up with the word *laigh*, Scots for "low-lying ground", which applied to the whole area. There are also some nice secluded spots along the shore for picnics and swims. To rent a fishing boat or a rod contact the Lake of Menteith Fisheries (April–Oct; ☎ 01877 385664).

Island of Inchmahome
Lake of Menteith • Daily: April–Sept 9.30am–4.30pm; Oct 9.30am–3.30pm • £5.50 including ferry • HS

From the northern shore of the lake, you can take a little ferry out to the **Island of Inchmahome** to explore the lovely, ruined Augustinian abbey. Founded in 1238, **Inchmahome Priory** is the most beautiful island monastery in Scotland, its remains rising tall and graceful above the trees. The masons employed to build the priory are thought to be those who built Dunblane Cathedral; certainly the western entrance there resembles that at Inchmahome. The nave of the church is roofless, but in the choir are preserved the graves of important families from the surrounding area. Most touching is a late thirteenth-century double effigy depicting Walter, the first Stewart earl of Menteith, and his countess, Mary, who, feet resting on lion-like animals, turn towards each other and embrace.

Also buried here is the adventurer and scholar Robert Bontine Cunninghame Graham, once a pal of Buffalo Bill and Joseph Conrad, and first president of the National Party of Scotland. Five-year-old Mary, Queen of Scots, was hidden at Inchmahome in 1547 before being taken to France, and there's a formal garden in the west of the island, known as Queen Mary's Bower, where legend has it she played. Traces remain of an orchard planted by the monks, but the island is thick now with oak, ash and Spanish chestnut. Visible on a nearby but inaccessible islet is the ruined castle of **Inchtalla**, the home of the earls of Menteith in the sixteenth and seventeenth centuries.

Lake of Menteith Hotel Port of Menteith ☎01877 385258, ⓦ www.lake-hotel.com. The Lake of Menteith is a beautiful place to stay: the hotel enjoys a lovely waterfront setting next to Port of Menteith's Victorian Gothic parish church, and also has a classy restaurant. **£120**

Queen Elizabeth Forest

David Marshall Lodge visitor centre daily: March–June, Sept & Oct 10am–5pm; July & Aug 10am–6pm; Nov & Dec 10am–4pm; Jan Sat & Sun 10am–4pm; Feb Thurs–Sun 10am–4pm · Car park £3 · ☎ 01877 382258

North of Aberfoyle, the A821 road to Loch Katrine winds its way into the Queen Elizabeth Forest, snaking up **Duke's Pass** (so called because it once belonged to the duke of Montrose). You can walk or drive the short distance from Aberfoyle to the park's excellent **visitor centre** at David Marshall Lodge, where you can pick up maps of the walks and cycle routes in the forest, get background information on the area's flora and fauna or settle into the **café** with its splendid views out over the tree tops.

The only road in the forest open to cars is the **Achray Forest Drive**, just under two miles further on from the centre, which leads through the park and along the western shore of **Loch Drunkie** before rejoining the main road.

Adjacent to the David Marshall Lodge is the **Go Ape adventure course** (April–Oct daily 9am–5pm; Feb & March Sat & Sun 9am–5pm; £30/£24 10–17-year-olds; bookings ☎08704 282710, ⓦgoape.co.uk), which involves an extended series of 40ft-high rope bridges, Tarzan swings and high-wire slides through the forest.

Loch Katrine

Cruises April–Oct daily · £13 return · ☎ 01877 376315, ⓦ lochkatrine.co.uk

Heading down the northern side of the Duke's Pass you come first to **Loch Achray**, tucked under Ben A'an. Look out across the loch for the small **Callander Kirk** in a lovely setting alone on a promontory. At the head of the loch a road follows the short distance through to the southern end of **Loch Katrine** at the foot of Ben Venue (2370ft).

The elegant Victorian passenger **steamer**, the SS *Sir Walter Scott*, has been plying the waters of Loch Katrine since 1900, chugging up to the wild country of Glengyle. It makes various cruises each day, but only the first (departing at 10.30am) stops off at Stronachlachar most days, though on Wednesdays and weekends there's a second trip to Stronachlachar departing at 2.30pm; the shorter one-hour cruises don't make any stops (£12). A popular combination is to **rent a bike** from the Katrinewheelz hut by the pier (☎01877 376366, ⓦkatrinewheelz.co.uk; £28 per day), take the steamer up to Stronachlachar, then cycle back by way of the road around the north side of the loch.

Brig o'Turk and Loch Venachar

From Loch Katrine the A821 heads due east past the tiny village of **Brig o'Turk**, where there are a couple of excellent eating options. From here, carry on along the shores of Loch Venachar, where *Venacher Lochside* houses an attractive café and a fishing centre offering boat rental and fly-fishing tuition.

Brig o'Turk Tea Room Glen Finglas Rd ☎01877 376283, ⓦbrigoturktearoom.co.uk. The cosy, wooden-clad little place is a good place to refresh after a walk or cycle. Good coffee and excellent home-made cakes dished up on retro crockery. Also serves appealing dinner options: try beef stew with dumplings (£9.50). Easter–Sept Mon, Tues & Thurs–Sun 10am–9pm.

★ **Byre Inn** Brig o'Turk ☎01877 376292, ⓦbyreinn .co.uk. A tiny country pub and classy restaurant offering mains such as fillet of cod for £10.95 and set in an old stone barn with wooden pews; it's the starting point for way-marked walks to lochs Achray, Drunkie and Venachar. Noon–late; food served noon–3pm & 6–9pm.

Callander and around

CALLANDER, on the eastern edge of the Trossachs, sits on the banks of the River Teith at the southern end of the **Pass of Leny**, one of the key routes into the Highlands. Significantly larger than Aberfoyle, it suffers in high season for being right on the main tourist trail from Stirling through to the west Highlands. Callander first came to fame during the "Scottish Enlightenment" of the eighteenth and nineteenth centuries, with the glowing reports of the Trossachs given by Sir Walter Scott and William Wordsworth. Development was given a further boost when Queen Victoria chose to visit, and then by the arrival of the train line – long since closed – in the 1860s. Tourists have arrived in throngs ever since, as the plethora of restaurants, tearooms, gift shops and shops selling woollens and crafts testifies.

2

Callander to Strathyre Cycleway

North of Callandar, you can walk or ride the scenic six-mile Callander to Strathyre (Route 7) Cycleway, which forms part of the network of cycleways between the Highlands and Glasgow. The route is based on the old Caledonian train line to Oban, which closed in 1965, and runs along the western side of Loch Lubnaig.

ARRIVAL AND INFORMATION

By bus Callander has bus connections with Loch Katrine (late June to mid-Oct Thurs–Tues 4 daily; 55min). First Group (☎01324 602200, ⓦfirstgroup.com) operates services between Callander and Stirling. There's a reduced service at weekends.

Tourist office In a converted church on Ancaster Square on the main street (March–Oct daily; ☎08707 200628).

CALLANDER AND AROUND

By bike Mounter Bikes, on Ancaster Square at the centre of Callander, offer rental, sales, repairs and accessories (☎01877 331052, ⓦmounterbikes.co.uk). Wheels Cycling Centre next to *Trossachs Tryst* (see below) a mile and a half southwest of Callander, is the best rental place in the area, with front- or full-suspension models available, as well as baby's and child's seats.

ACCOMMODATION

Arden House Bracklinn Rd ☎01877 330235, ⓦarden house.org.uk. A grand Victorian guesthouse in its own gardens with good views and woodland walks from the back door. April–Oct. **£85**

Callander Meadows 24 Main St ☎01877 330181, ⓦcallandermeadows.co.uk. Centrally located rooms in an attractive townhouse that has three comfortable en-suite rooms and a decent restaurant. Full board available. **£75**

Roman Camp Country House Hotel Main St ☎01877

330003, ⓦromancamphotel.co.uk. The town's most upmarket option is this romantic, turreted seventeenth-century hunting lodge situated in twenty-acre gardens on the River Teith. **£155**

Trossachs Tryst Invertrossachs Rd ☎01877 331200, ⓦscottish-hostel.com. A friendly, well-equipped and comfortable 32-bed hostel and activity centre with self-catering dorms and family rooms. It's located a mile southwest of town, down a turn-off from the A81 to Port of Monteith. Bike rental available. Dorms **£20**; doubles **£50**

EATING AND DRINKING

Lade Inn Kilmahog, a mile west of Callander ☎01877 330152, ⓦtheladeinn.com. Pub food such as beer-battered chicken goujons (£10.25) is served at this convivial inn where the owners are particularly keen on real ales; an on-site shop sells bottled beers from all over Scotland. Mon–Thurs noon–11pm, Fri & Sat noon–1am, Sun 12.30–10.30pm; food served Mon–Fri noon–2.30pm &

5.30–9pm, Sat noon–9pm, Sun 12.30–8pm.

★ **Mhor Fish** 75–77 Main St ☎01877 330213, ⓦmhor.net. One of a new breed of fish and chip shops; it has a sustainable fish policy, daily specials and everything from snacks to bistro-style seafood dishes – and you can get fish suppers, burgers, pies and haggis to take away for around £12. Daily 10am–10pm.

Balquhidder

Beyond the northern end of Loch Lubnaig is tiny **BALQUHIDDER**, most famous as the site of the **grave of Rob Roy** (see p.136), which you'll find in the small yard behind the ruined church. His grave is marked by a rough stone carved with a sword, a cross and a man with a dog.

On the road to the *Monachyle Mhor* hotel is the unexpected sight of the **Dhanakosa Buddhist retreat centre** (☎01877 384213, ⓦdhanakosa.com) – they run weekend or week-long retreats here, with courses ranging from t'ai chi to hillwalking.

ACCOMMODATION AND EATING	BALQUHIDDER
MHOR 84 Balquhidder Lochearnhead ☎01877 384622, ⓦmhor.net. An agreeable and stylish addition to the MHOR empire, this is a seven-room motel (with one family room and two dog-friendly ones). Their super-cool restaurant serves excellent seafood dishes (five-course dinner £55, two-course lunch £24). Daily noon–11pm. **£80** ★ **Monachyle MHOR** Loch Voil ☎01877 384622,	ⓦmhor.net. Drive 6 miles beyond the village to this much-acclaimed hotel/restaurant, set in an eighteenth-century farmhouse. It features chic modern rooms and a terrific restaurant (open to non-residents, but book ahead; set dinner £47). They specialize in locally sourced food, much of it from the family's farm and bakery, and there are views over Loch Voil. Food served noon–1.45pm & 7–9pm. **£195**

Perthshire

Genteel **Perthshire** is, in many ways, the epitome of well-groomed rural Scotland. First settled over eight thousand years ago, it was occupied by the Romans and then the Picts before Celtic missionaries established themselves, enjoying the amenable climate, fertile soil and ideal location for defence and trade. North and west of the county town of Perth, there are some magnificent landscapes to be discovered – snow-capped peaks falling away to forested slopes and long, deep lochs – topography that inevitably controls transport routes, influences the weather and tolerates little development. The various mountains, woods and lochs provide terrific walking and watersports, particularly through the **Strath Tay** area, dominated by Scotland's longest river, the **Tay**, which flows from **Loch Tay** past the attractive towns of **Dunkeld** and **Aberfeldy**. Further north, the countryside of **Highland Perthshire** becomes more sparsely populated and more spectacular, especially around the towns of **Pitlochry** and **Blair Atholl** and the wild expanses of **Rannoch Moor** to the west.

Dunkeld

DUNKELD, twelve miles north of Perth on the A9, was proclaimed Scotland's ecclesiastical capital by Kenneth MacAlpine in 850. Its position at the southern boundary of the Grampian Mountains made it a favoured meeting place for Highland and Lowland cultures, and the town is one of the area's most pleasant communities, with handsome whitewashed houses, appealing arts and crafts shops, and a charming cathedral.

Dunkeld cathedral

Cathedral St • Daily: April–Sept Mon–Sat 9.30am–6.30pm, Sun 2–4pm; Oct–March Mon–Sat 9.30am–4pm, Sun 2–4pm • Free • ⓦ dunkeldcathedral.org.uk

Dunkeld's partly ruined **cathedral** is on the northern side of town, in an idyllic setting amid lawns and trees on the east bank of the Tay. Construction began in the early twelfth century and continued throughout the next two hundred years, but the building was more or less ruined at the time of the Reformation. The present structure consists of the fourteenth-century choir and the fifteenth-century nave; the choir, restored in 1600 (and several times since), now serves as the parish church, while the nave remains roofless apart from the clock tower. Inside, note the leper's peep near the pulpit in the north wall, through which lepers could receive the sacrament without coming into contact with the congregation. Also look out for the effigy of the **Wolf of Badenoch**, Robert II's son, born in 1343. The Wolf acquired his name and notoriety when, after being excommunicated for leaving his wife, he took his revenge by burning the towns of Forres and Elgin and sacking the latter's cathedral.

ARRIVAL AND INFORMATION

DUNKELD

By train The nearest train station is in nearby Birnam.
By bus Buses travelling to and from Perth stop opposite the *Royal Dunkeld Hotel* on Atholl St, Dunkeld.
Destinations Inverness (5 daily; 2hr 30min); Perth (every 30min; 40min).

Tourist office The Visit Scotland information centre is on The Cross, in the middle of Dunkeld (April–June, Sept & Oct Mon–Sat 10am–4.30pm, Sun 11am–4pm; July & Aug Mon–Sat 9.30am–5.30pm, Sun 10.30am–5pm; Nov–March Fri–Sun 11am–4pm; ☎ 01350 727688).

ACCOMMODATION

Hilton Dunkeld House Blairgowrie Rd ☎ 01350 727771, ⊛ hilton.co.uk/dunkeld. Pricy and a little corporate but undeniably luxurious, this vast country estate house on the banks of the Tay has a spa, swimming pool and excellent facilities for outdoor pursuits. **£169**
The Pend 5 Brae St ☎ 01350 727586, ⊛ thepend.com. An elegantly furnished B&B just off the main street in Dunkeld, with three large rooms that share a couple of

bathrooms. Dinner is also available for residents. **£76**
Wester Caputh Independent Hostel Manse Rd, Caputh ☎ 01738 710449, ⊛ westercaputh.co.uk. Four miles downstream along the Tay from Dunkeld, this hostel offers small dorm rooms and there's also a self-catering house for rent. The convenient location and relaxing, welcoming atmosphere make this a great base. Dorms **£18**

EATING AND DRINKING

The Scottish Deli 1 Atholl St ☎ 01350 728028, ⊛ scottish-deli.com. Fill up on gourmet delights at this well-stocked deli, which also has its own wine room. There's also a counter selling eat-in salads for £4.50. Mon–Fri 9.30am–5.30pm, Sat 9am–5.30pm, Sun 10.30am–4.30pm.

★ **The Taybank** Tay Terrace ☎ 01350 727340, ⊛ the taybank.co.uk. A raggedy beacon for music fans, who come for the regular live sessions in the convivial bar. Fancy joining in? Wednesday night is open-mike night. Mon–Thurs 11am–11pm, Fri & Sat 11am–midnight, Sun noon–11pm.

Birnam

Dunkeld is linked to its sister community, **BIRNAM**, by Thomas Telford's seven-arched bridge of 1809. This little village has a place in history thanks to Shakespeare, for it was on Dunsinane Hill, to the southeast of the village, that Macbeth declared: "I will not be afraid of death and bane/Till Birnam Forest come to Dunsinane." The **Birnam Oak**, a gnarly old character propped up by crutches which can be seen on the waymarked riverside walk, is inevitably claimed to be a survivor of the infamous mobile forest.

Birnam Institute

Station Rd • Daily 10am–4.30pm • £3 • ⊛ birnaminstitute.com

Just like Shakespeare, children's author Beatrix Potter drew inspiration from the Birnam area, recalling her childhood holidays here when penning the Peter Rabbit stories. A Potter-themed exhibition and garden can be found in the impressive barrel-fronted **Birnam Institute**, a lively theatre, arts and community centre.

The Hermitage

Dunkeld and Birnam are surrounded by some lovely countryside, both along the banks of the Tay and in the deep surrounding forest. One of the most rewarding walks is the mile and a half from Birnam to **The Hermitage**, set in a grandly wooded gorge of the plunging River Braan. Here you'll find a pretty eighteenth-century folly, also known as Ossian's Hall, which was once mirrored to reflect the water – the mirrors were smashed by Victorian vandals and the folly was more tamely restored. The hall, appealing yet incongruous in its splendid setting, neatly frames a dramatic waterfall.

Loch of the Lowes

Just off the A923 • Visitor centre: March–Oct daily 10am–5pm; Nov–Feb Fri–Sun 10.30am–4pm • £4 • ☎ 01350 727337

Two miles east of Dunkeld, the **Loch of the Lowes** is a nature reserve that offers a rare chance to see breeding **ospreys** and other wildfowl; the visitor centre has video-relay screens and will point you in the direction of the best vantage points.

2

By train The Dunkeld and Birnam train station is just south of the A9 in Birnam.

Destinations Inverness (8 daily; 1hr 50min); Perth (10 daily; 20min).

By bus Direct services to Inverness leave from opposite the *Birnam Hotel* on Perth Rd.

Destinations Inverness (5 daily; 2hr 30min); Perth (every 30min; 40min).

ACCOMMODATION

Merryburn Hotel Station Rd ☎01350 727216, ⓦmerryburn.co.uk. An old ironmonger's shop converted into a small and inviting hotel, just across from the Birnam

Institute. Many of the building's original Victorian features are still intact. **£80**

Aberfeldy and around

From Dunkeld the A9 runs north alongside the Tay for eight miles to Ballinluig, a tiny village marking the turn-off along the A827 to **ABERFELDY**, a prosperous settlement of large stone houses that acts as a service centre for the wider Loch Tay area. Aberfeldy sits at the point where the Urlar Burn – lined by the silver birch trees celebrated by Robert Burns in his poem *The Birks of Aberfeldy* – flows into the River Tay.

Wade's Bridge

In Aberfeldy the Tay is spanned by the humpbacked, four-arch **Wade's Bridge**, built by General Wade in 1733 during his efforts to control the unrest in the Highlands, and one of the general's more impressive pieces of work. Overlooking the bridge from the south end is the **Black Watch Monument**, depicting a pensive, kilted soldier; it was erected in 1887 to commemorate the first muster of the Highland regiment gathered as a peacekeeping force by Wade in 1740.

Dewar's World of Whisky

Half a mile east of Aberfeldy, just off the A827 • April–Oct Mon–Sat 10am–6pm, Sun noon–4pm; Nov–March Mon–Sat 10am–4pm • £7; Cask Tasting Tour £18; Connoisseur Tour £25 • ⓦdewarswow.com

The main set-piece attraction in Aberfeldy is **Dewar's World of Whisky**, at the Aberfeldy Distillery, which puts on an impressive show of describing the process of making whisky. A **Cask Tasting Tour** and **Connoisseur Tour** are available for real aficionados, giving a more in-depth look around the distillery and a chance to taste (or "nose") the whisky at different stages in its life.

Castle Menzies

1 mile west of Aberfeldy, across Wade's Bridge • Easter to late Oct Mon–Sat 10.30am–5pm, Sun 2–5pm • £6 • ⓦcastlemenzies.co.uk

West of Aberfeldy, **Castle Menzies** is an imposing, Z-shaped, sixteenth-century tower house, which until the middle of the last century was the chief seat of the Clan Menzies (pronounced "Ming-iss "). With the demise of the line, the castle was taken over by the Menzies Clan Society, which since 1971 has been involved in the lengthy process of restoring it. Much of the interior is on view, and most of it is refreshingly free of fixtures and fittings, displaying an austerity that is much more true to medieval life than many grander, furnished castles elsewhere in the country.

By bus Buses stop on Chapel Street in Aberfeldy, near the junction with Dunkeld Street (the A827), with regular services to Perth (up to 12 daily; 1hr 25min).

Tourist office The Square in the town centre (April–June, Sept & Oct Mon–Sat 10am–5pm, Sun 10.30am–3.30pm;

July & Aug Mon–Sat 9.30am–5pm, Sun 10.30am–3.30pm; Nov–March Mon–Wed 10am–4pm; ☎01887 820276). Good for advice on local accommodation and details of nearby walking trails.

ACTIVITIES

Highland Safaris 2 miles west of Castle Menzies, off the B846 ☎ 01887 820071, ⓦ highlandsafaris.net. Near the hamlet with the unfortunate name of Dull (twinned with Boring, Oregon, USA), this adventure outlet arranges Land Rover trips into the heather-clad hills nearby in search

of eagles, red deer and grouse. At the lodge you can try your hand at gold and mineral panning (£5).
Bike rental If you want to rent a bike (£20/day), head to Dunolly Adventure Outdoors (☎ 01887 820298, ⓦ dunolly adventures.co.uk), close to the River Tay on Taybridge Drive.

ACCOMMODATION

Balnearn Guest House Crieff Rd ☎ 01887 820431, ⓦ balnearnhouse.co.uk. Stylish and unpretentious rooms close to the middle of town, with the added bonus of a drying room for your outdoor gear. **£65**
The Bunkhouse Glassie Farm, 3 miles from Aberfeldy along the winding track that starts near the footbridge ☎ 01887 820265, ⓦ thebunkhouse.co.uk. The closest bunkhouse to Aberfeldy has small rooms that share simple

showers, plus two self-catering kitchens and a communal area with magnificent views over the town. Popular with groups. Dorms **£17**
Coshieville House 5.5 miles west of Aberfeldy along the B846 ☎ 01887 830319, ⓦ aberfeldybandb.com. In peaceful surroundings, this 300-year-old inn provides modern accommodation with nice touches like fresh flowers brightening up the communal areas. **£40**

EATING AND DRINKING

Ailean Chraggan Across Wade's Bridge in Weem ⓦ aileanchraggan.co.uk. The long, regularly updated lunch and dinner menu at this hotel/restaurant include plenty of fishy mains (£11–16). Daily noon–2pm & 5.30–8/9pm.
★ **The Watermill** Mill Street ⓦ aberfeldywatermill

.com. Aberfeldy isn't short on cafés, but the best bet for a good cup of coffee, a bowl of lunchtime soup (£4.20) or after-noon tea, is this relaxed, superbly restored, early nineteenth-century mill, with a pretty riverside garden. There's also an inspiring bookshop. Daily 10/11am–5.30pm.

Loch Tay

Aberfeldy grew up around a crossing point on the River Tay, which leaves it six miles adrift of **Loch Tay**, a fourteen-mile-long stretch of fresh water connecting the western and eastern Highlands. Rising steeply above the loch's northern edge is Ben Lawers, the tenth-highest peak in Scotland, whose mineral-rich slopes support plant life more commonly seen in the Alps or Arctic.

Kenmore

Guarding the northern end of Loch Tay is **KENMORE**, where whitewashed estate houses and well-tended gardens cluster around the gate to the extensive grounds of **Taymouth Castle**, built by the Campbells of Glenorchy in the early nineteenth century. The rocket-like eighteenth-century **church** contains an ancient "poor box" for donations and memorials to soldiers of the Black Watch Regiment.

Scottish Crannog Centre

Around half a mile from Kenmore, along the southern shore of the loch • Daily: April–Oct 10am–5.30pm • £8 • ⓦ crannog.co.uk

The main attraction around Loch Tay is the **Scottish Crannog Centre**. Crannogs are Iron Age loch dwellings built on stilts over the water, with a gangway to the shore that could be lifted up to defy a hostile intruder, whether animal or human. Following underwater excavations in Loch Tay, the team here has superbly reconstructed a crannog, and visitors can now walk out over the loch to the thatched wooden dwelling, complete with sheepskin rugs, wooden bowls and other evidence of how life was lived 2500 years ago.

ACCOMMODATION AND EATING	LOCH TAY

The Courtyard Just off the A827 in the centre of Kenmore ☎ 01887 830756, ⓦ balnearnhouse.co.uk. For something to eat, head to this brasserie beside the Kenmore golf course, which does a good Moroccan-style

vegetable casserole (£11.95). There's also a deli/gift shop in the same complex (daily 9am–5pm). Daily 9am–late, last food orders 9pm.
Culdees Bunkhouse 4 miles along the loch's north shore

2

CLIMBING THE BEN LAWERS GROUP

Ordnance Survey Explorer map 378

Dominating the northern side of Loch Tay is moody Ben Lawers (3984ft), Perthshire's highest mountain; from the top there are incredible views towards both the Atlantic and the North Sea. The ascent – which shouldn't be tackled unless you're properly equipped for Scottish hillwalking (see p.42) – takes around three hours from the NTS car park, which you can reach by following a winding, hilly road off the A827.

The Ben Lawers range offers rich pickings for Munro-baggers, with nine hills over 3000ft in close proximity. The whole double-horseshoe-shaped ridge from Meall Greigh in the east to Meall a'Choire Leith in the northwest is too much for one day, though the eastern section from Meall Greigh (3284ft) to Beinn Ghlas (3619ft), taking in Ben Lawers, can be walked in eight to ten hours in good conditions. Standing on its own a little to the east is perhaps the prettiest of the lot, **Meall nan Tarmachan** ("The Hill of the Ptarmigan"); at 3427ft, a less arduous but rewarding four-hour round-trip from the roadside, a mile or so further on from the car park.

in Fearnan ☎ 01887 830519, ⓦ culdeesbunkhouse.co.uk. Family-friendly bunkhouse and B&B accommodation on a spectacularly located farm, where the emphasis is on perma-culture and spiritual values. Dorms **£18**; family room sleeping four/person (under-10s half-price) **£23**

Kenmore Hotel On the village square ☎ 01887 830205, ⓦ kenmorehotel.com. The nicest place to stay in Kenmore; it's well run and has pleasant rooms that each have a TV, DVD player and free wi-fi access. **£89**

Glen Lyon

North of the Ben Lawers range is **Glen Lyon** – at 34 miles long, the longest enclosed glen in Scotland – where, legend has it, the Celtic warrior Fingal built twelve castles. The narrow single-track road through the glen starts at **KELTNEYBURN**, near Kenmore, at the northern end of the loch, although a road does struggle over the hills to **Bridge of Balgie**, halfway down the glen. Either way, it's a long, winding journey.

Fortingall

A few miles from Keltneyburn, the village of **FORTINGALL** is little more than a handful of pretty thatched cottages, though locals make much of their 5000-year-old yew tree – believed (by them at least) to be the oldest living thing in Europe. The venerable tree can be found in the churchyard, with a timeline nearby listing some of the events the yew has lived through. One of these, bizarrely, is the birth of Pontius Pilate, reputedly the son of a Roman officer stationed near Fortingall.

ACCOMMODATION   **GLEN LYON**

Fortingall Hotel In the centre of Fortingall ☎ 01887 830367, ⓦ fortingallhotel.com. If you're taken by the peace and remoteness of Glen Lyon, you can stay at this attractive, ten-bedroom country house, which has an excellent restaurant; it also organizes fishing and walking packages. **£165**

Killin

The mountains of **Breadalbane** (pronounced "bred–albin", from the Gaelic "braghaid Albin" meaning "high country of Scotland") loom over the southern end of Loch Tay. Glens Lochay and Dochart curve north and south respectively from the small town of **KILLIN**, right in the centre of which the River Dochart comes rushing down over the frothy **Falls of Dochart** before disgorging into Loch Tay. A short distance west of Killin the A827 meets the A85, linking the Trossachs with Crianlarich (see p.135), an important waypoint on the roads to Oban, Fort William and the west coast.

There's little to do in Killin itself, but it makes a convenient base for some of the area's best walks.

INFORMATION AND ACTIVITIES **KILLIN**

Tourist information Located on the ground floor of the old watermill by the falls (daily: April–Oct 10am–4pm). **Killin Outdoor Centre and Mountain Shop** Main St ☎ 01567 820652, ⓦ killinoutdoor.co.uk. If you're interested in outdoor activities, make for this helpful and enthusiastic outdoor centre, which rents out mountain bikes, canoes and tents. Daily 8.45am–5.45pm.

ACCOMMODATION AND EATING

Falls of Dochart Inn Gray St ☎ 01567 820270, ⓦ falls-of-dochart-inn.co.uk. Killin's best place to grab a bite to eat is this attractive, stone-walled pub, right above the famous rapids; the varied menu includes braised lemon sole for £13.95. Daily noon–11pm.

The Old Smiddy Main St ☎ 01567 820619, ⓦ theold smiddykillin.co.uk. Offers three neat B&B rooms near the centre of the town, two of which have views of the river. The bistro-style café downstairs is a popular spot for cakes (£2.95) and ice cream. **£56**

Pitlochry

Just off the A9 and surrounded by mountains, **PITLOCHRY** is undoubtedly a useful place to find somewhere to stay or eat en route to or from the Highlands. However, there's little charm to be found on its main street, with crawling traffic and endless shops selling cut-price woollens and knobbly walking sticks to tourists, who use the town as a starting point for scenic hikes (see below). Far more appealing is the area south of the river, which is home to a renowned theatre and a serene botanical garden.

Explorers: the Scottish Plant Hunters' Garden

Across the river from the town centre, near the theatre • April–Oct daily 10am–5pm (last entry 4.15pm) • £4, tours £1 extra • ⓦ explorersgarden.com

If you want to escape the bustle of Pitlochry's main drag, it's worth having a wander around **Explorers: the Scottish Plant Hunters' Garden**, a garden and forest area that pays tribute to Scottish botanists and collectors who roamed the world in the eighteenth and nineteenth centuries in search of new plant species. An amphitheatre in the grounds is sometimes used for outdoor performances.

Pitlochry Power Station and Dam

A short stroll upstream to the west of the theatre is the **Pitlochry Power Station and Dam**, a massive concrete wall that harnesses the water of artificial Loch Faskally, just

---

WALKS AROUND PITLOCHRY

BEN VRACKIE

Pitlochry is surrounded by good walking country. The biggest lure has to be **Ben Vrackie** (2733ft; *Ordnance Survey Explorer map 386*), which provides a stunning backdrop for the town, and deserves better than a straight up-and-down walk. However, the climb should only be attempted in settled weather conditions and if you're properly prepared (see p.42).

The direct route up the hill follows the course of the Moulin burn past the inn of the same name. Alternatively, a longer but much more rewarding circular route heads northwest out of Pitlochry, along the edge of Loch Faskally, then up the River Garry to go through the **Pass of Killiecrankie**. This is looked after by the NTS, which has a visitor centre (see p.147) providing background on the famous battle here. From the NTS centre follow the route past Old Faskally to meet the main track at Loch a'Choire. Alternatively, you can turn back here and loop around Loch Faskally instead.

BLACK SPOUT

A lovely, short hillwalk from the south end of Pitlochry follows a path through oak forests along the banks of the **Black Spout** burn; when you emerge from the woods it's just a few hundred yards further uphill to the lovely Edradour Distillery (see p.146).

2

north of the town, for hydroelectric power. Near the base of the dam there's a small observation cabin where you can take a peek at the underwater workings of Pitlochry's **salmon ladder**, a staircase of murky glass boxes through which you might see some nonplussed fish making their way upstream past the dam. An electronic counter shows how many of them have successfully completed the climb.

With parking available at the theatre, nearby, the dam makes a good starting point for a complete loop of the loch (around nine miles to the Pass of Killiecrankie and back).

Edradour Distillery

2.5 miles east of Pitlochry • March & April Mon–Sat 10am–4pm, Sun noon–4pm; May–Oct Mon–Sat 10am–5pm, Sun noon–5pm; Nov–Feb Mon–Sat 10am–4pm • £7.50 • ⓦ edradour.com

The **Edradour Distillery** – Scotland's smallest – has an idyllic position tucked into the hills a couple of miles east of Pitlochry on the A924. Although the tour of the distillery itself isn't out of the ordinary, the lack of industralization and the fact that the whole traditional process is done on-site give Edradour more personality than many of its rivals.

ARRIVAL AND DEPARTURE
PITLOCHRY

By train Pitlochry is on the main train line to Inverness. The station is on Station Rd, just south of the centre. Destinations Inverness (every 1–2hr; 1hr 35min); Perth (every 1–2hr; 30min).

By bus Buses stop near the train station. Destinations Inverness (7 daily; 2hr 10min); Perth (every 1–2hr; 40min).

INFORMATION AND ACTIVITIES

Tourist office 22 Atholl Rd (March Mon–Sat 9.30am–4.30pm, Sun 11am–3pm; April–June Mon–Sat 9.30am–5.30pm, Sun 10am–4pm; July & Aug Mon–Sat 9.30am–6.30pm, Sun 9.30am–5.30pm; Sept & Oct Mon–Sat 9.30am–4.30pm, Sun 10am–4pm; Nov–Feb Mon–Sat 9.30am–4.30pm; ☏01796 472215). They can sell you a guide to walks in the surrounding area (£1) and also offer an accommodation booking service.

Bike rental For bike rental (£24/day), advice on local cycling routes, as well as general outdoor gear, try Escape Route, 3 Atholl Rd (Mon–Sat 9am–5.30pm, Sun 10am–5pm; ☏01796 473859, ⓦ escape-route.biz).

ACCOMMODATION

Craigatin House and Courtyard 165 Atholl Rd ☏01796 472478, ⓦ craigatinhouse.co.uk. On the northern section of the main road through town, this is an attractive, contemporary B&B with large beds, soothing decor and a pretty garden. **£87**

Fonab Castle Hotel Foss Rd, south of the river ☏01796 470140, ⓦ fonabcastlehotel.com. Once the headquarters of a power company, this turreted, waterside landmark has now been transformed into a luxury hotel with a spa and panoramic fine-dining restaurant. The interiors, with sparkly Swarovski wall coverings, may be a little bling for some tastes. **£170**

Moulin Hotel 11 Kirkmichael Rd, Moulin, on the outskirts of Pitlochry ☏01796 472196, ⓦ moulinhotel .co.uk. Pleasant old travellers' inn with a great bar and restaurant (see below) and its own brewery offering free guided tours (Thurs–Mon noon–3pm). **£77**

Pitlochry Backpackers Hotel 134 Atholl Rd ☏01796 470044, ⓦ pitlochrybackpackershotel.com. Right in the centre of town, this hostel is based in a former hotel, and offers dorms, twin and double rooms, and a communal lounge. Dorms **£18**; doubles **£52**

EATING AND DRINKING

Moulin Inn 11 Kirkmichael Rd, Moulin, on the outskirts of Pitlochry ☏01796 472196, ⓦ moulininn.co.uk. Joined to the hotel of the same name, this restaurant serves Scottish meals such as deep-fried haggis (£6.95) in a cosy, country pub setting at the foot of Ben Vrackie. Food served noon–9.30pm.

Scottish Deli 96 Atholl Rd ☏01796 473322, ⓦ scottish -deli.com. Busy deli with a few seats along one wall, where you can tuck into freshly made rolls, baguettes and ciabattas, with plenty of different fillings to choose from (from £3.25). Mon–Sat 8am–5.30pm, Sun 10am–5pm.

Strathgarry Hotel 113 Atholl Rd ☏01796 472469, ⓦ strathgarryhotel.co.uk. You'll find a range of moderately priced bistro food at this hotel on Pitlochry's main drag; expect to pay £5.95 for a bowl of soup and a sandwich. Daily 10am–10pm.

ENTERTAINMENT

Pitlochry Festival Theatre Port na Craig, on the south side of the river ☎ 01796 484626, ⓦ pitlochry.org.uk. On the southern edge of Pitlochry, just across the river, lies Scotland's renowned "Theatre in the Hills". A variety of productions – mostly mainstream theatre from the resident repertoire company, along with regular music events – are staged in the summer season and on ad hoc dates the rest of the year. Box office daily: May–Oct 9am–8pm; Nov–April 9am–5pm.

Pass of Killiecrankie

2

NTS visitor centre: 4 miles north of Pitlochry along the A9 • Daily: mid-March–Oct 10am–5.30pm • Free; parking £2

Four miles north of Pitlochry, the A9 cuts through the **Pass of Killiecrankie**, a breathtaking wooded gorge that falls away to the River Garry below. This dramatic setting was the site of the **Battle of Killiecrankie** in 1689, when the Jacobites crushed the forces of General Mackay. Legend has it that one soldier of the Crown, fleeing for his life, made a miraculous jump across the eighteen-foot **Soldier's Leap**, an impossibly wide chasm halfway up the gorge. Queen Victoria, visiting here 160 years later, contented herself with recording the beauty of the area in her diary.

Exhibits at the slick NTS **visitor centre**, which sits inside the boundaries of the Loch Tummel National Scenic Area, recall the battle and examine the gorge in detail. The surroundings here are thick, mature forest, full of interesting plants and creatures. If you visit during the springtime keep a lookout for the centre's webcams, which are trained on nearby nesting spots.

Blair Atholl

Three miles north of the Pass of Killiecrankie, the village of **BLAIR ATHOLL** makes for a much quieter and more idiosyncratic stop than Pitlochry. Understandably popular with day-trippers for the extravagant Blair Castle, there are also plenty of walks and bike rides to enjoy in the surrounding countryside.

Blair Castle

Just off the B8079, midway between the train station and the bridge over the River Tilt • April–Oct daily 9.30am–5.30pm (last admission 4.30pm); Nov–March occasional weekends only (see website for details) • Castle and grounds £9.80; grounds £5.40 • ⓦ blair-castle.co.uk

Seat of the Atholl dukedom, whitewashed, turreted **Blair Castle**, surrounded by parkland and dating from 1269, presents an impressive sight as you approach up the drive. A piper, one of the Atholl Highlanders, may be playing in front of the castle; this select group was retained by the duke as his private army – a unique privilege afforded to him by Queen Victoria, who stayed here in 1844.

Thirty or so rooms display a selection of paintings, antique furniture and plasterwork that is sumptuous in the extreme. Highlights are the soaring **entrance hall**, with every spare inch of wood panelling covered in weapons of some description, and the vast **ballroom**, with its timber roof, antlers and mixture of portraits.

As impressive as the castle's interior are its surroundings: Highland cows graze the ancient landscaped grounds and peacocks strut in front of the castle. There is a **riding stable** from where you can take treks, and formal woodland walks take you to various parts of the castle grounds, including the walled water garden and the towering giant conifers of Diana's Grove.

Atholl Country Life Museum

A 5min walk east of the train station along the B8079 • May–Sept daily 1.30–5pm; July & Aug Mon–Fri 10am–5pm • £3 • ☎ 01796 481232, ⓦ athollcountrylifemuseum.org

The modest **Atholl Country Life Museum** offers a homespun and nostalgic look at the history of life in the local glens. In among the old photos and artefacts, the star attraction is a stuffed, full-sized Highland cow; according to the owners, it's the only one of its kind.

Blair Atholl Watermill

Ford Road • April–Oct daily 9.30am–5pm; milling takes place Wed–Fri • Free • ⓦ blairathollwatermill.co.uk

Close to the River Tilt is Blair Atholl's **Watermill**, which dates back to 1613. During the summertime you can wander around and witness the mill in action. Better still is a trip to the pleasant timber-beamed tearoom (see below), where you can enjoy home-baked scones and light lunches (many items are made with the mill's own flour).

INFORMATION AND ACTIVITIES   BLAIR ATHOLL

Atholl Estates Information Centre Close to the bridge over the River Tilt, a 5min walk east of the train station (April–Oct daily 9am–4.45pm; ⓦ athollestates rangerservice.co.uk). Modern ranger station, where you can get details of the extensive network of local walks and bike rides, as well as information on surrounding flora and fauna.

Bike rental You can rent bikes (£17.50/day) from Blair Atholl Bike Hire (☎ 01796 481500, ⓦ blairathollbikehire .co.uk), near the Atholl Country Life Museum.

ACCOMMODATION AND EATING

Atholl Arms Hotel On the main road, near the train station ☎ 01796 481205, ⓦ athollarms.co.uk. Grand but reasonably priced hotel, and the best place in town for a drink or a bar meal. A tasty ham and haddie (smoked haddock and bacon with cheese sauce) costs £10.15. Food served daily noon–9.30pm. **£82**

★ **Blair Atholl Watermill** Ford Rd ☎ 01796 481321, ⓦ blairathollwatermill.co.uk. Blair Atholl's top spot for tea, tray bakes, toasties (from £4.65) and bagels (from £5.25), in a charming (and still functioning) old watermill. April–Oct daily 9.30am–5pm.

Blair Castle Caravan Park Within the grounds of Blair Castle ☎ 01796 481263, ⓦ blaircastlecaravanpark.co .uk. Busy but attractive campsite with laundry facilities, a games room and a shop selling the estate's own sausages. **£18**/pitch

Loch Tummel

West of Pitlochry, the B8019/B846 makes a memorably scenic, if tortuous, traverse of the shores of **Loch Tummel** and then Loch Rannoch. These two lochs and their adjoining rivers were much changed by the massive hydroelectric schemes built in the 1940s and 1950s, yet this is still a spectacular stretch of countryside and one that deserves leisurely exploration. **Queen's View** at the eastern end of Loch Tummel is an obvious vantage point, looking down the loch to the misty peak of **Schiehallion**; the name comes from the Gaelic meaning "Fairy Mountain".

Schiehallion

Rising cone-like southwest of Loch Tummel to a peak of 3553ft, **Schiehallion** is a popular, fairly easy and inspiring mountain to climb (3–4hr), with views on a good day to the massed ranks of Highland peaks. The path up starts at Braes of Foss, just off the B846 that links Aberfeldy with Kinloch Rannoch. You'll get a good view of the mountain from the cosy *Loch Tummel Inn* (see below), about halfway along Loch Tummel.

ACCOMMODATION AND EATING   LOCH TUMMEL

Loch Tummel Inn About halfway along Loch Tummel, on the B8019 ☎ 01882 634272, ⓦ lochtummelinn .co.uk. Beautiful stone-built inn serving real ale and rich meals like pan-fried red-deer venison (£15.95). The picnic benches out the front have magnificent views over the loch and Schiehallion. Food served Mon–Sat 12.15–2.30pm & 5.30–8.30pm; Sun 12.15–8pm. **£80**

Loch Rannoch

Beyond Loch Tummel, marking the eastern end of Loch Rannoch, the small community of **KINLOCH RANNOCH** doesn't see a lot of passing trade – fishermen and hillwalkers are the most common visitors. Otherwise, the only real destination here is **Rannoch Station**, a lonely outpost on the Glasgow–Fort William West Highland train line, sixteen miles

THE SPEYSIDE WAY

⬡ ◀ Tomintoul

2

RANNOCH MOOR

Rannoch Moor occupies roughly 150 square miles of uninhabited and uninhabitable peat bogs, lochs, heather hillocks, strewn lumps of granite and a few gnarled Caledonian pines, all of it over one thousand feet above sea level. Perhaps the most striking thing about the moor is its inaccessibility: one road, between Crianlarich and Glen Coe, skirts its western side, while another struggles west from Pitlochry to reach its eastern edge at Rannoch Station. The only regular form of transport is the **West Highland Railway**, which stops at **Rannoch** and, a little to the north, Corrour station, which has no road access at all. There is a simple tearoom in the station building at Rannoch, as well as a pleasant small hotel, the *Moor of Rannoch*, but even these struggle to diminish the feeling of isolation. **Corrour**, meanwhile, stole an unlikely scene in the film *Trainspotting* when the four central characters headed here for a taste of the great outdoors; a wooden SYHA hostel is located a mile away on the shores of **Loch Ossian** and is only accessible on foot, making the area a great place for hikers seeking somewhere genuinely off the beaten track. From Rannoch Station it's possible to catch the train to Corrour and walk the nine miles back; it's a longer slog west to the *Kingshouse Hotel* at the eastern end of Glen Coe, the dramatic peaks of which poke up above the moor's western horizon. Determined hillwalkers will find a clutch of Munros around Corrour, including remote Ben Alder (3765ft), high above the forbidding shores of Loch Ericht.

further on: the road goes no further. Here you can contemplate the bleakness of **Rannoch Moor** (see box above), a wide expanse of bog, heather and wind-blown pine trees that stretches right across to the imposing entrance of Glen Coe (see p.193).

ARRIVAL AND DEPARTURE   LOCH RANNOCH

By train The West Highland Railway stops at Rannoch and, a little to the north, Corrour station, which has no road access at all.

Destinations (from Rannoch station) Corrour (3–4 daily; 12min); Fort William (3–4 daily; 1hr); Glasgow Queen St (3–4 daily; 2hr 50min); London Euston (sleeper service Mon–Fri & Sun daily; 11hr–12hr 40min).

By bus A local bus service (Broons Bus #85; up to 4 daily; 40min) from Kinloch Rannoch provides connections with Rannoch railway station, 16 miles to the west.

ACCOMMODATION AND EATING

LOCH RANNOCH

Macdonald Loch Rannoch Half a mile west of Kinloch Rannoch along B846 ☎ 08448 799059, ⓦ macdonald hotels.co.uk. This large and rather plain hotel has a redeeming lochside location. Guests have access to a leisure complex with an indoor pool and gym. **£63**

RANNOCH MOOR

Moor of Rannoch Rannoch Station ☎ 01882 633238, ⓦ moorofrannoch.co.uk. If it's isolation you want, this is

the place to stay; there's no internet access, radio or TV. The five comfy en-suite rooms look out over the boggy moorland. **£104**

LOCH OSSIAN

Loch Ossian Youth Hostel A 1-mile walk northeast from Corrour's train station, on the shores of Loch Ossian ☎ 01397 732207, ⓦ syha.org.uk. Only accessible on foot, this is an excellent option for hikers seeking somewhere genuinely off the beaten track. Dorms **£19**

The Angus glens

The high country in the northern part of the county of **Angus**, east of the A9 and north of the Firth of Tay, holds some of the Central Highlands' most pleasant scenery and is relatively free of tourists, most of whom tend to bypass it on their way north. Here the long fingers of the **Angus glens** – heather-covered hills tumbling down to rushing rivers – are overlooked by the southern peaks of the Grampian Mountains. Each has its own feel and devotees, **Glen Clova** being, deservedly, one of the most popular, along with **Glen Shee**, which attracts large numbers of people to its ski slopes. Handsome market towns like **Kirriemuir** and **Blairgowrie** are good bases for the area, while the tiny village of **Meigle** at the southern end of Glen Isla has Scotland's finest collection of carved Pictish stones.

Glen Shee and around

The upper reaches of **Glen Shee**, the most dramatic and best known of the Angus glens, are dominated by its **ski fields**, ranged over four mountains above the Cairnwell mountain pass. The resorts here may not amount to much more than gentle training slopes in comparison with those of the Alps or North America, but they all make for a fun day out for everyone from beginners to experienced skiers. During the season (Dec–March), ski lifts and tows give access to gentle beginners' slopes, while experienced skiers can try the more intimidating Tiger run. In summer it's all a bit sad, although there are some excellent hiking and mountain-biking routes. Active types tend to overnight in Spittal of Glenshee, or twenty miles further south along the A93 in Blairgowrie, a small town at the southern end of the glen.

Spittal of Glenshee

The small settlement of **SPITTAL OF GLENSHEE** (the name derives from the same root as "hospital", indicating a refuge), though ideally situated for skiing, has little to commend it other than the busy *Gulabin Bunkhouse*. From Spittal the road climbs another five miles or so to the ski centre at the crest of the Cairnwell Pass.

ACTIVITIES SPITTAL OF GLENSHEE

Gulabin Lodge Outdoor Centre At Gulabin Lodge, Spittal of Glenshee ☎ 01250 885255, ⓦ gulabinoutdoors .co.uk. Snow sports are the big draw in winter, of course, but staff here can also arrange summer activities like archery and rock climbing. Pre-booking advised.

ACCOMMODATION

Dalmunzie Castle Tucked away among the hills behind Spittal ☎ 01250 885224, ⓦ dalmunzie.com. A lovely Highland retreat in a magnificent turreted mansion, with first-class dining and over sixty malt whiskies to enjoy by the fireside. **£135**

Gulabin Lodge On the A93 at Spittal of Glenshee, run by Gulabin Lodge Outdoor Centre ☎ 01250 885 255, ⓦ gulabinoutdoors.co.uk. Clean, basic accommodation in a nineteenth-century manse. Singles, doubles and family rooms also available. Twins **£45**; doubles **£50**

Blairgowrie

Travelling to Glen Shee from the south you'll pass through the well-heeled little town of **BLAIRGOWRIE**, set among raspberry fields on the glen's southernmost tip and a good place to pick up information and plan your activities. Strictly two communities – Blairgowrie and **Rattray**, set on either side of the River Ericht – the town's modest claim to fame is that St Ninian once camped at Wellmeadow, a pleasant grassy triangle in the town centre.

Cateran Trail

ⓦ caterantrail.org

The **Cateran Trail** is an ambitious, long-distance footpath that starts in Blairgowrie then heads off on a long loop into the glens to the north following some of the drove roads used by caterans, or cattle thieves. It's a four- to five-day tramp, though of course it's possible to walk shorter sections of the way (see the website for more information).

SKIING IN GLEN SHEE

For information on skiing in Glen Shee, contact **Ski Glenshee** (☎ 013397 41320, ⓦ ski -glenshee.co.uk), which also offers ski rental and lessons, as does the Gulabin Lodge Outdoor Centre (see above), at the Spittal of Glenshee. For the latest snow and **weather conditions**, phone Ski Glenshee or check out the Ski Scotland website (ⓦ ski.visitscotland.com).

2

By bus Blairgowrie is well linked by hourly bus #57 to both Perth and Dundee.

Tourist office 26 Wellmeadow (April–June, Sept & Oct Mon–Fri 10am–5pm, Sun 10.30am–3.30pm; July & Aug Mon–Sat 9.30am–5pm, Sun 10.30am–3.30pm; Nov–March Mon–Sat 10am–4pm; ☎01250 872960, ⓦperthshire.co .uk). Blairgowrie's friendly tourist office can help with accommodation.

ACCOMMODATION AND EATING

Bridge of Cally Hotel 6 miles north of town on the A93 ☎01250 886231, ⓦbridgeofcallyhotel.com. Welcoming roadside pub serving good grub throughout the day (steak-and-kidney pie £10.50), plus real ale by an open fire. Food served daily 10am–8.45pm.

Cargills By the river on Lower Mill St ☎01250 876735, ⓦcargillsbistro.com. Popular bistro serving inexpensive formal meals and civilized coffee and cakes. The menu includes good vegetarian options, such as mushroom risotto (£11.90). Daily 10.30am–9pm.

Heathpark House Coupar Angus Rd ☎01250 870700, ⓦheathparkhouse.com. Good, spacious en-suite rooms at a Victorian house south of the centre with two acres of gardens. No children under the age of 16. **£80**

SHOPPING

Blairgowrie Farm Shop 14–16 Reform St ☎01250 876528, ⓦblairgowriefarmshop.co.uk. Jams, vegetables, organic breads and frozen meats are all for sale at this well-stocked deli and farm shop. Mon–Sat 8.30am–5.30pm.

Meigle

Museum: Dundee Rd, Meigle • April–Sept daily 9.30am–5.30pm • £4.50; HS

Fifteen miles north of Dundee on the B954 lies the tiny settlement of **MEIGLE**, home to Scotland's most important collection of early Christian and Pictish **inscribed stones**. Housed in a modest former schoolhouse, the **Meigle Museum** displays some thirty pieces dating from the seventh to the tenth centuries, all found in and around the nearby churchyard. The majority are either gravestones that would have lain flat, or cross slabs inscribed with the sign of the cross, usually standing. Most impressive is the 7ft-tall great cross slab, said to be the gravestone of Guinevere, wife of King Arthur. The exact purpose of the stones and their enigmatic symbols is obscure, as is the reason why so many of them were found at Meigle. The most likely theory suggests that Meigle was once an important ecclesiastical centre that attracted secular burials of prominent Picts.

Glen Isla and around

Three and a half miles north of Meigle is **ALYTH**, near which, legend has it, Guinevere was held captive by Mordred. It's a sleepy village at the south end of **Glen Isla**, which runs parallel to Glen Shee and is linked to it by the A926. If you decide to stay in the area, the best options are in and around **Kirkton of Glenisla**, a small hamlet ten miles north of Alyth.

Reekie Linn

Close to the Bridge of Craigisla, which is a ten-minute drive north of Alyth along the B954, the River Isla narrows and then plunges some 60ft into a deep gorge to produce the classically pretty waterfall of **Reekie Linn**, or "smoking fall", so called because of the water mist produced when the fall hits a ledge and bounces a further 20ft into a deep pool known as the Black Dub. There's a car park beside the bridge, and the waterfall is a short walk away along the river's edge.

By bus Transport connections into the glen are limited: Alyth is on the main bus routes linking Blairgowrie with Dundee, while hourly bus #57 from Dundee to Perth passes through Meigle.

Glenmarkie Horse Riding and Trekking Centre Around 3 miles northeast of Kirkton of Glenisla

☎01575 582293, 🌐glenmarkie.co.uk. Beyond *West Freuchies*, a long and bumpy road leads to this remote

activity centre, where you can take horseriding lessons (£26/hr) in a spectacularly rural landscape.

ACCOMMODATION

Glenisla Hotel In Kirkton of Glenisla, 10 miles north of Alyth ☎01575 582223, 🌐glenisla-hotel.com. Cosy hotel, which doubles as a good place for classy home-made bar food and convivial drinking. Doubles **£77.50**

West Freuchies Just outside Kirkton of Glenisla ☎01575 582716, 🌐glenisla-westfreuchies.co.uk. A

comfortable bed and breakfast whose first-floor rooms have views over the hills. There's also self-catering accommodation nearby in a converted mill. Approaching from Alyth, a right-hand turn leads northeast to the B&B (signposted before you reach Kirkton of Glenisla). Doubles **£70**

Kirriemuir and around

The sandstone town of **KIRRIEMUIR**, known locally as Kirrie, is set on a hill six miles northwest of Forfar on the cusp of glens Clova and Prosen. Despite the influx of hunters up for the "season", it's still a pretty special place, a haphazard confection of narrow closes, twisting wynds and steep braes. The main cluster of streets have all the appeal of an old film set, with their old-fashioned bars, tiled butcher's shop, tartan outlets and haberdasheries somehow managing to avoid being contrived and quaint.

J.M. Barrie's birthplace

9 Brechin Rd • Mid-March till June Mon–Wed, Sat & Sun noon–5pm; July & Aug daily 11am–5pm; Sept–Oct Mon–Wed, Sat & Sun noon–5pm • £6.50; NTS

Kirrie was the birthplace of **J.M. Barrie**. A local handloom-weaver's son, Barrie first came to notice with his series of novels about "Thrums", a village based on his home town, in particular *A Window in Thrums* and his third novel, *The Little Minister*. The story of Peter Pan, the little boy who never grew up, was penned by Barrie in 1904 – some say as a response to a strange upbringing dominated by the memory of his older brother, who died as a child. **Barrie's birthplace**, a plain little whitewashed cottage, has a series of small rooms decorated as they would have been during Barrie's childhood, as well as displays about his life and works. The wash house outside was apparently the model for the house built by the Lost Boys for Wendy in Never-Never Land. Despite being offered a prestigious plot at London's Westminster Abbey, Barrie chose to be buried in Kirrie, and the unassuming family grave can be seen in the town cemetery.

Camera obscura

In the old cricket pavilion above town just off West Hill Rd • Mid-March till June: Sat noon–5pm, Sun 1–5pm; July–Sept: Mon–Sat noon–5pm, Sun 1–5pm • £3.50; NTS

One of the few camera obscuras still functioning in Scotland, this unexpected treasure was donated to the town in 1930 by Barrie, and offers splendid views of Strathmore and the glens. On a clear day it's possible to see as far as Ben Ledi, almost sixty miles to the west.

Gateway to the Glens Museum

32 High St • Tues–Sat 10am–5pm • Free • 🌐angus.gov.uk

J.M. Barrie is Kirriemuir's most famous son, but another man born in the town attracts a handful of rather different pilgrims. **Bon Scott** of the rock band AC/DC lived here before emigrating to Australia; more about him can be found at Kirriemuir's **Gateway to the Glens Museum**, in the old Town House on the main square. The oldest building in Kirrie, it has seen service as a tollbooth, court, jail, post office, police station and chemist; these days you can find two floors of interactive displays and exhibits on the town and the Angus glens, including a scale model of Kirrie in 1604.

ARRIVAL AND DEPARTURE   KIRRIEMUIR AND AROUND

By bus The hourly #20 bus runs from Kirriemuir High St to Forfar and Dundee.

2

ACCOMMODATION AND EATING

Falls of Holm 4 miles west of Kirriemuir in Kingoldrum ☎01575 575867, ⓦfallsofholm.com. Cosy and luxurious farmhouse B&B, which provides a peaceful alternative to staying in the middle of town. **£70**

Muirhouses Farm North of town on the way to Cortachy ☎01575 573128, ⓦmuirhousesfarm.co.uk. Offering a taste of the countryside, this is a working cattle farm with bright, plain rooms looked after by friendly owner Susan. Breakfast includes meat from the local butcher. Offers discounts for longer stays. **£75**

Thrums Hotel Bank St ☎01575 572758, ⓦthrums hotel.co.uk. Good central option for lunches and evening meals; the menu includes a succulent slow-roasted lamb shank (£8.50). There are also nine en-suite rooms available. Food daily noon–2pm & 5–8pm. **£80**

SHOPPING

Star Rock Shop 27–29 The Roods ☎01575 572579. Pretty, old-style shop specializing in Scottish confectionery, first opened in 1833. Nice place to try the hard, sweet and milky Scottish candy known as tablet (£2/bag). Tues–Sat 9/10am–5pm.

Glen Prosen

Five miles north of Kirriemuir, the low-key hamlet of **DYKEHEAD** marks the point where **Glen Prosen** and Glen Clova divide. A mile or so up Glen Prosen, you'll find the house where Captain Scott and fellow explorer Doctor Wilson planned their ill-fated trip to Antarctica in 1910–11, with a roadside **stone cairn** commemorating the expedition. From here on, Glen Prosen remains essentially a quiet wooded backwater, with all the wild and rugged splendour of the other glens but without the crowds. To explore the area thoroughly you need to go on foot, but a good road circuit can be made by crossing the river at the tiny village of **GLENPROSEN** and returning to Kirriemuir along the western side of the glen via Pearsie. Alternatively, the reasonably easy four-mile **Minister's Path** links Prosen with Clova. It is clearly marked and leaves from near the church in the village.

Glen Clova and around

With its stunning cliffs, heather slopes and valley meadows, **Glen Clova** – which in the north becomes **Glen Doll** – is one of the loveliest of the Angus glens. Although it can get unpleasantly congested in peak season, the area is still remote enough that you can leave the crowds with little effort. Wildlife is abundant, with deer on the mountains, wild hares and even grouse and the occasional buzzard. The meadow flowers on the valley floor and arctic plants (including great splashes of white and purple saxifrage) on the rocks make it a botanist's paradise.

Clova

The B955 from Dykehead and Kirriemuir divides at the Gella Bridge over the swift-coursing River South Esk. Around six miles north of Gella, the two branches of the road join up once more at the hamlet of **CLOVA**, little more than the hearty *Glen Clova Hotel*. An excellent, if fairly strenuous, four-hour walk from behind the old school at the back of the hotel leads up into the mountains and around the lip of **Loch Brandy**.

North from Clova village, the road turns into a rabbit-infested lane coursing along the riverside for four miles to the car park, a useful starting point for numerous superb **walks**. There are no other facilities beyond the village.

ACCOMMODATION AND EATING — GLEN CLOVA AND AROUND

Glen Clova Hotel In Glen Clova ☎01575 550350, ⓦclova.com. Inviting country hotel, which also has its own bunkhouse and a private fishing loch. The restaurant serves up traditional Scottish food, such as venison casserole and haggis. Restaurant: Mon–Thurs & Sun noon–7.45pm, Fri & Sat noon–8.45pm. Dorms **£17**; doubles **£90**

WALKS FROM GLEN DOLL
Ordnance Survey Explorer maps 388 & 387

These **walks** are some of the main routes across the Grampians from the Angus glens to Deeside, many of which follow well-established old drovers' roads. All three either fringe or cross the royal estate of Balmoral, and Prince Charles's favourite mountain – **Lochnagar** – can be seen from all angles. The walks all begin from the car park at the end of the tarred road where Glen Clova meets Glen Doll; all routes should always be approached with care, and you should follow the usual safety precautions.

CAPEL MOUNTH TO BALLATER
(15 miles; 7hr)
Initially, the path zigzags its way up fierce slopes before levelling out to a moorland plateau, leading to the eastern end of Loch Muick. It then follows the River Muick to Ballater.

CAPEL MOUNTH ROUND-TRIP
(15 miles; 8hr)
Follows the above route to Loch Muick, doubling back along the loch's southern shore. The dramatic Streak of Lightning path that follows Corrie Chash leads to a ruined stables below Sandy Hillock; the descent passes the waterfall by the bridge at Bachnagairn, where a gentle burn-side track leads back to Glen Doll car park.

JOCK'S ROAD TO BRAEMAR
(14 miles; 7hr)
A signposted path leads below Cairn Lunkhard and along a wide ridge towards the summit of Crow Craigies (3018ft). From here, the path bumps down to Loch Callater then follows the Callater Burn, eventually hitting the A93 two miles short of Braemar.

Brechin

Twelve miles or so northeast of Kirriemuir, **BRECHIN** is an attractive town whose red-sandstone buildings give it a warm, welcoming feel. The chief attraction is the old **cathedral**, a building that's emboldened some (including the local football team) to proudly describe Brechin – in line with the historic definition – as a fully fledged city.

The cathedral
On Bishop's Close, off the High St • Daily 9am–5pm • Free

There's been a religious building of sorts here since the arrival of evangelizing Irish missionaries in 900 AD, and the red-sandstone structure has become something of a hotchpotch of architectural styles. What you see today dates chiefly from an extensive rebuilding in 1900, with the oldest surviving part of the cathedral being the 106ft-high round tower, one of only two in Scotland. The cathedral's doorway, built 6ft above the ground for protection against Viking raids, has some notable carvings, while inside you can see various Pictish stones, illuminated by the jewel-coloured stained-glass windows.

Pictavia
Haughmuir, 1 mile west of Brechin • April–Oct Mon–Sat 9am–5pm, Sun 10am–5pm; Nov–March Sat 9am–5pm, Sun 10am–5pm • £3.25 • Ⓦ pictavia.org.uk

A mile from the town centre along the Forfar road in the expansive grounds of Brechin Castle (not generally open to the public) is **Pictavia**, a custom-built tourist attraction with the grandly titled Brechin Castle Centre (a garden centre) as its hub; this is also where you'll find Brechin's **tourist office**. Based on the history and heritage of the Picts, it's a little lacking in substance.

ARRIVAL, INFORMATION AND TOURS   BRECHIN

By bus Brechin is easy to get to and from; bus #30 runs at least once per hour to Montrose, 9 miles east.

Tourist office At Pictavia (April–Oct Mon–Sat 9am–5pm, Sun 10am–5pm; Nov–March Sat 9am–5pm, Sun

10am–5pm; ☎ 01356 623050).
Caledonian Railway tours ☎ 01356 622992, ⓦ caledonianrailway.com. Trains operate every weekend

(June–Aug), travelling along 4 miles of track from Brechin to the Bridge of Dun (£6 return). Diesel trains run on Saturdays, steam trains run on Sundays.

Edzell and around

Travelling around Angus, you can hardly fail to notice the difference between organic settlements and planned towns that were built by landowners who forcibly rehoused local people in order to keep them under control, especially after the Jacobite uprisings. One of the better examples of the latter, **EDZELL**, five miles north of Brechin on the B966, was cleared and rebuilt with Victorian rectitude a mile to the west of its original site in the 1840s. Through the Dalhousie Arch at the entrance to the village the long, wide and ruler-straight main street is lined with prim nineteenth-century buildings, which now do a roaring trade as genteel teashops and antiques emporia.

The original village (identifiable from the cemetery and surrounding grassy mounds) lay immediately to the west of the wonderfully explorable red-sandstone ruins of Edzell Castle, itself a mile west of the planned village.

Edzell Castle

1 mile west of Edzell • April–Sept daily 9.30am–5.30pm • £5.50; HS

The main part of the old castle is a good example of a comfortable tower house, where luxurious living rather than defence became a priority. However it's the **pleasance garden** overlooked by the castle tower that makes a visit to **Edzell Castle** essential, especially in late spring and early to mid-summer. The garden was built by Sir David Lindsay in 1604, at the height of the optimistic Renaissance, and its refinement and extravagance are evident. The walls contain sculpted images of erudition: the Planetary Deities on the east side, the Liberal Arts on the south and, under floods of lobelia, the Cardinal Virtues on the west wall. In the centre of the garden, low-cut box hedges spell out the family mottoes and enclose voluminous beds of roses.

The Caterthuns

Four miles southwest of Edzell, lying either side of the lane to Bridgend, which can be reached either by carrying on along the road past the castle or by taking the narrow road at the southern end of Edzell village, are the **Caterthuns**, twin Iron Age hillforts that were probably occupied at different times. The surviving ramparts on the White Caterthun (978ft) – easily reached from the small car park below – are the most impressive, and this is thought to be the later fort, occupied by the Picts in the first few centuries AD.

ARRIVAL AND DEPARTURE   EDZELL AND AROUND

By bus Edzell is 5 miles north of Brechin on the B966, and linked to it by buses #21, #29 and #30.

ACCOMMODATION

Alexandra Lodge Inveriscandye Rd ☎ 01356 648266, ⓦ alexandralodge.co.uk. Just a short walk east of the High Street, this is a friendly B&B located in a little Edwardian lodge built in 1907. April–Oct. **£75**
Panmure Arms 52 High St ☎ 01356 648950,

ⓦ panmurearmshotel.co.uk. The best of Edzell's hotels, offering sizeable, well-decorated rooms and fairly predictable bar meals. You'll find it close to the mini roundabout at the north end of the High Street. **£95**

Deeside

More commonly known as **Royal Deeside**, the land stretching west from Aberdeen along the River Dee revels in its connections with the Royal Family, who have

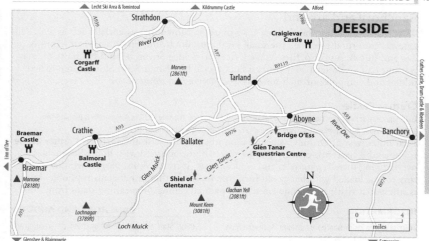

regularly holidayed here, at **Balmoral**, since Queen Victoria bought the estate. Eighty thousand Scots turned out to welcome her on her first visit in 1848. Victoria adored the place and the woods were said to remind Prince Albert of Thuringia, his homeland.

Deeside is undoubtedly handsome in a fierce, craggy, Scottish way, and the royal presence has helped keep a lid on any unattractive mass development. The villages strung along the A93, the main route through the area, are well heeled and have something of an old-fashioned air. Facilities for visitors hereabouts are first class, with a number of bunkhouses and hostels, some decent hotels and plenty of castles and grounds to snoop around. It's also an excellent area for **outdoor activities**, with hiking routes into both the Grampian and Cairngorm mountains, alongside good mountain biking, horseriding and skiing.

GETTING AROUND   DEESIDE

By bus Stagecoach Bluebird buses #201, #202 and #203 from Aberdeen regularly chug along the A93, serving most of the towns on the way to Braemar. Bus #201 runs to Crathes (45min), Banchory (50min), Ballater (1hr 45min), and Braemar (2hr 10min), while #202 and #203 stop at Lumphanan and Banchory respectively.

Drum Castle

Near Drumoak, 10 miles west of Aberbeen off the A93 • April–June & Sept Mon & Thurs–Sun 11am–4pm; July & Aug daily 11am–4pm; Garden of Historic Roses April–Oct daily 11am–4.15pm • £6, grounds only £2 • NTS

Ten miles west of Aberdeen, **Drum Castle** stands in a clearing in the ancient **woods of Drum**, made up of the splendid pines and oaks that covered this whole area before the shipbuilding industry precipitated mass forest clearance. The castle itself combines a 1619 Jacobean mansion with Victorian extensions and the original, huge thirteenth-century keep, which has been restored and reopened. Given by Robert the Bruce to his armour-bearer, William de Irvine, in 1323 for services rendered at Bannockburn, the castle remained in Irvine hands for 24 generations until the NTS took over in 1976. The main part of the house is Victorian in character, with grand, antique-filled rooms and lots of family portraits. The finest room is the library, within the ancient tower; you'll get an even better sense of the medieval atmosphere of the place by climbing up to the upper levels of the tower, with the battlements offering views out over the forest.

Banchory and around

BANCHORY, meaning "fair hollow", is a one-street town that essentially acts as a gateway into rural Deeside. The small local **museum** (Mon, Fri & Sat 11am–1pm & 2–4pm; July & Aug also Tues & Wed; free) on Bridge Street, behind High Street, may warrant half an hour or so if you're a fan of local boy James Scott Skinner, renowned fiddler and composer of such tunes as *The Bonnie Lass o'Bon Accord*.

Crathes Castle

Crathes, just east of Banchory • Jan–March Sat & Sun 10.30am–3.45pm; April–Oct daily 10.30am-4.45pm; Nov & Dec Sat & Sun 10.30am–3.45pm; last admission 45min before closing • £12 including access to the gardens; NTS

Four miles west of Drum Castle and around two miles east of Banchory, **Crathes Castle** is a splendid sixteenth-century granite tower-house adorned with flourishes such as overhanging turrets, gargoyles and conical roofs. Its thick walls, narrow windows and tiny rooms loaded with heavy old furniture make Crathes rather claustrophobic, but it is still worth visiting for some wonderful painted ceilings; the earliest dates from 1602.

INFORMATION   BANCHORY AND AROUND

Tourist office Inside Banchory museum (April–Oct Mon–Sat 10am–5pm; July & Aug also Sun 1–5pm; ☎01330 822000). Staff can provide information on walking and fishing in the area.

ACCOMMODATION

Raemoir House 2.5 miles north of Banchory ☎01330 824884, ⓦraemoir.com. Glamorous country-house hotel set in spacious parkland, complete with a decadent drawing room. The best rooms have four-poster beds. **£180**

Tor-Na-Coille Hotel Inchmarlo Rd, Banchory ☎01330 822242, ⓦtornacoille.com. Once a retreat for Charlie Chaplin and his family, *Tor-Na-Coille* has a scenic location on the town's southern edge. Some of the smart rooms overlook Banchory Golf Club's rolling fairways. **£125**

EATING AND DRINKING

The Milton Near the entrance to Crathes Castle ☎01330 844566, ⓦmiltonbrasserie.com. Smart restaurant just across from Crathes Castle, serving moderately priced à la carte meals such as a red pepper and star anise risotto (£12). Mon & Tues noon–3pm, Wed & Thurs noon–3pm & 6–9pm, Fri & Sat noon–3pm & 6–9.30pm, Sun noon–5pm.

Aboyne and around

Twelve miles west of Banchory on the A93, **ABOYNE** is a typically well-mannered Deeside village at the mouth of **Glen Tanar**, which runs southwest from here for ten miles or so deep into the Grampian hills. The glen, with few steep gradients and some glorious stands of mature Caledonian pine, is ideal for walking, mountain biking or horseriding.

ACTIVITIES   ABOYNE AND AROUND

Horseriding One- and two-hour horseriding lessons (from £36) are on offer at the Glen Tanar Equestrian Centre (☎01339 886448, ⓦglentanar.co.uk).

Gliding If you have a head for heights, consider taking a flight from the Deeside Gliding Club (trial lesson £75; ☎01339 853339, ⓦdeesideglidingclub.co.uk).

Kart racing and quad biking Family-oriented thrills such as kart racing and quad-bike trekking can be found at Deeside Activity Park (both activities £45/hr; ☎01339 883536, ⓦdeesideactivitypark.com), 4 miles northeast of Aboyne. The park is signposted off the A93.

Ballater

Ten miles west of Aboyne is the neat and ordered town of **BALLATER**, attractively hemmed in by the river and fir-covered mountains. The town was dragged from obscurity in the nineteenth century when it was discovered that waters from the local

EXPLORING GLEN TANAR

Ordnance Survey Explorer map 395

Lying to the south of the Deeside town of Aboyne, the easily navigated forest tracks of **Glen Tanar** offer a taste of the changing landscape of the northeastern Highlands, passing through relatively prosperous farmland along the River Dee, through ancient woodland and then to remote grouse moors and bleak hillsides in the heart of the Grampian Mountains. Flatter than Glen Muick and without its vehicle traffic, Glen Tanar is a great place to explore on mountain bike, although there is plenty of opportunity for walking and there's also an **equestrian centre** in the glen (see opposite), offering riding trips lasting from one hour to all day on riverside, mountain and forest horse-trails.

Leave the south Deeside road (B976) at **Bridge o'Ess**, one and a half miles southwest of Aboyne, and carry on along a tarred road on the west side of the Water of Tanar for two miles to a car park and the Braeloine Visitor Centre and **ranger information point** (April–Sept Mon & Wed–Sun 10am–5pm; Oct–March Mon & Thurs–Sun 10am–5pm; ☎01339 886072, ⓦglentanar .co.uk). Here you can pick up details on the various routes in the glen, as well as some background on the flora and fauna of the area including efforts to protect the habitat of the rare capercaillie. If you're on **foot**, the best idea is to strike out along the clear forest tracks that follow both sides of the river, connected at various points by attractive stone bridges, allowing for easy round-trips. Most of the time you are surrounded by superb old pine woodland, some of which is naturally seeded remnants of ancient Caledonian forest, with broadleafs in evidence along the river, as are wild flowers and fungi in season. The end of the glen, at **Shiel of Glentanar**, is eight miles from the car park, from where you can either retrace your path or take to the hills: **Mount Keen** (3081ft), the most easterly of Scotland's 3000ft-high mountains, looms ahead. The more ambitious can pick up the Mounth road at Shiel of Glentanar, which heads up and over Mount Keen to Invermark at the head of Glen Esk.

Pannanich Wells might be useful in curing scrofula. Deeside water is now back in fashion, though these days it's bottled and sold far and wide as a natural mineral water.

It was in Ballater that Queen Victoria first arrived in Deeside by train from Aberdeen back in 1848; she wouldn't allow a station to be built any closer to Balmoral, eight miles further west. Although the line has long been closed, the town's rather self-important royalism is much in evidence at the restored **train station** in the centre. The local shops that supply Balmoral with groceries and household basics also flaunt their connections, with oversized "By Appointment" crests.

If you prefer to discover the fresh air and natural beauty that Victoria came to love so much, you'll find Ballater an excellent base for local **walks and outdoor activities**. There are numerous hikes from Loch Muik (pronounced "mick"), nine miles southwest of town, including the Capel Mounth drovers' route over the mountains to Glen Doll (see p.155), and a well-worn but strenuous all-day trek up and around Lochnagar (3789ft), the mountain much painted and written about by the current Prince of Wales.

ARRIVAL AND DEPARTURE   BALLATER

By bus Buses stop at the northern end of Golf Road, near the A93.

Destinations Aboyne (hourly; 20min); Banchory (hourly; 40min); Braemar (9 daily; 35min).

INFORMATION AND ACTIVITIES

Tourist office In the renovated former train station on Station Square (daily: July & sAug 10am–6pm; Sept–June 10am–5pm; ☎01339 755306).

Bike rental Good-quality bikes, including mountain

bikes and tandems, can be rented from Cycle Highlands, at 13–15 Victoria Rd (from £18/day; ☎01339 755864, ⓦwww.cyclehighlands.com).

ACCOMMODATION

Auld Kirk Braemar Rd ☎01339 755762, ⓦtheauldkirk .co.uk. As the name suggests, this pleasingly unorthodox B&B

is based in a renovated church. All of the rooms are upstairs, leaving the ground floor free for a licensed lounge area. **£120**

Ballater Caravan Park South of Anderson Rd, close to the River Dee ☎01339 755727. Large campsite down by the water that mostly attracts touring caravans – tents are welcome too, though, and there are laundry and shower facilities. Easter–Oct. **£13.50**/pitch

Deeside Hotel Just west of the centre at 45 Braemar Rd ☎01339 755420, ⱳdeesidehotel.co.uk. Welcoming nineteenth-century house with relatively expensive doubles and twins, all of which are en-suite. The bar downstairs is stacked full of whisky and bottled ales, and there's also a restaurant in the large conservatory out the back. **£110**

Habitat @ Ballater Bridge Square ☎01339 753752, ⱳhabitat-at-ballater.com. Excellent and well-equipped hostel tucked away off the main road. Choose between a bunk bed with its own locker, or one of the private rooms. Dorms **£20**; doubles **£50**

EATING AND DRINKING

Barrel Lounge 6 Church Square ☎01339 755488, ⱳcrannach.com. If you fancy a wee dram with the locals, pop into this pub on the main green. There's an open fire and usually, the TV is on in the corner. Mon–Wed & Sun 11am–midnight, Thurs–Sat 11am–1am.

Crannach Bakery A couple of miles east of Ballater at Cambus O'May ☎01339 755126, ⱳcrannach.com. A cultured spot offering good coffees, snacks and light meals, as well as superb cakes (around £1.50) and bread from its in-house organic bakery. Tues–Sun 11am–5pm.

La Mangiatoia Bridge Square ☎01339 755999. Cheap and cheerful Italian place close to the middle of town and popular with families. A meat feast pizza here will cost you £9.20. Daily except Mon 5–9.30pm.

Rocksalt and Snails 2 Bridge St ☎07834 452583. The pick of Ballater's cafés, selling cupcakes, sharing platters and light bites, including veggie options like goat's cheese in a sweet chilli sauce (£6.50 with bread). Daily 10am–6pm, Thurs, Fri & Sat till 10pm.

Balmoral Estate and around

8 miles west of Ballater, off the A93 **Balmoral Castle** April–July daily 10am–5pm • £10; audio-tours included in admission price (£5 deposit required) • Land Rover safari £60/person for 3hr (min two people) • ☎01339 742534, ⱳbalmoralcastle.com **Tourist office** In the car park by the church on the main road • April–Oct daily 10am–5pm; Nov–March Mon–Fri 10am–noon • ☎01339 742414

Originally a sixteenth-century tower house built for the powerful Gordon family, **Balmoral Castle** has been a royal residence since 1852, when it was converted to the Scottish Baronial mansion that stands today. The Royal Family traditionally spend their summer holidays here each August, but despite its fame it can be something of a disappointment even for a dedicated royalist. For the three months when the doors are nudged open, the general riffraff are permitted to view only the ballroom, an exhibition room and the grounds. With so little of the castle on view, it's worth making the most of the grounds and larger estate by following some of the country walks, heading off on a Land Rover safari or allowing the free audio-tour to guide you.

Opposite the castle's gates on the main road, the otherwise dull granite church of **Crathie**, built in 1895 with the proceeds of a bazaar held at Balmoral, is the royals' local church.

DEESIDE AND DONSIDE HIGHLAND GAMES

Royal Deeside is the home of the modern **Highland Games**, claiming descent from gatherings organized by eleventh-century Scottish king Malcolm Canmore to help him recruit the strongest and fittest clansmen for his army. The most famous of the local games is undoubtedly the **Braemar Gathering**, held on the first Saturday in September, which can see crowds of 15,000 and usually a royal or two as guest of honour. Vying for celebrity status in recent years has been the **Lonach Gathering** in nearby Strathdon on Donside, held the weekend before Braemar, where local laird Billy Connolly dispenses drams of whisky to marching village men and has been known to invite some Hollywood chums along – Steve Martin has appeared dressed in kilt and jacket, while Robin Williams has competed in the punishing hill race. For a true flavour of the spirit of Highland gatherings, however, try to get to one of the events that take place in other local towns and villages at weekends throughout July and August, where locals outnumber tourists and the competitions are guaranteed to be hard-fought and entertaining.

Local tourist offices and the tourist board website (ⱳaberdeen-grampian.com) should be able to tell you what's happening where.

Braemar

West of Balmoral, the road rises to 1100ft above sea level in the upper part of Deeside and the village of **BRAEMAR**, situated where three passes meet and overlooked by an unremarkable **castle**. It's an invigorating, outdoor kind of place, well patronized by committed hikers, but probably best known for its Highland Games, the annual **Braemar Gathering**, on the first Saturday of September. Since Queen Victoria's day, successive generations of royals have attended and the world's most famous Highland Games have become rather an overcrowded, overblown event. You're not guaranteed to get in if you just turn up; the website (ⓦ braemargathering.org) has details of how to book tickets in advance.

Linn of Dee

A pleasant diversion from Braemar is to head six miles west to the end of the road and the **Linn of Dee**, where the river plummets savagely through a narrow rock gorge. From here there are countless walks into the surrounding countryside or up into the heart of the Cairngorms (see p.164), including the awesome Lairig Ghru pass which cuts all the way through to Strathspey.

ARRIVAL, INFORMATION AND ACTIVITIES   BRAEMAR

By bus Buses to and from Ballater (9 daily; 35min) stop on Auchendryne Square, while long-distance coaches drop package tourists on the lot opposite the *Fife Arms Hotel*.
Tourist office In The Mews, in the middle of the village on Mar Rd (daily: April–June, Sept & Oct 9.30am–5pm;

July & Aug 9.30am–6pm; Nov–March 9.30am–4.30pm; ☎ 01339 741600).
Outdoor activities Advice on outdoor activities, as well as ski, mountain-bike and climbing equipment rental, is available from Braemar Mountain Sports (daily 9am–6pm; ⓦ braemarmountainsports.com).

ACCOMMODATION

Braemar Lodge A quarter of a mile south of the village on Glenshee Rd ☎ 01339 741627, ⓦ braemar lodge.co.uk. Seven, tartan-accented hotel rooms and bunkhouse on the same plot, which has budget beds and laundry facilities. Double £120; bunkhouse £15
Clunie Lodge Guest House Clunie Bank Road ☎ 01339 741330, ⓦ clunielodge.com. Just south of the tourist office, close to the middle of the village, is this six-room B&B with lovely views up Clunie Glen. £70
Invercauld Caravan Club Park Half a mile south of the village off Glenshee Road ☎ 01339 741373. Year-round

caravan site which also has thirty camping pitches. Can get busy in the summer, so book ahead. £21.40/pitch
Rucksacks Tucked behind The Mews ☎ 01339 741517. Cheery, easy-going bunkhouse that's well equipped for walkers and backpackers – stay in one of the twin rooms, or crash out in the shared alpine-style hut. Dorms £10; twins £32
SYHA Braemar Corrie Feragie, 21 Glenshee Road ☎ 01339 741659, ⓦ syha.org.uk. SYHA hostel in a former shooting lodge with bike storage facilities and a big communal kitchen. It's also just a short stroll from the centre. £18

EATING AND DRINKING

When it comes to eating in Braemar the best advice is to avoid the large hotels, which tend to be filled with coach parties.

The Gathering Place Invercauld Rd, by Braemar Mountain Sports ☎ 01339 741234, ⓦ the-gathering -place.co.uk. Bistro in the heart of the village selling mouthwatering, though pricey, Scottish-based cuisine, including a game pie made with ale and red wine (£16.95). Tues–Sat 6pm–8.30pm.

Taste Airlie House, beside the Mar Rd roundabout ☎ 01339 741425, ⓦ taste-braemar.co.uk. Reliably good coffee shop and moderately priced contemporary restaurant doing home-made, gluten-free soups for £3.60. Tues–Sat 10am–5pm.

The Don Valley

The quiet countryside around the **Don Valley**, once renowned for its illegal whisky distilleries and smugglers, lies at the heart of Aberdeenshire's prosperous agricultural region. From Aberdeen, the River Don winds northwest through **Inverurie**, where it takes a sharp turn west to **Alford**, then continues past ruined castles through the **Upper Don Valley** and the heather moorlands of the eastern Highlands. This remote and under-visited area is positively littered with ruined castles, Pictish sites, stones and hillforts.

Alford and around

ALFORD (pronounced "aa-ford"), 21 miles northwest of Banchory, only exists at all because it was chosen, in 1859, as the terminus for the Great North Scotland Railway. A fairly grey little town now firmly within the Aberdeen commuter belt, it's still well worth making the trip here for the Grampian Transport Museum.

Grampian Transport Museum

Main St · Daily: April–Sept 10am–5pm; Oct 10am–4pm · £9.50 · ⓦ gtm.org.uk

The **Grampian Transport Museum** is home to a diverse display of transport through the ages, from old tramcars and pushbikes to modern, ecofriendly cars. Notable exhibits include the Craigevar Express, a strange, three-wheeled steam-driven vehicle developed by the local postman for his rounds, and that famous monument to British eccentricity and ingenuity, the Sinclair C5 motorized tricycle.

Alford Valley Railway

Just north of Main St, or a short walk east of the Grampian Transport Museum · April–June & Sept Sat & Sun 12.30–4pm; July & Aug daily 12.30–4pm · Return trip £4 · ☎ 07879 293934, ⓦ alfordvalleyrailway.org.uk

A couple of minutes' walk from Grampian Transport Museum is the terminus for the **Alford Valley Railway**, a narrow-gauge train that runs for about a mile from Alford Station through wooded vales to the wide open space of **Murray Park**. The return journey takes an hour.

Craigievar Castle

6 miles south of Alford · Castle: April–June & Sept Fri–Tues 11am–4.45pm; July & Aug daily 11am–4.45pm; grounds: daily 11am–5.30pm · £12; car parking £1; NTS · ☎ 08444 932174

Six miles south of Alford on the A980, **Craigievar Castle** is a fantastic pink confection of turrets, gables, balustrades and cupolas bubbling over from its top three storeys. It was built in 1626 by a Baltic trader known as Willy the Merchant, who evidently allowed his whimsy to run riot.

ARRIVAL AND INFORMATION — ALFORD AND AROUND

By bus Stagecoach Bluebird buses #218 and #220 link Aberdeen with Alford (1hr 10min).

Tourist office The Grampian Transport Museum is home to the helpful tourist office (April–Sept Mon–Sat 9am–5pm, Sun 12.45–5pm; ☎ 01975 562650).

Lumsden

The A944 heads west from Alford, meeting the A97 just south of the tiny village of **LUMSDEN**, an unexpected hot spot of Scottish sculpture. A contemporary **Sculpture Walk** – heralded by a fabulous skeletal black horse at its southern end – runs parallel to the main road, coming out near the premises of the widely respected **Scottish Sculpture Workshop**, 1 Main St (Mon–Fri 9am–5pm, or by arrangement; free; ⓦ ssw.org.uk), very much an active workshop rather than a gallery, at the northern end of the village.

Rhynie

The village of **RHYNIE**, folded beautifully into the hills four miles north of Lumsden up the A97, is forever associated with one of the greatest Pictish memorials, the

Rhynie Man, a remarkable 6ft-high boulder discovered in 1978, depicting a rare whole figure, clad in a tunic and holding what is thought to be a ceremonial axe. The original is in Woodhill House in Aberdeen, but there's a cast on display at the school in Rhynie, across the road from the church. A further claim to fame for the village is that the bedrock lying deep beneath it, known as **Rhynie Chert**, contains plant and insect fossils up to 400 million years old, making them some of the earth's oldest.

Tap o'Noth

A mile or so from Rhynie, along the A941 to Dufftown, a car park gives access to a path up the looming **Tap o'Noth**, Scotland's second-highest Pictish hillfort (1847ft), where substantial remnants of the wall around the lip of the summit show evidence of vitrification (fierce burning), probably to fuse the rocks together.

The Upper Don valley

Travelling west from Alford, settlements become noticeably more scattered and remote as the countryside takes on a more open, recognizably Highland appearance. The **Lecht Road**, crossing the area of bleak but wonderfully empty high country to the remote mountain village of Tomintoul (see p.179), passes the Lecht Ski Centre at 2090ft above sea level, but is frequently impassable in winter due to snow.

Kildrummy Castle

Kildrummy, 10 miles west of Alford off the A97 • **Castle** April–Sept daily 9.30am–5.30pm • £4.50; HS **Kildrummy Castle Gardens** April–Oct daily noon–5pm • £4.50

Ten miles from Alford stand the impressive ruins of the thirteenth-century **Kildrummy Castle**, where Robert the Bruce sent his wife and children during the Wars of Independence. The castle blacksmith, bribed with as much gold as he could carry, set fire to the place and it fell into English hands. Bruce's immediate family survived, but his brother was executed and the entire garrison hanged, drawn and quartered. Meanwhile, the duplicitous blacksmith was rewarded for his help by having molten gold poured down his throat. The sixth earl of Mar used the castle as the headquarters of the ill-fated Jacobite risings in 1715, but after that Kildrummy became redundant and it fell into disrepair. Beside the ruins, the separate **Kildrummy Castle Gardens** are quite a draw, boasting everything from swathes of azaleas in spring to Himalayan poppies in summer.

Lost Gallery

4 miles north of Strathdon • Mon & Wed–Sun 11am–5pm • Free • ⓦ lostgallery.co.uk

Ten miles west of Kildrummy Castle, the A944 sweeps round into the parish of **Strathdon**, little more than a few buildings scattered along the roadside. Four miles north of here, up a rough track leading into Glen Nochty, lies the unexpected **Lost Gallery**, which shows work by some of Scotland's leading modern artists in a wonderfully remote and tranquil setting.

Corgarff Castle

Corgarff, 10 miles southwest of Strathdon • April–Sept daily 9.30am–5.30pm; Oct–March Sat & Sun 9.30am–4.30pm • £5.50; HS

In Corgarff, just off the A939, lies **Corgarff Castle**, an austere tower house with an unusual star-shaped curtain wall and an eventful history. Built in 1537, it was turned into a barracks in 1748, in the aftermath of Culloden, by the Hanoverian government in order to track down local Jacobite rebels; a century later, English redcoats were stationed here with the unpopular task of trying to control whisky smuggling. Today the place has been restored to resemble its days as a barracks, with stark rooms and rows of hard, uncomfortable beds – authentic touches which also extend to graffiti on the walls and peat smoke permeating the building from a fire on the upper storey.

Allargue Arms Hotel Half a mile north of the castle ☎01975 651410, ⓦallarguearmshotel.co.uk. The nearest accommodation option to Corgaff Castle, offering simple B&B and good-value bar meals that include a half-pound steak burger. This old wayside inn overlooks the castle and is a cosy base for skiing, fishing or hiking trips. Daily noon–3pm & 7–9pm. **£60**

2 Strathspey

Rising high in the heather-clad hills above remote Loch Laggan, forty miles due south of Inverness, the **River Spey**, Scotland's second longest river, drains northeast towards the Moray Firth through one of the Highlands' most spellbinding valleys. Famous for its ancient forests, salmon fishing and ospreys, the area around the upper section of the river, known as **STRATHSPEY**, is dominated by the sculpted **Cairngorms**, Britain's most extensive mountain massif, unique in supporting subarctic tundra on its high plateau. Though the area has been admired and treasured for many years as one of Scotland's prime natural assets, the Cairngorms National Park was only declared in 2004. Outdoor enthusiasts flock to the area to take advantage of the superb hiking, biking, watersports and winter snows, aided by the fact that the area is easily accessible by road and rail from both the central belt and Inverness.

A string of towns and villages along the river provide useful bases for setting out into the wilder country, principal among them **Aviemore**, a rather ugly straggle of housing and hotel developments which nevertheless has a lively, youthful feel to it. It's also a good first stop for information, to sort out somewhere to stay or to find out about nearby outdoor

---

CAIRNGORMS NATIONAL PARK

The **Cairngorms National Park** (ⓦcairngorms.co.uk) covers almost 1750 square miles and incorporates the **Cairngorms massif**, the largest mountainscape in the UK and the only sizeable plateau in the country over 2500ft. It's the biggest national park in Britain, and while Aviemore and the surrounding area are regarded as the main point of entry, particularly for those planning outdoor activities, it's also possible to access the park from Perthshire as well as Deeside and Donside in Aberdeenshire. Crossing the range is a significant challenge: by road the only connection is the A939 Tomintoul to Cock Bridge, frequently impassable in winter due to snow. On foot the only way to avoid the high peaks is to follow the old cattle drovers' route called the **Lairig Ghru**, a very long day's walk between Inverdruie at the edge of Rothiemurchus and the Linn of Dee, near Inverey.

The name Cairngorm comes from the Gaelic *An Carm Gorm*, meaning "the blue hill" after the blueish-tinged stones found in the area, and within the park there are 52 summits over 2953ft, as well as a quarter of Scotland's native woodland and a quarter of the UK's threatened wildlife species. The conservation of the landscape's unique flora and fauna is, of course, one of the principal reasons national park status was conferred.

Vegetation in the area ranges from one of the largest tracts of ancient **Caledonian pine and birch forest** remaining in Scotland at Rothiemurchus, to subarctic tundra on the high plateau, where **alpine flora** such as starry saxifrage and the star-shaped pink flowers of moss campion peek out of the pink granite in the few months of summer that the ground is free of snow. In the pine forests of the river valleys, strikingly coloured **birds** such as crested tits, redwings and goldfinches can be observed, along with rarely seen **mammals** such as the red squirrel and pine marten. On the heather slopes above the forest, red and black grouse are often encountered, though their larger relative, the capercaillie, is a much rarer sight, having been reintroduced in 1837 after dying out in the seventeenth century. Birds of prey you're most likely to see are **osprey**, best seen at the **Abernethy Forest RSPB Reserve** (see p.171) at Loch Garten or fishing on the lochs around Aviemore, though golden eagles and peregrine falcons can occasionally be seen higher up. Venturing up to the plateau you'll have the chance of seeing the shy **ptarmigan**, another member of the grouse family, which nests on bare rock and has white plumage during winter, or even the dotterel and snow bunting, rare visitors from the Arctic.

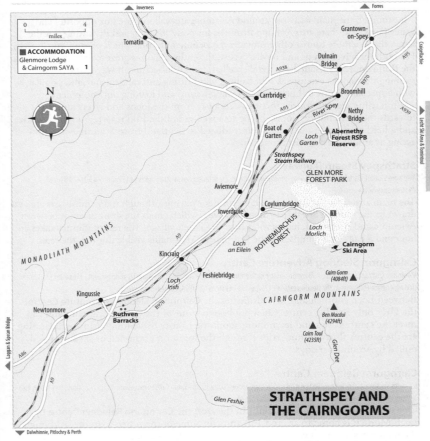

Map labels:
Inverness / Forres
Tomatin
Grantown-on-Spey
Dulnain Bridge
A938
Carrbridge
Broomhill
River Spey
A95
Nethy Bridge
Boat of Garten
Loch Garten
Abernethy Forest RSPB Reserve
Strathspey Steam Railway
GLEN MORE FOREST PARK
Aviemore
Coylumbridge
Inverdruie
Loch Morlich
ROTHIEMURCHUS FOREST
MONADLIATH MOUNTAINS
Loch an Eilein
Cairngorm Ski Area
Kincraig
Cairn Gorm (4084ft)
Feshiebridge
Loch Insh
CAIRNGORM MOUNTAINS
Kingussie
Newtonmore
Ben Macdui (4294ft)
Ruthven Barracks
Cairn Toul (4235ft)
Glen Dee
A86
A9
B970
Glen Feshie
Laggan & Spean Bridge
Dalwhinnie, Pitlochry & Perth

N

ACCOMMODATION
Glenmore Lodge & Cairngorm SAYA   **1**

0   4
miles

STRATHSPEY AND THE CAIRNGORMS

2

Grantulachie / A95
Lecht Ski Area & Tomintoul / A939

activities, which are likely to seem very enticing after a glimpse of the stunning mountain scenery provided by the 4000ft-summit plateau of the Cairngorms. South of Aviemore, the sedate villages of **Newtonmore** and **Kingussie** are older established holiday centres, more popular with anglers and grouse hunters than canoeists and climbers.

The planned Georgian town of **Grantown-on-Spey** is an attractive alternative base for outdoor activities, with solid Victorian mansions but fewer facilities for visitors than Aviemore, while smaller settlements such as **Boat of Garten** and **Kincraig** are quieter, well-kept villages. The whole area boasts a wide choice of good-quality accommodation, particularly in the budget market, with various easy-going hostels run by and for outdoor enthusiasts.

Aviemore and around

The once-sleepy village of **AVIEMORE** was first developed as a ski and tourism resort in the mid-1960s and, over the years, fell victim to profiteering developers with scant regard for the needs of the local community. Despite recent attempts to turn things around, it remains a soulless hotchpotch of retail outlets, café-bars and characterless housing developments. That said, Aviemore is undeniably well equipped with services and facilities and is the most convenient base for the Cairngorms.

In summer, the main activities around Aviemore are walking (see box opposite) and watersports, and there are great opportunities for pony trekking and fly-fishing (for the latter, the Aviemore tourist office provides a brochure outlining which permits you'll need). For both the adventurous and novice cyclist, the entire region is great for mountain biking; the Rothiemurchus Estate has several excellent (and non-technical) way-marked trails running through its extensive lands. Sailing, windsurfing and canoeing are also popular, with a specialist centre at Loch Insh providing lessons and loaning out equipment.

Wintertime sees the tourist focus switch away from the lochs and rivers and up towards the surrounding slopes, home to a well-established ski resort, a dogsled centre, and a herd of reindeer – a species reintroduced to Scotland from Scandinavia – now acting as an unlikely tourist attraction.

Strathspey Steam Railway

Aviemore Station, Dalfaber Rd • July & Aug three times daily; less regular service at other times • £13 return • ☎ 01479 810725, ⓦ strathspeyrailway.co.uk

The main attractions of Aviemore are its outdoor pursuits, though train enthusiasts are also drawn to the restored **Strathspey Steam Railway**, which chugs the short distance between Aviemore and Broomhill, just beyond Boat of Garten village. The return journey takes an hour and a half, with glimpses of the Cairngorm Mountains visible through the trees.

Cairngorm Sleddog Adventure Centre

Moormore Cottage, 3 miles east of Aviemore on the Rothiemurchus Estate • Sledding Oct–April, by appointment • **Museum** £8; 30min sled experience £60/person; 3hr sleddog safaris £175/person • ☎ 07767 270526, ⓦ sled-dogs.co.uk

Between Loch Morlich and Inverdruie lies the **Cairngorm Sleddog Adventure Centre**, the UK's only sleddog centre. On a pre-booked tour of the centre's museum you can meet the centre's dogs and learn more about the history of sledding. More exhilarating are the centre's thirty-minute trips through the forest on a wheeled or ski-based sled, pulled by around ten dogs.

Cairngorm Reindeer Centre

6.5 miles southeast of Aviemore, on the road to *Glenmore Lodge* • Daily 10am–5pm • Guided excursions 11am & 2.30pm; July & Aug also 3.30pm • £12 • ☎ 01479 861228, ⓦ cairngormreindeer.co.uk

One of the more unusual attractions in the area, the **Cairngorm Reindeer Centre** by Loch Morlich is home to around 140 animals, some of them free-roaming. Although the reindeer here today were all born in Scotland, they are descended from a small group brought to the area from Sweden and Norway in the 1950s and 1960s. Visitors can feed and pet the group of reindeer kept by the centre or, during summer, embark on a four-hour reindeer trek in the surrounding hills (£50).

Cairngorm Ski Area

9 miles southeast of Aviemore • Ski season Dec–April, but varies depending on snowfall • ☎ 01479 861319, ⓦ cairngormmountain.org • Buses from Aviemore wind past Inverdruie, stopping at the Coire Cas car park, near the funicular railway's base station

By continental European and North American standards it's all on a tiny scale, but occasionally snow and sun coincide at the **Cairngorm Ski Area** high above Loch Morlich in Glenmore Forest Park to offer beginner and expert alike a great day on the pistes. The ski area is well served by public transport; from the car park at Coire Cas (2150ft), the year-round **funicular railway** (see opposite) is the principal means of getting to the top of the ski slopes.

Base station

Accessed via the Coire Cas car park • Ranger office daily: April–Oct 8.30am–5pm; Nov–March 8.30am–4.30pm • Free

At the Cairngorm Ski Area base station there's a **ranger office** where you can find out about various trails, check the latest weather report and – on fine days between May and October – join guided walks. The "Guided Walk @ The Top" (£15.95; allow

2hr 30min) involves riding the funicular partway up the mountain, joining a guided walk to the summit, and then taking the funicular back down to the base station. Guided mountain-bike descents of the mountain can also be arranged (from £22.50).

Cairn Gorm Mountain Railway

Leaves from the base station • Daily: May–Oct 10.20am–4.30pm; Nov–April 9am–4.30pm; last train up 4pm; every 20min • £10.30

The Cairngorm Ski Area base station is the departure point for the **Cairn Gorm Mountain Railway**, a two-car funicular system that runs to the top of the ski area. A highly controversial £15 million scheme that was bitterly opposed by conservationists, the railway whisks skiers in winter, and tourists throughout the year, along a mile and a half of track to the top station at an altitude of 3600ft, not far from the summit of Cairn Gorm mountain (4085ft). The top station incorporates an exhibition/interpretation area and a café/restaurant from which spectacular views can be had on clear days. Note, there is no access beyond the confines of the top station and its open-air viewing terrace, so unless you're embarking on a winter skiing trip or a guided walk, you'll have to trudge up from the car park at the bottom.

ARRIVAL AND DEPARTURE | AVIEMORE AND AROUND

By train Aviemore's train station is on Grampian Rd, just south of the tourist office.

Destinations Edinburgh (Mon–Sat 12 daily, 6 on Sun; 3hr); Glasgow (11 daily, 6 on Sun; 2hr 50min); Inverness (Mon–Sat 11 daily, 7 on Sun; 40min).

By bus Buses arrive and depart from a stop outside the train station.

Destinations Cairngorm ski area (hourly; 30min); Edinburgh (6 daily; 3–4hr); Glasgow (5 daily; 2hr 40min–3hr 20min); Grantown-on-Spey (Mon–Sat 1–2/hr; 4 on Sun; 30min); Inverness (at least 11 daily; 45min).

INFORMATION AND GETTING AROUND

Tourist office 7 The Parade, Grampian Rd (April & May Mon–Sat 9am–5pm, Sun 10am–5pm; June Mon–Sat 9am–6pm, Sun 9.30am–5pm; July & Aug Mon–Sat 9.30am–6.30pm, Sun 9.30am–6pm; Sept–March 9am–5pm, Sun 10am–4pm; ☎ 01479 810930). Aviemore's business-like tourist office is in the heart of things. It offers an

---

WALKS AROUND AVIEMORE

Ordnance Survey Explorer maps 402 & 403

Walking of all grades is a highlight of the Aviemore area, though you should heed the usual safety guidelines (see p.42). These are particularly important if you want to venture into the subarctic climatic zone of the Cairngorms. However, as well as the high mountain trails, there are some lovely and well-signposted low-level walks in the area.

LOCH AN EILEAN

It takes an hour or so to complete the gentle circular walk around pretty **Loch an Eilean** with its ruined castle in the Rothiemurchus Estate, beginning at the end of the back road that turns east off the B970 a mile south of Inverdruie. The helpful estate visitor centres at the lochside and by the roadside at Inverdruie provide more information on other woodland trails.

RYVOAN PASS

Another good, shortish (half-day) walk leads along a well-surfaced forestry track from Glenmore Lodge up towards the **Ryvoan Pass**, taking in An Lochan Uaine, known as the "Green Loch" and living up to its name, with amazing colours that range from turquoise to slate grey depending on the weather.

MEALL A'BHUACHALLIE

The **Glenmore Forest Park Visitor Centre** (daily 9am–5pm; ☎ 01479 861220, ☒ forestry.gov .uk) by the roadside at the turn-off to *Glenmore Lodge* is the starting point for the three-hour round-trip climb of **Meall a'Bhuachallie** (2654ft), which offers excellent views and is usually accessible year-round. The centre has information on other trails in this section of the forest.

2

accommodation booking service and reams of leaflets on local attractions.

By bus The most useful local bus route is the #31, which runs hourly from Aviemore to the Cairn Gorm Mountain Railway (see p.167) via Rothiemurchus and Loch Morlich. The #34 service is also handy, running regularly (roughly hourly) to Grantown via Boat of Garten.

ACTIVITIES

SKIING

For an overview of skiing and snowboarding in the area, including the latest road and slope conditions, check out Visit Scotland's dedicated winter sports website (ⓦ ski .visitscotland.com).

G2 Outdoor Plot 10, Dalfaber Industrial Estate, Aviemore ☏ 01479 811008, ⓦ g2outdoor.co.uk. The experts at G2 Outdoor will provide one-to-one tuition in the art of telemarking (£120/2hr) and back-country skiing. In summer, they also run kayaking and canyoning trips.

Mountain Spirit 98 Grampian Rd ☏ 01479 811788, ⓦ mountainspirit.co.uk. If you want to buy or rent equipment, from ski boots and poles to mountaineering gear, pay a visit to this friendly and well-stocked shop in the centre of Aviemore. Daily 9am–5.30pm.

The Ski School In the Day Lodge, near the funicular railway's base station in the Cairngorm Ski Area ☏ 08455 191191, ⓦ theskischool.co.uk. A good bet for ski/board rental and lessons, not least because of its proximity to the funicular, which whizzes skiers up to the slopes. Courses run mid-Dec–early April.

CYCLING

Bothy Bikes 5 Granish Way, Dalfaber, half a mile north of Aviemore's train station ☏ 01479 810111, ⓦ bothy bikes.co.uk. For the best advice, including guiding, maps and high-quality (front suspension) bike rental (£20/day), stop in at Bothy Bikes. Daily 9am–5.30pm.

OUTDOOR TRAINING

National Outdoor Training Centre Glenmore Lodge,

8 miles east of Aviemore ☏ 01479 861256, ⓦ glenmore lodge.org.uk. For a crash course in surviving Scottish winters, you could do worse than try a week at the National Outdoor Training Centre, at the east end of Loch Morlich. This superbly equipped and organized centre (complete with cosy après-ski bar) offers winter and summer courses in hillwalking, mountaineering, alpine ski-mountaineering, avalanche awareness and much more.

HORSERIDING

Alvie Stables 5 miles south of Aviemore, near Kincraig ☏ 07831 495397, ⓦ alvie-estate.co.uk. Family-friendly riding centre set in superb countryside a short drive from Aviemore, offering 30-minute lessons and longer guided rides (£25/hr).

WATERSPORTS

Loch Insh Watersports Centre 6 miles up-valley near Kincraig ☏ 01540 651272, ⓦ lochinsh.com. Offers sailing, windsurfing and canoeing trips and rents mountain bikes (£19/day), as well as boats for fishing. To save visitors travelling back and forth from Aviemore, the centre also offers accommodation (see p.172).

FISHING

Rothiemurchus Estate Inverdruie ☏ 01479 810703, ⓦ rothiemurchus.com. Has a stocked rainbow trout-fishing loch, where success is virtually guaranteed. A one-hour lesson followed by an hour's fishing costs £45. July & Aug 9.30am–9pm; Sept–June 9.30am–5.30pm.

ACCOMMODATION

HOTELS AND B&BS

★ **Corrour House Hotel** Inverdruie, 2 miles southeast of Aviemore ☏ 01479 810220, ⓦ corrourhousehotel .co.uk. A secluded small hotel, surrounded by countryside, with a nice, classy vibe. Good choice if you want to avoid staying in the centre of town. **£96**

Glenmore Lodge 8 miles east of Aviemore ☏ 01479 861256, ⓦ glenmorelodge.org.uk. Specialist outdoor pursuits centre with excellent accommodation in en-suite twin rooms and self-catered lodges – guests can make use of the superb facilities, which include a pool, weights room, sauna and indoor climbing wall. Twin **£74**; 4-berth chalet **£545**/week

Ravenscraig Guest House 141 Grampian Rd ☏ 01479 810278, ⓦ aviemoreonline.com. This welcoming, family-friendly B&B has a handy central location. Single, double and family rooms available, plus a wide choice of breakfast options, including sausages bought from a local butcher. **£80**

HOSTELS AND BUNKHOUSES

Aviemore Bunkhouse Dalfaber Rd, next to the Old Bridge Inn ☏ 01479 811181, ⓦ aviemore-bunkhouse .com. A large modern place beside a cosy pub and within walking distance of the station, with 6- and 8-bed dorms, as well as private rooms. Dorms **£19**; doubles **£50**

CLOCKWISE FROM TOP CYCLISTS ON THE AVIEMORE TO BOAT OF GARTEN ROUTE (P.171); LAKE OF MENTEITH (P.137); FALLS OF DOCHART (P.144) >

2

Aviemore SYHA 25 Grampian Rd ☎01479 810345, ⓦsyha.org.uk. Aviemore's large SYHA hostel, with its own bike store and drying room, has rather plain rooms but is within easy walking distance of the town centre. Dorms £17; twins £45

Cairngorm Lodge 6.5 miles east of Aviemore, by Loch Morlich ☎01479 861238, ⓦsyha.org.uk. A SYHA hostel towards the Cairngorms at Loch Morlich, located in an old shooting lodge. Feb–Oct, plus weekends

in Jan. Dorms £17; twins £45

CAMPING

Rothiemurchus Caravan Park 2 miles southeast of Aviemore in Coylumbridge ☎01479 812800, ⓦrothiemurchus.net. Relaxed site for tents and caravans, nestled among tall pine trees at Coylumbridge on the way to Loch Morlich. £10/person

EATING AND DRINKING

★ **Mountain Café** 111 Grampian Rd ☎01479 812473. Above the Cairngorm Mountain Sports shop in the centre of town, Kiwi-run *Mountain Café* is reasonably priced, serving an all-day menu of wholesome snacks (scones cost £1.60) and freshly prepared meals. Specializes in wheat- and gluten-free food. Mon & Fri–Sun 8.30am–5.30pm, Tues–Thurs 8.30am–5pm.

Old Bridge Inn Dalfaber Rd, next to Aviemore Bunkhouse ☎01479 811137. Fire-warmed pub that hosts regular live music sessions and serves up decent

dinners; the menu includes a whole grilled sea bream with new potatoes and dressed leaves for £16. Mon–Thurs & Sun noon–midnight, Fri & Sat noon–1am.

Super Panther Bar & Kitchen 12–13 Aviemore Centre, Grampian Rd ☎01479 811670. Unexpectedly cool bar that wouldn't look out of place in Camden or Brooklyn, selling waffles, pancakes and smoothies (£3.50) as well as burgers (£10 with chips and a drink) and cocktails (£6.50). Mon–Thurs & Sun 10am–9.30pm, Fri & Sat 10am–1am.

Carrbridge

Worth considering as an alternative to Aviemore – particularly as a skiing base – **CARRBRIDGE** is a pleasant, quiet village about seven miles north. Look out for the spindly Bridge of Carr at the northern end of the village, built in 1717 and still making a graceful stone arch over the River Dulnain.

Landmark Forest Adventure Park

Just off the B9153 at the southern end of the village • Daily: April to mid-July 10am–5/6pm; mid-July to Aug 10am–7pm; Sept–March 10am–5pm • £11.55 • ☎08007 313446, ⓦlandmarkpark.co.uk

The main attraction in the village is the **Landmark Forest Adventure Park**, which offers families a host of excellent outdoor and indoor activities including forest walks, nature trails, water fun rides and a vertiginous wooden tower with 360-degree views of the surrounding mountains.

ARRIVAL AND DEPARTURE   CARRBRIDGE

By train The train station is around half a mile west of the village centre, served by trains from Aviemore (5–6 daily; 10min) and Inverness (4–5 daily; 30min).

By bus Frequent buses (every 1–2hr; 15min) connect Aviemore with the car park that lies 200m south of the river on the B9153.

ACCOMMODATION

MellonPatch Station Rd, roughly halfway between the train station and the Bridge of Carr ☎01479 841592, ⓦmellonpatch.com. Rambling house with good, large

rooms and friendly owners. The rates, including a full Scottish breakfast, are low for this area. £60

Boat of Garten

Seven miles northeast of Aviemore, close to the River Spey, is the attractive village of **BOAT OF GARTEN**, which has a number of good accommodation options. A short drive or pleasant walk away on the other side of the river is the northeastern shore of **Loch Garten**, famous as the nesting site of the osprey, one of Britain's rarest birds.

Abernethy Forest RSPB Reserve

2.5 miles east of Boat of Garten, on the northeastern shore of Loch Garten • Reserve open year-round; Visitor centre April–Aug daily 10am–6pm • £4 • 3hr guided walks late May to early Aug Wed 9.30am; £5 • ☎ 01479 831476, ⦿ rspb.org.uk

A little over fifty years ago, the **osprey**, known in North America as the fish hawk, had completely disappeared from the British Isles. Then, in 1954, a single pair of these exquisite white-and-brown raptors mysteriously reappeared and built a nest in a tree half a mile or so from Loch Garten, now the location of the **Abernethy Forest RSPB Reserve**. One year's eggs fell victim to thieves, and thereafter the area became the centre of an effective high-security operation. There are now believed to be up to three hundred pairs nesting across the UK. The best time to visit is between April and August, when the ospreys return from West Africa to nest and the RSPB opens an **observation centre**, complete with powerful telescopes and CCTV monitoring of the nest. The reserve is also home to several other rare species, including the Scottish crossbill, capercaillie, whooper swan and red squirrel. Once-weekly **guided walks** leave from the observation centre, while during the spring lekking season (April to mid-May) when male capercaillie gather and joust with each other, the centre opens at 5.30am for "Caperwatch".

ARRIVAL AND INFORMATION

BOAT OF GARTEN

By bus Buses from Aviemore run hourly to Boat of Garten, stopping outside the post office on Deshar Rd.

By train Strathspey Steam Railway trains (see p.166) stop at the attractive old station in the centre of the village (3 daily July & Aug, less frequent at other times; 15min to Aviemore; 25min to Broomhill).

Bike rental From Cairngorm Bike and Hire near the station (daily July & Aug 9.30am–5.30pm; limited hours at other times; ☎ 01479 831745, ⦿ cairngormbikeandhike .co.uk) for £16/day.

ACCOMMODATION AND EATING

Anderson's Deshar Rd, 300m west of the station ☎ 01479 831466, ⦿ andersonsrestaurant.co.uk. Attractive place for lunch or dinner, serving creative dishes based on local ingredients, like their Highland lamb, rosemary and root vegetable hotpot (£14.95). Daily noon–1.45pm & 6–9.30pm.

Boat Hotel Across from the train station ☎ 01479 831258, ⦿ boathotel.co.uk. The most elegant place to stay in the village, with fresh, airy bedrooms. The hotel also has a bistro serving its own interpretations of Scottish favourites – from Cullen skink to chicken tikka masala. **£110**

Fraoch Lodge 15 Deshar Rd ☎ 01479 831331, ⦿ scotmountainholidays.com. Excellent hostel providing high-quality home-cooked meals along with good facilities such as a purpose-built drying room. Enthusiastically run by experienced mountaineers, who also offer guided walking holidays. Minimum stay of two nights when booking in advance; please note that prices quoted here are per night, based on a two-night stay. Singles **£21**; twins **£42**

Old Ferryman's House Just east of the village, across the Spey ☎ 01479 831370. A wonderfully simple, and homely B&B, with an old-school approach: no TVs, lots of books, and delicious evening meals and breakfasts. **£70**

Kincraig

Around **KINCRAIG**, six miles southwest of Aviemore on the B9152 towards Kingussie, there are a couple of unusual encounters with animals which offer a memorable diversion if you're not setting off on outdoor pursuits.

Highland Wildlife Park

2 miles southwest of Kincraig • Daily: June–Aug 10am–6pm; April, May, Sept & Oct 10am–5pm; Nov–March 10am–4pm; last entry 1hr before closing • £14 • ☎ 01540 65127, ⦿ highlandwildlifepark.org

Run by the Royal Zoological Society of Scotland, the **Highland Wildlife Park** is a safari park and zoo, offering visitors the chance to see wolves and bison, as well as many rarely seen natives, including pine martens, capercaillie, wildcats and eagles. The park also runs photography tours and "keeper for a day" experiences with the chance to feed tigers.

2

Working Sheepdogs

Leault Farm, Kincraig • May–Oct Mon–Fri & Sun 4pm • £5 • ☎ 01540 651402, ⓦ leaultworkingsheepdogs.co.uk

Nearby, the engrossing **Working Sheepdogs** demonstrations at Leault Farm afford the rare opportunity to see a champion shepherd herd a flock of sheep with up to eight dogs, using whistles and other commands. The fascinating 45-minute-long display also includes a chance to see traditional hand-shearing, duck-herding and collie-pup training.

ACCOMMODATION AND EATING

Loch Insh Watersports Centre ☎ 01540 651272, ⓦ lochinsh.com. This popular activity centre (see p.168) has basic but practical B&B rooms, some with en-suite bathrooms, as well as an all-day restaurant serving burgers and the like for around £8. Daily 10am–8pm. **£36.25**

Grantown-on-Spey

Around fifteen miles northeast of Aviemore, the pretty town of **GRANTOWN-ON-SPEY** makes a good alternative base for exploring the Strathspey area. Local life is concentrated around the central square, with its attractive Georgian architecture, but there are plenty of opportunities for hiking and biking in the immediate area.

ARRIVAL AND INFORMATION

By bus Buses from Aviemore (roughly hourly; 35min) and Inverness (at least 2 per day Mon–Sat; 1hr 10min) stop on Grantown-on-Spey's High St.
Tourist office 54 High St (April–June, Sept & Oct Mon–Sat 9.30am–5pm, Sun 10am–3pm; July & Aug Mon–Sat 9am–5.30pm, Sun 10am–4pm; ☎ 01479 872242, ⓦ grantown

onspey.com). Grantown's seasonal tourist office has leaflets on local attractions, as well as maps of the area.
Bike rental Good bikes and decent coffee at BaseCamp Bikes (Mon–Sat 9.30am–5.30pm, Sun 10am–5pm; £25/day; ☎ 01479 870050, ⓦ basecampmtb.com), next door to the Co-op convenience store on the town's main square.

ACCOMMODATION

Dunallan House Woodside Ave ☎ 01479 872140, ⓦ dunallan.com. Large house with big double rooms, all en-suite or with private facilities, and comfy, welcoming lounges to relax in. The room on the top floor, with a free-standing bathtub across the landing, is the pick of the bunch. **£86**
Garth Hotel Castle Rd, north end of the town square ☎ 01479 872 836, ⓦ garthhotel.com. If you're after some reasonably swish accommodation head for the large

seventeenth-century *Garth Hotel,* where the restaurant serves respectable, traditional meat-based dinners. **£95**
Lazy Duck Hostel A few miles south of town, at Nethy Bridge ☎ 01479 821642, ⓦ lazyduck.co.uk. Tiny, eight-bed hostel with its own sauna. Makes a peaceful and comfortable retreat with woodland camping and great moorland walking on its doorstep. May–Oct. Dorms **£15**; camping **£15**/pitch

EATING

Craig Bar Woodside Ave ☎ 01479 872669. Snug pub full of military aviation memorabilia, from pictures of fighter planes to dangling model aircraft. Warm yourself by the fire with a pint of real ale, and choose some food. The choice is made easy: the jovial landlord only sells pies (£7.50). Mon–Fri 5pm–midnight, Sat & Sun 11am–midnight.

Revack Highland Estate 2 miles south of town on the B970 ☎ 01479 872234. At this café-cum-gift-shop on the 350-acre Revack estate you can watch red squirrels at play as you tuck into a fresh herring salad with mustard and dill (£7.95). Daily 10am–5pm.

Kingussie

Twelve miles southwest of Aviemore at the head of the Strathspey Valley, **KINGUSSIE** (pronounced "king-yoos-ee") is a pleasant village best known for the free-to-access ruins of Ruthven Barracks, which stand east across the river on a hillock. The best-preserved garrison built to pacify the Highlands after the 1715 rebellion, it makes for great exploring by day and is impressively floodlit at night.

ARRIVAL AND DEPARTURE
KINGUSSIE

By train Kingussie's train station is on Station Rd, just south of the A86.
Destinations Edinburgh (Mon–Sat 7 daily, 5 on Sun; 2hr 40min); Glasgow (Mon–Sat 4 daily, 2 on Sun; 2hr 30min); Inverness (Mon–Sat 12 daily, 7 on Sun; 55min); Newtonmore (Mon–Sat 5 daily, 3 on Sun; 5min).

By bus Buses arrive and depart from near the *Duke of Gordon Hotel*, on the High St.
Destinations Edinburgh (5 daily; 3hr 30min); Inverness (Mon–Sat 8 daily, Sun 5 daily; 1hr); Newtonmore (roughly hourly; 5min).

ACCOMMODATION

★ **The Cross** North of the centre off Ardbroilach Rd ☎01540 661166, ⓦthecross.co.uk. One of the most appealing places to stay in the whole of Speyside, this relaxed but stylish restaurant with rooms is located in a converted tweed mill on the banks of the River Gynack. The superb restaurant (see below) is open to non-residents. **£120**

The Laird's Bothy 68 High St ☎01540 661334, ⓦthetipsylaird.co.uk. For a cheap, comfortable bed try this hostel on the High St. It's attached to the *Tipsy Laird* pub, which hosts occasional jam sessions and karaoke nights. Dorms **£17**

EATING AND DRINKING

The Cross North of the centre off Ardbroilach Rd ☎01540 661166, ⓦthecross.co.uk. The most ambitious (and pricey) restaurant in the area, where a three-course meal carefully crafted from fresh Scottish ingredients like Shetland lobster and Perthshire lamb costs £50. Daily 7–8.30pm.

The Potting Shed 84 High St. Cute little tearoom with teacups hanging in the window. Good spot for a drink, but your main objective should be devouring one of the tasty, wheat-free cakes with fruity fillings (£4.50). Mon & Thurs–Sun 9.30am–5pm.

Tipsy Laird 68 High St ☎01540 661334. This pub is a good spot for a light lunch or an inexpensive evening meal; it's £6.75 for a plate of haggis, neeps and tatties with gravy and oatcakes. Mon–Wed noon–midnight, Thurs–Sat noon–1am, Sun 12.30pm–midnight.

Newtonmore

Kingussie's closest neighbour, **NEWTONMORE**, is also its biggest rival. The two villages, separated by a couple of miles of farmland, both have long-established shinty teams that battle for dominance in the game, a fierce indigenous sport from which ice hockey and golf evolved. Newtonmore itself is notable for its top-notch folk museum, and there are plenty of rough-and-ready mountain biking routes in the forests to the south.

Highland Folk Museum

Kingussie Rd • Daily: April–Aug 10.30am–5.30pm; Sept & Oct 11am–4.30pm • Free; donation requested • ⓦhighlandfolk.com

Newtonmore's chief attraction is the excellent **Highland Folk Museum**. The outdoor site is a living history museum, with reconstructions of a working croft, a water-powered sawmill and a church where recitals on traditional Highland instruments are given.

Laggan Wolftrax

8 miles southwest of Newtonmore on the A86, just beyond the junction with the A889 from Dalwhinnie • Free; car parking £3/day • ☎01463 791575, ⓦwww.forestry.gov.uk

Laggan Wolftrax is a superb, free facility with more than twenty miles of marked mountain-biking trails to suit all abilities. The three-mile-long green route is the best place for those starting out, but expert riders might prefer the gruelling black route, which traverses a steep and rocky staircase made up of uneven slabs.

ARRIVAL AND INFORMATION
NEWTONMORE

By train The train station is south of the centre on Station Rd.
Destinations Edinburgh (Mon–Sat 3 daily, 2 on Sun; 2hr 30min); Glasgow (Mon–Sat 2 daily, 1 on Sun; 2hr 20min); Inverness (Mon–Sat 5 daily, 3 on Sun; 55min); Kingussie (Mon–Sat 5 daily, 3 on Sun; 5min).

By bus Buses for Edinburgh and Inverness arrive and depart from Main St.
Destinations Edinburgh (Mon–Fri 5 daily; 3hr 25min); Inverness (Mon–Sat 8 daily, Sun 5 daily; 1hr 10min); Kingussie (roughly hourly; 5min).

2

Tourist information For information, including maps of walking trails that pass local waterfalls and forests, try the volunteer-run Wildcat Centre on Main St (June–Aug Mon & Thurs 9.30am–12.30pm, Tues & Sat 9.30am–12.30pm & 2–5pm; Sept–May Mon, Thurs & Sat 9.30am–12.30pm; ☎ 01540 673131).

ACCOMMODATION

Coig Na Shee Laggan Rd, a 10min walk west of Main St ☎ 01540 670109, ⓦ coignashee.co.uk. A soothingly decorated B&B in an old Edwardian hunting lodge. Bright rooms with free wi-fi and good en-suite facilities. **£75**

The Pottery Bunkhouse 8 miles south of Newtonmore at Laggan Bridge ☎ 01528 544231, ⓦ potterybunkhouse .co.uk. The most convenient accommodation for Laggan Wolftrax, with an excellent coffee shop, good-value rooms and even an outdoor hot tub (extra charge); bedding £4 extra. Dorms **£12**

Speyside

Strictly speaking, the term **Speyside** refers to the entire region surrounding the River Spey, but to most people the name is synonymous with the **"whisky triangle"**, stretching from just north of Craigellachie, down towards Tomintoul in the south and east to Huntly. Indeed, there are more whisky distilleries and famous brands (including Glenfiddich, Glenlivet and Macallan) concentrated in this small area than in any other part of the country. Running through the heart of the region is the River Spey, whose clean, clear, fast-running waters play a vital part in the whisky industry and are also home to thousands of salmon, making it one of Scotland's finest angling locations. Obviously fertile, the tranquil glens of the area have none of the ruggedness of other parts of the Highlands; tourism blends into a local economy kept healthy by whisky and farming, rather than dominating it.

At the centre of Speyside is the quiet market town of **Dufftown**, full of solid, stone-built workers' houses and dotted with no fewer than nine whisky distilleries. Along with the well-kept nearby villages of **Craigellachie** and **Aberlour**, it makes the best base for a tour of whisky country, whether on the official Malt Whisky Trail or more independent explorations. Fewer visitors take the chance to discover the more remote glens, such as **Glenlivet**, which push higher up towards the Cairngorm massif, nestled into which is Britain's highest village, **Tomintoul**, situated on the edge of both whisky country and a large expanse of wild uplands. The **Speyside Way**, one of Scotland's long-distance footpaths, offers the chance to enjoy the scenery of the region, as well as its whiskies, on foot.

Dufftown

The cheery community of **DUFFTOWN**, founded in 1817 by James Duff, fourth Earl of Fife, proudly proclaims itself "Malt Whisky Capital of the World" for the reason that it produces more of the stuff than any other town in Britain. A more telling statistic, perhaps, is that as a result Dufftown also reportedly raises more capital for the exchequer per head of population than anywhere else in the country. There are seven active distilleries around Dufftown, as well as a cooperage, and an extended stroll around the outskirts of the town gives a good idea of the density of whisky distilling going on, with glimpses of giant warehouses and whiffs of fermenting barley or peat smoke lingering on the breeze. On the edge of town along the A941 is the town's largest working distillery, **Glenfiddich** (see box, p.177).

There isn't a great deal to do in the town itself, but it's a useful starting point for orienting yourself towards the whisky trail. Dufftown's four main streets converge on its main square, scene of a lively annual party on Hogmanay when free drams are handed out to revellers. Another major event is the **Spirit of Speyside Whisky Festival** (ⓦ spiritofspeyside .com), which draws whisky experts and enthusiasts to the area in early May. A separate festival, marked by special "nosing" events, takes place at the end of September.

Whisky Museum

24 Fife St • Daily 10am–4/5pm • Free

The small, volunteer-run **Whisky Museum** has a slightly disorganized collection of illicit distilling equipment, most of it donated by local distilleries. There are also plenty of old books and photographs, which help to give visitors a flavour of the industry's humble beginnings.

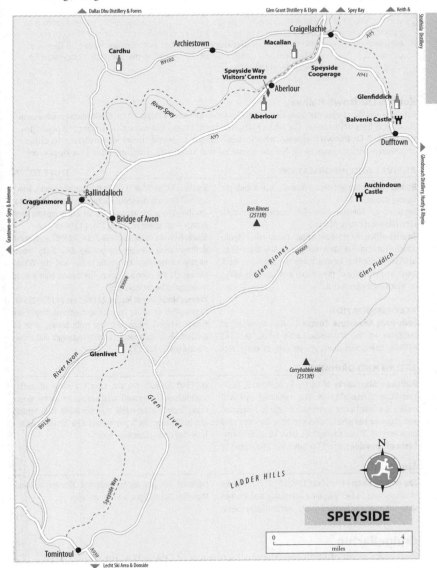

2

THE SPEYSIDE WAY

The **Speyside Way** (W speysideway.org), with its beguiling blend of mountain, river, wildlife and whisky, is fast establishing itself as an appealing and less taxing alternative to the popular West Highland and Southern Upland long-distance footpaths. Starting at **Buckie** on the Moray Firth coast, it follows the fast-flowing River Spey from its mouth at Spey Bay south to **Aviemore** (see p.165), with branches linking it to **Dufftown**, Scotland's malt whisky capital, and **Tomintoul** on the remote edge of the Cairngorm mountains. Some 65 miles long without taking on the branch routes, the whole thing is a five- to seven-day expedition, but its proximity to main roads and small villages means that it is excellent for shorter walks or even bicycle trips, especially in the heart of **distillery** country between Craigellachie and Glenlivet; Glenfiddich, Glenlivet, Macallan and Cardhu distilleries, as well as the Speyside Cooperage, lie directly on or a short distance off the route.

Keith & Dufftown Railway

Station Rd • April–Sept 3 trips on Sat & Sun; June–Aug also Fri • 40min • £10 return • ☎ 01340 821181, W keith-dufftown-railway.co.uk

Restored by enthusiasts, the old Dufftown train station is now the departure point for the **Keith & Dufftown Railway**, which uses various restored diesel locomotives to chug through whisky country to Keith, home of the Strathisla distillery (see box opposite).

ARRIVAL AND INFORMATION   DUFFTOWN

By bus Buses arrive and depart from the road outside the railway station.
Destinations Aberlour (Mon–Sat hourly; 10–15min); Elgin (Mon–Sat hourly; 50min).
Tourist office The small but helpful tourist office (April–June & Sept Mon–Sat 10am–4pm; July & Aug 10am–5pm; ☎ 01340 820501) is located inside the handsome clock tower at the centre of the square, and can offer advice on which distilleries to visit.

ACCOMMODATION

Loch Park Adventure Centre 3 miles northeast of Dufftown on the Drummuir Castle Estate ☎ 01542 810334, W lochpark.co.uk. It's possible to camp, rent

kayaks (£12) and fish (£18) at this outdoor centre, which has self-catering bunkhouse accommodation. Unfortunately there's no public transport this far, and groups are given priority – so call ahead. Dorms £15; £12/pitch
Morven On the main square ☎ 01340 820507, W morven dufftown.co.uk. Simple, inexpensive B&B that's conveniently located near the tourist office and the Whisky Museum in the middle of town. The owners offer a small reduction for longer stays. £50
Tannochbrae Guest House 22 Fife St ☎ 01340 820541, W tannochbrae.co.uk. Pleasant and enthusiastically run former provost's house near the main square, with six comfortable en-suite rooms, a lovely restaurant and a well-stocked whisky bar. £73

EATING AND DRINKING

Dufftown Glassworks 16 Conval St ☎ 01340 821534, W dufftownglassworks.com. This combined café and gallery is a smart place to sit with a latte or Americano and plan your trip around whisky country. The rocky road slices here (£1.80) are scrumptious. Daily 10.30am–5pm.
Taste of Speyside Just off The Square at 10 Balverie St

☎ 01340 820860. You can sample a range of quality Scottish food at the town's most popular restaurant, where mains include a vegetable crumble made with tomato and basil sauce. You'll pay around £20 for two courses. Tues–Sat noon–2pm & 6–9pm.

SHOPPING

The Whisky Shop 1 Fife St ☎ 01340 821 097, W whisky shopdufftown.co.uk. This mind-bogglingly well-stocked shop has over six hundred malts and umpteen beers,

produced not just on Speyside but all over Scotland. Mon–Sat 10am–6pm, Sun 10am–5pm.

Craigellachie

Four miles north of Dufftown, the small settlement of **CRAIGELLACHIE** (pronounced "Craig-*ell*-ach-ee") sits above the confluence of the sparkling waters of the Fiddich and the Spey. From the village, you can look down on a beautiful iron bridge over the Spey built by Thomas Telford in 1815. The local distillery isn't open to the public, though Glen Grant (see box below) with its attractive gardens is only a few miles up the road at Rothes.

Speyside Cooperage

Dufftown Rd • Mon–Fri 9am–4pm (last tour 3.30pm) • £3.50 • ⓦ speysidecooperage.co.uk

For an unusual alternative to a distillery tour, the **Speyside Cooperage** is well worth a visit. After a short exhibition explaining the ancient and skilled art of cooperage,

2

TOURING MALT WHISKY COUNTRY

Speyside is the heart of Scotland's **whisky** industry, and the presence of more than fifty distilleries is testimony to a unique combination of clear, clean water, benign climate and gentle upland terrain. Yet for all the advertising-influenced visions of timeless traditions, whisky is a multimillion-pound business dominated by huge corporations, and to many working distilleries visitors are an afterthought, if not a downright nuisance. That said, plenty are located in attractive historic buildings that now go to some lengths to provide an engaging experience for visitors. Mostly this involves a tour around the essential stages in the whisky-making process, though a number of distilleries now offer pricier connoisseur tours with a tutored tasting (or **nosing**, as it's properly called) and in-depth studies of the distiller's art. Some tours have restrictions on children.

There are eight distilleries on the official **Malt Whisky Trail** (ⓦ maltwhiskytrail.com), a clearly signposted seventy-mile meander around the region. These are Benromach, Cardhu, Dallas Dhu Historic Distillery, Glenfiddich, Glen Grant, Glenlivet, Glen Moray and Strathisla. Unless you're seriously interested in whisky, it's best to just pick out a couple that appeal. All offer a guided tour, and at most places – but not all – it's okay to turn up without booking. You could cycle or walk parts of the route, using the Speyside Way (see box opposite). The following is a list of selected highlights from the area; not all are on the official trail.

Cardhu On the B9102 at Knockando ☎ 01479 874635, ⓦ discovering-distilleries.com/cardhu. Established over a century ago, when the founder's wife would raise a red flag to warn crofters if the authorities were on the lookout for their illegal stills. With attractive, pagoda-topped buildings, it sells rich, full-bodied whisky with distinctive peaty flavours that comes in an attractive bulbous bottle; £5 including voucher. April & May Mon–Fri 10am–5pm; June–Aug Mon–Thurs & Sat 10am–5pm, Fri 10am–7pm, Sun 11am–4pm; Sept Mon–Sat 10am–5pm, Sun 11am–4pm; Oct–March Mon–Fri 11am–3pm; tours at 11am, noon, 1pm & 2pm.

Glen Grant Rothes ☎ 01340 832118, ⓦ glengrant .com. Makes a well-known, floral whisky aggressively marketed to the younger customer. The highlight here is the attractive Victorian gardens, a mix of well-tended lawns and mixed, mature trees which include a tumbling waterfall and a hidden whisky safe; £3.50 including voucher. Mid-Jan to mid-Dec Mon–Sat 9.30am–5pm, Sun noon–5pm.

Glenfiddich On the A941 just north of Dufftown ☎ 01340 820373, ⓦ glenfiddich.com. The biggest and slickest of all the Speyside distilleries, despite the fact that it's still owned by the same Grant family who founded it in 1887. It's a light, sweet whisky packaged in triangular bottles – unusually, the bottling is still done on the premises and is part of the tours (offered in various languages); free. Daily 9.30am–4.30pm.

Glendronach 8 miles northeast of Huntly ☎ 01466 730202, ⓦ glendronachdistillery.com. Off the official trail, this isolated distillery makes much of the fact that, uniquely, its stills are heated in the traditional method by coal fires; £5. Booking essential. May–Sept daily 10am–4.30pm; Oct–April Mon–Fri 10am–4.30pm.

Glenlivet On the B9008 to Tomintoul ☎ 01340 821720, ⓦ theglenlivet.com. A famous name in a lonely hillside setting. This was the first licensed distillery in the Highlands, following the 1823 act that aimed to reduce illicit distilling and smuggling. The Glenlivet 12-year-old malt is a floral, fragrant, medium-bodied whisky; free. April–Oct Mon–Sat 9.30am–5pm, Sun noon–5pm.

Speyside Cooperage See above.

Strathisla Keith ☎ 01542 783044. A small, old-fashioned distillery claiming to be Scotland's oldest (1786); it's certainly one of the most attractive, with the River Isla rushing by. Inside there's an old-fashioned mashtun and brass-bound spirit safes. You can arrive here on one of the restored trains of the Keith & Dufftown Railway (see opposite); £6. Booking advised. April–Oct Mon–Sat 9.30am–5pm, Sun noon–5pm.

Macallan Near Craigellachie ☎ 01340 872 280, ⓦ themacallan.com. Small tours, and a classy whisky aged in sherry casks to give it a rich colour and flavour. £10. Booking essential. April–Aug Mon–Sat 9.30am–4.30pm; Sept & Oct Mon–Fri 9.30am–4.30pm; Nov–March Mon–Fri 11am–3pm.

you're shown onto a balcony overlooking the large workshop where the oak casks for whisky are made and repaired.

ARRIVAL AND DEPARTURE   CRAIGELLACHIE

By bus Buses for Dufftown (hourly; 10min) arrive and depart from Edward Avenue (the A941) in Craigellachie.

ACCOMMODATION AND EATING

Archiestown Hotel In Archiestown, a few miles west of Craigellachie ☎01340 810218, ⓦarchiestownhotel .co.uk. This traditional place serves good evening meals and has some comfy rooms upstairs. In good weather, it's also a fine spot for alfresco dining. **£180**

Craigellachie Hotel Victoria St ☎08431 787114, ⓦbespokehotels.com/craigellachiehotel. Near the River Spey, this grand nineteenth-century hotel is the epitome of sumptuous Scottish hospitality, with classy cuisine and a bar lined with whisky bottles. **£140**

Fiddichside Inn On the A95 just outside Craigellachie ☎01340 881239. A wonderfully original and convivial pub with a garden by the river; quite unfazed by the demands of fashion, it has been in the hands of the same family since 1919. You'll pay about £3.10 for a pint of ale. Mon–Fri 11am–2.30pm & 5–11pm, Sat 11am– midnight, Sun 12.30–11pm.

Highlander Inn On Victoria St in Craigellachie ☎01340 881446, ⓦwhiskyinn.com. Upscale pub grub is served at basement level in this tartan-strewn pub, including locally "caught" haggis for £10. There are reasonable rooms on the ground floor, though the decor is a little old-fashioned. Food served daily 5.30–9.30pm. **£103**

Aberlour

Two miles southwest from Craigellachie is **ABERLOUR**, officially "Charlestown of Aberlour". Founded in 1812 by Charles Grant, its long main street, neat, flower-filled central square and well-trimmed lawns running down to the Spey have all the markings of a planned village. Though you can visit the distillery here, it's another local product – **shortbread** – that is exported in greater quantity around the world, mostly in tartan tins adorned with kilted warriors. A local baker, **Joseph Walker**, set up shop here at the turn of the twentieth century, quickly gaining a reputation for the product which seems to epitomize the Scottish sweet tooth. If you're keen, you can join the coachloads who visit the factory shop on the outskirts of the village. The town is also right on the Speyside Way (see box, p.176).

ARRIVAL AND ACTIVITIES   ABERLOUR

By bus Local buses stop on The Square, just off the High Street.
Destinations Craigellachie (every 30min; 5min); Dufftown (hourly; 15min).
Moray Monster Trails Ben Aigan car park, off the A95 near Mulben ☎01466 794161, ⓦforestry.gov.uk. Aberlour is just a few miles from the entrance to the extensive Moray Monster (Mountainbike) Trails at Ben Aigen, on which you can test your skills on a variety of challenging single-track bike routes.

ACCOMMODATION AND EATING

Aberlour Gardens Caravan Park ☎01340 871586, ⓦaberlourgardens.co.uk. Though the campsite here is the most pleasant in the area, with its own shop specializing in local produce, it's a walk of a mile and a half from either Aberlour or Craigellachie. March–Dec. **£9.90**/pitch

Mash Tun 8 Broomfield Square ☎01340 881771, ⓦmashtun-aberlour.com. The best place to eat and drink is this pleasant, traditional pub, which serves up freshly prepared bar meals (pan-fried pork steak £9.95), real ales and all the local whiskies in the heart of Aberlour near the Spey; it also has cosy rooms and a luxury suite. Mon–Fri noon–2pm & 6–9pm, Sat & Sun noon–9pm. **£97**

Spey Larder 96 High St ☎01340 871243. There's a good range of produce on offer at this well-stocked deli, right by the village square, including olives, herbs, locally made shortbread and big bottles of ginger ale (£4.95). Mon–Sat 9am–5pm.

Glenlivet

Beyond Aberlour, the Spey and the main road both head generally southwest to Ballindalloch and, a dozen miles beyond that, Grantown-on-Spey, at the head of the

Strathspey region (see p.172). South from Ballindalloch are the quieter, remote glens of the Avon (pronounced "*A'an*") and Livet rivers. Allegedly, in the days of the despised tax excisemen, the Braes of Glenlivet once held over one hundred illicit whisky stills. The (legal) distillery at **GLENLIVET** (see p.177), founded in 1824 by George Smith, is one of the most famous on Speyside, and certainly enjoys one of the more attractive settings.

ARRIVAL AND DEPARTURE	GLENLIVET
By car Public transport in this area is extremely limited, which makes having your own wheels a must. To reach the distillery from Aberlour, follow the A95 south as far as	Ballindalloch (around 8 miles) and then swing left onto the B9008 for the final 4 miles.

2

Tomintoul

Deep into the foothills of the Cairngorms, **TOMINTOUL** (pronounced "*tom*-in-towel") is, at 1150ft, the highest village in the Scottish Highlands, and the northern gateway to the **Lecht Ski Area** (see below). Its long, thin layout is reminiscent of a Wild West frontier town; Queen Victoria wrote that it was "the most tumble-down, poor looking place I ever saw". A spur of the Speyside Way connects Ballindalloch through Glenlivet to Tomintoul, and there are plenty of other terrific walking opportunities in the area, as well as some great routes for mountain biking.

Glenlivet Crown Estate

If you've come this far it's worth exploring the **Glenlivet Crown Estate**, an extensive tract of carefully managed land abutting Tomintoul; information and useful maps about its wildlife (including reindeer) and the numerous paths and bike trails are available from the tourist office or the estate **ranger's office** at the southern end of the long main street.

ARRIVAL AND INFORMATION	TOMINTOUL
By car The only reliable way to reach Tomintoul is by car; from Grantown-on-Spey the A939 snakes east, passing Tomintoul on the way to Ballater.	farm kitchen and a smithie.
Tourist office On the central square, the helpful tourist office (April–Oct Mon–Sat 10am–5pm; ☎ 01309 696261) also acts as the local museum, with mock-ups of an old	**Estate ranger's office** At the southern end of Main St (Mon–Fri 9am–5pm; ☎ 01479 870070, ⓦ glenlivetestate .co.uk). The place to come for information on local walks and events.

ACCOMMODATION

Camping at Glenlivet It is possible to camp beside the Glenlivet Estate ranger's office for free, though there are no facilities here whatsoever.

The Bunkhouse Near the tourist office on the central square ☎ 01807 590752, ☎ 07711 466340. Long, white hut with clean and cheap (if cramped) bunk rooms that share a small kitchen. If no one is around, call for the access

code. Dorms £17

Glenavon On the main square ☎ 01807 580218, ⓦ glenavon-hotel.co.uk. The most convivial of the hotels gathered around the main square, with en-suite rooms above a bar that screens football matches and does cheap lunchtime meals (two for £10). £70

Lecht Ski Area

7 miles southeast of Tomintoul along the A939 • Open year-round • Full-day pass £28; ski rental costs £20/day from the ski school at the base station • For information on skiing and road conditions, call the base station on ☎ 01975 651440 or check ⓦ lecht.co.uk or ⓦ ski.visitscotland.com

The Lecht is the most remote of Scotland's ski areas, but it works hard to make itself appealing with a range of winter and summer activities. While its runs include some gentle beginners' slopes there's little really challenging for experienced skiers other than a Snowboard Fun Park, with specially built jumps and ramps. Snow-making equipment helps extend the snow season beyond January and February, while downhill bike tracks open in the summer (no bike hire on site).

The Great Glen

BUACHAILLE ETIVE MHÒR, GLEN COE

The Great Glen

The Great Glen, a major geological faultline cutting diagonally across the Highlands from Fort William to Inverness, is the defining geographic feature of the north of Scotland. A huge rift valley was formed when the northwestern and southeastern sides of the fault slid in opposite directions for more than sixty miles, while the present landscape was shaped by glaciers that retreated only around 8000 BC. The glen is impressive more for its sheer scale than its beauty, but the imposing barrier of loch and mountain means that no one can travel into the northern Highlands without passing through it. With the two major service centres of the Highlands at either end, it makes an obvious and rewarding route between the west and east coasts.

3

Of the Great Glen's four elongated lochs, the most famous is **Loch Ness**, home to the mythical monster; lochs **Oich**, **Lochy** and **Linnhe** (the last of these a sea loch) are less renowned though no less attractive. All four are linked by the **Caledonian Canal**. The southwestern end of the Great Glen is dominated by the town of **Fort William**, the self-proclaimed "Outdoor Capital of the UK". Situated at the heart of the Lochaber area, it is a utilitarian base, with plenty of places to stay and excellent access to a host of adventure sports. While the town itself is charmless, the surrounding countryside is a magnificent blend of rugged mountain terrain and tranquil sea loch. Dominating the scene to the south is **Ben Nevis**, Britain's highest peak, best approached from scenic Glen Nevis. The most famous glen of all, **Glen Coe**, lies on the main A82 road half-an-hour's drive south of Fort William, the two separated by the coastal inlet of **Loch Leven**. Nowadays the whole area is unashamedly given over to tourism, with Fort William swamped by bus tours throughout the summer, but take a short drive from town and solitude is easy to find.

At the northeastern end of the Great Glen is the capital of the Highlands, **Inverness**, a sprawling city with some decent places to eat; it's most often used as a springboard to remoter areas further north. Inevitably, most transport links to the northern Highlands, including Ullapool, Thurso and the Orkney and Shetland islands, pass through Inverness.

GETTING AROUND THE GREAT GLEN

By car The main A82 road runs the length of the Great Glen, although relatively high traffic levels mean that it's not a fast or particularly easy route to drive.

By bus The Great Glen is reasonably well served by buses, with several daily services between Inverness and Fort William.

By boat The traditional and most rewarding way to travel through the Great Glen is by boat: a flotilla of kayaks, small yachts and pleasure vessels take advantage of the Caledonian Canal and its old wooden locks during the summer.

By bike Well-marked routes make it possible to cycle all the way from Fort William to Inverness.

On foot The 79-mile Great Glen Way links Fort William with Inverness, and takes five to six days to walk in full (see box, p.187).

CRUISE BOAT ON LOCH NESS

Highlights

❶ Commando Memorial An exposed but dramatic place to take in sweeping views over Scotland's highest ben (Nevis) and its longest glen (the Great Glen). **See p.191**

❷ Glen Coe Spectacular, moody, poignant and full of history – a glorious place for hiking or simply absorbing the atmosphere. **See p.193**

❸ Cruise Loch Ness Chances of seeing the famous monster Nessie aren't high, but the on-board sonar images are intriguing and the scenery's fine. **See p.197 & p.199**

❹ Glen Affric Some of Scotland's best-hidden scenery, with ancient Caledonian forests and gushing rivers. **See p.200**

❺ Culloden battlefield Experience the cannon-fire in a "battle immersion theatre" and tramp the heather moor where Bonnie Prince Charlie made his last stand. **See p.208**

❻ Dolphins of the Moray Firth Europe's most northerly school of bottle-nosed dolphin can be seen from the shore or on a boat trip. **See p.208**

HIGHLIGHTS ARE MARKED ON THE MAP ON P.184

Fort William

With its stunning position on Loch Linnhe, tucked in below the snow-streaked bulk of Ben Nevis, **FORT WILLIAM** (known by the many walkers and climbers who come here as "Fort Bill") should be a gem. Sadly, the same lack of taste that nearly saw the town renamed "Abernevis" in the 1950s is evident in the ribbon bungalow development and ill-advised dual carriageway – complete with grubby pedestrian underpass – which have

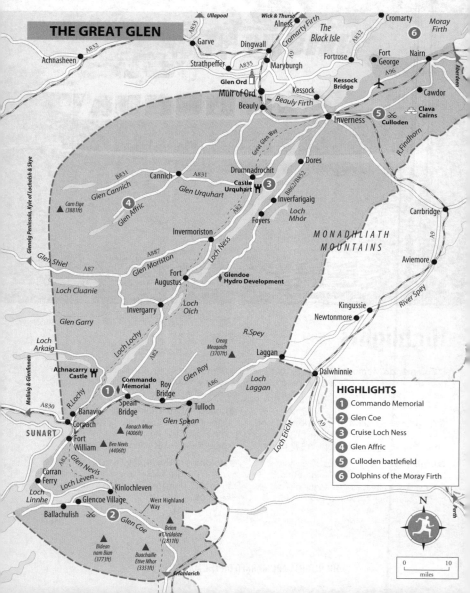

THE GREAT GLEN

HIGHLIGHTS

1. Commando Memorial
2. Glen Coe
3. Cruise Loch Ness
4. Glen Affric
5. Culloden battlefield
6. Dolphins of the Moray Firth

BLOODY TALES BEYOND THE BEAUTY

Although best known for its windswept slopes and glassy lochs, the Great Glen has a turbulent and bloody **history**. Founded in 1655 and named in honour of William III, the town of Fort William was successfully held by government troops during both of the Jacobite risings. The country to the southwest, meanwhile, is inextricably associated with Bonnie Prince Charlie's flight after **Culloden** (see p.208). **Glen Coe** is another historic site with a violent past, renowned as much for the infamous massacre of 1692 as for its magnificent scenery.

---

wrecked the waterfront. The main street and the little squares off it are more appealing, though occupied by some decidedly tacky tourist gift shops. Other than the excellent **museum**, the town is short on must-sees, but it's undeniably a convenient base for outdoor activities – most notably walking. Several cruises leave from the town pier every day, offering the chance to spot the marine life of Loch Linnhe, which includes seals and seabirds. Shops rent out kayaks and mountain bikes for independent exploration of the surrounding area, and local guides run mountaineering courses (in summer and winter) on the slopes of nearby munros.

West Highland Museum

Cameron Square, just off the High St • March, Nov & Dec Mon–Sat 10am–4pm; April–Oct Mon–Sat 10am–5pm • Free • ☎ 01397 702169, ⊚ westhighlandmuseum.org.uk

Collections at the splendid and idiosyncratic **West Highland Museum** cover virtually every aspect of Highland life and the presentation is traditional, but very well done, making a refreshing change from the state-of-the-art heritage centres popping up across Scotland. There's a secret portrait of Bonnie Prince Charlie and the long Spanish rifle used in the famous Appin Murder, and even a 550kg slab of aluminium, the stuff that's processed into silver foil just five miles north of town (you'll see the huge pipes running down the mountainside).

The Jacobite Steam Train

Mid-May to Oct Mon–Fri; mid-June to mid-Sept also Sat & Sun • Departs Fort William 10.20am, return 2.10pm; June–Aug only additional afternoon service departs Fort William 2.30pm, with return at 6.40pm • Return £33 (£56 for first class) • ☎ 0844 850 4685, ⊚ westcoastrailways.co.uk

One enjoyable excursion from town is the 84-mile round-trip to Mallaig (see p.224) on the **West Highland Railway Line** aboard the **Jacobite Steam Train**. Heading along the shore of Loch Eil to the west coast via historic Glenfinnan (see p.221), the train passes through some of the region's most spectacular scenery, though these days it's as popular for its role as the locomotive used in the *Harry Potter* films.

ARRIVAL AND INFORMATION   FORT WILLIAM

By train Just across the A82 dual carriageway from the north end of the High Street you'll find Fort William's train station (one of the stops on the scenic West Highland Railway from Glasgow).

Destinations Crianlarich (Mon–Sat 4 daily, 3 on Sun; 1hr 50min); Glasgow Queen Street (Mon–Sat 3 daily, 2 on Sun; 3hr 50min); London (1 nightly; 12hr); Mallaig (Mon–Sat 4 daily, 3 on Sun; 1hr 20min).

By bus Intercity coaches from Glasgow and Inverness stop outside the train station on MacFarlane Way.

Destinations Drumnadrochit (9 daily; 1hr 25min); Edinburgh (1 daily; 4hr); Fort Augustus (9 daily; 50min);

Glasgow (8 daily; 3hr); Inverness (9 Mon–Sat, 6 Sun; 2hr); Mallaig (Mon–Fri 3 daily; 1hr 20min); Oban (Mon–Sat 3 daily; 1hr 30min); Portree, Skye (4 daily; 3hr).

Tourist office 15 High St (April & May Mon–Sat 9am–5pm, Sun 10am–5pm; June Mon–Sat 9am–6pm, Sun 9.30am–5pm; July & Aug Mon–Sat 9am–6.30pm, Sun 9am–6pm; Sept & Oct Mon–Sat 9am–5pm, Sun 10am–4pm; Nov–March Mon–Sat 9am–5pm, Sun 10am–3pm; ☎ 01397 701801, ⊚ visithighlands.com). Busy and very helpful tourist office, which stocks an excellent selection of maps and guidebooks on exploring the Great Glen. Upstairs you can surf the net (£1/20min).

3

BOAT TOURS AND ACTIVITIES

BOAT TOURS

Crannog Cruises Town Pier ☎01397 703786, ⓦcrannog
.net/cruises. Runs cruises down Loch Linnhe, where you'll
have the chance to spot porpoises and grey seals. Daily trips
(April–Sept; 90min; £12.50) depart from the town pier at
10am, noon, 2pm and 4pm, with additional evening cruises at
7.30pm every Tues, Thurs and Sun during July & Aug at 7.30pm.
Seaventures 3 Kincardine Place ☎01397 701687,
ⓦseaventuresscotland.co.uk. Seaventures offers exhilarating fast boat trips, plus three-and-a-half-hour wildlife cruises
to nearby islands (Mon, Wed & Fri from June–Aug; £30).

MOUNTAIN BIKING

Alpine Bikes 117 High St ☎01397 704008, ⓦalpine
bikes.com; at Nevis Range ☎01397 705825. High-spec
mountain bikes are available for rent at Alpine Bikes (from
£15/day). Staff here know the best routes and can issue
free maps. There's a second branch at the Nevis Range
gondola base station (see p.190) – a location that boasts
forest rides and a world-championship-standard downhill
track. April–Oct: Mon–Sat 9am–5.30pm, Sun 10am–
5.30pm; Nov–March Mon–Sat 9am–5.30pm.

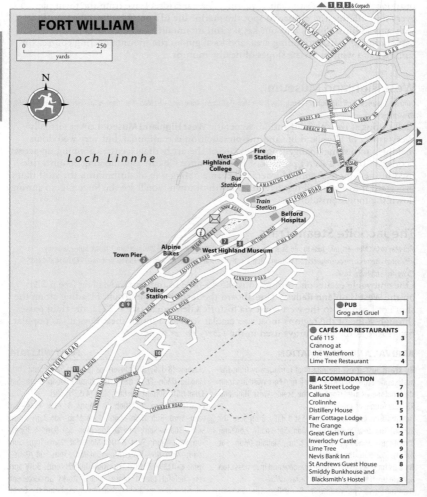

FORT WILLIAM

● PUB

Grog and Gruel	1

● CAFÉS AND RESTAURANTS

Café 115	3
Crannog at the Waterfront	2
Lime Tree Restaurant	4

■ ACCOMMODATION

Bank Street Lodge	7
Calluna	10
Crolinnhe	11
Distillery House	5
Farr Cottage Lodge	1
The Grange	12
Great Glen Yurts	2
Inverlochy Castle	4
Lime Tree	9
Nevis Bank Inn	6
St Andrews Guest House	8
Smiddy Bunkhouse and Blacksmith's Hostel	3

THE GREAT GLEN WAY AND CYCLE PATH

Ordnance Survey Landranger maps 41, 34 and 26

The enormous cleft of the Great Glen is the most obvious – and by far the flattest – way of traversing northern Scotland from coast to coast. Stretching 79 miles, the **Great Glen Way** long-distance footpath is a relatively undemanding five- to six-day hike that uses a combination of canal towpath and forest- and hill-tracks between Fort William and Inverness. Accommodation is readily available all the way along the route in campsites, hostels, bunkhouses and B&Bs, though in high season you should book ahead and if you know you're going to arrive late somewhere it's worth checking that you can still get a meal either where you're staying or somewhere nearby. There are various **guidebooks** that describe the route, including *The Great Glen Way*, published by Rucksack Readers (£10.99). For the best selection of guides, plus the relevant Ordnance Survey Landranger maps (£6.99 each) head to the tourist office in Fort William. Note, however, that forestry work can see the route diverted at short notice, so it's wise to check the official website (ⓦ greatglenway.com) before setting off.

Cyclists with mountain bikes or hybrids can also use the Great Glen Way, which offers a tranquil alternative to the hazardous A82 (currently the only option for those with road bikes). The route is well signposted and can be pedaled in one long day or two easier days, though of course you can tackle shorter sections. Bikes can be rented at Fort William, Banavie, Drumnadrochit and Inverness.

Whether you're cycling or walking, the suggested **direction** for following the route is from west to east, to take advantage of the prevailing southwesterly wind.

3

MOUNTAINEERING

Snowgoose Mountain Centre Station Rd, Corpach ☎ 01397 772467, ⓦ highland-mountain-guides.co.uk. Set beside *Smiddy Bunkhouse and Blacksmith's Hostel*, this activity centre offers instruction, rental and residential courses for activities such as mountaineering, ice-climbing and dinghy sailing.

West Coast Mountain Guides ☎ 01397 719120, ⓦ west coast-mountainguides.co.uk. Long-established group of experienced guides, who run climbing and mountaineering courses throughout the year. A two-day introduction to winter mountaineering costs £120 per person. Trips to Skye (and even the Swiss Alps) can also be arranged.

CANOEING AND KAYAKING

Rockhopper Unit 17, Annat Industrial Estate, Corpach ☎ 07739 837344, ⓦ rockhopperscotland.co.uk. Get in touch with Rockhopper for sea-kayak coaching, including half-day excursions (£40) and two-day camping trips with meals provided (£195 per person).

ACCOMMODATION

The town itself isn't the most exciting place to base yourself, but Fort William's plentiful accommodation ranges from large luxury hotels to budget hostels and bunkhouses. Numerous **B&Bs** are also scattered across town, many of them in the suburb of Corpach on the other side of Loch Linnhe, three miles along the Mallaig road (served by regular buses), where you'll also find a couple of good **hostels**.

HOTELS AND B&BS

Crolinnhe Grange Rd ☎ 01397 703795, ⓦ crolinnhe .co.uk. Beautifully appointed guesthouse overlooking Loch Linnhe, with elegant French furniture in the rooms and attractive landscaped gardens outside. Quite grand and upmarket. Easter–Oct. **£120**

Distillery House North Rd ☎ 01397 700103, ⓦ stayin fortwilliam.co.uk. Very comfortable upper-range guesthouse a 10min walk north of the town centre near the Glen Nevis turn-off, with singles, doubles and more expensive "superior" rooms with king-sized beds. **£99.50**

The Grange Grange Rd ☎ 01397 705516, ⓦ grange fortwilliam.com. Top-grade accommodation in a striking old stone house, with log fires, views towards Loch Linnhe and luxurious en-suite doubles. Vegetarian breakfasts on request. April–Oct. **£116**

Inverlochy Castle Torlundy, 3 miles north of the town centre on the A82 ☎ 01397 702177, ⓦ inverlochy castlehotel.co.uk. Built on the site of a thirteenth-century fortress, this is one of Scotland's grandest and most luxurious country-house hotels with fantastic accommodation and Michelin-star food. **£440**

★ **Lime Tree** Achintore Rd ☎ 01397 701806, ⓦ limetreefortwilliam.co.uk. A stylish and relaxing option in an old manse, with a great modern restaurant and an excellent gallery; they've also got the practicalities covered with a drying room, map room and bike storage. **£110**

3

Nevis Bank Inn Belford Rd ☎ 01397 705721, ⓦ nevis bankinn.co.uk. The small, functional hotel rooms here are a little on the plain side, but they're comfortable and quiet – and the attached restaurant is a convenient place to grab some pasta or a steak. **£144**

St Andrews Guest House Fassifern Rd ☎ 01397 703038, ⓦ standrewsguesthouse.co.uk. Comfortable and very reasonable B&B in a converted granite choir school 5min walk uphill from the High St, featuring various inscriptions and stained-glass windows. **£60**

HOSTELS AND CAMPSITES

Bank Street Lodge Bank St ☎ 01397 700070, ⓦ bank streetlodge.co.uk. A clean and bright 43-bed hostel handy for transport and the town centre. Choose between dorm accommodation and a good range of en-suite rooms. Dorms **£17**; doubles **£55**; singles **£25**

Calluna Heathercroft, Connachie Rd ☎ 01397 700451, ⓦ fortwilliamholiday.co.uk. Well-run self-catering and hostel accommodation a 10min walk from the centre of town, configured for individual, family and group

stays. On-site laundry facilities and a bouldering wall. The owners can also organize mountaineering trips. Dorms **£16**

Farr Cottage Lodge 3.5 miles from Fort William in Corpach, on the main A830 ☎ 01397 772315, ⓦ farr cottage.co.uk. Well-equipped, lively place with range of dorms and double/twin rooms. Offers a multitude of outdoor activities including canyoning and sea-fishing. Dorms **£15**; doubles **£34**

Great Glen Yurts 3 miles northeast of Fort William off A82 (signposted from Torlundy) ⓦ greatglenyurts.com. Rotund and spacious, these luxury yurts occupy a magnificently peaceful setting with views of Ben Nevis. There's an open-sided kitchen for sociable evening meals. April– Oct. **£90**

Smiddy Bunkhouse and Blacksmith's Hostel Snowgoose Mountain Centre, Station Rd, Corpach ☎ 01397 772467, ⓦ highland-mountain-guides.co.uk. Alpine hostel and bunkhouse on the site of an old blacksmith's workshop. It's 4 miles from Ben Nevis at the southwestern end of the Caledonian Canal. Dorms **£16**

EATING AND DRINKING

CAFÉS AND RESTAURANTS

Café 115 115 High St ☎ 01397 702500. A decent, cheap and central place to stop for coffee and a snack. A toasted bagel with cheddar and red onion will cost you £3.95. Mon–Sat 10am–4pm.

Crannog at the Waterfront Town Pier ☎ 01397 705589, ⓦ crannog.net. Red-roofed restaurant with lochside views and fresh seafood, including steamed clams and mussels with tomato and chilli (£17.50), plus a reasonable wine list. Located at the pier just off the bypass on entering Fort William. Daily noon–2.30pm & 6–9pm.

Lime Tree Restaurant The Old Manse, Achintore Rd

☎ 01397 701806, ⓦ limetreefortwilliam.co.uk. Serves an excellent selection of contemporary Scottish food. The three-course meal (£29.95) includes a roast rack of lamb wrapped in a rosemary crust. Daily 6–9pm.

PUB

Grog and Gruel 66 High St ☎ 01397 705078. Loud and friendly, the downstairs alehouse at *Grog and Gruel* is a good bet for Scottish beer. The upstairs restaurant is more relaxed, doing mostly Mexican mains, including a spicy "inferno burger" for £10.95. Mon–Wed & Sun noon– midnight, Thurs–Sat noon–1am.

Around Fort William

Any disappointment you harbour about the dispiriting flavour of Fort William town should be offset by the wealth of scenery and activities in its immediate vicinity. Most obvious – on a clear day, at least – is **Ben Nevis**, the most popular, though hardly the most rewarding, of Scotland's high peaks. The path up leaves from **Glen Nevis**, also a starting point for some other excellent walks of various lengths and elevations. The mountain abutting Ben Nevis is **Aonach Mhòr**, home of Scotland's most modern ski resort and an internationally renowned honey-pot for downhill mountain-bike enthusiasts. Some of the best views of these peaks can be had from **Corpach**, a small village opposite Fort William that marks the start of the **Caledonian Canal** (see p.197).

The main road travelling up the Great Glen from Fort William towards Inverness is the A82, ten miles along which is the small settlement of **Spean Bridge**, a good waypoint for getting to various remote and attractive walking areas with several backpacker hostels, notably glens **Spean** and **Roy**, along the A86 trunk road, which links across the central highlands to the A9 and the Speyside region.

Glen Nevis

A ten-minute drive south of Fort William, **GLEN NEVIS** is indisputably among the Highlands' most impressive glens: a classic U-shaped glacial valley hemmed in by steep bracken-covered slopes and swathes of blue-grey scree. With the forbidding mass of Ben Nevis rising steeply to the north, it's not surprising that the valley has served as a location in the films *Rob Roy* and *Braveheart*. Apart from its natural beauty, Glen Nevis is also the starting point for the ascent of Ben Nevis.

A great **low-level walk** (six miles round-trip) runs from the end of the road at the top of Glen Nevis. The good but very rocky path leads through a dramatic gorge with impressive falls and rapids, then opens out into a secret hanging valley, carpeted with wild flowers, with a high waterfall at the far end. If you're really energetic (and properly equipped) you can walk the full twelve miles on over **Rannoch Moor** to **Corrour Station** (see p.150), where you can pick up one of four daily trains to take you back to Fort William (50min).

ARRIVAL AND INFORMATION

GLEN NEVIS

By bus Bus #42 runs from the High St in Fort William, past the Glen Nevis Visitor Centre, campsite and SYHA hostel to the Lower Falls car park (3 daily; 25min) almost 5 miles up the Glen Nevis road.

Visitor Centre A mile and a half southeast of Fort William along the Glen Nevis road; take bus #42 from Fort William (daily 8.30am–6pm; ☎01397 705922). Staff here can give advice on climbing the mountain. It's also worth asking for a copy of the useful leaflet *Ben Nevis: Safety information for walking the mountain track.*

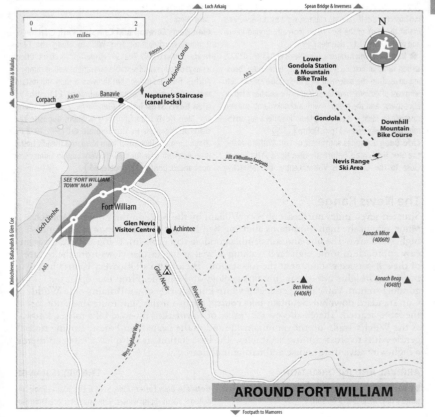

AROUND FORT WILLIAM

ASCENT OF BEN NEVIS

Of all the walks in and around Glen Nevis, the **ascent of Ben Nevis** (4406ft), Britain's highest summit, inevitably attracts the most attention. In high summer the trail is teeming with hikers – around 100,000 summit each year. However, this doesn't mean that the mountain should be treated casually. It can snow at the summit any day of the year and people die on the slopes, so take the necessary precautions (see p.42); in winter, of course, the mountain should be left to the experts. The most obvious **route**, a Victorian pony-path up the whaleback south side of the mountain, built to service the observatory that once stood on the top, starts from the helpful Glen Nevis Visitor Centre, a mile and a half southeast of Fort William along the Glen Nevis road. Return via the main route or, if the weather is settled and you're confident enough, make a side-trip from the wide saddle into the **Allt a'Mhuilinn glen** for spectacular views of the great cliffs on Ben Nevis's north face. Allow a full day for the climb (8hr) and check the weather forecast before setting out (Ⓦ bennevisweather.co.uk is useful).

Maps One of the best maps of the mountain is *Harvey's Ben Nevis Superwalker Map*, available from Fort William's tourist office and most local bookshops and outdoor stores.

Equipment You can buy mountain equipment and last-minute supplies at the Glen Nevis Visitor Centre.

ACCOMMODATION AND EATING

Achintee Farm Guest House Glen Nevis ☎01397 702240, Ⓦachinteefarm.com. Friendly B&B with adjoining hostel and self-catering cottage, right by the *Ben Nevis Inn* at the start of the Ben Nevis footpath. Drying rooms and wi-fi. Dorms £17; doubles £45

★ **Ben Nevis Inn** Achintee, Glen Nevis ☎01397 701227, Ⓦben-nevis-inn.co.uk. A basic and cosy bunkhouse (booking advised) in the basement of a lively 250-year-old pub, 50m east of *Achintee Farm Guest House*. The pub has a terrific atmosphere and the menu – with a chunky lamb and veg casserole for £9.85 – is especially tempting after a day on the mountain. Daily noon–11pm. Dorms £15.50

Café Beag 2.5 miles southeast of Fort William along the Glen Nevis road, before the Glen Nevis SYHA hostel. Close to the Glen Nevis Visitor Centre, this attractive wood-panelled café sells hearty soups (£3.50) and big cooked breakfasts (£6). Mon–Thurs 8am–6pm, Fri–Sun 8am–8pm.

Glen Nevis Caravan and Camping Park Glen Nevis, 2 miles southeast of Fort William along the Glen Nevis road ☎01397 702191, Ⓦglen-nevis.co.uk. Offers a range of lodges and rentable caravans as well as camping pitches. Facilities include hot showers, a shop and restaurant, and wheelchair-accessible bathrooms. £11/pitch

Glen Nevis SYHA hostel Glen Nevis, 2.5 miles along the Glen Nevis road from Fort William, opposite the start of the path to the summit ☎01397 702336, Ⓦsyha.org.uk. Though far from town, this friendly hostel is an excellent base for walkers. Very busy in summer, so book ahead. Dorms £22; doubles £50

The Nevis Range

Situated seven miles northeast of Fort William by the A82, on the slopes of **Aonach Mhòr**, one of the high mountains abutting Ben Nevis, the **Nevis Range** is Scotland's highest ski area. The one-and-a-half-mile gondola trip (15min), rising 2000ft, gives an easy approach to some high-level walking as well as spectacular views from the terrace of the self-service restaurant at the top station. There's also a Discovery Centre here, providing insights into the mountain's geology and wildlife. From the top of the gondola station, you can experience a white-knuckle ride down Britain's only World-Cup standard **downhill mountain-bike course**, a hair-raising 3km route that's not for the faint-hearted. There's also over 25 miles of waymarked off-road bike routes, known as the Witch's Trails, on the mountainside and in the Leanachan Forest, ranging from gentle paths to cross-country scrambles. The base station area also has a café and there's a high-wire adventure course and nature trail nearby.

ARRIVAL AND INFORMATION

THE NEVIS RANGE

By bus Bus #41 runs from Fort William's bus station four times a day (Mon–Sat; 2 on Sun).

Gondola Daily Easter–June, Sept & Oct 10am–5pm; July & Aug 9.30am–6pm; winter: 9am–sunset (closed mid-Nov to mid-Dec); £11.50 return.

Tourist information In the Mountain Discovery Centre, at the top gondola station (daily June–Aug 9.30am–6pm, Sept & Oct 10am–sunset; ☎01397 705825, ⦿nevis -range.co.uk). Has information on the history and ecology of the area.

ACTIVITIES

Mountain-bike courses Nevis Bike School (☎01397 705825, ⦿bike.nevisrange.co.uk) runs 2hr 30min training courses for £33 per person (minimum 3 people). Depending on the trail you choose, you may also need to buy a gondola pass.

Bike rental At the entrance to the lower gondola station, Alpine Bikes (☎01397 705825, ⦿alpinebikes.com) rents general mountain bikes (from £15) as well as full-suspension ones for the downhill course. Daily May–Oct 9am–5pm.

Neptune's Staircase

In the suburb of **Banavie**, three miles north of the centre of Fort William along the A830 to Mallaig, the **Caledonian Canal** (see p.197) climbs 64ft in less than half a mile via a punishing but picturesque series of eight locks known as **NEPTUNE'S STAIRCASE**. There are stunning views from here of Ben Nevis and its neighbours, and it's a popular point from which to walk or cycle along the canal towpath.

ARRIVAL AND ACTIVITIES NEPTUNE'S STAIRCASE

By bus Stagecoach bus #45A (every 15–30min; 10min) runs from Middle Street in Fort William to Banavie.
By bike You can rent a bike (£15/day) at *Farr Cottage Lodge* in Corpach (see p.189); from there it's a short ride northeast along the canal towpath to Neptune's Staircase.

ACCOMMODATION AND EATING

Chase the Wild Goose Hostel Locheil Crescent, Banavie ☎01397 772531, ⦿great-glen-hostel.com. A small, comfortable hostel close to Neptune's Staircase and handy for the Great Glen Way. Has a barbecue area for use in summer. Dorms **£17**

The Eagle Inn Laggan Locks, at the northern end of Loch Lochy ☎07789 858567. If you do choose to cycle along the Caledonian Canal, look out for this unusual pub, where mains like peat-smoked salmon (£17.80) and real ale are offered aboard a wonderful 1920s Dutch barge. Easter–Oct Mon & Thurs–Sun noon–11pm.

Moorings Hotel Beside the staircase in Banavie ☎01397 772797, ⦿moorings-fortwilliam.co.uk. This mid-sized hotel near the canal serves curries and other pub staples in its bar, as well as classier Scottish dinners (£30 for three courses) in the main restaurant. Daily: bar noon–9.30pm; restaurant 7–9.30pm. **£123**

Spean Bridge and around

Ten miles northeast of Fort William, the village of **SPEAN BRIDGE** marks the junction of the A82 with the A86 from Dalwhinnie and Kingussie (see p.172). If you're here, it's well worth heading a mile out of the village on the A82 towards Inverness to the **Commando Memorial** (see box, p.192), a group of bronze soldiers commemorating the men who trained in the area during World War II. The statue looks out on an awesome sweep of moor and mountain that takes in the wider Lochaber area and the Ben Nevis massif.

Glen Roy

Three miles east of Spean Bridge, a minor road turns north off the A86 and up **Glen Roy**. Drive a couple of miles along the glen and you'll see the so-called "parallel roads": not roads at all, but ancient beaches at various levels along the valley sides, which mark the shorelines of a loch confined here by a glacial dam in the last Ice Age.

Tulloch and Loch Laggan

Four miles east of the turn-off to Glen Roy along the A86, just before **Tulloch**, the train line and the main road part company. From Tulloch's small railway station, accessible

3

THE COMMANDO TRAIL

From 1942 until the end of World War II, the Lochaber district around the southern part of the Great Glen was used as a training area by the elite **commando** units of the British army. Below are some of the key spots along the trail; a **leaflet** giving a fuller description of the trail and the commandos' activities in the area can be obtained from local tourist information offices.

MEMORIAL AND EXHIBITION

A striking **memorial** depicting a group of bronze soldiers, sculpted in 1952 by Scott Sutherland, stands overlooking an awesome sweep of moor and mountain beside the A82 just to the north of Spean Bridge. In a room inside the *Spean Bridge Hotel*, a mile south along the A82 in Spean Bridge (daily 7am–10pm; free; ☎01397 712250, ⓦcommando.speanbridgehotel.co.uk), the proudly assembled **Commando Exhibition** has impressive displays of photos, medals and memorabilia.

ACHNACARRY

The soldiers' base was at **Achnacarry Castle**, hereditary seat of the Clan Cameron, around which there's an interesting five-mile **walk** retracing many of the places used by them during their training. To get here, follow the minor B8004 beside the memorial, which branches down to Gairlochy by the canalside at Loch Lochy's southern tip, then follow the signs for the small **Clan Cameron museum** (April to mid-Oct daily 1.30–5pm; July & Aug 11am–5pm; £3.50; ⓦclan-cameron.org), located in the old post office near the castle still occupied by the clan chief Cameron of Lochiel. The museum tells the clan history, including its involvement in the 1745 rebellion, and has memorabilia relating to the commandos' residency.

LOCH ARKAIG AND LOCH LOCHY

You can park your car at the Clan Cameron museum and walk to the eastern end of **Loch Arkaig**, one of Scotland's most ruggedly wild and remote stretches of water, then walk down the tree-lined **Mile Dorcha**, or Dark Mile. Around here there are various caves and small bothies used by **Bonnie Prince Charlie** when he was on the run after Culloden, dodging government troops, and desperately hoping for the arrival of a French ship to carry him to safety. The road leads to the shores of **Loch Lochy**, where the commandos would practise opposed landings, often using live ammunition to keep them on their toes. After a mile by the lochside, turn right back along the road that leads to the Clan Cameron museum.

only by a single-track road and served by Caledonian sleeper services from London, trains swing south to pass Loch Treig and cross Rannoch Moor (see p.150). Beyond the turn off to Tulloch station, the A86 runs alongside the artificial **Loch Laggan** with the picturesque Ardverikie Castle on its southern shore and the attractive walking area of **Creag Meagaidh National Nature Reserve** to the north.

ARRIVAL AND DEPARTURE

SPEAN BRIDGE AND AROUND

By bus Buses bound for Spean Bridge depart Fort William's bus station a couple of times per hour, taking 15–30min to arrive in the centre of the village.

ACCOMMODATION AND EATING

Àite Cruinnichidh 3.5 miles west of Tulloch railway station, just south of A86 ☎01397 712315, ⓦhighland-hostel.co.uk. A comfortable wood-lined bunkhouse in a beautiful setting, with good facilities including family rooms and a sauna, as well as local advice for walkers and cyclists. Dorms £16.50

Old Pines Hotel and Restaurant A few hundred yards northwest of the Commando Memorial, on the B8004 to Gairlochy ☎01397 712324, ⓦoldpines.co.uk. At this welcoming and upmarket hotel and restaurant, guests are treated to locally sourced game and shellfish (seared scallop starter £8.50) as well as home-baking, pasta and ice cream. Lunch: Tues–Sat noon–3pm; dinner: daily 6.30–9pm.

Station Lodge At Tulloch station ☎01397 732333, ⓦstationlodge.co.uk. The station building at Tulloch is now a friendly and well-equipped hostel, which can provide breakfasts and dinners with advance notice. Dorms £17

Glen Coe and around

Glen Coe, half-an-hour's drive south of Fort William on the main A82 road to Glasgow, is one of Scotland's most inspiring places, a breathtakingly beautiful mountain valley between velvety-green conical peaks, their tops often wreathed in cloud, their flanks streaked by cascades of rock and scree. Arriving from the south across the desolate reaches of Rannoch Moor, you're likely to find the start of the glen – with **Buachaille Etive Mhòr** to the south and **Beinn a'Chrùlaiste** to the north – little short of forbidding. By the time you've reached the heart of the glen, with the three huge rock buttresses known as the **Three Sisters** on one side and the Anoach Eagach ridge on the other combining to close up the sky, you'll almost certainly want to stop. Added to the compelling emotional mix is the story of the notorious **massacre of Glen Coe** in 1692, nadir of the long-standing enmity between the clans MacDonald and Campbell (see box, p.194). At its western end, Glen Coe meets Loch Leven: the main road goes west and over the bridge at Ballachulish en route to Fort William.

At the eastern end of Glen Coe, meanwhile, beyond the looming massif of Buachaille Etive Mhòr, the landscape opens out onto vast Rannoch Moor (see p.150). From the **Glencoe Mountain Resort** (see p.194) a chairlift climbs 2400ft to Meall a Bhuiridh, giving spectacular views over Rannoch Moor and to Ben Nevis. At the base station, there's a simple but pleasant café. Beyond the mountains at the eastern end of Loch Leven is the slowly reviving settlement of **Kinlochleven**, site of the world's largest indoor ice-climbing centre and a waypoint on the West Highland Way long-distance footpath (see box, p.133).

3

WALKS AROUND GLEN COE

Ordnance Survey Explorer map 384

Flanked by the sheer-sided Munros, **Glen Coe** offers some of the Highlands' most challenging **hiking** routes, with long steep ascents over rough trails and notoriously unpredictable weather conditions that claim lives every year. The walks outlined below number among the glen's less-ambitious routes, but still require a map. It's essential that you take the proper precautions (see p.42), and stick to the paths, both for your own safety and the sake of the landscape, which has become badly eroded in places. For a broader selection of walks, get hold of the Ordnance Survey *Pathfinder Guide: Fort William and Glen Coe Walks*.

DEVIL'S STAIRCASE

A good introduction to the splendours of Glen Coe is the half-day hike over the **Devil's Staircase**, which follows part of the old military road that once ran between Fort William and Stirling. The trail, part of the West Highland Way (see p.133), starts at the village of **Kinlochleven** and is marked by thistle signs, which lead uphill to the 1804ft pass and down the other side into Glen Coe.

ALLT COIRE GABHAIL

Set right in the heart of the glen, the half-day **Allt Coire Gabhail** hike starts at the car park opposite the distinctive Three Sisters massif on the main A82. This explores the so-called "Lost Valley" where the Clan MacDonald fled and hid their cattle when attacked. Once in the valley, there are superb views of the upper slopes of Bidean nan Bian, Gearr Aonach and Beinn Fhada, which improve as you continue on to its head, another twenty- to thirty-minute walk.

BUACHAILLE ETIVE BEAG

Undoubtedly one of the finest walks in the Glen Coe area that doesn't entail the ascent of a Munro is the **Buachaille Etive Beag** circuit, which follows the textbook glacial valleys of Lairig Eilde and Lairig Gartain, ascending 1968ft in only nine miles of rough trail. Park near the waterfall at **The Study** – the gorge part of the A82 through Glen Coe – and walk up the road until you see a sign pointing south to "Loch Etiveside".

> ### VALLEY OF WEEPING
>
> In 1692 Glen Coe (literally "valley of weeping") was the site of a notorious massacre, in which the MacDonalds were victims of an abiding government desire to suppress the clans. Fed up with what they regarded as unacceptable lawlessness, and a groundswell of Jacobitism and Catholicism, the government offered a general pardon to all those who signed an oath of allegiance to William III by January 1, 1692. When clan chief **Alastair MacDonald** missed the deadline, a plot was hatched to make an example of "that damnable sept", and **Campbell of Glenlyon** was ordered to billet his soldiers in the homes of the MacDonalds, who for ten days entertained them with traditional Highland hospitality. In the early morning of February 13, the soldiers turned on their hosts, slaying around forty and causing more than three hundred to flee in a blizzard.

Glencoe Village and around

Tucked between steep mountains, Loch Leven and the grassy banks of the River Coe, **GLENCOE VILLAGE** is an attractive place to spend a couple of days. There's a good choice of accommodation in the area, and if you fancy a break from walking, the village museum and nearby visitor centre make for pleasant distractions. Beyond the small village at the western end of the glen, the glen itself (a property of the NTS since the 1930s) is virtually uninhabited, and provides outstanding climbing and walking.

Glencoe Folk Museum

Easter–Aug Mon–Sat 10am–4.30pm (last admission at 4pm) • £3 • ⓦ glencoemuseum.com

If you have an hour to spare in Glencoe Village, you can pay a visit to the delightful heather-roofed **Glencoe Folk Museum**. Various games and activities for kids can be enjoyed within this cosy 1720 croft where items include a chair that reputedly once belonged to Bonnie Prince Charlie.

NTS visitor centre

Feb–Easter Thurs–Sun 10am–4pm; Easter–Oct daily 9.30am–5.30pm; Nov–Jan Thurs–Sun 10am–4pm • NTS • £5.50 • **Guided walks** Easter & June–Sept • From £5; book ahead • ⓦ glencoe-nts.org.uk

The attractive NTS **visitor centre** sits in woodland a mile south of Glencoe Village. It has a good exhibition, with film, giving a balanced account of the massacre, plus information about the area's natural history and conservation issues, and some entertaining material on rock- and hill-climbing through the years. There's also a cabin area providing information on the local weather and wildlife, and you may be able to join a ranger-led **guided walk**.

ARRIVAL AND ACTIVITIES   GLENCOE VILLAGE AND AROUND

By bus To get to the NTS visitor centre or Glencoe Mountain Resort from Fort William's bus station, hop on one of the Glasgow-bound Scottish Citylink coaches (up to 8 daily; 30–45min); Bus #44 from Fort William also stops at least 10 times a day (3 on Sun) at Glencoe Village en route to Kinlochleven.

Glencoe Mountain Resort Half a mile south of the A82 at the foot of the mountain ☎01855 851226, ⓦ glencoemountain.co.uk. Skiing, snowboarding and mountain-biking sessions can be arranged at this spectacularly located resort. The chairlift (£10) runs throughout the year. Jan–Oct Mon–Thurs & Sun 9am–8.30pm, Fri & Sat 9am–10.30pm; Nov & Dec daily 9am–4.30pm.

ACCOMMODATION

Glencoe Independent Hostel North of the river, halfway between Glencoe Village and the Clachaig Inn ☎01855 811906, ⓦ glencoehostel.co.uk. Cheap independent hostel in rustic whitewashed buildings, offering free wi-fi, hot showers and a laundry service. Dorms £17 **Red Squirrel** 150m south of the turn-off to Glencoe Independent Hostel ☎01855 811256, ⓦ redsquirrel campsite.co.uk. Sylvan year-round campsite, just south of the SYHA hostel on the road to *Clachaig Inn*. Campfires and pets permitted. **£19**/pitch

Scorry Breac A short walk from the centre of Glencoe Village, on the north side of the river ☎ 01855 811354, ⓦ scorrybreac.co.uk. Secluded and friendly, *Scorry Breac* guesthouse has five affordable en-suite rooms. The best have views over the mountains. **£60**

EATING AND DRINKING

★ **Clachaig Inn** 2.5 miles south of Glencoe Village on the minor road off the A82 ☎ 01855 811252, ⓦ clachaig .com. The liveliest, best-known hotel in the area is a great place to reward your exertions with cask-conditioned ales and heaped platefuls of food (venison casserole £10.95); it's an easy stroll away from the campsite and hostel listed here. Mon–Thurs & Sun 8am–11pm, Fri 8am–midnight, Sat 8am–11.30pm.

Kinlochleven

At the easternmost end of Loch Leven, the settlement of **KINLOCHLEVEN** is, thanks to its location on the West Highland Way, steadily reviving its fortunes. For many years it was a tourism backwater best known as the site of a huge, unsightly aluminium smelter built in 1904. The tale of the area's industrial past is told in **The Aluminium Story** (same hours as tourist information centre; free), a small series of displays in the same corrugated-metal building as the post office and tourist information centre. As well as being close to Glen Coe, Kinlochleven stands at the foot of the Mamore hills, popular with Munro-baggers; Fort William is a day's walk away.

The Ice Factor

Leven Rd • Mon, Wed & Fri–Sun 9am–7pm, Tues & Thurs 9am–10pm • 2hr 30min ice-climbing course £48 • ☎ 01855 831100, ⓦ ice-factor.co.uk

Kinlochleven's disused aluminium smelter is now the home of an innovative indoor mountaineering centre called **The Ice Factor**. The facility includes the world's largest artificial ice-climbing wall (13.5m) as well as a range of more traditional climbing walls plus equipment rental, and a steam room and sauna. There's a bar upstairs and food is available.

ARRIVAL AND INFORMATION

KINLOCHLEVEN

By bus The hourly #44 bus from Fort William runs to the centre of Kinlochleven (50min), passing Glencoe (15min) en route.

Tourist information In The Aluminium Story building on Linnhe Rd, in the centre of the village (Mon, Tues, Thurs & Fri 9am–12.30pm & 1.30–5.30pm, Wed & Sat 9am–1pm; ☎ 01855 831021). Staff at the combined post office, museum and information point can give tips on local attractions. Look out for the useful leaflet, published by Kinlochleven Community Trust, which details local walking routes.

ACCOMMODATION AND EATING

Blackwater Hostel Beside the river on Lab Rd ☎ 01855 831253, ⓦ blackwaterhostel.co.uk. A decidedly upmarket hostel, with en-suite dorms and Hobbit-sized two-bed "micro lodges" available for rent. You can also camp here. Dorms **£16.50**; micro lodge **£35**; camping **£7**/person

Edencoille Guest House Garbhein Rd ☎ 01855 831358, ⓦ kinlochlevenbedandbreakfast.co.uk. There's fine hospitality at this Edwardian-built house where, with notice, they can organize packed lunches, evening meals and guided walking trips. **£72**

Lochleven Seafood Café A few miles west of Kinlochleven on the B836 (north side of the loch) ☎ 01855 821048, ⓦ lochlevenseafoodcafe.co .uk. The best place to eat near Kinlochleven, this is a relaxed restaurant with an attractive outdoor terrace. Specializes in local shellfish such as whole brown crab cooked in sea water (£12.75). Daily noon–3pm & 6–9pm.

MacDonald Hotel Fort William Rd ☎ 01855 831539, ⓦ macdonaldhotel.co.uk. This central hotel has ten reasonable en-suite bedrooms, but is best visited for its *Bothy Bar*, where you can join fellow walkers for fish and chips (£8.90) and other pub meals. Bar: Mon–Wed 12.30–11.30pm, Thurs–Sat 12.30pm–12.30am, Sun 12.30–11.15pm. **£84**

3

Loch Ness and around

Twenty-three miles long, unfathomably deep, cold and often moody, **LOCH NESS** is bound by rugged heather-clad mountains rising steeply from a wooded shoreline, with attractive glens opening up on either side. Its fame, however, is based overwhelmingly on its legendary inhabitant, Nessie, the "Loch Ness monster" (see box below), who encourages a steady flow of hopeful visitors to the settlements dotted along the loch, in particular **Drumnadrochit**. Nearby, the impressive ruins of **Castle Urquhart** – a favourite monster-spotting location – perch atop a rock on the lochside and attract a deluge of bus parties during the summer. Almost as busy in high season is the village of **Fort Augustus**, at the more scenic southwest tip of Loch Ness, where you can watch queues of boats tackling one of the Caledonian Canal's longest flight of locks. You'll need your own **car** to complete the whole loop around the loch, a journey that includes an impressive stretch between Fort Augustus and the high, hidden Loch Mhòr, overlooked by the imposing Monadhliath range to the south.

Away from the lochside, and seeing a fraction of Loch Ness's visitor numbers, the remote glens of **Urquhart** and **Affric** make an appealing contrast, with Affric in particular boasting narrow, winding roads, gushing streams and hillsides dotted with ancient Caledonian pine forests. The busiest of these glens to the north is the often bleak high country of Glen Moriston, a little to the southeast of Glen Affric, through which the main road between Inverness and Skye passes.

3

GETTING AROUND

LOCH NESS AND AROUND

By bus Using the A82, buses can travel the entire length of Loch Ness, from Inverness to Fort Augustus. On the eastern side of the loch, however, regular bus services are limited to the stretch between Inverness and Foyers.

By car Although most visitors drive along the tree-lined

A82 road, which runs along the western shore of Loch Ness, the sinuous, single-track B862/B852 (originally a military road built to link Fort Augustus and Fort George) that skirts the eastern shore is quieter and affords far more spectacular views.

NESSIE

The world-famous **Loch Ness monster**, affectionately known as **Nessie** (and by serious aficionados as *Nessiteras rhombopteryx*), has been a local celebrity for some time. The first mention of a mystery creature crops up in St Adamnan's seventh-century biography of **St Columba**, who allegedly calmed an aquatic animal that had attacked one of his monks. Present-day interest, however, is probably greater outside Scotland than within the country, and dates from the building of the road along the loch's western shore in the early 1930s. In 1934 the *Daily Mail* published London surgeon R.K. Wilson's sensational photograph of the head and neck of the monster peering up out of the loch, and the hype has hardly diminished since. Recent encounters range from glimpses of ripples by anglers to the famous occasion in 1961 when thirty hotel guests saw a pair of humps break the water's surface and cruise for about half a mile before submerging.

Photographic evidence is showcased in two separate exhibitions located at **Drumnadrochit**, but the most impressive of these exhibits – including the renowned black-and-white movie footage of Nessie's humps moving across the water, and Wilson's original head-and-shoulders shot – have now been exposed as fakes. Indeed, in few other places on earth has watching a rather lifeless and often grey expanse of water seemed so compelling, or have floating logs, otters and boat wakes been photographed so often and with such excitement. Yet while even high-tech sonar surveys carried out over the past two decades have failed to come up with conclusive evidence, it's hard to dismiss Nessie as pure myth. After all, no one yet knows where the unknown layers of silt and mud at the bottom of the loch begin and end: best estimates say the loch is over 750ft deep, deeper than much of the North Sea, while others point to the possibilities of underwater caves and undiscovered channels connected to the sea. What scientists have found in the cold, murky depths, including pure white eels and rare arctic char, offers fertile grounds for speculation, with different theories declaring Nessie to be a remnant from the dinosaur age, a giant newt or a huge, visiting Baltic sturgeon.

LOTS AND LOTS OF LOCHS AND LOCKS

Surveyed by James Watt in 1773, the **Caledonian Canal** was completed in the early 1800s by Thomas Telford to enable ships to pass between the North Sea and the Atlantic without having to navigate Scotland's treacherous northern coast. There are sixty miles between the west-coast entrance to the canal at Corpach, near Fort William, and its exit onto the Moray Firth at Inverness, although strictly speaking only 22 miles of it are bona fide canal – the other 38 exploit the Great Glen's natural string of **freshwater lochs** of Lochy, Oich and Ness.

The most famous piece of canal engineering in Scotland is the series of eight **locks** at Banavie, about a mile from the entrance at Corpach, known as Neptune's Staircase (see p.191). While the canal was originally built for freight-carrying ships and large passenger-steamers, these days it is almost exclusively used by small yachts and pleasure boats. Good spots to watch their leisurely progress are Neptune's Staircase and Fort Augustus, where four locks take traffic through the centre of the village into Loch Ness.

If you're interested in the history of the waterway, it's worth taking a look at the small **Caledonian Canal Visitor Centre**, beside the locks in Fort Augustus (see below). For more active encounters with the canal, you can set off along a section of the Great Glen Way footpath or Great Glen cycleway, both of which follow the **canal towpath** for part of their length (see box, p.187).

3

Fort Augustus

FORT AUGUSTUS, a tiny, busy village at the scenic southwestern tip of Loch Ness, was named after George II's son, the chubby lad who later became the "Butcher" duke of Cumberland of Culloden fame; it was built as a barracks after the 1715 Jacobite rebellion. Today, it's dominated by comings and goings along the **Caledonian Canal**, which leaves Loch Ness here, and by its large former **Benedictine abbey**, a campus of grey Victorian buildings founded on the site of the original fort in 1876. Until relatively recently this was home to a small but active community of monks, but it has now been converted into luxury flats. There are some good cycling routes locally, notably along the Great Glen cycle route.

ARRIVAL AND INFORMATION

FORT AUGUSTUS

By bus Frequent buses ply the A82, linking Fort Augustus with Inverness and Drumnadrochit to the north and Fort William, 30 miles south.

Destinations Drumnadrochit (up to 10 daily; 35min); Fort William (up to 9 daily; 1hr); Inverness (up to 9 daily; 1hr).

Tourist office The car park, north of the canal (April & May Mon–Sat 9.30am–5pm, Sun 10am–4pm; June Mon–Sat 9am–5pm, Sun 10am–4pm; July & Aug Mon–Sat 9am–6pm, Sun 10am–4pm; Sept & Oct Mon–Sat 9.30am–5pm, Sun 10am–3pm; Nov–March daily 10am–3pm; ☎01320 366779). The very helpful tourist office hands out useful free walking leaflets and stocks maps of the Great Glen Way (see box, p.187).

Caledonian Canal Visitor Centre Ardchattan House, Canalside, by the locks (Easter–Oct daily 10am–1.30pm & 2–5.30pm; ☎01320 366493). Houses a small exhibition showing why, when and how the Caledonian Canal was built. Black-and-white pictures reveal how the canal looked in the nineteenth century, but aside from these (and a dusty old telescope) there's little in the way of proper exhibits.

TOURS AND ACTIVITIES

Boat tours From its berth by the Clansman Centre, near the swing bridge, Cruise Loch Ness sails 5 miles up Loch Ness (daily; 1hr; £13; ☎01320 366277, ⊛cruiselochness .com), using sonar technology to provide passengers with impressive live 3D imagery of the deep where underwater cave systems, salmon, cannibalistic trout (and, some would speculate, Nessie) are to be found.

Fishing The tourist office (see above) can advise you on how to obtain permits to fish the loch or nearby river.

ACCOMMODATION

Corrie Liath Market Hill, half a mile south of the centre along A82 ☎01320 366409, ⊛corrieliath.co.uk. Small, thoughtfully managed B&B whose comfortable rooms have books and DVDs for guests to enjoy. The garden has a barbecue hut for use in the summertime. **£65**

Cumberlands Campsite Glendoe Rd, by Stravaigers

Lodge ☎ 01320 366257, ⊛ cumberlands-campsite.com. Spacious campsite with good facilities, a 5min walk from the loch and a short stroll from the shops and pubs of Fort Augustus. **£16**/pitch

Lovat Arms Hotel On the A82 in the centre of Fort Augustus ☎ 01456 490000, ⊛ thelovat.com. Expensive hotel refurbished along ecofriendly principles and built on the site of the 1718 Kilwhimen Barracks. The hotel's restaurant and brasserie serve inventive (and costly) dishes with a local focus. **£121**

Morag's Lodge Bunoich Brae, on the Loch Ness side of town ☎ 01320 366289, ⊛ www.moragslodge.com. The atmosphere at this well-equipped hostel – with four- and six-bed dorms – livens up with the daily arrival of backpackers' minibus tours. Dorms **£21**; doubles **£50**

Stravaigers Lodge Glendoe Rd, a short walk south of the centre ☎ 01320 366257, ⊛ highlandbunkhouse .co.uk. Basic hostel with a mix of twin rooms and cheaper bunk rooms, split between two separate buildings, each with its own kitchen. Dorms **£18**; twins **£46**

EATING AND DRINKING

The Lock Inn Canalside, opposite the Caledonian Canal Visitor Centre ☎ 01320 366302. With attractive wood-panelled interiors and a wider selection of pub meals (such as chicken curry, £11.95), *The Lock* is a slightly better choice than its neighbour, *The Bothy*. Daily 11am–11pm.

The Scots Kitchen Opposite the tourist office. One of the few cheap spots for a coffee in Fort Augustus. Also sells moderately priced breakfasts, lunches and dinners (June–Oct only), including vegetarian haggis (£9.25). Daily 8am–8pm.

The east side of Loch Ness

The tranquil and scenic **east side** of Loch Ness is skirted by General Wade's old military highway, now the B862/B852. From Fort Augustus, the narrow single-track road swings up, away from the lochside through the near-deserted **Stratherrick** valley, dotted with tiny lochans. To the southeast of Fort Augustus you'll pass the massive earth workings of the Glendoe Hydro Station. From here, the road drops down to rejoin the shores of Loch Ness at **FOYERS**, where there are numerous marked forest trails and an impressive waterfall.

Past **Inverfarigaig** – where a road up a beautiful, steep-sided river valley leads east over to Loch Mhòr – is the sleepy village of **DORES**, nestled at the northeastern end of Loch Ness, the whitewashed *Dores Inn* providing a pleasant pit-stop.

ARRIVAL AND DEPARTURE   EAST SIDE OF LOCH NESS

By bus Local buses run up and down part of the east side of the loch, connecting Inverness with Foyers (Mon–Fri up to 5 daily, Sat 2; 45min).

ACCOMMODATION AND EATING

Dores Inn 11 miles north of Foyers in the village of Dores ☎ 01463 751203. Only 9 miles southwest of Inverness, this old lochside pub is popular with Invernessians, who trickle out here on summer evenings for a stroll along the grey pebble beach and some monster-spotting. The barley paella with seafood, garlic and paprika costs £11.95. Mon–Thurs 10am–11pm, Fri & Sat 10am–midnight, Sun 10am–10pm.

Foyers House In Upper Foyers, up the track next to Waterfall Café ☎ 01456 486405, ⊛ foyershouse-lochness

.com. Out of the way, adults-only B&B with fabulous views of the loch from its terrace. Has a self-catering kitchen and dining room. **£50**

Waterfall Café In Upper Foyers village, opposite the footpath to the waterfall ☎ 01456 486233. Previously known as the *Red Squirrel Café*, this friendly tea shop still runs a live webcam of red squirrels nesting across the road – and does delicious tray bakes (£1.50) to boot. April–Oct Mon–Thurs 9am–5pm, Fri & Sat 9am–8pm, Sun 10am–3pm; Nov–March Fri & Sat 9.30am–7pm, Sun 10am–2pm.

Drumnadrochit and around

Situated above a verdant, sheltered bay of Loch Ness fifteen miles southwest of Inverness, **DRUMNADROCHIT** is the southern gateway to remote Glen Affric and the centre of Nessie-hype, complete with a rash of tacky souvenir shops and two rival monster exhibitions whose head-to-head scramble for punters occasionally erupts into acrimonious exchanges, detailed with relish by the local press.

Loch Ness Centre & Exhibition

On the main A82 • Daily: Easter–June, Sept & Oct 9.30am–5pm; July & Aug 9.30am–6pm; Nov–Easter 10am–3.30pm • £6.95 • ☎ 01456 450573, Ⓦ lochness.com

Of the two major monster hubs in Drumnadrochit (the other being the Nessieland Monster Centre), the **Loch Ness Centre & Exhibition** is the better bet, offering an in-depth rundown of eyewitness accounts and information on various Nessie research projects.

Nessieland Monster Centre

Just west of the Loch Ness Centre & Exhibition on the A831 • Sept–June 9am–5pm; July & Aug 9am–9pm • £6 • ☎ 01456 450342, Ⓦ nessieland.co.uk

Aimed mainly at families, the **Nessieland Monster Centre** has an exhibition on monster sightings, a plastic model of Nessie for kids to clamber on, plus its own adventure playground. Couples and solo travellers might prefer a quiet drink at the adjacent *Loch Ness Lodge Hotel*, whose wood-panelled and heavily tartanized interior is said to harbour a resident ghost.

Castle Urquhart

Beside the loch: 2 miles southeast of Drumnadrochit and just off the A82 • Daily: April–Sept 9.30am–6pm; Oct 9.30am–5pm; Nov–March 9.30am–4.30pm • £7.90; HS

The thirteenth-century ruined lochside **Castle Urquhart**, a couple of miles from Drumnadrochit, was built as a strategic base to guard the Great Glen. The castle was taken by Edward I of England and later held by Robert the Bruce against Edward III, only to be blown up in 1692 to prevent it from falling to the Jacobites. Today it's one of Scotland's classic picture-postcard ruins, particularly splendid at night when it's floodlit and the crowds have gone. In the small visitor centre, a short film highlights the turbulent history of the castle.

ARRIVAL AND DEPARTURE DRUMNADROCHIT AND AROUND

By bus Drumnadrochit is served by frequent buses from Inverness, Fort William and Fort Augustus, which arrive and depart from near the post office, on the A82.

Destinations Fort Augustus (up to 10 daily; 35min); Fort William (up to 9 daily; 1hr 30min); Inverness (at least hourly; 30min).

INFORMATION AND ACTIVITIES

Tourist information In the middle of the main car park in the village (April & May Mon–Sat 9.30am–5pm, Sun 10am–3pm; June Mon–Sat 9am–5pm, Sun 10am–6pm; July & Aug Mon–Sat 9am–6pm, Sun 10am–4pm; Sept & Oct Mon–Sat 9.30am–5pm, Sun 10am–3pm; Nov–March

Tues–Sat 9.30am–3.30pm; ☎ 01456 459086).

Boat tours The sonar-equipped *Nessie Hunter* (Easter–Oct hourly 9am–6pm; £15; ☎ 01456 450395, Ⓦ loch-ness-cruises.com) runs hour-long cruises on the loch, which can be booked at the Nessieland Monster Centre.

ACCOMMODATION

Benleva Kilmore Rd, Kilmore ☎ 01456 450080, Ⓦ benleva.co.uk. Small, basic hotel in Kilmore, a 15min walk from the monster centres of Drumnadrochit. The six en-suite rooms have tartan bedspreads and free wi-fi. __£70__

Borlum Farm A mile southeast of central Drumnadrochit, off the A82 ☎ 01456 450220, Ⓦ borlum.com. Attractive campsite overlooking the village, with space for caravans and tents. The site is part of a popular riding school offering lessons, rides and treks (from £15/hr). __£12__/pitch

Glenkirk B&B 300m west of Nessieland Monster

Centre along the A831 ☎ 01456 450802, Ⓦ lochness bandb.com. Bright, friendly B&B in a former church located just a few minutes' walk from the centre, with simple yet smartly decorated bedrooms. __£80__

Loch Ness Backpackers Lodge Coiltie Farmhouse, Lewiston; follow the signs to the left when coming from Drumnadrochit ☎ 01456 450807, Ⓦ lochness-backpackers.com. For a cheap bed for the night, head for this immaculate and friendly hostel, which has dorms, private rooms and good facilities including a bar and two lounges. Dorms __£18__; doubles __£52__

EATING AND DRINKING

Benleva Kilmore Rd, Kilmore ☎01456 450080. One of many hotels doing bar food, *Benleva* sets itself apart by using local beer in some of its dishes, including the steak and ale pie with chips and seasonal veg (£10.50). Mon–Thurs noon–midnight, Fri noon–1am, Sat noon–11.45pm, Sun noon–11pm.

Fiddlers' Just south of the village green on the A82 ☎01456 450678, ⓦfiddledrum.co.uk. Busy, friendly bar with plenty of outside seating and, it's claimed, more than

500 single malt whiskies. The mostly meaty menu has a couple of veggie options, including a falafel and spinach burger (£7.95). Daily 12.30–2.30pm & 6–9.30pm.

Glen Café On the village green, just off the A82 ☎01456 450282. This inexpensive café does reasonable lunches and snacks. A baked potato stuffed with chilli con carne costs £5.50. Mon–Sat 9am–6.30pm, Sun 10am–6.30pm.

Glen Affric

Due west of Drumnadrochit lies a vast area of high peaks, remote glens and few roads. The reason most folk head this way is to explore the picturesque native forests and grand mountains of **Glen Affric**, heaven for walkers, climbers and mountain-bikers. Munro-baggers (see p.40) are normally much in evidence, and it is possible to tramp 25 miles all the way through Glen Affric to Shiel Bridge, on the west coast near Kyle of Lochalsh.

Cannich and Loch Affric

The main approach to Glen Affric is through the small settlement of **CANNICH**, thirteen miles west of Drumnadrochit on the A831. Cannich is a quiet and uninspiring village, but it has an excellent campsite where mountain bikes can be rented. From the car park at the head of the single-track road along the glen, ten miles southwest of Cannich, there's a selection of **walks**: the trip around **Loch Affric** will take you a good five hours but allows you to appreciate the glen, its wildlife and Caledonian pine and birch woods in all their remote splendour.

ARRIVAL AND INFORMATION   GLEN AFFRIC

By bus Ross's Minibuses (☎01463 761250, ⓦross -minibuses.co.uk) runs scheduled services to the car park at Glen Affric (July–Sept; its vehicles will also carry bikes if given advance notice) from Cannich (4 on Mon, Wed & Fri; 30min); Drumnadrochit (3 on Mon, Wed & Fri; 1hr 35min) and Inverness (2 on Mon, Wed & Fri; 2hr 10min).

Tourist information Notice boards are dotted around

the glen; the Forestry Commission website (ⓦforestry.gov .uk/glenaffric) includes an interactive map showing where they're located.

Volunteering For details of volunteer work in Glen Affric helping with the restoration of the woodland, get in touch with Trees for Life (ⓦtreesforlife.org.uk).

ACCOMMODATION AND EATING

Bog Cotton Café At Cannich Camping & Caravan Park. The best option for food in Cannich, this welcoming chalet-like café has large windows overlooking the campsite. Planning a hike? You can buy takeaway sandwiches here for £3 too. Daily 9am–5pm.

Cannich Camping & Caravan Park In the centre of Cannich ☎01456 415364, ⓦhighlandcamping.co.uk. Mountain bikes can be rented (£17/day) at this pretty, well-shaded campsite, which has good facilities, including

wi-fi and a TV room. **£7**/person

Glen Affric Youth Hostel Allt Beithe, 20 miles southwest of Cannich ☎0845 293 7373, ⓦsyha.org.uk. Utterly remote, this SYHA hostel near the head of Glen Affric makes a convenient if rudimentary stopover on the 25-mile hike through Glen Affric to Shiel Bridge. A wind turbine and solar panels provide the hostel with electricity, but note that you'll need to bring all your own food. Dorms **£22**; twins **£47**

Inverness

Straddling a nexus of major road and rail routes, **INVERNESS** is the busy hub of the Highlands, and an inevitable port of call if you're exploring the region by public transport. Over a hundred miles from any other major settlement yet with a population rapidly approaching 100,000, Inverness is the only city in the Highlands. Crowned by a pink crenellated **castle** and lavishly decorated with flowers, the city centre still has some hints of its medieval street layout, though unsightly concrete blocks do an efficient job of masking it. Within walking distance of the centre are peaceful spots along by the Ness, leafy parks and friendly B&Bs located in prosperous-looking stone houses.

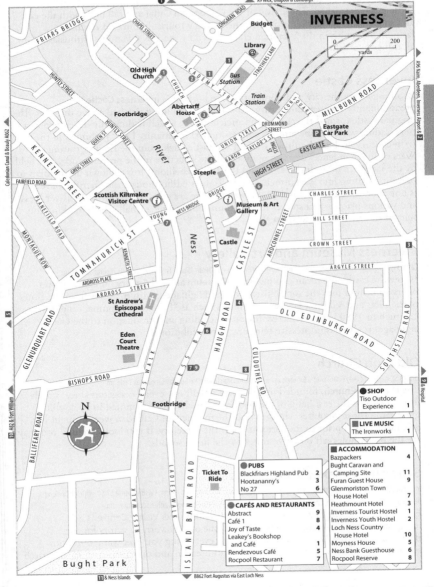

INVERNESS

● SHOP	
Tiso Outdoor Experience	1

■ LIVE MUSIC	
The Ironworks	1

■ ACCOMMODATION	
Bazpackers	4
Bught Caravan and Camping Site	11
Furan Guest House	9
Glenmoriston Town House Hotel	7
Heathmount Hotel	3
Inverness Tourist Hostel	1
Inverness Youth Hostel	2
Loch Ness Country House Hotel	10
Moyness House	5
Ness Bank Guesthouse	6
Rocpool Reserve	8

● PUBS	
Blackfriars Highland Pub	2
Hootananny's	3
No 27	6

● CAFÉS AND RESTAURANTS	
Abstract	9
Café 1	8
Joy of Taste	4
Leakey's Bookshop and Café	1
Rendezvous Café	5
Rocpool Restaurant	7

The sheltered **harbour** and proximity to the open sea made Inverness an important entrepôt and shipbuilding centre during medieval times. David I, who first imposed a feudal system on Scotland, erected a castle on the banks of the Ness to oversee maritime trade in the early twelfth century, promoting it to royal burgh status soon after. Bolstered by receipts from the lucrative export of leather, salmon and timber, the town grew to become the kingdom's most prosperous northern outpost, and an obvious target for the marauding Highlanders who plagued this remote border area. A second wave of growth occurred during the eighteenth century as the Highland cattle trade flourished. The arrival of the **Caledonian Canal** and **rail** links with the east and south brought further prosperity, heralding a tourist boom that reached a fashionable zenith in the Victorian era, fostered by the Royal Family's enthusiasm for all things Scottish.

Inverness Castle

Looming above the city and dominating the horizon is **Inverness Castle**, a predominantly nineteenth-century red-sandstone building perched above the river. The original castle formed the core of the ancient town, which had rapidly developed as a port trading with Europe after its conversion to Christianity by St Columba in the sixth century. Robert the Bruce wrested the castle back from the English during the Wars of Independence, destroying much of the structure in the process, and while held by the Jacobites in both the 1715 and the 1745 rebellions, it was blown up by them to prevent it falling into government hands. Today's edifice houses the Sheriff Court and is not open to the general public. However, there are good views down the River Ness and various plaques and statues in the grounds including a small plinth marking the start of the 73-mile Great Glen Way.

Inverness Museum and Art Gallery

Castle Wynd • April–Oct Tues–Sat 10am–5pm; Nov–March Thurs–Sat 10am–5pm • Free • ⦿ inverness.highland.museum

Below the castle, the revamped **Inverness Museum and Art Gallery** on Castle Wynd offers an insight into the social history of the Highlands, with treasures from the times of the Picts and Vikings, taxidermy exhibits such as "Felicity" the puma, caught in Cannich in 1980, and interactive features including an introduction to the Gaelic language. It also has impressive temporary art exhibitions.

Old High Church

Church St, next to Leakey's bookshop • Grounds open to public; church open for Sunday services at 11.15am

The **Old High Church**, founded in 1171 and rebuilt on several occasions since, stands just back from the east bank of the river on Church Street, hemmed in by a walled graveyard. Those Jacobites who survived the massacre of Culloden were brought here and incarcerated prior to their execution in the cemetery. If you look carefully you may see the bullet holes left on gravestones by the firing squads.

Scottish Kiltmaker Visitor Centre

In the Highland House of Fraser shop, on the west bank, 4–9 Huntly St • Daily 9am–10pm • Visitor centre £2.50, with kilt-making demonstrations daily 9am–5pm, English-language film shown on the hour • ⦿ highlandhouseoffraser.com

Entered through the factory shop, the **Scottish Kiltmaker Visitor Centre** is an imaginative small attraction, complete with the outfits worn by actors for the *Braveheart* and *Rob Roy* films, which sets out everything you ever wanted to know about tartan. There's an interesting seven-minute film and on weekdays you can watch

THE TRUTH ABOUT TARTAN

To much of the world, **tartan** is synonymous with Scotland. It's the natural choice for packaging for Scottish exports from shortbread and Sean Connery, and when the Scottish football team travels abroad, the high-spirited "Tartan Army" of fans is never far behind. Tartan is big business for the tourist industry, yet the truth is that romantic fiction and commercial interest have enclosed this ancient Highland art form within an almost insurmountable wall of myth.

The original form of tartan, the kind that long ago was called **Helande**, was a fine, hard and almost showerproof cloth spun in Highland villages from the wool of the native sheep, dyed with preparations of local plants. It was worn as a huge single piece of cloth, or **plaid**, which was belted around the waist and draped over the upper body, like a knee-length toga. The natural colours were clear but soft, and the broken pattern gave superb camouflage, unlike modern versions, where garish, clashing colours are often used to create impact.

TRANSFORMING TARTAN

The myth-makers were about four centuries ahead of themselves in dressing up the warriors of the film *Braveheart* in plaid: in fact tartan did not become popular in the Lowlands until the beginning of the eighteenth century, when it was adopted as the anti-Union badge of the **Jacobites**. After Culloden, a ban on the wearing of tartan in the Highlands lasted some 25 years; in that time it became a fondly held emblem for emigrant Highlanders in the colonies and was incorporated into the uniforms of the new Highland regiments in the British Army. Then **Sir Walter Scott** set to work glamorizing the clans, dressing George IV in a kilt for his visit to Edinburgh in 1822. By the time Queen Victoria set the royal seal of approval on both the Highlands and tartan with her extended annual holidays at Balmoral, the concept of tartan as formal dress rather than rough Highland wear was assured.

With the gentrification of the kilt came "rules" about the correct form of attire and the idea that every clan had its own distinguishing tartan. To have the right to wear tartan, one had to belong, albeit remotely, to a clan, and so the way was paved for the "what's-my-tartan?" lists that appear in Scottish souvenir shops. Great feats of genealogical gymnastics were performed: where lists left gaps, a marketing phenomenon of themed tartans developed, with new patterns made for different districts, companies and even football teams.

Scotsmen today will commonly wear the kilt for weddings and other formal occasions; properly made kilts, however – comprising some four yards of one hundred percent wool – are likely to set you back £300 or more, with the rest of the regalia at least doubling that figure. If the contents of your sporran don't stretch that far, most places selling kilts will rent outfits on a daily basis. The best place to find better-quality material is a recognized Highland outfitter rather than a souvenir shop: in Inverness, try the **Scottish Kiltmaker Visitor Centre** at the Highland House of Fraser shop (see opposite).

various tartan products being made in the workshop. The finished products are, of course, on sale in the showroom downstairs, along with all manner of Highland knitwear, woven woollies and Harris tweed.

Ness Islands

From **St Andrews Episcopal Cathedral**, on the west bank of the river, you can wander a mile or so upriver to the peaceful **Ness Islands**, an attractive, informal public park reached and linked by footbridges. Laid out with mature trees and shrubs, the islands are the favourite haunt of local anglers.

Caledonian Canal

Half a mile upstream from the Ness Islands park, the River Ness runs close to the **Caledonian Canal**, designed by Thomas Telford in the early nineteenth century as a link between the east and west coasts, joining lochs Ness, Oich, Lochy and Linnhe. Today its main use is recreational, and there are cruises through part of it to Loch Ness (see p.197), while the towpath provides relaxing walks with good views.

ARRIVAL AND DEPARTURE INVERNESS

By plane Inverness Airport (☎01667 464000) is at Dalcross, 7 miles east of the city; from here, bus #11 (every 30min, 6am–11pm; 25min; £3.75; ⊛stagecoachbus.com) goes into town, while a taxi (try Tartan Taxis on ☎01463 222777) costs around £14.

Destinations Belfast (6 weekly; 1hr 5min); Birmingham (Mon–Fri & Sun 1 daily; 1hr 30min); Bristol (1–2 daily; 1hr 5min); Kirkwall (Mon–Sat 1–2 daily; 45min); London Gatwick (4–5 daily; 1hr 50min); Luton (1 daily; 1hr 20min); Manchester (Mon–Fri 2 daily, Sat & Sun 1 daily; 1hr 30min); Stornoway (Mon–Fri 3–4 daily, Sat, & Sun 1 daily; 40min).

By train The train station is on Station Square, just off Academy St, to the northeast of the centre.

Destinations Aberdeen (Mon–Sat 11 daily; Sun 5 daily; 2hr 15min); Aviemore (Mon–Sat 11 daily, Sun 7 daily; 40min); Edinburgh (Mon–Sat 8 daily, Sun 5 daily; 3hr

30min); Glasgow Queen St (3–4 daily; 3hr 20min); Kyle of Lochalsh (Mon–Sat 4 daily, Sun 2 daily; 2hr 30min); London King's Cross (Mon–Fri & Sun 2 daily, Sat 1 daily; 8hr–12hr 45min); Thurso (Mon–Sat 2 daily, Sun 1 daily; 3hr 45min); Wick (Mon–Sat 4 daily, Sun 1; 4hr 20min).

By bus The main bus hub is just north of the train station, close to the public library.

Destinations Aberdeen (hourly; 3hr 50min); Aviemore (every 1–2hr; 45min); Drumnadrochit (1–2/hr; 30min); Fort Augustus (up to 9 daily; 1hr); Fort William (up to 9 daily; 2hr); Glasgow (5 daily; 3hr 25min–4hr); Kyle of Lochalsh (3 daily; 2hr); Nairn (up to 3/hr; 45min); Perth (7 daily; 2hr 50min); Portree (3 daily; 3hr 15min); Thurso (Mon–Sat 5 daily, Sun 3 daily; 3hr); Ullapool (2–4 daily; 1hr 25min).

INFORMATION AND ACTIVITIES

Tourist office The tourist office is in an unsightly 1960s block on Castle Wynd, just 5min walk from the train station (April & May Mon–Sat 9am–5pm, Sun 10am–5pm; June Mon–Sat 9am–6pm, Sun 9.30am–5pm; July & Aug Mon–Sat 9am–6.30pm, Sun 9.30am–6pm; Sept & Oct Mon–Sat 9am–5pm, Sun 10am–4pm; Nov–March Mon–Sat 9am–5pm, Sun 10am–3pm). It stocks a wide range of literature, including free maps of the city and its environs, and the staff can book local accommodation for a £4 fee. There's also a CalMac ferry booking office in the building (⊛calmac.co.uk).

Left luggage Train-station lockers cost £3/5 for 24hr, depending on size (Mon–Sat 6.40am–7.50pm, Sun

10.40am–6.20pm); the left-luggage room in the bus station costs £4 per item per day (Mon–Sat 8.30am–5.30pm, Sun 9am–5.30pm).

Bike rental Ticket to Ride at The Pavilion, Bellfield Park (daily 9am–6pm; ☎01463 419160, ⊛tickettoride highlands.co.uk) rents out decent hybrid bikes for £20/day.

Equipment Tiso Outdoor Experience at 2 Henderson Rd, on the Longman Estate (Mon, Tues, Fri & Sat 9am–6pm, Wed 9.30am–6pm, Thurs 9am–7pm, Sun 10am–5pm; ☎01463 729171, ⊛tiso.com) has a large range of outdoor gear to hire or buy. There's also an indoor climbing wall and a path for testing walking boots before you buy.

TOURS AND CRUISES

Inverness is the departure point for a range of day-tours and cruises to nearby attractions, including Loch Ness, Skye, Orkney and the Moray Firth, where there's a chance to spot dolphins (see p.208). Inverness is also one of the few places where transport connections allow you to embark on a major grand tour of the Highlands.

THE HIGHLANDS AND SKYE

For exploring the northwest, ScotRail (☎0845 755 0033, ⊛scotrail.co.uk) sells a Highland Rover pass (£81.50), offering four days of unlimited travel over eight consecutive days, with many train, ferry and coach routes included.

LOCH NESS

Loch Ness cruises typically incorporate a visit to a monster exhibition at Drumnadrochit and Urquhart Castle. Jacobite Cruises (☎01463 233999, ⊛jacobite.co.uk) runs a 3hr

30min coach trip (£30) to Loch Ness, including a 30min cruise and admission to the Loch Ness Centre & Exhibition (see p.199).

ORKNEY

From June to August, John O' Groats Ferries (☎01955 611353, ⊛jogferry.co.uk) runs day-trips to Orkney (£68), including visits to Kirkwall, Scapa Flow and the Ring of Brodgar. Departures daily from Inverness at 7.30am.

FROM TOP DOLPHINS IN THE MORAY FIRTH (P.208); LEANACH COTTAGE, CULLODEN (P.209) >

ACCOMMODATION

HOTELS

Glenmoriston Town House Hotel 20 Ness Bank ☎01463 223777, ⓦ www.glenmoristontownhouse.com. A smart contemporary hotel by the riverside just a few minutes' walk from the town centre, with muted decor and a good dining experience on offer at *Abstract* (see below). **£130**

Heathmount Hotel Kingsmill Rd ☎01463 235877, ⓦ heathmounthotel.com. Reasonably central boutique hotel with blingy but comfortable rooms, some of which have four-poster beds; all come with Sky TV and an iPod dock. **£95**

Loch Ness Country House Hotel Off the A82 Fort William Rd ☎01463 230512, ⓦ lochnesscountryhouse hotel.co.uk. Luxurious country-house hotel, 3 miles south-west of central Inverness. Offers modern Scottish food, fine wines and more than two hundred malts, as well as very comfortable and spacious rooms. **£169**

★ **Rocpool Reserve** Culduthel Rd ☎01463 240089, ⓦ rocpool.com. Only a 10min walk south of the castle, this acclaimed hotel and restaurant has tastefully decorated rooms (think white-cotton bed sheets and subtle splashes of colour), plus a swanky, French-inspired restaurant. **£210**

B&BS

Furan Guest House 100 Old Edinburgh Rd ☎01463 712094, ⓦ furan.co.uk. Good-value B&B a mile south of the centre, run by former hoteliers. Has a good choice of spotlessly clean rooms and a friendly resident cat. Book direct for the best rates. **£75**

Moyness House 6 Bruce Gardens ☎01463 233836, ⓦ moyness.co.uk. Warm, welcoming, upmarket B&B on the west side of Inverness, with original Victorian features (it was built in 1880) and a nice walled garden. **£78**

Ness Bank Guesthouse 7 Ness Bank ☎01463 232939, ⓦ nessbankguesthouse.co.uk. Five comfortable if slightly dated rooms in a lovely Grade II-listed Victorian house on the river; the in-room information packs have handy tips on the local area. **£76**

HOSTELS

Bazpackers 4 Culduthel Rd ☎01463 717663, ⓦ bazpackershostel.co.uk. The most cosy and relaxed of the city's hostels, with more than thirty beds, including three doubles and two twins; some dorms are mixed. Good location, great views and a garden, which is used for barbecues. Dorms **£17**; twins/doubles **£40**

Inverness Tourist Hostel 24 Rose St ☎01463 241962, ⓦ invernesshostel.com. Cheap, conveniently located hostel near the bus station, with cheery, helpful staff. The downside is that the dorms are a little musty, and there's a slightly institutional feel to the place. Dorms **£10**

Inverness Youth Hostel Victoria Drive, off Millburn Rd, about three-quarters of a mile east of the centre ☎01463 231771, ⓦ syha.org.uk. Big SYHA hostel with large kitchens and communal areas, plus six-bed family rooms and cheap singles in addition to the usual dorms. However, it's quite far from the centre, and the building is devoid of character. Dorms **£20**; singles **£22**; twins **£46**; family room **£138**

CAMPSITE

Bught Caravan and Camping Site Bught Park, a mile south of the centre ☎01463 236920, ⓦ inverness caravanpark.com. Inverness's main campsite on the west bank of the river near the sports centre. Has good facilities, but it can get very crowded at the height of the season. Easter to Sept. **£8**/person

EATING

CAFÉS

★ **Leakey's Bookshop and Café** Church St ☎01463 239947. Prise yourself away from the old books and maps at Scotland's largest used bookshop to enjoy a cup of tea or a warming bowl of soup (£3.30) at the upstairs café. Mon–Sat 10am–5.30pm.

Rendezvous Café 14A Church St ☎01463 718444. Good lattes (£2.40) are served inside and out at this café, one of the more relaxed places for coffee and a snack in the city centre. Mon–Sat 8am–5pm, Sun 9am–4pm.

RESTAURANTS

Abstract 20 Ness Bank ☎01463 223777, ⓦ abstract restaurant.com. This award-winning French restaurant within the *Glenmoriston Town House Hotel* (see above) stylishly serves unexpected combinations of flavours – like

wild hake with smoked mashed potato. Mains start at £16.50. Tues–Sat 6pm–10pm.

Café 1 75 Castle St ☎01463 226200, ⓦ cafe1.net. You'll find contemporary cooking – like grilled chicken with rocket, pineapple and balsamic vinegar – in a bistro-style setting here. The restaurant's beef, lamb and pork is reared on a croft 8 miles north of Inverness. At £12.50 for two courses, the "early bird" menu (Mon–Fri noon–6.45pm & Sat noon–2.30pm) is good value. Mon–Fri noon–9.30pm, Sat noon–2.30pm & 6–9.30pm.

Joy of Taste 25 Church St ☎01463 241459, ⓦ thejoyof taste.co.uk. Sparkly green cloths cover *Joy of Taste*'s tables, which are worked by a team of volunteers, each of whom has a stake in the restaurant's success. The lunch menu, with pork sausages and mash for £5.95, represents superb value. Refreshingly different. Daily: noon–3pm & 5pm–late.

Rocpool Restaurant 1 Ness Walk ☎01463 717274. One of the city's excellent, smartish dining options, with a contemporary setting, attentive staff and deliciously rich food. The escalope of calves liver with roasted purple figs is £19.95. Mon–Sat noon–2.30pm & 5.45–10pm.

DRINKING AND ENTERTAINMENT

PUBS

Blackfriars Highland Pub 93–95 Academy St. Popular pub where you can enjoy folk music most Friday and Saturday nights, plus a selection of real ale, cheap steak and gravy pies (£2.25), and bigger pub meals. Mon–Thurs 11am–midnight, Fri 11am–1am, Sat 11am–12.30am & Sun 12.30–11pm; food served daily 11am–9pm.

Hootananny's 67 Church St ☎01463 233651. Lively watering hole with hearty food (including a butternut squash and chickpea casserole served with cheese scones). On Saturday afternoons there are ceilidhs (2.30–4.30pm).

Mon–Thurs noon–1am, Fri & Sat noon–3am, Sun 6.30pm–midnight.

No 27 27 Castle St. Skinny bar/restaurant with a wide range of beers (there's a new guest ale every Sunday) and salmon fishcakes for £8.50. Mon–Thurs 11am–11pm, Fri & Sat 11am–midnight, Sun 12.30–11pm.

LIVE MUSIC

The Ironworks 122b Academy St ⊛ironworksvenue .com. Large live venue with space for a thousand music fans. The place to come for touring bands, stand-up comedy and the occasional club night (see website for events).

DIRECTORY

Car rental Budget, Railway Terrace, behind the train station (☎01463 713333).

Hospital Raigmore Hospital (☎01463 704000) is at Old Perth Rd on the southeastern outskirts of town, close to the A9.

Internet Inverness Library, near the bus station, offers free internet access (ID required). Mon & Tues 9am–6.30pm,

Wed 10am–6.30pm, Thurs 9am–8pm, Fri 9am–6.30pm, Sat 9am–5pm.

Laundry New City Laundrette, 17 Young St ☎01463 242507.

Post office 14–16 Queensgate (Mon & Wed–Sat 9am–5.30pm, Tues 9.30am–5.30pm).

Around Inverness

A string of worthwhile sights punctuates the approach to Inverness along the A96, the main route from Aberdeen. The low-key resort of **Nairn**, with its long white-sand beaches and championship golf course, stands within striking distance of several monuments, including whimsical **Cawdor Castle**, best known for its role in Shakespeare's *Macbeth*, and **Fort George**, one of several impressive Hanoverian bastions erected in the wake of the Jacobite rebellion. The infamous battle and ensuing massacre that ended Bonnie Prince Charlie's uprising took place on the outskirts of Inverness at **Culloden**, where a visitor centre and memorial stones beside a heather-clad moor recall the gruesome events of 1746.

Northeast of Inverness is the **Moray Firth**, one of the UK's best locations for spotting dolphins (see p.108). Closer to the city, where this inlet merges with the River Ness, is the start of the Beauly Firth, a sheltered sea loch bounded by the Black Isle in the north and the wooded hills of the Aird to the south. Heading northwest from Inverness, most traffic uses Kessock Bridge (the A9) to cross the Moray Firth; the A862, which skirts the shoreline and the mud flats, offers a slower, more scenic alternative.

Craig Phadrig

3 miles west of the city centre • Stagecoach bus #2 from Church St to Scorguie (Mon–Sat every 20min; 10min) then walk the final half-mile west

West of the town, on the top of **Craig Phadrig** hill, there's a vitrified **Iron Age fort**, reputed to be where the Pictish king Brude received St Columba in the sixth century.

The walls of the fort were built of stone laced with timber and, when the timber was set alight, some of the stone fused to glass, becoming "vitrified". Waymarked forest trails start from the car parks at the bottom of the hill and lead up to the fort, though only the outlines of its perimeter defences are now visible, and tree planting is beginning to block some of the views.

Culloden

6 miles east of Inverness off B9006 • Visitor centre daily: April, May, Sept & Oct 9am–5.30pm; June–Aug 9am–6pm, Nov, Dec, Feb & March 10am–4pm; closed Jan • £10.50, including audio guide of the site; NTS • W nts.org.uk/culloden • Hourly Stagecoach buses run from Falcon Square near Inverness train station to the visitor centre (35min)

The windswept moorland of **CULLODEN** witnessed the last-ever battle on British soil when, on April 16, 1746, the Jacobite cause was finally subdued – a turning point in the history of the Scottish nation. Today, this historic site attracts more than 200,000 visitors annually. Your first stop should be the superb **visitor centre**, which hosts costumed actors and state-of-the-art audiovisual and interactive technology, all employed to tell the tragedy of Culloden through the words, songs and poetic verse of locals and soldiers who experienced it. The *pièce de résistance* is the powerful "battle immersion theatre" where visitors are surrounded by lifelike cinematography and the sounds of the raging, bloody fight.

> ### THE DOLPHINS OF THE MORAY FIRTH
>
> The **Moray Firth**, a great wedge-shaped bay forming the eastern coastline of the Highlands, is one of only three areas of UK waters that support a resident population of **dolphins**. Around 200 of these beautiful, intelligent marine mammals live in the estuary, the most northerly breeding ground in Europe for this particular species – the bottle-nosed dolphin (*Tursiops truncatus*) – and you stand a good chance of spotting a few, either from the shore or a boat.
>
> One of the best places in Scotland, if not in Europe, to look for them is **Chanonry Point**, on the Black Isle – a spit of sand protruding into a narrow, deep channel, where converging currents bring fish close to the surface, and thus the dolphins close to shore; a rising tide is the most likely time to see them.
>
> Several companies run dolphin-spotting **boat trips** around the Moray Firth. However, researchers claim that the increased traffic is causing the dolphins unnecessary stress, particularly during the all-important breeding period when passing vessels are thought to force calves underwater for uncomfortably long periods. So if you decide to go on a cruise to see the dolphins, which also sometimes provides the chance of spotting minke whales, porpoises, seals and otters, make sure that the operator is a member of the Dolphin Space Programme's accreditation scheme (W dolphinspace.org).
>
> Trips with accredited operators, most of which run between April and October, are especially popular in July and August, so be sure to book them well in advance. To get from Inverness to Avoch (20min) or Cromarty (50min) with public transport, take Stagecoach bus #26 from the bus station (at least hourly) – not all services run as far as Cromarty, so check before boarding.
>
> #### BOAT TOURS
>
> **Dolphin Trips Avoch** On the northern side of the firth in Avoch T 01381 622383, W dolphintripsavoch.co.uk. Hourly sailings from Avoch's harbour, at the eastern end of the village, with trips lasting one hour (£14).
>
> **Ecoventures** Victoria Place, Cromarty T 01381 600323, W ecoventures.co.uk. Based on the Black Isle, on the northern side of the firth, *Ecoventures* runs two-hour wildlife cruises (£25) with the chance to spot dolphins, harbour porpoises and grey seals.
>
> **Phoenix Boat Trips** T 07703 168097, W inverness-dolphin-trips.co.uk. Runs one-hour trips (£16) from Inverness Marina at 10.30am, noon, 1.30pm and 3pm. When demand warrants it, they also run a 2hr 30min cruise to Fort George (see p.210) and Chanonry Point (£25).

Every April, on the Saturday closest to the date of the battle, there's a small commemorative service at Culloden. The visitor centre has a reference library and will check for you if you think you have an ancestor who died here.

Brief history

The second Jacobite rebellion had begun on August 19, 1745, with the raising of the Stuarts' standard at **Glenfinnan** on the west coast (see p.221). Shortly after, Edinburgh fell into Jacobite hands, and Bonnie Prince Charlie began his march on London. The ruling Hanoverians had appointed the ambitious young Duke of Cumberland to command their forces, which included troops from the Lowlands and Highlands. The duke's pursuit, together with bad weather and lack of funds, eventually forced the Jacobite forces – mostly comprised of Highlanders – to retreat north. They ended up at Culloden, where, ill fed and exhausted after a pointless night march, they were hopelessly outnumbered by the government forces. The open, flat ground of Culloden Moor was totally unsuitable for the Highlanders' style of courageous but undisciplined fighting, which needed steep hills and lots of cover to provide the element of surprise, and they were routed.

The end of the clan system

After the battle, in which 1500 Highlanders were slaughtered (many of them as they lay wounded on the battlefield), Bonnie Prince Charlie fled west to the hills and islands, where loyal Highlanders sheltered and protected him. He eventually escaped to France, leaving his supporters to their fate – and, in effect, ushering in the end of the clan system. The clans were disarmed, the wearing of tartan and playing of bagpipes forbidden, and the chiefs became landlords greedy for higher and higher rents. The battle also unleashed an orgy of violent reprisals on Scotland, as unruly government troops raped and pillaged their way across the region; within a century, the Highland way of life had changed out of all recognition.

The battlefield

Flags mark out the positions of the two armies while simple headstones mark the **clan graves**. The **Field of the English**, for many years unmarked, is a mass grave for the fifty or so government soldiers who died (though as this government force also included Scottish infantry regiments, the term "English" is a misnomer). Half a mile east of the battlefield, just beyond the crossroads on the main road, is the **Cumberland Stone**, thought for many years to have been the point from where the duke watched the battle. It is more likely, however, that he was much further forward and simply used the stone for shelter. Elsewhere, the restored **Leanach cottage** marks the spot where thirty injured Jacobites were burnt alive.

Cawdor Castle

14 miles northeast of Inverness off the A96 • May–Oct daily 10am–5pm • £9.75; gardens & nature trails only £5.50 • ☎ 01667 404401, ⓦ cawdorcastle.com • From Nairn (see p.210), take a taxi for the 6 miles (around £14; book with Taxi 24/7 Nairn ☎ 01667 459595) or book Nairn's Dial-a-Bus service by 6pm the day before (☎ 01667 456066)

The pretty village of **CAWDOR**, eight miles east of Culloden, is the site of **Cawdor Castle**, a setting intimately linked to Shakespeare's *Macbeth*: the fulfilment of the witches' prediction that Macbeth was to become thane of Cawdor sets off his tragic desire to be king. Though visitors arrive here in their droves each summer because of the site's literary associations, the castle, which dates from the early fourteenth century, could not possibly have witnessed the grisly historical events on which the Bard's drama was based. However, the immaculately restored monument – a fairy-tale affair of towers, turrets, hidden passageways, dungeons, gargoyles and crenellations whimsically shooting off from the original keep – is still well worth a visit.

Fort George

13 miles northeast of Inverness, near Ardersier • Daily: April–Sept 9.30am–5.30pm; Oct–March 9.30am–4.30pm • £8.90; HS • ☎ 01667 460 232 • As with Cawdor Castle (see p.209), book a taxi or Dial-a-Bus service to take you from Nairn

Eight miles of undulating coastal farmland separate Cawdor Castle from **Fort George**, an old Hanoverian bastion with walls a mile long, considered by military architectural historians to be one of the finest fortifications in Europe. Crowning a sandy spit that juts into the middle of the Moray Firth, it was built between 1747 and 1769 as a base for George II's army, in case the Highlanders should attempt to rekindle the Jacobite flame. By the time of its completion, however, the uprising had been firmly quashed and the fort has been used ever since as barracks; note the armed sentries at the main entrance and the periodic crack of live gunfire from the nearby firing ranges.

Walking on the northern, grass-covered casemates, which look out into the estuary, you may be lucky enough to see a school of bottle-nosed **dolphins** (see p.208) swimming in with the tide. This is also a good spot for birdwatching: a colony of kittiwakes occupies the fort's slate rooftops.

Nairn

One of the driest and sunniest places in the whole of Scotland, **NAIRN**, sixteen miles east of Inverness, began its days as a peaceful community of fishermen and farmers. The former spoke Gaelic, the latter English, allowing James VI to boast that a town in his kingdom was so large that people at one end of the main street could not understand those at the other end. Nairn became popular in Victorian times, when the train line offered a convenient link to its revitalizing sea air and mild climate, and today the 11,000-strong population still relies on tourism, with all the ingredients for a traditional seaside holiday – sandy beach, ice-cream shops and fish-and-chip stalls. The town has two championship golf courses, and Thomas Telford's **harbour** is filled with leisure craft rather than fishing boats.

Nairn Museum

Viewfield House, King St • May–Oct Mon–Fri 10am–4.30pm, Sat 10am–1pm (last admission 30min before closing) • £3 • ☎ 01667 456791, Ⓦ nairnmuseum.co.uk

The **Nairn Museum** provides a general insight into the history and prehistory of the area; the **Fishertown Room** illustrates the parsimonious and puritanical life of the fishing families, while the weapon-filled **Military Room** includes information on the battles of Culloden and Auldearn.

ARRIVAL AND INFORMATION   NAIRN

By bus Buses arrive and depart from King St, just south of the police station.
Destinations Aberdeen (hourly; 3hr 15min); Elgin (every 30min; 45min); Forres (every 30min; 25min); Inverness (up to 3/hr; 45min).
By train Nairn's station is just south of the centre, where Chattan Drive meets Cawdor St.
Destinations Aberdeen (every 1–2hr; 2hr); Elgin (every 1–2hr; 25min); Forres (every 1–2hr; 10min); Inverness (every 1–2hr; 20min).

Bike rental Bikes are available from Bike and Buggy, 6A Falconers Lane (Mon, Tues, Thurs & Fri 9.30am–5pm, Sat 9.30am–4pm; ☎ 01667 455416, Ⓦ bikeandbuggy.co.uk), for £15/day.
Information There's a tourist information point within the Nairn Community & Arts Centre on King St (Mon–Thurs 8.30am–10pm, Fri 8.30am–late, depending on events, Sat 8.30am–5pm, Sun 9am–1pm & 5–9pm; ☎ 01667 453476, Ⓦ nairncommunitycentre.co.uk). Their handy *Welcome to Nairn* map is worth picking up.

ACCOMMODATION

Boath House In the village of Auldearn, 2 miles east of Nairn ☎ 01667 454896, ⓦ boath-house.com. The most luxurious place to stay in the area is this fine Georgian country house set in magnificent gardens, with its own Michelin-starred restaurant (see below). **£265**

Cawdor House 7 Cawdor St ☎ 01667 455855, ⓦ cawdor housenairn.co.uk. A bright and attractive B&B, conveniently located between the train station and the main shopping street. Good choice of breakfasts, with vegetarians well catered for. **£82**

EATING AND DRINKING

Boath House At Boath House (see above) ☎ 01667 454896. Mouthwatering, pricey, Michelin-starred cooking that draws upon organic produce and regional dairy, fish and meat suppliers. For an affordable taste of such luxury, book a lunchtime table (three courses for £30). Note that there is only one sitting for dinner. Daily: lunch 12.30–1.15pm; dinner served at 7.30pm.

The Classroom 1 Cawdor St ☎ 01667 455999. Nairn's most popular bar/restaurant, serving tasty light bites, lunches and dinners. Try the house salad with sun-blushed tomatoes and char-grilled chicken (£7.50). Mon–Sat 10am–late, Sun 11am–late.

3

The north and northwest Highlands

SURFER NEAR THURSO

The north and northwest Highlands

Come to the north and northwest Highlands, the area beyond the Great Glen, to sample the soul of the Highlands. This is a region of spectacular scenery: a combination of bare mountains, remote glens, dark lochs and tumbling rivers surrounded on three sides by a magnificent coastline. Although the inspiring landscape, along with its tranquility and space, are the main attractions, so too is the sense of remoteness, even today. The vast peat bogs in the north are among the most extensive and unspoilt wilderness areas in Europe and some of the west coast crofting villages can still be reached only by boat.

Different weather conditions and cultural histories give each of the three coastlines a distinct character. For many visitors, the Highlands' **west coast** is the reason to visit Scotland. The Vikings, who ruled the region in the ninth century, called it the "South Land", from which the modern district of Sutherland takes its name. After Culloden, the Clearances emptied most of the inland glens of the far north, and left the population clinging to the coastline, which is the main reason to come. Cut by fjord-like **sea lochs**, it is scalloped by white-sand **beaches** or **waterfalls** in high, shattered cliffs, with **mountains** sweeping up from the shoreline. Weather fronts roll over rapidly but when the sun shines, the sparkle of the sea, the rich colours in the clear light and the clarity of the views to the Hebrides are pure magic. With exhilarating scenery everywhere you look, this is superb touring country. It also provides some of the best **cycling**, **walking** and **sea-kayaking** in Britain, superlative trout and salmon **fishing**, and wildlife by the tonne. In fact the only issues are the west coast's predictably unpredictable **weather**, and **midges** that drive even the locals to distraction from June to August.

The most visited part of the west coast is the stretch between Kyle of Lochalsh and Ullapool. This is **Wester Ross**, with quintessentially west-coast scenes and beautiful coast set against some of Scotland's most impressive mountains and Skye and the Western Isles on the horizon. The obvious highlights are the mountainscape of **Torridon**, **Gairloch**'s sandy beaches, the botanic gardens at **Inverewe**, and **Ullapool** itself, a bustling fishing town and launchpad for the Outer Hebrides. However, press on north or south and you get a truer sense of the isolation that makes this coast so special. Traversed by few roads, the remote northwest is wild and bleak. Villages in the southwest tend to be more sheltered, but they are separated by some of the most extensive wilderness areas in Britain – lonely peninsulas like **Ardnamurchan**, **Glenelg** or **Knoydart**, a magical place with no road access and the remotest pub in mainland Britain.

The other coasts receive fewer visitors and of the two the north coast is more popular. Stretching from **Cape Wrath** at the very northwest tip of the mainland to **John O'Groats**,

APPLECROSS PENINSULA, WESTER ROSS

Highlights

❶ West Highland Railway Ride the rails of Britain's most scenic train journey from Glasgow to Mallaig via Fort William for scenery that's more magical by the mile. **See p.222**

❷ Knoydart Thrilling remoteness is not the only reason to visit Britain's last wilderness – there's a so its most isolated pub. **See p.225**

❸ Wester Ross Arguably Scotland's finest scenery – a heady mix of high mountains, sea lochs, sweeping bays, scattered islands and icyllic Applecross. **See p.231**

❹ Ceilidhs An impromptu night of music and song in the pub best expresses the vitality of modern Highland culture – try *Ceilidh Place* in Ullapool or Knoydart's *Old Forge*. **See p.242**

❺ Suilven The fantastical sugarloaf outline of this iconic mountain is reason enough to travel to Assynt. **See p.244**

❻ Sandwood Bay It's a two-hour walk – or the start of a two-day hike around Cape Wrath – to this glorious beach at the tip of Britain. **See p.248**

❼ Dunnet Head Come to the true tip of mainland Britain, all remote red cliffs and empty seascapes to Orkney. **See p.254**

❽ Cromarty A mix-and-match of handsome Georgian townhouses and cute cottages all packaged up in a friendly coastal town. **See p.257**

HIGHLIGHTS ARE MARKED ON THE MAP ON PP.216–217

THE NORTH & NORTHWEST HIGHLANDS

HIGHLIGHTS

1. West Highland Railway
2. Knoydart
3. Wester Ross
4. Ceilidhs
5. Suilven
6. Sandwood Bay
7. Dunnet Head
8. Cromarty

Hoy

Pentland Firth

Stroma

Duncansby Head

John O'Groats

Ness Head

Sinclair's Bay

Wick

Loch of Yarrows

Lybster

Hill o' Many Stanes

Grey Cairns of Camster

Dunnet Head

Dunnet Bay

Thurso

Scrabster

Dounreay

Melvich

Strathy Pt.

Halkirk

A9

Dunbeath

Badbea

Helmsdale

Morven (2316ft)

FLOW COUNTRY

Forsinard

A897

Kinbrace

Kildonan

Brora

Dunrobin Castle

Golspie

Dornoch

Dornoch Firth

Tarbat Ness

Portmahomack

Tain

Bettyhill

BORGIE FOREST

Strath Naver

Syre

Loch Naver

Rogart

L. Fleet

Bonar Bridge

A9

Kyle of Tongue

Tongue

Ben Loyal (2509ft)

Ben Hope (3040ft)

Altnaharra

Loch Shin

Laing

Fall of Shin

A838

Carbisdale Castle

Croick

Ben Wyvis

Smoo Cave

Kyle of Durness

Durness

Keodale

Kinlochbervie

Loch Eriboll

Foinaven (2980ft)

Eas-Coul-Aulin Falls

Inchnadamph

Ben More Assynt (3273ft)

A837

Corrieshalloch Gorge

Braemore

Corrieshalloch Gorge

Cape Wrath

Sandwood Loch

Sandwood Bay

Sheigra

Loch Laxford

Handa Island

Tarbet

Scourie

Laxford Bridge

A894

Kylestrome

Kylesku

Loch Assynt

Canisp (2779ft)

Suilven (2398ft)

A835

Ullapool

Loch Broom

A835

Drumbeg

B869

Achmelvich

Lochinver

Eddrachillis Bay

Pt. of Stoer

Altandhu

Achiltibuie

COIGACH

Little Loch Broom

Summer Isles

Scoraig

Gruinard Bay

Gruinard Island

Inverewe

Loch Ewe

Poolewe

Cove

Rua Reidh

NORTH MINCH

Lewis

Stornoway

it is even more rugged than the west, its sheer cliffs and white-sand bays bearing the brunt of frequently fierce Atlantic storms. The only town here is **Thurso**, jumping-off point for the main ferry service to Orkney.

All of this makes the fertile **east coast** of the Highlands such a surprise. Stretching north from Inverness to the old herring port of **Wick**, it is a place of rolling moors, green fields and woodlands which run down to the sandy beaches of the **Black Isle** and **Cromarty** and **Dornoch firths**. If the west coast is about raw nature, the east is one of human history: **Golspie**'s Sutherland Monument and castle, **Dornoch**'s fourteenth-century sandstone cathedral, relics of the **Picts** and several sites linked to the **Clearances**.

GETTING AROUND
THE HIGHLANDS

Getting around the **Highlands**, particularly the remoter parts, can be tricky without your own transport. **Bus services** are sporadic and often cease entirely on Sunday. And a word of advice if you are **driving**: fuel supplies are few and far between in the west and north, so fill up early and be prepared for higher prices. Bear in mind, too, that the Highlands' single-track roads are far from fast. See that as a good thing.

Morvern to Knoydart: the "Rough Bounds"

Its Gaelic name *Garbh-chiochan* translates as the "**Rough Bounds**", implying a region geographically and spiritually apart, and the southwest corner of the Highlands is indeed remote and sparsely populated. From the empty district of **Morvern** to the isolated **Knoydart** peninsula are lonely mountains and moors, a rocky, indented coast studded by white beaches and wonderful views to Mull, Skye and other islands. It's scenery that begs you to spend time exploring on foot.

Morvern

Bounded on three sides by sea lochs and in the north by desolate Glen Tarbet, the mountainous **Morvern peninsula** lies at the southwest corner of the Rough Bounds. Many inhabitants of St Kilda were settled here when the island was abandoned (see p.310) and the landscape can seem bleak until the coast reveals views to Mull.

Lochaline

Most visitors only travel through the Morvern peninsula to get to **LOCHALINE** (pronounced "loch-*aa*lin") on the **Sound of Mull**, little more than a scattering of houses around a small pier built as a work-for-food scheme during famine in 1846. From here, a small ferry chugs to **Fishnish** – the shortest crossing to Mull from the mainland and cheaper than the Oban–Craignure crossing with a car.

ARRIVAL AND DEPARTURE
MORVERN

By bus Shiel Buses (☎01967 431272, ☜shielbuses.co.uk) runs a single service between Morvern and Fort William on Tues, Thurs and Fri, plus a Sat service from mid-June to early Sept. By request, the bus goes as far as the road end at Drimnin (3h 10min), at the northwest corner of Morvern, for ferries to Tobermory.

By ferry To save the long journey around Loch Eil into the peninsula, a ferry nips across to Ardgour from

Corran Ferry, 9 miles south of Fort William, every 20–30min (Mon–Sat 6.30am–9.20pm, Sun 8.30am–9.20pm; 10min). In addition, two services link the peninsula to Mull: a car ferry from Lochaline to Fishnish (Mon–Sat 6.30am–9.20pm, Sun 8.30am–9.20pm; 15min) and a passenger-only charter service from Drimnin to Tobermory, run by Ardnamurchan Charters (☎01972 500208, ☜west-scotland-marine.com).

ACTIVITIES

Lochaline Dive Centre Lochaline ☎01967 421627, ☜lochalinedivecentre.co.uk. Based in the village centre, this outfit specializes in underwater archeology on local

wrecks, and provides drift, shallow, scenic and shore dives. Also offers air filling and cylinder hire.

EATING

★ **Whitehouse Restaurant** Lochaline ☎ 01967 421777, ⓦ thewhitehouserestaurant.co.uk. Arguably the best reason to visit Morvern, this is one of the Highlands' finest restaurants. Simple style belies outstanding modern European cooking that showcases local meat and seafood like fresh mussels and crab. Booking recommended. Easter–Oct Tues–Sat noon–9pm.

The Ardnamurchan peninsula

The **Ardnamurchan peninsula** is the most westerly point on the British mainland. Once ruled by Norse invaders, the peninsula lost most inhabitants during the Clearances and only a handful of crofting settlements cling to the coastline, making this one of the west coast's backwaters. Yet with its empty beaches and sea vistas, Ardnamurchan is an inspiring place. A single-track road threads down its length, a superb route with a real sense of transition from ancient mossy oak forest to salt-sprayed moorland as you approach the sea. It's not fast, but this is slow travel at its best, with a huge variety of wildlife and scenery to make **walking** a pleasure; pick up a locally produced guide from tourist offices and most shops.

Strontian and Salen

Actually part of the near-roadless regions of **Sunart** and **Ardgour**, STRONTIAN serves as a gateway base for the peninsula. The village's moment of fame came in 1722, when local lead mines yielded the first-ever traces of **strontium**, which was named after the village. Don't get too excited.

The hamlet of **SALEN**, spread around another sheltered notch on the loch's shore, marks the turn-off for Ardnamurchan Point: from here it's 25 miles of scenic driving beside Loch Sunart – slow and all the better for it. A turf-roofed Garbh Eilean **hide** (free access) five miles west of Strontian is an opportunity to peer for seals, seabirds and the occasional eagle.

Nàdurra

Glenborrodale • April–Oct Mon–Sat 10am–5.30pm, Sun 11.30am–5pm; Nov, Feb & March Tues–Fri 10am–4pm, Sun noon–3.30pm • £4.50 • ☎ 01972 500209, ⓦ nadurracentre.co.uk

Nàdurra, a small, child-friendly natural history centre just west of **Glenborrodale** (5 miles down the road from Salen), introduces the flora, fauna and geology of Ardnamurchan. Named after the Gaelic word for "nature", the centre is in a timber "Living Building" designed to allow in wildlife – pine martins nest within the walls, long-eared bats occasionally hang from the rafters and a glass wall descends into a wildlife pond. Otherwise there are the usual wildlife displays and a film, plus cameras trained on whatever's most interesting – the pine martins, perhaps, or a heronry opposite.

Kilchoan and Ardnamurchan Lighthouse

KILCHOAN is Ardnamurchan's main village – a modest crofting settlement which straggles along the Sound of Mull. From here, the road continues to **Ardnamurchan Point**, the most westerly point in mainland Britain, marked by a 118ft-high **lighthouse**. The lighthouse buildings house a small café and an **exhibition** on local history, while tours go up the tower to see the lighting mechanism (exhibition April–Oct daily 10am–5pm; £3; tour April–Oct daily 11am–4pm; £6; ☎ 01972 510210, ⓦ ardnamurchanlighthouse.com).

Sanna Bay

Explore the area around Kilchoan to find myriad coves, beaches and headlands. The finest beach is **Sanna Bay**, about three miles north of the lighthouse, a white strand with unforgettable views of the Small Isle. Incidentally, the road there crosses the crater of what was the largest volcano in prehistoric Britain, still visible on a map in the northwest peninsula.

4

ARRIVAL AND DEPARTURE

By bus A single service (Mon–Sat; ☎ 01967 431272) that begins at Fort William (currently 1.25pm) goes via Corren Ferry to reach Strontian (1hr) before continuing to Kilchoan (3hr).

By ferry A CalMac (ⓦ calmac.co.uk) car ferry operates

THE ARDNAMURCHAN PENINSULA

between Tobemory (Mull) and Kilchoan (Mon–Sat 7 daily, plus Sun May–Aug 5 daily; 35min).

By car The single-track road from Salen to Ardnamurchan Point is 25 miles long; allow about 1hr 30min in each direction.

INFORMATION AND ACTIVITIES

Strontian tourist office On the village green (Easter–Oct daily 10am–5pm; ☎ 01967 402382).

Kilchoan tourist office In the community centre (Mon–Sat: Easter–Oct 9am–5pm; Nov–March 10am–4pm; ☎ 01972 510711, ⓦ ardnamurchan.com).

Ardnamurchan Charters ☎ 01972 500208, ⓦ west-scotland-marine.com. Based in Laga, near Lochaline, but operates boat trips out of Kilchoan to observe wildlife, including dolphins, seals, basking sharks, whales and possibly sea eagles.

ACCOMMODATION AND EATING

Accommodation isn't plentiful and in summer you're advised to **book** through local tourist offices for **B&Bs**. **Food** options are also limited; Strontian has two modest cafés. The Ferry Stores in Kilchoan carries fresh local produce when available – ideal for the most westerly picnic tables on mainland Britain at Ardnamurchan Point.

STRONTIAN

Ariundle Centre ☎ 01967 402279, ⓦ ariundlecentre.co.uk. Part of a pleasant craft centre and café serving cheap fresh lunches and dinner such as tagines and burgers – a godsend for walkers and cyclists – this modern bunkhouse has dorms, family rooms and twins, all en suite. It's set among woods a mile from the centre – turn right across Strontian bridge. Food served noon–8pm. Dorms **£18**

SALEN

Resipole Farm 2 miles east of Salen ☎ 01967 431235, ⓦ resipole.co.uk. This is a well-maintained spot, with a camping and caravan park plus year-round self-catering accommodation (one week min). Facilities include a laundry and a basic store. Easter–Oct. **£14**/pitch

Salen Hotel ☎ 01967 431661, ⓦ salenhotel.co.uk. Less a small hotel than a restaurant with three smart rooms above – tastefully furnished where modern flair meets antiques – and simpler comfy rooms in a chalet. The restaurant offers

a Scottish gastropub menu: pâtés of smoked mackerel, whisky and tomatoes, local venison or steak-and-ale pies for around £12–15. Daily 11.30am–2pm & 6–9pm. **£60**

GLENBORRODALE

Nàdurra ☎ 01972 500209. The simple café of the natural history centre rustles up home-made soups and sandwiches plus a blackboard menu of dishes such as casseroles and goulash for under a tenner. April–Oct Mon–Sat 10am–5.30pm, Sun 11.30am–5pm; Nov, Feb & March Tues–Fri 10am–4pm, Sun noon–3.30pm.

KILCHOAN

★ **Ardnamurchan Campsite** Ormsaigbeg ☎ 01972 511 0766, ⓦ ardnamurchanstudycentre.co.uk. Views to inspire poetry plus campfires on the beach of a laudably back-to-basics campsite behind the loch – pure magic at sunset and usually spared summer midges by a breeze. Find it past the Ferry Stores. Easter–Sept. **£7.50**/person

Acharacle and Glenulig

At the eastern end of Ardnamurchan, just north of Salen where the A861 heads north towards the district of Moidart, the main settlement is **ACHARACLE**, a nondescript crofting village set back from **Loch Shiel**. The reason to swing through is **Castle Tioram** (pronounced "cheerum"), one of Scotland's most atmospheric monuments. Perched on a promontory above **Loch Moidart** and accessed via a sandy causeway (its Gaelic name means "dry land"), the thirteenth-century fortress was the seat of the MacDonalds of Clanranald until it was destroyed by their chief in 1715 to prevent it falling into Hanoverian hands. There's no entry into the castle, but for a slice of picture-postcard romantic Scotland, it's hard to beat. It's located a mile north of Acharacle via a side road off the A861.

Keep going north on the A861 and you'll roll through woods to arrive at **GLENULIG**, gathered on a picturesque inlet on the Sound of Arisaig. Barely a hamlet, it makes a fine base for walking, sea-kayaking (see opposite) – or partying, when the community centre hosts gigs every fortnight (listings on ⓦ glenulig.com).

ARRIVAL AND DEPARTURE	ACHARACLE AND GLENULIG

By bus Buses go from Fort William (Mon–Sat 1–2 daily) to Acharacle (1hr 30min) and Glenulig (1hr 10min).

By boat Loch Shiel Cruises runs trips to Acharacle from

Glenfinnan at the head of Loch Shiel (Easter to mid-Oct Wed only; £17 single, £26 return; ☎01687 470322, ⓦhighlandcruises.co.uk).

ACCOMMODATION, EATING AND ACTIVITIES

Glenuig Arms Glenuig ☎01687 470219, ⓦglenuig.com. A refurbished inn that ticks all boxes: an excellent hostel with single beds, not bunks; modest motel-style rooms in an annexe; and local beers plus well-priced

bar-food – posh kebabs, wraps, home-made burgers, all around £12. A sea-kayak guide, the owner runs half- and full-day trips in the Sound of Arisaig from £50. Daily noon–9pm. Dorms **£25**; doubles **£100**

The Road to the Isles

The "**Road to the Isles**" from Fort William to Mallaig, followed by the West Highland Railway and the winding A830, traverses the mountains and glens of the Rough Bounds before breaking out near **Arisaig** onto a spectacular coast of sheltered inlets, white beaches and wonderful views to the islands of Rùm, Eigg, Muck and Skye. This is a country commonly associated with **Bonnie Prince Charlie**, whose adventures of 1745–46 began on this stretch of coast with his gathering of the clans at **Glenfinnan** and ended here too, when he embarked near Arisdale and fled into French exile.

Glenfinnan

GLENFINNAN may be spectacularly sited at the head of Loch Shiel, yet it's Scottish history that draws most visitors since it was here that Bonnie Prince Charlie raised his standard and rallied forces before the ill-fated march on London (see p.223).

Glenfinnan Visitor Centre and monument

The spot where the Young Pretender raised his battle standard on August 19, 1745, is marked by a column crowned with a Highland clansman in full battle dress, erected as a tribute by Alexander Macdonald of Glenaladale in 1815. It's a beautiful, brooding spot at the head of the loch that's best appreciated from a viewpoint behind a visitor centre (daily April, May, June, Sept & Oct 10am–5pm; July & Aug 9.30am–5.30pm; £3; NTS; ☎0844 493 2221, ⓦnts.org.uk), which gives an account of the '45 uprising through to the rout at Culloden (see p.208).

Glenfinnan Station Museum

Centre of the village • Daily April to mid-Oct 9am–5pm • 75p • ☎01397 722295, ⓦglenfinnanstationmuseum.co.uk

The town's second claim to fame is for one of the most spectacular parts of the **West Highland Railway** line (see p.222), which chuffs over the 21-arched Loch nan Uamh **viaduct** built in 1901. You might recognize it from *Harry Potter* films, in which it is crossed by the *Hogwart's Express* – Loch Shiel itself serves as the "Dark Lake" seen from the ramparts of Hogwart's.

Head to the **Glenfinnan Station Museum** in the village centre to learn more about the history of this section of the railway in a modest museum in the old booking office – no surprise that the gift shop is stuffed with Harry Potter merchandise. Enthusiastic rail buffs can stay the night or dine here (see p.222).

ARRIVAL AND DEPARTURE	GLENFINNAN

By train A direct service links Fort William to Glenfinnan (Mon–Sat 3–4 daily; 35min).

INFORMATION AND TOURS

Tourist information ⓦroad-to-the-isles.org.uk.

Loch Shiel Cruises ☎01687 470322, ⓦhighlandcruises.co.uk. Runs boat trips to view the superb scenery

between Easter and Sept. Cruises embark from a jetty near *Glenfinnan House Hotel*, signposted off the main road half a mile from the monument.

THE WEST HIGHLAND RAILWAY

A fixture in lists of the world's most scenic train journeys, the brilliantly engineered **West Highland Railway** runs from Glasgow to Mallaig via Fort William. The line is in two sections: the southern part travels from **Glasgow** Queen Street station, up the banks of Loch Lomond to **Crianlarich**, then around Beinn Odhar on a horseshoe of viaducts to cross **Rannoch Moor**, where the track had to be laid on a mattress of tree roots, brushwood and thousands of tonnes of earth and ashes. You're out in the wilds here, the line long having diverged from the road. The route then swings into Glen Roy, passing through the **Monessie Gorge** to enter **Fort William**.

Leg two, from Fort William to Mallaig, is even more spectacular. Shortly after leaving Fort William the railway crosses the Caledonian Canal beside Neptune's Staircase at **Benavie**, before travelling along Locheil and crossing the 21-arch viaduct at **Glenfinnan**, where passengers get to live out *Harry Potter* fantasies. Then it's on to the coast, with views of the Small Isles and Skye before journey's end at **Mallaig**. Between May and October, this leg of the route is also served by the **Jacobite Steam Train** (ⓦsteamtrain.info).

ACCOMMODATION AND EATING

Prince's House Glenfinnan ☎01397 722246, ⓦglenfinnan.co.uk. This former seventeeth-century coaching inn offers comfy rooms – the best at the front nod to Highlands tradition. The fine restaurant offers a seasonal, fresh menu or there's gastropub grub in the bar; expect West Coast scallops, lamb and venison. Mains average £12–16. March–Dec; food served Easter–Sept daily 11am–3pm & 6–10pm. **£120**

Sleeping Car Glenfinnan station ☎01397 722295, ⓦglenfinnanstationmuseum.co.uk. A 1958 camping coach is now a mini-hostel with three twin compartments (bunk beds), a family compartment for four, plus a kitchen, lounge and bathroom – a memorable if slightly cramped place to stay. The adjacent *Dining Car* is open for light lunches from April to Sept (daily 10am–5pm; phone ahead for evening meals). Dorms **£14**; doubles **£28**

Arisaig to Morar

Though short, this is a superb coast – all white sands, turquoise seas and rocky islets draped with orange seaweed. Better still, thanks to a bypass road to Mallaig, the spectacular coast road (signposted "Alternative Coastal Route") is fairly quiet – touring heaven.

First stop is **ARISAIG**, an appealingly drowsy place scattered around a sandy bay. The only specific attraction in the village is the **Land, Sea and Islands Visitor Centre** (Easter to mid-Oct Mon–Fri 10am–6pm, Sat 10am–4pm, Sun 2pm–5pm; donations; ☎01687 450771, ⓦarisaigcentre.co.uk), a volunteer-run community project with displays on crofting life, local characters and the area's role as a base for Special Operations during World War II. There's also a small research library of wildlife and walks – gen up before walking to a seal colony at nearby **Rhumach**, reached via a single-track lane heading west out of Arisaig.

Stretching for eight miles or so north of Arisaig is a string of stunning white-sand, azure-water **beaches**: summer holiday favourites backed by flowery machair and with views out to Eigg and Rùm. Pretty **Traigh** beach is your spot to collect cowrie shells, but larger and more celebrated is **Camusdarach Beach** a mile or so north, where the beach scenes of *Local Hero* and *Highlander* were shot. If it's busy, two intimate beaches lie over the headlands on either side.

Morar village, which bookends this route, is dowdy stuff after such a glorious coast. It lies a short way west of **Loch Morar**, rumoured to be the home of a monster called Morag, a lesser-known rival to Nessie.

ARRIVAL AND DEPARTURE

ARISAIG TO MORAR

By train Direct services (Mon–Sat 3–4 daily, Sun 1–2 daily) run from Fort William to Arisaig (1hr 5min) and Morar (1hr 15min).

By boat Arisaig Marine (☎01687 450224, ⓦarisaig .co.uk) sails from Arisaig marina to the Small Isles (see p.285) at 11am daily, from late April to late Sept.

ACTIVITIES

Arisaig Sea Kayak Centre ☎ 07858 214985, ⓦ arisaig seakayakcentre.co.uk. Based at the *Arisaig Hotel*, this operator offers trips several times a week in season for all levels (day-trips £70 or private guiding £250 for two people). You can also rent craft here (from £25/day) – a superb way to experience this coastline.

West Coast Cycles ☎ 07769 901823, ⓦ westcoast cyclehire.co.uk. Rents mountain bikes by the day (£20) or up to a week. Collect bikes from *Arisaig Hotel*.

ACCOMMODATION AND EATING

Arisaig Hotel Arisaig ☎ 01687 450210, ⓦ arisaighotel .co.uk. Enthusiastic new management has pepped up a tired hotel since 2013. It now prepares a solid pub menu at good prices plus Highland real ales on draught. A revamp of accommodation (Easter–Oct) is promised. Daily 12.30–2.30pm & 6–9pm.

The Boatyard Arisaig marina ☎ 01687 450224. Although more of a gift shop/chandlery than a café, this is a splendid spot – with floor-to-ceiling windows offering mesmerizing views down the loch – for coffees, simple toasties and baked potatoes priced around a fiver. Mon–Sat 9am–4pm.

★ **Camusdarach Campsite** Camusdarach ☎ 01687 450221, ⓦ camusdarachcampsiteandbeach.co.uk. By far the loveliest campsite in the area, its neat fields a pleasing balance of eco-emptiness and facilities, all spread behind sands so white they've featured in films. A campsite café is promised from 2014. Late March to early Oct. **£12**/pitch

Cnoc-na-Faire Back of Keppoch, 1 mile north of Arisaig ☎ 01687 450249, ⓦ cnoc-na-faire.co.uk. Highlands meets Art Deco in a hotel with smart modern-country rooms of tartan fabrics, stainless steel and blond wood. It also prepares breakfasts, light lunches and dinners, all of fine Scottish cuisine: expect venison and sloe gin jus, seafood pastas or fresh fish priced around £14–18. Daily 8.30–9.30am, 11.30am–2.30pm & 6–10pm. **£110**

4

IN THE FOOTSTEPS OF BONNIE PRINCE CHARLIE

The Road to the Isles is steeped in the tragic tale of **Bonnie Prince Charlie**'s failed rebellion. Having landed on the Western Isles (see p.294), he set foot on the Scottish mainland on the sands of **Borrodale** at Loch nan Uamh (Loch of Caves) near Arisaig on July 25, 1745. He had been promised ten thousand French troops to back a claim to the British throne on behalf of his father, the Old Pretender. Instead he arrived with only seven companions – the "Seven Men of Moidart", commemorated at Kinlochmoidart by a line of beech trees (now reduced in number). For a week he gauged support, then took an old hill route to **Dalilea**, on the north shore of Loch Shiel, and on August 19 rowed to the head of the loch at **Glenfinnan**. At a position marked by the Glenfinnan monument, the young rebel prince, surrounded by two hundred loyal clansmen, waited to see if the Cameron of Loch Shiel would arrive. Without the support of this powerful chief, the Stuarts' claim to the throne would have been folly. Late in the day, Cameron backed the uprising with eight hundred men. The prince raised his red-and-white silk colours, proclaimed his father as King James III of England and marched on London. Only a handful of the soldiers would return.

If Charles's original visit to Arisaig and Moidart was full of optimism, his return was desperate. By summer 1746 he was on the run, his armies routed at Culloden and a £30,000 bounty on his head. Yet none of the Highlanders the prince called on for food, favours or hiding turned him in, and his fortitude and bravery in those months earned much respect. Fleeing from Culloden down the Great Glen, he passed through Arisaig en route to the Western Isles, desperately hoping for a French ship to rescue him. On South Uist, **Flora MacDonald** extracted him from a tight squeeze (see p.283), but still on the run he landed back on the mainland again at **Mallaigvaig**, near Mallaig.

It was swarming with soldiers, so he returned to **Borrodale**, this time hiding in a large cave, then fled to Lochaber, dodging patrols and hiding in caves near **Loch Arkaig** (see p.192) and on the slopes of Ben Alder, by **Loch Ericht** (see p.150). Finally, some hope: a French frigate, *L'Heureux*, was off the west coast. Charles dashed back to Arisaig and from a promontory in **Loch nan Uamh** on September 19, 1746, half a mile east of where he'd landed fourteen months before, he clambered into the French shoreboat. It was his last footfall in Scotland and he died, an embittered alcoholic, in Rome. A cairn on the shore between Lochailort and Arisaig village (on A380) marks the spot.

The best place to learn more of the prince's doomed campaign is on the site of his final defeat, **Culloden** (see p.208).

Old Library Lodge and Restaurant Arisaig ☎01687 450651, ⓦoldlibrary.co.uk. The best rooms overlook the bay; those in a garden annexe are modest motel numbers with mod cons like flatscreen TVs and wi-fi. The dining room offers Scottish dishes: cullen skink or delicious crab sandwiches for lunch (around £8), venison pie or sea bass for dinner (average £13). Feb & March Tues–Sat noon–2.30pm (except early season) & 6–9.30pm. **£96**

Mallaig

The fate of **MALLAIG**, 47 miles west of Fort William, is to be seen as somewhere to go through, not to. Before the railway arrived in 1901 it consisted of a few cottages. Now in season it's full of visitors as the main embarkation point for ferries to Skye, the Small Isles and Knoydart. Mallaig is nothing if not well-placed for day-trips and even if not especially pretty, it is a solid wee town given a workaday honesty by its local **fishing** industry – it once had one of Europe's busiest herring ports and the harbour remains the source of the village's wealth.

Mallaig Heritage Centre

Beside the train station • April, May & Oct Mon–Fri 11am–4pm, Sat noon–4pm; June–Sept Mon–Fri 9.30am–4.30pm, Sat & Sun noon–4pm • £2 • ☎01687 462085, ⓦmallaigheritage.org.uk

Apart from the hubbub of the harbour, the town's only sight is **Mallaig Heritage Centre** – nothing to quicken the pulse but worth a browse for displays on the area's past and information about lifeboats, fishing and the highland galleys that once plied the waters of the Inner Hebrides and descend directly back to Viking longships.

4

ARRIVAL AND DEPARTURE

MALLAIG

BY TRAIN

A direct service arrives from Fort William (Mon–Sat 3–4 daily, Sun 4 daily; 1hr 25min) and Glasgow (Mon–Sat 3 daily; 5hr 15min), via Glenfinnan and Arisaig.

BY BUS

There are regular buses from Fort William to Mallaig via Glenfinnan and Arisaig (Mon–Fri 3 daily, Sat 1 daily; 1hr 20min).

BY FERRY

The CalMac ticket office (☎01687 462403, ⓦcalmac.co.uk) is just west of the harbour.

To/from Skye Regular services shuttle between Mallaig and Armadale (Mon–Sat 8 daily; also mid-May to mid-Sept Sun 6 daily; 30min). Reservations are recommended in peak season.

To/from the Small Isles There are services between Mallaig and Eigg (Mon, Thurs, Sat & Sun 1 daily; 1hr 15min); Rùm (Mon, Wed, Fri, Sat & Sun 1 daily; 1hr 20min); Muck (Tues, Thurs, Fri, Sat & Sun 1 daily; 2hr 5min); and Canna (Mon, Wed, Fri, Sat & Sun; 1 daily; 2hr 30min).

To/from Knoydart Bruce Watt Cruises (☎01687 462320, ⓦknoydart-ferry.co.uk) sails from Mallaig to Inverie every morning and afternoon (mid-May to mid-Sept Mon–Fri; mid-Sept to mid-May Mon, Wed & Fri; 45min).

INFORMATION

Tourist office Beside the harbour (Easter–Oct daily 8am–8pm; Nov–Easter 9am–4pm; ☎01687 462883, ⓔmallaigvisitorcentre@btconnect.com).

ACCOMMODATION

Mallaig Backpackers' Lodge Main St ☎01687 462764, ⓦmallaigbackpackers.co.uk. There are two mixed dorms, a small kitchen and a lounge in this relaxed, independent modern hostel. "Reception" is in the *Tea Garden* restaurant opposite the harbour. March–Dec. Dorms **£17**

Seaview Main St ☎01687 462059, ⓦseaview guesthousemallaig.com. Snug dimensions and surprisingly smart decor – tasteful shades of taupe and grey with a leaning towards modest boutique – set the tone in this central B&B, which has harbour views from the front. Note that only one room is en-suite. March–Oct. **£65**

West Highland Hotel ☎01687 462210, ⓦwest highlandhotel.co.uk. Uphill from the harbour, this traditional pile is slowly being upgraded since 2008. Rooms don't live up to the promise of the public areas but are spacious, the best with bespoke furnishings and king-size beds. "Deluxe" ones provide sea or harbour views. March to mid-Oct. **£110**

EATING AND DRINKING

Cornerstone Main St ☎ 01687 462306. A simple first-floor restaurant that's the locals' choice for classic seafood – expect a daily soup and a blackboard menu of fresh fish, simply but excellently prepared and fairly priced at around £12–16. March to mid-Oct daily noon–2.30pm & 5–9.30pm.

Island View ☎ 01687 462210, ⓦ westhighlandhotel .co.uk. In the *West Highland Hotel*, this is Mallaig's fine-dining address, with modern Scottish cooking: fish and

seafood feature plus well-aged steaks priced around £15 a main. Start (or end) with one of over a hundred whiskies in the bar. March to mid-Oct daily 6.30–9pm.

Tea Garden Main St ☎ 01687 462764. As central as it gets, with a terrace to watch the world pass by and a relaxed dining room with a traditional bistro menu of Cullen skink, pints of prawns or home-made scones for under £10. Mid-March to mid-Nov daily 9am–9pm.

The Knoydart peninsula

For many, the **Knoydart peninsula** is mainland Britain's most captivating wilderness area. The fact that it is inaccessible by car is part of the allure – to reach the heart of the peninsula, you either catch a **boat** from Mallaig or **hike** across rugged moorland, sleeping in stone bothies (marked on OS maps). The scenery is superb, flanked by **Loch Nevis** ("Loch of Heaven") and the fjord-like **Loch Hourn** ("Loch of Hell") and three Munros sweeping straight up from the sea. Unsurprisingly, the peninsula has long attracted walkers. But with increasingly comfortable accommodation, it is also gaining a cachet among holiday-makers in search of escapism: a place to slow down for a few days' self-imposed exile from modernity.

Brief history

At the end of the eighteenth century, around a thousand people eked out a living from this inhospitable terrain through crofting and fishing. **Evictions** in 1853 began a dramatic decrease in the population, which continued to dwindle through the twentieth century as a succession of landowners ran the estate as a hunting and shooting playground, prompting a famous land raid in 1948 by a group of crofters known as the "**Seven Men of Knoydart**", who claimed ownership of portions of the estate. Although their bid failed, their cause was invoked when the crofters of Knoydart finally achieved a **community buyout** in 1998. An offer to provide the money from theatre impresario Cameron Mackintosh was rejected because locals were wary of giving up control.

Inverie

Most of the peninsula's hundred or so occupants live near the hamlet of **INVERIE**. Spread along Loch Nevis, it has a pint-sized post office and shop (with internet access), a ranger post with tips on local walks and wildlife, and mainland Britain's most remote pub, *The Old Forge*. You're here for scenery, for walks and for the thrill of dropping off the radar – unless, that is, your visit coincides with that of seven hundred revellers for the Knoydart Festival (ⓦ knoydartfestival.co.uk) every other April.

WALKING INTO KNOYDART
Ordnance Survey Explorer maps 413 and 398

There are two main **hiking routes** into Knoydart. The trailhead for the first is **Kinloch Hourn** at the far-east end of Loch Hourn (turn south off the A87 six miles west of Invergarry). From Kinloch Hourn, a well-marked path winds around the coast to Barisdale, where there's a year-round bothy and wild camp (bothy £3, campsite £1; ⓦ barisdale.com), before continuing ten miles to Inverie; expect 18–20 hours' walk in total. The second path into Knoydart starts from the west end of **Loch Arkaig**, approaching the peninsula via Glen Dessary. Hardened walkers reckon on knocking off the 18-mile journey in one long summer's day. The rest of us should set aside two. Either way, take wet-weather gear, a good map, plenty of food, warm clothes and a good sleeping bag, and leave your name and expected time of arrival with someone when you set off.

ARRIVAL AND DEPARTURE

By boat Bruce Watt Cruises (☎01687 462320, ⓦknoydart -ferry.co.uk) sail from Mallaig to Inverie every morning and afternoon (mid-May to mid-Sept Mon–Fri; mid-Sept to mid-May Mon, Wed & Fri; 45min). A ferry from Arnisdale, Glenelg peninsula, across Loch Hourn to Barisdale (and

THE KNOYDART PENINSULA

Kinlochhourn) in northern Knoydart was suspended at the time of writing; for updates call ☎01599 522247 or visit ⓦarnisdaleferry.com.

On foot It's a two-day hike into Knoydart; our box (see p.225) gives details.

INFORMATION AND ACTIVITIES

Tourist information A ranger post (☎01687 462242) beside *The Old Forge* has information on the Knoydart Foundation, and on local walks and wildlife.

Knoydart Pony Trekking Inverie ☎01687 462830, ⓦknoydartponytrekking.co.uk. Based at stables near the *Knoydart Foundation Bunkhouse*, this operator provides

beginners' treks plus overnight rides with a wild camp for more experienced riders.

Mountain biking Two mountain-bike trails – a 1.5-mile red-grade route and 500yd blue-grade – loop around Inverie. You'll need to bring a bike, however, unless you're staying at *Knoydart Lodge* (see below), which rents bikes to guests.

ACCOMMODATION

Most beds are in Inverie. You can **wild camp** (albeit with a compost toilet and water supply) on "long beach", east of Inverie centre, for a £4 donation to the Knoydart Foundation – pay the ranger or leave it in an honesty box at the campsite. Showers (£4) are available in *The Old Forge* pub.

HOTELS AND B&BS

★ **Doune Stone Lodges** ☎01687 462667, ⓦdoune -knoydart.co.uk. No roads, no stress – this may be the ultimate Scottish getaway, with en-suite doubles in restored pine-clad crofts behind a bay. As well as isolation and views, its lovely owners provide superb cooking. Minimum three nights. Full board. Easter–Sept. **£156**

The Gathering Inverie ☎01687 460051, ⓦthegathering knoydart.co.uk. Relaxed sophistication in a modern B&B just west of the wharf that feels like self-contained accommodation (the owner lives opposite). Superb views and sensational breakfasts. Also rents mountain bikes to guests. **£99**

Knoydart Lodge Inverie ☎01687 460129, ⓦknoydart lodge.co.uk. Near the beach and beside the community allotment, this airy wooden house provides a warm

welcome and modest luxury in en-suite rooms with the full complement of mod cons and a shared veranda. **£94**

HOSTELS

Knoydart Foundation Bunkhouse Inverie ☎01687 462163, ⓦknoydart-foundation.com. The community hostel is on an old farm west of the pier, near the beach. Dorms are large, facilities include a kitchen and laundry, and there's internet access in a lofty lounge with a wood-burner. Rather dated but perfectly comfy. Dorms **£17**

Torrie Shieling Inverie ☎01687 462669, ✉torrie cottage@gmail.com. Fine self-catering facilities, comfort-able four-bunk rooms and open fires in a living room in an independent hostel east and above the village. Close to hillside trails, but less handy for the pub – the owner collects arrivals off the ferry. Dorms **£25**

EATING AND DRINKING

Knoydart Pottery & Tearoom Inverie ☎01687 460191. A lovely spot to lose a few hours (or a long wet day): choose from sofas or a long communal table with the best loch view in Knoydart. Breakfasts plus home-made soups and gluten-free home-baking for around £5–8. Easter–Oct Mon–Fri 9am–5pm, Sat 11am–3pm.

★ **The Old Forge** Inverie ☎01687 462267. Though far

more modern than you'd expect, this remains one of Scotland's finer pubs fuelled by a convivial atmosphere and sense of remoteness. Generous bar meals feature local seafood – specials are around £16, fish and chips £11 – and terrific loch views. Mon–Thurs & Sun 11am–midnight, Fri & Sat 11am–1am; food served noon–3pm & 6.30–9.30pm.

Kyle of Lochalsh and around

Once the main gateway to Skye, **Kyle of Lochalsh** has been left as a mere terminus for the train route from Inverness since the construction of the Skye Bridge in 1995. Of more interest is nearby **Eilean Donan Castle** on the shores of **Loch Duich**. Both are fixtures on the tourist trail, which makes the remote **Glenelg** peninsula to the south side of Loch Duich all the more inspiring. A few miles north of Kyle of Lochalsh, the village of **Plockton** is a lovely spot, with a superb setting on **Loch Carron**, a long inlet which acts as a dividing line between Kyle of Lochalsh and the splendours of Wester Ross to the north.

Kyle of Lochalsh

Moribund since the opening of the Skye Bridge, **KYLE OF LOCHALSH** is not particularly attractive and traffic has little reason to stop, especially since Skye or Plockton nearby offer more appealing accommodation. A great café aside, the only reason to pause is the *Atlantis*, the UK's only semi-submersible **glass-bottom boat** (☎01471 822716 or ☎0800 980 4846, ⓦseaprobeatlantis.com), which offers trips to protected seal and bird colonies on Seal Island (£12.99) or over the World War II wreck of HMS *Port Napier* (£15.99).

ARRIVAL AND DEPARTURE
KYLE OF LOCHALSH

By train It's a glorious journey from Inverness to Kyle of Lochalsh (Mon–Sat 4 daily, Sun 2 daily; 2hr 30min); trains stop at Plockton (15min from Kyle) en route.

By bus Reservations are recommended for all services (☎0870 550 5050, ⓦcitylink.co.uk). Buses stop on the waterfront at the old slipway.

Destinations Fort William via Invergarry (3 daily; 1hr 50min); Glasgow (3 daily; 5hr); Inverness via Invermoriston (3 daily; 2hr 10min); Kyleakin, Skye (every 45min; 10min).

EATING

Buth Bheay By the old ferry wharf. A takeaway shack where fish and seafood from the owner's boat goes into big sandwiches and salad boxes – a bargain at £2–3. Also prepares Cullen skink, and home-baking. Mid-Feb to Christmas Tues–Fri 10am–5pm, Sat 11am–3pm.

Loch Duich

Skirted on its northern shore by the A87, **Loch Duich** features prominently on the tourist trail: coach tours from all over Europe thunder down from **SHIEL BRIDGE** en route to Skye and one of Scotland's most iconic castles, Eilean Donan. Not that it's just the happy hordes who visit: at the end of the loch is Glen Shiel, flanked by the **Five Sisters of Kintail** – a classic tough trek that ticks off three Munros (see box, p.40).

Eilean Donan Castle
Beside A87 near the village of Dornie • Feb–Christmas daily 10am–6pm • £6.50 • ☎01599 555202, ⓦeileandonancastle.com

After Edinburgh's fortress, **Eilean Donan Castle** has to be the most photographed monument in Scotland. Located on the A87 guarding the confluence of lochs Alsh, Long and Duich, its tower rises on an islet, joined to the shore by a stone bridge and set against a backdrop of mountains. Small wonder it has featured in *Highlander* and the James Bond adventure *The World is Not Enough*. The castle was established in 1230 by Alexander II to protect the area from the Vikings but was destroyed during the Jacobite uprising of 1719. It was rebuilt between 1912 and 1932 by a British army officer, John Macrae-Gilstrap, because of the Macrae clan's ancestral links to the area. So, its three floors, including the banqueting hall, the bedrooms and the troops' quarters, are re-creations rather than originals. The Jacobite and clan relics on display are all original.

ACCOMMODATION AND EATING
LOCH DUICH

Grants at Craigellachie Ratagan, 2 miles south of Shiel Bridge ☎01599 511331, ⓦhousebytheloch.co .uk. You'll find B&B charm and hotel quality in the three modern en-suites plus a suite with kitchenette. The owner's intimate restaurant serves first-class modern Scottish dishes like pot-roast pheasant with wild boar, leek and tarragon stuffing (mains average £16). Reservations essential. Easter–Oct Tues–Sat from 7pm. **£115**

Kintail Lodge Hotel Shiel Bridge ☎01599 511275, ⓦkintaillodgehotel.co.uk. A Victorian pile on the loch's east shore with twelve hotel rooms plus dorm-style hostel accommodation in the well-named *Wee Bunkhouse* plus simple twins and singles in the *Trekkers' Lodge*. Its *Kintail Bar* serves good pub-grub such as steak-and-ale pies or fish and chips (£10). Hotel doubles £130; lodge twins £30; dorms £15

Ratagan SYHA Ratagan, 2 miles south of Shiel Bridge ☎01599 511243, ⍟syha.org.uk. Superbly sited on the loch, with views across to the Five Sisters. Traditional in public areas but dorms are more IKEA-esque. It also

runs guided walks and beginners' sea-kayaking sessions. March–Oct. Dorms £17; doubles £44.20

Shielbridge Caravan Park & Campsite Shiel Bridge ☎01599 511221, ⍟shielbridgecaravanpark.co.uk. A minor legend among hikers thanks to its superb location at the west end of Glen Shiel beneath the Five Sisters. Find it off the A87 behind the garage. Late March to Oct. £6/person

The Glenelg peninsula

In contrast to Loch Duich, the **Glenelg peninsula** is one of the region's more remote areas. Even though summer traffic trickles through for the Kylerhea ferry to Skye, this little-known crofting area remains a quiet backwater jutting into the Sound of Sleat – one benefit of being on a road to nowhere. Indeed, the peninsula has probably changed little since Gavin Maxwell wrote about it in his otter novel *Ring of Bright Water* and he disguised its pristine coast by calling it "Camusfearnà". The landward approach is equally impressive on a road that switchbacks over the Mam Ratagan Pass (1115ft) with a spectacular view over the **Five Sisters** massif. The main village, **GLENELG**, is an appealingly soporific spot – a row of whitewashed houses, surrounded by trees, that shows little indication of its time as a strategic centre in the 1700s, when a large barracks kept clans in check. The ruins of Bernera Barracks are on the left as you drive to the ferry.

Glenelg Brochs

Nearly two miles south of Glenelg, a left turn up Glen Beag leads to the **Glenelg Brochs**, one of the best-preserved Iron Age monuments in Scotland. Its spectacular circular towers – Dun Telve and Dun Troddan – in a sheltered valley are thought to have been erected around two thousand years ago to protect surrounding settlements from raiders.

Arnisdale

A lonely backroad beyond Glenelg village snakes southeast through a scattering of old crofting hamlets, timber forests and views that grow more spectacular at each bend. Eventually you drop down to the shore of Loch Hourn at **ARNISDALE**, actually two hamlets in the bosom of the mountains: **Camusbane**, a traditional crofting settlement ranged behind a pebble beach; and **Corran** a mile further, a minuscule, whitewashed fishing hamlet huddled around a river mouth. Display boards in the latter's **Ceilidh House and Heritage Centre** (always open; free) relate local history, including that of Mansion House between the hamlets, built by Valentine Fleming, father of James Bond author Ian. Other than that, there's no reason to come except to see the most jaw-dropping sea loch in Scotland. Keep it quiet.

HIKING IN GLEN SHIEL

Ordnance Survey Explorer map 414

The mountains of **Glen Shiel**, rising dramatically from sea level to over 3000ft in less than a couple of miles, offer some of the best hiking routes in Scotland. Taking in a bumper crop of Munros, the classic **Five Sisters traverse** is claimed by some walkers to be the best day-walk in Scotland. Allow ten hours to complete the whole 19km route, which starts at a lay-by off the A87 in Glen Shiel. The distinctive chain of mountains across the glen from the Five Sisters is the **Kintail Ridge**, with breathtaking views south across Knoydart and the islands of the west. It's another full-day trek, beginning from the *Cluanie Inn* on the A87.

Don't underestimate either of these two routes: walkers come unstuck here every year, so only attempt them if you're confident in your walking experience, and have a map and a compass.

ARRIVAL AND DEPARTURE

THE GLENELG PENINSULA

GLENELG

By bus The post bus and Skyeways bus service (both Mon–Fri 1 daily; 50min) operate from Kyle of Lochalsh via Shiel Bridge.

By ferry The six-car Glenelg–Kylerhea ferry (daily: Easter–Oct 9am–6pm; June–Aug 10am–7pm; ☎01599 522313, ⍟ skyeferry.co.uk) shuttles to and from Skye every 15min, taking 5min.

ARNISDALE

By bus In a word, tricky. The MacRae Kintail community bus from Kyle of Lochalsh goes to Arnisdale on request via Shiel Bridge, *Ratagan Youth Hostel* and Glenelg (1 daily Mon–Fri). Booking required on ☎01599 511384.

ACCOMMODATION AND EATING

★ **The Glenelg Inn** Glenelg ☎01599 522273, ⍟ glenelg-inn.com. Snug, eclectic, with a fire in the grate and the occasional fisherman at the bar, this is all you could want of a Highland pub, with a spectacular lochside setting to boot. Luxurious rooms and a top-notch gastropub menu that showcases local seafood from that fisherman – fish, crabcakes, mussels (mains average £14) – confirm this is a class act. Feb–Nov Mon–Thurs 11.30am–11pm, Fri & Sat 11.30am–midnight; food served noon–2.30pm & 6–9.30pm. **£120**

Plockton

With its picture-postcard cottages curved behind a tiny harbour and views across Loch Carron to mountains, **PLOCKTON** is one of the most picturesque settlements of the west coast. Until the end of the eighteenth century, Am Ploc, as the settlement was then known, was just another crofting hamlet. Then a local laird transformed it with a prosperous fishery, funding a planned village that was renamed "Plocktown". It's packed in high season with tourists, yachties – a popular regatta fills the bay over a fortnight from late July – and second-home owners, and the brilliance of the light has made it something of an artists' hangout. It may look familiar to first-time visitors – its flower and palm-filled seafront featured in cult horror film *The Wicker Man* and BBC's *Hamish Macbeth* series.

ARRIVAL AND DEPARTURE

PLOCKTON

By train Trains from Inverness (2hr 15min) to Kyle of Lochalsh (13min) also stop in Plockton (Mon–Sat 3–4 daily, Sun 1–2 daily).

INFORMATION AND ACTIVITIES

Information ⍟ plockton.com.

Calum's Seal Trips ☎01599 544306 or ☎07761 263828, ⍟ calums-sealtrips.com. This outfit promises "better views than the QE2" aboard its pretty, traditional cruiser. Perhaps true if you like seals (1hr; £10 or free if no seals) or dolphins (2hr; £16) on an evening sail.

Plockton Boat Hire 33 Harbour St ☎01599 544306 or ☎07584 044241, ⍟ plocktonboathire.co.uk. Rents rowing boats and canoes as well as offering dinghy sailing tasters and two-day courses provided by an accredited RYA instructor.

ACCOMMODATION

An Caladh 25 Harbour St ☎01599 544356, ⍟ plockton .uk.com. Anna MacAulay's whitewashed fisherman's cottage is one of the best of Plockton's many B&Bs, boasting a central location, sea views from front rooms and mod cons like wi-fi – though not en suites in all. **£65**

Duncraig Castle Turn-off midway between Duirnish and Plockton ☎01599 544295, ⍟ duncraigcastle .com. On the opposite side of the bay from Plockton village, this Scots Baronial pile reopened in spring 2014 after top-to-bottom renovation to restore its former Victorian grandeur. It now has grand rooms, shabby-chic decor, chandeliers, roll-top baths and stone floors, befitting of its romantic location opposite Plockton. April–Sept. **£149**

Plockton Hotel 41 Harbour St ☎01599 544274, ⍟ plocktonhotel.co.uk. This friendly, small hotel provides cosy, contemporary-cottage decor in rooms, of which the best come with a view at the front. A four-room annexe on the harbour appeals for its shared kitchen as much as its cheaper rates that still include breakfast. Closed first fortnight in Jan. Annexe **£80**; doubles **£130**

Station Bunkhouse Opposite train station ☎01599 544235, ✉ mickcoe@btinternet.com. A pleasant wee bunkhouse bang opposite the railway station, with rather cramped six-bed dorms and better four-bed dorms popular with families, all below a pleasant open-plan kitchen and living area. Check-in is at the same owner's *Nessun Dorma* B&B next door. Dorms **£14**

EATING AND DRINKING

Plockton Inn Innes St ☎01599 544222. The locals' choice offers excellent lunches like watercress and sweet-potato soup or smoked trout pâté, then a fine evening menu of fresh seafood, often from the inn's own smokery. Good vegetarian options and music on Tues and Thurs evenings. Daily noon–2.30pm & 6–11.30pm; food served noon–2.30pm & 6–9pm.

Plockton Shores 30 Harbour St ☎01599 544263. Metropolitan-styled café-restaurant that starts the day as a relaxed coffee and lunch-stop, then shifts up a gear for Modern Scottish, European-flavoured dishes like monkfish in a light Talisker whisky-and-fennel sauce. Tues–Sun 9.30am–9pm (closed Sun eve Nov–Easter).

Loch Carron

North of Plockton are the twin sea lochs of **Loch Kishorn**, so deep it was once used as an oil-rig construction site, and **Loch Carron**, which cuts far inland to **STRATHCARRON**, a useful rail link between Kyle of Lochalsh and Torridon, but little else. If you're arriving from the south by car, however, you pass **Attadale Gardens** (April to mid-Oct Mon–Sat 10am–5.30pm; £6; ☎01520 722603, ⍈attadalegardens.com), made up of twenty artistically landscaped acres ranked among Scotland's finest gardens by horticultural aficionados.

Lochcarron

With supermarkets, cafés, a bank and fuel, **LOCHCARRON** represents a major hub hereabouts. While it's of more use than interest, two crafty sights warrant a pause. A mile north of town on the main road, the **Lochcarron Old Smiddy Heritage Centre** (Easter–Oct Mon–Sat 10am–5pm), a nineteenth-century smithy and forge, is open erratically in season but has become a focus for local **crafts collectives**, with two halls displaying and selling weaving and quilting, pottery, painting and woodwork. More celebrated are the tartans of **Lochcarron Weavers** (☎01520 722212, ⍈lochcarronweavers.co.uk). You can see weaving demonstrations (and buy fabrics and clothing) in its workshop a mile south of Lochcarron towards Strome Castle.

ARRIVAL AND INFORMATION LOCHCARRON

By rail Strathcarron is on the Kyle–Inverness line (Mon–Sat 4 daily, Sun 2 daily): trains run from/to Inverness (1h 45m) and Kyle (40min).

By bus Timetables are coordinated so that buses meet train arrivals at Strathcarron. Services run to Lochcarron from Shieldaig (Mon–Fri 1 daily; 1hr) and Torridon (Mon–Sat 1 daily; 1hr).

Tourist information Due to move on our last visit, the information point should be in the crafts collective at the Old Smiddy by the time you read this (Easter–Oct Mon–Sat 10am–5pm).

ACCOMMODATION AND EATING

★ **Kishorn Seafood Bar** Kishorn, 6 miles north of Lochcarron ☎01520 733240. A bright, informal café named in the top-ten British seafood restaurants by one national newspaper for local and fresh seafood. Come for sharing platters (£25 for two), Skye mussels or just garlic scallops and a croissant (£8). March–June, Oct & Nov Mon–Thurs, Sat & Sun 10am–5pm, Fri 10am–9pm; July–Sept Mon–Sat 10am–9pm, Sun 10am–5pm.

Old Manse Church St, Lochcarron ☎01520 722208, ⍈theoldmanselochcarron.com. Floral fabrics, pine furniture and wrought-iron beds – country style rules in the five spacious rooms of the *Old Manse*, on the road to Strome Castle. Perhaps its real appeal is the location before the loch – £10 extra buys you a room with a view. **£60**

Rockvilla Hotel Main St, Lochcarron ☎01520 722379, ⍈therockvilla.com. Refurbished in 2013 to offer smart (if slightly bland) small-hotel decor, this is far better than a tired pebble-dashed exterior suggests – spotless, comfortable en-suites, posh toiletries plus mod cons like flatscreen TVs, iPod docks and wi-fi. It also has a licensed restaurant. Easter–Sept. **£79**

Wester Ross

Wester Ross, the western seaboard of the old county of Ross-shire, is where the west coast ups the ante. Here, all the classic elements of Scotland's **coastal scenery** – craggy mountains, sandy beaches, whitewashed crofting cottages and shimmering island views – come together. Settlements such as **Applecross** and the peninsulas north and south of **Gairloch** maintain a simplicity and sense of isolation outside of peak season. There is some tough but wonderful **hiking** in the mountains around **Torridon** and **Coigach**, while **boat trips** and the prolific sea- and birdlife draw nature-lovers. The hub of life is **Ullapool**, a proper wee fishing town and ferry port whose modest size ranks as a metropolis in these parts.

The Applecross peninsula

The **Applecross peninsula** sounds bucolic; the English-sounding name is a corruption of the Gaelic *Apor Crosan*, meaning "estuary". Yet the approach from the south – up a glacial U-shaped valley and over the **Bealach na Bà** ("Pass of the Cattle") at 2054ft – is one of the classic drives and cycle pistes of the Highlands. A former drovers' road provides the greatest road ascent in the UK, with a 1:5 gradient and switchbacks worthy of the Alps. Views across the Minch to Raasay and Skye more than compensate – assuming the weather plays ball. The other way in from the north is a beautiful coast road that meanders from Shieldaig on Loch Torridon, past scattered crofting villages and with gorgeous seascapes.

Applecross

The sheltered, fertile coast around **APPLECROSS** village, where an Irish missionary Maelrhuba founded a monastery in 673 AD, is a surprise after experiencing the wilds that surround it. Though popular in peak season, it feels exhilaratingly remote, with little to do but potter along lanes, paddle a kayak or build sandcastles on the beach. A small **Heritage Centre** (April–Oct Mon–Sat noon–4pm; ⊚ applecrossheritage.org.uk) near the site of St Maelrhuba's monastery, and beside Clachan church, showcases local history and several **waymarked trails** along the shore are great for walking off lunch.

ARRIVAL AND DEPARTURE   APPLECROSS

By bus The Dial-A-Bus (☏ 01520 722205) between Strathcarron and Achasheen calls at Applecross.

INFORMATION AND ACTIVITIES

Tourist information There's an info point maintained by the campsite opposite the fuel pumps in the centre of the village (Easter–Oct; opening times erratic). Village websites are ⊚ applecross.info and ⊚ applecross .uk.com.

Applecross Mountain & Sea ☏ 01520 744394, ⊚ applecross.uk.com. Located by the fuel pumps, this company organizes mountain walking and climbing adventures, plus sea-kayaking, from half-day tasters to overnight wild-camping trips.

ACCOMMODATION AND EATING

Applecross Campsite East of the centre ☏ 01520 744268, ⊚ applecross.uk.com/campsite. A popular, well-run two-field site above the village – the furthest field is the quietest. It also provides basic cabins that sleep four, has a buzzy bar and rustles up breakfasts and a menu of stone-baked pizzas and bistro staples like venison casserole or home-made fishcakes in the on-site café (mains £8–12). March–Oct; food served May to mid-Sept daily 9am–9pm. Camping **£9**/person; cabins **£48**

Applecross Inn On the waterfront ☏ 01520 744262, ⊚ applecross.uk.com. The heart of the community provides pretty, cottagey en-suites in the eaves, all with

sea views. In the lively bar downstairs are Highland ales and freshly prepared classic pastas and pies plus Applecross Bay prawns and crab (mains around £10–14). Reservations recommended in season. Daily noon–11pm; food served noon–9pm. **£120**

The Potting Shed Signed from back of the bay ☏ 01520 744440. Head here to enjoy delicious food in the laidback atmosphere of a walled Victorian garden. It's fairly inexpensive as a daytime café, but pricier in the evening, when dishes like chicken-and-thyme casserole, local lobster and local crab in a herb pancake cost around £8–16. March–Oct daily 11am–8.30pm.

4

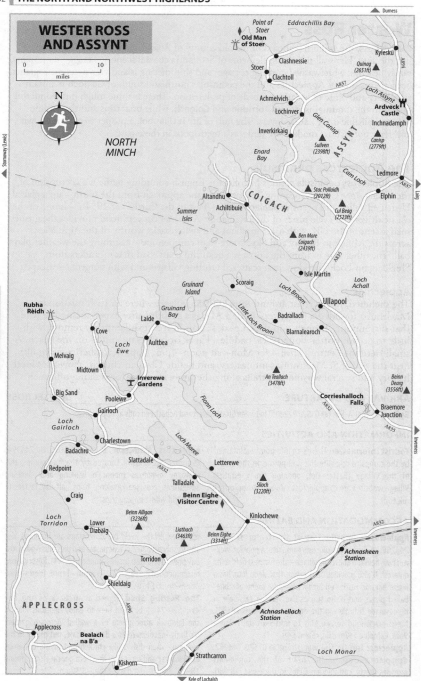

WESTER ROSS
AND ASSYNT

0   10
miles

N

NORTH
MINCH

Stornoway (Lewis)

4

Durness

Point of
Stoer
Old Man
of Stoer

Eddrachillis Bay

Kylesku

A894

Clashnessie

Quinag
(2651ft)

Stoer

Loch Assynt

Clachtoll

A837

Ardveck
Castle

Achmelvich

Glen Canisp

Inchnadamph

Lochinver

ASSYNT

Inverkirkaig

Canisp
(2779ft)

Sullven
(2398ft)

Enard
Bay

Cam Loch

Ledmore

A837

Laing

Stac Pollaidh
(2012ft)

Elphin

Altandhu

COIGACH

Achiltibuie

Cul Beag
(2523ft)

Summer
Isles

Ben More
Coigach
(2439ft)

A835

Loch
Achall

Isle Martin

Scoraig

Loch Broom

Gruinard
Island

Ullapool

Rubha
Rèidh

Gruinard
Bay

Laide

Badrallach

Little Loch Broom

Beinn
Dearg
(3556ft)

Cove

Aultbea

Loch
Ewe

Blarnalearoch

An Teallach
(3478ft)

Corrieshalloch
Falls

A832

Melvaig

Midtown

Inverewe
Gardens

Braemore
Junction

A835

Inverness

Big Sand

Poolewe

Fionn Loch

Gairloch

Loch
Gairloch

Loch Maree

Charlestown

Letterewe

Badachro

Slattadale

A832

Redpoint

Talladale

Slioch
(3220ft)

Kinlochewe

A832

Inverness

Craig

Beinn Eighe
Visitor Centre

Loch
Torridon

Beinn Alligan
(3236ft)

Lower
Diabaig

Liathach
(3463ft)

Beinn Eighe
(3314ft)

Achnasheen
Station

Torridon

Shieldaig

A896

APPLECROSS

A890

Achnashellach
Station

Applecross

Bealach
na B'a

Loch Monar

Kishorn

Strathcarron

Kyle of Lochalsh

Loch Torridon

Loch Torridon marks the northern boundary of the Applecross peninsula and a transition into some awe-inspiring scenery. From the water rise the mountains of **Liathach** and **Beinn Eighe**, shapely hulks of reddish 750-million-year-old Torridonian sandstone-tipped white quartzite. Around fifteen thousand acres of the massif are under the protection of the National Trust for Scotland, which makes this superb walking country, with a trio of Munros to bag.

Shieldaig

Smuggled off the main road on the shore of Loch Torridon, pretty **SHIELDAIG** ("herring bay") is a gentle spot – until the Shieldaig Fete livens things up with some wacky boat races over the first weekend in August. A track winding north up the peninsula from the village makes for an enjoyable stroll. Otherwise, simply enjoy the view to **Shieldaig Island**, managed by the National Trust.

Torridon

TORRIDON village, at the east end of the loch, marks where the road heads inland through spectacular Glen Torridon to Kinlochewe (see p.234). The village itself – thirty or so houses and a shop – straggles along the loch beneath the mountains, making it a fine launchpad for hikes (see below). A **Countryside Centre** (Easter–Sept Sun–Fri 10am–5pm; £3.50 donation requested; ☎0844 493 2229, ⓦnts.org.uk/Property /Torridon) at the turning into the village provides advice on mountain walks plus information on geology, flora and fauna.

4

ARRIVAL AND DEPARTURE   LOCH TORRIDON

By bus The Dial-A-Bus (☎01520 722205) between Strathcarron and Achasheen also calls at Shieldaig and Torridon (Mon–Sat 1 daily).

ACTIVITIES

Torridon Activities 1 mile south of turn-off into village ☎01445 791242, ⓦthetorridon.com. An operator based at the *Torridon* hotel (see p.234) provides the full range of local fun: guided walks, gorge scrambling and climbing, plus kayaking and even clay pigeon shooting.

Torridon Sea Tours Shieldaig ☎01520 755353, ⓦtorridonseatours.com. Luxury boat tours reveal the superb scenery and wildlife in the area: half-day loch trips, full-day journeys to Isle of Rona or Skye, plus a sunset trip with wine and nibbles.

WALKS AROUND TORRIDON

Ordnance Survey Explorer map 433

The Torridon area offers a wealth of fantastic **walks**. If you're relatively inexperienced but want to do the magnificent ridge walk along the **Liathach** (pronounced "lee-ach") massif, or the strenuous traverse of **Beinn Eighe** (pronounced "ben ay"), you can join a National Trust Ranger Service guided hike (July & Aug weekdays via Torridon Countryside Centre; ☎01445 791221).

For those confident to go it alone, one of many possible routes takes you behind Liathach and down the pass, **Coire Dubh**, to the main road in Glen Torridon. This covers thirteen miles and takes in superb landscapes: weather permitting, you can make the rewarding diversion up to the **Coire Mhic Fhearchair**, widely regarded as the most spectacular corrie in Scotland. Allow the whole day.

Even in rough weather, the seven-mile hike up the coast from **Lower Diabaig**, ten miles northwest of Torridon village, to **Redpoint** is a rewarding one, and on a clear day the views across to Raasay and Applecross are wonderful. For any of these walks, ensure you are properly equipped with waterproofs, warm clothing, provisions and a map.

ACCOMMODATION AND EATING

SHIELDAIG

Camping area A designated campsite with no facilities but superb views of the loch is above the waterfront near the primary school at the village's north end.

★ **Tigh-an-Eilean** ☎ 01520 755251, ⓦ tighaneilean .co.uk. Faultless service and utter relaxation in a lovely small hotel on the waterfront with classy country accommodation plus a sensational restaurant (reservation essential); expect the likes of West Coast sea bream with a Provençal tomato confit on innovative daily menus (£45 for three courses). The attached *Shieldaig Bar and Coastal Kitchen* rustles up top-notch bistro dishes like seafood stews and posh pizzas (£8–12). Bar Feb–New Year daily 11am–11pm; food served March–Oct daily 6–9pm. **£150**

TORRIDON

Camping area A wild camp is located beside the turning into the village beside the SYHA hostel. Dishwashing and a shower is in an adjacent public toilet. Beware the midges in summer, though.

Torridon 1 mile south of turn-off into village ☎ 01445 791242, ⓦ thetorridon.com. This Victorian hunting lodge is one of the west coast's grandest stays. Sympathetically styled where boutique meets baronial in public areas and Master rooms; Classics are more up to date. A fine-dining restaurant (£55 for three courses) is splendidly elegant for daily menus of seasonal modern European cuisine, the whisky bar with 350-plus malts a delight. **£230**

Torridon Inn 1 mile south of turn-off into village ☎ 01445 791242, ⓦ thetorridon.com. Adjacent to and run by the *Torridon* hotel, this is more cyclist- and walker-friendly, with neat, plain en-suites. Its moderately priced bar-bistro serves regional ales and good gastropub cooking – salmon, fish and chips or steak-and-ale pie (around £10–12). Jan–March & Dec Thurs–Sun 8am–11pm; food served 8–10am & noon–9pm; April–Nov daily, same hours. **£104**

SYHA Torridon Start of village, 100m from turn-off ☎ 01445 791284, ⓦ syha.org.uk. Though the Seventies-vintage municipal building is no looker, this hostel is spacious and a popular choice with hikers and bikers thanks to a location beneath the peaks. Provides the usual laundry and drying room, plus very cheap meals daily. Closed three weeks in Jan. Dorms **£18**; doubles **£46**

Loch Maree

About eight miles north of Loch Torridon, **Loch Maree**, dotted with Caledonian-pine-covered islands, is one of the area's scenic highlights, best viewed from the A832 road that drops down to its southeastern tip through Glen Docherty. At the southeastern end of the loch, the A896 from Torridon meets the A832 from Achnasheen at small **KINLOCHEWE**, a good base if you're heading into the hills.

Beinn Eighe Nature Reserve

The A832 skirts the southern shore of Loch Maree, passing the **Beinn Eighe Nature Reserve**, Britain's oldest wildlife sanctuary, set up in 1951. Parts of the reserve are forested with Caledonian pine, which once covered the whole country, and it is home to pine martens, wildcats, buzzards and golden eagles. A mile north of Kinlochewe, the **Beinn Eighe Visitor Centre** (Easter & May–Oct daily 10am–5pm; ☎ 01445 760254, ⓦ nnr-scotland.org.uk/beinn-eighe), on the A832, informs visitors about the rare species and offers several "talking trails" for children. Two **walks** start from the Coille na Glas-Leitir car park a mile north of the visitor centre: a mile-long trail into ancient pine woodland and a 3.5-mile track into the mountains.

ACCOMMODATION AND EATING

Kinlochewe Hotel A832 ☎ 01445 760253, ⓦ kinlochewehotel.co.uk. A traditional hotel with a warm welcome and decent line in regional beers and daily good-value soups and casseroles. Rooms are modest but comfy enough, though en-suites cost another £20. An annexe holds a very basic twelve-bed bunkhouse, with triple-deck bunks in one room. Doubles **£75**; dorm **£15.50**

Whistle Stop Café Torrisdale Rd ☎ 01445 760423. The old village hall is always a good stop before or after the hills, preparing hearty breakfasts and a modern-European bistro menu, that swings from sandwiches and wraps to salads of scallops and bacon (£6–14). Easter–Oct Mon–Thurs 9am–7pm, Fri & Sat 9am–9pm; Nov–Easter same hours but closed Mon.

Gairloch and around

Cheerful and unpretentious, **GAIRLOCH** thrives as a low-key holiday resort, with several sandy beaches for the bucket and spade brigade, some good coastal walks within easy reach and an abundance of wildlife cruise operators that pray for passing minke whales. The township is divided into distinct areas spread along Loch Gairloch: to the south, in **Flowerdale Bay**, is Charlestown with the harbour; west, at the turn-off to Melvaig, **Achtercairn** is the centre of Gairloch; and along the north side of the bay is the crofting area of **Strath**. Near the *Old Inn* in Charlestown, the **Sòlas Gallery** (Easter–Oct daily 9am–5pm; ☎01445 712626, ⓦsolasgallery.co.uk) is worth a stop for its ceramics and watercolours inspired by the Highlands landscapes. While you're there, a 1.5-mile walk (round trip) tracks the Flowerdale River through a woodland glen to a waterfall.

Gairloch Heritage Museum

By the turn-off from the A832 into Achtercairn • April–Oct Mon–Sat 10am–5pm • £4 • ☎ 01445 712287, ⓦ gairlochheritagemuseum.org

The **Gairloch Heritage Museum** houses eclectic displays of traditional Highland life, from a mock-up crofthouse to an early knitting machine, plus a small gallery of folk art. Probably the most interesting section is the archive made by elderly locals – an array of photographs, maps, genealogies and taped recollections, albeit mostly in Gaelic.

Big Sand and Melvaig

The area's real attraction is its **coastline**. There's a **beach** just north of the harbour in Charlestown, a crescent of pure sand, or a more impressive stretch a few miles around the north side of the bay at **Big Sand** – it's cleaner, quieter and a mite more pebbly. The B8021 terminates at the crofting hamlet of **Melvaig** – a pint and meal await you in the eccentric *Melvaig Inn* (see p.236).

Ruba Reidh and around

From Melvaig, a private track heads three miles to **Rubha Reidh** (pronounced "roo-a-ray"), where a fully operational lighthouse houses a hostel in its keepers' quarters (see p.236). Only guests are permitted to drive along the track, but visitors are welcome to walk or cycle to the lighthouse.

Around the headland lies beautiful **Camas Mòr** beach, from where a marked footpath tracks inland (southeast) beneath a sheer scarp slope, past a string of lochans and ruined crofts to **MIDTOWN** on the east side of the peninsula, four miles north of Poolewe on the B8057. Allow half a day, though be aware that few buses travel back from Poolewe (currently Mon, Wed & Sat; 7.45pm; check times on ☎01445 712255).

Badachro and Redpoint

On the south side of Loch Gairloch, a single-track lane (built with the Destitution Funds raised during the nineteenth-century potato famine) winds past wooded coves and inlets along the loch to **BADACHRO**, a secluded, former fishing village with a wonderful pub (see p.236).

Beyond Badachro, the road winds five miles further to **REDPOINT**, with beautiful beaches of peach-coloured sand on either side of the headland and great views to Raasay, Skye and the Western Isles. It also marks the trailhead for the wonderful coast walk to Lower Diabaig (see p.233). Even if you don't fancy a full-blown hike, follow the path a mile or so to find an exquisite **beach** on the south side of the headland.

4

ARRIVAL AND INFORMATION GAIRLOCH AND AROUND

By bus Public transport is minimal and requires careful planning. Bus stops for all services are at the *Old Inn*, Charlestown, as well as Achtercain and Strath.
Destinations Inverness (Mon–Sat 1 daily; also ScotBus June–Sept Mon–Sat 1 daily; 2hr 45min); Poolewe (Mon,

Wed & Sat 1 daily; 15min); Ullapool (Mon, Wed, Thurs & Sat 1 daily; 1hr 10min).
Tourist information In community centre Gale Centre in Achtercairn (Mon–Fri 9.30am–5pm, Sat 10am–4pm, Sun 11am–3pm; ☎ 01397 874543, ⓦ galeactionforum.co.uk).

ACTIVITIES

BOAT TRIPS

Gairloch prides itself on wildlife cruises from its harbour. Orcas and minke whales migrate past from late spring to late summer; porpoise, dolphins and seals are common year-round. All operators are located on the harbour at Charlestown.

Gairloch Marine Life Centre & Cruises Charlestown ☎01445 712636, ⍟porpoise-gairloch.co.uk. Up to three trips (Easter–Oct; £20) a day run by the largest operator, which deploys a mini-sub for underwater pictures and a hydrophone to pick up audio. Its visitor centre (Easter–Oct Mon–Fri 10am–3pm, Sat & Sun 11am–3pm) has displays of local sea life.

Hebridean Whale Cruises Charlestown ☎01445 712458, ⍟hebridean-whale-cruises.co.uk. As well as in-shore cruises, the longest established operator runs trips (Easter–Oct; call for winter cruises; from £45) in a high-speed RIB that allow it to reach further off-shore into the North Minch out to the Shiant Isles off Lewis.

PONY TREKKING

Gairloch Trekking Centre 1 Flowerdale Mains, Charlestown ☎01445 712652, ⍟gairlochtrekking centre.co.uk. Lead-rein rides for young or inexperienced riders, plus longer hacks through pretty Highland scenery, between March and Oct.

ACCOMMODATION

GAIRLOCH

Kerrysdale House Charlestown ☎01445 712292, ⍟kerrysdalehouse.co.uk. Marie Macrae's atmospheric and tastefully furnished B&B is set back from the road in its own gardens before the turn-off to Badachro. One room stands out for its cool, contemporary decor; most are relaxed and homely. **£72**

Old Inn Charlestown ☎01445 712006, ⍟theoldinn .net. Country character abounds in the rooms of this former coaching inn set off the main road beside the Flowerdale River. Expect pretty patchwork-style quilts or tartan headboards in cosy en-suite rooms, along with hotel-standard facilities like wi-fi, and tea- and coffee-making facilities. **£104**

BIG SAND

Gairloch Carn Dearg SYHA ☎01445 712219, ⍟syha .org.uk. This former hunting lodge is spectacularly sited above the foreshore, with vast views to Skye from its

lounge. It's also one of the oldest hotels in the network and rather shows its age. April–Sept. Dorms **£18**; doubles **£40**

Sands Caravan and Camping ☎01445 712152, ⍟sandscaravanandcamping.co.uk. The best of the area's campsites, with pitches behind the dunes for sea views. Also rents "wigwams" – actually Scandi-style cabins for up to five with a barbecue and fire pit. Offers laundry facilities, plus kayak and bike rental. April–Oct. **£14.50**/pitch; wigwams for two **£32**

RUBHA REIDH

Rua Reidh Lighthouse ☎01445 771263, ⍟stayata lighthouse.co.uk. Epic seascapes to the Hebrides in the only lighthouse hostel on Britain's west coast, recently redecorated and with private bathrooms throughout – check website to confirm winter openings (undecided on our last visit). Breakfasts, packed lunches and dinner available at bargain prices. **£40**

EATING AND DRINKING

GAIRLOCH

Mountain Coffee Company Achtercairn ☎01445 712316. Here's an unusual find for a small Highlands town – a relaxed café with a global backpacker vibe. Coffees, home-baking and bagels with fresh fillings, plus a good bookshop on-site. Easter–Nov daily 9am–5pm; Dec–Easter Mon–Sat 10am–3pm.

Old Inn Charlestown ☎01445 712006. Flagstone floors and stone walls provide character in a sympathetically modernized coaching inn. Posh-pub specials such as pheasant in pastry, pork roasts and venison steaks, plus beers of the on-site microbrewery, provide the sustenance. Mains average £13. Daily 11am–11pm; food served noon–2.30pm & 6–9pm.

MELVAIG

Melvaig Inn ☎01445 771212. Beyond the pebbledash

this is more quirky youth club than Highlands pub – the owner's past was with Seventies and Eighties rock bands. In the restaurant, spectacular sea views, local seafood and venison casseroles (£13) are specialities. Feb–Oct Tues–Sun noon–11pm, Nov–Dec Sat & Sun same hours; food served noon–3pm & 6–8pm.

BADACHRO

★ **Badachro Inn** ☎01445 771212. Settle onto the terrace with a plate of pork belly or creel-caught langoustine (£10–13) and this pub by the old harbour is as fine a place as you'll find for a sunny afternoon. Inside are real ales, excellent malts and a fire for chill evenings. April–Oct daily noon–midnight, Sun noon–11pm; Nov–March Wed–Sun same hours; food served weekdays noon–3pm & 6–9pm, Sat & Sun noon–3pm.

Poolewe

It's a short hop over the headland from Gairloch to the village of **POOLEWE** at the sheltered southern end of Loch Ewe. During World War II, the Arctic convoy embarked from here and the deep-water loch remains one of only three berths for nuclear submarines. One of the area's best **walks** begins nearby, signposted from the lay-by viewpoint on the A832, a mile south. It takes a couple of hours to follow the easy trail across open moorland to the shores of **Loch Maree** (see p.234), then the car park at Slattadale, seven miles southeast of Gairloch. Double check timetables (☎01445 712255), but you should be able to continue along the loch shore to catch the Wester bus from Inverness back to Poolewe from the *Loch Maree Hotel* at 7pm (Tues, Thurs & Fri only).

Inverewe Gardens

Half a mile north of Poolewe on A832 • Daily April, May & Sept 9.30am–5pm; June–Aug 9.30am–6pm; Oct 10am–4pm; Nov–March 10am–3pm • £10 • ☎0844 493 2225, ⓦnts.org.uk

Most visitors arrive in Poolewe for **Inverewe Gardens**, an oasis of foliage and riotously colourful compared to the wild coast. The gardens were the brainchild of **Osgood MacKenzie** who collected plants from all over the world for his walled garden, which still forms the nucleus of the complex. Protected from Loch Ewe's salt breezes by Scots pine, rowan, oak, beech and birch trees, the fragile plants flourished on rich soil brought as ballast on Irish ships and by the time MacKenzie died in 1922, his garden sprawled over the peninsula, surrounded by a hundred acres of woodland. Today a network of paths and walkways wander through more than a dozen gardens featuring exotic plant collections from as far afield as Chile, China, Tasmania and the Himalayas. Mid-May to mid-June is the best time to see the rhododendrons and azaleas, while the herbaceous garden reaches its peak in July and August, as does the wonderful Victorian vegetable and flower garden beside the sea. Free **guided walks** depart from the visitor centre.

ARRIVAL AND DEPARTURE   POOLEWE

By bus There's a daily bus to Poolewe from Gairloch (15min), currently at 7.45am.

ACCOMMODATION AND EATING

Bridge Cottage Café and Gallery Main road ☎01445 781335. Delicious home-baking and freshly prepared snacks like scrambled eggs and smoked salmon (£7) and soups (£3–4) have earned this welcoming café a superb local reputation. The gallery part upstairs displays art and crafts too. Easter–Oct daily 10.30am–4.30pm.

Inverewe Gardens Camping & Carvanning Main road ☎01445 781249. As trim a site as usual from a member of the Camping & Carvanning Club and largely occupied by motorhomes. Facilities are well maintained and a few pitches in a shady corner allow campers to wake up to loch views. Easter–Oct. **£16.75**/pitch

⭐ **Pool House Hotel** Main road ☎01445 781272, ⓦpoolhousehotel.co.uk. Once the residence of Inverewe Gardens' Osgood MacKenzie, the Harrison family home remains one of the Highlands' most romantic small hotels – think rich fabrics, family antiques and art, loch views and a serene sense of calm. Don't be surprised if you struggle to leave the lounge. Easter–Oct. **£160**

Poolewe to Ullapool

At **LAIDE**, ten miles north of Poolewe, the road skirts the shores of **Gruinard Bay**. It's a great drive, offering fabulous views and, at the inner end of the bay, some excellent sandy beaches before you swing east, tracking high above Little Loch Broom, with gorgeous views to mountains opposite – **Badrallach**, seven miles from a left-turn at the head of the loch, is a magical spot to drop off the radar.

Inland, the route joins the A835 at **Braemore Junction**, above the head of Loch Broom. Easily accessible from a lay-by on the A835, the spectacular 160ft **Falls of Measach** plunge through the mile-long **Corrieshalloch Gorge**, formed by

4

glacial meltwaters. A Victorian suspension bridge spans the chasm for a view of the falls and gorge, whose 197ft vertical sides are draped in wych elm, goat willow and bird cherry.

ACCOMMODATION
POOLEWE TO ULLAPOOL

Badrallach Croft 9, Badrallach ☎01854 633281, ⓦbadrallach.com. Views, space and pure escapism literally at the end of the road. Alongside the campsite are beds in a superb bothy, a 1960s caravan, B&B in an Airstream caravan and a sweet two-bedroom cottage (week minimum). With fishing rod and kayak hire, too, this deserves a few days. **£13**/pitch; bothy **£6**; caravan **£45**

Northern Lights Badcaul, near Dundonnell ☎01697 371379. While this basic campsite may not have the facilities of Gruinard Bay campsite 10 miles west, nor does it have the caravans. This is a true campers' site, its small sloping field all about views to inspire poetry: sea, mountains, sky, space. Magic. **£10**/pitch

Ullapool

ULLAPOOL, the northwest's principal town, was founded by the British Fisheries Society at the height of the herring boom in 1788. Spread across a sheltered arm of land in Loch Broom, the grid-plan town remains an important fishing centre, which gives it a salty authenticity despite the hundreds of visitors who pass through in high season, bound north or to catch the **ferry** to Stornoway on Lewis (see p.300). And even

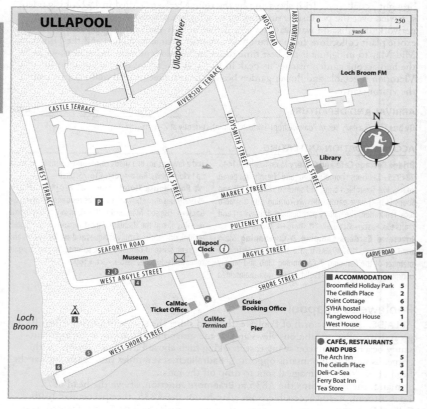

ULLAPOOL

■ ACCOMMODATION

Broomfield Holiday Park	5
The Ceilidh Place	2
Point Cottage	6
SYHA hostel	3
Tanglewood House	1
West House	4

● CAFÉS, RESTAURANTS AND PUBS

The Arch Inn	5
The Ceilidh Place	3
Deli-Ca-Sea	4
Ferry Boat Inn	1
Tea Store	2

WALKS AND HIKES AROUND ULLAPOOL

Ordnance Survey Explorer maps 439, 436 & 435

Ullapool lies at the start of several excellent **hiking trails**, from sedate shoreside ambles to strenuous ascents of Munros. As ever, be aware the weather here changes quickly, so take necessary precautions (see p.42). Northwest Outdoors on West Argyle Street stocks a fair selection of kit, plus OS maps. More detailed descriptions of the routes below are available from the hostel on Shore Street.

An easy **half-day ramble** begins at the north end of Quay Street: cross the walkway/footbridge and follow the river beyond towards the sea. Walk past the golf course and follow the shore for around two miles to reach a hilltop lighthouse for fine views across to the Summer Isles. For a harder **half-day hike**, head north along Mill Street on the east edge of town to Broom Court retirement home, trailhead for the Ullapool hillwalk. A rocky path zigzags steeply up to the summit of **Meall Mòr** (886ft) for great views of the area's major peaks. Botanists love the place for its insect-eating sundews and butterworts. The path then drops sharply down the northeast side into **Glen Achall**, where you turn left onto a surfaced road running past a limestone quarry; the main road back to Ullapool lies thirty minutes' walk west.

A right turn where the path meets the road takes you through the **Rhidorroch** estate to Loch Achall, the start of a **two-day wilderness hike** along an old drovers' trail to **Croick**. Don't tackle this alone or without proper gear, and provide details of your route to someone before setting off – and call them to confirm your safe arrival. Start off at *East Rhidorroch Lodge* and camp halfway at **Knockdamph bothy** by Loch nan Daimh.

when holiday-makers throng its streets, Ullapool remains an appealing place – a good base for exploring the northwest Highlands with all the cultural life of the only town worth the name in the region.

Ullapool Museum

7–8 West Argyle St • Easter–Oct Mon–Sat 10am–5pm; by prior arrangement in winter • £3 • ☎ 01854 612987, ⓦ ullapoolmuseum.co.uk

The only conventional attraction in town, the **Ullapool Museum**, in the old parish church, uses photographs, audiovisual and touch-screen displays to provide an insight into crofting, fishing, local religion and emigration. During the Clearances, Ullapool was one of the ports through which evicted crofters left to start new lives abroad – it also has some genealogy resources.

Isle Martin

Isle Martin Trust, 26 Argyle St • ☎ 01854 612937, ⓦ islemartin.co.uk • Ferries May–Sept, dependent on weather (£6; contact Ullapool tourist office for times)

Three miles from Ullapool in Loch Broom, **Isle Martin** was inhabited on and off for a few thousand years – they say it was named after a follower of St Colomba, who may be under a fifth-century gravestone in the old graveyard – until the last crofting families called it a day in 1949. Gifted to the RSPB in 1999, the four-hundred-acre island is a romantic spot to be a temporary castaway, with beaches, walks and views to the cliffs of Beinn Mhor Coigach and the Summer Isles. Accommodation overnight is available in two bothies (£35).

Summer Isles

During summer, the *Summer Queen* steamer (May to early Sept Mon–Sat; from £20; ☎01854 612472, ⓦsummerqueen.co.uk) and the *Centaur* (Easter–Sept depending on weather; £28; ☎01854 633708, ⓦsea-scape.co.uk), a fast speedboat, run wildlife cruises and trips to the **Summer Isles**, twelve miles west of Ullapool, to view seabird colonies, grey seals, dolphins, porpoises and the occasional whale. Whether slow and stately or fast and full-on in caves, it's a superb trip in good weather.

ARRIVAL AND DEPARTURE

ULLAPOOL

By bus Buses stop at the pier, near the ferry dock. Destinations Durness (May–Sept Mon–Sat 1 daily, plus Sun 1 daily in July & Aug; 3hr); Inverness (Mon–Sat 3 daily, Sun 1 daily; 1hr 30min).

By ferry CalMac (☎01854 612358, ⊛calmac.co.uk) sails to Stornaway, Lewis (Mon–Sat 2 daily, Sun 1 daily; 2hr 45min); an extra sailing runs on Sun during summer school holidays.

INFORMATION

Tourist office Argyle St (Easter–May & Sept Mon–Sat 9.30am–5pm, Sun 10am–3pm; June–Aug Mon–Sat 9am–6pm, Sun 9.30am–4.30pm; ☎01854 612486,

⊛ullapool.co.uk). This well-run tourist office also offers an accommodation booking service.

ACCOMMODATION

Ullapool is busy from Easter through until September – **booking in advance** is recommended.

HOTELS, GUESTHOUSES AND B&BS

★ **The Ceilidh Place** West Argyle St ☎01854 612103, ⊛theceilidhplace.com. Antique beds or old books on vintage cabinets add character to rooms of this lovely small hotel. Some are pepped up with stylish wallpaper, otherwise modern-rustic rules. The cheapest rooms share bathrooms. Also manages a small two-room bunkhouse (£20) directly opposite. **£90**

Point Cottage West Shore St ☎01854 612494, ⊛ullapoolbedandbreakfast.co.uk. A seafront former fisherman's cottage with loch views from its two pretty front rooms, finished, like the rear double, in soft natural shades and subtle tartans for a homely atmosphere. **£75**

★ **Tanglewood House** 1 mile south off A835 ☎01854 612059, ⊛tanglewoodhouse.co.uk. Charm and character in an extraordinary house built by a sailor that's full of art and antiques. Superb rooms are individually furnished, the best with a terrace to enjoy the position above Loch Broom – worth its extra £14. Factor in a beach beneath for a dip and this is a truly memorable stay. Closed Easter,

Christmas and New Year. **£96**

West House West Argyle St ☎01854 613126, ⊛west housebandb.co.uk. A former manse, with all the handsome proportions that suggests, plus charming owners who spoil you with fresh bread and cakes. Relaxing modern rooms and a pre-stocked fridge in each room means a continental breakfast at your leisure. All in all a bargain. **£60**

HOSTEL AND CAMPSITE

Broomfield Holiday Park West Shore St ☎01854 612020, ☎broomfieldhp.com. Hurrah: a campsite in the centre of town with great loch views and space galore at the tip of Ullapool, plus good facilities and all close to the pub. Easter–Sept. **£16**/pitch

SYHA Hostel Shore St ☎01854 612254, ⊛syha.org.uk. Busy hostel bang on the seafront, where prints and murals of seaside scenes help add a cheerful holiday atmosphere. There are dorms of various sizes, doubles, twins, two lounges, internet access and laundry plus lots of good information about local walks. April–Oct. Dorms **£18**; doubles **£44**

EATING AND DRINKING

For a waterfront picnic, pick up fine regional nosh at the **West Coast Delicatessen**, 5 Argyle St.

The Arch Inn West Shore St ☎01854 612454. Ullapool's liveliest pub divides between a popular bar and informal restaurant with Scottish-French cooking: starters like pan-fried scallops with curry oil or Cullen skink, then home-made fishcakes or duck confit alongside the usual fish and chips. Mon–Thurs 11am–11pm, Fri & Sat 11–1am, Sun 12.30–11pm; food served noon–2pm & 6–9pm.

The Ceilidh Place West Argyle St ☎01854 612103. Though locals warn quality can be erratic, this hall-like venue remains one of the best in town. After breakfasts, it shifts into a bistro menu – home-made burgers, salads, schnitzels, plus daily specials like risotto and fish casseroles – and its bar hosts live music. Daily 9am–10pm.

Deli-ca-sea West Shore St (opposite ferry terminal) ☎01854 612141. Come here for the best takeaway fish

and chips to eat by the harbour; all fish is prepared to order and sourced that morning direct from local boats. Mon–Thurs & Sun noon–9pm, Fri & Sat noon–10pm.

Ferry Boat Inn Shore St ☎01854 612366. The interior is nothing special – all character of the eighteenth-century pub ripped out by some bland, modern café furnishings – but the *FBI* remains a choice spot to swig a pint of ale at the lochside (midges permitting) and watch the boats. Daily 11am–11pm.

Tea Store Argyle St ☎01854 612995. Fabulous fry-up breakfasts with black pudding and haggis, home-baked cakes and scones, soups and baked potatoes and a refreshing cuppa at prices around £5 – small wonder this unpretentious wee café is popular with locals. Mon–Sat 8am–5pm, Sun 9am–4pm.

CLOCKWISE FROM TOP LIGHTHOUSE, CAPE WRATH (P.249); SANDWOOD BAY (P.248); EILEAN DONAN CASTLE (P.227) >

CEILIDHS

The **ceilidh** is essentially an informal, homespun kind of entertainment, the word being Gaelic for a "visit". In remote Highland communities, talents and resources were pooled, people gathering to play music, sing, recite poems and dance. The dances themselves are thought to be ancient in origin; the Romans wrote that the Caledonians danced with abandon round swords stuck in the ground, a practice echoed in today's traditional sword dance, where the weapons are crossed on the floor and a quick-stepping dancer skips over and around them.

Highland ceilidhs, fuelled by whisky and largely extemporized, must have been an intoxicating, riotous means of fending off winter gloom. Like much of clan culture, however, the traditions died or were forced underground after the defeat of the Highlanders at **Culloden** and the passing of the 1747 Act of Proscription, which forbade the wearing of the plaid and other expressions of Highland identity.

Ceilidhs were enthusiastically revived in the reign of tartan-fetishist **Queen Victoria**, and in the twentieth century became the preserve of the village hall and hotel ballroom, buoyed to some extent by the popularity of jaunty 1950s TV programmes. More recently, though, the ceilidh has thrown off its dated associations, with places such as *The Ceilidh Place* in Ullapool (see p.240) and the *Taybank Hotel* in Dunkeld (see p.141) restoring some of its spontaneous, infectious fun to a night of Scottish music and dancing.

Whether performed by skilled traditional musicians or in more rollicking form by younger players, ceilidh music is irresistible, and it's common to find all generations gathering. Ceilidh dances look complex. Actually most are reasonably simple and are explained or "called" beforehand by the bandleader. We find a whisky or two earlier on helps.

4

ENTERTAINMENT AND FESTIVALS

The liveliest pub around, the *Arch Inn* (see p.240), hosts live bands, and live Scottish **folk music** is a feature at *The Ceilidh Place* (see p.240). The town's musical highlight, however, is the excellent **Loopallu rock festival** (ⓦ loopallu.co.uk), which takes place on the third weekend in Sept; past acts have included Franz Ferdinand, Echo and the Bunnymen, Mumford and Sons and Paolo Nutini. On a different track, the **Ullapool Book Festival** (ⓦ ullapoolbookfestival.co.uk) is the Highlands' answer to Hay-on-Wye.

Assynt

If the landscape before Ullapool was impressive, the **Assynt** region just north has an epic, almost cinematic quality. Marking the transition from Wester Ross into Sutherland, this region is one of the least populated areas in Europe and its landscape consists not of mountain ranges but extraordinary peaks which rise individually from the moorland. See a mountain like **Suilven** and you understand why the name is said to derive from "A-ssynt", meaning seen from afar, or "ass" – Old Norse for rocky. Certainly, Assynt boasts some of the world's oldest rock formations and roadside signs highlight the region's geological importance as the **Northwest Highlands Geopark** (ⓦ northwest-highlands-geopark.org.uk).

Lochinver, the main settlement, makes a fine base – it puts peaks like Suilven within reach and is also acquiring a foodie reputation. Without your own transport it's almost your only option. With wheels, this is splendid touring country: an area of peaceful backroads which twist past crofts to deserted beaches or windswept headlands with superb views to the Outer Hebrides and those shapely mountains. There are appealing crofting villages to discover around **Achiltibuie**, scenic backroads to tour and two Munros to bag above **Inchnadamph**.

Coigach

Coigach is the peninsula immediately north of Loch Broom, accessible via a road off the A835. It's a beautiful drive, squeezing between the northern shore of Loch Lurgainn and mountains like mammoths, including **Cul Beag** (2523ft), craggy **Stac Pollaidh** (2012ft) and the awesome bulk of **Ben More Coigach** (2439ft), southeast, which presides over the area. There's some spectacular coastal scenery too. It's a place to unwind, with gorgeous views of the Summer Isles scattered offshore and signposted trails along coastal moors and mountains. If the steep Ben More Coigach–Sgurr an Fhidhleir horseshoe (7 miles; 7hr) seems too tough, the Culnacraig circuit (5 miles; 2hr) between Achduart and Culnacraig offers great views. Coigach's main settlement is **ACHILTIBUIE**, a crofting village spread above beaches and rocks. Sunsets here can be astonishing.

Tanera Mor

A mile offshore, **Tanera Mor** is the largest island of the **Summer Isles**. It briefly hit the headlines in May 2013 when its family custodians put it up for sale – a snip at £2.5 million. Presumably the new owner will continue to allow **boat** trips (Easter–Oct Mon–Sat; 2hr 15min; £25; ☎01854 622200 or ☎07927 920592, ⓦsummerisles -seatours.co.uk) round the isles to put ashore on Tanera Mor for an hour, allowing visitors to potter up to the post office to buy "Summer Isles" stamps or have a cuppa in a small café by the pier.

Achiltibuie Artists' Gallery

Coigach Community Hall, Achiltibuie • Easter–Oct daily 10am–5pm • ☎01854 622409, ⓦfacebook.com/scotlandgallery

Whether working in jewellery, pottery, painting, prints, textiles or knits, a love of nature inspires the work of the local artists who display and sell work at the community-run **Achiltibuie Artists' Gallery**. These are individual pieces, so don't expect any bargains, but quality is excellent.

ARRIVAL AND INFORMATLION   COIGACH

By bus The Scotbus service from Ullapool (Mon–Fri 2–3 daily, Sat 1 daily; 1hr 10min) doubles as the school bus, so services are scheduled around the start and end of the school day.

Tourist information Useful websites include ⓦcoigach .com, or ⓦsummer-isles.com for Tanera Mor.

ACCOMMODATION AND EATING

Achininver SYHA Achininver, 2 miles south of Achiltibuie ☎01854 622482, ⓦsyha.org.uk. Twenty-bed hostel with dorms and twin rooms which retains all the stone walls, wood panelling and rustic character of the original croft. It makes a fine base for mountain hikes – Ben Mor Coigach ridge rises directly behind. May–Aug. Dorms __£17__; twins __£75__

Am Fuaran Althandhu ☎01854 622339. A lovely wee pub whatever the exterior suggests, as cosy as a cabin inside and with a fine (if pricey) menu – steak-and-ale pies, chickpea tagine, scallops in ginger and lemon butter. Most mains are around £15–18. Daily noon–11pm; food served 12.30–2.30pm & 6–8pm.

★ **Port A Bhaigh Campsite** Althandhu ☎01854 622339, ⓦportabhaigh.co.uk. Spread behind the beach with mesmerizing sea views and sunsets and excellent facilities that include a laundry, this is as fine a campsite as

you'll find in the Highlands. Midges can be horrendous but the Am Fuaran bar is literally over the road. __£9__/pitch

Summer Isles Bar Achiltibuie ☎01854 622449, ⓦsummerisleshotel.co.uk. This former crofters' pub is run by the Summer Isles Hotel and food is correspondingly high-end – sourdough baguettes for around £10 and seafood sharing platters – to go with regional beer and the occasional music. Easter–Oct noon–11pm, Nov–Easter eve only (times vary).

Summer Isles Hotel Achiltibuie ☎01854 622282, ⓦsummerisleshotel.co.uk. A stylish hideaway with a superb setting, fresh modern-country decor and lovely simple rooms, most in adjoining annexes. Its restaurant (£58 menu; reservation essential) is no longer Michelin-starred but seasonal modern British menus still dazzle with plates such as scallops or langoustine. Easter–Oct daily 6–9pm. __£155__

Lochinver and around

It's hard to think of a more beautiful route than the single-track road that wriggles north from Coigach towards Inverkirkaig. Unremittingly spectacular, the journey is the Highlands in miniature, threading through stunted beech woods, heaving valleys, open moorland and bare rock, past the startling shapes of Cul Beag (2523ft),

WALKS IN COIGACH AND ASSYNT
Ordnance Survey Explorer map 442

Of Coigach's and Assynt's spectacular array of idiosyncratic peaks, **Stac Pollaidh** (2011ft) counts as the most accessible and popular hike – so much so that the path is often repaired and re-routed up the mountain from a car park on the Achiltibuie road. It now leads walkers around the northern side of the hill before climbing steeply. You'll need a head for heights on the jagged summit ridge – turn back from the summit if you feel uncertain about basic rock-climbing.

Suilven (2398ft) is the most memorable of the Assynt peaks – "one sandstone chord that holds up time in space", said poet Norman McCaig of its weird sugarloaf profile. The ascent is a tough eight-hour trip that starts with a boggy five-mile walk to the base. From the A837 at Elphin, head around the north of Cam Loch then through the glen between Canisp and Suilven, to pick up a path that aims for the saddle – Bealach Mor – in the middle of Suilven's summit ridge, from where the path to the top is straightforward. The return is by the same route, although at the saddle you could choose to turn southwest for the route to Inverkirkaig.

The highest peaks in Assynt are **Conival** (3238ft) and **Ben More Assynt** (3274ft), often climbed as Munros (see p.40) even though they're less distinctive than their neighbours, and are known for their bleak landscapes. The route follows the track up Glen Dubh from Inchnadamph; stay to the north of the river and aim for the saddle between Conival and the peak to the north, Beinn an Fhurain. On the ridge, turn southeast to climb to the summit of Conival then east along a high ridge to the top of Ben More. The entire walk, including the return to Inchnadamph, takes five to six hours.

For something less testing there are some classic **coastal walks** immediately north of Lochinver. From **Baddidarrach**, a path with fantastic views of the Assynt peaks leads over heather slopes to Loch Dubh and down to **Achmelvich** (1hr). From here there's a sporadically signposted but reasonable path to **Clachtoll** (about 2hr) past delightful sandy coves, grassy knolls, old water mills and rocks at low tide. More dramatic still is the ninety-minute clifftop circuit from Stoer lighthouse to the famous stack, **The Old Man of Stoer**.

Cul Mor (2785ft) and the distinctive sugar-loaf **Suilven** (2398ft) until it slaloms along the sea shore to Inverkirkaig, the start of two fantastic walks (see below). **LOCHINVER**, another two miles north, marks the return to civilization. One of the busier fishing harbours in Scotland, the small town (oversized village, really) has a pleasingly down-to-earth atmosphere. Factor in good accommodation and a growing reputation for food, and it makes a natural base for the area.

Inverkirkaig Falls and Suilven

A car park in Inverkirkaig, two miles south of Lochinver, marks the start of a **walk** upriver to **Falls of Kirkaig**, itself the start of a long but gentle walk to the base of **Suilven** – its huge sandstone dome is as much of a landmark today as it was for Viking sailors. Serious hikers use the path as an approach to scale the peak (10–12hr), but you can also follow it for an easy five-mile, three-hour (return) ramble, taking in a waterfall and a secluded loch.

ARRIVAL AND INFORMATION

By bus Lochinver may be large by local standards, but connections are not great.

Destinations Inverness (May–Sept Mon–Sat 1 daily, plus Sun 1 daily in July & Aug; 3hr 10min); Ullapool (Mon–Sat 2 daily school term-time only; 1hr).

Tourist information The Assynt Visitor Centre in central

LOCHINVER AND AROUND

Lochinver (Easter to mid-June & Sept–Oct Mon–Sat 10am–4pm; mid-June to Aug Mon–Sat 9.30am–5pm, Sun 11am–3pm; ☎01571 844194, ⊕lochinver.org.uk) has displays on geology, wildlife and history and is stuffed with local tourist information, including the booklet *Walks around Assynt* (£2).

ACCOMMODATION AND EATING

Some of the local accommodation is in a conjoined village, **Baddidarrach**, on the north side of the loch; from Lochinver, cross the bridge and turn left.

★ **The Albannach** Baddidarrach ☎ 01571 844407, ⓦ thealbannach.co.uk. Lesley Crosfield and Colin Craig's Victorian house provides a stay of exquisite taste and astonishing views of Suilven. Individually decorated rooms vary from romantic to hip, with great bathrooms. The couple also possess Britain's most northerly Michelin star: six-course set menus (dinner included for residents; £65 for non-residents) of modern European food created from local and home-grown ingredients are brilliant without ever showing off. No children under 12. Food served from 6pm: mid-March to Oct & Dec Tues–Sun; Nov Thurs–Sun. **£295**

Inver Lodge Signed off Main St, Lochinver ☎ 01571 844496, ⓦ inverlodge.com. Refurbishment of a hillside hotel has created a five-star stay, featuring relaxed contemporary decor with a nod to Highlands country style and loch views. The latter are at their best from the restaurant, an outpost of *Chez Roux*, with fresh seafood plus rich French country dishes like confit pork belly; menus start at £43. April–Oct daily 6–10pm. **£215**

★ **Lochinver Larder** Main Street, near bridge ☎ 01571 844356. Sensational home-made pies, including exotics like wild boar, port and prune, have made it famous, but this fine bistro prepares other food too: think seafood linguini, home-made fishcakes (£13) or langoustine in lime, ginger and chilli butter (£19). Superb takeaways too: those pies, focaccia and baked potatoes. Daily: Easter–Oct 10am–8pm; Nov–Easter 11am–3pm. Closed first fortnight in Jan.

Lochinver Mission Lochinver harbour ☎ 01571 844324, ⓦ lochinvermission.org.uk. New in 2011, the former seamen's mission by the harbour is now a community-run bunkhouse. It has three modern dorms – spotless if a wee bit bare and tight for space in the six-bed – plus a good kitchen and laundry facilities. The price includes breakfast in the café beneath. Dorms **£18**

Veyatie Baddidarrach ☎ 01571 844424, ⓦ veyatie -scotland.co.uk. Gorgeous views across the loch and a warm welcome in a B&B of immaculate rooms with excellent new showers. Patterned bedspreads and local pottery soften modern furnishings and hotel-quality extras with homely charm. Two nights min April–Sept is no great hardship. **£86**

North of Lochinver

There are two routes **north** from Lochinver: the fast A837 along the shore of Loch Assynt (see p.246) to join the A894, or the scenic B869 coast road. Hugging the indented shoreline, the latter offers coastal views, superb **beaches** and high cliff walks. The first village worth a detour is **ACHMELVICH**, three miles northwest of Lochinver, where a tiny bay cradles a white-sand beach lapped by azure water. It's popular (relatively speaking), but there are equally seductive beaches up the coast, including a tiny, hidden cove, **Port Alltan na Bradhan**, a mile north, plus a beautiful strand at **CLACHTOLL** a couple of miles beyond.

Old Man of Stoer

A side road that branches north off the B869 between **STOER** and **CLASHNESSIE** ends abruptly by a lighthouse at **Raffin**. The reason to come is a two-mile stroll along a boggy track to reach the **Old Man of Stoer**, a 197ft rock stack just off the headland's tip, surrounded by sheer cliffs and occasionally scaled by climbers. It's worth a circuit around the south side of the headland to return with a vast view of the mountains of Assynt, after which you'll deserve a cuppa in the tea van at the car park (Easter–Sept 9am–5pm except in high winds and heavy rain).

POWER TO THE PEOPLE

Unusually, most of the land and lochs north of Lochinver are owned by local crofters rather than wealthy landlords. Helped by grants and private donations, the **Assynt Crofters' Trust** (ⓦ assyntcrofters.co.uk) made history in 1993 when it pulled off the first-ever **community buyout** of estate land in Scotland. Subsequent agreements have now given Little Assynt Estate over nine thousand hectares of the Assynt hinterland to manage. The Trust owns the lucrative fishing rights to the area, too, selling permits through local post offices and the Lochinver tourist office. The tourist office also sells permits for the lochs managed by the Assynt Angling Group on parcels of land to the south of the Assynt Crofters' Trust.

Achmelvich Beach SYHA Achmelvich ☎01571 844480, ⓦsyha.org.uk. Although the open-plan lounge-kitchen of this 27-bed hostel in a former school and cottage struggles when full, most people are outside anyway – just 100yd away are the white sands of the beach. Dorms and private twins are available. Closed mid-Sept to Easter, as well as weekdays Sept & Easter. Dorms **£18**; twins **£42**

Clachtoll Beach Campsite Clachtoll ☎01571 855377, ⓦclachtollbeachcampsite.co.uk. Less is often more in campsites – less concrete, more nature – and this simple,

neat site at the heart of the crofting village is all about its location right behind one of the most appealing stretches of powder white sand on the west coast. Easter–Sept. **£14**/pitch

Split Rock Croft 145 Clachtoll ☎01571 855215, ⓦsplitrockcroftbb.co.uk. B&B on a new-build working croft that's as welcoming as its young owners. Has spacious, quietly luxurious en-suites – the Skye Room has sea views, the suite-style Garden Terrace has a kitchenette. Breakfasts are all home-grown. **£80**

Loch Assynt and around

Bounded by peaks of the Ben More Assynt massif, the area inland from Lochinver is a wilderness of mountains, moorland, mist and scree. Anglers love it because of the brown trout in its lochs and lochans, while the toothy remains of **Ardveck Castle**, a MacLeod stronghold from 1597 that fell to the Seaforth Mackenzies after a siege in 1691, add romance. The region's other claim to fame is **Knockan Crag** (Creag a' Chnocain; ⓦknockan-crag.co.uk), thirteen miles south of Loch Assynt on the A835 to Ullapool, one of the world's most important geological sites. In 1859 geologist James Nicol came up with the theory of thrust faults from its geology. Two interpretive **trails** (15min and 1hr) highlight the movement of rock plates for novices and there's information on the area in an unstaffed **visitor centre**.

Kylesku and around

Until a road bridge swept over the mouth of lochs Glencoul and Glendhu, **KYLESKU**, 33 miles north of Ullapool, was the embarkation point for a ferry that was the only link to north Scotland. Off the main road since the bridge's construction in 1984, it's now a beautiful, soporific spot, where interlocking slopes plunge into the deep waters. Marking a last hurrah before the Assynt's sharp sandstone gives way to rounded quartzite, Kylesku is popular with walkers due to its proximity to **Quinag** (2651ft), less a single Munro than several peaks reached by a **ridge-walk**. The easiest ascent is from a car park on the A894 a few miles south of Kylesku. Also in the area is Britain's highest waterfall, **Eas a Chùal Aluinn** (650ft) at the head of Loch Glencoul. It's five miles return east of a car park two miles south of Kylesku or a full day on a track around the north side of both lochs. Alternatively boat tours run from the wharf.

By bus D&E Coaches' (☎01463 222444) summer-only service from Inverness to Durness via Ullapool and Lochinver stops at Kylesku. It can carry bikes with a reservation.
Destinations Inverness (late May to Sept 1 daily Mon–Sat, plus Sun 1 daily in July & Aug; 4hr); Lochinver (same times; 30min).

Tours Alongside boat trips to Eas a Chùal Aluinn aboard the *Rachael Clare* (Easter–Sept 2–3 daily; round trip 1.5hr; £25; ☎01971 502239 or ☎0792 114 9086, ⓦrachaelclare .com), the operator also runs a number of specials afloat, including wildlife safaris, geography tours with a geologist and evening mackerel-fishing.

★ **Kylesku Hotel** Kylesku ☎01971 502231, ⓦkylesku hotel.co.uk. Refurbishment over 2012–13 has created a small hotel of crisp, modern style – soft natural tones, tweed headboards – beside the loch. It provides by far the

best food in the area, all sourced locally. Expect the likes of turbot with vermouth and chive sauce (£14), well-hung steak and home-made fish pie. March–Oct. **£92.50**

The far northwest coast

The Sutherland coast north of Kylesku is a trip too far for some. Others find that the **far northwest coast** captures the stark, elemental beauty of the Highlands like nowhere else. Here, as the geology shifts into ice-scoured pinkish quartzite barely covered by a thin skin of moorland, peaks become more widely spaced and settlements smaller and fewer, linked by twisting roads and shoreside footpaths. Up here, life feels exhilaratingly on the edge of civilization. The flip side is that accommodation and food are sparse, particularly out of season.

Scourie and around

Ten miles north of Kylesku, **SCOURIE** lies among a landscape marbled with lochs and lochans. This is prime Scottish **fly-fishing** territory; permits (£5–10) are available from the Fishing Tackle Shop in the garage. There's also some terrific **walking** hereabouts up mountains like Ben Stack (2359ft) – locals yarn that its pyramidal peak inspired a visiting Hollywood executive to create the logo for Paramount Pictures – and a beautiful beach makes it a small-fry family resort.

Handa Island

Owned by the Scottish Wildlife Trust (W swt.org.uk) • No charge to visit, but donations encouraged • Ferries operate April–Sept Mon–Sat 9am–2pm, every 20–30min (£12.50)

Reason enough to come through Scourie is **Handa Island**, the huge chunk of red Torridon sandstone just offshore. Carpeted with machair and purple heather, the island is maintained as a **wildlife reserve** by the Scottish Wildlife Trust and supports one of the largest seabird colonies in northwest Europe – razorbills and Britain's largest breeding colony of guillemots on ragged sandstone cliffs during summer, and puffins in clifftop burrows from late May to mid-July. Until the mid-nineteenth century, Handa supported a community of crofters who survived on fish, potatoes and seabirds and devised their own government system, with a "queen" (Handa's oldest widow) and male "parliament" who met each morning. Uprooted by potato famine in 1847, most villagers emigrated to Cape Breton, Canada.

Ferries shuttle regularly in summer from **Tarbet**, six miles north of Scourie. Allow three hours at least to follow a **footpath** around the island – an easy and enjoyable walk taking in Great Stack, a 361ft rock pillar on the north shore, and fine views across the Minch.

ARRIVAL AND DEPARTURE   **SCOURIE AND AROUND**

By bus Scourie is on the summer-only bike-carrying Inverness–Durness service of D&E Coaches (☎ 01463 222444) via Ullapool and Lochinver. The Durness–Lairg service of Durness Bus links to Durness.

Destinations Durness (Mon–Sat 1 daily; 1hr); Inverness (late May to Sept Mon–Sat 1 daily, plus Sun 1 daily in July & Aug; 4hr 10min); Lochinver (same times; 50min); Ullapool (same times; 1hr 10min).

ACCOMMODATION AND EATING

Scourie Caravan and Camping Park Scourie ☎ 01971 502060. Spread behind the beach, this well-maintained site provides sea views to go with its flat pitches and tidy amenities block. An on-site café-bar (daily May–Sept 8am–10pm), rustles up food and drinks and has a lounge area in case of bad weather. April to early Oct. **£15**/pitch

Scourie Hotel Scourie ☎ 01971 502396, W scourie-hotel.co.uk. A traditional coaching inn whose fishing obsession only adds character. There are plaster trout in trophies on the walls, squishy sofas, creaky floorboards and comfortable en-suite rooms that make a virtue of simplicity; room 18 is the pick. April–Sept. **£90**

★ **Shorehouse** Tarbert wharf ☎ 01971 502251. With its views of pristine shore, this feels like the restaurant at the end of the world. Simple decor matches excellent, unfussy seafood: home-made soups and sandwiches, plus mains of fresh salmon, hot mackerel and seafood platters, around £13. Mon–Sat noon–7pm, until 8pm July & Aug.

Kinlochbervie

North of Scourie, the road sweeps through the Highlands at its starkest – rocks piled on rocks, bog and water, and a bare, stony coastline that looks increasingly inhospitable. For some that's a call to adventure: sailor and adventurer John Ridgway established an outdoor school on an isolated sea loch off **Loch Laxford** in the 1960s (see below). The largest settlement here, reached on the B801, is **KINLOCHBERVIE**, where a huge fish market and harbour reveal this as the premier fishing port in the area, reduced in stature since its heyday in the late 1980s, but still serviced by trucks from all over Europe. Otherwise it's a scruffy, utilitarian place, usually visited only as a launchpad for Sandwood Bay (see p.248).

ARRIVAL AND DEPARTURE   KINLOCHBERVIE

By bus Kinlochbervie is on the summer-only Inverness–Durness service of D&E Coaches (☎01463 222444) via Ullapool and Lochinver.

Destinations Scourie (late May to Sept 1 daily Mon–Sat, plus Sun 1 daily in July & Aug; 40min); Ullapool (same times; 3hr).

ACTIVITIES

Cape Adventure International ☎01971 521006, ⓦ capeventure.co.uk. Your place for proper adventure in the company of Rebecca Ridgway, the first woman to canoe around Cape Horn. It operates sea-kayaking day and weekend trips plus courses, and runs guided walking weekends around Cape Wrath (p.249) from Sandwood Bay.

ACCOMMODATION AND EATING

Old School Restaurant and Rooms Inshegra, 1 mile before Kinlochbervie on B801 ☎01971 521383, ⓦ old schoolklb.co.uk. By far the most comfortable accommodation option in the area, with a handful of rather smart rooms, including a cute separate en-suite single. Guests are treated to good-value evening meals of home-cooking: expect haddock chowder then braised lamb shank, venison casserole or veggie lasagne (£12–16). May–Aug. **£60**

Sandwood Bay

A single-track road continues northwest of Kinlochbervie through **OLDSHOREMORE**, an isolated crofters' village above a stunning white-sand beach (a magic spot to wild camp), then on to **BLAIRMORE**, start of the four-mile walk to **Sandwood Bay**. The shell-white **beach** beyond the peat moors is one of the most beautiful in Scotland, flanked by rolling dunes and lashed by gales for much of the year. Vikings beached their longships here over a millennium ago – the name is a corruption of "sand" and "vatn", meaning sand and water. A later bearded mariner who perished on this dangerous coast (undercurrents are too treacherous for swimming) is said to haunt the beach – two crofters in the early 1940s said he tramped across the sand in a buttoned tunic and bellowed at them that the beach was his – and Britain's most recent sighting of a mermaid was recorded here in 1900; apparently she had red hair, green-blue eyes and a 7ft yellow body. Good luck with them both if you decide to wild camp here.

It's possible to trek overland from Sandwood Bay north to Cape Wrath (see p.249), the northwestern tip of mainland Britain, a full day's walk away. If you're planning to meet the Cape Wrath minibus to Durness (see opposite) contact them first since it won't run if the weather turns bad.

The north coast

A stream of sponsored walkers, cyclists and tour groups makes it to **John O'Groats**, yet few visitors travel the length of the wild **north coast**. Those who do rarely return disappointed. Scotland's rugged northern shore is backed by superb mountains in the west and by lochs and open rolling grasslands in the east. Between them is mile upon mile of crumbling cliffs, sheer rocky headlands and perfect white beaches that are nearly always deserted except for intrepid surfers who come for the best waves in Scotland. Visit in January and there's a chance you might witness the Northern Lights, too.

Only a small place, **Durness** is a good jumping-off point for **Cape Wrath**, the windswept promontory at Scotland's tip which has retained an end-of-the-world mystique lost long ago by John O'Groats. Continuing east, **Tongue** enjoys an attractive setting and a Munro to climb nearby while **Thurso**, the largest town on the north coast, is acclaimed by surfers. For everyone else it's a gateway to seabird colonies around **Dunnet Head** and **Duncansby Head**.

Durness and around

Scattered over sheltered sandy coves and grassy clifftops, **DURNESS** is the most northwesterly village on the British mainland, straddling the point where the road swings from peat bogs to the fertile limestone machair of the north coast. The village sits above Sango Sands bay, whose fine beach has made it a modest resort. Beatle **John Lennon** came here as a teenager on family holidays to stay with his Auntie Lizzie (Elizabeth Parkes) – his memories later went into the song *In My Life* and he revisited in 1969 with Yoko. Parkes is buried in the graveyard at Balnakiel.

Smoo Cave

1 mile east of Durness • Always open • Free

A mile east of the village is **Smoo Cave**, a gaping hole in a limestone cliff created by the sea and a small burn. Tucked at the end of a narrow sea cove, the main chamber is accessible via steps from the car park. The much-hyped rock formations are less memorable than a short trip by rubber dinghy (run on demand May–Sept; £3; ☏01971 511704) into two further caverns, not least after heavy rain causes a waterfall through the middle of the cavern.

Balnakiel

The white sands of **Balnakiel Bay** are stunning in any weather, but especially spectacular when sunny days turn the sea a brilliant turquoise. A path winds north through the dunes behind to reach **Faraid Head** – fine views east to the mouth of Loch Eriboll and west to Cape Wrath make this circuit (3–4hr) the best in the area.

Cape Wrath

The headland takes its name not from stormy seas but the Norse word *hvarf* ("turning place"), a throwback to the days when Viking warships passed en route to raid the Scottish coast. Yet **Cape Wrath** still exudes a powerful sense of nature in the raw. The British mainland's most northwesterly point – and one of only two capes in the country – is tipped by a Stevenson lighthouse and stands above **Clo Mor cliffs**, the highest sea cliffs in Britain and a prime breeding site for seabirds. On a good day you'll gaze out to Orkney and the Outer Hebrides.

The surprise is that Cape Wrath is so easily reached on a day-trip from Durness. The journey begins two miles southwest at **Keoldale**. A foot-passenger **ferry** crosses the Kyle of Durness estuary to link with a **minibus** for the fourteen-mile run to Cape Wrath and the *Ozone* café at the lighthouse (open daily year-round). With two to three days to spare, you could catch the ferry then walk a circuit to Sandwood Bay, catching a bus back to Durness from Kinlochbervie. There's a basic free bothy at Kearvaig. Note that the Ministry of Defence maintains Garvie Island (An Garbh-eilean) as an air bombing range and so occasionally closes the road to Cape Wrath. Indeed, at the time of research it hoped to buy up the peninsula.

ARRIVAL AND DEPARTURE

DURNESS AND AROUND

DURNESS

By bus Public transport is sparse; the key service is the D&E Coaches (May–Sept Mon–Sat 1 daily; also Sun 1 daily in July & Aug). It goes from Inverness (5hr 15min) via Ullapool (3hr 40min), Lochinver (2hr) and Scourie (1hr 10min) and has a cycle carrier.

CAPE WRATH

By ferry and minibus The foot-passenger ferry from Keoldale runs from April to Sept (in theory daily at 11am, plus June–Aug 9.30am; ☏01971 511246, ☏07719 678729); call to confirm tides and Ministry of Defence schedules. It drops you on the opposite bank of the kyle to connect with a minibus to Cape Wrath (£10 return; ☏07742 670196).

INFORMATION AND ACTIVITIES

Tourist office Just east of the centre of Durness (April, May & Oct daily 10am–4.30pm; June–Aug daily 9.30am–5pm; Nov–March currently Tues & Thurs 10am–12.30pm; ☏01972 511368, ⓦ durness.org). This helpful tourist office can provide information about walks and cycle tracks, including guided ranger walks. Information on Cape Wrath is at ⓦ capewrath.org.uk.

Bike rental Available from community operator Bike Hub on the car park in the centre of Durness (£12/day); contacts and opening times posted on door.

Golf Durness golf course (☏01971 511364, ⓦ durness golfclub.org), the most northwesterly course on mainland Britain, is a nine-hole with two tee-off options per hole to create 18 holes (£20). Closed to visitors Sun morning, equipment rental from clubhouse (from £5).

ACCOMMODATION AND EATING

DURNESS

Lazy Crofter Bunkhouse ☏01971 511202, ⓦ durness hostel.com. Run year-round by *Mackay's* next door, this is the finest bunkhouse on the north coast, far more appealing than the SYHA hostel by Smoo Cave. Has a snug cabin atmosphere and gets extra marks for individual reading lights in compact twins and two dorms. Nice terrace too, if the weather and midges allow. Dorms **£17**

★ **Mackay's** ☏01971 511202, ⓦ visitmackays.com. Handmade and vintage furniture, luxury linen, natural colours and genuine hospitality make this one of the best stays on the north coast. It also manages weekly self-catering options: from a sweet cabin to Croft 103's eco-chic. Food at their on-site restaurant is excellent if you can get a table, with continental flavours added to local seafood, lamb and beef (booking essential; mains £11–16). March/ April & Oct daily 6–10pm; May–Sept noon–2.30pm & 6–10pm. **£125**

Sango Sands Oasis ☏01971 511726, ⓦ sangosands .com. This flat, spacious site spreads over cliffs above the turquoise waters of its namesake and beside the pub that manages it. Campers get premier pitches, so wake to a vast seascape. Free out of season, though cold-water showers only. April–Oct. **£13.50**/pitch

BALNAKIEL

Cocoa Mountain Balnakiel Craft Village ☏01971 511233. A rich bitter-sweet hot chocolate topped off by white chocolate is the speciality in the bright modern café of this chocolatier, which sells snacks (£5–7) plus its chocolates and truffles. A treat after time in the wilds. March–Oct daily 9am–6pm.

NORTH-COAST WALKING AND CYCLING

Ordnance Survey Explorer maps 447 & 448

Rising up from the southern end of the Kyle of Tongue, Ben Hope and Ben Loyal offer moderate-to-hard walks, rewarded on a decent day by vast views over the empty landscape. **Ben Hope** (3041ft), which was given its name ("Hill of the Bay") by the Vikings, is the most northerly of Scotland's Munros – they say that from its summit at the summer equinox, the sun never vanishes entirely beneath the horizon. It's suprisingly accessible – the best approach is a four-hour round-trip from the road that runs down the west side of Loch Hope. Start at a sheep shed by the roadside, just under two miles beyond the southern end of Loch Hope.

   Ben Loyal (2506ft), though lower, is a longer hike at around six hours. To avoid the worst of the bogs, follow the northern spur from Ribigill Farm, a mile south of Tongue. At the end of the southbound farm-track, a path emerges; follow this up a steepish slope to gain the first peak on the ridge from where the walking to the top is easier.

   For **shorter walks** or **cycles**, there are well-marked woodland trails at **Borgie Forest**, six miles west of Tongue, and **Truderscraig Forest** by Syre, twelve miles south of Bettyhill on the B871. Near the entrance to Borgie Forest is the *a'chraobh*, a spiral feature created using native trees and carved local stone. If you follow the signs to **"Rosal Pre-Clearance Village"**, a stop on the Strathnaver Trail (see p.252), you'll find an area clear of trees with what little remains of the village – fifteen families were evicted between 1814 and 1818. Information boards explain the crofters' lifestyles in the eighteenth century before the upheavals of the Highland Clearances.

JACOBITES IN THE KYLE OF TONGUE

The Kyle of Tongue was the location of the naval engagement reputed to have sealed the fate of Bonnie Prince Charlie's **Jacobite rebellion** in 1746. In response to pleas for help from the prince, the King of France dispatched a sloop, *Hazard*, and £13,600 in gold coins to Scotland. However, the Jacobite ship was spotted by the English frigate HMS *Sheerness* and fled into the Kyle, where it was forced aground. Pounded by English cannons, the Jacobite crew slipped ashore at night in an attempt to smuggle the treasure to Inverness. However, the rebels were ambushed by the anti-Jacobite MacKay clan, and threw the gold into **Lochan Hakel**, southwest of Tongue. On the prince's behest, Lord Cromartie sent 1500 men to rescue the treasure. They too were defeated and taken prisoner. Historians still debate whether the extra men might have altered the outcome of the Battle of Culloden three weeks later. The gold, meanwhile, was recovered later. Or most of it – they say cows still wander out of the loch's shallows with gold pieces stuck in their hooves.

Tongue to Thurso

Vast and empty, there's drama in the landscape between Tongue and Thurso. It's a bleak moorland intercut with sandy sea lochs and with few inhabitants: tiny **Tongue** is pleasant enough, as is **Bettyhill**, further east. But the real reason to venture this far is the landscape: a dead-end **coast road** west of Tongue; **Ben Hope** (3040ft), the most northerly Munro; or the blanket bog of the **Flow Country** inland.

Tongue and around

4

Having taken a slow, circuitous route around Loch Eriboll and east over the moors of A'Mhoine, you roll finally into the pretty crofting township of **TONGUE**. Dominated from a hillside spur by the ruins of **Castle Varrich** (Caisteal Bharraich), a medieval stronghold of the Mackays (three-mile return walk), the village is strewn above the east shore of the **Kyle of Tongue**, which you can cross either via a causeway or by a longer and more scenic single-track road around its southern side. When the tide recedes, this shallow estuary becomes a mass of golden sand flats, superb on sunny days, with the sharp profiles of **Ben Hope** (3040ft) and **Ben Loyal** (2509ft) looming like twin sentinels to the south, and the Rabbit Islands a short way out to sea. A dead-end road offers views of the islands, plus superb seascapes and scenery as it threads through Talmine towards a beach at **Strathan**; take the left turn to Melness before Tongue causeway.

ACCOMMODATION AND EATING — TONGUE AND AROUND

Ben Loyal Tongue ⊕01847 611216. Seafood fresh off the owner's boat is served in a relaxed pub along with favourites such as steak pie or home-made burgers. With decent prices (£8–14 main) and live music most Saturdays, this is the choice of many locals. Daily 11.30am–3pm & 5–11.30pm; food served noon–2.30pm & 6–9pm.

Cloisters Talmine ⊕01847 601286, ⓦcloistertal.demon.co.uk. *Cloisters* provides a relaxing stay in homely rooms – think wicker furniture and peach and cream colours – plus beautiful views towards the Orkney Islands outside. Breakfast (and dinner at weekends) is in the owners' converted church alongside. £65

The Craggan Talmine ⊕01847 601278. Ignore the tired pebbledash exterior – this pub has proper restaurant cooking; fresh mackerel with mustard mash, lemon and samphire are typical of mains created from fresh ingredients (average £17–18). Lunches such as ciabatta sandwiches are simpler and half the price. Daily 11.30am–3pm & 6–11pm; food served noon–2pm & 6–9pm.

Tongue Hotel ⊕01847 611206, ⓦtonguehotel.co.uk. This nineteen-bedroom small hotel marries relaxed modern taste with the architectural heritage of a former ducal hunting lodge. There are antiques in the best rooms, even the odd marble washstand, and spacious proportions throughout. £110

Tongue SYHA ⊕01847 611789, ⓦsyha.org.uk. Another Victorian pile of the Duke of Sutherland, this large well-equipped hostel has spacious dorms and family rooms, plus great mountain views from its position beside the causeway, on the Kyle's east shore. Mid-April to Sept. Dorms £18; twins £45

THE FLOW COUNTRY

A detour inland on the A897 east of Bettyhill towards Helmsdale heads south into the **Flow Country**. The name (pronounced to rhyme with "now") derives from *flói*, an Old Norse word meaning "marshy ground" and this 1544-mile squared expanse of "blanket bog" – the largest in the world, says Unesco, which has it filed under "possible" on its World Heritage status – is both a valuable carbon sink and a home to a wide variety of birdlife. The RSPB's **Forsinard Flows Visitor Centre** (Easter–Oct daily 9am–5pm; free; ☎01641 571225, ⊕rspb.org.uk reserves) at the train station in **FORSINARD**, is the gateway to the so-called Forsinard Flows. Pick up a leaflet then follow the mile-long **Dubh Lochan Trail** over flagstones to learn about its blanket bog being restored from forestry use. En route, you get to see bog asphodel, bogbean, and insect-trapping sundew and butterwort; you've also got a good chance of spotting greenshanks, golden plovers and hen harriers. The visitor centre runs twice-weekly **guided walks** through the area (May–July, currently Mon & Tues 2–5pm; 3hr walk; £5) to explain the wonders of peat; wellies or walking boots are recommended.

Bettyhill and around

Twelve miles east of Tongue, **BETTYHILL** is a major crofting village, set among rocky green hills. In Gaelic it was known as *Am Blàran Odhar* ("Little Dun-coloured Field"). The origins of the English name are unknown but it was definitely not named after Elizabeth, Countess of Sutherland, who presided over the Strathnaver Clearances whose sorry tale is told in the town museum. The village is also surrounded on either side by beautiful beaches: **Farr beach**, a splendid crescent of white sand, is behind the museum, while the unbroken arc of **Torrisdale Bay** sweeps west of the town beyond the Naver River. Both receive good surf. For more cerebral stuff, the 24-mile **Strathnaver Trail** runs south along the B873 to Altnaharra, past historical sites from the Neolithic, Bronze and Iron Age periods, not to mention the remains of crofting villages cleared in the early 1800s. Pick up guide leaflets (£2) from the museum.

Strathnaver Museum

In the old Farr church, east of the main village • April–Oct Mon–Sat 10am–5pm • £2 • ☎ 01971 521418, ⊕ strathnavermuseum.org.uk

The volunteer-run **Strathnaver Museum** houses the usual exhibits of ethnological and archeological interest – crofting items including a bizarre fishing buoy made from a dogskin, Pictish stones and a 3800-year-old early Bronze-Age beaker – and also narrates the Sutherland Clearances through a short film. It's most famous item is free to view – the **Farr stone**, a ninth-century engraved Pictish gravestone, is in the west end of the graveyard.

ACCOMMODATION AND EATING   BETTYHILL AND AROUND

Bettyhill Hotel Main road ☎01641 521202, ⊕bettyhill-hotel.com On our last visit, the *Bettyhill Hotel* was in the process of being renovated; standard rooms were expected to go for **£90**, budget ones for **£70**

Café at Bettyhill Beside Strathnaver Museum, east of the main village ☎01641 521244. One of the only options in Bettyhill, this small, simple café is all about home-cooking, whether daily specials like fisherman's pie (£8) or filled baked potatoes or cakes. It serves fish and chips year-round at weekends (Fri & Sat 5–7pm). April–Oct daily 10.30am–4.30pm.

Thurso

THURSO feels like a metropolis after the wild west. In reality it's a modest administrative service centre, most of whose visitors only pause before catching the ferry to Orkney from its port, **Scrabster**. Yet it makes a good base for the area and is legendary among British **surfers**, drawn to a wave which barrels off a reef just east of the harbour. One of the most powerful waves in Europe, "Thurso East" is not a break for beginners.

The town's name derives from the Norse word *Thorsa*, literally "River of the God Thor", and in Viking times this was a major gateway to the mainland. Later, ships set sail for the Baltic and Scandinavian ports loaded with meal, beef, hides and fish. Much of the town, however, dates from the 1790s, when Sir John Sinclair built a large new extension to the old fishing port. Consequently, Thurso's grid-plan streets have some rather handsome Victorian architecture in local, greyish sandstone. There's little sign of those older roots except **Old St Peter's Church** up the High Street, a substantial ruin with origins in the thirteenth century.

Caithness Horizons

High St • April–Sept Mon–Sat 10am–6pm, Sun 11am–4pm; Oct–March Mon–Sat 10am–6pm • Free • ☎ 01847 896508,
ⓦ caithnesshorizons.co.uk

Caithness Horizons, a local museum in a revamped Victorian town hall, is more modern than any other museum on the coast, using interactive technology as well as old photos to explore local geology, history, farming and fishing. Treasures include a Bronze Age beaker and a Viking brooch. The centre also hosts temporary art exhibitions in a gallery and has a café.

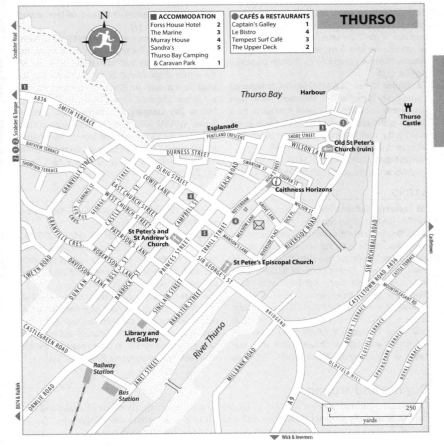

THURSO

■ ACCOMMODATION	
Forss House Hotel	2
The Marine	3
Murray House	4
Sandra's	5
Thurso Bay Camping & Caravan Park	1

● CAFÉS & RESTAURANTS	
Captain's Galley	1
Le Bistro	4
Tempest Surf Café	3
The Upper Deck	2

4

ARRIVAL AND DEPARTURE

THURSO

By train Trains to Thurso leave from Inverness and go up the east coast via Lairg. The following services are all Mon–Sat 4 daily, Sun 1 daily.

Destinations Inverness (4hr); Lairg (2hr 10min); Wick (30min).

By bus Buses depart from the train station, Olrig St and Sir George's St.

Destinations Inverness (4–5 daily; 3hr 30min); John O'Groats (Mon–Fri 6–10 daily, Sat 5 daily; 1hr); Wick (Mon–Fri 8 daily, Sat 4 daily; 35min).

By ferry NorthLink ferries (⍟northlinkferries.co.uk) operate ferries to Stromness, Orkney (4–6 daily; 90min) from Scrabster, a mile west of town, linked by buses from the train station.

INFORMATION AND ACTIVITIES

Tourist office Located in the foyer of Caithness Horizons, on the High St (April–Sept Mon–Sat 10am–6pm, Sun 11am–4pm; Oct–March Mon–Sat 10am–6pm; ☎01847 896508).

Tempest Surf Riverside Rd, by Thurso harbour ☎01847 892500. Offers equipment hire, including boards (£20/day), wetsuits (£20/day), and boots and gloves (£5/day).

ACCOMMODATION

Forss House Hotel 3 miles west of Thurso on A836 ☎01847 861201, ⍟forsshousehotel.co.uk. Built in 1810 as a hunting lodge, this thirteen-bedroom hotel offers an upmarket stay, with a choice of traditional accommodation in the main house or more modern rooms in annexes. The Forss River, which wends through the grounds, offers fine salmon fishing – the hotel can provide a ghillie. **£130**

The Marine 38 Shore St ☎01847 890676, ⍟themarinethurso.co.uk. Opened in 2013, the newest B&B in town has modern furnishings and tweed headboards for a relaxed, contemporary style. More appealing than the rooms is the small conservatory off the breakfast room with superb sea views – surfers take note. **£90**

Murray House 1 Campbell St ☎01847 895759, ⍟murrayhousebb.com. Central, comfortable and friendly, this B&B is a proper home from home, with five cottagey rooms of floral wallpaper and warm saffron and cream colours, all en suite. Mod cons include flatscreen TVs and wi-fi. Off-street parking available for residents. **£70**

Sandra's 24–26 Princes St ☎01847 894575, ⍟sandras-backpackers.co.uk. The only hostel in town is a clean and well-run 26-bed place that's managed by the owners of the popular chippy downstairs. Refurbished in 2013, its small but neat rooms are all en suite. Free internet access and discount bike rental. Dorms **£16**; doubles **£38**

Thurso Bay Camping & Caravan Park Scrabster Terrace ☎01847 892244, ⍟thursobaycamping.co.uk. Large, trim site a 5min walk west from the town centre. As well as views to Dunnet Head and Orkney, it has an on-site café with free wi-fi and a laundry. April–Sept. **£15.50**/pitch

EATING

★ **Captain's Galley** Harbour, Scrabster ☎01847 894999. Fish fresh off the boat is the speciality – unfussy dishes like roast hake with borlotti broth and mussels – on three-course menus (£49) that win awards for sustainability as much as flavour. Also offers takeaway fish and chips of whatever's freshest (Tues–Sat 12.30–6.30pm). Reservations essential. Easter–Oct Tues–Sat 6–10pm; Nov–Easter Thurs–Sat 6–10pm.

Le Bistro 2 Traill St ☎01847 893737. An ever-popular option in Thurso even though it can feel cramped at peak times. The reason is reliable bistro dishes with a Scottish twist such as chicken stuffed with local haggis or Orkney herring. Mains £12–16. June–Aug

Tues–Sat 10am–9pm; Sept–May Tues–Wed 10am–3pm, Thurs–Sat 10am–9pm.

Tempest Surf Café Riverside Rd ☎01847 892500. Home-baking, toasties and home-made burgers (£5–8) served in a harbourside café with a laidback surf-shack vibe: think surfboards and surf posters and driftwood art on the walls. Daily 10am–5pm.

The Upper Deck The Ferry Inn, Scrabster ☎01847 872814. The place to head for a huge Aberdeen Angus steak – choose your cut and select your size – plus traditional dishes like pork in Dijon mustard and surf'n'turf classics; mains average £15. It's above a popular pub which locals swear by for afternoon tea. Daily 6.30–9pm.

Dunnet and around

Despite the publicity given to John O'Groats, the most northerly point of mainland Britain is actually **Dunnet Head** four miles north of the unremarkable village of **DUNNET**. It's a far more evocative spot too, covered in heather and bog and plummeting in red cliffs at the headland, marked by a Stevenson lighthouse, and with the whole north coast spread out before you from Cape Wrath to Duncansby Head on a clear day.

Dunnet Bay

Just south of Dunnet lies **Dunnet Bay**, a vast, golden beach backed by huge dunes. Surfers come for a smattering of reef breaks plus a beach break that offers shelter for beginners depending on whereabouts on the bay you tuck in. At the northeast end of the bay, the **Seadrift Visitor and Ranger Centre** (April–Sept Tues, Thurs, Fri & Sun 2–5pm; free; ☎01847 821531) holds an exhibition about the fauna of the northwest coast and ecology of its sand dunes. It also stocks information leaflets on local history and nature walks.

Mary-Ann's Cottage

South end of Dunnet • June–Sept Tues–Sun 2–4.30pm • £3 • ☎ 01847 851765

Signposted off the through road in Dunnet, **Mary-Ann's Cottage** is a farming croft vacated in 1990 by the then 93-year-old Mary-Ann Calder. Her grandfather built the cottage and today it is maintained as she left it, full of mementoes of the three generations who lived and worked there over 150 years. With its antique rocking chair before a blackened hearth, still with its old metal teapot, and family photos, it's a very intimate portrait of a recent past that already feels distant.

Castle of Mey

5 miles east of Dunnet • May–July & mid-Aug to Sept daily 10.20am–4pm • £10.50, gardens only £6 • ☎ 01847 851473, ⓦ castleofmey.org.uk

The village of Mey whizzes past in just a few houses – yet it was here that the late Queen Mother had her Scottish home. The original **Castle of Mey** was a sixteenth-century Z-plan affair, owned by the earls of Caithness until 1889, and bought in a state of disrepair in 1952, the year the Queen Mother's husband, George VI, died. She spent her summer holidays here each August, which may help explain why it's a modest wee place, unstuffy inside despite the facade that bristles with turrets. The walls are hung with works by local amateur artists and watercolours by Prince Charles (who still visits in late July, when it's closed for two weeks) and personal mementoes of the Queen Mum remain on show – guides are more than happy to explain their significance. The **gardens** outside are a lovely spot for an amble on a sunny day, not least for their views across the Pentland Firth.

THE PENTLAND FIRTH AND STROMA

All along the Caithness coastline you see Orkney. Between you and it, however, is the **Pentland Firth**, one of the world's most treacherous waterways. Only seven miles across, it forms a narrow channel between the Atlantic Ocean and North Sea, and for fourteen hours each day the tide rips west to east at ten knots or more, flooding back in the opposite direction for the remaining ten hours. Combined with the rocky seabed and a high wind, this creates deep whirlpools and serious waves even on calm days as the ebb rips against the shore. Both are the subject of old mariners' myths – the Vikings said the sea-king Mysing caused the whirlpools by grinding salt to keep the seas saline. Many oil tankers brave the Pentland Firth to save time on the longer passage north of Orkney – an environmental catastrophe waiting to happen, say some locals.

Obstructing the flow of the Pentland Firth is **Stroma** (from the Norse *staum-øy* or "tidal stream"), a flat island visible a few miles north of Gills Bay. Officially part of Caithness rather than the Orkney islands, Stroma had a population of well over three hundred in the late nineteenth century. It had dwindled to around eighty by the 1950s, so to help stem depopulation a new harbour was constructed in 1955. A bad move, it turned out. The islanders earned such good wages through labouring that many moved to the mainland. Within a few years, only the lighthouse keepers remained. Even they left in 1997 and only sheep use the buildings.

4

By bus Bus #80 between Thurso (stops at train station and Olrig St) and John O'Groats passes through Dunnet and Mey (Mon–Fri 8 daily, Sat 5 daily).

ACCOMMODATION AND EATING

Castle Arms Hotel Mey ☎01847 851244, ⓦcastle armshotel.co.uk. A simple but comfortable stay almost opposite the castle entrance; all rooms are en suite, family-size suites are good value. The restaurant prepares good pub-grub such as local steak and fish and chips (£9) plus daily specials. Daily noon–2pm & 6–9pm. **£90**

Dunnet Bay Carvan Club Dunnet Bay ☎01847 721319, ⓦcaravanclub.co.uk. On the plus side are the position behind the dunes – a surfer's paradise when waves are firing – and immaculate facilities. The bad news is it's geared to motorhomes and is expensive due to a surcharge for non-Caravan Club members. April–Sept. **£27**/pitch

John O'Groats and around

Don't expect a magical meeting of land and water at **JOHN O'GROATS** – this is an uninspiring tourist trap. While the views to Orkney are fine, the village is effectively a car park ringed by pebbledashed souvenir shops. Who knows what Jan de Groot, the Dutchman who operated a ferry to Orkney from 1496, would think. Come to tick a box or embark on a wildlife cruise, but that's all.

Duncansby Head

Far more appealing than John O'Groats, **Duncansby Head**, a couple of miles east, has the lonely lighthouse and spectacular cliffs everyone wants from a mainland tip. What it lacks is commercialism. The birdlife here is prolific and south of the headland lie spectacular 200ft-high cliffs, cut by sheer-sided clefts known locally as *geos*, and several impressive sea stacks.

By bus Thanks to its fame, John O'Groats has regular bus services from Thurso (Mon–Fri 6–10 daily, Sat 5 daily; 1hr) and Wick (Mon–Fri 6 daily, Sat 5 daily; 50min).

By ferry The John O'Groats passenger ferry (☎01955 611353, ⓦjogferry.co.uk) sails to Burwick, Orkney (May–Sept 2–3 daily; 40min). It also offers afternoon cruises around the seabird colonies and stacks of Duncansby Head or the seal colonies of Stroma (mid-June to Aug daily 2.30pm; 1hr 30min; £17).

Tourist office Beside the main car park (March–Oct daily 9am–5pm; ☎01847 89237, ⓦvisitjohnogroats.com).

The Black Isle and around

The **east coast** of the Highlands is nowhere near as spectacular as the west, and feels more lowland than highland. Heading north from Inverness, you're soon into the **Black Isle** – not an island at all, but a peninsula whose rolling hills, prosperous farms and deciduous woodland make it more reminiscent of Dorset or Sussex than the Highlands. It probably gained its name because of its mild climate: there's rarely frost, which leaves the fields "black" all winter. Another explanation is that the name derives from the Gaelic word for black, *dubh* – a possible corruption of St Duthus (see p.259).

The Black Isle is littered with **prehistoric sites**, but the main incentive to detour east off the A9 is **Cromarty**, a picturesque fishermen's town that is arguably the highlight of the entire Highlands' east coast. If you're heading this way with your own transport, a string of villages along the south coast are worth a stop en route for a modest cultural fix, while **Chanonry Point** is among the best **dolphin-spotting** sites in Europe. In a lay-by just across the Kessock Bridge from Inverness, the small **Dolphin and Seal Centre** (June–Sept daily 9.30am–12.30pm & 1–4.30pm; free; ☎01343 820339, ⓦwdcs.org) provides the chance to observe (and listen to) the creatures.

Fortrose and Rosemarkie

FORTROSE, ten miles northeast of Inverness, is a quietly elegant village dominated by the beautiful ruins of a once huge, early thirteenth-century **cathedral** (daily 9.30am–5.30pm; free) founded by King David I. It languishes on a pretty green bordered by red-sandstone and colourwashed houses. **ROSEMARKIE** a mile on is equally appealing, with its neat high street of stone houses.

Groam House Museum

High St, Rosemarkie • March–Oct Mon–Fri 11am–4.30pm, Sat 2–4.30pm; Nov–early Dec Sat 2–4pm • Free • ☎ 01381 620961, ⓦ groamhouse.org.uk

Located at the lower end of Rosemarkie's high street, **Groam House Museum** displays fifteen intricately carved **Pictish standing stones** (among them the famous Rosemarkie Cross Slab) dating from as early as the eighth century. It also screens a video that highlights other sites in a region that was a stronghold of Pictish culture – a primer to tempt any history buff into a visit to Portmahomack (p.260).

ARRIVAL AND DEPARTURE   FORTROSE AND ROSEMARKIE

By bus Stagecoach buses #23 and #26 from Inverness to Cromarty stop at both Fortrose and Rosemarkie   (Mon–Sat every 30min, Sun 4 daily; 30–35min).

Cromarty

An appealing jumble of handsome Georgian townhouses and pretty workers' cottages knitted together by a cat's-cradle of lanes, **CROMARTY**, the Black Isle's main settlement, is simply a joy to wander. An ancient ferry crossing on the pilgrimage trail to Tain, it became a prominent port in 1772, fuelling a period of prosperity that gave Cromarty some of the Highlands' finest Georgian houses. The railways poached that trade in the nineteenth century – a branch line to the town was begun but never completed – but the flip side of stagnation is preservation. Out of town, there's a fine four-mile circular coastal **walk**: leave town to the east on Miller Road and turn right when the lane becomes "The Causeway". For a simpler shoreline walk, turn left here, following the path to the water.

Cromarty Courthouse

Church St • April–Sept Sun–Thurs noon–4pm • £2 • ☎ 01381 600418, ⓦ cromarty-courthouse.org.uk

The streets are gorgeous, but to help bring Cromarty's past alive try this child-friendly **museum** in the old **Courthouse**, which tells the history of the courthouse and town using audiovisuals and "talking" mannequins in period costume. You are also issued with an audio handset and a map for an excellent **walking tour** around the town.

Hugh Miller's birthplace

Church St • Late March to Sept daily noon–5pm; Oct Tues, Thurs & Fri noon–5pm • £6.50; NTS • ☎ 01381 600245, ⓦ hughmiller.org

Cromarty's most celebrated son is **Hugh Miller**, a nineteenth-century stonemason turned author, journalist, geologist, folklorist and Free Church campaigner. His thatched cottage **birthplace** has been restored to give an idea of what Cromarty must have been like in his day, with decor that swings between cosy rustic and rather formal Victoriana, and displays that highlight his efforts as a social reformer. Friendly staff and a pretty garden add to the appeal.

ARRIVAL AND DEPARTURE   CROMARTY

By bus Stagecoach buses #23 and #26 run from Inverness main bus station (Mon–Sat every 30min, Sun 5 daily; 1hr).
By ferry Scotland's smallest ferry, the two-car service between Nigg and Cromarty (late July to Sept daily 8am–6.15pm, until 7.15pm July & Aug; £2.50; ☎ 01381 610269 or ☎ 07879 401659, ⓦ cromarty-ferry.co.uk) sails from the jetty near the lighthouse.

ACTIVITIES

EcoVentures Off Bank Street, opposite Sutor Creek ☎ 01381 600323, ⓦ ecoventures.co.uk. Sails from the harbour in a powerful RIB out through the Sutor stacks to the Moray Firth to see the resident bottlenose dolphins and other wildlife up to three times daily (2hr; £25).

ACCOMMODATION AND EATING

Royal Hotel Marine Terrace ☎ 01381 600217, ⓦ royal cromartyhotel.co.uk. On the seafront just behind the harbour, this traditional inn provides fairly bland but perfectly acceptable rooms which overlook the Firth. Superiors provide the most character through a mix and match of antique furnishings and more modern decor. **£110**

★ **Sutor Creek** 21 Bank St ☎ 01381 600855, ⓦ sutor creek.co.uk. A lovely café-restaurant full of laidback seaside charm. It focuses on local and seasonal food, whether light lunches (£6–10) or excellent dinners like Shetland scallops with black pudding. The same ethos carries into posh pizzas, best washed down with Black Isle Brewery beers. A gem. May–Aug daily 11am–9pm; Sept–April Wed–Sun 11am–9pm.

Sydney House High St ☎ 01381 600451, ⓦ sydney house.co.uk. Antique wood or iron beds and pretty dressing tables are typical of the furnishings picked up over the years by the owners to lend character to the three en-suites in their smart redbrick house just off High St. The best rooms look out over the rear gardens. **£70**

Strathpeffer

Visitors first came to this leafy Victorian spa town to take the waters. In the 1970s and 1980s they arrived with coach tours to wallow in its faded glamour. Now **STRATHPEFFER** is restyling itself again as a place for activities in the surrounding hills, with a focus – ironically – on "wellbeing" that sees it return to its origins as a renowned European **health resort**. All manner of guests disembarked from the *Strathpeffer Spa Express* train: George Bernard Shaw, Emmeline Pankhurst (who caused a scandal with a lecture on women's rights) and Franklin and Eleanor Roosevelt on honeymoon.

Renovation has transformed the town's Victorian grand hall into an arts centre and upgraded the adjacent **Upper Pump Room** (April–Sept Mon–Sat 10am–6pm, Sun 2–5pm; donation), where displays narrate the spa's history.

For all the appeal of the village's faded grandeur, it's the hills that will make you stay. Within striking distance is **Ben Wyvis**, an approachable Munro usually scaled without complication from **GARBAT**, six miles west of Strathpeffer, in five hours. Another excellent

---

WALKS AND RIDES AROUND STRATHPEFFER

Ordnance Survey Explorer map 437

From the southern end of Strathpeffer, a two- to three-hour walk leads to the remains of a vitrified Iron-Age fort at **Knock Farril**. The first part of the walk is through woodland; after a mile, turn up onto the ridge above and follow it northeast along the crest of the hill known as the Cat's Back. The trees thin out to offer great views of the Cromarty Firth as you reach the hillfort. Before you get to the ridge is **Touchstone Maze**, built as a local arts project in 1992 – its eighty stones are intended to represent the rock types of the Highlands. A path also leads directly to the maze from near the old train station in Strathpeffer.

The **Rogie Falls** are two miles north of Contin on the main A835 to Braemore. They're well signposted and it's a short walk from the car park to where the Black Water froths down a stretch of rocks and mini-gorges, in one place plunging 26ft. Salmon leap upriver in high summer, particularly at a fish ladder built by the toughest rapids. A suspension bridge over the river leads to some waymarked forest trails, including a five-mile loop to **View Rock**, at a point only 160ft above sea level, but which has great views of the local area. Contin Forest holds several fun **mountain-bike trails** too, including a rooty, rocky, red-grade ten-mile track.

The most ambitious hike in this area is up **Ben Wyvis**, a huge mass of mountain just north. The high point is Glas Lethad Mor (3432ft), which means, rather prosaically, "Big Greenish-Grey Slope". The most common route is through Garbat Forest, leaving the road just south of Garbat itself, staying on the north bank of the Allt a'Bhealaich Mhoir stream to get onto the southwestern end of the long summit ridge at the minor peak of An Cabar.

hike in the area is up Cnoc Mor hill, where the Iron Age hillfort of **Knock Farril** affords superb panoramic views to the Cromarty Firth and surrounding mountains.

ARRIVAL AND ACTIVITIES   STRATHPEFFER

By bus Stagecoach bus #27 from Inverness drops passengers in the town square (Mon–Sat 12 daily, Sun 5 daily; 50min).

Bike rental The excellent Square Wheels (☎01997 421000, ⓦsquarewheels.biz; closed Mon) on the main square rents out bikes and offers good advice on local trails.

ACCOMMODATION AND EATING

Craigvar The Square ☎01997 421622, ⓦcraigvar.com. Good breakfasts set you up for a day in the hills and a relaxing atmosphere to settle into afterwards. As central as it gets, this B&B provides modern decor that refers to the early Victorian house (love the roll-top baths) yet includes flatscreen TVs and wi-fi throughout. **£90**

Linnmhor House Park Road ☎01997 420072, ⓦlinnmhor-house.co.uk. Another relaxing and rather luxurious stay, this B&B boasts the period features of an Edwardian villa in en-suite rooms, all tastefully and

sympathetically furnished. Great breakfasts and delicious dinners for guests upon request. **£100**

Red Poppy Main St ☎01997 423332. By spring 2014, this casual, modern place should have shifted from the exhibition hall to new premises opposite the Pump Room. The bistro menu – Cullen skink and pastas, burgers and beef Stroganoff priced around £6–12 – is expected to remain the same. Tues–Sat 11am–8.30pm, Sun noon–3.30pm.

The Dornoch Firth and around

For centuries, visitors on the pilgrim trail to the **Fearn peninsula** came from the south by ferry from Cromarty. Nowadays the area north of **Dornoch Firth** is linked by the A9, skirting past the quiet town of **Tain**, best known as the home of Glenmorangie whisky, and the neat town of **Dornoch** itself, an unexpected pleasure known for its cathedral and golf courses.

4

Tain

There's a sense of having arrived somewhere as you swing through the handsome buildings of central **TAIN**. Reputedly Scotland's oldest Royal Burgh, it was the birthplace of **St Duthus**, an eleventh-century missionary. Many a medieval pilgrim came to venerate his miracle-working relics enshrined first in a sanctuary then in fourteenth-century **St Duthus Collegiate Church**. James IV visited annually, usually fresh from the arms of his mistress, Janet Kennedy, whom he had installed in nearby Moray.

Tain Through Time

Tower St • April–Oct Mon–Fri 10am–5pm, June–Aug also Sat & Sun 10am–5pm • £3.50 • ☎01862 894089, ⓦtainmuseum.org.uk

Installed in three buildings of St Duthus church and graveyard, the town museum, **Tain Through Time**, is a good place to gen up on the Fearn peninsula's Pictish past and Tain's pilgrimage history, the latter taking in King James's guilty conscience. There's also a dressing-up box if you have kiddies to entertain. The ticket price also includes an audio **walking tour** of the town; set aside twenty minutes. The same ticket gets you into a neighbouring **museum** with a dry display of Tain silver, alongside clan memorabilia.

Glenmorangie distillery

Beside the A9, 1.5 miles northwest of central Tain • Tours Mon–Fri 10.30am–3.30pm, Sat 10.30am–2.30pm, Sun 12.30–2.30pm; shop Mon–Fri 9am–5pm, June–Aug also Sat 10am–4pm & Sun noon–4pm • £5 (book ahead) • ☎01862 892477, ⓦglenmorangie.com

Whatever the history, Tain's most popular attraction is the **Glenmorangie whisky distillery**. Tours of the distillery and warehouses explain the alchemic process that ferments mashed malt, distills the liquid in Scotland's tallest stills then matures it in oak casks to create a delicate, vanilla-y malt. There's a dram or two to finish, naturally.

By train Tain is on the Inverness–Thurso North Highlands line (4 daily; Inverness, 1hr 10min; Thurso 2hr 30min).
By bus Stagecoach east coast buses from Inverness to

Thurso (#X99) stop in Tain (Mon–Fri every 30min–1hr, Sun hourly; Inverness 40min–1hr 10min; Thurso 2hr 10min).

ACCOMMODATION

Golf View House 13 Knockbreck Rd ☎01862 892856, ⓦ golf-view.co.uk. Just south of the centre, this former manse offers a lovely B&B stay in its five rooms. Decor is

relaxed contemporary Scottish with a touch of romance and en-suite bathrooms are excellent. Factor in fine views to the Dornoch Firth and full Scottish breakfasts. **£80**

Portmahomack and around

The fishing village of **PORTMAHOMACK**, strung out around a curving sandy beach, is a surprise after the rolling fields of the **Fearn peninsula** east of Tain. Though empty nowadays, this was a heartland of eighth-century Picts before Viking raids became too much.

Tarbat Discovery Centre

Tarbatness Rd • April Mon–Sat 2–5pm; May Mon–Sat 10am–5pm; June–Sept Mon–Sat 10am–5pm, Sun 2–5pm; Oct daily 2–5pm • £3.50 • ☎01862 871351, ⓦ tarbat-discovery.co.uk

Archeological digs in the church at the edge of the village have unearthed sculpted artefacts, including some fine gravestones decorated with Celtic animals or mythical beasts, all well presented in the church as the **Tarbat Discovery Centre**. It marks the first stop on a trail of other Pictish sites south on the peninsula – pick up the *Highlands Pictish Trail* leaflet to locate other impressive Pictish standing stones, including those at Hilton and Shandwick.

Tarbat Ness

North of Portmahomack lies **Tarbat Ness**, a gorse-covered point with one of the highest lighthouses in Britain at its tip. Come for sea views and a seven-mile stroll (2–3hr round trip). The **walk** heads south from Tarbat Ness for three miles, following a narrow passage between the cliffs and foreshore, to the hamlet of Rockfield. A road leads past fishermen's cottages to Portmahomack to rejoin the road back to the lighthouse.

By bus Buses from Tain, Lamington St, go east to Portmahomack (Mon–Fri 7 daily; 20min), and to Shandwick, Hill

and Fearn (Mon–Fri 7 daily, Sat 6 daily).

ACCOMMODATION AND EATING

Oystercatcher Main St, Portmahomack ☎01862 871560, ⓦ the-oystercatcher.co.uk. This pretty place in a harbour-side cottage prepares bistro lunches, then dinner menus specializing in seafood, including a cheeky house Bloody Mary – crab with spiced tomato frappé with a zing

of vodka; two courses £29. Bed and outstanding breakfast is available in three pretty en-suites above. Reservations recommended. Thurs–Sun 12.15–2.45pm, Wed–Sat 6.30–11pm. **£108**

SHOPPING

Anta Fearn ☎01862 832477, ⓦ anta.co.uk. While you're in the area, pay a visit to Fearn village (signposted) for the workshop outlet of Anta, manufacturer of contemporary

fine tweeds and tartans plus pottery and homeware; entertain the kids on a rainy day with painting mugs. Mon–Sat 9.30am–5.30pm, Sun 10am–5pm.

Bonar Bridge and around

The A9 across the Kyle of Sutherland has left **BONAR BRIDGE** out on a limb. Yet in the fifteenth century this was a heart of industry because of a large iron foundry. James IV

A SCOTTISH SAFARI PARK

The Clearances, rampant forestry and sheep-grazing have conspired to change much of the Highlands beyond recogniton. Though not, perhaps, permanently, believes **Paul Lister**, a millionaire entrepreneur turned conservationist who hopes to return the great Caledonian woodland that existed two thousand years ago to his estate near Croik. His high-profile plan to reintroduce predators such as **wolves**, **bears** and **lynx** ran up against local opposition when he bought the £3.2m, 23,000-acre estate in 2003, yet the **Alladale Wilderness Reserve** (☎ 01463 716416, ⓦ alladale.com) has enjoyed some success as a conservation project. Alongside a **reforestation** programme, it nutrures iconic **Highland species** such as red and roe deer, red squirrel, Scottish wildcats, otters and golden eagles as well as reintroduced elk and bison. The estate is run as a Scottish safari park for well-funded guests or groups and provides activities such as fly-fishing, 4WD tours, pony trekking, or survival camps set up by adventurist Bear Grylls. If you're interested in its conservation programme, call to see if you can join a group tour with a ranger.

passed through and was so shocked to find the forest virtually clear-felled he ordered oak saplings be planted – the ancient woodland east of Bonar Bridge dates from this era. Bring a bike – several miles of **mountain-biking trails** run through nearby Forestry Commission woodland, blue and black grade at Balblair two miles north, and blue and red beneath Carbisdale Castle (see below).

Croik

CROIK is well worth a detour for its humble **church**, which illuminates the tragedy of the Clearances. Evicted from their homes in 1845, ninety villagers from Glencalvie took shelter in the churchyard and scratched poignant messages on the east window of the church. Inside is a facsimile of a contemporary report of their plight by a *Times* journalist.

Carbisdale Castle

A daunting neo-Gothic pile northwest of Bonar Bridge, **Carbisdale Castle** was erected between 1906 and 1917 for the dowager Duchess of Sutherland; it is designed in three styles to give an impression of long heritage. It was eventually acquired by a Norwegian shipping magnate in 1933 until gifted with all its marble statues and gilt mirrors to the SYHA as one of the most opulent **hostels** in the world. The duchess would've been livid. However, protracted expensive repairs have seen it closed for years and at the time of writing its future was uncertain.

Lairg and around

North of Bonar Bridge, the A836 parallels the River Shin to **LAIRG**, scattered at the eastern end of **Loch Shin**. It's predominantly a transport hub, with little of interest unless your visit coincides with the annual lamb sale in mid-August, one of the largest one-day markets in Europe.

Falls of Shin

4 miles south of Lairg • Daily mid-May to Oct 9am–5pm; Nov to mid-May 10am–4pm • Free • ☎ 01549 402231, ⓦ fallsofshin.co.uk

The reason to come this way is the **Falls of Shin** in Achany Glen: one of the best places in Scotland to see **salmon** leap on their upstream migration between March and November; the 12ft cascade is on the cusp of the maximum leap for a fish and most tumble back into the river. A platform provides a front-row view of the action, which peaks from late July to September, and the site offers a restaurant and an excellent adventure playground for the kiddies. Incidentally, the life-size Mohamed Al-Fayed waxwork in the visitor centre is a homage to the local laird – the Harrod's owner bought the estate in 1972 and saved the centre from closure in 2002.

Dornoch

DORNOCH, a genteel, villagey town eight miles north of Tain, lies on a headland overlooking the **Dornoch Firth**. Blessed with good looks and a sunny climate (by Scottish standards) and surrounded by sand dunes, it has morphed into a modest upmarket resort: all antiques shops and fine accommodation in the historic sandstone centre, a championship **golf course** plus miles of sandy beaches just outside. So, it was a crowning achievement when in 2002 Dornoch hosted Scotland's most rock'n'roll wedding of recent times – Madonna married Guy Ritchie at nearby **Skibo Castle** and had her son baptized in Dornoch Cathedral.

The Cathedral

Castle St • Visitor times mid-May to mid-Sept Mon–Fri 10am–4pm; services Sun 11am • ☎ 01862 810296

Dating from the twelfth century, Dornoch became a royal burgh in 1628. Pride of place among its oldest buildings grouped around the square is the **Cathedral** founded in 1224 and built of local sandstone. The original was horribly damaged by marauding Mackays in 1570, and much of what you see today was restored by the Countess of Sutherland in 1835, though the worst of her Victorian excesses were removed in the twentieth century, when the interior stonework was returned to its original state. The stained-glass windows in the north wall were later additions. The counterpart to the cathedral is the fortified sixteenth-century **Bishop's Palace** opposite, now refurbished as a hotel (see below).

Historylinks

The Meadows • 10am–4pm: April, May & Oct Mon–Fri; June–Sept daily; Nov–March Wed & Thurs • £2.50 • ☎ 01862 811275, ⓦ historylinks.org.uk

A block behind the Bishop's Palace on the high street, **Historylinks** is a small museum which tells the story of Dornoch, from local saints and the last witch burning in Scotland, which occurred here in 1727, to golfers and Madonna herself, with the usual exhibits, plus three films.

ARRIVAL AND DEPARTURE
DORNOCH

By bus Stagecoach's Inverness–Thurso service (via Helmsdale) stops at Dornoch.

Destinations Inverness (Mon–Sat 6 daily, Sun 4 daily; 1hr 10min); Thurso (Mon–Sat 5 daily, Sun 4 daily; 1hr 45min).

INFORMATION AND ACTIVITIES

Tourist office In the courthouse building next to the *Castle Hotel* (Mon–Fri 9am–4pm, plus Sat June–Aug and Sun July & Aug, same hours; ☎ 01862 810594).

Royal Dornoch Golf Club Golf Rd ☎ 01862 810219, ⓦ royaldornoch.com. Opened four hundred years ago, this golf club maintains a par 70 Championship links course (£110) rated among the world's best by many golf media and the easier par 71 Struie course (£40). Booking is essential to play. Note that it has a dress code of no T-shirts (except polo shirts).

ACCOMMODATION

★ **2 Quail** Castle St ☎ 01862 811811, ⓦ 2quail.com. What it lacks in size this three-room B&B makes up in traditional country character and charm. Decor is beautiful, featuring tartan fabrics and paint-shades of mossy green and soft mustard, old pine furnishings and oil paintings by local artists. The owner is a chef so breakfasts are excellent. **£100**

Dornoch Castle Hotel Castle St ☎ 01862 810216, ⓦ dornochcastlehotel.com. For a splurge, choose the fabulous historic Deluxe rooms in the turreted tower of the Bishop's Palace. Elsewhere this smart hotel is more modern – spacious Superiors with pillow chocolates and whisky miniatures or comfy but bland Garden rooms that overlook the rear garden. **£136**

Trevose Main square ☎ 01862 810269. With the central location of the *Dornoch Castle Hotel* directly opposite for a fraction of the price, this detached B&B swathed in roses beside the cathedral is all warm golds and creams in its two rooms, decorated with country style. May–Sept. **£60**

EATING AND DRINKING

Dornoch Castle Hotel Castle Street ☎ 01862 810216. Two dining options in the former bishop's palace: bar food served in the former bishopric kitchen, or modern British mains like Highland venison (mains £18–24) in *The Garden*

restaurant – a three-course table d'hôte (£33) is better value. Daily noon–3pm & 6.30–9.30pm.
Luigi's Castle St ☏ 01862 810893. A modern metropolitan-styled bistro with modern European dishes like bream with lemon risotto – but the stress on fresh seasonal produce means you may also find mussels in a red Thai broth or crab fishcakes. Mains £10–18. Easter–June, Sept & Oct lunch daily (11am–2pm) & dinner (6.45–9pm) Wed–Sun; July & Aug lunch and dinner daily; rest of year lunch daily, dinner Sat & Sun.

North to Wick

North of Dornoch, the A9 hugs the coast for most of the sixty miles to **Wick**, the principal settlement in the far north of the mainland. The most telling landmark in the stretch is the **Sutherland Monument** near Golspie, erected to the first duke of Sutherland, the landowner who oversaw the eviction of thousands of tenants during the Clearances. That bitter memory haunts the small towns and villages of this stretch, including **Brora**, **Dunbeath**, **Lybster** and pretty **Helmsdale**. Nonetheless, many of these settlements went on to flourish through a thriving fishing trade, none more so than Wick, once the busiest herring port in Europe.

Golspie and around

Ten miles north of Dornoch the A9 rolls through the red-sandstone town of **GOLSPIE**. It's a pleasantly bustling if fairly forgettable place, and for most visitors serves only as a gateway to good mountain-bike trails or the grandest castle of this coastline.

Highland Wildcat Trails

ⓦ highlandwildcat.com

One of the best reasons to stop is the **Highland Wildcat Trails** within the hills west of Golspie. Named the best **mountain-bike** rides in the UK by one magazine in 2008, the black-, red- and blue-graded trails include a huge descent from the summit of Ben Bhraggie to sea level. All trails are accessed from the end of Fountain Road.

Dunrobin Castle

A9, 1 mile north of Golspie • April, May, Sept & early Oct Mon–Sat 10.30am–4.30pm, Sun noon–4.30pm; June–Aug daily 10.30am–5.30pm • £10 • ☏ 01408 633177, ⓦ dunrobincastle.co.uk

Mountain-biking aside, the reason to stop in Golspie is to tour the largest house in the Highlands, **Dunrobin Castle**, north of the centre. Modelled on a Loire chateau by Sir Charles Barry, the architect behind London's Houses of Parliament, it is the seat of the Sutherland family, once Europe's biggest landowners with a staggering 1.3 million acres. They were also the driving force behind the Clearances here – it's worth remembering that such extravagance was paid for by evicting thousands of crofters.

Only a tenth of the 189 furnished rooms are visited on tours of the **interior**, as opulent as you'd expect with their fine furniture, paintings (including works by Landseer, Allan Ramsay and Sir Joshua Reynolds), tapestries and objets d'art. Alongside, providing a venue of falconry displays (11.30am & 2pm), the attractive **gardens** are pleasant to wander en route to Dunrobin's **museum**, housed in the former summerhouse and the repository of the Sutherlands' hunting trophies – heads and horns on the walls plus displays of everything from elephants' toes to rhinos' tails – and ethnographic holiday souvenirs from Africa.

The last extravagance is that the castle has its own **train** station (summer only) on the Inverness–Wick line; no surprise, considering the duke built the railway.

The Sutherland Monument

Approaching Golspie, you can't miss the **monument** to the first duke of Sutherland on the summit of **Beinn a'Bhragaidh** (Ben Bhraggie). A 30ft-high statue on a 79ft column,

4

it bears an inscription which recalls its creation in 1834 by "a mourning and grateful tenantry [to] a judicious, kind and liberal landlord", and quietly overlooks the fact that the duke forcibly evicted fifteen thousand crofters from his million-acre estate. A campaign to destroy the statue has died down, unlike the duke's reputation as Scotland's Josef Stalin. The stiff **climb** to the monument (round-trip 1hr 30min) provides vast coast views but the steep path is tough going and there's little view until the top. Head up Fountain Road and pass (or park) at Rhives Farm, then pick up signs for the Beinn a'Bhragaidh footpath (BBFP).

ARRIVAL AND DEPARTURE   GOLSPIE AND AROUND

By bus Stagecoach's Inverness–Thurso service stops at Golspie.
Destinations Inverness (Mon–Sat 6 daily, Sun 4 daily; 1hr 15min); Thurso (Mon–Sat 5 daily, Sun 4 daily; 1hr 40min).

By train Dunrobin Castle is a summer stop on the Inverness–Thurso line (April–Oct Mon–Sat 3 daily; 2hr 10min from Inverness, 1hr 35min from Thurso).

ACCOMMODATION AND EATING

Coffee Bothy Fountain Rd ☎01408 633022. A cabin-style café popular with bikers and walkers. Fill up on all-day breakfasts, fresh soups and baked potatoes before (£5–8), and reward yourself with home-baking afterwards. Feb–Dec Mon–Fri 9am–5pm, Sat 10am–5pm.

Granite Villa Fountain Rd ☎01408 633146, ⊛granite villa.co.uk. A floral overload – wallpaper and bedspreads – brings country charm and keeps to the period style of this late Victorian house. Accommodation is spacious and comfortable in all en-suites; the twin is more restrained in decor. **£80**

Sleeperjazz Rogart, 8 miles west of Golspie ☎01408 641343, ⊛sleeperzzz.com. Sleep in the quirkiest accommodation for miles around: a first-class railway carriage parked in a siding beside the Inverness–Thurso line; a 1930s' showman's caravan; or a Bedford bus. March–Sept. **£16**/person

Helmsdale

HELMSDALE is one of the largest villages between Golspie and Wick. It's certainly the most picturesque: a tight little grid of streets set above a river-mouth harbour. Romantic novelist Barbara Cartland was a frequent visitor and must have looked as exotic as a flamingo in its grey stone streets. For all its charm, it's a newcomer, founded in the nineteenth century to house the evicted inhabitants of Strath Kildonan, which lies behind it, and which subsequently flourished as a herring port.

Timespan Heritage Centre

Drunrobin St • March–Oct Mon–Sat 10am–5pm, Sun noon–5pm; Nov–Feb Tues 2–4pm, Sat & Sun 11am–4pm • £4 • ☎01431 821327, ⊛timespan.org.uk

Good looks and sleepy ambience aside, the appeal of Helmsdale is the **Timespan Heritage Centre** beside the river. An ambitious venture for a place this size, the modern museum tells the story of Viking raids, crofting in re-created houses, the Kildonan Gold Rush, the Clearances, and fishing through high-tech displays, including Wii-based games to navigate animations of local yarns, and audio-tours. It also has an art gallery.

ARRIVAL AND INFORMATION   HELMSDALE

By train On the Inverness–Thurso line (Mon–Sat 3 daily, Sun 2 daily; 2hr 20min from Inverness, 1hr 15min from Thurso).
Tourist information Strath Ullie Crafts on the harbour

doubles as a source of tourist information (Mon–Sat 10am–5.30pm; ☎01431 821402). Otherwise, visit ⊛helmsdale.org.

ACCOMMODATION AND EATING

On our last visit the once-excellent **Bridge Hotel** was awaiting sale. Hopefully a new owner will restore its restaurants and accommodation.

Helmsdale Hostel Stafford St ☎ 08701 553255, ⓦ helmsdalehostel.co.uk. Snug from panelled walls and wood floors – a legacy of former use as a gym – as much as a woodburner in the lounge, this is a friendly wee hostel with room for fourteen guests in two dorms or two rooms, most with single beds. Easter–Sept. Dorms **£17**; twins **£45**

La Mirage Dunrobin St ☎ 01431 821615. Not quite "The North's Premier Restaurant" as it claims, but possibly the most bizarre due to the tastes in decor of a former proprietor who styled herself after Barbara Cartland. The menu, although as dated as Babs herself, is solid: fish or scampi and chips, gammon steaks, even chicken Kiev (average £9). Daily 11am–9pm.

Dunbeath and around

The landscape becomes wilder north of Helmsdale. Once over the long haul up the **Ord of Caithness** – a steep hill which used to be a major obstacle and is still blocked by snowstorms – the scenery switches from heather-clad moors to treeless grazing lands, dotted with derelict crofts and dry-stone walls.

Badbea

As you come over the Ord of Caithness, look for signs to the ruined village of **Badbea**, reached via a walk from the car park beside the A9. Built by tenants cleared from nearby Ousdale, the settlement is now deserted, although its ruined hovels (and information boards) show the hardships crofters endured – the cottages stood so near the cliff-edge that children were tethered to prevent them from being blown over.

Dunbeath

DUNBEATH was another village founded to provide work in the wake of the Clearances, laid along the glen beside the river. The local landlord built a harbour at the river mouth in 1800, at the start of the herring boom, and the settlement briefly flourished. It now suffers the indignity of an A9 flyover soaring over much of the village.

The novelist Neil Gunn was born in one of the terraced houses under the flyover and his tale is told in the **Dunbeath Heritage Centre** (April–Sept Mon–Fri 10am–5pm, Sun 10am–4pm; £2.50; ☎ 01593 731233, ⓦ dunbeath-heritage.org.uk) alongside exhibits of local Pictish and Viking history.

Laidhay Croft Museum

May–Sept Mon–Sat 10am–5pm • £3.50 • ☎ 07563 370231, ⓦ laidhay.co.uk

Just north of Dunbeath is the simple **Laidhay Croft Museum**, housed in an eighteenth-century longhouse which encorporated dwelling, stable and byre. Restored from a ruin in 1971, its re-creation of life in the early 1900s offers a useful riposte to the often over-romanticized life of a Highlander before the Clearances.

Lybster and around

Another neat planned village, **LYBSTER** (pronounced "libe-ster") was established at the height of the nineteenth-century herring boom. Two hundred boats once worked out of its picturesque small harbour, a story told in the **Water Lines** heritage centre here (May–Sept daily 11am–5pm; £2.50 donation requested) – there are modern displays about the "silver darlings" and the fishermen who pursued them, plus a café.

Grey Cairns of Camster

7 miles north of Lybster on a side road (to Roster)

Prehistoric sites litter the coast north to Wick – evidence of a past as fertile farmland before it was smothered by a blanket of peat bog in the Bronze Age. The most impressive are the **Grey Cairns of Camster**: surrounded by moorland, these two enormous reconstructed burial chambers were originally built five thousand years ago with corbelled dry-stone roofs in their hidden chambers.

4

Hill o'Many Stanes

East Clyth, two miles north of Lybster, is the stop for a path to the "**Hill o'Many Stanes**". Some two hundred boulders are set in 22 rows that run north to south. Why is a mystery – an ancient observatory is one theory – although archeological studies suggest they were set around 2000 BC and are just a fraction of the six hundred stones originally in place.

Whaligoe staircase

On the A99, at the north end of Ulbster

Go ten miles north of Lybster to the north end of the village of **Ulbster**, then turn towards the sea opposite a sign to "Cairn o'Get" to find the little-known **Whaligoe staircase**. Its 365 uneven steps lead steeply down from beside a car park to a natural harbour surrounded by high cliffs. It's an atmospheric spot that feels far more remote than the road suggests, all wheeling seabirds and empty sea. Just be glad you don't have to haul baskets full of herring back up as the village's fisherwomen once did.

Wick

Since it was founded by Vikings as *Vik* (meaning "bay"), **WICK** has lived by the sea. It's actually two towns: Wick proper and, south across the river, **Pultneytown**, created by the British Fisheries Society in 1806 to encourage evicted crofters to take up fishing. By the mid-nineteenth century, Wick was the busiest herring port in Europe, with a fleet of more than 1100 boats, exporting tonnes of fish to Russia, Scandinavia and the West Indian slave plantations. Robert Louis Stevenson described it as "the meanest of man's towns, situated on the baldest of God's bays". The demise of its fishing trade has left Wick down at heel, reduced to a mere transport hub. Yet the huge harbour in Pultneytown and a walk around the surrounding area – scruffy rows of fishermen's cottages, derelict net-mending sheds and stores – gives an insight into the scale of the former fishing trade.

Wick Heritage Centre

Bank Row, Pultneytown • Easter–Oct Mon–Sat 10am–5pm, last entry 3.45pm • £4 • ☎ 01955 605393, ⓦ wickheritage.org

The volunteer-maintained **Wick Heritage Centre** is the best place to evoke the heyday of the fishing boom. Larger than it looks, it contains a fascinating array of artefacts from the old days, including fully rigged boats, boat models and reconstructed period rooms, plus a superb archive of photographs captured by three generations of a local family between 1863 and 1975.

Old Pulteney Distillery

Huddart St • Mon–Fri 10am–4pm, May–Sept Sat 10am–4pm; tours at 11am & 2pm or by arrangement (from £6) • ☎ 01955 602371, ⓦ oldpulteney.com

Until city fathers declared Wick dry in the 1920s, fishermen consumed three hundred gallons of whisky a day. The last distillery in town – and most northerly in Scotland – distils more refined malts nowadays; most are light or medium-bodied, with a hint of sea salt. Much is made of maritime character on tours which end, needless to say, with a dram or full tastings.

ARRIVAL AND DEPARTURE   **WICK**

The train station and bus stops are immediately south and west of the central bridge.

By plane Wick Airport (☎ 01955 602215, ⓦ wickairport .com), just north of town, has flights to and from Edinburgh (Mon, Wed–Fri & Sun 1 daily; 1hr) and Aberdeen (Mon–Fri 3 daily; 35min) with Flybe and Eastern Airways respectively.

By train Trains from Inverness (Mon–Sat 4 daily, 2 on Sun; 4hr 15min) make a long but scenic journey via Lairg, Helmsdale, then the Flow Country inland.

WALKING AND CYCLING AROUND WICK

Ordnance Survey Explorer map 450

There's a good **clifftop walk** to the ruins of **Sinclair** and **Girnigoe castles** on a needle-thin promontory three miles north of Wick. They functioned as a single stronghold for the earls of Caithness – in 1570 the fourth earl, suspecting his son of trying to murder him, imprisoned him in the dungeon until he starved. From the harbour of fishing hamlet **Staxigoe**, head north to Field of Noss farm and follow the line of the cliffs. At Noss Head lighthouse, an access road leads to a car park, from where a path leads to the castles on the north coastline. It's a great **cycling** route: the roads near Noss Head are flat and straight, though can be buffeted by strong winds.

By bus Local buses run to John O'Groats then Thurso; long-distance routes to and from Inverness involve a coordinated change at Durneath.

Destinations Inverness (Mon–Sat 4 daily, Sun 3 daily; 3hr); John O' Groats (Mon–Fri 6 daily, Sat 4 daily; 30–35min); Thurso (Mon–Fri 6 daily, Sat 4 daily; 30–35min).

ACTIVITIES

Caithness Sea Coast ☎01955 609200, ❶caithness-seacoast.co.uk. Harbour tours (30min; £10) plus longer tours to spot wildlife and admire the high cliffs south (from £17) in a fast RIB. The operator also runs longer trips to Lybster (3hr; £45), including one-way trips in either direction (£28). All April–Oct.

ACCOMMODATION AND EATING

The Clachan 13 Randolph Place ☎01955 605384, ⓦtheclachan.co.uk. A four-star B&B on the main road south of Wick, a 5min walk from the centre. So, easy to find and easy to enjoy in spotless modern rooms in a private section of the house, all simply but tastefully furnished by an owner who goes the extra mile to help. **£80**

Mackays River St ☎01955 602323, ⓦmackayshotel .co.uk. On-going renovation has introduced fresh contemporary cool – oversized headboards, streamlined oak furnishings and iPod docks. First-floor rooms are brightest. Its *No.1 Bistro* serves the likes of lemon-and-garlic roast chicken with Moroccan spices plus fish and chips (mains average £14). Daily 10.30am–9pm. **£107**

4

Skye and the Small Isles

TROTTERNISH PENINSULA

5

Skye and the Small Isles

For many visitors the Isle of Skye (An t-Eilean Sgiathanach) is the Highlands in miniature. With its shapely summits and shifting seascapes, its superb hiking routes, wildlife and crofting villages, it crams much of the region's appeal into one manageable island. It even has classic Highlands weather. According to one theory, Skye is named after the Old Norse for "cloud" (*skuy*), earning itself the Gaelic moniker *Eilean a' Cheò* (Island of Mist). Despite unpredictable weather, tourism has been an important part of the economy since the railway reached Kyle of Lochalsh in 1897. The Edwardian bourgeoisie swarmed to its mountains, whose beauty had been proclaimed by the Victorians ever since Sir Walter Scott visited in 1814, arguably the most successful tourism PR campaign in Scottish history. People still come in droves, yet Skye is deceptively large. You'll get the most out of it – and escape the worst crowds – if you explore the remoter parts of the island.

The Clearances saw an estimated thirty thousand indigenous *Sgiathanachs* (pronounced "ski-anaks") emigrate in the mid-nineteenth century; today, the population is just over nine thousand. Tourism is now by far the island's biggest earner and has attracted hundreds of incomers from the rest of Britain over the last couple of decades, including an increasing quota of artists. Nevertheless, Skye remains the most important centre for **Gaelic culture** and language outside the Western Isles. Over a third of the population is fluent in Gaelic, the Gaelic college on Sleat is the most important in Scotland, and the Free Church maintains a strong presence.

In contrast to the crowds on Skye, the so-called **Small Isles** – the improbably named Rùm, Eigg, Muck and Canna – to the south only receive a trickle of visitors. Each with a population of fewer than a hundred and with its own identity, they are easily accessible by ferry from Mallaig and Arisaig, though limited accommodation means an overnight visit requires planning.

Skye

Skye ranks among Scotland's most visited destinations, with all the summer coach tours that suggests. Yet the island also has twenty Munros to bag and year-round hikers and climbers pay homage to the **Cuillin** ridge, whose peaks dominate the island; you'll need experience and determination to explore them. For years, the hiking-and-heather view of Skye was all you'd get, but over the last decade a new generation of islanders, including an influx of younger settlers, has introduced a vibrant arts and crafts scene and updated the food and accommodation. Nowadays, Skye holds its own against anywhere in Scotland. In fact, so sophisticated is some of the relaxation on offer that the island is no longer the preserve of hikers and coach tours. The former congregate around Cuillin or the impressive rock formations of the **Trotternish** peninsula, the

Walking in the Cuillin p.276	**Raasay in history** p.285
Flora MacDonald p.283	**Hiking in the Rùm Cuillin** p.288

BUTCHER, SKYE

Highlights

❶ Skye Cuillin Countless lochans, eleven Munros, one challenging 12km ridge trail – and the mountains are almost as impressive seen on the road to Glenbrittle as up on the trail. **See p.275**

❷ Loch Coruisk Few sights in Scotland prepare you for the drama of this glacial loch in the Cuillin – the boat ride there from Elgol just adds to the fun. **See p.275**

❸ Trotternish Take a walk into the bizarre, Tolkeinesque landscapes of the Quiraing or say hello to the Old Man; this peninsula has some of Skye's most distinctive scenery. **See p.282**

❹ Food on Skye Whether in a flagship restaurant like *Three Chimneys* (p.279), the lovely *Glenview* (p.284) or just an arty wee café such as the *Red Roof Gallery* (p.279), you'll eat well on Skye.

❺ Kinloch Castle, Isle of Rùm Visit this frankly bonkers Edwardian pile to discover the decadence of the contemporary landed gentry. **See p.287**

❻ Isle of Eigg Sample off-grid island living in the most vibrant of the Small Isles, with sandy beaches, an easy climb and peace everywhere. **See p.288**

HIGHLIGHTS ARE MARKED ON THE MAP ON P.272

5

latter **Dunvegan** and its castle or **Portree**, the island's capital, with modest charm and amenities. And if the summer crush really gets too much there's always the **Isle of Raasay** off the east coast.

ARRIVAL AND DEPARTURE   SKYE

By car The Skye Bridge sweeps across from Kyle of Lochalsh. If driving, don't underestimate the size of Skye.

Fuel is available 24hr at Broadford, as well as at Portree, Armadale, Dunvegan and Uig.

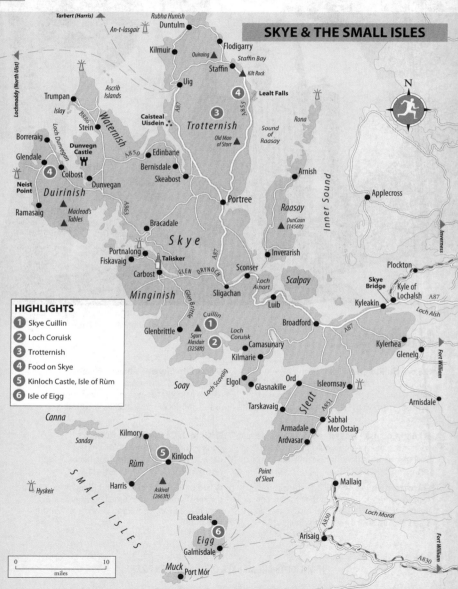

SKYE & THE SMALL ISLES

HIGHLIGHTS
1. Skye Cuillin
2. Loch Coruisk
3. Trotternish
4. Food on Skye
5. Kinloch Castle, Isle of Rùm
6. Isle of Eigg

0 — 10 miles

By ferry From Mallaig, Caledonian MacBrayne (℡0800 C66 5000, ⓦcalmac.co.uk) operates regular car ferries across to Armadale on the Sleat peninsula (Mon–Sat 8 daily, Sun 4–6 daily; 30min). In addition, a tiny community-run car ferry (℡01599 522313, ⓦskyeferry.co.uk) hops across to Kylerhea from Glenelg, south of Kyle of Lochalsh (Easter to mid-Oct daily 10am–6pm every 15min; 5min).

By train and ferry or bus Mallaig (departure point for ferries to Skye – see p.224) is served by direct trains from Fort William (4–5 daily; 1hr 20min) and Glasgow Queen St

(Mon–Sat 3 daily, Sun 1 daily; 5hr 10min). There are also trains from Inverness to Kyle of Lochalsh (Mon–Sat 3–4 daily, Sun 1–2 daily; 2hr 30min) where you can catch a bus over the Skye Bridge to Kyleakin (every 45min; 10min) and up to Portree (1 daily; 1hr 10min).

Moving on to the Western Isles It's 57 miles from Armadale and 49 miles from Kyleakin to Uig, from where ferries leave for Tarbert on Harris and Lochmaddy on North Uist.

GETTING AROUND AND INFORMATION

By bus Bus services peter out in more remote areas and don't run on Sundays. Skye Dayrider tickets for unlimited one-day travel cost £8.

Tourist information The best tourist office on the island is at Portree (see p.280). A useful website about the island is ⓦskye.co.uk.

The Sleat peninsula

Thanks to the CalMac ferry from Mallaig to **ARMADALE**, many people's introduction to Skye is the **Sleat** (pronounced "Slate") **peninsula** at the southern tip of the island. The irony is that it's unlike almost anywhere else hereabouts – an uncharacteristically fertile area branded "The Garden of Skye".

Clan Donald Skye

On A851 • Late March to Oct daily 9.30am–5.30pm, gardens year-round same hours or till dusk • £7.50 • ℡01471 844305, ⓦclandonald.com

Branded as **Clan Donald Skye** on account of its former inhabitants, **Armadale Castle**, a mile north of the ferry terminal, is the shell of the neo-Gothic seat of the MacDonald clan – the laird moved into the gardeners' cottage when the kelp fertilizer market collapsed in the 1920s. Intended as an account of the clan, its modern **Museum of the Isles** is actually more interesting for its perspectives on Highland history, with sections on the Jacobite period and its aftermath, featuring Bonnie Prince Charlie keepsakes such as his shoe buckles worn in battle at Culloden and a couple of cannonballs fired at the castle by HMS *Dartmouth*, sent by William III. Just as appealing is the castle's forty-acre wooded **garden**.

Isleornsay

Having retired as Skye's main fishing port, **ISLEORNSAY** (Eilean Iarmain), six miles north of Armadale, is these days just a pretty, secluded village. Come for views: out across the bay to a necklace of seaweed-encrusted rocks and the tidal **Isle of Ornsay**, and behind it all a panorama of peaks on the mainland.

The west coast of Sleat

A single-track road loops off the A851 to access the wilder west coast of Sleat. Turning at Kilbeg, you ascend over moorland then arrive finally into **TARSKAVAIG**, scattered behind a little beach. Further up the coast, the stony beach at **TOKAVAIG** is overlooked by ruined Dunscaith Castle and enjoys views over the Cuillin range – this, and neighbouring **ORD**, with a sandy beach, offer a superb panorama of the mountains (if the weather plays ball).

ARRIVAL AND DEPARTURE

THE SLEAT PENINSULA

By ferry Reservations are recommended in peak season (ⓦ0800 066 5000, ⓦcalmac.co.uk) for the Mallaig–Armadale crossing (Mon–Sat 8 daily, Sun 4–6 daily; 30min).

By bus All bus services from/to Armadale are via Broadford.

Destinations Broadford (Mon–Fri 5 daily, Sat 2 daily; 30min); Portree (Mon–Fri 2 daily; 1hr 20min); Sligachan (Mon–Fri 2 daily; 1hr).

5

ACTIVITIES

Bike rental You can rent bikes from Armadale Bikes (☎01471 844241 or ☎07919 278871, ⓦarmadalebikes.co.uk), in Ardvasar, half a mile south of the ferry terminal, or bikes can be collected from the ferry terminal with notice.

Seafari ☎01471 833316, ⓦseafari.co.uk. Wildlife and scenery trips in a high-speed RIB from Armadale to spot dolphins and minke whales in summer.

ACCOMMODATION, EATING AND DRINKING

ARMADALE AND ARDVASAR

Ardvasar Hotel Ardvasar, 0.5 miles south of Armadale ☎01471 844223, ⓦardvasarhotel.com. This pretty little inn has benefitted from refurbishment to create comfortable, contemporary accommodation as well as a smart restaurant specializing in local seafood – lobster, scallops and crab, plus Speyside beef for around £13. **£130**

Flora MacDonald Hostel Kilmore, 4 miles north of Armadale ☎01471 844272, ⓦskye-hostel.co.uk. Turn opposite Kilmore church to find the community-run hostel. Decor is of the granny's armchair variety – adding character or dated depending on your view. Bunks are in mixed dorms or a family/group lodge. Dorms **£16**; twins **£42**

Rubha Phoil Entry at ferry terminal, Armadale ☎01471 844700, ⓦskye-permaculture.org.uk. Just ten pitches plus two cute cabins in a 16-acre woodland campsite affiliated to an organic nursery. Alongside green credentials, you get eggs from free-range hens (with honesty box), yoga classes, communal campfires and, if you're keen, astounding sunrises. Camping **£7.50**/person; cabins (for two) **£30**

ISLEORNSAY AND AROUND

★ **Eilean Iarmain** Isleornsay ☎01471 833332, ⓦeileaniarmain.com. This small hotel is a charmer, romantically furnished in cosy country style: antiques, pretty fabrics, awesome views and not a TV in sight. The restaurant serves fine dining menus such as venison with garlic and white truffle mash, or there's informal eating in the bar (mains average £13). Daily noon–2.30pm & 6–9pm. **£170**

Napier Cottage 1 mile south of Isleornsay ☎01471 833461, ⓦnapiercottage.co.uk. Underfloor heating, Scandinavian woodburners and views to the Knoydart peninsula in the lounge, modern wood furnishings in tasteful rooms and lovely owners who can't do enough to help combine to make a luxury B&B stay. **£120**

Kinloch Lodge 1 mile south of Isleornsay ☎01471 833333, ⓦkinloch-lodge.co.uk. One of the island's leading small hotels, this remains the home of Lord and Lady Macdonald of Macdonald and as such is furnished with antiques and clan mementos. As famous is the Michelin-starred food of Claire Macdonald; seasonal tasting menus or succinct set menus showcase super-fresh island ingredients. Two courses from £30. Daily noon–2pm & 6–9pm. **£300**

Kyleakin

The **Skye Bridge** that rendered the ferry crossing redundant has been a mixed blessing for the old port of **KYLEAKIN** (pronounced "ka*la*kin", with the stress on the second syllable). On one hand it's now bypassed; on the other, that leaves its neat centre that bit quieter, even in high season. Bizarrely, it's also evolved into a backpackers' hangout.

The bridge has been less kind to **Eilean Bàn**, an island from which the bridge leapfrogs to cross Loch Alsh. From 1968 to 1969, its lighthouse keeper's cottage was briefly the home of Gavin Maxwell, author of *Ring of Bright Water* and *Tarka the Otter*. The island now serves as a nature reserve and can be visited on tours booked through the Bright Water Visitor Centre (see below) in Kyleakin.

ARRIVAL AND INFORMATION   KYLEAKIN

By bus There are buses from and to Kyle of Lochalsh (Mon–Sat hourly; 10min) and Portree via Broadford (1 daily; 55min).

Tourist information Available in the Bright Water Visitor Centre, The Pier (Easter–Sept, generally 10am–4pm but phone for times; ☎01599 530040, ⓦeileanban.org).

ACCOMMODATION AND EATING

Saucy Mary's Kyleakin ☎01599 534845, ⓦsaucymarys.com. The largest hostel in the village has loch views and is popular with backpackers for its location above the pub – quieter accommodation for families is in an annexe, and the same owners also manage a B&B next door. Dorms **£18.50**; doubles **£49**

Broadford

Skye's second-largest village, **BROADFORD** (An t-Àth Leathann), strung out along the main road, has a traffic problem and a charm bypass. That said, Broadford is handy for its full quota of facilities – not least a large supermarket and 24-hour fuel – and has one of the island's few wet-weather retreats. The **Skye Serpentarium** (Easter–Oct Mon–Sat 10am–5pm; July & Aug daily; £4.50; ☎01471 822 2209, ⓦskyeserpentarium.org.uk), just off the main road, has around fifty reptiles on display, all abandoned or rescued, ranging from tiny tree frogs to large iguanas. There's usually a snake to handle too – handy if you have children to entertain when the heavens open.

ARRIVAL AND INFORMATION

BROADFORD

By bus Broadford is served by local buses from and to Kyle of Lochalsh (Mon–Sat hourly; 25min), Kyleakin (Mon–Fri 1 daily, Sat 2 daily; 15min) and Portree (Mon–Sat 5–6 daily; 40min).

Tourist information A friendly independent info point is by the 24hr garage and supermarket in the centre (May–Oct Mon–Sat 9.30am–5.30pm, Sun 10am–4pm, April till 4pm; no tel).

ACTIVITIES

Skyak Adventures Lower Breakish ☎01471 820002, ⓦskyakadventures.com. Based outside Broadford at

Lower Breakish, this experienced company runs sea-kayaking trips and courses for all abilities.

ACCOMMODATION AND EATING

Berabhaigh 3 Limepark ☎01471 822372, ⓦisleofskye .net/berabhaigh. This relaxed B&B behind the Serpentarium, run by a hugely hospitable couple, represents great value for money considering the spotlessly clean en-suite rooms, both with loch views. March–Oct. **£76**

Broadford Hotel Torrin Rd ☎01471 822372, ⓦbroadfordhotel.co.uk. A rather smart four-star hotel with tweedy carpets, russet- and chocolate-toned fabrics and neat extras like iPod docks. Its *Spinnaker* restaurant serves mains like sea trout on baby leeks (£13), while the bar offers pub food under £10 and Skye Brewery beers. Daily noon–3pm & 5.30–9.30pm. **£130**

Creelers Seafood Restaurant Lower Harrapool ☎01471 822281, ⓦskye-seafood-restaurant.co.uk. No fuss, no highfalutin' foams, this wee restaurant is all about local seafood simply but superbly prepared – a rich bouillabaisse or mussels in dry white wine, butter, garlic and parsley (mains average £17). March–Oct Mon–Sat noon–9.30pm.

★ **Tigh an Dochais** 13 Harrapool ☎01471 820022, ⓦskyebedbreakfast.co.uk. Jaw-dropping views down Broadford Bay through walls of glass are the draw at this striking B&B, although streamlined contemporary style and a calm, grown-up vibe are just as good reasons to check in. March–Nov. **£90**

The Cuillin and Red Hills

They have razor-edge ridges, the slopes plummet in scree fields and the lonely lochs are imbued with an almost tangible magic. Small wonder that for many people, the spectacular **Cuillin** range is the sole reason to visit Skye. When – if – the cloud disperses, these spectacular peaks dominate the island. There are three **approaches**: from the south, by foot or by boat from Elgol; from *Sligachan Hotel* to the north; or from Glen Brittle to the west of the mountains. Glen Sligachan is one of the most popular routes as it divides the granite of the round-topped **Red Hills** (sometimes referred to as the Red Cuillin) to the east from the Cuillin themselves – sometimes known as the **Black Cuillin** on account of the colour of their coarse-grained jagged gabbro. With twenty Munros between them, these are mountains to take seriously. There are around five fatalities a year here and many routes are for experienced climbers only. If you're unsure, hire a guide.

Elgol, Loch Coruisk and Glen Sligachan

The road to **ELGOL** (Ealaghol) at the tip of the Strathaird peninsula is one of the most impressive on Skye, swooping into the heart of the Red Hills to culminate in beautiful views of the Small Isles above Elgol pier.

5

WALKING IN THE CUILLIN
Ordnance Survey Explorer map 411

For many walkers and climbers, there's nowhere in Britain to beat **the Cuillin**. The main ridge is just eight miles long, but with its immediate neighbours it is made up of over thirty peaks, twelve of them Munros. Those intent on doing a complete traverse of the Cuillin ridge usually start at **Gars-bheinn**, at the southeastern tip, and finish off at **Sgùrr nan Gillean** (3167ft), descending on the famous *Sligachan Hotel* for a well-earned pint. The entire journey takes a minimum of sixteen hours, which either means a very long day or two days and a bivouac. A period of settled weather is pretty much essential, and only experienced walkers and climbers should attempt it. Take note of all the usual safety precautions and be aware that **compasses** are unreliable in the Cuillin, due to the magnetic nature of the rocks.

If you're based in Glen Brittle, one of the easiest walks is the five-mile round trip from the campsite up **Coire Làgan**, to a crystal-cold lochan squeezed in among the sternest of rockfaces. If you simply want to bag one or two of the peaks, several corries provide relatively straightforward approaches to the central Munros. From the SYHA hostel, a path heads west along the southern bank of the stream that tumbles down from the **Coire a' Ghreadaidh**. From the corrie, you can climb up to An Dorus, the obvious gap in the ridge, then ascend **Sgùrr a' Mhadaidh** (3012ft) or **Sgùrr a' Ghreadaidh** (3192ft) to the south. Alternatively, before Coire a' Ghreadaidh, you can head south to the Coir' an Eich, from which you can easily climb **Sgùrr na Banachdaich** (3166ft) via its western ridge. To the south of the youth hostel, the road crosses another stream, with another path along its southern banks. This path heads west past the impressive **Eas Mòr** (Great Waterfall), before heading up to the **Coire na Banachdaich**. The pass above the corrie is the main one over to Loch Coruisk, but also gives access to Sgùrr Dearg, best known for its great view of the **Inaccessible Pinnacle** or "In-Pin" (3235ft) – it doesn't actually live up to the name, but Scotland's most difficult Munro requires good rock-climbing skills. Back at Eas Mòr, paths head off for Coire Làgan, by far the most popular corrie thanks to its steep sides and tiny lochan. If you're unsure about any hike or want help, hire a guide: try Skye Guides (☎01471 822116, ⊛skyeguides.co.uk).

The chief reason for visiting Elgol is to take a boat, whether a wildlife cruise or a trip across Loch Scavaig to visit **Loch Coruisk**. This isolated, glacial loch lies beneath the highest peaks of the Cuillin and is a superb trip, about an hour by boat then up to a half-day ashore. **Walkers** use the boat simply to begin hikes in the Red Hills or over the pass into **Glen Sligachan**. Alternatively, you can walk round the coast to the bay of **Camasunary**, over two miles to the east – a difficult walk that involves a tricky river crossing and negotiating "The Bad Step", an overhanging rock with a 30ft drop to the sea – and head north to Glen Sligachan. Conversely, a time-honoured approach into Glen Sligachan is from the north via the *Sligachan Hotel* (see opposite), a popular hikers' base.

Glen Brittle
Yet another route into the peaks is from **Glen Brittle** on the west side. The valley edges the most spectacular peaks of the **Cuillin**, a semicircle of mountains which ring Loch Coruisk, before it runs to a beach at Loch Brittle. One of the easiest walks is a five-mile round trip (3hr) from *Glenbrittle* campsite (see opposite) up **Coire Làgan** to a lochan squeezed among stern rockfaces. An equally good reason to come is the **Fairy Pools**, one of Britain's most celebrated wild swimming destinations. The scenery is superb as the river tumbles beneath peaks – the downside is water temperature of 8–10°C at best. The pools are signposted from Glumagan Na Sithichean car park, five miles from the Glen Brittle turn.

ARRIVAL AND DEPARTURE	THE CUILLIN AND RED HILLS

By bus Elgol is accessed most easily from Broadford (Mon–Fri 5 daily, Sat 2 daily; 30min). Sligachan is a stop on the Portree–Broadford route (Mon–Sat 6–7 daily; Broadford 35min, Portree 20min).

5

ACTIVITIES

Boat trips From Easter to Oct, two operators offer superb trips from Elgol to Loch Coruisk, taking 1hr each way, with up to half a day ashore: the *Bella Jane* (daily; £14 single, £24 return; ☎ 0800 731 3089, ⓦ bellajane.co.uk) and the *Misty Isle* (Mon–Sat; £12.50 single, £20 return; ☎ 01471 866288, ⓦ mistyisleboattrips.co.uk). The owner of *Bella Jane* also runs wildlife-watching and walking trips to the Small Isles in a fast RIB as Aquaxplore (Easter–Oct daily; from £16).

ACCOMMODATION AND EATING

★ **Coruisk House** Elgol ☎ 01471 866330, ⓦ coruisk house.com. A taste of Skye on unfussy super-fresh menus – squat lobster in hazelnut butter, a famous fish pie, Soay lamb or rich Mull beef stews – with two courses from £20. Above are two beautiful cottage rooms of understated luxury: expect dinner, a relaxing night and an awesome breakfast. Perfect. Reservations essential. Daily 7–10pm. **£100**

Glenbrittle Campsite End of road, Glenbrittle ☎ 01478 640404. With sea views and the beach in front, and mountains behind, this spacious, natural site is the best of both worlds. The bad news is midges. Thousands of them, though they vanish with a breeze. April–Sept. **£7**/person

Glenbrittle SYHA Glenbrittle ☎ 01478 640278, ⓦ syha.org.uk. Refurbished in 2013 has reduced the bed quota, opened up the lounge arrangement, modernized facilities and sensitively updated the mountain chalet vibe; its old wood panelling and new leather sofas now combine into a sort of rugged Scandi chic. Offers frozen prepared meals. April–Sept. Dorms **£17**; doubles **£45**

Rowan Cottage Glasnakille, 1 mile east of Elgol ☎ 01471 866287, ⓦ rowancottage-skye.co.uk. Go across the moors from Elgol pier then left at the T-Junction to find Christine and Jim's place – the end of the road bar 100 yards. It's a homely B&B with a big welcome and sea views to Sleat from rooms – free wi-fi too. **£72**

Sligachan Bunkhouse On A87 ☎ 01478 650458, ⓦ sligachanselfcatering.co.uk. There are peaks just beyond the back door from this modern, clean, no-frills bunkhouse adjacent to the *Sligachan Hotel*. Within are large dorm rooms with some of the largest bunks you'll see plus a laundry, a spacious kitchen and a small lounge with a fireplace. Dorms **£16**

Sligachan Hotel and Campsite On A87 ☎ 01478 650204, ⓦ sligachan.co.uk. This longstanding launchpad for hikers is almost embraced beneath Cuillin's peaks. Alongside dated but comfy enough en-suite rooms, it maintains the barn-like *Seamas' Bar* which serves breakfasts plus dishes like venison and chestnut stew or haggis, neaps and tatties (£8–12). A campsite is over the road (no telephone) – the midges in summer are as famous as the view. Hotel: March–Oct; campsite: year-round. **£130**; camping **£6**/person

Minginish

If the Cuillin has disappeared into the mist for the day and you have your own transport, you can while away a happy afternoon exploring the nearby **Minginish** peninsula, north of Glen Brittle.

Talisker whisky distillery

By Loch Harport, Carbost • April, May & Oct Mon–Sat 9.30am–5pm; June Mon–Fri 9.30am–5pm, Sun 11am–5pm; July & Aug Mon–Sat 9.30am–5.30pm, Sun 11am–5pm; Nov–March Mon–Fri 10am–4.30pm • Tours from £7 • ☎ 01478 614308

One ideal wet-weather activity is a guided tour of the **Talisker whisky distillery**, which produces a sweet full-bodied single malt with a whiff of smoke and peat. Skye's only distillery is situated on the shores of Loch Harport at **CARBOST**, not at the village of Talisker itself, which lies on the west coast of Minginish.

ACCOMMODATION AND EATING   MINGINISH

Old Inn and Waterfront Bunkhouse Carbost ☎ 01478 640205, ⓦ theoldinnskye.co.uk. A chalet-style building and lochside location lend this bunkhouse a cheerful holiday atmosphere. It's managed by the historic *Old Inn* next door, which provides good bar meals – fresh local seafood plus cheaper staples like haggis, neaps and tatties in a whisky cream sauce – for around £10 a main. Daily 11–9pm. Dorms **£16**

★ **Skyewalker Hostel** Portnalong, 2 miles north of Carbost ☎ 01478 640250, ⓦ skyewalkerhostel.com. Not just the best hostel on Skye but awarded the best in Scotland in 2012. Housed in a converted school, it's an appealing blend of the practical – solid bunks, an outstanding modern kitchen – and the charming – pretty vintage-style bathroom, a lounge that hosts the occasional music evening, a garden solar dome and marvellous owners. Easter–Sept. Dorms **£16**; doubles **£36**

5

Dunvegan

DUNVEGAN (Dùn Bheagain) is something of a letdown after the route there, skirting the bony sea cliffs and stacks of the west coast. Yet it has one of Skye's most famous traditional sights, plus two of the island's more interesting peninsulas, Duirinish and Waternish, in its backyard.

Dunvegan Castle

1 mile north of Dunvegan • Easter to mid-Oct daily 10am–5pm • £9.50, or £6 for gardens only • ☎ 01470 521206, ⓦ dunvegancastle.com

Just north of the village, **Dunvegan Castle** sprawls over a rocky outcrop, sandwiched between the sea and several acres of attractive **gardens**. It's been the seat of the Clan MacLeod since the thirteenth century, but the present facade is a product of Victorian romanticism. Older architecture remains inside, where you get the usual furniture and oil paintings alongside some more noteworthy items. The most intriguing is the scrappy remnants of the **Fairy Flag**, carried back to Skye, they say, by the Gaelic boatmen of King Harald Hardrada after the Battle of Stamford Bridge in 1066. MacLeod tradition states the flag was the gift of a fairy to protect the clan – as late as World War II, MacLeod pilots carried pictures of it for luck.

Claigan Coral Beaches

3 miles north of Dunvegan

Keep it quiet but these **beaches** in Claigan, three miles north of Dunvegan, might be as good a reason to visit as the castle. The strands are not coral but calcified maerl (seaweed) and tiny sea shells, but on a sunny day, their white sand and aqua water could almost be the Caribbean. Almost.

ARRIVAL AND ACTIVITIES   DUNVEGAN

By bus Dunvegan is served by buses that loop around northern Skye from Portree (Mon–Fri 6 daily, Sat 3 daily; 45min); about half of them stop at the castle.

Boat trips Seal-watching trips (mid-April to Sept 10am–5pm; £6) in a rowing boat embark from a quay beneath Dunvegan Castle's garden.

ACCOMMODATION

★ **Greshornish House** Greshornish, 6 miles east of Dunvegan ☎ 01470 582266, ⓦ greshornishhouse.com. This wonderful small hotel – half country hotel, half family home of its charming owners – has cosy, traditional rooms, period charm and a relaxed atmosphere that's difficult to leave. April–Nov. **£130**

Kinloch Campsite Loch Dunvegan ☎ 01470 521531, ⓦ kinloch-campsite.co.uk. Spreads across the head of Loch Dunvegan just as its name (literally "loch head")

suggests, although motorhomes and caravans claim the prime waterfront – campers pitch at the sides and on a low hill. April–Oct. **£7**/person

Roskhill House Ose, 3 miles south of Dunvegan ☎ 01470 521317, ⓦ roskhillhouse.co.uk. Stone walls, crafts and home-made cake bring charm to this old croft house, whose modern oak furnishings and bed throws over crisp white linen lend understated style to your stay. Great breakfasts too. **£78**

EATING

Edinblaine Inn Edinblaine, 8 miles east of Dunvegan ☎ 01470 582414. Proper restaurant dishes such as herb-crust lamb with a root veg terrine and red wine jus (average £16) meets local vibe in a pub that wins plaudits from locals. Music on Wed evenings and Sun afternoons. Mon–Sat 6–9pm, Sun noon–3pm; closed Thurs Oct–June.

Jann's Cakes Dunvegan. This tiny place on the high street is a Skye legend for its cakes and home-made chocolates,

and also prepares fresh sandwiches and soups. Not cheap – £5 a slice of cake or £6 for scallop chowder – but quality is high. Mon–Sat 10am–5pm.

The Old School Dunvegan ☎ 01470 521421. Offers upmarket cooking such as venison haunch with whisky and honey sauce or hake with langoustine bisque (average £17). Raw stone walls add character to a lofty and rather smart dining room. April–Oct daily 6–10pm; Nov–March Sat & Sun same hours.

The Duirinish peninsula

5

Much of the **Duirinish peninsula**, west of Dunvegan, is inaccessible to all except walkers prepared to scale or skirt the area's twin flat-topped basalt peaks: Healabhal Bheag (1600ft) and Healabhal Mhor (1538ft). The mountains are better known as **MacLeod's Tables** – the story goes that the MacLeod chief held a royal feast on the lower of the two for James V.

Glen Dale

West from Loch Dunvegan, the broad, green sweep of **Glen Dale** feels instantly wilder after Dunvegan. Its moment in history came in 1882, when local crofters staged a rent strike against their landlords, the MacLeods. Five locals, who became known as the "Glen Dale Martyrs", were given two-month prison sentences and in 1904 the crofters became the first owner-occupiers in the Highlands.

Colbost Folk Museum

Colbost village • Easter–Oct daily 10am-6pm • £1.50 • ☎ 01470 521 2016

Local history plus information about nineteenth-century crofting is told through news cuttings in this restored blackhouse, four miles up the road from Dunvegan. A guide is usually on hand to answer questions and the peat fire is often lit.

The west coast of Duirinish

A bumpy road leads up the west coast of Duirinish to Ramasaig, continuing five miles to the deserted village of **Lorgill** where, on August 4, 1830, every crofter was ordered to board the *Midlothian* in Loch Snizort to go to Nova Scotia or go to prison (those over the age of 70 were sent to the poorhouse). It's a great place for walkers, though, with easy, blustery footpaths to **Neist Point**, Skye's most westerly spot, a spectacular end-of-the-world headland with high sea cliffs, and wonderful views to the Western Isles.

ARRIVAL AND INFORMATION	THE DUIRINISH PENINSULA

By bus Buses go to Colbost from Portree via Dunvegan (Mon–Fri 2 daily; 1hr 15min).

Tourist information A useful website on the area is ⓦ glendaleskye.com.

ACCOMMODATION AND EATING

Carter's Rest 8/9 Upper Milovaig, 4 miles west of Colbost ☎ 01470 511272, ⓦ cartersrestskye.co.uk. Little touches like a digital radio impress almost as much as furnishings such as a wooden sleigh bed in this luxury four-star B&B with astonishing coast views. It prepares evening meals for guests in shoulder months. **£85**

★ **Red Roof Gallery** Holmisdale, 3 miles west of Colbost ☎ 01470 511766. This award-winning little café owned by an artist-musician couple has a loyal fan base for its superb lunches (average £5–8) of local cheese or seafood platters with home-made breads, plus home-baking with great coffee. Sun–Fri 11am–5pm.

★ **Three Chimneys** Colbost ☎ 01470 511258, ⓦ three chimneys.co.uk. A gourmet restaurant at the vanguard of Skye's foodie revolution which has been ranked among the world's best dining experiences. Seven Courses of Skye menus (£90) offer exquisite seafood plus unfussy mains like blackface lamb with rosemary maize. Shorter, cheaper menus also available. Reservations essential. Mid-March to Oct Mon–Sat 12.15–1.45pm & 6–9pm; also open for Sun lunch in high season. Doubles **£295**

Waternish

Waternish is a backwater by Skye's standards. Though not as spectacular as Duirinish or Trotternish it provides equally good views over to the Western Isles, and with fewer visitors, feels appealingly remote. To reach the peninsula, you cross the **Fairy Bridge** (Beul-Ath nan Tri Allt or "Ford of the Three Burns"), at the junction of the B886. Legend has it the fourth MacLeod clan chief was forced to say farewell to his fairy wife here when she had to return to her kind – her parting gift was the Fairy Flag (see p.278).

5

Stein

STEIN, looking out over Loch Bay to the Western Isles, is Waternish's prettiest village, a row of whitewashed cottages built in 1787 by the British Fisheries Society. The place never really took off and was more or less abandoned within a couple of generations. Today it's a little livelier, thanks to its lovely restaurant and pub – there are few nicer places on Skye for a pint on a sunny summer evening.

Trumpan Church

At the end of the road that continues north from Stein is the medieval shell of **Trumpan Church**. Its beautiful location belies one of the bloodiest episodes in Skye's history. In a revenge attack in 1578, the MacDonalds of Uist set fire to the church while numerous MacLeods were attending a service within. Everyone perished except one young girl, who squeezed through a window and raised the alarm. The MacLeods rallied and slaughtered the MacDonalds, then threw their bodies into a nearby dyke. In the graveyard is the **Trial Stone** – in the fourteenth century, accused criminals were blindfolded and if they could fit their fingers in its hole they were deemed innocent. Otherwise, ouch.

ACCOMMODATION   WATERNISH

★ **Loch Bay Seafood Restaurant** Stein ☎ 01470 592235. Tiny, romantic, fabulous, with super-fresh seafood in a dining room full of art. Blackboard menus list the day's catch alongside regulars like peat-smoked salmon or oysters; mains are around £18. Reservations highly recommended. Easter to mid-Oct Tues, Fri & Sat 7–10pm, Wed & Thurs noon–3pm & 7–10pm.

★ **Stein Inn** Stein ☎ 01470 592362, ⊛ steininn.co.uk. A sixteenth-century waterfront inn that's as traditional as you'd hope: local ales, 125 malts and home-made dishes like pork Stroganoff (average £12). Above are five cheerful en-suite rooms; simple, clean and you wake to sea views. Mon–Thurs 11am–11pm/midnight, Fri & Sat 11am–midnight/1am; food served Easter–Oct noon–4pm & 6–9pm; Oct–Easter noon–2.30pm & 5.30–8pm. **£74**

Portree

PORTREE is the only town on Skye, with a population of around 2500. It's also one of the most attractive ports in northwest Scotland, its deep, cliff-edged harbour filled with fishing boats and circled by multicoloured houses. Originally known as Kiltaraglen, it takes its current name – some say – from Port Rìgh (Port of the King), after the state visit James V made in 1540 to assert his authority over the chieftains of Skye.

The focus of activity for many visitors is the **harbour**, with an attractive wharf that dates from the early nineteenth century and a fishing fleet that still lands a modest catch. Looming behind is **The Lump**, a steep and stumpy peninsula on which public hangings once attracted crowds of up to five thousand. The tidy town centre spreads around **Somerled Square**, built in the late eighteenth century as the island's administrative and commercial centre. A shame that it now serves as Portree's bus station and car park.

ARRIVAL AND DEPARTURE   PORTREE

By bus Portree is the hub of all transport on the island and has mainland connections from Glasgow with CityLink.
Destinations Broadford via Sligachan (Mon–Sat 4–6 daily;

50min); Dunvegan (Mon–Sat 3–5 daily; 45min); Glasgow (Mon–Sat 3 daily; 6hr 15min); Glen Brittle (Mon–Fri 2 daily; 50min); Trotternish circuit via Old Man of Storr, Staffin and Uig (Mon–Sat 6 daily; 2hr total circuit).

INFORMATION AND ACTIVITIES

Tourist office Just off Bridge St (Mon–Sat 9am–5pm, plus Sun 10am–4pm April–Oct; ☎ 01478 612992). The best tourist office on the island can book accommodation and has internet terminals.

Bike rental Island Cycles, accessed off The Green or above the long-stay car park (Easter–Oct Mon–Sat 9am–5pm, call other months; ☎ 01478 613121).

FROM TOP SEA-KAYAKER, LOCH SCAVAIG (P.276); WALKERS, GLEN BRITTLE (P.276) >

5

ACCOMMODATION

★ **Ben Tianavaig** 5 Bosville Terrace ☎01478 612152, ⊚ben-tianavaig.co.uk. The best B&B in the centre, with a warm welcome from your hosts and cottagey en-suites that are modern and bright, with art on the walls and unrestricted harbour views for an extra £10. Good breakfasts whatever the tariff. Reservations recommended. **£70**

Cuillin Hills Hotel Turn left at end of Bosville Terrace ☎01478 612003, ⊚cuillinhills-hotel-skye.co.uk. Lord Macdonald's old hunting lodge secluded in fifteen acres is the smartest formal hotel in Portree, and with views over the Sound of Raasay makes a luxurious country stay with town facilities to hand. Accommodation is spacious and comfortable, refurbished into a sort of Highlands chic. **£210**

★ **The Spoons** 75 Aird Bernisdale, near Skeabost Bridge, 6 miles north of Portree ☎01478 532217, ⊚thespoonskye.com. This epitomizes the new breed of stylish B&B: chalky grey walls, crisp linen and wool throws, an eclectic mix of antique and modern furnishings, and outstanding breakfasts. A very grown-up, relaxing stay. **£140**

Torvaig Campsite 2 miles north of Portree on A855 ☎01478 611849, ⊚portreecampsite.co.uk. Views of mountains and flat pitches appeal at this family-run site on the road to Staffin. Alongside the usual amenities and electricity hook-ups, handy extras include a laundry with tumble driers and wi-fi. Easter–Oct. **£7/person**

★ **Viewfield House** Signposted off A87 ☎01478 612217, ⊚viewfieldhouse.com. The last word in Scots Baronial style is this pile on the southern edge of town. It's almost eccentric in its Victorian grandeur, all fabulous floral wallpaper, hunting trophies, stuffed polecats and antiques. Rooms are individually furnished; some tranquil, some gloriously over the top. Great fun. Easter to early Oct. **£116**

EATING AND DRINKING

Café Arriba Quay Brae ☎01478 611830. This local institution packs in the punters. They come for a gossip over the best coffee in town or tea served in large china pots as much as the globe-trotting café menu of home-made soups, wraps, pastas or posh lamb kebabs for around £8. Easter–Oct daily 7am–6pm.

Harbour View 7 Bosville Terrace ☎01478 612069. As cosy as the fisherman's front room it once was, Portree's most romantic restaurant prepares the likes of seared hake on puy lentils (£17) or Loch Eihort *moules marinière* on a seafood menu. Tues–Sun: March, April, Nov & Dec 5.30–10pm; May–Oct noon–2.30pm & 5.30–10pm.

Isles Inn Somerled Square ☎01478 612129. With its log fire and flagstone floors, this is the most appealing of Portree's pubs; it also has the occasional ceilidh band. Alongside Skye ales, it has a no-nonsense menu of fish and chips, venison burgers or local haggis, neeps and tatties (£7–12). Mon–Thurs 11am/noon–midnight, Fri & Sat till 1am, Sun till 11pm.

Sea Breezes 2 Marine Buildings ☎01478 612016. A modern, informal restaurant on the harbour that specializes in local fish – such as Uist scallops with crayfish or local seafood pasta – but finds space for steak and chicken with Toulouse sausage. Mains £10–20. April to late Oct daily noon–2pm & 5–9.30pm.

Trotternish

Protruding twenty miles north of Portree, the **Trotternish peninsula** has some of the island's most bizarre scenery, particularly on the east coast, where volcanic basalt has pressed down on softer sandstone and limestone, causing massive landslides. These, in turn, have created sheer cliffs, peppered with outcrops of hard, wizened basalt – pinnacles and pillars that are at their most eccentric in the **Quiraing**, above Staffin Bay, a long arc of beach just north of Staffin village.

Old Man of Storr

6 miles north of Portree along the A855

The most celebrated column of rock on Skye, the **Old Man of Storr** is all that is left after one massive landslip. Huge blocks of stone still occasionally break off the cliff of the Storr (2358ft) above. A half-hour trek from a car park ascends to the pillar but don't expect to have it to yourself – this is one of the island's signature sights.

Lealt Falls

Off the A855, east of Lealt

Five miles north of the Old Man, a signposted turn goes west to the **Lealt Falls**, at the head of a gorge which is largely in shadow (and home to crack squadrons of midges).

The views across to Raasay and Rona from the first stage of the path can be spectacular. The coast here is worth exploring, too, especially the track leading to **Rubha nam Brathairean** (Brothers' Point).

Kilt Rock
Off the A855, southeast of Staffin

With spectacular tubular, basalt columns that plummet sheer into the sea – like the folds in a kilt, apparently – and cliffs dotted with fulmar and kittiwake, it's little surprise **Kilt Rock** is a popular call on the tourist route. A waterfall which falls 170ft to the sea only adds to the appeal. The car park is a few miles north of the Lealt Falls turn.

Quiraing

Just past Staffin Bay, a single-track road cuts east across the peninsula into the **Quiraing**, a spectacular area of rock pinnacles, sheer cliffs and strange rock formations produced by rock slips. There are two **car parks**: from the first, beside a cemetery, it's a steep half-hour climb to the rocks; from the second, on the saddle, it's a longer but more gentle traverse. Once you're among the rocks, you can make out "The Prison" to your right, and the 131 ft "Needle", to your left. "The Table", a sunken platform where locals used to play shinty, lies a further fifteen-minute scramble up the rocks.

Duntulm

Beyond Flodigarry, four miles further along the A855, lies **DUNTULM** (Duntuilm), whose heyday as a MacDonald power base is recalled by the shattered remains of a headland fortress abandoned by the clan in 1732; they say a clumsy nurse dropped the baby son and heir from a window onto the rocks below. They also say you can see the keel marks of Viking longships scoured into the rocks.

Skye Museum of Island Life
On the A855, 2 miles west of Duntulm • Easter–Oct Mon–Sat 9.30am–5pm • £2.50 • ☎ 01470 552206, ⓦ skyemuseum.co.uk

It's a short trip from Duntulm to the best of the island's folk museums. Run by locals, the **Skye Museum of Island Life** – an impressive pair of thatched blackhouses decorated with home furnishings and farming tools – provides an insight into a way of life commonplace only a century ago. Behind the museum are the graves of **Flora MacDonald**, heroine during Bonnie Prince Charlie's flight, and her husband. Such was her fame the original mausoleum fell victim to souvenir hunters and had to be replaced. The Celtic cross headstone is inscribed with a tribute by Dr Johnson, who visited her in 1773: "Her name will be mentioned in history, if courage and fidelity be virtues mentioned with honour."

FLORA MACDONALD

Perhaps the strangest moment in the tale of Bonnie Prince Charlie came after the Battle of Culloden when he fled in a frock disguised as the Irish maid of **Flora MacDonald**. Born in South Uist in 1722 to a family sympathetic to the Jacobites, she rowed the fugitive prince to Skye in 1746. While he fled to France, Flora was arrested en route home and jailed in the Tower of London, which must have been a shocking experience for a 24-year-old from the Outer Hebrides. She was already a Highlands heroine when she was released in 1747 and, back on Skye, went on to have nine children with her new husband, Allan Macdonald. Samuel Johnson praised her courage and fidelity after his visit in 1773, a year before the couple emigrated to North Carolina, then Nova Scotia. They returned in 1779 and Flora died in 1790, back in her old bed, a symbol of Highlands pluck whose funeral attracted a procession a mile long.

5

Uig

Skye's chief ferry port for the Western Isles is **UIG** (Uige; pronounced "oo-ig"), which curves its way round a dramatic, horseshoe bay. Most folk are just passing through, but if you've time to kill, take the lovely, gentle **walk** up Glen Uig, better known as the **Faerie Glen**, a Hobbity landscape of miniature hills at the east end of the bay.

ARRIVAL AND GETTING AROUND
TROTTERNISH

By ferry CalMac (☎ 0800 066 5000, ⓦ calmac.co.uk) sails between Uig and Tarbert on the Isle of Harris (1–2 daily; 1hr 40min).

By bus The North End Circular bus (service #57A and #57C) loops around the peninsula from Portree via Old Man of Storr, Staffin and Uig (Mon–Sat 6 daily; 2hr total circuit).

ACCOMMODATION AND EATING

STAFFIN

Small & Cosy Teahouse 4 Digg, 2 miles south of Staffin ☎ 01470 562471. The Czech owner's fascination with her grandmother's herbal teas has morphed into a menu of up to fifty leaf teas plus interesting cakes and home-made soups in a lovely wee café with a touch of bygone tea parlour. Tues–Sun noon–6pm.

Staffin Campsite Staffin ☎ 01470 562213, ⓦ staffin campsite.co.uk. A spacious site with a relaxed vibe and a good location spread beneath the Totternish Ridge, with glimpses of the sea a 10min walk away. There's plenty of flat ground and a simple amenities block. £5/person

QUIRAING AND AROUND

Dun Flodigarry Hostel ☎ 01470 552212, ⓦ hostel flodigarry.co.uk. What were the servants' quarters for a grand country hotel is now a spacious if fairly dated independent hostel on the loch; rooms and dorms could do with an update. You can also camp on the lawn and use facilities. Camping £9/pitch; dorms £17; twins £45

Ellishadder Art Café Culnacnoc, 3 miles south of Staffin ☎ 01470 562734. Superb light lunches of savoury tarts like courgette, fennel and goats' cheese plus exquisite cakes for afternoon nibbles in a gallery/café that sells the owners' beautiful hand-weavings and paintings. Feb, March, Nov & Dec Fri & Sat 10.30am–5.30pm; Easter–Oct daily same hours.

Flodigarry Country House Hotel Flodigarry ☎ 01470 552203, ⓦ flodigarry.co.uk. Beautifully sited on the loch, this is every inch the traditional country hotel, all soporific ticking grandfather clock and squishy sofas in the lounge.

Rooms are in the main hotel or a cottage behind where Flora MacDonald lived out her days. £160

★ **Glenview Hotel** Culnacnoc, 3 miles south of Staffin ☎ 01470 562248, ⓦ glenviewskye.co.uk. Quirky vintage-style accommodation – all Bakelite radios, naïve paintings and painted floorboards – and sensational cooking in a restaurant with rooms. Short menus (two courses £30) created from super-fresh produce might include nettle and parsley soup with scallops, sole with local mussel sauce or venison in a red wine and tarragon sauce. March–Nov Tues–Sat 7–10pm. £110

UIG

The Sheiling & Ella's Café ☎ 01470 542797. Within a former crofters' warehouse behind Uig garage, Ella serves home-made toasted focaccia, smoked salmon and crowdie pâté and delicious baking (£5–8). It doubles as a local crafts outlet to feel like a village hall on fête day. Easter–Oct Mon 2–5pm, Tues–Sat 9am–5pm; Nov–Easter Tues–Sat 10am–4pm.

Uig SYHA ☎ 01470 542746, ⓦ syha.co.uk. Great views over the bay from the south side of the village and lovely staff, but a 20min walk from the centre and the simple if spacious dorms are rather tired. Bear in mind too that, like all SYHA hostels, it's locked between 10.30am and 5pm. April–Sept. Dorms £17; twins £44.20

Woodbine House ☎ 01470 542243, ⓦ skyeactivities .co.uk. The pick of Uig's accommodation, this B&B is in a tasteful house on the Duntulm road. Front rooms benefit from sea views, and all are en-suite. The owners (hugely helpful) also rent mountain bikes. Two nights minimum June–Aug. March–Oct. £68

Isle of Raasay

The hilly, fourteen-mile island of **Raasay** (Ratharsair) sees few visitors. Yet in many ways it's the ultimate Skye escape, with plenty of walks – intimate strolls compared to the wide spaces of Skye – and rich flora and fauna, including golden eagles, snipe, orchids and the unique Raasay vole, not to mention the castaway thrill of a small island. Most visitors come on foot – if you come by car be aware there's no petrol. The ferry docks in Churchton Bay, near **INVERARISH**, the island's tiny village set within thick woods on the southwest coast.

RAASAY IN HISTORY

Raasay's woes began after the staunchly Jacobite MacLeods of Lewis sent a hundred local men and 26 pipers to Culloden. Bonnie Prince Charlie later spent a miserable night on Raasay in a "mean low hut" during his flight and swore to replace the turf cottages with proper stone houses (he never did). Raasay was practically destroyed by **government troops** in the aftermath of the 1745 uprising, then when the MacLeods were forced to sell up in 1843, the Clearances started in earnest. In 1921, seven ex-servicemen and their families from neighbouring **Rona** illegally squatted crofts on Raasay, and were imprisoned, causing a public outcry. As a result, both islands were **bought** by the government the following year. Rona now has one permanent resident while Raasay's population stands at around two hundred.

Dun Caan

Most visitors come to walk into the island's interior – a rugged terrain of sandstone in the south and gneiss in the north. The obvious destination is the flat-top volcanic plug of **Dun Caan** (443m) where Boswell "danced a Highland dance" when he visited with Dr Johnson in 1773. The five-mile trail to the top is easy to follow; a splendid trek along the burn through forest behind Inverarish. The quickest return is down the northwest slope but you can also get back to the ferry along the path by the southeast shore, passing the abandoned crofters' village of Hallaig.

North Raasay

On a fine day the north provides fine views across to the Cuillin, Portree and the Trotternish peninsula. Where the road dips to the east coast the stark remains of fifteenth-century **Brochel Castle** stand overlooking the shore. The final two-mile stretch of the road to Arnish is known as **Calum's Road**: in the 1960s the council refused to extend the road, so Calum MacLeod decided to build it himself. It took him ten years, and by the time he'd finished he and his wife were the only people left in the village.

ARRIVAL AND INFORMATION   ISLE OF RAASAY

By ferry The CalMac ferry (Mon–Sat 8–10 daily, Sun 2 daily; 25min; ☎ 0800 066 5000, ⓦ calmac.co.uk) to Raasay departs from Sconser, 3 miles east of *Sligachan Hotel* (see p.277). **Tourist information** ⓦ raasay.com.

ACCOMMODATION

Raasay House ☎ 01478 660300, ⓦ raasay-house .co.uk. The MacLeods' rebuilt manor serves as an outdoor centre. Accommodation ranges from B&B in simple modern bunkrooms to large Deluxe rooms with balconies and views to the Cuillins, via hotel-style four-stars that overlook the garden. It also has camping. Among activities on offer (Easter–Oct, weather-dependent other months) are guided walks and canyoning, coasteering, kayaking and sailing. Camping £6/person; dorms £25; doubles £125

Raasay SYHA ☎ 01478 660240, ⓦ syha.org.uk. A two-mile track from the wharf cuts up behind the village to Raasay's hostel, small and simple throughout – just one loo and one shower – but with beautiful views to the Skye Cuillin and well-placed to explore the island. A superb getaway. Late May to Aug. Dorms £17.50; doubles £39

The Small Isles

Seen from southern Skye or the west coast of the Highlands, the **Small Isles** – **Rùm**, **Eigg**, **Muck** and tiny **Canna** – lie scattered in a silver-grey sea like a siren call to adventure. After centuries of being passed between owners, most islands have stabilized into tight-knit communities of crofters. While Muck is still privately owned, Eigg was bought out by its islanders in 1997, ending more than 150 years of property speculation, while other islands have been bequeathed to national agencies: Rùm, by far the largest and most visited of the group, passed to the Nature Conservancy Council (now Scottish Natural Heritage) in 1957; and Canna has been in the hands of the National Trust for Scotland since 1981.

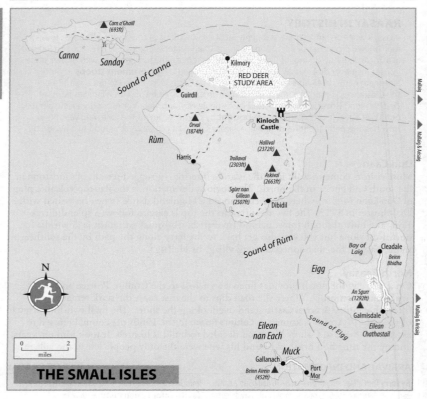

THE SMALL ISLES

Many people come on a day-trip from Mallaig. Yet the Small Isles deserve longer. They are an opportunity to experience some off-grid island life while walking, birdwatching or simply admiring seascapes. Accommodation requires **forward planning** and public transport on the islands is nonexistent. But regular ferries mean you're not as cut off as the atmosphere suggests. Better still, services link all islands for a happy week of island-hopping.

Brief history

The history of the Small Isles is typical of the Hebrides: early Christianization, followed by Norwegian rule, ending in 1266 when the islands fell into Scottish hands. Their support for the Jacobites resulted in hard times after the failed 1745 rebellion, but the biggest problems came in the mid-eighteenth century. The success of potatoes grown with traditional cereals eliminated famine at a stroke, prompting a population explosion. In 1750, there were a thousand islanders. By 1800 that number had almost doubled. At first, the problem of **overcrowding** was camouflaged by a kelp boom, but the economic bubble burst with the end of the Napoleonic Wars and, to maintain profit margins, the owners resorted to drastic action. The first to **sell** was Alexander MacLean. Having acquired quotations to ship its people to Nova Scotia, he gave islanders a year's notice and sold Rùm as grazing land. He also cleared Muck to graze cattle, as did the MacNeills on Canna. Only on Eigg was compassion shown: the new owner, a certain Hugh MacPherson, who bought the island in 1827, offered some tenants extended leases.

Be aware that boats are frequently cancelled by bad **weather**, so check forecasts.

By ferry CalMac (☎ 01687 462403, ⓦ calmac.co.uk) sails from Mallaig (late March to mid-Oct daily, otherwise Mon–Sat), although doesn't sail to all islands each day. Long day-trips are possible on Sat. Sheerwater (☎ 01687 450224, ⓦ arisaig.co.uk) sails daily from Arisaig (see p.222) to Eigg plus Rùm or Muck from late April to late Sept. The ride doubles as a wildlife cruise, so while enjoyable is more expensive than travelling with CalMac.

Rùm

After almost a century as the "Forbidden Isle" – the exclusive sporting estate of self-made Lancastrian industrialists the Bulloughs – **Rùm** has opened up. Indeed since it passed to Scottish Natural Heritage in 1957, visitors are positively encouraged. Many come to hike the eight-mile **Rùm Cuillin Ridge Walk**, tracking a crown of peaks that are modest by Skye's standards – the summit of Askival is only 812m – but every bit as impressive in looks. And in recent years, crofting land has been released as Scottish Natural Heritage (SNH) tries to encourage a community. Most of the island's forty inhabitants live around **KINLOCH** on the east coast, and many are employed by SNH, which runs the island as a National Nature Reserve. SNH have reintroduced native woodland and **white-tailed (sea) eagles**, most of which promptly flew to neighbouring islands. Of its wildlife, Rùm is most famous for its **Manx shearwaters**, which nest in burrows of high peaks. You can learn more about the flora and fauna in an unmanned **visitor centre** halfway between the wharf and castle.

The best **beach** is **Kilmory** in the north of the island, a flattish walk on tracks through Kinloch then Kilmory glens (10 miles, 5hr return from Kinloch). Bear in mind that Rùm is the wettest of the Small Isles, and is infamous for **midges** (see p.41) – come prepared.

Kinloch Castle

Kinloch • March–Oct guided tours coincide with the ferry • £9 • ☎ 01687 462037

Most day-trippers to Rùm head straight for **Kinloch Castle**, a squat, red-sandstone edifice. Built at huge expense in 1900 – the red sandstone was shipped in from Dumfriesshire and the soil for the gardens from Ayrshire – its interior is a perfectly preserved example of Edwardian decadence. It's also appealingly bonkers. From the galleried hall, with its tiger rugs, stags' heads and giant Japanese incense burners, to the Soho snooker table in the Billiard Room, the interior is packed with technical gizmos accumulated by **Sir George Bullough** (1870–1939), the spendthrift son of self-made millionaire, Sir John Bullough, who bought the island as a sporting estate in 1888. It was only really used for a few weeks each autumn, when guests were woken at eight each morning by a piper; later, an orchestrion (an electrically driven barrel organ) that was made for Queen Victoria would grind out pre-dinner ditties like *The Ride of the Valkyries* and *Ma Blushin' Rosie*.

Walks from Kinloch

Two gentle waymarked **walks** head from Kinloch into the surrounding countryside. The **Northside nature trail** (1hr) circuits via Kinloch Glen and is signposted from the visitor centre. In addition, a lochside trail from the ferry dock reaches an **otter hide** (30min return walk) then continues to the abandoned hamlet of Port na Caranean (40min on from the hide). The goal for hardened hikers is the Rùm Cuillin Ridge Walk (see box, p.288).

Bullough Mausoleum

Harris, 8 miles southwest of Kinloch

When the island's headcount peaked at 450 in 1791, the hamlet of **HARRIS** on the southwest coast (a 3–4hr walk from Kinloch), housed a crofting community. All that

5

HIKING IN THE RÙM CUILLIN

Ordnance Survey Explorer map 397

Rùm's **Cuillin** may not be as famous as Skye's, but in fine weather offers equally exhilarating **hiking** possibilities. Whatever route you choose, be sure to take all the usual safety precautions (see p.42).

The most popular walk is to traverse most or part of the **Cuillin Ridge**, around a twelve-hour round-trip from Kinloch. The most frequent route is via Coire Dubh, then on to the saddle of Bealach Bairc-mheall. From here, you can either climb Barkeval to the west, or go for **Hallival** (2372ft) southeast, which looks daunting but is only a mild scramble. South of Hallival, the ridge is grassy, but the north ridge of **Askival** (2663ft) needs to be taken carefully, sticking to the east side. Askival is the highest mountain on Rùm, and if you're thinking of heading back, or the weather's closing in, Glen Dibidil provides an easy descent.

To continue along the ridge, head west to the double peak of **Trollaval** (or Trallval). The descent to Bealach an Fhuarain is steep, after which it's another scramble to reach the top of **Ainshval** (2562ft). Depending on the time and weather, you can continue along the ridge to **Sgùrr nan Gillean**, descend via Glen Dibidil and take the coastal path back to Kinloch, or skip the Sgùrr and go straight on to the last peak of the ridge, **Ruinsival**.

remains are ruined blackhouses, which makes the Neoclassical **Bullough Mausoleum** all the more extraordinary. It was built by Sir George for his father and is actually the second family mausoleum here: the first was lined with Italian marble, but dynamited after a friend remarked it looked like a public lavatory.

ARRIVAL AND INFORMATION RÙM

By ferry The longest day-trip possibilities from Mallaig are on Sat (11hr). Note that overnight visitors cannot bring dogs, but day-trippers can. Summer timetables are: Arisaig–Rùm (Tues, Thurs & Sat 1 daily; 2hr 30min); Canna–Rùm (Mon, Wed, Fri & Sat 1 daily; 55min); Eigg–Rùm (Mon & Sat 1 daily; 1hr–3hr 30min); Mallaig–Rùm (Mon, Wed, Fri, Sat & Sun 1 daily; 1hr 20min–2hr 30min); Muck–Rùm (Sat 1 daily; 1hr 10min).

Tourist information ⓦ isleofrum.com.

ACCOMMODATION AND EATING

Visitors are permitted to **wild camp** and there are two simple **bothies** (three nights maximum) in Dibidil, on the southeast coast, and Guirdil, on the northwest coast. You'll find a shop/post office/off-licence in Kinloch, beside the community hall, which serves **teas** and **snacks** (April–Sept Mon–Sat noon–4pm).

Ivy Cottage Kinloch ☎ 01687 462744, ✉ fliss@isleofrum .com. Delivers loch views from two pleasant en-suite rooms and the conservatory where you breakfast, plus a relaxed atmosphere in the first B&B on Rùm, in a modern house on the loch in front of the castle. Its young owners prepare dinners for guests and non-residents on request. **£90**

Kinloch Campsite ☎ 01687 460328. A community-run campsite with an appealing location spread along the shore on the south side of Kinloch Bay. Also on site are four tiny, insulated camping cabins with four beds each. Camping **£5**/person; cabins for two **£20**

Kinloch Castle Hostel ☎ 01687 462037. This hostel was in transition on our last visit; dormitories have moved to timber-clad Porta-kabins on the lawn before a new bunkhouse is built by the campsite (by around 2015). It currently has four-bed rooms (one bunk, two singles) plus a shared kitchen and lounge. April–Oct. Dorms **£18.50**

Eigg

Eigg – which measures just five miles by three – does little to conceal its volcanic origins. It is made of a basalt plateau and a great stump of pitchstone lava, known as An Sgùrr, rises in the south. Active geology aside, Eigg is by far the most vibrant of the Small Isles, with a strong sense of community among the hundred residents. This was given an enormous boost in 1997 when they (alongside the Scottish Wildlife Trust) pulled off the first **buyout** of a Highlands estate, thereby ending Eigg's unhappy history of private ownership, most recently by Keith Schellenberg, an Olympic bobsleigher and

5

motor magnate. The anniversary is celebrated with an all-night **ceilidh** on the weekend nearest June 12. Its other world-first is that its electricity grid is the first powered entirely by renewable sources.

Galmisdale

Ferries arrive into **Galmisdale Bay**, in the southeast corner of the island. If time is limited, you could head up through woods for superb sea views, or track the shore south to see crofting ruins before the Sgùrr cliffs – the remains of Upper and Lower Grulin settlements. If the tide is low you can scramble along the shore into Cathedral Cave or Massacre Cave (**Uamh Fhraing**), where all but one of Eigg's 396 inhabitants died in 1577, suffocated by the MacLeods of Skye, who lit a fire in the cave mouth. Bring a torch and prepare to feel spooked.

An Sgùrr

The largest piece of pitchstone in the UK, **An Sgùrr** (393m) is the obvious destination for a hike. Actually, the route up is not as daunting as the cliffs suggest; the path is signposted left from the main road, crossing boggy moor to approach the summit from the north via a saddle (3–4hr return). The rewards are wonderful views to Muck and Rùm.

Cleadale

For an easy stroll, strike out to **CLEADALE**, the main crofting settlement in north Eigg. It's spectacularly sited beneath the island's basalt ridge, **Ben Bhuidhe**, and above a beach known as Camas Sgiotaig, or the **Singing Sands**, because the quartz grains squeak underfoot.

ARRIVAL AND DEPARTURE   EIGG

By ferry Summer timetables are: Canna–Eigg (Mon & Sat 1 daily; 2hr 10min); Mallaig–Eigg (Mon, Tues Eigg–Mallaig only 1 daily, Thurs, Sat 1 daily; 1hr 15min); Muck–Eigg (Thurs 1 daily; 35min); Rùm–Eigg (Mon & Sat 1 daily; 1hr–3hr 30min).

GETTING AROUND AND INFORMATION

By minibus or bike A minibus is scheduled around ferries (☎01687 482494; £2), or Charlie's taxi can be booked in advance (☎01687 482494). Bike rental is available from Eigg Adventures (late April–Sept; ☎01687 315012, ⓦeigg adventures.co.uk), based near the harbour. **Tourist information** ⓦisleofeigg.org.

ACCOMMODATION AND EATING

There's an excellent **wild camp** on north Galmisdale Bay. A craft and produce **market** in the community hall uphill from Galmisdale (June–Aug Mon noon–4pm) is a great spot to pick up lunch.

An Laimhrig Harbour. Island ingredients go into home-made soups, quiche, pizza, lamb or venison burgers, plus blackboard specials such as fishcakes – all for under a tenner. Mon 10am–1pm, Wed & Fri 10am–10pm, Sat 1–10pm, winter open around ferry schedules.
Glebe Barn Galmisdale ☎01687 482417. Eigg's hostel on the hill above the harbour has a rather stylish, spacious lounge with awesome coast views and pleasant wee dorm rooms. Better still is the self-contained cottagey Tigh Ard Beag annexe – a superb stay for up to five people. April–Oct. Dorms **£17**; twins **£40**; annexe from **£52**
Kildonan House Galmisdale Bay ☎01687 482446, ⓦkildonanhouseeigg.co.uk. A traditional stay in an eighteenth-century farmhouse on the north side of Galmisdale Bay. Marie offers three pleasingly simple pine-panelled rooms, one with an en-suite shower, all with sea views and dinners included. **£120**
★ **Lageorna** Cleadale ☎01687 460081, ⓦlageorna .com. Beautiful, modern rooms full of contemporary crafts – think rustic wood beds and knitted throws – and astonishing views, plus a lovely vintage cottage that sleeps four. The owner also prepares good-value dishes such as salmon on a bed of spicy puy lentils; reservations recommended. Easter–Sept Mon–Wed & Fri noon–4pm, dinner by arrangement; other months by arrangement. Doubles **£140**; cottage **£500**
Sue Holland's Croft Cleadale ☎01687 482480, ⓦeiggorganics.co.uk. On an organic croft, this is the only designated campsite and it's a belter, with views and sunsets to inspire poetry. The old cowshed is now a basic bothy for up to four or for considerably more comfort choose a yurt. Camping **£5**/person; bothy and yurt **£40**

5

Muck

Barely two miles long, tiny **Muck** is the smallest and most southerly of the Small Isles. Low-lying and almost treeless, it is extremely fertile, so has more in common with Coll and Tiree (see p.88) than its neighbours. Its name derives from *muc*, the Gaelic for "pig" (or possibly *muc mara*, "sea pig" or porpoise, which are plentiful) and has long caused embarrassment to lairds – they preferred to call it the "Isle of Monk" because it briefly belonged to the medieval church.

PORT MÓR is the hub of all activity, where visitors arrive and the thirty or so residents live – a tenth of the 320 of the early 1800s. A mile-long road connects Port Mór with the island's main farm, **Gallanach**, which overlooks rocky skerries on the north side. The nicest sandy **beach** is Camas na Cairidh, to the east of Gallanach. For a stiffer challenge, **Beinn Airein** (2hr return), in the southwest corner of the island, is worth climbing, despite being only 450ft above sea level, for a 360-degree panorama of surrounding islands from its summit.

ARRIVAL AND INFORMATION   MUCK

By ferry Summer timetables are: Canna–Muck (Sat 1 daily; 1hr 35min); Eigg–Muck (Tues, Thurs & Sat 1 daily; 35min); Mallaig–Muck (Tues & Thurs–Sun 1 daily; 1hr 40min–4hr 20min); Rùm–Muck (Sat 1 daily; 2hr 45min).

Tourist information The Craft Shop (see below) doubles as an information point. See also ⓦisleofmuck.com, a useful website.

ACCOMMODATION AND EATING

To **wild camp** on the island, check in at the Craft Shop to find out about any areas currently off-limits.

The Craft Shop Port Mór ☎01687 462990. The only shop on the island prepares daily soups and sandwiches made from fresh home-baked bread, plus afternoon teas and dinners of tasty Scottish home-cooking prepared on request. April, May & Sept hours vary; June–Aug daily 11am–4pm.

Gallanach Lodge Gallanach Bay ☎01687 462365, ⓔlodge@isleofmuck.com. A purpose-built luxury lodge opened in 2013 that takes full advantage of a superb position above the beach to provide fantastic views to Rùm. The style is island boutique – rustic, handmade beds in rooms with hotel-style mod cons. Full board only. **£170**

Isle of Muck Bunkhouse Port Mór ☎01687 462042. Just six beds in three rooms and not a bunk in sight in the island's simple wee bothy, sited near the port. Life revolves around the Raeburn stove in the simple living room and the kitchen. Hardly luxurious but full of character. Dorms **£12**

Port Mór House Port Mór ☎01687 460089, ⓔewenandjudy@gmail.com. The MacEwen family, who have owned the island since 1896, now let their nine-bedroom house as a self-catering property, but provide B&B in its pine-clad rooms plus dinner for guests (or £18 to non-guests) when the house is not booked exclusively for a week. Phone for rates.

Canna

Measuring a mere five miles by one, **Canna** is managed as a **bird sanctuary** by the National Trust for Scotland (NTS). There are no roads, just open moorland stretched over a basalt ridge, and few people now the population has dwindled to eight. While Canna doesn't receive many visitors by ferry, plenty come by yacht for the best harbour in the Small Isles, a sheltered bay off Canna's main hamlet, **A'Chill**. Notwithstanding walks (see below), you come to Canna for birdlife; this has been a sanctuary since 1938 and 157 species have been recorded, including golden and white-tailed eagles, and Manx shearwaters, razorbills and puffins on cliffs at the western end.

Although less obviously scenic than other Small Isles, the flat(ish) terrain makes for enjoyable **walks**. You can circuit the entire island on a long day (10hr; 12 miles), or from the dock it's about a mile across a grassy plateau to the cliffs on the north shore and Compass Hill, named because its high iron content distorts compasses. A mile west is Carn a'Ghaill, Canna's summit at a heady 688ft.

ARRIVAL AND INFORMATION
CANNA

By ferry Summer timetables are: Eigg–Canna (Mon & Sat; 1 daily; 2hr 10min); Mallaig–Canna (Mon, Wed & Fri–Sun 1 daily; 2hr 30min–3hr 50min); Muck–Canna (Sat 1 daily; 1hr 35min); Rùm–Canna (Mon, Wed & Fri–Sun 1 daily; 55min).

Tourist information ⓦ thesleofcanna.com.

ACCOMMODATION

With permission from the NTS, you may **wild camp** on Canna, though bring supplies.

Tighard ☎ 01687 462474, ⓦ tighard.co.uk. The Sanday room is the pick – spacious, traditional and with sweeping sea views – in the only B&B on Canna. Its other two smaller and simpler twins also enjoy sea views. Also offers packed lunch and dinner with notice. **£90**

The Western Isles

UIG SANDS (TRÀIGH UUIGE)

The Western Isles

Beyond Skye, across the unpredictable waters of the Minch, lie the wild and windy Outer Hebrides, officially known as the Western Isles. A 130-mile-long archipelago stretching from Lewis and Harris in the north to the Uists and Barra in the south, the islands appear as an unbroken chain when viewed from across the Minch – hence their nickname, the Long Isle. In reality there are more than two hundred islands, although only a handful are inhabited, with the total population around 28,000. This is truly a land on the edge, where the turbulent seas of the Atlantic smash up against a geologically complex terrain whose coastline is interrupted by a thousand sheltered bays and, in the far west, a long line of sweeping sandy beaches. The islands' interiors are equally dramatic, veering between flat, boggy, treeless peat moor and bare mountain tops soaring high above a host of tiny lakes, or lochans.

The major difference between the Western Isles and much of the Hebrides is that the islands' fragile economy is still mainly concentrated around crofting, fishing and weaving, and the percentage of incomers is low. In fact, the Outer Hebrides remain the heartland of **Gaelic** culture, with the language spoken by the majority of islanders, though its everyday usage struggles due to the national dominance of English. Its survival is thanks partly to the efforts of the Western Islands Council, the Scottish parliament, and the influence of the Church in the region: the Free Church and its various offshoots in Lewis, Harris and North Uist, and the Catholic Church in South Uist and Barra.

Lewis and Harris form two parts of the same island. The interior of the northernmost part, **Lewis**, is mostly peat moor, a barren and marshy tract that gives way to the bare peaks of **North Harris**. Across a narrow isthmus lies **South Harris**, with wide beaches of golden sand trimming the Atlantic in full view of the rough boulder-strewn mountains to the east. Across the Sound of Harris, to the south, a string of tiny, flatter isles – **North Uist**, **Benbecula**, **South Uist** – linked by causeways, offer breezy beaches, whose fine sands front a narrow band of boggy farmland which, in turn, is bordered by a lower range of hills to the east. Finally, tiny **Barra** contains all the above landscapes in one small Hebridean package.

In contrast to their wonderful surroundings, villages in the Western Isles are seldom very picturesque in themselves, and are usually made up of scattered, relatively modern crofthouses dotted about the elementary road system. **Stornoway**, the only real town in the Outer Hebrides, rarely impresses. Many visitors, walkers and nature-watchers forsake the main settlements altogether and retreat to secluded cottages, simple hostels and B&Bs.

TOMB OF ALASDAIR CROTACH, ST CLEMENT'S CHURCH (TUR CHLIAMAINN)

Highlights

❶ **Garenin (Gearrannan), Lewis** An abandoned crofting village whose thatched blackhouses have been beautifully restored: some are now self-catering cottages, one is a café, and a couple have been left as they were when they were last inhabited. **See p.307**

❷ **Callanish (Calanais) standing stones** Scotland's finest standing stones are in a serene lochside setting on the west coast of the Isle of Lewis. **See p.307**

❸ **Beaches** The western seaboard of the Outer Hebrides, particularly on South Harris and the Uists, is strewn with stunning, deserted beaches backed by flower-strewn machair. **See p.314**

❹ **Rodel (Roghadal) Church, Harris** Rodel's pre-Reformation St Clement's Church, at the southernmost tip of Harris, boasts the most ornate sculptural decoration in the Outer Hebrides. **See p.315**

❺ **Barra** Barra is a great introduction to the Western Isles: a Hebridean island in miniature, with golden sands, crystal-clear rocky bays and mountains of Lewissian gneiss. **See p.324**

HIGHLIGHTS ARE MARKED ON THE MAP ON P.296

THE WESTERN ISLES

0 _____ 25
miles

HIGHLIGHTS

1 Garenin (Gearrannan), Lewis
2 Callanish (Calanais) standing stones
3 Beaches
4 Rodel (Roghadal) Church, Harris
5 Barra

N

Flannan Isles

Sula Sgeir
Butt of Lewis
Port of Ness

A857

Garenin 1
Arid Uig
Bernera
Carloway 2
Callanish Standing Stones
A858
Barvas
A857
A858
Stornoway
A859
A866
A859

L e w i s

Scarp

An Cliseam (2619ft) ▲

A859

Taransay

Shiant Isles

Tarbert
3
H a r r i s
A859
Scalpay

Leverburgh
Rodel (Roghadal) 4 †
Church, Harris

Berneray

W E S T E R N   I S L E S

North Uist
A867
3
Lochmaddy

Monach Islands

Benbecula

Neist Point

3
A865

South Uist

Beinn Mhor (2034ft) ▲

Lochboisdale

T h e   M i n c h

Ullapool

T h e   L i t t l e   M i n c h

Uig

Portree

S k y e

Raasay

A87

Broadford

Canna

Hyskeir

S M A L L   I S L E S

Rùm

Armadale

Mallaig

Eriskay

Barra
5
Castlebay
Vatersay
Sandray
Pabbay
Mingulay
Barra Head

Eigg

Muck

Arisaig

▼ Tiree   ▼ Oban

GAELIC IN THE WESTERN ISLES

All Ordnance Survey maps and many **road signs** are exclusively in **Gaelic**, a difficult language to the English-speaker's eye, with complex pronunciation (see p.421), though the English names sometimes provide a rough guide. If you're driving, it's a good idea to pick up a bilingual Western Isles **map**, available at most tourist offices. We've put the English equivalent first in the text, with the Gaelic in parentheses.

Brief history

The Western Isles were first settled by Neolithic farming peoples around 4000 BC. They are remembered by scores of remains, from passage graves through to stone circles – most famously at **Callanish** (Calanais) on Lewis. Viking colonization gathered pace from 700 AD onwards – as evidenced by the islands' place names, the majority of which are of Norse, not Gaelic, origin – and it was only in 1266 that the islands were returned to the Scottish Crown. James VI (and I of England), a Stuart and a Scot, though no Gaelic-speaker, was the first to put forward the idea of clearing the Hebrides, though it wasn't until after the Jacobite uprisings, in which many Highland clans disastrously backed the wrong side, that the **Clearances** began in earnest.

The isolation of the Outer Hebrides exposed them to the whims and fancies of merchants and aristocrats who caught "island fever" and bought them up. From the mid-eighteenth century onwards, the land and its people have been sold to the highest bidder. Some proprietors have been well-meaning but insensitive – like **Lord Leverhulme**, who had no time for crofting and wanted to turn Lewis into a centre of the fishing industry in the 1920s. Others have simply been autocratic, such as **Colonel Gordon of Cluny**, who bought Benbecula, South Uist, Eriskay and Barra, and forced the inhabitants onto ships bound for North America at gunpoint. Almost everywhere crofters were driven from their ancestral homes, robbing them of their particular sense of place. Today, memorials and cairns dot the landscape, commemorating the often violent struggle which accompanied this period.

ARRIVAL AND DEPARTURE
THE WESTERN ISLES

By plane There are scheduled flights from Glasgow, Edinburgh, Inverness and Aberdeen to Stornoway on Lewis, and to Barra and Benbecula. Be warned: weather conditions are notoriously changeable, making flights prone to delay and even cancellation. On Barra, the plane lands on the beach, so the timetable is adjusted with the tides.

By ferry CalMac car ferries run daily from Ullapool to Stornoway; from Uig, on Skye, to Tarbert and Lochmaddy; and from Oban to South Uist and Barra, via Coll and Tiree (Thurs only). The timetables quoted in the text are summer frequencies – check ⓦ calmac.co.uk for the latest and always book ahead.

GETTING AROUND

By car and by ferry A series of causeways makes it possible to drive from one end of the Western Isles to the other with just two interruptions – the ferry from Harris to Berneray, and from Eriskay to Barra. If you're going to take the ferry, it's advisable to book in advance.

By bus The islands have a decent bus service, though there are no buses on Sundays.
By bike The wind makes cycling something of a challenge – head south to north to catch the prevailing wind.

Lewis (Leodhas)

Shaped rather like the top of an ice-cream cone, **Lewis** is the largest and most populous of the Western Isles. Nearly half of the island's inhabitants live in the crofting and fishing villages strung out along the northwest coast, between **Callanish** (Callanais) and **Port of Ness** (Port Nis), in one of the country's most densely populated rural areas. On this coast you'll also find the best-preserved **prehistoric remains** – Dun Carloway (Dùn Charlabhaigh) and the Callanish standing stones – as well as a smattering of ancient

6

RELIGION IN THE WESTERN ISLES

It's difficult to overestimate the importance of **religion** in the Western Isles, which are divided – with very little enmity – between the **Catholic** southern isles of Barra and South Uist, and the **Protestant** islands of North Uist, Harris and Lewis. Church attendance is higher than anywhere else in Britain and in fact, Barra, Eriskay and South Uist are the only parts of Britain where Catholics are in a majority, and where you'll see statues of the Madonna by the roadside. In the Presbyterian north, the creed of **Sabbatarianism** is strong. Here, Sunday is the Lord's Day, and the whole community (irrespective of their degree of piety) stops work – shops close, pubs close, garages close and there's very little public transport. Visitors should check whether it's OK to arrive at or leave their accommodation on a Sunday, to avoid causing offence.

The main area of division is, paradoxically, within the Protestant Church itself. Scotland's national church, the **Church of Scotland**, is Presbyterian (ruled by the ministers and elders of the church) rather than Episcopal (ruled by bishops). At the time of the main split in the Presbyterian Church – the so-called **1843 Disruption** – a third of its ministers left the Church of Scotland, protesting at a law that allowed landlords to impose ministers against parishioners' wishes, and formed the breakaway **Free Church of Scotland** – sometimes referred to as the "**Wee Frees**", though this term is also used for members of the Free Presbyterian Church of Scotland. Since those days there have been several amalgamations and reconciliations with the Church of Scotland, as well as further splits.

The various brands and subdivisions of the Presbyterian Church may appear trivial to outsiders, but to the churchgoers of Lewis, Harris and North Uist (as well as much of Skye and Raasay) they are still keenly felt. In part, this is due to social and cultural reasons: Free Church elders helped organize resistance to the Clearances, and the Wee Frees have contributed greatly to preserving the **Gaelic language**. A Free Church service is a memorable experience – there's no set service or prayer book and no hymns, only biblical readings, psalm singing and a sermon; the pulpit is the architectural focus of the church, not the altar, and communion is taken only on special occasions. If you want to attend a service, the Free Church on Kenneth Street in Stornoway has one of the UK's largest Sunday-evening congregations, with up to 1500 people attending.

---

crofters' houses in various stages of abandonment. The landscape is mostly flat peat bog – hence the island's Gaelic name, from *leogach* (marshy) – but the shoreline is more dramatic, especially around Butt of Lewis (Rubha Robhanais), the island's northernmost tip. The other half of the island's population lives in **Stornoway**, on the east coast, the only real town in the Western Isles. To the south, where Lewis is physically joined with Harris, the land rises to over 1800ft, providing an exhilarating backdrop for the excellent beaches that pepper the isolated western coastline around **Uig**.

Brief history

After Viking rule ended in 1266, Lewis became a virtually independent state, ruled over by the **MacLeod clan** for several centuries. In 1610, however, King James VI declared the folk of Lewis to be "void of religion", and attempted to establish a colony, as in Ulster, by sending Fife Adventurers to attack Lewis. They were met with armed resistance by the MacLeods, so, in retaliation, James VI granted the lands to their arch rivals, the MacKenzies of Kintail. The MacKenzie chiefs – the Earls of Seaforth – chose to remain absentee landlords until 1844, when they sold Lewis to **Sir James Matheson**, who'd made a fortune from pushing opium on the Chinese. Matheson was relatively benevolent when the island was hit by potato famine in the mid-1840s, but ultimately opted for solving the problem through eviction and emigration. His chief factor, Donald Munro, was utterly ruthless, and was only removed after the 1874 Bernera Riot (see p.308). The 1886 Crofters' Act greatly curtailed the power of the Mathesons; it did not, however, right any of the wrongs of the past. Protests, such as the 1887 Pairc Deer Raid, in which starving crofters killed two hundred deer from one of the sporting estates, and the Aignish land raids of the following year, continued against the Clearances of earlier that century.

When **Lord Leverhulme**, founder of the soap empire Unilever, acquired the island (along with Harris) in 1918, he was determined to drag Lewis out of its cycle of poverty by establishing an integrated fishing industry. To this end he founded MacFisheries, a nationwide chain of retail outlets for the fish which would be caught and processed on the islands: he built a cannery, an ice factory, roads, bridges and a light railway; he bought boats, and planned to use spotter planes to locate the shoals of herring. But the dream never came to fruition. Unfortunately, Leverhulme regarded the island's centuries-old tradition of crofting as inefficient and "an entirely impossible way of life". In 1923, financial difficulties prompted Leverhulme to pull out of Lewis and concentrate on Harris. He gifted Lews Castle and Stornoway to its inhabitants and offered free crofts to those islanders who had not been involved in land raids. In the

6

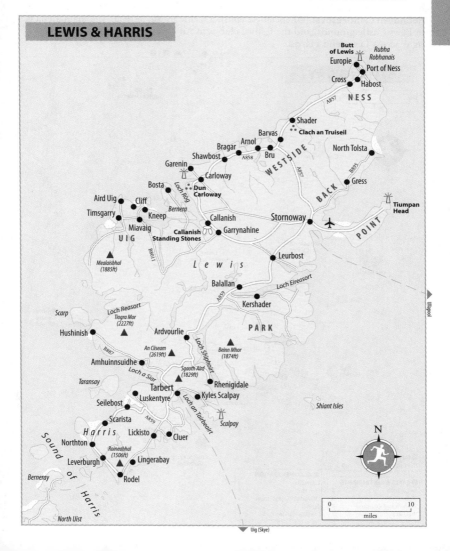

LEWIS & HARRIS

event, few crofters took up the offer – all they wanted was security of tenure, not ownership. Whatever the merits of Leverhulme's plans, his departure left a huge gap in the non-crofting economy, and between the wars thousands emigrated.

Stornoway (Steòrnabhagh)

In these parts, **STORNOWAY** is a buzzing metropolis, with around nine thousand inhabitants, a one-way system, a pedestrian precinct and all the trappings of a large town. It's a centre for employment, a social hub for the island and home to the Western Isles Council, or **Comhairle nan Eilean Siar**, set up in 1974, which has done so much to promote Gaelic language and culture. Aesthetics are not its strong point, however, and the urban pleasures on offer are limited, but in July Stornoway hosts the **Hebridean Celtic Festival** (w hebceltfest.com), a Celtic music festival. The main arena is in Lews Castle grounds, and the festival club is in An Lanntair, but events are held right across Lewis and Harris.

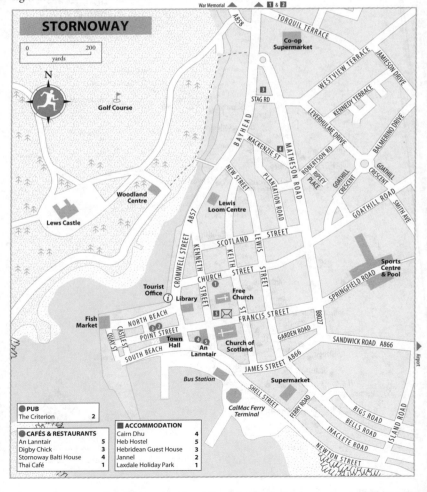

● PUB	
The Criterion	2

● CAFÉS & RESTAURANTS	
An Lanntair	5
Digby Chick	3
Stornoway Balti House	4
Thai Café	1

■ ACCOMMODATION	
Cairn Dhu	4
Heb Hostel	5
Hebridean Guest House	3
Jannel	2
Laxdale Holiday Park	1

6

THE IOLAIRE DISASTER

Of the 6200 men from the Western Isles who served in World War I, around a thousand died – the highest casualty rate per capita in the British Empire. Yet, on **New Year's Day 1919**, in the single most terrible tragedy to befall Lewis, another 208 perished. Some 530 servicemen were gathered at Kyle of Lochalsh to return home to Lewis and their families on the mailboat. As there were so many of them, an extra boat was called into service, the **Iolaire**, originally built as a luxury yacht in 1881. The boat left at 7.30pm heavily overloaded, carrying 284 men, young men and veterans, friends and relatives, to cross the Minch. In the early hours of the morning as the boat approached Stornoway harbour, it struck a group of rocks called Blastan Thuilm (Beasts of Holm). In the darkness, it was impossible for those on board to see that they were in fact only twenty yards from the shore.

One man, a boatbuilder from Ness (Nis), a village that was to lose 21 men that night, fought his way ashore with a lifeline which saved the lives of forty others. Another was saved by clinging to the mast for seven hours, but he lost his elder brother, who'd postponed his return so that they could come back together. Another man, on active service, had spent 36 hours in the sea, the sole survivor of his torpedoed ship; now he drowned within sight of his home. Every village in Lewis lost at least one returning loved one, and this, together with the losses in the war and the mass emigration that followed, cast a shadow over life on Lewis for many years. It was the worst peacetime shipping disaster in home waters that century. There's a **monument** at Holm Point (Rubha Thuilm), overlooking the rocks, and the ship's bell is in the Museum nan Eilean in Stornoway.

For centuries, life in Stornoway has focused on its **harbour**, whose quayside was once filled with barrels of pickled herring, and whose deep and sheltered waters were thronged with coastal steamers and fishing boats in their nineteenth-century heyday, when over a thousand boats were based at the port. Today, most of the catch is landed on the mainland, and, despite the daily comings and goings of the CalMac ferry from Ullapool, the harbour is a shadow of its former commercial self – the nicest section is Cromwell Street Quay, by the tourist office, where the remaining fishing fleet ties up for the night.

Stornoway's commercial centre, to the east, is little more than a string of unprepossessing shops and bars. The one exception is the old **Town Hall** on South Beach, a splendid Scots Baronial building from 1905, its rooftop peppered with conical towers, above which a central clocktower rises. One block east along South Beach, and looking rather like a modern church, you'll find **An Lanntair** (Gaelic for "lantern"), Stornoway's modern cultural centre (see p.302).

Lews Castle

Across the bay from the town centre • Castle interior closed until 2015 • Grounds open 24hr • Woodland Centre Mon–Sat 9am–5pm • Free • ☎ 01851 706916, ⓦ stornowaytrust.org.uk

The castellated pomposity of **Lews Castle** was built by Sir James Matheson in 1863 after resettling the crofters who used to live here. As the former laird's pad, it has long been seen as a symbol of old oppression by many: it was here, in the house's now-defunct conservatory, that Lady Matheson famously gave tea to the Bernera protesters, when they marched on Stornoway prior to rioting (see p.308); when the eccentric Lord Leverhulme took up residence, he had unglazed bedroom windows which allowed the wind and rain to enter, and gutters in the asphalt floor to carry off the residue.

The building – closed for over 25 years – is having a £14 million makeover to transform it into a state-of-the-art bilingual museum, due to open in 2015. This will be the new **Museum nan Eilean**, telling the story of the islands' geology, its Gaelic culture, the struggles of the nineteenth century and the Leverhulme era – the museum is even hoping to get six Lewis Chessmen on long-term loan from the British Museum. For the moment, however, Lews Castle's chief attraction is its mature wooded grounds, a unique sight on the Western Isles, for which Matheson had to import thousands of tonnes of soil. Hidden among the trees is the **Woodland Centre**, which has a straightforward exhibition on the history of the castle and the island upstairs, and a decent **café** serving soup, salads and cakes downstairs.

ARRIVAL AND DEPARTURE — STORNOWAY

By plane Stornoway Airport (☎01851 707400, ⟨w⟩hial .co.uk) is 4 miles east of the town centre: the hourly bus takes 15min (Mon–Sat only), or it's a £5 taxi ride into town.

By ferry Ferries between Stornoway and Ullapool (Mon–Sat 2–3 daily, Sun 1 daily; 2hr 45min; ☎01851 702361) run from the octagonal CalMac ferry terminal on South Beach, near the bus station.

By bus The bus station (☎01851 704327) is on South Beach in the town centre.

Destinations Arnol (Mon–Sat 6–8 daily; 35min); Barvas (Mon–Sat 6–9 daily; 25min); Callanish (Mon–Sat 4–6 daily; 40min); Carloway (Mon–Sat 5–6 daily; 45min); Garenin (Mon–Sat 3–4 daily; 1hr); Great Bernera (Mon–Sat 4 daily; 1hr); Leverburgh (Mon–Sat 4–5 daily; 2hr); Port of Ness (Mon–Sat 6–8 daily; 1hr); Shawbost (Mon–Sat 6–9 daily; 45min); Tarbert (Mon–Sat 5 daily; 1hr); Tolsta (Mon–Sat hourly; 40min); Uig (Mon–Sat 4 daily; 1hr–1hr 30min).

GETTING AROUND AND INFORMATION

By car Car rental is available from Mackinnon Self-Drive, 18 Inaclete Rd (☎01851 702984, ⟨w⟩mackinnonselfdrive .co.uk), from around £25/day – they're based in Stornoway but will deliver locally for free.

By bike Alex Dan's Cycle Centre, 67 Kenneth St (☎01851 704025, ⟨w⟩stornowaycyclehire.co.uk; closed Sun), offers

bike rental from £20/day to £60/week; panniers and car racks are also available.

Tourist office 26 Cromwell St (April–Sept Mon–Sat 9am–6pm; Oct Mon–Sat 9am–5pm; Nov–March Mon–Fri 9am–5pm; ☎01851 703088, ⟨w⟩visithebrides.com).

ACCOMMODATION

Cairn Dhu 18a Matheson Rd ☎01851 701611, ⟨w⟩lewis apartments.co.uk. Superbly equipped contemporary apartment, with leather upholstery, a fully equipped modern kitchen and free wi-fi, in a Victorian villa on the town's nicest leafy street. **£140**

Heb Hostel 25 Kenneth St ☎01851 709889, ⟨w⟩heb hostel.co.uk. A clean, centrally located terrace house in salmon pink, converted into a simple hostel, with free wi-fi, laundry and kitchen facilities and run by a friendly resident warden. **£16**/person

Hebridean Guest House 61 Bayhead St ☎01851 702268, ⟨w⟩hebrideanguesthouse.co.uk. Whitewashed property containing a whole range of en-suite rooms

with attractive wood furnishings, including an annexe with a couple of self-catering apartments. Free wi-fi available. **£90**

Jannel 5 Stewart Drive ☎0800 634 3270, ⟨w⟩jannel -stornoway.co.uk. A short walk from the town centre, this B&B is run by a delightful landlady, and offers five spacious, immaculate rooms, with free wi-fi. **£75**

Laxdale Holiday Park Laxdale Lane ☎01851 703234, ⟨w⟩laxdaleholidaypark.com. The well-equipped campsite has caravans, a self-catering bungalow and a purpose-built bunkhouse, as well as a sheltered spot for tents. It lies a mile or so along the road to Barvas. Bunkhouse **£16**/person; camping **£24**/pitch

EATING AND DRINKING

CAFÉS AND RESTAURANTS

★ **An Lanntair** Kenneth St ☎01851 703307, ⟨w⟩lanntair.com. Stylish café-restaurant in the An Lanntair arts centre which does decent sandwiches and lighter dishes during the day, as well as more imaginative stuff, like black pudding-stuffed chicken wrapped in bacon, in the evening (mains £8–18). Free wi-fi. Mon–Sat food served 10am–noon, 12.30–2.30pm & 5.30–8.30pm.

Digby Chick 5 Bank St ☎01851 700026, ⟨w⟩digbychick .co.uk. Smart, modern, buzzy little bistro with a real emphasis on using local produce, such as the famous Stornoway black pudding. Sandwiches available at lunchtimes or two courses for around £13; three-course dinners for under £30. Mon–Sat noon–2pm & 5.30–9pm.

Stornoway Balti House 24 South Beach ☎01851 706116. Family-run restaurant that's been in Stornoway

for over 25 years. The curries are the real thing and the service great, but the real boon is that it's open on Sundays. Daily noon–2pm & 5–11pm.

Thai Café 27 Church St ☎01851 307181, ⟨w⟩thai-cafe -stornoway.co.uk. Despite the name, this is actually a restaurant, serving authentic Thai food (mains around £8). No licence so bring your own bottle (50p corkage). Mon–Sat noon–2.30pm & 5–11pm.

PUBS

The Criterion 32 Point St ☎01851 701990. A tiny, wee, authentic no-frills Stornoway pub, where they have regular informal (music) sessions – if nothing's going down, try nearby *MacNeill's*. Mon–Thurs 11am–11pm, Fri & Sat 11–1am.

Back (Am Bac)

The dead-end B895 that runs along Lewis's east coast, north of Stornoway – an area known as **Back** – boasts excellent golden beaches and marks the starting point of a lovely coastal walk to Ness.

Griais Memorial

The legacy of Lord Leverhulme's brief ownership of Lewis is recalled by the striking **Griais Memorial** to the Lewis land-raiders, situated by Griais Bridge, above Gress Sands. It was here that Leverhulme's plans came unstuck: he wanted to turn the surrounding crofting land into three big farms, which would provide milk for the workers of his fish-canning factory; the local crofters just wanted to return to their traditional way of life. Such was Leverhulme's fury at the land-raiders from Gress (Griais) and nearby Coll (Col), a mile to the south, that, when he offered to gift the crofts of Lewis to their owners, he made sure the offer didn't include Gress and Coll. The stone-built memorial is a symbolic croft split asunder by Leverhulme's interventions.

The path to Ness

Further north, beyond Tolsta (Tolastadh), is the finest of the coast's sandy **beaches**, Garry (Gheardha), and the beginning of the footpath to Ness. Shortly after leaving the bay, the path crosses the **Bridge to Nowhere**, built by Leverhulme as part of an unrealized plan to forge a new road along the east coast to Ness. Further along the track, there's a fine waterfall on the River of Stones (Abhainn na Cloich). The makeshift road peters out, but a waymarked path continues for another ten miles via the old sheiling village of Diobadail, to Ness (see p.304). It's very boggy, and badly churned up in places, so make sure you've got proper footwear.

ARRIVAL AND DEPARTURE **BACK**

By bus There's a regular bus from Stornoway (Mon–Sat hourly; 40min).

ACCOMMODATION

Broad Bay House ☎ 01851 820990, ⓦ broadbayhouse .co.uk. This place has raised the bar exponentially both in terms of standards and price, with quality furnishings, patio doors leading to private decking areas, free wi-fi, free bike hire and exceptionally good home-cooking. **£180**

Seaside Villa ☎ 01851 820208, ⓦ seasidevilla.co.uk. At the other end of the extreme, this is a simple, comfortable B&B with no pretensions at all. Comes with free wi-fi, a real peat fire and a friendly Gaelic welcome. **£66**

The road to Barvas (Barabhas)

The A857 crosses the vast, barren **peat** bog (see box, p.304) that characterizes the interior of Lewis, an empty, undulating wilderness riddled with stretchmarks formed by peat cuttings and pockmarked with freshwater lochans. The whole area was once covered by forests, but these disappeared long ago, leaving a deposit of peat that continues to serve as a valuable energy resource, with each crofter being assigned a slice of the bog.

Twelve miles across the peat bog the road approaches the west coast of Lewis and divides, heading southwest towards Callanish, or northeast through **BARVAS** (Barabhas), which has a handy shop. Just beyond Barvas, a signpost points to the pleasant **Morven Gallery** (Easter–Sept Mon–Sat 10.30am–5pm; free; ⓦ morvengallery .com), which hosts exhibitions by local artists and photographers and has a handy café, serving great coffee, where you can hole up during bad weather. Three miles further up the road, you pass the 20ft monolith of **Clach an Truiseil**, the first of a series of prehistoric sights between the crofting and weaving settlements of **Ballantrushal** (Baile an Truiseil) and **Shader** (Siadar).

6

PEAT

One of the characteristic features of the landscape of the Highlands and Islands is **peat** (*mòine*) – and nowhere is its presence more keenly felt than on Lewis. Virtually the whole interior of the island is made up of one, vast blanket bog, scarred with lines of peat banks old and new, while the pungent smell of peat smoke hits you as you pass through the villages. Peat is made up of **dead vegetation** that has failed to rot completely because the sheer volume of rainfall has caused the soil acidity to reach a level that acts as a preservative. In other words, organic matter – such as sphagnum moss, rushes, sedges and reeds – is dying at a faster rate than it is decomposing. This means, of course, that peat is still (very slowly) forming in certain parts of Scotland, at an inch or less every fifty years. In the (mostly treeless) islands, peat provided an important source of fuel, and the cutting and stacking of peats in the spring was part of the annual cycle of crofting life. Peat cutting remains embedded in the culture, and is still practised on a large scale, particularly in the Hebrides. It's a social occasion as much as anything else, which heralds the arrival of the warmer, drier days of late spring.

Great pride is taken in the artistry and neatness of the **peat banks and stacks**. In some parts, the peat lies up to 30ft deep, but peat banks are usually only cut to a depth of around 6ft. Once the top layer of turf has been removed, the peat is cut into slabs between two and four peats deep, using a traditional *tairsgeir* (pronounced "tushkar"). Since peat is **ninety percent water** in its natural state, it has to be carefully "lifted" in order to dry out. Peats tend to be piled up either vertically in "rooks", or crisscrossed in "windows"; either way the peat will lose three quarters of its water content, and shrink by about a quarter. Many folk wonder how on earth the peat can dry out when it seems to rain the whole time, but the wind helps, and eventually a skin is formed that stops any further water from entering the peats. After three or four weeks, the peats are skilfully "grieved", like the slates on a roof, into round-humped stacks or onto carts that can be brought home. Traditionally, the peat would be carried from the peat banks by women using "creels", baskets that were strapped on the back. Correctly grieved peats allow the rain to run off, and therefore stay dry for a year or more outside the croft.

White House 11 Upper Shader (Siadar Uarach) ☎01851 820990, ⓦwhitehousebb.co.uk. Ignore the tartan carpeting, the rooms themselves are very tastefully furnished and well equipped. There's free wi-fi and their hens provide the eggs for breakfast. **£60**

Ness (Nis)

The main road continues through a string of densely populated, fervently Presbyterian villages that make up **NESS** (Nis), at the northern tip of Lewis. Ness has the highest percentage of Gaelic speakers in the country (75 percent), but the locals are perhaps best known for their annual culling of young gannets on **Sula Sgeir** (see box opposite). These scattered settlements have none of the photogenic qualities of Skye's whitewashed villages: the churches are plain and unadorned; the crofters' houses relatively modern and smothered in grey pebble-dash rendering or harling; the stone cottages and enclosures of their forebears often lie half-abandoned in the front garden: a rusting assortment of discarded cars and vans store peat bags and the like. The road terminates at the fishing village of **PORT OF NESS** (Port Nis), with a tiny harbour and lovely golden beach. It's worth noting that there are few shops (other than mobile ones) in these parts, so it's as well to stock up in Stornoway before you set out.

Comunn Eachdraidh Nis

Cross School, North Dell (Dail bho Thuath) • March–Oct Mon–Fri 10am–4pm; Nov–Feb Mon–Fri noon–4pm • £2 • ☎01851 810377, ⓦcenonline.org

For an insight into the social history of the area, take a look inside Ness Heritage Centre or **Comunn Eachdraidh Nis** in **CROSS** (Cros). The museum, housed in the village school, contains a huge collection of photographs, but its prize possession is a diminutive sixth- or seventh-century cross from the Isle of Rona (see box below), decorated with a much-eroded nude male figure, and thought by some to have been St Ronan's gravestone; you can have tea and coffee here too.

Europie (Eoropaidh)

Shortly before you reach Port of Ness, a minor road heads two miles northwest to the hamlet of **EUROPIE** (Eoropaidh) – pronounced "Yor-erpee". By the road junction that leads to the Butt of Lewis stands the simple stone structure of **St Moluag's Church** (Teampull Mholuaidh), amid the runrig fields, now acting as sheep runs. Thought to date from the twelfth century, when the islands were still under Norse rule, but restored in 1912 (and now used once a month by the Scottish Episcopal Church for sung Communion), the church features a strange south chapel with only a squint window connecting it to the nave. In the late seventeenth century, the traveller Martin Martin noted: "They all went to church… and then standing silent for a little time, one of them gave a signal… and immediately all of them went into the fields, where they fell a drinking their ale and spent the remainder of the night in dancing and singing, etc." Church services aren't what they used to be.

OFFSHORE ISLANDS

Though three men dwell on Flannan Isle
To keep the lamp alight,
As we steer'd under the lee, we caught
No glimmer through the night.   Flannan Isle by Wilfred Wilson Gibson

On December 15, 1900, a passing ship reported that the lighthouse on the **Flannan Isles** 21 miles west of Aird Uig on Lewis, was not working. The lighthouse had been built the previous year by the Stevenson family (including the father and grandfather of author Robert Louis Stevenson). Gibson's poem goes on to recount the arrival of the relief boat from Oban on Boxing Day, whose crew found no trace of the three keepers. More mysteriously still, a full meal lay untouched on the table, one chair was knocked over, and only two oilskins were missing. Subsequent lightkeepers doubtless spent many lonely nights trying in vain to figure out what happened, until the lighthouse went automatic in 1971.

Equally famous, but for different reasons, is the tiny island of **Sula Sgeir**, also known as "The Rock", 41 miles north of the Butt of Lewis. Every August, the men of Ness (known as Niseachs) have set sail from Port of Ness to harvest the young gannet or guga that nest in their thousands high up on the islet's sea cliffs. It's a dangerous activity, but boiled gannet and potato are a popular Lewis delicacy (the harvest is strictly rationed), and there's no shortage of volunteers for the annual two-week cull. For the moment, the Niseachs have a licence to harvest up to two thousand birds, granted by Scottish Natural Heritage who manage the island.

Somewhat incredibly, the island of **Rona** (sometimes referred to as North Rona), ten miles east of Sula Sgeir, was inhabited on and off until the nineteenth century, despite being less than a mile across, with up to thirty inhabitants at one time. The island's St Ronan's Chapel is one of the oldest Celtic Christian ruins in the country. St Ronan was, according to legend, the first inhabitant, moving here in the eighth century with his two sisters, Miriceal and Brianuil, until one day he turned to Brianuil and said, "My dear sister, it is yourself that is handsome, what beautiful legs you have." She apparently replied that it was time for her to leave the island, and made her way to neighbouring Sula Sgeir where she was later found dead with a shag's nest in her ribcage. The island is now owned by Scottish Natural Heritage and is an important breeding ground for Leach's storm petrel.

Clearly visible from the ferry to Lewis and Harris, the **Shiant Isles** (ⓦ shiantisles.net), whose name translates as "the enchanted islands", sit in the middle of the Minch, five miles off the east coast of Lewis. Inhabited on and off until the beginning of the last century, the islands were bought by the author Compton MacKenzie in 1925, and then sold on to the publisher Nigel Nicolson, whose family still owns them. The Shiants have wonderful cliffs of fluted basalt columns that shelter thousands of seabirds, including puffin, in the breeding season.

Butt of Lewis (Rubha Robhabais)

From Eoropaidh, a narrow road twists to the bleak and blustery northern tip of the island, **Rubha Robhanais** – well-known to devotees of the BBC *Shipping Forecast* as the **Butt of Lewis** – where a redbrick lighthouse sticks up above a series of sheer cliffs and stacks, alive with kittiwakes, fulmars and cormorants, with skuas and gannets feeding offshore; it's a great place for spotting marine mammals. The lighthouse is closed to the public, and there's no way down to the sea, but backtrack half a mile or so, and there's a path down to the tiny sandy bay of **Port Sto**, a more sheltered spot for a picnic than the Butt itself.

ARRIVAL AND DEPARTURE   NESS

By bus There's a regular bus service from Stornoway to Port of Ness (Mon–Sat 6–8 daily; 1hr).

ACCOMMODATION

Galson Farm South Galson (Gabhsann Bho) ☎01851 850492, ⓦgalsonfarm.co.uk. An attractive converted eighteenth-century farmhouse, which offers generous portions of Aga-cooked dinner, bed and breakfast, and runs a six-bunk bunkhouse close by. Bunkhouse **£17**/person; doubles **£86**

Loch Beag 19 Fivepenny (Coig Peighinnean) ☎01851 810405, ⓦlochbeag.co.uk. A typically dour-looking B&B on the final stretch of road to Butt of Lewis, with a much more cheerful interior run by a very friendly local Gaelic-speaking couple. **£60**

EATING AND DRINKING

Café Sonas Port of Ness ☎01851 810222. Simple comfort food for the most part, but with a few local specialities thrown in – local fish pie, crab salad and Barra scampi (all under £7). Great views over the bay. Mon noon–5pm, Tues–Sat 10am–8pm.

Cross Inn Cross (Cros) ☎01851 810152. Pubs are few and far between in these parts so the *Cross Inn* is a real find, and has a peat fire to warm yourself by. Mon 5–11pm, Tues & Wed noon–2.30pm & 5–11pm, Thurs & Fri noon–2.30pm & 5pm–1am, Sat 11.30–1am, Sun 12.30–2.30pm & 6–11pm.

Westside (An Toabh Siar)

Heading southwest from the crossroads near Barvas (see p.303) brings you to the **Westside**. The main road lies a mile or so inland from the coast, but several villages meander down towards the sea. At **Arnol** and **Garenin** (Gearrannan) there are beautifully preserved blackhouses to explore, and at **Callanish** (Calanais), the islands' justifiably popular standing stones.

Arnol Blackhouse

42 Arnol • Mon–Sat: April–Sept 9.30am–5.30pm; Oct–March 9.30am–4.30pm • £4.50; HS • ☎01851 710395, ⓦhistoric-scotland .gov.uk

In Arnol, the remains of numerous blackhouses lie abandoned by the roadside. One, however, has been very carefully preserved to show exactly how a true blackhouse, or *taigh-dubh*, would have been. The dark interior is lit and heated by a small peat fire, kept alight in the central hearth of bare earth; smoke drifts up through the thatch, helping to keep out the midges and turn the heathery sods and oat-straw thatch itself into next year's fertilizer. The animals would have slept in the byre, separated only by a low partition, while potatoes and grain were stored in the adjacent barn. The old woman who lived here moved out very reluctantly in 1964, only after the council agreed to build a house with a byre for her animals (the building now houses the ticket office). Across the road is a ruined blackhouse, abandoned in 1920 when the family moved into no. 39, the white house, or *taigh-geal*, next door. A little beyond the blackhouse, a path leads down to **Loch na Muilne**, where you've a good chance of spotting the very rare red-necked phalarope (May–Aug).

Shawbost (Siabost) museum
Old School Centre, Shawbost • April–Sept Mon–Sat 11am–4pm • Free • ☎ 01851 710212

Two miles on from Bragar, at **SHAWBOST** (Siabost) – home to one of the main Harris Tweed mills in the Outer Hebrides – there's a tiny **museum** in the **Old School Centre**, across the road from the new school. The exhibits – most of them donated by locals – include a rare Lewis brick from the short-lived factory set up by Lord Leverhulme.

Norse Mill and Kiln
Signposted off the A858 • Open 24hr • Free

Just outside Shawbost, to the west, there's a sign to the restored **Norse Mill and Kiln**. It's a ten-minute walk over a small hill to the two thatched bothies beside a little stream; the nearer one's the kiln, the further one's the horizontal mill. Mills and kilns of this kind were common in Lewis up until the 1930s, and despite the name are thought to have been introduced here from Ireland as early as the sixth century.

Garenin (Gearrannan)
5a Garenin • May–Sept Mon–Sat 9.30am–5.30pm • £2.50 • ☎ 01851 643416, ⓦ gearrannan.com

In the parish of Carloway (Carlabhagh), with its crofthouses, boulders and hillocks rising out of the peat moor, a mile-long road leads off north to the beautifully remote coastal settlement of **GARENIN** (Gearrannan). Here, rather than re-create a single museum-piece blackhouse as at Arnol, a whole cluster of nine thatched crofters' houses – the last of which was abandoned in 1974 – have been restored and put to a variety of uses. As an emsemble, they also give a great impression of what a **Baile Tughaidh**, or blackhouse village, must have been like. The first house you come to houses the ticket office and **café**. The second house has been restored to its condition at the time of abandonment, so there's electric light, but no running water, lino flooring, but a peat fire and box beds – and a weaving machine in the byre. The third house has interpretive panels and a touch-screen computer telling the history of the village and the folk who lived there. Next door, there are toilets, while several others have been converted into **self-catering** houses.

Dun Carloway (Dùn Charlabhaigh)
Signposted off the A858 • Open 24hr • Free • ☎ 01851 710395, ⓦ historic-scotland.gov.uk

Just beyond Carloway village, **Dun Carloway** (Dùn Charlabhaigh) perches on top of a conspicuous rocky outcrop overlooking the sea. Scotland's west coast is strewn with over five hundred **brochs**, or fortified towers, but this is one of the best preserved, its dry-stone circular walls reaching a height of more than 30ft on one side. The broch consists of two concentric walls, the inner one perpendicular, the outer one slanting inwards, the two originally fastened together by roughly hewn flagstones, which also served as lookout galleries reached via a narrow stairwell. The only entrance to the roofless inner yard is through a low doorway set beside a crude and cramped guard cell. As at Callanish (see below), there have been all sorts of theories about the purpose of the brochs, which date from between 100 BC and 100 AD; the most likely explanation is that they were built to provide protection from Roman slave-traders.

Callanish (Calanais) standing stones
Loch Roag • **Stones** Open 24hr • Free • **Callanish Visitor Centre** April, May, Sept & Oct Mon–Sat 10am–6pm; June–Aug Mon–Sat 10am–8pm; Oct–March Tues–Sat 10am–4pm • £2.50 • ☎ 01851 621422, ⓦ callanishvisitorcentre.co.uk

Overlooking the sheltered, islet-studded waters of Loch Roag (Loch Ròg), on the west coast, are the islands' most dramatic prehistoric ruins, the **Callanish standing stones**. These monoliths – nearly fifty slabs of gnarled and finely grained gneiss up to 15ft high – were transported here between 3000 BC and 1500 BC, but their exact function remains a mystery. No one knows for certain why the ground plan resembles a colossal Celtic cross, nor why there's a central burial chamber. It's likely that such a massive endeavour was prompted by the desire to predict the seasonal cycle upon which these early farmers were entirely dependent, and indeed many of the stones are aligned with the positions of the sun and the stars. Whatever the reason for their existence, there's certainly no denying the powerful primeval presence, not to mention sheer beauty, of the stones.

You can visit the stones at any time, but if you need shelter or some simple sustenance, head to the nearby **Callanish Visitor Centre**, which has a small museum that explores the theories about the stones. If you want to commune with standing stones in solitude, head for the smaller circles in more natural surroundings a mile or two southeast of Callanish, around Garynahine (Gearraidh na h-Aibhne).

ARRIVAL AND DEPARTURE   WESTSIDE

By bus There are regular buses between Stornoway and Callanish (Mon–Sat 4–6 daily; 40min); Carloway (Mon–Sat 5–6 daily; 45min); Garenin (Mon–Sat 3–4 daily; 1hr); and Great Bernera (Mon–Sat 4 daily; 1hr).

ACCOMMODATION

Eilean Fraoich campsite Shawbost (Siabost) ☏ 01851 710504, ⍵ eileanfraoich.co.uk. Located behind the old village church, the campsite is a pristine, flat, grassy field in complete contrast with the surrounding undulating landscape. Kitchen and laundry facilities available. April–Oct. £15/pitch

Leumadair 7A Callanish (Calanais) ☏ 01851 612706, ⍵ leumadair.co.uk. A purpose-built modern guesthouse owned by a very friendly Lewis couple who have a pet hawk. Free wi-fi is available and dinner can be provided on request. £80

Bernera (Bearnaraigh)

Dividing Loch Roag (Loch Ròg) in two is the island of Great Bernera, usually referred to simply as **Bernera**. Joined to the mainland since 1953 via a narrow bridge that spans a small sea channel, Bernera is a rocky island, dotted with lochans, fringed by a few small lobster-fishing settlements and, until recently, owned by Robin Ian Evelyn Milne Stuart le Comte de la Lanne Mirrlees, the Queen's former herald, who also claimed the title Prince of Incoronata (an area of former Yugoslavia gifted to the count by King Peter II).

Bernera has an important place in Lewis history due to the **Bernera Riot** of 1874, when local crofters successfully defied the eviction orders delivered to them by the landlord, Sir James Matheson. In truth, there wasn't much of a riot, but three Bernera men were arrested and charged with assault. The crofters marched on the laird's house, Lews Castle in Stornoway, and demanded an audience with Matheson, who claimed to have no knowledge of what his factor, Donald Munro, was doing. In the subsequent trial, Munro was exposed as a ruthless tyrant, and the crofters were acquitted. A stone-built cairn now stands as a memorial to the riot, at the crossroads beyond the central settlement of **BREACLETE** (Brecleit), which sits beside one of the island's many lochs.

Bernera Museum

Breaclete Community Centre • May–Sept Mon–Fri noon–4pm • Free • ☎ 01851 612285

Housed in the local community centre, the **Bernera Museum** has a small exhibition on lobster fishing, a St Kilda mailboat and a mysterious five-thousand-year-old Neolithic stone tennis-ball, and, of course, a genealogy section.

Iron Age House

Bosta (Bostadh) • For times contact the Stornoway tourist office • ☎ 01851 703088

Much more interesting than the Bernera Museum is the replica **Iron Age House** that's been built above a precious little bay of golden sand beyond Bosta (Bostadh) cemetery, three miles north of Breaclete – follow the signs "to the shore". In 1992, gale-force winds revealed an entire late Iron Age or Pictish settlement hidden under the sand; due to its exposed position, the site has been refilled with sand, and a full-scale mock-up built instead, based on the "jelly baby" houses – after the shape – that were excavated. Inside, the house is incredibly spacious, and very dark, illuminated only by a central hearth and a few chinks of sunlight. If the weather's fine and you climb to the top of the nearby hills, you should get a good view over the forty or so islands in Loch Roag (Loch Ròg), and maybe even the Flannan Isles (see p.305) on the horizon.

ARRIVAL AND DEPARTURE BERNERA

By bus There are regular buses from Stornoway to Bernera (Mon–Sat 4 daily; 1hr).

6

Uig (Uuige)

It's a long drive along the partially upgraded B8011 to the remote region of **Uig** (Uuige), one of the areas of Lewis that suffered very badly from the Clearances. The landscape here is hillier and more dramatic than elsewhere, a combination of myriad islets, wild cliff scenery and patches of pristine golden sand.

The main road into the area takes you through the narrow canyon of Glen Valtos (Glèann Bhaltois) to **TIMSGARRY** (Timsgearraidh), which overlooks **Uig Sands** (Tràigh Uuige), the largest and most prized of all the golden strands on Lewis, where the sea goes out for miles at low tide; the best access point is from the car park near the cemetery in Ardroil (Eadar Dha Fhadhail), a couple of miles south of Timsgarry.

To the west of the Uig Sands is the tiny settlement of **MANGERSTA** (Mangurstadh), and a coastline of spectacular stacks and cliffs. A mile or so to the north, the old RAF radio station on the headland of **Aird Mòr** is the chosen site for a new **St Kilda Centre**, which one day will tell the fascinating story of the remote archipelago (see p.310), and – on fine days – afford views of it.

Uig Museum

Uig Community Centre, Timsgarry • Mon–Fri noon–5pm • £1 • ☎ 01851 672456

A giant wooden statue of one of the **Lewis Chessmen**, which were found in a local sandbank in 1831, heralds the **Uig Museum** in Timsgarry. Inside, you can see some replicas of the twelfth-century Viking chesspieces, which were carved from walrus ivory and whale teeth and now reside in Edinburgh's Royal Museum of Scotland and the British Museum in London. As well as putting on some excellent temporary exhibitions, the museum has bits and bobs from blackhouses and is staffed by locals, who are happy to answer any queries you have; there's also a welcome **tearoom** in the adjacent nursery during the holidays.

ARRIVAL AND DEPARTURE UIG

By bus There are regular buses from Stornoway to Uig (Mon–Sat 4 daily; 1hr–1hr 30min).

ACCOMMODATION

Ardroil campsite Ardroil (Eadar Dha Fhadhail) ☎ 01851 672248. The location, by one of the most remote and incredible sandy beaches in the Western Isles, is unbeatable, but be warned, there's only a toilet block and

---

BOAT TRIPS

There's a wide choice of **boat trips** offered around the Western Isles. Prices start at around £45 per person for a short RIB wildlife cruise to around £200 for a day-trip to St Kilda. Sea Trek (☎ 01851 672469, ⊛ seatrek.co.uk), who leave from Miavaig (Miabhaig) in Uig, go regularly to St Kilda (and occasionally to Sula Sgeir and Rona), as do Kilda Cruises (☎ 01859 502060, ⊛ kildacruises.co.uk), who operate a 55ft motor cruiser from West Tarbert on Harris, and also offer shorter trips to the likes of the Shiant Isles. For longer trips around the islands, contact Island Cruising (☎ 01851 672381, ⊛ island-cruising.com), based at Miavaig (Miabhaig) in Uig.

6

> ## ST KILDA (HIORT)
>
> Britain's westernmost island chain is the NTS-owned **St Kilda** (ⓦ kilda.org.uk) archipelago, forty miles from its nearest landfall, Griminish Point on North Uist. Dominated by the highest cliffs and sea stacks in Britain, Hirta, St Kilda's main island, was occupied on and off for two thousand years, with the last 36 Gaelic-speaking inhabitants evacuated at their own request in 1930. Immediately after evacuation, the island was bought by the Marquess of Bute, to protect the island's millions of puffins, gannets, petrels and other seabirds. In 1957, having agreed to allow the army to build a missile-tracking radar station here linked to South Uist, the marquess bequeathed the island to the NTS. St Kilda is one of only two dozen **UNESCO World Heritage Sites** with a dual status reflecting its natural and cultural significance. Despite its inaccessibility, several thousand visitors make it out here each year; if you get to land, you can see the museum, send a postcard and enjoy a drink at the army's pub, the *Puff Inn*. Between mid-May and mid-August, the NTS organizes volunteer **work parties**, which either restore and maintain the old buildings or take part in archeological digs – for more information, contact the NTS (☎0844 493 2100, ⓦnts.org.uk). For the armchair traveller, the best general book on St Kilda is Tom Steel's *The Life and Death of St Kilda*, or else there's the classic 1937 film *The Edge of the World* by Michael Powell (which was actually shot on Foula in Shetland). Several companies offer **boat day-trips** for around £200 per person (see p.309). The sea journey (8hr return) is not for the faint-hearted and there's no guarantee that you'll be able to land.

a cold water tap. For very slightly more facilities, head for nearby Kneep (Cnìp). **£6**/person

Auberge Carnish 5 Carnish (Carnais) ☎01851 672459, ⓦaubergecarnish.co.uk. A new-build guesthouse on the far side of the stunning Uig Sands. The rooms are spacious and tastefully furnished and the restaurant's food – like the owners – is Franco-Hebridean. Mid-March to mid-Nov daily 6.30–8.30pm. **£120**

Baile na Cille Timsgarry (Timsgearraidh) ☎01851 672242, ⓦbailenacille.co.uk. A chaotic kind of place, run by an eccentric couple who are very welcoming to families and dogs and dish up wonderful set-menu dinners for £30

a head. Free wi-fi. Mid-April to mid-Sept. **£110**

Kneep campsite Kneep (Cnìp) ☎01851 672265. Informal camping beside the wonderful sandy beach of Reef Beach (Tràigh na Beirghe). It's run by the local community and the only facilities are a small unisex toilet block with coin-operated showers. Mid-April to mid-Sept. **£6**/person

Suainaval 3 Crowlista (Cradhlastadh) ☎01851 672386, ⓦsuainaval.com. The best B&B in the whole area, run by a truly welcoming couple; rooms have pine floors and furnishings and fabulous views over the golden sands of Uig. **£75**

Harris (Na Hearadh)

Harris, whose name derives from the Old Norse for "high land", is much hillier, more dramatic and much more immediately appealing than Lewis, its boulder-strewn slopes descending to aquamarine bays of dazzling white sand. The shift from Lewis to Harris is almost imperceptible, as the two are, in fact, one island, the "division" between them embedded in a historical split in the MacLeod clan, lost in the mists of time. The border was also, somewhat crazily, a county boundary until 1975, with Harris lying in Invernessshire, and Lewis belonging to Ross and Cromarty. Nowadays, the dividing line is rarely marked even on maps; for the record, it comprises Loch Reasort in the west, Loch Seaforth (Loch Shìphoirt) in the east, and the six miles in between. Harris itself is more clearly divided by a minuscule isthmus, into the wild, inhospitable mountains of **North Harris** and the gentler landscape and sandy shores of **South Harris**.

Brief history

Along with Lewis, Harris was purchased in 1918 by **Lord Leverhulme**. In contrast to Lewis, though, Leverhulme and his ambitious projects were broadly welcomed by the

CLOCKWISE FROM TOP KISIMUL CASTLE (P.324); BLACKHOUSE, GARENIN (GEARRANNAN) (P.307); GIANT WOODEN CHESSMAN OUTSIDE UIG MUSEUM (P.309) >

people of Harris. His most grandiose plans were drawn up for Leverburgh (see p.315), but he also purchased an old Norwegian whaling station in Bunavoneadar (Bun Abhàinn Eadarra) in 1922, built a spinning mill at Geocrab and began the construction of four roads. Financial difficulties, a slump in the tweed industry and the lack of market for whale products meant that none of the schemes was a wholehearted success, and when he died in 1925 the plug was pulled on all of them by his executors.

Since the Leverhulme era, unemployment has been a constant problem in Harris. Crofting continues on a small scale, supplemented by the Harris Tweed industry, though the main focus of this has, in fact, shifted to Lewis. Fishing continues on **Scalpay**, while the rest of the population gets by on whatever employment is available: roadworks, crafts, hunting and fishing and, of course, the one growth industry, tourism.

Tarbert (An Tairbeart)

Sheltered in a green valley on the narrow isthmus, **TARBERT** (An Tairbeart) is the largest settlement on Harris and a wonderful place to arrive by boat. The port's mountainous backdrop is impressive, and the town is attractively laid out on steep terraces sloping up from the dock.

ARRIVAL AND INFORMATION TARBEART

By ferry There are CalMac car ferries to and from Uig on Skye (Mon–Sat 1–2 daily; 1hr 45min).

By bus Tarbert is served by regular buses from and to Stornoway, as well as a few other places.

Destinations Hushinish (schooldays Mon–Fri 2–3 daily; school holidays Tues & Fri 3 daily; 45min); Leverburgh (Mon–Sat 6–8 daily; 45min–1hr); Leverburgh via the Bays (Mon–Sat 2–4 daily; 1hr); Rhenigdale (by request ☎01463 731280; Mon–Sat 2 daily; 30min); Scalpay (Mon–Sat 4–6 daily; 20min).

Tourist office Harris's tourist office is close to the ferry terminal (April–Oct Mon–Sat 9am–6pm; open to greet the evening ferry; ☎01859 502011).

HARRIS TWEED

Far from being a picturesque cottage industry, as it's sometimes presented, the production of **Harris Tweed** is vital to the local economy, with a well-organized and unionized workforce. Traditionally the tweed was made by women, from the wool of their own sheep, to provide clothing for their families, using a 2500-year-old process. Each woman was responsible for plucking the wool by hand, washing and scouring it, dyeing it with lichen, heather flowers or ragwort, carding (smoothing and straightening the wool, often adding butter to grease it), spinning and weaving. Finally the cloth was dipped in stale urine and "waulked" by a group of women, who beat the cloth on a table to soften and shrink it while singing Gaelic waulking songs. Harris Tweed was originally made all over the islands, and was known simply as *clò mór* (big cloth).

In the mid-nineteenth century, Catherine Murray, **Countess of Dunmore**, who owned a large part of Harris, started to sell surplus cloth to her aristocratic friends; she then sent two sisters from Strond (Srannda) to Paisley to learn the trade. On their return, they formed the genesis of the modern industry, which continues to serve as a vital source of employment, though demand (and therefore employment levels) can fluctuate wildly as fashions change. To earn the official **Harris Tweed Authority (HTA)** trademark of the Orb and the Maltese Cross – taken from Lady Dunmore's coat of arms – the fabric has to be hand-woven on the Outer Hebrides from 100 percent pure new Scottish wool, while the other parts of the manufacturing process must take place only in the local mills.

The main **mills** are actually in Carloway and Shawbost, in Lewis, where the wool is dyed, carded and spun. In the last few decades, there has been a revival of traditional tweed-making techniques, with several small producers following old methods, using indigenous plants and bushes to **dye** the cloth: yellow comes from rocket and broom; green from heather; grey and black from iris and oak; and, most popular of all, reddish brown from crotal, a flat grey lichen scraped off rocks.

ACCOMMODATION

Coel na Mara 7 Direcleit ☎ 01859 502464, ⓦ coelna mara.com. With your own transport, this secluded B&B, across the bay from Tarbert, is a good choice: nicely furnished throughout, with great views over East Loch Tarbert. The smallest and cheapest room doesn't have en-suite facilities. **£90**

Harris Hotel Scott Rd ☎ 01859 502154, ⓦ harrishotel .com. Just a 5min walk from the harbour, this is Tarbert's longest-established and largest hotel. It's been refurbished fairly recently so it's a solid choice, with 23 en-suite rooms, some with sea views, and all with free wi-fi – also serves food, even on a Sunday. **£100**

No. 5 hostel 5 Drinishader (Drinisiadar) ☎ 01851 511255, ⓦ number5.biz. A converted cottage, 3 miles south of Tarbert, offering bed linen and laundry service along with canoes, kayaks and cycles for hire. Beds are in dorms, plus one twin. March–Oct. **£20**/person

EATING AND DRINKING

First Fruits Pier Road Cottage ☎ 01859 502439. Very pleasant tearoom behind the tourist office, housed in an old stone-built cottage and serving real coffee, home-made cakes, toasties and so forth. April & May Mon, Wed & Fri 10.30am–4pm, Thurs & Sat 10.30am–3pm; June–Sept Mon–Fri 10am–4pm, Sat 10am–3pm.

Isle of Harris Inn Scott Rd ☎ 01859 502566. A lively pub, next door to the *Harris Hotel*, offers very good fish and chips (under £10) and the occasional seafood special. Mon–Sat 11am–11pm; food served noon–9.30pm.

North Harris (Ceann a Tuath na Hearadh)

Mountainous **North Harris** was run like some minor feudal fiefdom until 2003, when the locals managed to buy the land for a knock-down £2 million. If you're coming from Stornoway on the A859, it's a spectacular introduction to Harris, its bulging, pyramidal mountains of ancient gneiss looming over the dramatic fjord-like **Loch Seaforth** (Loch Shìphoirt). From **ARDVOURLIE** (Aird a' Mhulaidh), you weave your way over a boulder-strewn saddle between mighty **Sgaoth Aird** (1829ft) and An Cliseam or the **Clisham** (2619ft), the highest peak in the Western Isles. This bitter terrain, littered with debris left behind by retreating glaciers, offers but the barest of vegetation, with an occasional cluster of crofters' houses sitting in the shadow of a host of pointed peaks, anywhere between 1000ft and 2500ft high.

The road to Hushinish (Huisinis)

The winding, single-track B887, which clings to the northern shores of West Loch Tarbert (Loch a Siar), gives easy access to the awesome mountain range of the (treeless) Forest of Harris to the north. Immediately as you turn down the B887, you pass through **Bunavoneadar** (Bun Abhàinn Eadarra), where some Norwegians established a short-lived whaling station – the slipways and distinctive redbrick chimney can still be seen. Seven miles further on, you pass **Abhainnsuidhe Castle** (pronounced "avan-soo-ee"), designed by David Bryce in Scottish Baronial style in 1865 for the Earl of Dunmore. The main road takes you through right past the front door, much to the annoyance of the castle's successive owners – as you do, be sure to admire the lovely salmon-leap waterfalls and pristine castle grounds. It's another five miles to the end of the road at the small crofting community of **Hushinish** (Huisinis), where you are rewarded with a south-facing beach of shell sand that looks across Hushinish Bay to South Harris.

Scarp

A slipway north of Hushinish Bay serves the nearby island of **Scarp**, a hulking mass of rock rising over 1000ft, once home to over two hundred people but abandoned in 1971 (it's now a private holiday hideaway). The most bizarre moment in its history – subject of the 2002 film *The Rocket Post* – was undoubtedly in 1934, when the German scientist **Gerhardt Zucher** experimented in sending mail by rocket. Zucher made two attempts at launching his rocket from Scarp, but the letter-laden missile exploded before it got off the ground, and the idea was shelved.

6

SCALPAY (SCALPAIGH)

A high-flying, single-track bridge, erected in 1997, now connects Harris to the island of **Scalpay** (Scalpaigh) – from the Norse *skalp-ray* (the island shaped like a boat), off the east coast of Harris. Scalpay is the place where Bonnie Prince Charlie is thought to have tried unsuccessfully to get a boat to take him back to France after the defeat at Culloden. On a good day, it's a pleasant and fairly easy three-mile hike along the island's north coast to the **Eilean Glas** lighthouse, which looks out over to Skye. This was the first lighthouse to be erected in Scotland, in 1789, though the present Stevenson-designed granite tower dates from 1824.

ACCOMMODATION	NORTH HARRIS

Rhenigidale (Reinigeadal) SYHA Hostel 4 miles off the A859 ⓦ gatliff.org.uk. Simple hostel in an isolated coastal community – there's a (request-only) bus connection, or else it's a magnificent six-mile (3hr) hike over the rocky landscape from Tarbert: ask at the tourist office for directions. No advance booking and no phone. £12/person

South Harris (Ceann a Deas na Hearadh)

The mountains of **South Harris** are less dramatic than in the north, but the scenery is equally breathtaking. There's a choice of routes from Tarbert to the ferry port of **Leverburgh**, which connects with North Uist: the east coast, known as **The Bays** (Na Baigh), is rugged and seemingly inhospitable, while the **west coast** is endowed with some of the finest stretches of golden sand in the whole of the archipelago, buffeted by the Atlantic winds.

The Bays (Na Baigh)

Paradoxically, most people on South Harris live along the harsh eastern coastline of **The Bays** rather than the more fertile west side. But not by choice – they were evicted from their original crofts to make way for sheep-grazing. Despite the uncompromising lunar landscape – mostly bare grey gneiss and heather – the crofters managed to establish "lazybeds" (small labour-intensive, raised plots between the rocks fertilized by seaweed and peat), a few of which are still in use even today. The narrow sea lochs provide shelter for fishing boats, while the interior is speckled with freshwater lochans, and the whole coast is now served by the endlessly meandering **Bays Road**, often wrongly referred to as the "Golden Road", though this, in fact, was the name given to the sideroad to Scadabay (Scadabhagh), coined by a local councillor who disapproved of the expense.

The west coast

The main road from Tarbert into South Harris snakes its way west for ten miles across the boulder-strewn interior to reach the coast. Once there, you get a view of the most stunning **beach**, the vast golden strand of **Luskentyre** (Tràigh Losgaintir). The road continues to ride above a chain of sweeping sands, backed by rich **machair**, that stretches for nine miles along the Atlantic coast. In good weather the scenery is particularly impressive, foaming breakers rolling along the golden sands set against the rounded peaks of the mountains to the north and the islet-studded turquoise sea to the west – and even on the dullest day the sand manages to glow beneath the waves. A short distance out to sea is the island of **Taransay** (Tarasaigh), which once held a population of nearly a hundred, but was abandoned as recently as 1974. Beyond lies **Scarista** (Sgarasta), where one of the first of the Hebridean Clearances took place in 1828, when thirty families were evicted and their homes burnt.

Seallam!

Northton (Taobh Tuath) • Mon–Sat 10am–5pm • £2.50 • ☎ 01859 520258, ⓦ seallam.com

There's loads of information on local history, geology, flora and fauna to be found at **Seallam!**, a purpose-built heritage centre close to the village of Northton (Taobh Tuath), overlooked by the round-topped hill of Chaipabhal at the westernmost tip of South Harris. As well as detailing the area's history of emigration, it's a useful centre for ancestor-hunters, and there's a good section on St Kilda (see p.310).

Leverburgh (An t-Ob)

From Northton the road veers to the southeast to trim the island's south shore, eventually reaching the sprawling settlement of **LEVERBURGH** (An t-Ob). Named after Lord Leverhulme, who planned to turn the place into the largest fishing port on the west coast of Scotland, it's the terminal for the CalMac **car ferry** service to Berneray and the Uists. The hour-long journey across the skerry-strewn Sound of Harris is one of Scotland's most tortuous ferry routes, with the ship taking part in a virtual slalom-race to avoid numerous hidden rocks – it's also a great crossing from which to spot seabirds and sea mammals.

Rodel (Roghadal)

A mile or so from Renish Point (Rubha Reanais), the southern tip of Harris, is the old port of **RODEL** (Roghadal), where a smattering of picturesque ancient stone houses lies among the hillocks. Down by the old harbour where the ferry from Skye used to arrive, you'll find the *Rodel Hotel*, a solid, stone-built, family-run hotel originally erected in 1781.

St Clement's Church (Tur Chliamainn)

For opening times phone ahead • ☎ 01851 710395, ⍟ historic-scotland.gov.uk

On top of one of the grassy humps, with sheep grazing in the graveyard, is **St Clement's Church** (Tur Chliamainn), burial place of the MacLeods of Harris and Dunvegan in Skye. Dating from the 1520s – in other words pre-Reformation, hence the big castellated tower (which you can climb) – the church was saved from ruination in the eighteenth century, and fully restored in 1873 by the countess of Dunmore. The bare interior is distinguished by its wall tombs, notably that of the founder, Alasdair Crotach (also known as Alexander MacLeod), whose heavily weathered effigy lies beneath an intriguing backdrop and canopy of sculpted reliefs depicting vernacular and religious scenes – elemental representations of, among others, a stag hunt, the Holy Trinity, St Michael and the devil, and an angel weighing the souls of the dead. Look out, too, for the *sheila-na-gig* halfway up the south side of the church tower; unusually, she has a brother displaying his genitalia, below a carving of St Clement on the west face.

ARRIVAL AND INFORMATION   SOUTH HARRIS

By ferry There's a daily ferry between Leverburgh and Berneray, North Uist (3–4 daily; 1hr).

By bus There's a regular bus service along the west coast between Leverburgh and Tarbert (Mon–Sat 6–8 daily; 45min–1hr), and a less frequent one via The Bays on the east coast (Mon–Sat 2–4 daily; 1hr).

Tourist information On the north side of the bay is the An Clachan co-op store which houses a small information office (Mon–Sat 9am–6pm; ☎ 01859 520370).

ACCOMMODATION AND EATING

THE BAYS

★ **Lickisto Blackhouse Camping** Lickisto (Liceasto) ☎ 01851 530485, ⍟ freewebs.com/vanvon. There's fresh bread and eggs available, a peat fire to warm you in the kitchen blackhouse and toilets in the byres. Yurts also available. March–Oct. Yurts £70; camping £24/pitch

★ **Old School House** Finsbay (Fionnsbhagh) ☎ 01859 530420, ⍟ theoldschoolhousefinsbay.com. A very friendly couple run this nicely converted Victorian former village schoolhouse, which comes with free wi-fi, good home-cooking and huge portions for dinner (£20–30) and breakfast. £70

Skoon 4 Geocrab ☎ 01851 530268, ⍟ skoon.com. There aren't too many places to stop and have a bite to eat, so *Skoon* is something of a boon: home-made soup, baguettes, cakes and good coffee on offer. April–Sept Tues–Sat 10am–4.30pm; Oct–March Fri & Sat same hours.

6

THE WEST COAST

Beul-na-Mara Seilebost ☎01859 550205, ⓦbeulna
mara.co.uk. This is a perfectly decent B&B run by a local
couple, but what makes it particularly special is the stunning location, overlooking the golden sands of Luskentyre
(Tràigh Losgaintir). **£90**

★ **Pairc an t-Srath** Borve (Na Buirgh) ☎01859 550386,
ⓦpaircant-srath.co.uk. A working crofthouse, with beautiful Harris Tweed furnishings – there's a superb view from the
dining room and the food is both filling and beautifully
prepared (three-course dinners for £35 a head). **£100**

Temple Café Northton (Taobh Tuath) ☎01859 550205,
ⓦbeulnamara.co.uk. Great little "Hobbit House" café in
the former MacGillivray Centre – expect butternut squash
soup, roast peppers and veggie burgers (all under £10)
and great views over the machair. April–Sept Wed–Sun
10.30am–5.30pm (also some eves until 9pm); Oct–
March same hours, Sat & Sun only.

LEVERBURGH

★ **Am Bothan** Ferry Rd ☎01859 520251, ⓦambothan
.com. Quirky, bright-red timber-clad bunkhouse that makes
for a pretty luxurious, very welcoming hostel close to the
ferry. Lovely big kitchen/living room, plus laundry and drying
facilities too. **£20**/person

The Anchorage Ferry Terminal ☎01859 520225.
For local venison and beef burgers, langoustines, black
pudding with poached egg on muffins (£10–15), head for
this lively bar/restaurant by the ferry slipway – great views
and occasional live music. Mon–Sat noon–11pm; food
served noon–9pm.

Carminish House 1A Strond ☎01859 520400,
ⓦcarminish.com. Modern, double-glazed guesthouse
with light, airy rooms, free wi-fi and some fabulous views
over the Sound from the residents' lounge, which has an
open fire. **£80**

North Uist (Uibhist a Tuath)

Compared to the mountainous scenery of Harris, **North Uist** – seventeen miles long
and thirteen miles wide – is much flatter and for some comes as something of an
anticlimax. Over half the surface area is covered by water, creating a distinctive
peaty-brown lochan-studded "drowned landscape". Most visitors come here for the
trout- and salmon-fishing and the deerstalking, all of which (along with poaching) are
critical to the survival of the island's economy. Others come for the smattering of
prehistoric sites, the birds, or the sheer peace of this windy isle and the solitude of
North Uist's vast sandy beaches, which extend – almost without interruption – along
the north and west coasts.

Lochmaddy (Loch nam Madadh) and around

Despite being situated on the east coast, some distance away from any beach, the ferry
port of **LOCHMADDY** – "Loch of the Dogs" – makes a good base for exploring the
island. Occupying a narrow, bumpy promontory, overlooked by the brooding
mountains of North Lee (Lì a Tuath) and South Lee (Lì a Deas) to the southeast,
it's difficult to believe that this sleepy settlement was a large herring port as far back as
the seventeenth century. While there's not much to see in Lochmaddy itself, there are
several prehistoric sites in the surrounding area.

Taigh Chearsabhagh

Mon–Sat 10am–5pm · £3 · ☎01876 603970, ⓦtaigh-chearsabhagh.org

The only thing to keep you in Lochmaddy is **Taigh Chearsabhagh**, a converted
eighteenth-century merchant's house, now home to a community arts centre, with
a simple airy café, post office, shop and excellent museum, which puts on some
worthwhile exhibitions. Taigh Chearsabhagh was one of the prime movers behind the
commissioning of a series of seven sculptures dotted about the Uists. Ask at the arts
centre for directions to the ones in and around Lochmaddy, the most interesting of
which is the **Both nam Faileas** (Hut of the Shadow), 1km north of the town. The hut is
an ingenious dry-stone, turf-roofed camera obscura built by sculptor Chris Drury that
projects the nearby land-, sea- and skyscape onto its back wall – take time to allow your

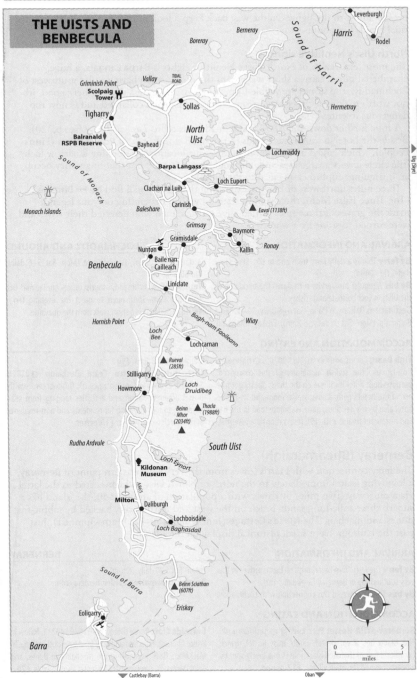

**THE UISTS AND
BENBECULA**

Leverburgh

Harris

Rodel

Sound of Harris

Berneray

Boreray

Hermetray

Sound of Skye

6

Vallay

TIDAL
ROAD

Griminish Point
**Scolpaig
Tower**

Sollas

North
Uist

Tigharry

**Balranald
RSPB Reserve**

Bayhead

A867

Lochmaddy

Sound of Monach

Barpa Langass

Loch Euport

Clachan na Luib

Monach Islands

Baleshare

Carinish

Eaval (1138ft)

Grimsay

Baymore

Gramisdale

Nunton

Kallin

Baile nan
Cailleach

Ronay

Benbecula

Liniclate

Bagh-nam Faoileann

Wiay

Hornish Point

Loch
Bee

Lochcarnan

Rueval
(285ft)

Stilligarry

Howmore

Loch
Druidibeg

Beinn
Mhor
(2034ft)

Thacla
(1988ft)

Rudha Ardvule

South Uist

Loch Eynort

**Kildonan
Museum**

Milton

Daliburgh

A865

Lochboisdale

Loch Baghasdail

Sound of Barra

Beinn Sciathan
(607ft)

Eriskay

Eoligarry

Barra

N

0   5
miles

Castlebay (Barra)

Oban

eyes to adjust to the light. On the way back keep a look out for otters, which love the tidal rapids hereabouts.

North Uist's Neolithic sights

The most remarkable of North Uist's Neolithic sights is **Barpa Langais**, a huge, chambered burial cairn a short walk from the A867, seven barren miles southwest of Lochmaddy. The stones are visible from the road and, unless the weather's good, it's not worth making a closer inspection as the chamber has collapsed and is now too dangerous to enter.

A mile further down the A867, a side road leads off to *Langass Lodge* (see p.320). Beside the hotel, a rough track leads to the small stone circle of **Pobull Fhinn** (Finn's People), which enjoys a much more picturesque location overlooking a narrow loch. The circle covers a large area and, although the stones are not that huge, they occupy an intriguing amphitheatre cut into the hillside.

Three miles northwest of Lochmaddy along the A865 you'll find **Na Fir Bhreige** (The Three False Men), three standing stones which, depending on your legend, mark the graves of three spies buried alive or three men who deserted their wives and were turned to stone by a witch.

ARRIVAL AND INFORMATION

LOCHMADDY AND AROUND

By ferry There's a daily ferry from and to Uig, Skye (1–2 daily; 1hr 40min).

By bus A regular bus service runs down the backbone of the Uists to Lochboisdale and Eriskay.
Destinations Balivanich (Mon–Sat 6–8 daily; 30–45min); Balranald (Mon–Sat 3 daily; 50min); Eriskay (Mon–Sat

3 daily; 2hr 20min); Lochboisdale (Mon–Sat 5–6 daily; 1hr 30min).

Tourist office Lochmaddy's tourist office (April to mid-Oct Mon–Sat 9am–5pm; open to greet the evening ferry; ☎01876 500321) is a short walk from the quayside.

ACCOMMODATION AND EATING

Tigh Dearg Lochmaddy ☎01876 500700, ⓦ tighdearg hotel.co.uk. The stylish modernity of this cherry-red, purpose-built hotel is unique on the Uists; guests get free use of the hotel's gym, sauna, steam room and wi-fi. The hotel also serves delicious, quite elaborate food in the bar and restaurant (mains £10–15); reservations are essential.

Daily 6.30–8.30pm. **£90**
Uist Outdoor Centre Cearn Dusgaidh ☎01876 500480, ⓦ uistoutdoorcentre.co.uk. Outdoor centre with hostel accommodation and activities ranging from sea-kayaking to rock climbing for residents and non-residents alike. March to early Dec. **£10**/person

Berneray (Bhearnaraigh)

The ferry connection with Harris leaves from the very southeastern point of **Berneray**, a low-lying island immediately to the north of North Uist and connected to the latter via a causeway. Two miles by three, with a population of around 140, the island has a superb three-mile-long sandy beach on the west and north coast, backed by rabbit-free dunes and machair. The **Nurse's Cottage** (June–Aug Mon–Fri 11am–3pm; £1), just past the harbour, has a small historical display on the island.

ARRIVAL AND INFORMATION

BERNERAY

By ferry The ferry from Leverburgh on Harris arrives at the very southern tip of Berneray (3–4 daily; 1hr).

By bus There's a decent bus connection with Lochmaddy.

(Mon–Sat 5–6 daily; 20min).
Tourist information ⓦ isleofberneray.com.

ACCOMMODATION AND EATING

Berneray SYHA Hostel Port Ludaig ⓦ gatliff.org.uk. The island has a wonderful Gatliff Trust hostel, which occupies a pair of thatched blackhouses in a lovely spot by a beach, beyond the main village. **£12**/person

Burnside Croft Borve (Borgh) ☎01876 540235. Follow in Prince Charles's footsteps and stay (and help out) at "Splash" MacKillop's B&B, overlooking the machair and dunes, and enjoy "storytelling evenings"; bike rental also available. **£70**

The Lobster Pot Borve (Borgh) ☎01876 540288. A tearoom (and shop) on the main road, near the ferry terminal, serving toasties and soup and simple summer evening meals (all under £10). Mon–Sat 9am–8.30pm; closes 5.30pm in winter.

The coastal road via Sollas (Solas)

In just six miles, the A867 will take you quickly from Lochmaddy to Clachan via several Neolithic sites (see opposite), but the A865, which skirts the northern and western shoreline of North Uist for more than thirty miles, takes you through the most scenic sections of the island.

Sollas (Solas)

Once you've left the boggy east coast and passed the turning to Berneray and the Harris ferry, the road reaches the parish of **SOLLAS** (Solas), which stands at the centre of a couple of superb tidal strands – sea green at high tide, sandy and golden at low tide – backed by large tracts of machair that are blanketed with wild flowers in summer. A new memorial opposite the local co-op recalls the appallingly brutal Clearances undertaken by Lord MacDonald of Sleat in Sollas.

Vallay (Bhalaigh)

Visible across the nearby sandy strand is the tidal island of **Vallay** (Bhalaigh), on which stands the ruined mansion of wealthy textile manufacturer and archeologist Erskine Beveridge (cousin of Lord William) – check tide times before setting out.

Scolpaig Tower and Griminish Point

Beyond Solas, the rolling hills that occupy the centre of North Uist slope down to the sea. Here, in the northwest corner of the island, you'll find **Scolpaig Tower**, a castellated folly on an islet in Loch Scolpaig, erected as a famine-relief project in the nineteenth century – you can reach it, with some difficulty, across stepping stones. A tarmac track leads down past the loch and tower to Scolpaig Bay, beyond which lies the rocky shoreline of **Griminish Point** (Rubha Griminis), the closest landfall to St Kilda (see box, p.310), clearly visible on the horizon in fine weather, looming like some giant dinosaur's skeleton emerging from the sea.

Balranald RSPB Reserve

Visitor centre April–Aug daily 9am–6pm

Roughly three miles south of Scolpaig Tower, through the sand dunes, is the **Balranald RSPB Reserve** where, if you're lucky, you should be able to encounter corncrakes, once common throughout the British countryside, but now among the country's rarest birds. Unfortunately, the birds are very good at hiding in long grass, so you're unlikely to see one; however, the males' loud "craking" is relatively easy to hear from May to July throughout the Uists and Barra. In fact, there are usually one or two making a loud noise right outside the RSPB **visitor centre**, from which you can pick up a leaflet outlining a two-hour walk along the headland, marked by posts. A wonderful carpet of flowers covers the machair in summer, and there are usually corn bunting and arctic tern inland, and gannet, Manx shearwater and skua out to sea.

ACCOMMODATION   THE COAST ROAD VIA SOLLAS

Balranald Hebridean Holidays Hougharry (Hogha Gearraidh) ☎01876 510304, ⓦbalranaldhebridean holidays.com. Lovely campsite by the RSPB reserve, surrounded by fields of wild flowers and close to a sandy beach – as well as the usual facilities, there's free wi-fi.

March–Sept. £20/pitch

Wheelhouse Airigh Mhic Ruairidh, Griminish (Griminis) ☎07952 163080, ⓦhebrides-holidays.co.uk. Eco-yurts and huts, powered with solar power and candlelight, on a spot looking across the tidal flats to Vallay. Two nights'

6

minimum (and bring your own bedding) or stay in the hostel hut or camp. Bike hire and activities from peat cutting to seashore foraging also on offer. April–Oct. Huts for two £50; hostel £16/person

Clachan (Clachan na Luib) and around

CLACHAN (Clachan na Luib), centred on the main crossroads of the A865 and the A867 from Lochmaddy, has a post office and general store. Offshore, to the southwest, lie two flat, tidal, dune and machair islands, the largest of which is **Baleshare** (Baile Sear), with its fantastic three-mile-long beach, connected by causeway to North Uist. In Gaelic the island's name means "east village", its twin "west village" having disappeared under the sea during a freak storm in the fifteenth or sixteenth century. The storm also isolated the **Monach Islands** (also known by their old Norse name of Heisker or Heisgeir in Gaelic), once joined to North Uist at low tide, now eight miles out to sea. The islands, which are connected with each other at low tide, were inhabited until the 1930s, when the last remaining families moved to Sollas.

Eabhal

For a superb overview of North Uist's watery landscape, it's a boggy, but relatively straightforward climb up the island's highest hill, **Eabhal** (1138ft). The best starting-point is the end of the B894 to Loch Euphoirt: skirt round the east side of Loch Obasaraigh and approach the summit from the northeast (return trip 3–4hr).

ACCOMMODATION
CLACHAN AND AROUND

★ **Bagh Alluin** 21 Baleshare (Baile Sear) ☎ 01876 580370, ⌨ jacvolbeda.co.uk. A secluded, beautifully designed modern B&B with fantastic views over the island run by a Dutch artist, who is a genuinely warm and friendly host. **£85**

Langass Lodge Loch Eport ☎ 01876 580285, ⌨ langass lodge.co.uk. From the A867, a side road leads off to this venerable hotel, which has a stylish modern extension, and a restaurant and bar that serve excellent local seafood (£30 for two courses); reservations advised. Daily 6–8.30pm. **£110**

Moorcroft Holidays 17 Carinish (Cairinis) ☎ 01876 580305, ⌨ moorcroftholidays.com. An exposed, but flat and very well equipped campsite, with sea views; the bunkhouse has just six beds, lovely wooden floors and furnishings and a modern kitchen. April–Oct. Bunkhouse **£18**/person; camping **£13**/pitch

EATING AND DRINKING

Claddach Kirkibost Centre Claddach Kirkibost (Cladach Chireboist) ☎ 01876 580390. Community-centre café in a conservatory with sea views, which uses local produce to make soups, sandwiches and simple dishes, even the occasional curry or Tex-Mex dish (£6–7). Mon–Sat 11am–4pm; closed Sat in winter.

Westford Inn Claddach Kirkibost (Cladach Chireboist) ☎ 01876 580653, ⌨ j7mis.co.uk/westfordinn. North Uist's only pub is housed in the eighteenth-century factor's house. There's a wood-panelled bar plus several smaller rooms with real fires in bad weather, Skye ales on tap and pub food until 9pm. May–Sept daily noon–11pm.

Benbecula (Beinn na Faoghla)

Blink and you could miss the pancake-flat island of **Benbecula** (put the stress on the second syllable), sandwiched between Protestant North Uist and Catholic South Uist. Most visitors simply trundle along the main road that cuts across the middle of the island in less than five miles – not such a bad idea, since the island is scarred from the postwar presence of the Royal Artillery, who once made up half the local population. The only reason to come to **BALIVANICH** (Baile a Mhanaich), Benbecula's grim, grey capital, is if you're flying into or out of **Benbecula Airport**, need an ATM, the laundry (behind the bank) or a supermarket.

Museum nan Eilean

Lniclate School (Sgoil Lionacleit) • Mon–Sat; phone for times • ☎ 01870 602864

The only secondary school (and public swimming pool) on the Uists and Benbecula is in Lionacleit (Liniclate), in the south of the island. The school is home to a small **Museum nan Eilean**, which puts on temporary exhibitions on the history of the islands, as well as occasional live music and other events.

ARRIVAL AND DEPARTURE   BENBECULA

By plane Benbecula Airport (⊛ hial.oc.uk) is just a 10–15min walk north of Balivanich. There's a small café inside the airport building.

By bus Buses en route to and from South or North Uist stop at Balivanich's airport and post office.

Destinations Berneray (Mon–Sat 5–7 daily; 1hr 10min); Eriskay (Mon–Sat 5–7 daily; 1hr 30min); Lochboisdale (Mon–Sat 7–8 daily; 1hr); Lochmaddy (Mon–Sat 6–7 daily; 30min).

ACCOMODATION AND EATING

Kyles Flodda Kyles Flodda (Caolas Fhlodaigh) ☎ 01870 603145, ⊛ kylesflodda.com. Secluded, picturesque, beautifully converted Victorian B&B halfway down the dead-end road in the northeast corner of the island. Free wi-fi. £80

Nunton House Hostel Nunton ☎ 01870 602017, ⊛ nuntonhousehostel.com. Four small dorm rooms in the former clan chief's house, where Bonnie Prince Charlie dressed up in drag before his escape over the sea to Skye. Free wi-fi and a free terminal. £20/person

Shell Bay campsite Liniclate (Lionacleit) ☎ 01870

602447. Flat grassy field right next to the main school (and museum) on Benbecula – facilities are good (including laundry) though it's not the most romantic of spots. April–Oct. £21/pitch

Stepping Stone Balivanich (Baile a Mhanaich) ☎ 01870 603377, ⊛ steppingstone10.tripod.com. A modern café-restaurant that serves chips with everything during the day (mains £7–8), and more varied dishes in the evening, such as local scallops and lamb burgers (mains £14–17). Mon–Fri 9am–9pm, Sat 11am–9pm, Sun noon–9pm.

South Uist (Uibhist a Deas)

To the south of Benbecula, the island of **South Uist** is the largest and most varied of the southern chain of islands. The west coast boasts some of the region's finest machair and beaches – a necklace of gold and grey sand strung twenty miles from one end to the other – while the east coast features a ridge of high mountains rising to 2034ft at the summit of Beinn Mhòr. The Reformation never took a strong hold in South Uist (or Barra), and the island remains Roman Catholic, as is evident from the various roadside shrines. The only blot on South Uist's landscape is the old Royal Artillery missile range, which dominates the northwest corner of the island. Whatever you do, however, don't make the mistake of simply driving down the main A865 road, which runs down the centre of the island like a backbone.

The north

The northern half of the island contains the best of the mountains and the beaches. To climb the mountains in the east, you need a detailed 1:25,000 Explorer map, in order to negotiate the island's maze of lochans; to reach the beaches (or even see them), you have to get off the main road and pass through the old crofters' villages that straggle along the west coast.

One of the best places to gain access to the sandy shoreline is at **HOWMORE** (Tobha Mòr), a pretty little crofting settlement with a fair number of restored houses, many still thatched, including one distinctively roofed in brown heather. It's an easy walk from the village church across the flower-strewn machair to the gorgeous beach. In among the crofts are the shattered, lichen-encrusted remains of no fewer than four medieval churches and chapels, and a burial ground now harbouring just a few scattered graves. The sixteenth-century **Clanranald Stone**, carved with the arms of the clan who ruled over South Uist from 1370 until 1839, used to lie here, but is now displayed in the nearby Kildonan Museum (see below).

ACCOMMODATION   THE NORTH

Howmore (Tobha Mòr) SYHA hostel Howmore (Tobha Mòr) ⓦ gatliff.org.uk. Simple Gatliff Trust hostel occupying a lovely thatched crofthouse near the village church, and just a short walk from the beach. **£10**/person
Kinloch Grogarry (Groigearraidh) ☎ 01870 620316, ⓦ kinlochuist.com. A fine, modern B&B sheltered by a little patch of woodland and overlooking freshwater Loch Druidibeg – run by a very keen angler, who will do evening

meals on request. **£90**
Orasay Inn Lochcarnan (Loch a' Charnain) ☎ 01870 610298, ⓦ orasayinn.co.uk. A modern purpose-built hotel off the main road; rooms are pretty standard, but the location is peaceful and the food is good – if you're coming to eat in the restaurant, book ahead. Daily noon–2.30pm & 6–8.30pm. **£85**

Lochboisdale (Loch Baghasdail) and around

LOCHBOISDALE occupies a narrow, bumpy promontory on the east coast, but, despite being South Uist's chief settlement and ferry port, has only very limited facilities. If you're arriving here late at night on the boat from Oban (or from Barra or Tiree), you should try to book accommodation in advance; otherwise, head for the tourist office.

Kildonan Museum (Taigh-tasgaidh Chill Donnain)

5 miles north of Lochboisdale • April–Oct daily 10am–5pm • £2 • ☎ 01878 710343, ⓦ kildonanmuseum.co.uk

At the **Kildonan Museum** (Taigh-tasgaidh Chill Donnain) you'll find mock-ups of Hebridean kitchens through the ages, two lovely box beds and an impressive selection of old photos, accompanied by an unsentimental yet poetic text on crofting life in the last two centuries. Pride of place goes to the sixteenth-century **Clanranald Stone**, carved with the arms of the clan who ruled over South Uist from 1370 to 1839. The museum café serves sandwiches and home-made cakes, and has a choice of historical videos for those really wet and windy days. A little south of the museum, the road passes a cairn that sits among the foundations of **Flora MacDonald**'s childhood home (see box, p.414); she was born nearby, but the house no longer stands.

ARRIVAL AND INFORMATION   LOCHBOISDALE AND AROUND

By ferry There's a ferry to and from Oban (Tues, Thurs, Sat & Sun; 5hr 20min–6hr 30min), which goes via Tiree on Thurs and links with Castlebay on Barra.
By bus There's a regular bus service along the spine road (as they call it) to North Uist (Mon–Sat only). Destinations Balivanich (Mon–Sat 2–5 daily; 1hr);

Berneray (Mon–Sat 1 daily; 2hr 50min); Eriskay (Mon–Sat 4–6 daily; 40min); Lochmaddy (Mon–Sat 1–2 daily; 1hr 30min).
Tourist office Pier Rd (Easter–Oct Mon–Sat 9am–5pm; also open for an hour to meet the ferry; ☎ 01878 700286).

ACCOMMODATION AND EATING

Heron Point Lochboisdale ☎ 01878 700073, ⓦ heron point.co.uk. This is a really tastefully furnished B&B, very efficiently run by an extremely friendly host, and just a mile up the road from the Lochboisdale ferry terminal. **£70**
Lochboisdale Hotel Lochboisdale ☎ 01878 700332, ⓦ lochboisdale.com. The town's long-established hotel is a convenient place to shelter if you're waiting for a ferry and it does decent bar meals, occasionally featuring local seafood. **£80**
Polochar Inn Polochar (Poll a' Charra) ☎ 01878 700215, ⓦ polocharinn.com. One of the best places to

hole up in, right on the south coast overlooking the Sound of Barra, and with its own sandy beach close by; the rooms all have sea views, and on the ground floor is a genuine pub, serving decent bar meals. Mon–Thurs 11am–11pm, Fri & Sat 11am–1am, Sun 12.30–11pm; food served 12.30–2.30pm & 5.30–9pm. **£70**
Uist Bunkhouse Daliburgh (Dalabrog) ☎ 01878 700566, ⓦ uistbunkhouse.co.uk. Clean and modern hostel three miles from the Lochboisdale ferry terminal, offering plain, simple en-suite singles, doubles and family rooms as well as dorms with bunks. **£15**/person

> **SS POLITICIAN**
>
> Eriskay's greatest claim to fame came in 1941 when the **SS Politician** or "Polly" as it's fondly known, sank on its way from Liverpool to Jamaica, along with its cargo of bicycle parts, £3 million in Jamaican currency and 264,000 bottles of whisky, inspiring *Whisky Galore*, Compton MacKenzie's book, and the Ealing comedy (filmed on Barra in 1948 and released as *Tight Little Island* in the US). The real story was somewhat less romantic, especially for the 36 islanders who were charged with illegal possession by the Customs and Excise officers, 19 of whom were found guilty and imprisoned in Inverness. The ship's stern can still be seen at low tide northwest of Calvay Island in the Sound of Eriskay, and one of the original bottles (and other memorabilia) can be viewed at *Am Politician* (see below).

Eriskay (Eiriosgaigh)

Famous for its patterned jerseys and a peculiar breed of pony, originally used for carrying peat and seaweed, the barren, hilly island of **Eriskay** has been connected by a causeway to the south of South Uist since 2001. The island, which measures just over two miles by one, and shelters a small fishing community of about 150, makes an easy day-trip from South Uist.

For a small island, Eriskay has had more than its fair share of historical headlines. The island's main beach on the west coast, Coilleag a Phrionnsa (Prince's Cockle Strand), was where **Bonnie Prince Charlie** landed on Scottish soil on July 23, 1745 – the sea bindweed that grows here to this day is said to have sprung from the seeds Charles brought with him from France. The prince, as yet unaccustomed to hardship, spent his first night in a local blackhouse and ate a couple of flounders, though he apparently couldn't take the peat smoke and chose to sleep sitting up rather than endure the damp bed.

St Michael's Church

Near the causeway

Built in 1903, in a vaguely Spanish style on raised ground in the northwest corner of the island, by the causeway, is the Roman Catholic **St Michael's Church**. Its most striking features are the bell, which sits outside the church and comes from the World War I battle cruiser *Derfflinger*, the last of the scuttled German fleet to be salvaged from Scapa Flow (see p.345), and the altar, which is made from the bow of a lifeboat.

Ben Sciathan

The walk (2hr return from the causeway) up to the island's highest point, **Ben Sciathan** (607ft), is well worth the effort on a clear day, as you can see the whole island, plus Barra, South Uist, and across the sea to Skye, Rùm, Coll and Tiree. On the way up or down, look out for the diminutive Eriskay ponies, which roam free on the hills but tend to graze around Loch Crakavaig, the island's freshwater source.

ARRIVAL AND DEPARTURE ERISKAY

By ferry CalMac runs a small car ferry between Barra (4–5 daily; 40min) and Ardmhor (Àird Mhòr), on the southwest coast of Eriskay.

By bus There's a regular bus between Eriskay and Lochboisdale (Mon–Sat 4–6 daily; 40min).

ACCOMMODATION AND EATING

Am Politician Rubha Ban ☎01878 720246. The island's purpose-built pub, near the two cemeteries on the west coast, offers an extensive bar menu, as well as home-made cakes and coffee, and great views out to sea from its conservatory. Easter–Oct Mon–Sat 11am–11pm (sometimes later), Sun noon–11pm; Oct–Easter open some weekends 11am–11pm; food served noon–7.45pm.

Oir na Mara ☎01878 720216. This plain, modern bungalow B&B is better inside than out. It's situated near Eriskay's pub, around a 15min walk from the Barra–Eriskay ferry terminal. Free wi-fi. **£80**

Barra (Barraigh)

Just four miles wide and eight miles long, **Barra** is like the Western Isles in miniature: sandy beaches, backed by machair, mountains of Lewisian gneiss, prehistoric ruins, Gaelic culture and a laidback, welcoming Catholic population of around 1200. Like some feudal island state, it was ruled over for centuries, with relative benevolence, by the MacNeils. Unfortunately, the family sold the island in 1838 to Colonel Gordon of Cluny, who had also bought Benbecula, South Uist and Eriskay. The colonel deemed the starving crofters "redundant", and offered to turn Barra into a state penal colony. The government declined, so the colonel called in the police and proceeded with some of the cruellest forced Clearances in the Hebrides. In 1937, the 45th chief of the MacNeil clan bought back most of the island, and in 2003 gifted the estate to the Scottish government.

Castlebay (Bàgh a Chaisteil)

The only settlement of any size on Barra is **CASTLEBAY** (Bàgh a Chaisteil), which curves around the barren, rocky hills of a beautiful wide bay on the south side of the island. It's difficult to imagine it now, but Castlebay was a herring port of some significance in the nineteenth century, with up to four hundred boats in the harbour and curing and packing factories ashore. Barra's religious allegiance is immediately announced by the large Catholic church, Our Lady, Star of the Sea, which overlooks the bay; to underline the point, there's a Madonna and Child statue on the slopes of **Sheabhal** (1260ft), the largest peak on Barra, and a fairly easy hike from the bay.

Kisimul Castle

April–Sept daily 9.30am–noon & 1.30–4.30pm • £5.50; HS • ☎ 01871 810313 • Access by ferry (every 30min), weather permitting

As its name suggests, Castlebay has a castle in its bay, the picturesque medieval islet-fortress of Caisteal Chiosmuil, or **Kisimul Castle**, ancestral home of the MacNeil clan. The castle burnt down in the eighteenth century, but when the 45th MacNeil chief – conveniently enough, a wealthy American and trained architect – bought the island back in 1937, he set about restoring the castle. There's nothing much to see inside, but the whole experience is fun – head down to the slipway at the bottom of Main Street, where the ferryman will take you over.

Dualchas

The Square • March, April & Sept Mon, Wed & Fri 10.30am–4.30pm; May–Aug Mon–Sat same hours • £2 • ⓦ barraheritage.com

The Barra Heritage Centre, known as **Dualchas**, is on the road that leads west out of town. It's an unpretentious little museum, housing the odd treasure like the monstrance from St Barr's Church in Northbay. There are lots of old newspapers, photo archives and local memoirs to trawl through; the museum also has a handy **café** serving soup, toasties and cakes.

The north

If you head to the north end of the island from Castlebay, you have a choice of taking the west- or east-coast road. The west-coast road takes you past the island's finest sandy beaches, particularly those at **Halaman Bay** and near the village of Allasdale (Allathasdal). The east-coast road winds its way in and out of various rocky bays, one of which, **Northbay** (Bàgh a Tuath), shelters a small fishing fleet and a little island sporting a statue of St Barr, better known as Finbarr, the island's Irish patron saint.

Cockle Strand

At the north end of the island, Barra is squeezed between two sandy bays: the dune-backed west side takes the full force of the Atlantic breakers, while the east side boasts the crunchy shell sands of Tràigh Mhòr, better known as **Cockle Strand**. The beach is also used as the island's **airport**, with planes landing and taking off according to the tides, since at high tide the beach (and therefore the runway) is covered in water. As its name suggests, the strand is also famous for its cockles and cockleshells, the latter being used to make harling (the rendering used on most Scottish houses).

Eòlaigearraidh (Eoligarry)

To the north of the airport is the scattered settlement of **EOLIGARRY** (Eòlaigearraidh), which boasts several sheltered sandy bays. Here, too, is **St Barr's Church** (Cille-Bharra), burial ground of the MacNeils (and the author Compton MacKenzie). The ground lies beside the ruins of a medieval church and two chapels, one of which has been reroofed to provide shelter for several carved medieval gravestones and a replica of an eleventh-century rune-inscribed cross, the original of which is in the National Museum of Scotland in Edinburgh.

6

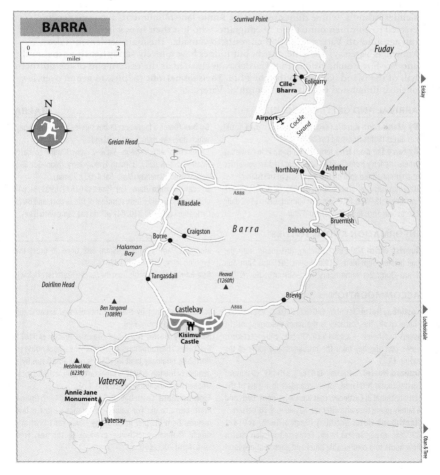

BARRA

0 ————— 2
miles

N

Scurrival Point

Fuday

Cille-
Bharra   Eoligarry

Airport   Cockle
            Strand

Greian Head

Enilay

Northbay   Ardmhor

A888

Allasdale

Bruernish

Borve   Craigston   *Barra*   Bolnabodach

Halaman
Bay

Doirlinn Head   Tangasdail   Heaval
                                 (1260ft)

Ben Tangaval   Castlebay   A888   Brevig
(1089ft)
                 Kisimul
                 Castle

Lochboisdale

Heishival Mòr
(623ft)   Vatersay

Annie Jane
Monument

Vatersay

Oban & Tiree

6

BOAT TO MINGULAY

Several of the Bishop's Isles to the south of Vatersay were inhabited until just before World War II. The largest of the islands is **Mingulay** (Miùghlaigh), which once had a population of 160 and with its large sea-bird colonies, spectacular sea cliffs and stacks, is often compared to St Kilda (see p.310). The crofters of Mingulay began a series of land raids on Vatersay from 1906 and by 1912 the island had been abandoned, with none of the publicity later given to St Kilda. The most southerly of the Western Isles is Berneray (Bearnaraigh) – not to be confused with the Berneray north of North Uist – best known for its lighthouse, **Barra Head**, which stands on cliffs over 620ft high. For details of boat trips to the island, phone Donald (☎01871 890384, 🌐barrafishingcharters.com) or contact the tourist office.

Vatersay (Bhatarsaigh)

To the south of Barra is the island of **Vatersay** (Bhatarsaigh), shaped rather like an apple core, and since 1991 linked to its neighbour by a causeway – a mile or so southwest of Castlebay. The island is divided into two peninsulas connected by a slender isthmus, whose dunes feature the **Annie Jane Monument**, a granite needle erected to commemorate the 350 emigrants who lost their lives when the *Annie Jane* ran aground off Vatersay in 1853 en route to Canada. The main settlement (also known as Vatersay) has little charm, but it does have a lovely **sandy beach** to the south; another fine beach, visible from Castlebay, is situated at the eastern end of the northern half of the island. Climb up the chief hill, **Theiseabhal Mòr** (623ft), to get an overview of the uninhabited islands to the south of Vatersay.

ARRIVAL AND GETTING AROUND　　　　　　　　　　　　　　　　　BARRA

By plane Barra Airport (☎01871 890212, 🌐hial.oc.uk) has direct flights from and to Glasgow.

By ferry The main ferry terminal on Barra is in Castlebay where the ferry from Oban arrives: from Eriskay, you arrive at an uninhabited spot on the northeast of the island. Destinations Coll (Thurs; 4hr); Eriskay (5 daily; 40min); Lochboisdale (Wed, Fri & Sun; 1hr 40min); Oban (1–2 daily except Sat; 5hr); Tiree (Thurs; 2hr 45min).

By bus There's a fairly decent bus service out of Castlebay, which does the rounds of the island. Destinations Airport (Mon–Sat 4–7 daily; 30min); Eoligarry (Mon–Sat 3–6 daily; 35min); Eriskay ferry (Mon–Sat 3–5 daily; 25min); Vatersay (Mon–Sat 4 daily; 20min)

By car or bike Barra Car Hire (☎01871 890313) will deliver cars to either ferry terminal or the airport, and Barra Cycle Hire (☎01871 810284) will do the same with bikes.

INFORMATION AND ACTIVITIES

Tourist office Main St, Castlebay, just round from the pier (Easter–Sept Mon–Fri 9am–6pm, Sat 9am–5pm, Sun 11am–3pm; Oct same hours Mon–Sat only; Nov & Dec Mon–Sat 9am–1pm & 2–5pm; also open to greet the evening ferry; ☎01871 810336).

Sea-kayaking Available from the *Dunard Hostel* (see below).

ACCOMMODATION

Castlebay Hotel Castlebay ☎01871 810223, 🌐castlebay -hotel.co.uk. The *Castlebay* is the more welcoming of the town's two hotels – a solid Victorian pile, with spectacular views over the bay from the restaurant and some of the rooms. **£105**

Dunard Hostel Castlebay ☎01871 810443, 🌐dunard hostel.co.uk. A relaxed, family-run place just west of the ferry terminal in Castlebay, that has twins, dorm beds and a family room; they also offer sea-kayaking. **£18**/person

Heathbank Hotel Northbay (Bagh a Tuath) ☎01871 890266, 🌐barrahotel.co.uk. Converted mission church now home to a comfortable hotel and unpretentious local

watering hole run by the very friendly and experienced local MacLeod family. **£96**

Northbay House Northbay (Bagh a Tuath) ☎01871 890266, 🌐barraholidays.co.uk. The old school house in Northbay, originally built in 1888, is now a B&B run by a genuinely friendly couple – breakfast menu includes local smoked haddock and poached egg. **£76**

Tigh-na-Mara Castlebay ☎01871 810304, 🌐tighna mara-barra.co.uk. For value and location – just a few minutes from the pier in Castlebay – you can't beat this simple Victorian guesthouse overlooking the sea. Free wi-fi. April–Oct. **£60**

CAMPING

Croft 183 Buaile nam Bodach (Bolnabodach) ☎ 01871 810846, ⓦ croft183.com. A well-equipped campsite on the rocky, eastern side of the island, with kitchen and laundry facilities, plus a small hostel. Free wi-fi. Hostel __£16__/person; doubles __£30__; camping __£12__/pitch

Scurrival campsite 3 Eoligarry (Eòlaigearraidh) ☎ 01871 890292. Very convenient for the Eriskay ferry, this is a lovely, simple site with showers and toilet facilities, overlooking the sea and close to the wide sandy beach of Scurrival (Tràigh Sgurabhal). April–Oct. __£5__/person

EATING AND DRINKING

★ **Café Kisimul** Main St ☎ 01871 810645, ⓦ cafe kisimul.co.uk. As well as offering Italian comfort food and playing great music, the *Kisimul* also cooks up the best curry in northwest Scotland (mains £12–15) – try the unique, local scallop pakora and make sure you book ahead. Daily morning until late.

Castlebay Hotel Castlebay ☎ 01871 810223, ⓦ castlebay -hotel.co.uk. The *Castlebay* has a cosy bar, which regularly has cockles, crabs and scallops on its menu (mains £12–16), and good views out over the bay. Daily noon–2pm & 6–9pm.

ENTERTAINMENT AND SPORT

Films are occasionally shown on Saturday evenings at the **local school** – look out for the posters – where there is also a **swimming pool** (Tues–Sun), **library** and **sports centre**, all of which are open to the general public.

Orkney

STROMNESS

Orkney

Orkney is a captivating and fiercely independent archipelago made up of seventy or so mostly low-lying islands, with a population of around twenty thousand. The locals tend to refer to themselves first as Orcadians, regarding Scotland as a separate entity, and proudly flying their own flag. For an Orcadian, the Mainland invariably means the largest island in Orkney rather than the rest of Scotland, and throughout their distinctive history the islands have been linked to lands much further afield, principally Scandinavia.

7

The islands offer excellent coastal **walking**, abundant birdlife and beautiful white-sand beaches. It has two chief settlements: **Stromness**, an attractive old fishing town on the far southwestern shore, and the capital, **Kirkwall**, at the dividing point between East and West Mainland. The Mainland is relatively heavily populated and farmed throughout, its green fields dotted with sandstone farmhouses. To the southeast, it's joined by causeways to a string of islands, the largest of which is **South Ronaldsay**. The island of **Hoy**, the second largest in the archipelago, south of Mainland, presents a superbly dramatic landscape, with some of the highest sea cliffs in the country. Hoy, however, is atypical: Orkney's smaller, much quieter **northern islands** are low-lying, fertile outcrops of rock and sand, scattered across the ocean.

Brief history

Small communities began to settle in the islands by 4000 BC; **Skara Brae** on the Mainland is one of the best-preserved Stone Age settlements in Europe. Elsewhere the islands are scattered with chambered tombs and stone circles, proof of the well-developed religious and ceremonial practices taking place here from around 2000 BC. More sophisticated **Iron Age** inhabitants built fortified villages incorporating stone towers known as brochs, the finest of which is the **Broch of Gurness**. Later, **Pictish** culture spread to Orkney and the remains of several early Christian settlements can be seen, the best at the **Brough of Birsay**. Around the ninth century, settlers from Scandinavia arrived and the islands became **Norse** earldoms, forming outposts of a powerful, expansive culture. The last of the Norse earls was killed in 1231, but their lasting legacy was not only their language but also Kirkwall's great medieval **St Magnus Cathedral**.

Sea trading and whaling

After Norse rule, the islands became the preserve of **Scottish earls**, who exploited and abused the islanders, although a steady increase in sea trade did offer some chance of escape. French and Spanish ships sheltered here in the sixteenth century, and the ships of the **Hudson's Bay Company** recruited hundreds of Orcadians to work in the Canadian fur trade. The islands were also an important staging-post in the **whaling industry** and the herring boom, which drew great numbers of Dutch, French and Scottish boats. The choice of **Scapa Flow**, Orkney's natural harbour, as the Royal Navy's

Orkney festivals p.333	**The Churchill Barriers** p.347
Kitchener Memorial p.340	**North Ronaldsay sheep** p.367
Scapa Flow p.345	

ST MAGNUS CATHEDRAL, KIRKWALL

Highlights

❶ Maes Howe Orkney's – and Europe's – finest Neolithic chambered tomb. **See p.337**

❷ Skara Brae Mesmerizing Neolithic homes, crammed with domestic detail. **See p.338**

❸ St Magnus Cathedral, Kirkwall Beautiful red-sandstone cathedral built by the Vikings. **See p.343**

❹ Tomb of the Eagles Privately owned Neolithic site on South Ronaldsay where you slide in on a trolley to view inside. **See p.348**

❺ Rackwick Experience splendid isolation, rumbling rocky beach and the famous Old Man of Hoy. **See p.350**

❻ Scapa Flow Visitor Centre Learn about the wartime history of Orkney's great natural harbour and the scuttling of the German Fleet. See p.352

❼ Westray Thriving Orkney island with sea-bird colonies, sandy beaches and a ruined castle. See p.357

❽ North Ronaldsay Orkney's northernmost island features a bird observatory, seaweed-eating sheep and Britain's tallest land-based lighthouse. **See p.366**

HIGHLIGHTS ARE MARKED ON THE MAP ON P.332

main base brought plenty of money and activity during both world wars, and left the clifftops dotted with gun emplacements and the sea bed scattered with wrecks – which today make for wonderful diving opportunities.

The oil boom

After the war, things quietened down, although since the mid-1970s the large **oil terminal** on the island of Flotta, the establishment of the Orkney Islands Council (OIC), combined with EU development grants, have brought surprise windfalls, stemming the exodus of young people. Meanwhile, many disenchanted southerners

ORKNEY

0 ——————— 10
miles

N

Mull Head

Papa Westray

North Ronaldsay ⑧

Noup Head
Pierowall

Westray ⑦

Rapness

Sanday

Kettletoft

Rousay

Eday

Egilsay

Wyre

Whitehall

Stronsay

Brough Head
Birsay

Evie

Tingwall

Lamb Head

Dounby

Mainland

Auskerry

Skara Brae ②

Balfour

Shapinsay

Wide Firth

Maes Howe ① Finstown

Kirkwall ③

Stromness

Mull Head

Graemsay
Hoy

Houton Orphir

Copinsay

Old Man of Hoy

Ward Hill (1577ft) ▲

Scapa Flow

St Mary's

Rackwick ⑤

Hoy

Lyness ⑥

Flotta

Churchill Barriers

Burray

Scrabster

Longhope

St Margaret's Hope

South Ronaldsay

Swona

Burwick Tomb ④ of the Eagles Brough Ness

Pentland Firth

Dunnet Head

Stroma

Gill's Bay John O'Groats

Pentland Skerries

Thurso

Duncansby Head
Wick

Aberdeen

Lerwick

HIGHLIGHTS

① Maes Howe
② Skara Brae
③ St Magnus Cathedral, Kirkwall
④ Tomb of the Eagles
⑤ Rackwick
⑥ Scapa Flow Visitor Centre
⑦ Westray
⑧ North Ronaldsay

ORKNEY FESTIVALS

Kirkwall's chief cultural bash is the week-long **St Magnus Festival** (Ⓦstmagnusfestival.com), a superb arts festival held in the middle of June, with some events in Stromness. July is peppered with several Island regattas and agricultural shows, culminating in the agricultural **County Show** held in Kirkwall in the middle of August.

To find out **what's on** (and the weather forecast), tune in to Radio Orkney on 93.7FM, buy yourself a copy of *The Orcadian*, which comes out on Thursdays, or log on to Ⓦorkneynews today.co.uk.

have become "ferryloupers" (incomers), moving to Orkney in search of peace and the apparent simplicity of island life.

ARRIVAL AND DEPARTURE

By plane Ⓦhial.co.uk. Flybe (Ⓣ0871 700 2000, Ⓦflybe .com) operate direct flights to Kirkwall from Inverness, Aberdeen, Edinburgh, Glasgow and Sumburgh in Shetland. Be warned: weather conditions are notoriously changeable, making flights prone to delay and even cancellation.

By ferry Northlink runs car ferries daily from Scrabster (with a shuttle bus from Thurso) to Stromness and less

frequently from Aberdeen and Lerwick (in Shetland) to Kirkwall; Pentland Ferries runs car ferries from Gills Bay (near John O'Groats) to St Margaret's Hope; and John O'Groats Ferries runs a small passenger ferry to Burwick. The timetables in the text are summer frequencies – check the internet for the latest sailing schedule and always book ahead.

GETTING AROUND AND TOURS

By plane Ⓣ01856 872494, Ⓦloganair.co.uk. Loganair run flights from Kirkwall to most of the outer isles, using an eight-seater plane, with discounted fares to North Ronaldsay and Papa Westray and between the islands, if you stay over.

By ferry Ⓣ01856 872044, Ⓦorkneyferries.co.uk. Getting to the other islands by ferry from the Mainland isn't difficult, but travel between individual islands isn't straightforward. However, a careful study of timetables may reduce the need to travel via Kirkwall. It's worth enquiring from Orkney Ferries about its additional Sunday sailings in summer, which often make useful interisland connections. Be warned, ticket prices on Orkney Ferries are expensive, and it's essential to book your passage in advance if you're taking a vehicle.

By bus Ⓦorkney.gov.uk. The bus service on Orkney

Mainland is pretty good during the week, but skeletal on Sundays – a free timetable is available from the tourist office. Except in Stromness and Kirkwall, there are no scheduled bus stops so just stand at a safe, visible spot and flag the bus down. On the smaller islands, a minibus usually meets the ferry and will take you to your destination.

By bike Cycling is an option if the weather holds, since there are few steep hills and distances are modest, though the wind can make it hard going.

Tours There's a whole range of escorted tours around the Mainland, which are great for those without a vehicle. Wildabout Orkney (Ⓣ01856 877737, Ⓦwildaboutorkney .com) offer a variety of tours of the Mainland, with departures from Stromness and Kirkwall, and there are several other companies specializing in particular islands and mentioned in the relevant text.

Stromness

STROMNESS is a quite enchanting port at which to arrive by boat, its picturesque waterfront a procession of tiny sandstone jetties and slate roofs nestling below the green hill of Brinkies Brae. It's well worth spending a day exploring, or using as a base in preference to Kirkwall. Its natural sheltered harbour (known as Hamnavoe) was probably used in Viking times, but the town itself only really took off in the eighteenth century when the **Hudson's Bay Company** made Stromness its main base from which to make the long journey across the North Atlantic. Crews from Stromness were also hired for herring and whaling expeditions – and press-ganged into the Royal Navy.

By 1842, the town boasted forty or so pubs, and reports circulated of "outrageous and turbulent proceedings of seamen and others who frequent the harbour". The **herring boom** brought large numbers of small boats, along with thousands of young

STROMNESS

N

0	200
	yards

Hoy, Graemsay & Scrabster ▼

women who gutted, pickled and packed the fish in barrels. Things got so rowdy by World War I that the town voted in a referendum to ban the sale of alcohol, leaving Stromness dry from 1920 until 1947. Nowadays, Stromness is very quiet, though it remains an important fishing port and **ferry terminal** and is the focus of the popular four-day **Orkney Folk Festival**, held at the end of May.

Unlike Kirkwall, the old town of Stromness still hugs the shoreline, its one and only street a narrow winding affair, paved with great flagstones and fed by a tight network of alleyways or closes. The central section, which begins at the imposing sandstone *Stromness Hotel*, is known as **Victoria Street**, though in fact it takes on several other names as it threads its way southwards. On the east side of the street the houses are gable-end-on to the waterfront, and originally each one would have had its own pier, from which merchants would trade with passing ships.

Pier Arts Centre

Victoria St • Tues–Sat 10.30am–5pm • Free • ☎ 01856 850209, ⓦ pierartscentre.com

A warehouse on one of the old jetties forms half of the **Pier Arts Centre**; the other half is a modern glass-and-steel structure which offers views of the harbour. The gallery has a remarkable permanent collection of twentieth-century British art, most notably by members of the Cornish school such as Barbara Hepworth, Ben Nicholson, Terry Frost, Patrick Heron, Eduardo Paolozzi and the self-taught Alfred Wallis, recently augmented by contemporary works, many by northern and Scandinavian artists, which continue the marine themes of the original collection.

Stromness Museum

52 Alfred St • April–Sept daily 10am–5pm; Oct–March Mon–Sat 11am–3.30pm • £4.50 • ☎ 01856 850025, ⓦ orkneycommunities.co.uk /stromnessmuseum

At the junction of Alfred Street and South End stands the **Stromness Museum**, built in 1858, partly to house the collections of the local natural-history society. The natural-history collection is still here – don't miss the pull-out drawers of birds' eggs, butterflies and moths. Look out for the Halkett cloth boat, an early inflatable like the one used by John Rae, the Stromness-born Arctic explorer, whose fiddle, octant and shotgun are also on display. Amid the beaver furs and model boats are numerous salty artefacts gathered from shipwrecks, including some barnacle-encrusted crockery from the German High Seas Fleet that was sunk in Scapa Flow in 1919.

7

Ness Battery

Guided hour-long tours all year, see website for details • £4.50 • ☎ 07759 857298, ⓦ nessbattery.co.uk

Just a short walk south of Stromness is **Ness Battery**, erected in World War I to guard the western entrance to Scapa Flow, and one of the most interesting of Orkney's coastal gun emplacements. On the tour you hear stories of the lives of the soldiers who manned the six-inch guns, and see several of the original wooden huts, one of which served as the Mess Hall and retains the idiosyncratic wartime murals painted there during World War II.

ARRIVAL AND DEPARTURE   STROMNESS

By ferry ☎ 0845 600 0449, ⓦ northlinkferries.co.uk. Car ferries arrive in the centre of Stromness from Scrabster (2–3 daily; 1hr 30min), which is connected to nearby Thurso by shuttle bus. The tiny passenger ferry to Moaness Pier on Hoy (via Graemsay) departs from the old harbour in Stromness (Mon–Fri 4–5 daily, Sat & Sun 2 daily; 25min).

By bus ☎ 01856 870555, ⓦ stagecoachbus.com. Buses depart from Stromness ferry terminal.
Destinations Houton (Mon–Fri 2 daily; 20min); Kirkwall (Mon–Sat hourly, Sun every 2hr; 30min); Skara Brae (Mon, Thurs & Sat 1 daily; 20min); St Margaret's Hope (10 daily; 1hr 5min).

INFORMATION AND ACTIVITIES

Tourist office Stromness ferry terminal houses the tourist office (March–Oct daily; ☎ 01856 850716, ⓦ visitorkney .com).

Orkney Cycle Hire 54 Dundas St ☎ 01856 850255, ⓦ orkney cyclehire.co.uk. Hybrids and mountain bikes from just £7.50 a day – panniers available and delivery/collection.

ACCOMMODATION

Brinkies Guest House Innertown ☎ 01856 850661. A substantial double-bay-fronted Victorian guesthouse located a 10min walk up from the town. Rooms enjoy fantastic views, the residents' lounge has loads of reading matter and there's free wi-fi. **£70**

Brown's 47 Victoria St ☎ 01856 850661, ⓦ brownshostel .co.uk. A family-run place, right in the centre of town, with bunk beds in very small, shared rooms – it's pretty clean, Mrs Brown is friendly and there's free internet access. **£18**/person

Burnside Farm ☎ 01856 850723, ⓦ burnside-farm

.com. A cracking B&B run by a local couple on a working farm about a mile out of town on the road to Kirkwall. The views are great, and the furnishings and facilities are truly top-notch: en-suite wet rooms and free wi-fi, plus bere bannocks for breakfast. **£70**

Hamnavoe Hostel 10a North End Rd ☎ 01856 851202, ⓦ hamnavoehostel.co.uk. A good 10min walk from the ferry terminal and no beauty from the outside, but inside it's all spotlessly clean, welcoming and well equipped. **£17**/person

Miller's House 13 John St ☏ 01856 851969, ⊚ millers houseorkney.com. Modern pine furnishings predominate in this B&B, housed in the town's oldest property (and a nearby annexe) in the heart of Stromness – great home-cooking, too. **£65**

Point of Ness Campsite ☏ 01856 873535. Busy camp-site in a superb (though extremely exposed) setting a mile south of the ferry terminal at Point of Ness, with great views over to Hoy; facilities include a TV lounge and a washing machine. May to mid-Sept. **£7**/pitch

EATING AND DRINKING

Ferry Inn 10 John St ☏ 01856 850280, ⊚ ferryinn.com. Situated opposite the ferry terminal, this is the most popular and welcoming pub in town, serving up classic pub grub as well as local scallops, Grimbister cheese and spicy Orkney crab cakes, all for under £10. Daily 9am–midnight; food served until 9.30pm.

Hamnavoe Restaurant 35 Graham Place ☏ 01856 850606. Offers the town's most ambitious cooking, concen-trating on local produce, such as grilled sole or peppered

monkfish – main courses start at around £15 and booking is essential. May–Sept Tues–Sun only.

Julia's Café and Bistro 20 Ferry Rd ☏ 01856 850904. Daytime café right opposite the ferry terminal, with a sunny conservatory and tables outside if the weather's good enough. It's comfort food for the most part, but you can get a decent fish pie, all for under £10. Mon–Sat 9am–5pm, Sun 10am–5pm.

West Mainland

The great bulk of the **West Mainland** – west of Kirkwall, that is – is fertile farmland, fenced off into a patchwork of fields used either to produce crops or for cattle-grazing. Fringed by a spectacular western coastline, West Mainland is littered with some of the island's most impressive prehistoric sites, such as the village of **Skara Brae**, the standing **Stones of Stenness**, the chambered tomb of **Maes Howe** and the **Broch of Gurness**, as well as one of Orkney's best-preserved medieval castles at **Birsay**. Despite the intensive farming, some areas are too barren to cultivate, and the high ground and wild coastline include several interesting **wildlife reserves**.

Stenness

The parish of **Stenness**, northeast of Stromness along the main road to Kirkwall, slopes down from Ward Hill (881ft) to the lochs of Stenness and Harray; the first is tidal, the second is a freshwater trout loch. The two lochs are joined by a short causeway that may well have been a narrow isthmus around 3000 BC, when it stood at the heart of Orkney's most important Neolithic ceremonial complex, centred on the burial chamber of **Maes Howe**.

Stones of Stenness

Guided tours June–Aug Mon, Wed & Fri 10am • Free; HS • ☏ 01856 841732

The most visible part of the complex between lochs Stenness and Harray is the **Stones of Stenness**, originally a circle of twelve rock slabs, now just four, the tallest of which is a real monster at over 16ft, and remarkably slender. A broken table-top lies within the circle, surrounded by a much-diminished henge (a circular bank of earth and a ditch) with a couple of entrances.

Ring of Brodgar

Guided tours June–Aug daily 1pm • Free; HS • ☏ 01856 841732

Less than a mile to the northwest of the Stones of Stenness, past the huge **Watch Stone** which stands beside the road, at over 18ft in height, the **Ring of Brodgar** is a much wider circle dramatically sited on raised ground. There were originally sixty stones, 27 of which now stand; of the henge, only the ditch survives. At the height of summer, it's best to go early (or late), so as to avoid the coach parties – or arrive in time for one of the guided tours.

Maes Howe

April–Sept daily 9.30am–5pm, June–Aug until 8pm; Oct–March Mon–Sat 9.45am–4.30pm • £5.50; HS • ☎ 01856 761606

Several large burial mounds are visible to the south of the Ring of Brodgar, but these are eclipsed by one of Europe's most impressive Neolithic burial chambers, **Maes Howe**, less than a mile northeast of the Stones of Stenness. Dating from 3000 BC, its excellent state of preservation is partly due to its construction from massive slabs of sandstone weighing up to thirty tonnes. Visitors must first buy a **timed ticket** for a guided tour, in advance or direct from Tormiston Mill by the main road, which houses the **ticket office**, toilets and interpretive display.

You enter the **central chamber** of Maes Howe down a low, long passage, one wall of which consists of a single immense stone. Once inside, you can stand upright and admire the superb masonry of the lofty corbelled roof. Remarkably, the tomb is aligned so that the rays of the winter solstice sun hit the top of the Barnhouse Stone, half a mile away, and reach right down the passage of Maes Howe to the ledge of one of the three cells built into the walls of the tomb. When Maes Howe was opened in 1861, it was virtually empty, thanks to the work of generations of grave-robbers, who had left behind only a handful of human bones. The Vikings entered in the twelfth century,

7

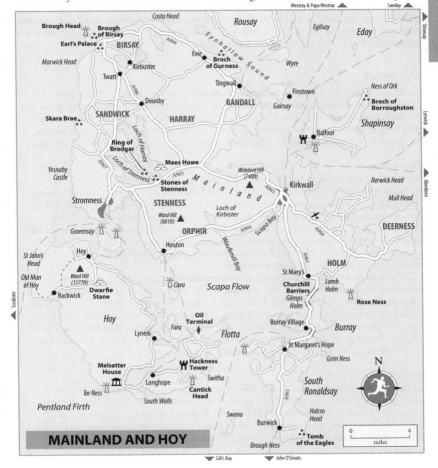

MAINLAND AND HOY

probably on their way to the Crusades, leaving copious runic graffiti, including cryptographic twig runes, cut into the walls of the main chamber. They include phrases such as "Many a beautiful woman has stooped in here, however pompous she might be", and the more prosaic "Thor and I bedded Helga".

ARRIVAL AND DEPARTURE
STENNESS

By bus Buses from Stromness to Kirkwall (Mon–Sat hourly, Sun every 2hr; 30min) can drop you off at Tormiston Mill by Maes Howe – under a mile from the Stones of Stenness and the same again from the Ring of Brodgar.

ACCOMMODATION

★ **Holland House** ☎ 01856 771400, ⓦ hollandhouse orkney.co.uk. A beautiful, solidly-built manse in Harray, set back from the A986. The house is filled with artworks, there's a peat fire and the home-cooking, including freshly baked scones for breakfast, is outstanding. **£96**

Mill of Eyrland ☎ 01856 850136, ⓦ millofeyrland .co.uk. Carefully converted former mill in a delightful setting on the A964 to Orphir; it's filled with wonderful antiques and old mill machinery, as well as all mod cons; free wi-fi and enormous breakfasts. **£80**

EATING AND DRINKING

Merkister Hotel Harray Loch ☎ 01856 771366, ⓦ merkister.com. Substantial hotel on the northeastern shore of the Loch of Harray, popular with the locals and visiting anglers. The bar's lively and does fairly predicatble

bar meals such as (local) fish and chips (around £10) but there's a restaurant, too, whose menu features more local seafood (mains £13–20). Food served daily noon–2pm & 6–9pm.

Sandwick

North of Stromness, the parish of **Sandwick** contains the best known of Orkney's prehistoric monuments, **Skara Brae**, beautifully situated beside the white curve of the Bay of Skaill. In addition, the cliffs either side of the bay provide some of the most spectacularly rugged **coastal walks** on Orkney's Mainland. The other good reason for exploring Sandwick is to visit the wonderful **Orkney Brewery** in the old schoolhouse in Quoyloo.

Skara Brae

Daily: April–Sept 9.30am–5.30pm; Oct–March 9.30am–4.30pm • £7.10; HS • ☎ 01856 761606

At **Skara Brae**, the extensive remains of a small Neolithic fishing and farming village, dating back to 3000 BC, were discovered in 1850 after a fierce storm ripped off the dunes covering them. The village is amazingly well preserved, its houses huddled together and connected by narrow passages, which would originally have been covered over with turf. The houses themselves consist of a single, spacious living room, filled with domestic detail, including dressers, fireplaces, built-in cupboards, beds and boxes, all ingeniously constructed from slabs of stone.

The **visitor centre** houses an excellent **café/restaurant**, where you can also get takeaway sandwiches to order. You can take in the small introductory **exhibition**, with a few replica finds, and some hands-on stuff for kids. You then proceed to a full-scale replica of House 7 (the best-preserved house), complete with a fake wood and skin roof. It's all a tad neat and tidy, with fetching uplighting – rather than dark, smoky and smelly – but it gives you the general idea, and makes up for the fact that, at the site itself, you can only look down on the houses from the outer walls.

Skaill House

In the summer months, your ticket also covers entry to nearby **Skaill House**, an extensive range of buildings 300yd inland, home of the laird of Skaill. The original house was a simple two-storey block, built for Bishop George Graham in the 1620s, but it has since been much extended. The house's prize possession is Captain Cook's dinner service from the *Resolution*; it was delivered after Cook's death when the *Resolution* and the *Discovery* sailed into Stromness in 1780.

Yesnaby

At **Yesnaby**, to the south of the Bay of Skaill, the sandstone cliffs have been savagely eroded into stacks and geos by the force of the Atlantic. Come here during a westerly gale and you'll see the waves sending sea spray shooting over the wartime buildings and the neighbouring fields. The clifftops support a unique plantlife, which thrives on the salt spray, including the rare, and very small, purple Scottish primrose, which flowers in May and from July to late September. The walk south along the coast from here is exhilarating: the Old Man of Hoy is visible in the distance and, after a mile and a half, you come to an impressive sea stack known as Yesnaby Castle.

ARRIVAL AND DEPARTURE   SANDWICK

By bus Services to Skara Brae are limited (Mon, Thurs & Sat only), albeit supplemented by extra services on schooldays and a flexible Octobus service from Finstown, which you must pre-book (☎01856 871536, ⍈octocic.co.uk). Alternatively, since it's only 7 miles from Stromness, you could just hire a bike.

ACCOMMODATION

Hyval Farm ☎01856 841522, ⍈hyval.co.uk. A working beef cattle farm in Quoyloo within walking distance of Skara Brae, the seaside and Orkney Brewery. There's a guests' lounge, and breakfast is taken in the little conservatory with great views over the Bay of Skaill. April–Oct. **£50**

EATING AND DRINKING

★ **Orkney Brewery, Quoyloo** ☎01856 841777, ⍈sinclairbreweries.co.uk. The old schoolhouse in Quoyloo has been tastefully converted into a state-of-the-art microbrewery, with tasting tours (£5) and also a great café where local produce is very much to the fore – try the beef and beer sausages – and all dishes are under £10. Mon–Sat 10am–4.30pm, Sun noon–4.30pm.

Birsay and around

Occupying the northwest corner of the Mainland, the parish of **BIRSAY** was the centre of Norse power in Orkney for several centuries before Kirkwall got its cathedral.

Earl's Palace

A tiny cluster of homes is gathered around the imposing sandstone ruins of the **Earl's Palace**, built in the late sixteenth century by Robert Stewart, Earl of Orkney, using the forced labour of the islanders, who weren't even given food and drink for their work. By all accounts, it was a "sumptuous and stately dwelling", built in four wings around a central courtyard, its upper rooms decorated with painted ceilings and rich furnishings; surrounding the palace were flower and herb gardens, a bowling green and archery butts. The palace appears to have lasted barely a century before falling into ruin; the crumbling walls and turrets retain much of their grandeur, although inside there is little remaining domestic detail. However, its vast scale makes the Earl's Palace in Kirkwall seem almost humble in comparison.

Brough of Birsay

Accessible 2hr either side of low tide • Tide times available at Stromness and Kirkwall tourist offices and on Radio Orkney (93.7FM; Mon–Fri 7.30–8am)

Just over half a mile northwest of Birsay village is the **Brough of Birsay**, a substantial Pictish settlement on a small tidal island. On the island, by St Peter's Church, is a small ticket office (see below), where you have to pay an entrance fee in season.

St Peter's Church

Mid-June to Sept daily 9.30am–5.30pm • £4.50; HS

The focus of the village of Brough of Birsay was – and still is – the sandstone-built twelfth-century **St Peter's Church**, which stands slightly higher than the surrounding buildings; the stone seating along the walls is still in place, and there are a couple of semicircular recesses for altars, and a semicircular apse. The church is thought to have stood at the centre of a monastic settlement. Close by are remains of a large complex of Viking-era buildings, including several houses, a sauna and some sophisticated stone drains. At the ticket office, you can inspect a few artefacts gathered from the site, including a game made from whalebone and an antler pin.

The northern coastline

The Brough of Birsay is a popular day-trip, partly due to the fun of dodging the tides, but few bother to explore the rest of the island, whose gentle green slopes, as viewed from the mainland, belie the dramatic, rugged cliffs that characterize the rest of the coastline. In winter, sea spray from the crashing waves can envelop the entire island. In summer, the cliffs are home to various seabirds, including a few puffins, making the half-mile walk to the island's castellated **lighthouse** and back along the northern coastline well worth the effort. While there, spare a thought for the lighthouse keepers on the **Sule Skerry** lighthouse from 1895 to 1982 – the most isolated in Britain – which lies on a piece of bare rock just visible some 37 miles west across the sea, and whose only contact with the outside world was via carrier pigeon.

Barony Mills
May–Sept daily 10am–1pm & 2–5pm • Free • ☎ 01856 721439

Half a mile southeast of Birsay, up the burn, is the **Barony Mills**, Orkney's only working nineteenth-century water mill. The mill specializes in producing traditional stone-ground beremeal, essential for making bere bannocks. Bere is a four-kernel barley crop with a very short growing season, perfectly suited for the local climate and once the staple diet in these parts. The miller on duty will give you a guided tour and show you the machinery going through its paces, though milling only takes place in the autumn.

Kirbuster Farm Museum
Birsay • April–Oct Mon–Sat 10.30am–1pm & 2–5pm, Sun 2–5pm • Free • ☎ 01856 771268

Lying between the Loch of Boardhouse and the Loch of Hundland, the **Kirbuster Farm Museum** offers an insight into life on an Orkney farmstead in the mid-nineteenth century. Built in 1723, the farm is made up of a typical, though substantial, collection of flagstone buildings, with its own, very beautiful garden. Ducks, geese and sheep wander around the grassy open yard, entered through a whalebone archway. The farm has retained its firehoose, in which the smoke from the central peat fire was used to dry fish fillets, before drifting up towards a hole in the ceiling.

ARRIVAL AND DEPARTURE   BIRSAY AND AROUND

By bus Bus services from Kirkwall (Mon, Thurs & Sat only) get you to Evie, supplemented by the Octobus service from Finstown (pre-book 24hr before; ☎ 01856 871536, ⊛ octocic.co.uk).

KITCHENER MEMORIAL

Marwick Head, an RSPB reserve renowned as a seabird nesting spot, is clearly visible to the south of Birsay Bay thanks to the huge castellated tower of **Kitchener Memorial**. Raised by the people of Orkney, it commemorates the Minister of War, Lord Kitchener, who drowned along with all but 12 of the 655 men aboard the cruiser *HMS Hampshire* when the ship struck a mine just off the coast on June 5, 1916. There has been much speculation about the incident over the years, because Kitchener was on a secret mission to Russia to hold talks with the Tsar. A German spy claimed to have sabotaged and sunk the ship, and rumours abounded that Kitchener had been deliberately sent to his death (he was extremely unpopular at the time). In reality, it appears to have been a simple case of naval incompetence: the weather forecast of severe northwesterly gales was ignored, as were the reports of submarine activity in the area.

ACCOMMODATION

Birsay Outdoor Centre 0.5 miles south of the Barony Mills ☎ 01856 873535 ext 2415, ⊛ orkney.gov.uk. A large refurbished hostel with a fully equipped kitchen and a drying room; there's also a campsite alongside. Check-in from 6pm. April–Sept only. Dorms __£16__; camping __£6.25__/pitch

EATING AND DRINKING

Barony Hotel ☎ 01856 721327, ⊛ baronyhotel.com. The only watering hole in Birsay is the bar of the *Barony* overlooking the Loch of Boardhouse, to the southeast of Birsay village. Daily noon–11pm; food served 12.30–2pm & 6.30–8.30pm.

Birsay Tea Room ☎ 01856 721399, ⊛ birsaybaytea room.co.uk. For light snacks and home-made cake, head for the modern tearoom, at the southern edge of the village, which boasts superb views of the Brough (binoculars provided). Wed–Sun 11am–5pm.

Broch of Gurness

Evie • April–Sept daily 9.30am–5.30pm • £5.50; HS • ☎ 01856 751414

Near the village of Evie, on the north coast, is the **Broch of Gurness** (also known as Aikerness Broch), the best-preserved broch on Orkney, still surrounded by a remarkable complex of later buildings. The sea has eaten away half the site, but the broch itself, dating from around 100 BC, still stands, its walls reaching a height of 12ft in places, its inner cells still intact. Clustered around the broch, the compact group of homes has also survived amazingly well, with much of their original and ingenious stone shelving and fireplaces still in place. The best view of the site is from the east, where you can clearly make out the "main street" leading towards the broch. Also worth a look is the **visitor centre** where you can try your hand at the quernstone corn grinder. The broch is clearly signposted from Evie, the road skirting the pristinely white **Sands of Evie**, a perfect picnic spot in fine weather, with great views across the turbulent waters of Eynhallow Sound towards the island of Rousay.

ARRIVAL AND DEPARTURE

BROCH OF GURNESS

By bus Bus services from Kirkwall will get you to Evie (Mon–Sat 4–5 daily; 30min), from which it's a 30min walk to the broch. There's also the Octobus service from Finstown (pre-book the day before on ☎ 01856 871536).

ACCOMMODATION

Castlehill Evie ☎ 01856 751228, ⊛ castlehillorkney .co.uk. This modern crofthouse under Burgar Hill looks nothing special from the outside but it's very well decked out inside, with pleasant wooden furnishings and quality bedding. Great views and top-notch home cooking. __£85__

Eviedale Campsite Evie ☎ 01856 751270, ⊛ creviedale .orknet.co.uk. Situated in a sheltered spot right by the junction of the road to Dounby, this is a small, simple campsite tucked in among a handful of self-catering cottages. Free wi-fi. April–Oct. __£7__/person

Orphir

The southern shores of the West Mainland, overlooking Scapa Flow, are much gentler than the rest of the coastline, and have fewer of Orkney's premier-league sights. However, if you've time to spare, or you're heading for Hoy from the car ferry terminal at Houton, there are a couple of points of interest in the neighbouring parish of **ORPHIR**.

Orkneyinga Saga Centre

Gyre Rd • April–Oct daily 9am–6pm • Free

Beside the parish cemetery in Orphir, you'll find the **Orkneyinga Saga Centre**, containing a small exhibition with a fifteen-minute audiovisual show which gives you a taste of the *Orkneyinga Saga*, the bloodthirsty Viking tale written around 1200 AD by an unnamed Icelandic author, which described the conquest of the Northern Isles by the Norsemen. The **Earl's Bu** at Orphir features in the saga as the home of Earl Thorfinn the Mighty, Earl Paul and his son, Håkon, who ordered the murder of Earl (later St) Magnus on

Egilsay (see p.356). The foundations of what was probably the Earl's Bu have been uncovered just outside the cemetery gates, while inside the cemetery is a section of the round church, built by Håkon after his pilgrimage in penance to Jerusalem.

Kirkwall

Initial impressions of **KIRKWALL**, Orkney's capital, are not always favourable. It has nothing to match the picturesque harbour of Stromness, and its residential sprawl is far less appealing. However, it does have one great redeeming feature – its sandstone **cathedral**, without doubt the finest medieval building in the north of Scotland. In any case, if you're staying any length of time on Orkney you're bound to find yourself in Kirkwall at some point, as it's home to the islands' better-stocked shops, including the only large supermarket, and is the departure point for most of the ferries to Orkney's northern isles.

7

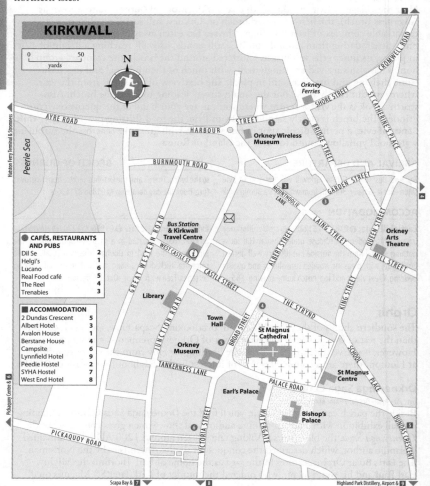

KIRKWALL

0   50
yards

N

● **CAFÉS, RESTAURANTS AND PUBS**
Dil Se	2
Helgi's	1
Lucano	6
Real Food café	5
The Reel	4
Trenabies	3

■ **ACCOMMODATION**
2 Dundas Crescent	5
Albert Hotel	3
Avalon House	1
Berstane House	4
Campsite	6
Lynnfield Hotel	9
Peedie Hostel	2
SYHA Hostel	7
West End Hotel	8

Nowadays, the town is very much divided into two main focal points: the old harbour, at the north end of the town, where visiting yachts moor and the small interisland ferries come and go all year round; and the flagstone **main street**. Despite the latter taking four different names as it winds through the town, orientation is easy with the prominent spire of St Magnus Cathedral clearly marking the town centre.

St Magnus Cathedral

Broad St • April–Sept Mon–Sat 9am–6pm, Sun 2–5pm; Oct–March 9am–1pm & 2–5pm • Free • Guided upper level tours Tues & Thurs 11am & 2pm • £6.85 • ☎ 01856 874894, Ⓦ stmagnus.org

Standing at the very heart of Kirkwall, **St Magnus Cathedral** is the town's most compelling sight. This beautiful red-sandstone building was begun in 1137 by the Orkney Earl Rögnvald (aka St Ronald), who decided to make full use of a growing cult surrounding the figure of his uncle Magnus, killed on the orders of his cousin Håkon in 1117 (see p.356). When Magnus's body was buried in Birsay, a heavenly light was said to have shone overhead, and his grave soon drew pilgrims from far afield. When Rögnvald took over the earldom, he built the cathedral in his uncle's honour, moving the centre of religious and secular power from Birsay to Kirkwall, before he himself was murdered.

Built using yellow sandstone from Eday and red sandstone from the Mainland, the cathedral has been added to and extended over the centuries. Today much of the detail in the soft sandstone has worn away – the capitals around the main doors are reduced to artistically gnarled stumps – but it's still an immensely impressive building, its shape and style echoing the great cathedrals of Europe. Inside, the atmosphere is surprisingly intimate, the bulky sandstone columns drawing your eye up to the exposed brickwork arches, while around the walls is a series of mostly seventeenth-century tombstones, many carved with a skull and crossbones and other emblems of mortality, alongside chilling inscriptions calling on the reader to "Remember death waits us all, the hour none knows".

In the square pillars on either side of the high altar, the bones of Magnus and Rögnvald are buried. In the southeastern corner of the cathedral lies the tomb of the Stromness-born Arctic explorer John Rae, who tried to find Sir John Franklin's expedition; he is depicted asleep, dressed in moleskins and furs, his rifle and Bible by his side. Beside Rae's tomb is Orkney's own Poets' Corner, with memorials to, among others, George Mackay Brown, Eric Linklater, Edwin Muir and Robert Rendall (who was also an eminent conchologist). Another poignant monument is the one to the dead of HMS *Royal Oak*, which was torpedoed in Scapa Flow in 1939 with the loss of 833 men (see p.347).

Bishop's and Earl's palaces

Palace Rd • April–Oct daily 9.30am–5.30pm • £4.50; HS • ☎ 01856 871918

South of the cathedral are the ruined remains of the **Bishop's Palace**, traditional residence of the Bishop of Orkney from the twelfth century. Here, the Norwegian king Håkon died in 1263 on his return from the Battle of Largs. Most of what you see now, however, dates from the time of Bishop Robert Reid, founder of Edinburgh University, in the mid-sixteenth century. The walls still stand, as does the tall round tower housing the bishop's private chambers. The ticket for the Bishop's Palace also covers entry to the neighbouring **Earl's Palace** – better preserved and more fun to explore – built by the infamous Earl Patrick Stewart around 1600 using forced labour. With its grand entrance, fancy oriel windows, dank dungeons, massive fireplaces and magnificent central hall, it has a confident solidity, and is a fine example of Scottish Renaissance architecture. The roof is missing but many domestic details remain, including a set of toilets and the stone shelves used by the clerk to do his filing. Earl Patrick enjoyed his palace for only a very short time before he was imprisoned and charged with treason.

The earl might have been acquitted, but he foolishly ordered his son, Robert, to organize an insurrection; he held out four days in the palace against the Earl of Caithness, before being captured and sent to Edinburgh to be hanged; his father was beheaded there five weeks later.

Orkney Museum

Broad St • Mon–Sat: May–Sept 10.30am–5pm; Oct–April 10.30am–12.30pm & 1.30–5pm • Free • ☎ 01856 873535

Opposite the cathedral stands the sixteenth-century **Tankerness House**, a former home for the clergy, and now home to the **Orkney Museum**. A couple of rooms have been restored as they would have been in 1820, when it was the Baikie family's private home. The rest houses some of the islands' most treasured finds, among the more unusual of which are a witch's spell box and a lovely whalebone plaque from a Viking boat grave discovered on Sanday. On a warm summer afternoon, the museum **gardens** are thick with the buzz of bees and vibrantly coloured flora.

Orkney Wireless Museum

Kiln Corner, Junction Rd • April–Sept Mon–Sat 10am–4.30pm, Sun 2.30–4.30pm • £3 • ☎ 01856 871400, ⊛ owm.org.uk

At the harbour end of Junction Road, you can browse around the tiny **Orkney Wireless Museum**, a single room packed to the roof with every variety of antique radio equipment imaginable. The museum is particularly strong on technical flotsam from the two world wars, and there's even a working crystal set that you can listen to.

Highland Park distillery

Holm Rd • April & Sept Mon–Fri 10am–5pm hourly tours; May–Aug Mon–Sat 10am–5pm, Sun noon–5pm hourly tours; Oct–March Mon–Fri tours at 2 & 3pm • £6 • ☎ 01856 874619, ⊛ highlandpark.co.uk

A mile or so south of Kirkwall along the A961 to South Ronaldsay is the **Highland Park distillery**. It's been in operation for more than two hundred years, and still has its own maltings, although it was closed during World War II, when the army used it as a food store and the huge vats served as communal baths.

Scapa Bay

If the weather is unusually good and you're moved to consider a swim, follow the locals and head a mile south of town on the B9148 to **Scapa Bay**, Kirkwall's very own sandy beach. Briefly a naval headquarters at the outbreak of World War I, Scapa's pier is now used by the council tugs and pilot launches servicing the oil tankers out in Scapa Flow. Visible from the beach is the green Admiralty wreck buoy marking the position of **HMS Royal Oak**, torpedoed by a German U-boat on October 14, 1939, with the loss of 833 men (out of a total crew of around 1400). A small display shed at the eastern end of the bay tells the full story, and has photos of the wreck (still an official war grave) as it looks today.

ARRIVAL AND DEPARTURE   KIRKWALL

By plane ☎ 01851 707400, ⊛ hial.co.uk. Kirkwall airport is 3 miles southeast of town on the A960; the hourly bus takes 15min, or else it's a £5 taxi ride into town. Destinations within Orkney Eday (Mon & Wed 1–2 daily; 10–30min); North Ronaldsay (Mon–Sat 3 daily, 2 on Sun; 20–30min); Papa Westray (Mon–Fri 3 daily, Sat & Sun 2 daily; 15–35min); Sanday (Mon–Fri 2 daily, 1 on Sat; 15min); Stronsay (Mon–Fri 2 daily, 1 on Sat; 10–25min);

Westray (Mon–Fri 2 daily, Sat & Sun 1 daily; 15–25min).
By ferry ☎ 0845 600 0449, ⊛ northlinkferries.co.uk. Ferries from Shetland (3 weekly; 5hr 30min) and Aberdeen (3 weekly; 6hr), and all cruise ships, dock at the Hatston terminal, a mile northwest of town; a shuttle bus will take you into Kirkwall (or to Stromness if you prefer). Ferries for the other islands within Orkney leave from the town pier in Kirkwall.

SCAPA FLOW

Apart from a few oil tankers, there's very little activity in the great natural harbour of **Scapa Flow**, yet for the first half of the twentieth century, it served as the main base of the Royal Navy, with over a hundred warships anchored here at any one time. The coastal defences required to safeguard Scapa Flow as the country's chief naval headquarters were considerable and many are still visible all over Orkney, ranging from half-sunk blockships to the **Churchill Barriers** (see p.347) and the gun batteries that pepper the coastline. Unfortunately, these defences weren't sufficient to save **HMS Royal Oak** from being torpedoed by a German U-boat in October 1939 (see p.347), but they withstood several heavy German air raids during the course of 1940. Ironically, the worst disaster the Flow ever witnessed was self-inflicted, when **HMS Vanguard** sank on July 9, 1917, after suffering an internal explosion, killing 843 crew and leaving only two survivors.

Scapa Flow's most celebrated moment in naval history, however, was when the entire **German High Seas Fleet** was interned here immediately after World War I. A total of 74 ships, manned by several thousand German sailors, was anchored off the isle of Cava awaiting the outcome of the Versailles Peace Conference. At around noon on Midsummer's Day 1919, believing either that the majority of the German fleet was to be handed over, or that hostilities were about to resume, the commanding officer, Admiral von Reuter, ordered the fleet to be scuttled. By 5pm, every ship was beached or had sunk and nine German sailors had lost their lives, shot by outraged British servicemen. The British government was publicly indignant, but privately relieved since the scuttling avoided the diplomatic nightmare of dividing the fleet among the Allies.

Between the wars, the largest **salvage operation** in history took place in Scapa Flow, with the firm of Cox & Danks alone raising 26 destroyers, one light cruiser, four battlecruisers and two battleships. Despite this, seven large German ships – three battleships and four light cruisers – remain on the sea bed of Scapa Flow, along with four destroyers and a U-boat. For more on Scapa Flow's wartime role, visit the museum on Hoy (see p.352). Scapa Flow is also considered one of the world's greatest dive sites and Scapa Scuba (☎01856 851218, Ⓦscapascuba.co.uk), based in Stromness, offer one-to-one scuba-diving tuition from £70 for half a day. If you don't want to get your feet wet, *Dawn Star II* (☎01856 876743, Ⓦorkneyboattrips.co.uk; May–Sept) will take you close to the Admiralty buoys and give you a history tour of the harbour; tours begin at St Mary's, by the Churchill Barriers, take three hours and cost £90 for two.

7

Destinations within Orkney Eday (2–3 daily; 1hr 15min–2hr 25min); North Ronaldsay (Tues & Fri; 2hr 40min); Papa Westray (Tues & Fri; 2hr 15min); Sanday (2 daily; 1hr 25min); Shapinsay (4–5 daily; 45min); Stronsay (2 daily; 1hr 40min–2hr); Westray (2–3 daily; 1hr 25min).

By bus ☎01856 870555, Ⓦstagecoachbus.com. The bus station is behind the Kirkwall Travel Centre on West Castle St.

Destinations Birsay (Mon–Sat 2–3 daily; 45min); Burwick (2–3 daily; 40min); Deerness (Mon–Sat 3–4 daily; 30min); Evie (Mon–Sat 4–5 daily; 30min); Houton (Mon–Fri 7 daily, 3 on Sat; 35–40min); Kirkwall Airport (Mon–Sat every 30min–hourly, 9 on Sun; 15min); Skara Brae (June–Aug Mon, Thurs & Sat 1 daily; 50min); St Margaret's Hope (Mon–Sat hourly; 30min); Stromness (Mon–Sat hourly, Sun every 2hr; 30min); Tingwall (Mon–Sat 4–5 daily; 25min).

INFORMATION

Tourist office The helpful tourist office is in Kirkwall Travel Centre, by the bus station: April–Sept Mon–Sat

9am–6pm, Sun 10am–2pm; Oct–March Mon–Sat only (☎01856 872856, Ⓦvisitorkney.com).

ACCOMMODATION

HOTELS AND B&BS

2 Dundas Crescent ☎01856 874805, Ⓦtwodundas .co.uk. Run by an Orcadian couple and situated just behind the cathedral, this former manse is a grand, and tastefully decorated, Victorian house, with four spacious rooms and period fittings intact. __£75__

Albert Hotel Mounthoolie Lane ☎01856 876000, Ⓦalberthotel.webeden.co.uk. Great central location,

lively *Bothy Bar* (with disco attached) and contemporary furnishings: this is Kirkwall's hippest hotel. Wi-fi in public areas. __£100__

Avalon House Carness Rd ☎01856 876665, Ⓦavalon -house.co.uk. Don't judge a B&B by its drab, modern exterior; this is a comfortable, purpose-built guesthouse run efficiently by a very welcoming couple, and situated a pleasant 20min coastal walk from the town centre. __£72__

Berstane House 1.5 miles southeast of town down Berstane Rd ☎01856 876277, ⓦberstane.co.uk. The B&B rooms and self-catering flats are a steal at this handsome Victorian pile, set in its own wooded grounds with sea views – best with your own transport. **£50**

Lynnfield Hotel Holm Rd ☎01856 872505, ⓦlynnfield .co.uk. Small ten-room hotel in a quiet spot a mile or so out of town near the distillery – the dark wood furnishings make the place seem really quite grand in style and the food is excellent. **£115**

West End Hotel 14 Main St ☎01856 872368, ⓦwest endkirkwall.co.uk. Orkney's first hospital is now a good, old-fashioned hotel located in a quiet street, just a few minutes' walk south of the centre. **£99**

HOSTELS AND CAMPSITES

Peedie Hostel 1 Ayre Houses ☎01856 875477, ⓦkirkwallpeediehostel.com. Centrally located overlooking the old harbour and out to sea, this is a clean and comfortable hostel with just eight beds. Washing machine and tumble dryer available, plus free wi-fi. April–Oct. Dorms **£15**

Pickaquoy Campsite Ayre Rd ☎01856 879900, ⓦpickaquoy.net. Central and well-equipped, since it is behind (and run by) the local leisure centre, but not exactly picturesque. April–Oct. **£7.15**/pitch

SYHA Hostel Old Scapa Rd ☎01856 872243, ⓦsyha .org.uk. A good 10min walk out of the centre on the road to Orphir – friendly enough, but no beauty outside or in. April–Oct. **£17**/person

EATING AND DRINKING

Dil Se 7 Bridge St ☎01856 875242, ⓦdilserestaurant .co.uk. Kirkwall's Indian restaurant has won numerous awards since it opened – tandooris and baltis predominate, with lots of veggie options (sides £3–4, mains £6–10). Daily 4–11pm.

Helgi's 14 Harbour St ☎01856 879293, ⓦhelgis.co.uk. A popular modern pub on the harbour front which serves nicely presented bar food, from burger/fish and chips to fajitas (all for under £10). Free wi-fi. Mon–Wed 11am–midnight, Thurs–Sat 11am–1am, Sun 12.30pm–midnight; food served Mon–Sat noon–2pm & 5–9pm, Sun 12.30–2.30pm & 5–9pm.

Lucano 31 Victoria St ☎01856 875687, ⓦlucanokirkwall .com. Busy, bright, modern, authentic Italian – a real find in Kirkwall – offering pizza, pasta and risotto with an Orcadian angle. It's popular so book ahead. Daily 9am–9pm.

Real Food Café 25 Broad St ☎01856 874225,

ⓦwww.judithglue.com. Cheery cream and sky-blue wood-panelling decor at this small snacky café at the back of Judith Glue's gift shop opposite the cathedral. Try the Westray crab claws and bere bannocks (all dishes under £10). June–Sept daily 9am–10pm; shorter hours in the low season.

★ **The Reel** 6 Broad St ☎01856 871000, ⓦwrigley andthereel.com. The old customs house near the cathedral is now a fabulous, laidback self-service café, run by the musical Wrigley Sisters, serving great coffee, sandwiches, pizzas and cakes, and offering free wi-fi and regular live music (Wed, Thurs & Sat). Mon–Fri 8.30am–6pm, Sat 9am–1am; in summer also Sun 10am–5pm.

Trenabies Bistro Albert St ☎01856 874336, ⓦtrenabiesfairtrade.co.uk. This cosy, old-fashioned café with booths is a classic Kirkwall institution – order Cajun fries and a panini for around £5. Mon–Sat 8.30am–5.30pm, Sun noon–4pm.

NIGHTLIFE AND ENTERTAINMENT

Phoenix Cinema Pickaquoy Centre ☎01856 879900, ⓦpickaquoy.net. Known locally as the "Picky", this is a short walk west of the town centre, up Pickaquoy Rd

past the supermarket. As well as serving as one of the town's main large-scale venues it also contains the New Phoenix cinema.

East Mainland and South Ronaldsay

Southeast from Kirkwall, the **East Mainland** juts out into the North Sea, its northern coastline consisting of three exposed peninsulas that jut out like giant claws. The East Mainland is joined, thanks to the remarkable Churchill Barriers, to several smaller islands, the largest of which are **Burray** and **South Ronaldsay**. The heavily farmed land contains few of Orkney's more famous sights but there are some good coastal walks and several unusual prehistoric sites, in particular the **Tomb of the Eagles** near Burwick.

Deerness

The easternmost peninsula of **Deerness** is joined to the Mainland only by a narrow, sandy isthmus. From the car park at its northeastern corner, a short walk eastwards will

THE CHURCHILL BARRIERS

The southeastern corner of Orkney Mainland is connected to the islands of Burray and South Ronaldsay by four causeways known as the **Churchill Barriers**, built during World War II as anti-submarine barriers. It was an astonishing feat of engineering considering the strength of Orkney tides, and also an extremely expensive undertaking, costing an estimated £2.5 million. The Admiralty (under Churchill) were only prompted into action by the sinking of the battleship HMS *Royal Oak* on October 14, 1939. Despite the presence of blockships, deliberately sunk during World War I in order to close off the eastern approaches, one German U-boat captain managed to get through and torpedo the *Royal Oak*, before returning to a hero's welcome in Germany. As you cross the barriers – don't cross them during high winds – you can still see the rusting blockships, even at low tide, an eerie reminder of Orkney's important wartime role.

bring you to **The Gloup**, an impressive collapsed sea-cave, whose name stems from the Old Norse *gluppa*, or "chasm"; the tide still flows in and out through a natural arch, making strange gurgling noises. From here, you can walk along the tops of the collapsing sandstone coastline half a mile north to the **Brough of Deerness**, a grassy promontory now accessible only via a precipitous path; the ruins are thought to have once been a Norse or Pictish monastic site. Another half-mile will bring you to the sea cliffs of **Mull Head**, home to nesting seabirds from May to August, including fulmars, kittiwakes, guillemots, razorbills and puffins, plus, inland, arctic terns that swoop and screech threateningly.

7

ACCOMMODATION   DEERNESS

★ **Northfield** ☎ 01856 741353, ⍟ orkneybedand breakfast.com. Large, purpose-built, modern farmhouse B&B in a wonderfully isolated location, with exposed oak timber beams, tasteful furnishings, free wi-fi and fabulous sea views out to Copinsay. **£70**

Lamb Holm: the Italian Chapel

Daily dawn–dusk • Free

Special camps were built on the uninhabited island of Lamb Holm, to accommodate the 1700 men involved in building the Churchill Barriers, 1200 of whom were Italian POWs. The camps have long since disappeared, but the Italians left behind the extraordinary **Italian Chapel** on **Lamb Holm**, by the main road (A961). This, the so-called "Miracle of Camp 60", must be one of the greatest adaptations ever, made from two Nissen huts, concrete, barbed wire and parts of a rusting blockship. It has a great false facade, and colourful trompe-l'oeil decor, lovingly restored by the chapel's original architect, Domenico Chiocchetti, in 1960.

Burray

Largest of the little islands between the Mainland and South Ronaldsay, **Burray** has a population of around 400. The main village expanded enormously in the nineteenth century during the boom years of the herring industry, but was badly affected by the sinking of the blockships during World War I. The two-storey warehouse, built in 1860 in order to cure and pack the herring, has since been converted into the *Sands Hotel* (see p.348).

Orkney Fossil and Heritage Centre

April–Sept daily 10am–4pm • £4 • ☎ 01856 731255, ⍟ orkneyfossilcentre.co.uk

The **Orkney Fossil and Heritage Centre** is in a converted farm on the main road that crosses the island. Most of the fossils downstairs have been found locally, and largely feature fish and sea creatures, since Orkney was at the bottom of a tropical sea in Devonian times. The UV "glow room", where the rocks reveal their iridescent colours, is a hit with kids, though be sure to show them the coprolite (fossilized poo) among the main displays, too. Upstairs, there's much wartime memorabilia and a whole section on the Churchill Barriers – kids can build their own – while the ground floor has a community-run café.

ARRIVAL AND DEPARTURE   BURRAY

Buses from Kirkwall to St Margaret's Hope call in at Burray village shop (Mon–Sat hourly; 30min).

ACCOMMODATION AND EATING

Sands Hotel 14 Main St ☎ 01856 731298, ⍟ thesands hotel.co.uk. An imposing stone-built former fish warehouse overlooking Burray harbour – now a hotel with simple pine furnishings and a few original features. The bar menu features the usual dishes (all under £10), plus herring in oatmeal, and mince and tatties; the restaurant will serve up local scallops and black pudding (mains £12–16). Food served Mon–Sat noon–2pm & 6–9pm, Sun noon–2pm & 5.30–8.30pm. __£99__

South Ronaldsay

At the southern end of the barriers is low-lying **South Ronaldsay**, the largest of the islands linked to the Mainland and, like the latter, rich farming country. It was traditionally the chief crossing-point to the Scottish mainland, as it's only six miles across the Pentland Firth from Caithness. Today, car **ferries** arrive at St Margaret's Hope, and a small passenger ferry links John O'Groats with Burwick, on the southernmost tip of the island (see opposite for details).

St Margaret's Hope

The main settlement on South Ronaldsay is **ST MARGARET'S HOPE**, which local tradition says takes its name from Margaret, the Maid of Norway, daughter of the king of Norway, who is thought to have died here aged 8 in November 1290. As granddaughter of Alexander III, Margaret had already been proclaimed queen of Scotland and was on her way to marry the English prince Edward (later Edward II), thereby unifying the two countries. Today, St Margaret's Hope – or "The Hope", as it's known locally (from the Norse *hyop* meaning "bay") – is a peaceful little gathering of pleasant stone-built houses overlooking a sheltered bay, and is by far the best base from which to explore the area.

Smiddy Museum
Cromarty Square • May–Aug daily 2–4.30pm • Free • ☎ 01856 831440

The village smithy on Cromarty Square has been turned into the **Smiddy Museum**, particularly fun for kids who enjoy getting hands-on with the old tools, drills and giant bellows. There's a small exhibition on the annual **Boys' Ploughing Match**, in which local boys compete with miniature hand-held ploughs on the third Saturday in August, at the beautiful golden beach at the **Sands O'Right** in Hoxa, a couple of miles west of The Hope. Simultaneously a **Festival of the Horse** takes place, with the local children, mostly girls, dressed in spectacular costumes and harnesses.

Tomb of the Eagles
Daily: March 10am–noon; April–Sept 9.30am–5.30pm; Oct 9.30am–12.30pm; Nov–Feb by appointment • £7 • ☎ 01856 831339, ⍟ tomboftheeagles.co.uk

One of Orkney's most enjoyable archeological sights is the Isbister Chambered Cairn at the southeastern corner of South Ronaldsay, also known as the **Tomb of the Eagles**. The cairn was discovered in 1958 and excavated by a local farmer, Ronald Simison of Liddle, who still owns it, so a visit here makes a refreshing change from Historic

Scotland sites. First, you get to look round the family's private museum of prehistoric artefacts; you can actually touch and admire the painstaking craftsmanship of Neolithic folk, and pick up a skull. Next there's a brief guided tour of a nearby Bronze-Age **burnt mound**, which is basically a prehistoric rubbish dump. Finally you get to walk the mile or so out to the Neolithic **chambered cairn**, by the cliff's edge, where human remains were found alongside talons and carcasses of sea eagles. To enter the cairn, you must lie on a trolley and pull yourself in using an overhead rope – something guaranteed to put a smile on every visitor's face. The cairn's clifftop location is spectacular, and walking along the coast in either direction is rewarding.

Tomb of the Otters
April–Oct daily 10am–5pm • £5 • ☎ 01856 831605, ⊕ bankschamberedtomb.co.uk

A Neolithic stone's throw from the Tomb of the Eagles, another Neolithic chambered cairn was discovered in 2010 near Banks farmhouse by local farmer Hamish Mowatt. The Banks Chambered Cairn or **Tomb of the Otters** as it's been dubbed, is unique on Orkney as it was cut directly into the bedrock, and had lain undisturbed for five thousand years. Layers of human bones within the tomb were found to be mixed with vast quantities of otter spraint, hence the name. You can examine some of the skulls and teeth found, and, if possible you get to crawl into the waterlogged tomb – waterproofs and boots are a good idea.

7

ARRIVAL AND DEPARTURE

SOUTH RONALDSAY

By ferry Pentland Ferries (☎ 01856 831226, ⊕ pentland ferries.co.uk) operates car catamarans from Gill's Bay (3 daily; 1hr), near John O'Groats (linked by bus to Wick and Thurso). John O'Groats Ferries (☎ 01955 611353, ⊕ jog ferry.co.uk) runs a passenger ferry from John O'Groats to Burwick at the southern tip of South Ronaldsay (May & Sept 2 daily; June–Aug 4 daily; 40min). Its departure is timed to connect with the arrival of the Orkney Bus from

Inverness; there's also a free shuttle service from Thurso train station for certain sailings. The ferry is small and, except in fine weather, is recommended only for those with strong stomachs.

By bus A regular bus service links Kirkwall with St Margaret's Hope (Mon–Sat hourly; 30min), and a summer-only one to Burwick connects with the John O'Groat's ferry (May–Sept 2–3 daily; 40min).

TOURS

Pettlandssker Boat Trip ☎ 01856 831605, ⊕ boattrips -orkney.co.uk. Daily trips to Pentland Skerries or Swona (puffins and seals guaranteed) from Burwick harbour

– the boat is an ex-lifeboat, the skipper is Hamish from the *Skerries Bistro* and tours cost around £30 and last up to 3 hours.

ACCOMMODATION AND EATING

ST MARGARET'S HOPE

The Creel Front Rd ☎ 01856 831311, ⊕ thecreel.co.uk. While the cooking here is really classy, the restaurant itself, in a sandstone house on the harbour front, is pleasantly informal. The short and seasonal menu regularly features local beef and seafood, with three-course dinners for around £30. The rooms are beautifully furnished and the breakfasts are among the best on Orkney. Food served April–Oct Tues–Sat 7pm. __£110__

★ **Roeberry House** ☎ 01856 831228, ⊕ roeberryhouse .com. Spacious rooms in a beautiful Victorian mansion in Hoxa. There are dogs, cats, chickens and peacocks, spectacular views and a genuinely warm welcome plus a small kitchen for guests' use, a billiard room and free wi-fi throughout the house. __£110__

St Margaret's Cottage ☎ 01856 831637, ⊕ stmargarets cottage.com. Handsome sandstone house on the edge of

The Hope, run by a genuine Orcadian couple; free wi-fi and very handy for the Pentland ferry. __£60__

St Margaret's Hope Backpackers Hostel Back Rd ☎ 01856 831225, ⊕ orkneybackpackers.com. Simple hotel, with a number of small rooms with double bunks – singles, doubles and family rooms available. There's a kitchen/lounge and a nice adjacent café with sofas and free wi-fi. Dorms __£15__

Wheems ☎ 01856 831556, ⊕ wheemsorganic.co.uk. Rambling old crofthouse and organic farm, 1.5 miles east of the main road, with a couple of wooden huts for hire, a sloping field for camping, all the usual facilities, plus a communal yurt. April–Oct. __£7__/pitch

BURWICK

Eastward Guest House ☎ 01856 831551, ⊕ eastward house.com. Housed in a tastefully converted former church on the main road to Burwick, this B&B has bags of character – reclaimed maple-wood flooring, Gothic windows. They also offer guests themed culinary evenings, specializing in Japanese food (ⓦmissingbell.com). **£90**

Skerries Bistro Banks ☎01856 831605, ⓦskerries

bistro.co.uk. Fabulous 180-degree view over the Pentland Firth and Skerries, with local fish and king scallops as big as steaks (mains around £15), plus delicious home-made puddings and cakes. April–Oct daily 11am–10pm.

Hoy

Hoy, Orkney's second-largest island, rises sharply out of the sea to the southwest of the Mainland. The least typical Orkney island, but certainly the most dramatic, it has north and west sides made up of great glacial valleys and mountainous moorland rising to over 1500ft, dropping into the sea off red sandstone cliffs, and forming the landmark sea stack known as the **Old Man of Hoy**. The northern half of Hoy is virtually uninhabited, with just the tiny village of Hoy opposite Stromness, and the cluster of houses at **Rackwick** nestling dramatically in a bay between the cliffs. Meanwhile, most of Hoy's four hundred or so residents live on the gentler, more fertile land in the southeast, in and around the villages of **Lyness** and **Longhope**. This part of the island is littered with buildings dating from the two world wars, when Scapa Flow served as the main base for the Royal Navy (see p.351).

North Hoy

Much of **North Hoy**'s magnificent landscape is made up of rough grasses and heather, which harbour a cluster of arctic plants (and a lot of midges) as well as a healthy population of mountain hares and birdlife. Facilities are minimal, however, with the nearest shop in Longhope (see p.352), and both Hoy and Rackwick absolutely tiny, with very little in the way of transport. If you're walking to Rackwick from Hoy, take the well-marked footpath past Sandy Loch and along the large open valley of **Berriedale** (1hr 30min).

Dwarfie Stane

Halfway along the road from Hoy to Rackwick, duckboards head across the heather to the **Dwarfie Stane**, Orkney's most unusual chambered tomb, cut from a solid block of sandstone and dating back to 3000 BC. The tomb is decorated with copious Victorian graffiti, the most interesting of which is on the northern exterior, where Major Mouncey, a former British spy in Persia and a confirmed eccentric who dressed in Persian garb, carved his name backwards in Latin and also carved in Persian the words "I have sat two nights and so learnt patience".

Rackwick

RACKWICK is an old crofting and fishing village squeezed between towering sandstone cliffs on the west coast. In an area once quite extensively cultivated, Rackwick went into a steady decline in the middle of the twentieth century: its school closed in 1953 and the last fishing boat put to sea in 1963. Electricity finally arrived in 1980 but these days only a few of the houses are inhabited all year round (the rest serve as holiday homes), though the savage isolation of the place has provided inspiration for a number of artists and writers, including Orkney's George Mackay Brown, who wrote "When Rackwick weeps, its grief is long and forlorn and utterly desolate". A small farm building beside the hostel has a tiny **museum** with a brief rundown of Rackwick's rough history, but for a deeper insight into how folk used to live in these parts, head over to the **Craa Nest**, the oldest crofthouse in the village, just up the path to the Old Man; last occupied in 1940, the place still has its box beds, barn and kiln intact. A short stroll away is the sandy beach, backed by giant sandstone pebbles washed smooth by the sea, which make a thunderous noise when the wind gets up.

The Old Man of Hoy

Rackwick has a steady stream of walkers and climbers passing through en route to the **Old Man of Hoy**, a great sandstone stack 450ft high, perched on an old lava flow which protects it from the erosive power of the sea. The Old Man is a popular challenge for rock-climbers, and a 1966 ascent, led by the mountaineer Chris Bonington, was the first televised climb in Britain. The well-trodden footpath from Rackwick is an easy three-mile walk (3hr round trip) – although the great skuas will dive-bomb you during the nesting season (May–Aug) – and rewards you with a great view of the stack. The surrounding cliffs provide ideal rocky ledges for thousands of nesting seabirds, including guillemot, kittiwake, razorbill, puffin and shag.

Continuing north along the clifftops from the Old Man, the path peters out before **St John's Head** which, at 1136ft, is one of Britain's highest sea cliffs. Another, safer, option is to hike to the top of **Ward Hill** (1577ft), the highest mountain in Orkney, from which on a fine day you can see the whole archipelago.

7

ARRIVAL AND GETTING AROUND   NORTH HOY

By ferry The passenger ferry runs from Stromness to Moaness pier, by Hoy village (Mon–Fri 4–5 daily, Sat & Sun 2 daily; 25min; ☎01856 850624), and also serves the island of Graemsay en route.

By bus A minibus usually meets the ferry and will take folk over to Rackwick or further afield. A Hoy Hopper bus service (mid-May to mid-Sept Wed–Fri only), which departs from Kirkwall, also calls at Moaness.

ACCOMMODATION

Burnside Bothy ☎01856 791316. You can camp in the dry-stone-walled field beside this beautiful but basic heather-thatched bothy by the beach – toilets, cold water and a driftwood fire available inside the bothy. Donations box

Hoy Centre ☎01856 873535 ext 2417. A council-run, SYHA-affiliated hostel in an old school. Situated in Hoy village, this place is large and modern, with a well-equipped

kitchen, washing and drying facilities and all rooms en suite. **£17**/person

Rackwick Outdoor Centre ☎01856 873535 ext 2417. Housed in Rackwick's tiny little former school-house, this simple hostel has just eight beds in two rooms and a small kitchen, but has a great situation in Rackwick village itself – camping permitted. April–Sept. **£13.50**/person

EATING AND DRINKING

Beneth'ill Café ☎01856 791119. Even if you've just come for a day-trip, you'll want to check out this really friendly, simple café, a short walk from Moaness pier. Expect Cullen skink, fresh local crab, home-made puddings

and proper coffee – they'll even do you a packed lunch and an evening meal on a Friday. May–Sept daily 10am–6.30pm.

Lyness

Along the sheltered eastern shore of Hoy, high moorland gives way gradually to a gentler environment. Hoy defines the western boundary of Scapa Flow, and **LYNESS** played a major role for the Royal Navy during both world wars. Most of the old wartime buildings have been cleared away, but the harbour and hills around Lyness are still scarred with scattered concrete structures that once served as hangars and storehouses, and are now used as barns and cowsheds. Among these are the remains of what was – incredibly – once the largest cinema in Europe, but perhaps the most unusual building is the monochrome Art-Deco facade of the old **Garrison Theatre** (now a private home) where the troops were entertained, on the main road to the south. Lyness also has a large **naval cemetery**, where many of the victims of the various disasters that have occurred in the Flow, such as the sinking of the *Royal Oak* (see p.345), now lie, alongside a handful of German graves.

Scapa Flow Visitor Centre and Museum

May–Sept Mon–Sat 9am–4.30pm, Sun open according to ferry; March, April & Oct Mon–Fri 9am–4.30pm • Free • ☎ 01856 791300, ⓦ scapaflow.co.uk

The old oil pumphouse, standing opposite Lyness ferry terminal, has been turned into the **Scapa Flow Visitor Centre**, giving a fascinating insight into wartime Orkney – even the **café** has an old NAAFI feel about it. As well as the usual old photos, torpedoes, flags, guns and propellers, there's a paratrooper's folding bicycle, and a whole section devoted to the scuttling of the German High Seas Fleet and the sinking of the *Royal Oak*. The pumphouse itself retains much of its old equipment used to pump oil from tankers into sixteen tanks, and into underground reservoirs cut into the neighbouring hillside. You can also wander over to the Romney Hut, where Admiral von Reuter's *Chefboot* resides along with engines from the old wartime railway, and to the air-raid shelter beyond.

ARRIVAL AND DEPARTURE   LYNESS

By ferry The roll-on/roll-off car ferry to/from Houton on the Mainland (Mon–Fri 6 daily, Sat & Sun 2–5 daily; 35min–1hr; ☎ 01856 811397) sometimes calls in at the oil terminal island of Flotta, and begins and ends its daily schedule at Longhope.

ACCOMMODATION

★ **Wild Heather B&B** ☎ 01856 791098, ⓦ wildheather bandb.co.uk. The most outstanding accommodation on Hoy lies just beyond the naval cemetery. It's a converted mill with just two en-suite rooms, both with sea views and a lovely breakfast conservatory – they provide evening meals, too, on request. **£65**

ENTERTAINMENT

Gable End Theatre ⓦ hoyorkney.com/getco.html. Established in the old North Walls school buildings, this community-run theatre (with its own wind turbine) shows regular films and puts on the occasional theatre piece and music gig – check their Facebook page for the latest.

Melsetter House

4 miles southwest of Lyness • Thurs by appointment • ☎ 01856 791352

The finest architecture on Hoy is to be found at **Melsetter House**, overlooking the deep inlet of North Bay. Originally built in 1738, it was bought by Thomas Middlemore, heir to a Birmingham leather tycoon, who commissioned Arts and Crafts architect William Lethaby to transform the house in 1898. The owners will happily take you round a handful of rooms in the house itself, all of which are simply decorated with white wood panelling, floral plasterwork and William Morris-style fabrics, and leave you to wander freely around the very beautiful grounds. Don't miss the little **Chapel of St Margaret and St Colm** that Lethaby fashioned from the Melsetter outhouses, which features, four tiny, stained-glass windows by, among others, Ford Madox Brown and Burne-Jones.

Longhope

East of Melsetter House, a causeway built during World War II connects Hoy with South Walls (pronounced "Waas"), a fertile tidal island which is more densely populated than Hoy. Along the north coast is the main settlement of **LONGHOPE**, an important safe anchorage even today.

Longhope Lifeboat Museum

By appointment • Free • ☎ 01856 701332, ⓦ longhopelifeboat.org.uk

Near the causeway the **Longhope Lifeboat Museum** houses the *Thomas McCunn*, a lifeboat in service from 1933 to 1962 and still launched for high days and holidays.

The Longhope Lifeboat capsized in strong gale-force winds in 1969 on its way to the aid of a Liberian freighter. The entire eight-man crew died, leaving seven widows and ten fatherless children; the crew of the freighter, by contrast, survived. There's a moving memorial to the men – six of whom came from just two families – in **Kirkhope churchyard** on the road to Cantick Head Lighthouse.

Hackness Martello Tower
April–Oct daily 9.30am–5.30pm • £4.50; HS • ☎ 01856 701727

Longhope's strategic importance during the Napoleonic Wars is evident at the Point of Hackness, where the **Hackness Martello Tower** stands guard over the entrance to the bay, with a matching tower on the opposite promontory of Crockness. Built in 1815, these two circular, sandstone Martello towers are the northernmost in Britain, and protected merchant ships from American and French privateers. You enter Hackness Tower via a steep ladder connected to the upper floor, where nine men and one officer shared the circular room. The walls are up to 9ft high on the seaward side, and the tower even had its own water supply.

7

ARRIVAL AND DEPARTURE　　　　　　　　　　　　　　　　　　　　LONGHOPE

By ferry The car ferry from Houton on the Mainland to Lyness begins and ends its daily schedule at Longhope.

ACCOMMODATION

Stromabank Hotel ☎ 01856 701494, ⦿ stromabank .co.uk. This small, unpretentious hotel is housed in an old schoolhouse on the hill above Longhope, with views over the Pentland Firth. Bar food available in the evening (closed Thurs). **£64**

Shapinsay

Just a few miles northeast of Kirkwall, **Shapinsay** is the most accessible of Orkney's northern isles. A gently undulating grid-plan patchwork of rich farmland, it's a bit like an island suburb of Kirkwall, which is clearly visible across the bay.

Balfour

The only village on Shapinsay is **BALFOUR**, named after the family who owned the local castle and the island, reformed the island's agricultural system and rebuilt the village – previously known as Shoreside – as a neat and disciplined cottage development, to house their estate workers. The family's grandiose efforts in estate management have left some appealingly eccentric relics around the village. Melodramatic fortifications around the harbour include the huge and ornate **gatehouse**, which now serves as the local pub. There's also a stone-built coal-fired **gasometer**, which once supplied castle and harbour with electricity and, southwest of the pier, the castellated **Douche** or Dishan Tower, a seventeenth-century doocot, converted into a saltwater toilet and shower in Victorian times.

Balfour Castle
Guided tour and tea Sun afternoons in Aug • £22 • ☎ 01856 711282

Shapinsay's chief landmark is **Balfour Castle**, an imposing baronial pile visible as you approach on the ferry and a short walk from the village. Designed by David Bryce, it was completed in 1848 by the Balfour family of Westray, who had made a small fortune in India the previous century. The Balfours died out in 1960 and nowadays the castle is an exclusive-use holiday retreat, but open for guided tours and afternoon teas on Sundays in August.

Shapinsay Heritage Centre

The Smithy • May–Sept daily 2–5pm • Free • ☎ 01856 711246

The old smithy, halfway along Balfour's main street, houses the **Shapinsay Heritage Centre**, where you can learn everything you ever wanted to know about the island, before availing yourself of its excellent café (see below).

ARRIVAL AND DEPARTURE   SHAPINSAY

By ferry Less than 30min from Kirkwall by ferry (4–5 daily), Shapinsay is an easy day-trip.

By bus There's a Dial-a-Bus service around the island, which must be booked in advance (☎ 0791 575162).

ACCOMMODATION AND EATING

Hilton Farmhouse ☎ 01856 711239, ⊕ hiltonorkney farmhouse.co.uk. This whitewashed farmhouse, less than a mile from Balfour, has just two sunny, south-facing bedrooms (one of which is en suite), and a restaurant in the conservatory (booking ahead essential) and offers optional full board. **£70**

The Smithy ☎ 01856 711269. Even if you're just coming for the day, it's worth popping into the wonderfully cosy licensed café below the heritage centre, which serves a simple menu during the day, and delicious, fresh, locally sourced fish and meat dishes in the evening (mains around £15). Evening boat charter from Mainland also available (£7 a head). May–Sept: Mon, Wed & Fri–Sun 9.30am–9pm, Tues & Thurs 9.30am–5pm.

Rousay, Egilsay and Wyre

Just over half a mile from the Mainland's northern shore, the hilly island of **Rousay** is one of the more accessible northern isles as well as being home to a number of intriguing prehistoric sites. The group of a dozen or so houses above the ferry terminal is the only settlement of any size, but a single road runs around the edge of the island,

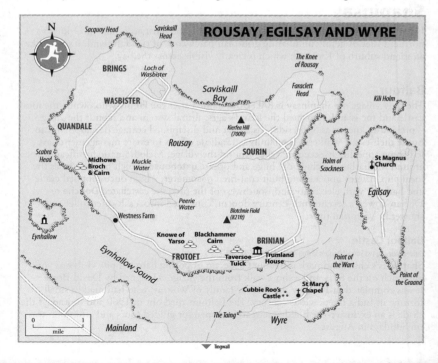

connecting a string of small farms which make use of the more cultivable coastal fringes. Many visitors come on a day-trip, as it's easy enough to reach the main points of archeological interest on the south coast by foot from the ferry terminal.

Rousay's diminutive neighbours, **Egilsay** and **Wyre**, contain a few medieval attractions of their own, which can either be visited on a day-trip from Rousay itself, or from the mainland.

Rousay

Despite its long history of settlement, **Rousay** today is home to little more than two hundred people (many of them incomers), as this was one of the few parts of Orkney to suffer Highland-style Clearances, initially by George William Traill at Quandale in the northwest. His successor and nephew, Lieutenant General Sir Frederick William Traill-Burroughs, built a wall to force crofters onto a narrow coastal strip and eventually provoked so much distress and anger that a gunboat had to be sent to restore order. You can learn about the history and wildlife of the island from the well-laid-out display room of the **Rousay Heritage Centre** housed in the back of the ferry waiting room.

7

Trumland House

Gardens May–Oct daily 10am–5pm • £2 • ☎ 01856 821322, ⓦ trumlandhouse.org

The island's laird, Lieutenant General Traill-Burroughs, built **Trumland House**, the forbidding Jacobean-style pile designed by David Bryce in the 1870s, hidden in the trees half a mile northwest of the ferry terminal. The house is currently undergoing much-needed restoration, as are the landscaped **gardens**: the rhododendrons have been pushed back and there are now lovely wooded walks and a walled garden.

The three cairns

The road west from Trumland House is bordered over the next couple of miles by a trio of intriguing prehistoric cairns, starting with **Taversoe Tuick**. Dating back to 3500 BC, it's remarkable in that it exploits its sloping site by having two storeys, one entered from the upper side and one from the lower.

A little further west is the **Blackhammar Cairn**, which is more promising inside than it looks from the outside. You enter through the roof via a ladder; the long interior is divided into "stalls" by large flagstones, rather like the more famous cairn at Midhowe (see p.356).

Finally, there's the **Knowe of Yarso**, another stalled cairn dating from the same period. It's worth the stiff climb up the hill from the road, if only for the magnificent view. The remains of 29 individuals were found inside, with the skulls neatly arranged around the walls; the bones of 36 deer were also buried here.

Trumland RSPB reserve

A footpath sets off from beside the Taversoe Tuick tomb into the **RSPB reserve** that encompasses most of the nearby heather-backed hills, the highest of which is **Blotchnie Field** (821ft). This high ground offers good hillwalking, with superb panoramic views of the surrounding islands, as well as excellent birdwatching. If you're lucky, you may well catch a glimpse of merlins, hen harriers, short-eared owls and red-throated divers, although the latter are more widespread just outside the reserve on one of the island's three freshwater lochs, which also offer good trout-fishing.

Westness Walk

The southwestern side of Rousay is home to the most significant and impressive of the island's archeological remains, strung out along the shores of Eynhallow Sound, which runs between the island and the Mainland. Most lie on the mile-long **Westness Walk** that begins at Westness Farm, four miles west of the ferry terminal. This scramble along the shore is rewarded with a kaleidoscope of history, with remains of an Iron Age cairn, a Viking farm, a post-Reformation church, a medieval tower, and crofts from which the tenants were evicted in the nineteenth century. Half a mile further, you'll reach the impressive clifftop scenery around **Scabra Head**, where numerous seabirds nest in summer.

Midhowe Cairn

Towards the end of the walk, **Midhowe Cairn** comes as something of a surprise, both for its immense size – it's known as "the great ship of death" and measures nearly 100ft in length – and because it's now entirely surrounded by a stone-walled barn with a corrugated roof. Unfortunately, you can't actually explore the roofless communal burial chamber, dating back to 3500 BC, but only look down from the overhead walkway. The central corridor, 25yd long, is partitioned with slabs of rock, with twelve compartments on each side, where the remains of 25 people were discovered in a crouched position with their backs to the wall.

Midhowe Broch

A couple of hundred yards beyond Midhowe Cairn is Rousay's finest archeological site, **Midhowe Broch**, whose compact layout suggests that it was originally built as a sort of fortified family house, surrounded by a complex series of ditches and ramparts. The broch itself looks as though it's about to slip into the sea: it was obviously shored up with flagstone buttresses back in the Iron Age, and has more recently been given extra sea defences by Historic Scotland. The interior of the broch, entered through an impressive doorway, is divided into two separate rooms, each with its own hearth, water tank and quernstone, all of which date from the final phase of occupation around the second century AD.

Egilsay

Egilsay, the largest of the low-lying islands sheltering close to the eastern shore of Rousay, makes an easy day-trip. Egilsay is almost entirely inhabited by incomers, and a large slice of the island's farmland is managed by the RSPB in a vain attempt to encourage corncrakes. If you're just here for the day, walk due east from the ferry terminal to the coast, where there's a beautiful sandy bay overlooking Eday.

St Magnus Church

The island is dominated by the ruins of **St Magnus Church**, with its distinctive round tower, venue for Egilsay's ever more popular summer-solstice celebrations. Built around the twelfth century in a prominent position in the middle of the island, probably on the site of a much earlier version, the roofless church is the only surviving example of the traditional round-towered churches of Orkney and Shetland. It is possible that it was built as a shrine to Earl (later Saint) Magnus, who arranged to meet his cousin Håkon here in 1117, only to be treacherously killed on Håkon's orders by the latter's cook, Lifolf.

Wyre

The tiny island of **Wyre**, to the southwest of Egilsay and directly opposite Rousay's ferry terminal, is another possible day-trip, and is best known for **Cubbie Roo's Castle**, the "fine stone fort" and "really solid stronghold" mentioned in the *Orkneyinga Saga*, and built around 1150 by local farmer Kolbein Hruga. The castle gets another mention in *Håkon's Saga*, when those inside successfully withstood all attacks. The outer defences have survived well on three sides of the castle, which has a central keep, with walls to a height of around 6ft, its central water-tank still intact. Close by the castle stands **St Mary's Chapel**, a roofless twelfth-century church founded either by Kolbein or his son, Bjarni the Poet, who was Bishop of Orkney. Kolbein's permanent residence or **Bu** is recalled in the name of the nearby farm, the Bu of Wyre, where the poet **Edwin Muir** (1887–1959) spent his childhood, described in detail in his autobiography. To learn more about Muir, Cubbie Roo or any other aspect of Wyre's history, pop into the **Wyre Heritage Centre**, near the chapel.

ARRIVAL AND GETTING AROUND

ROUSAY, EGILSAY AND WYRE

By ferry Rousay makes a good day-trip from the Mainland, with regular car ferry sailings from Tingwall (5–6 daily; 30min), linked to Kirkwall by bus (Mon–Sat 4–5 daily; 25min). Most ferries also call in at Egilsay and Wyre, but some are request journeys and must be booked the day before with Tingwall (☎ 01856 751360).

By bus A bus service runs every Thursday (7am–7pm), but must be booked in advance (☎ 01856 821360, ⓦ around rousay.co.uk/bus). There are also minibus tours available on demand (☎ 01856 821234; £30), which set off from the ferry terminal on Rousay (5–7hr).

ACCOMMODATION AND EATING

ROUSAY

Accommodation and eating options on Rousay are very limited. If you're coming for the day or self-catering, don't arrive expecting to be able to buy yourself many provisions, either, as Marion's Shop, the island's main general store, is in the northeastern corner of the island. Free wi-fi is available throughout the island – phone the Manse (☎ 01856 821229).

The Pier ☎ 01856 821359, ⓦ pierrestaurantorkney.com. A simple pub, right beside the ferry terminal, that serves bar meals (all under £10) and Orkney beers, and will serve up lobster or make up some fresh crab sandwiches if you phone in advance. May–Sept daily; shorter hours in winter.

The Taversoe ☎ 01856 821325, ⓦ taversoehotel.co .uk. Three miles west of the ferry terminal, the *Taversoe* offers unpretentious accommodation in three rooms (two with sea views) and does classic pub meals – fish and chips, scampi or burgers (all under £10). **£75**

Trumland Farm ☎ 01856 821252. Just half a mile west of the ferry terminal, this working organic farm has a couple of dorms and a family room – you can also camp here, and they offer bike rental. Dorms **£12**; camping **£5**/person

Westray

Although exposed to the full force of the Atlantic weather in the far northwest of Orkney, **Westray** shelters one of the most tightly knit, prosperous and independent island communities, numbering some six hundred Old Orcadian families who give the island a strongly individual character. Fishing, farming and tourism are the mainstays of the economy. The landscape is very varied, with sea cliffs and a trio of hills in the west, and rich low-lying pastureland and sandy bays elsewhere. However, given that it's about twelve miles from the ferry terminal in the south to the cliffs of Noup Head in the far northwest – and that the boat from Kirkwall takes nearly an hour and a half, Westray is an island that repays a longer stay, especially as there's lots of good accommodation and the locals are extremely welcoming.

Pierowall

The main village and harbour is **PIEROWALL**, set around a wide bay in the north of the island, eight miles from Rapness ferry terminal on the island's southernmost tip. Pierowall is a place of some considerable size, relatively speaking, with a school, several shops and a bakery (Orkney's only one off the Mainland).

Westray Heritage Centre

May–Sept Mon 11.30am–5pm, Tues–Sat 10am–noon & 2–5pm, Sun 1.30–5pm • £2.50 • ☎ 01857 677414, ⓦ westrayheritage.co.uk

The village's **Westray Heritage Centre** is a very welcoming wet-weather retreat, and a great place to gen up on (and with any luck catch a glimpse of) the Westray Wife or

Orkney Venus – a remarkable, miniature Neolithic female figurine found in 2009 in the dunes to the northwest of Pierowall – along with her incomplete companion, and the recently discovered Grobust Grandad.

Noltland Castle

Pick up the key, which hangs outside the back door of the nearby farm

The island's most impressive ruin is the colossal sandstone hulk of **Noltland Castle**, which stands above the village half a mile west up the road to Noup Head. This Z-plan castle, pockmarked with over seventy gun loops, was begun around 1560 by Gilbert Balfour, a shady character from Fife, who was Master of the Household to Mary, Queen of Scots, and was implicated in the murder of her husband, Lord Darnley, in 1567. When Mary was deposed, Balfour joined an unsuccessful uprising in favour of

7

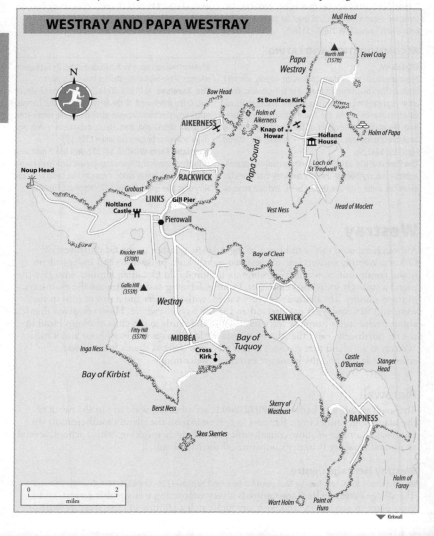

WESTRAY AND PAPA WESTRAY

the exiled queen and was forced to flee to Sweden. There he was found guilty of plotting to murder the Swedish king and was executed in 1576. The most striking features of the interior are the huge, carved stone newel at the top of the grand, main staircase, and the secret compartments built into the sills of two of the windows.

Noup Head

The northwestern tip of Westray rises up sharply, culminating in the dramatic sea cliffs of **Noup Head**, particularly spectacular when a westerly swell is up. During the summer months the guano-covered rock ledges are packed with over 100,000 nesting guillemots, razorbills, kittiwakes, fulmars and puffins: a heady sensation of sight, sound and smell. The open ground above the cliffs, grazed by sheep, is superb maritime heath and grassland, carpeted with yellow, white and purple flowers, and a favourite breeding-ground for arctic tern and arctic skua.

The south of the island

The four-mile coastal walk in the **south** of Westray, along the top of red-sandstone cliffs from Noup Head south to the Bay of Kirbist is thoroughly recommended, as is a quick ascent of nearby **Fitty Hill** (557ft), Westray's highest point. Also in the south of the island is the tiny **Cross Kirk** which, although ruined, retains an original Romanesque arch, door and window. It's right by the sea, and on a fine day the nearby sandy beach is a lovely spot for a picnic, with views over to the north side of Rousay. The sea cliffs in the southeast of the island around **Stanger Head** are not quite as spectacular as at Noup Head, but it's here that you'll find **Castle o'Burrian**, a sea stack, the best place on Westray at which to see **puffins** nesting – there's even a signpost from the main road.

ARRIVAL AND DEPARTURE
WESTRAY

By plane You can fly from Kirkwall (Mon–Fri 2 daily, Sat & Sun 1 daily; 15min) and go on the world's shortest scheduled flight between Westray and Papa Westray (Mon–Sat 1 daily; 2min).

By ferry Westray is served by car ferry from Kirkwall (2–3 daily; 1hr 25min; ☎01856 872044) and there's a passenger ferry between Pierowall (Westray) and Papa Westray (Mon–Thurs 6 daily, Fri & Sat 4 daily, 3 on Sun; 25min).

GETTING AROUND

By bus A minibus (May–Sept; at other times phone ☎01857 677758) meets the ferry and connects with the Papa Westray ferry at Gill Pier in Pierowall; book a seat for the bus on the ferry.

INFORMATION AND TOURS

Tourist information ⊛ westraypapawestray.co.uk.
Tours and bike rental Westray ☎01857 677777, ⊛ westraak.co.uk. Guided tours of the island by minibus can be arranged with Westraak, who will meet you at the ferry. They also offer bike rental.

ACCOMMODATION AND EATING

★ **The Barn** ☎01857 677214, ⊛ thebarnwestray .co.uk. A converted farm hostel at the southern edge of Pierowall; it's luxurious inside, with family rooms and twin bunks available, has a small campsite adjacent to it and a games room and genuinely friendly hosts. Dorms **£20**; camping **£5**/person.

Haf Yok ☎01857 677777. Café in a little shed in Pierowall itself (opposite the Lady Kirk) owned by the couple who also run Westraak tour company. Great for soup, toasties and cakes, with a few tables in a south-facing suntrap. Mid-May to Sept: Mon–Sat

10.30am–5pm, Sun noon–4pm.
No. 1 Broughton ☎01857 677726, ⊛ no1broughton .co.uk. Top-notch, good-value B&B in a renovated mid-nineteenth-century house with views across the bay, a lovely conservatory and even a small sauna. **£60**

Pierowall Hotel ☎01857 677472, ⊛ pierowallhotel .co.uk. The social hub of Pierowall itself, is unpretentious and very welcoming – the cheaper rooms have shared facilities. The popular bar has a well-justified reputation for excellent fish and chips, fresh off the boats (much of the catch you're unlikely to have heard of). **£76**

7

Papa Westray

Across the short Papa Sound from Westray is the island of **Papa Westray**, known locally as "Papay". With a population hovering around 90, Papay has had to fight hard to keep itself viable over the last couple of decades, helped by a hefty influx of outsiders. With one of Orkney's best-preserved Neolithic settlements, and a large nesting sea-bird population, Papay is worthy of a stay in its own right or an easy day-trip from its big neighbour.

As the name suggests – *papøy* is Old Norse for "priest" – the island was once a medieval pilgrimage centre, focused on a chapel dedicated to **St Tredwell**, now reduced to a pile of rubble on a promontory on the loch of the same name just inland from the ferry terminal. St Tredwell (Triduana) was a plucky young local girl who gouged out her eyes and handed them to the eighth-century Pictish king Nechtan when he attempted to rape her. By the twelfth century, the chapel had become a place of pilgrimage for those suffering from eye complaints.

Holland House

Farm buildings always open • Free

The island's visual focus is **Holland House**, occupying the high central point of the island and once seat of the local lairds, the Traill family, who ruled over Papay for three centuries. The main house, with crow-stepped gables, is still in private hands, but the owners are happy for visitors to explore the old buildings of the home farm, on the west side of the road, which include a kiln, a doocot and a horse-powered threshing mill. An old bothy for single male servants, decorated with red horse-yokes, has been restored and made into a small **museum** filled with bygone bits and bobs, from a wooden flea-trap to a box bed.

Knap of Howar

From Holland House, it's around half a mile to the western shore, and to Papay's prime prehistoric site, the **Knap of Howar**. Dating from around 3500 BC, this Neolithic farm building makes a fair claim to being the oldest-standing house in Europe. It's made up of two roofless buildings, linked by a little passageway; one has a hearth and copious stone shelves, and is thought to have been some kind of storehouse.

St Boniface Kirk

St Boniface Kirk is a pre-Reformation church three-quarters of a mile north of the Knap of Howar. Inside, it's beautifully simple, with a bare flagstone floor, dry-stone walls, a little wooden gallery and just a couple of surviving box pews. The church is known to have seated at least 220, which meant they would have been squashed in, fourteen to a pew. In the graveyard is a Viking **hogback grave**, decorated with carvings imitating the wooden shingles on the roof of a Viking longhouse.

North Hill

Escorted walks May–Aug Wed & Sat; meet at Rose Cottage • Free • ☎ 01857 644240

The northern tip of the island around **North Hill** (157ft) is an RSPB reserve. During the breeding season you're asked to keep to the coastal fringe, where razorbills, guillemots, fulmars, kittiwakes and puffins nest, particularly around Fowl Craig on the east coast, where you may spot the rare Scottish primrose, which flowers in May and from July to late September. If you want to explore the interior of the reserve, which has one of the largest arctic tern colonies in Europe as well as numerous arctic skuas, contact the warden, who conducts regular escorted walks.

Holm of Papa

To arrange a boat Community Co-operative • ☎ 01857 644321

If you're here for more than a day, it's worth considering renting a boat to take you over to the **Holm of Papa**, an islet off the east coast. Despite its tiny size, the Holm boasts several Neolithic chambered cairns, one of which, occupying the highest point, is extremely impressive. Descending into the tomb via a ladder, you enter the main rectangular chamber, which is nearly 70ft in length, with no fewer than twelve side-cells, each with its own lintelled entrance.

ARRIVAL AND DEPARTURE   PAPA WESTRAY

By plane You can fly direct from Kirkwall to Papa Westray (Mon–Sat 2–3 daily, 1 on Sun; 25min) for a special return fare of £21 if you stay overnight. Papay is also connected to Westray by the world's shortest scheduled flight (Mon–Sat 1 daily) – 2min in duration, or less with a following wind.

By ferry Papay is an easy day-trip from Westray, with a passenger ferry service from Gill Pier in Pierowall (3–6 daily; 25min), which also takes bicycles.

Car ferries On Tuesdays, the car ferry goes from Kirkwall to Papa Westray via North Ronaldsay, which means it takes over four hours; on Fridays, the car ferry from Kirkwall to Westray continues on to Papa Westray; at other times, you have to catch a bus to connect with the Papa Westray ferry from Pierowall. The bus should be booked ahead, while on the Westray ferry (☎ 01857 677758); it accepts a limited number of bicycles.

GETTING AROUND AND INFORMATION

By minibus Papay's Community Co-operative (☎ 01857 644321) has a minibus, which will take you from the pier to wherever you want on the island on request, and can

arrange a "Peedie Package" tour including lunch (Wed & Sat; £30) – you can even do it from Kirkwall as a 12hr day-trip.

Tourist information ⓦ papawestray.co.uk.

ACCOMMODATION AND EATING

Beltane House ☎ 01857 644224, ⓦ papawestray.co .uk. The island Co-op offers B&B, a two-room, sixteen-bed hostel, a place to camp, and a shop, all housed within the old estate-workers' cottages at Beltane, east of Holland

House. *Beltane House* opens its "bar cupboard" every Saturday night from 9pm, with bar meals available – a great way to meet the locals. **£70**; hostel **£13.50**/person; camping **£5**/person

Eday

A long, thin island at the centre of Orkney's northern isles, **Eday** shares more characteristics with Rousay and Hoy than with its immediate neighbours, dominated as it is by heather-covered upland, with farmland confined to a narrow strip of coastal ground. However, Eday's hills have proved useful in their own way, providing huge quantities of peat, which has been exported to other peatless northern isles for fuel, and was even, for a time, exported to various whisky distillers. Eday's yellow sandstone has also been extensively quarried, and was used to build the St Magnus Cathedral in Kirkwall.

Eday is sparsely inhabited, with a population of around 160, the majority of them incomers, and there's no main village as such; the island post office, petrol pump and community shop all cluster in Hammerhill. The ferry terminal is at the south end of the island, whereas the chief points of interest (and most of the amenities) are all in the northern half, about four miles away. The name Eday comes from the Norse for "isthmus" and, indeed, the island is almost divided in two by its thin waist. On either side are sandy bays, between which lies the airfield (known as London Airport). To the south, around Flaughton Hill (328ft), there's a large breeding population of whimbrels.

Eday Heritage Centre and HMS Otter

April–Oct daily 9am–6pm; Nov–March Sun 10am–5pm • Free • ☎ 01857 622263

Eday Heritage Centre, in an old Baptist chapel a mile north of the island's airport, has historical displays on Eday, with information on the island's tidal energy testing centre in the Fall of Warness, as well as a café. Perhaps the most unusual attraction, however, is in the hall of the former North School, almost opposite the island shop, where several internal sections of the Cold War-era **submarine** HMS *Otter* have been reassembled – a truly eerie experience.

Eday Heritage Walk: Mill Loch to Red Head

The clearly marked **Eday Heritage Walk** (4hr return) begins at **Mill Loch**, where a bird hide looks over the loch, where several pairs of **red-throated divers** regularly breed.

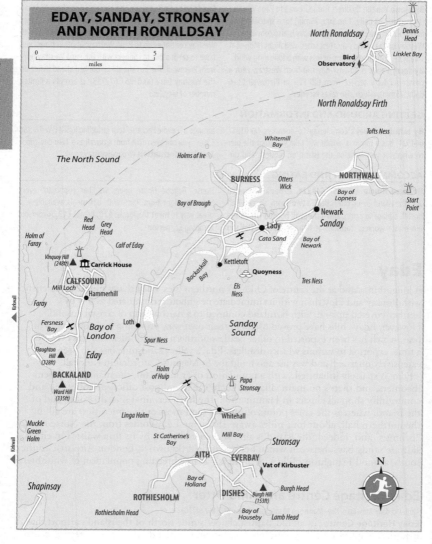

EDAY, SANDAY, STRONSAY AND NORTH RONALDSAY

Clearly visible over the road is the 15ft **Stone of Setter**, Orkney's most distinctive standing stone, weathered into three thick, lichen-encrusted fingers. From here, passing the less spectacular Braeside and Huntersquoy chambered cairns en route, you can climb the hill to reach Eday's finest, the **Vinquoy Chambered Cairn**, which has a similar structure to that of Maes Howe (see p.337). You can crawl into the tomb through the narrow entrance: a skylight lets light into the main, beehive chamber, now home to some lovely ferns, but not into the four side-cells. From the cairn, you can continue north to the viewpoint on **Vinquoy Hill** (248ft), and to the very northernmost tip of the island, where the dramatic red-sandstone sea cliffs of **Red Head** are a summer nesting place for numerous seabirds.

Redhouse Croft Restoration Project

June to mid-Sept Tues–Fri 11am–5pm • Free • ☎ 01857 622217

The **Redhouse Croft Restoration Project**, to the west of Vinquoy Hill, is where you can explore the evocative remains of a large nineteenth-century farm, complete with kiln, water-wheel and byre. There's a tearoom at the foot of the hill, offering soup, sandwiches and home-baked cakes.

Carrick House

Mid-June to Aug Sun 2–5pm or by appointment • ☎ 01857 622260

Visible on the east coast is **Carrick House**, the grandest home on Eday. Built by the Laird of Eday in 1633, it was extended in the original style by successive owners, but is best known for its associations with the pirate **John Gow** – on whom Sir Walter Scott's novel *The Pirate* is based – whose ship *The Revenge* ran aground on the **Calf of Eday** in 1725. He asked for help from the Laird, but was taken prisoner in Carrick House, before being sent off to London, where he was tortured and executed. The highlight of the tour is the bloodstain on the floor of the living room, where John Gow was detained and stabbed while trying to escape.

ARRIVAL AND INFORMATION
EDAY

By plane You can make a day-trip by plane from Kirkwall to Eday on Wednesdays (1 on Mon, 2 on Wed; 10min).

By ferry Eday is served by regular car ferry from Kirkwall

(2 daily; 1hr 15min–2hr).

Tourist information ⓦ visiteday.com.

GETTING AROUND AND TOURS

By car, taxi or minibus Car rental, taxis or minibus tours (May–Aug Mon, Wed & Fri; £12) can be organized through J&J by the pier (☎ 01857 622206).

Tours The island's ferry terminal is at Backaland pier in the south, not ideal for visiting the more interesting northern section of the island, although you should find it fairly easy to get a lift with someone off the ferry. The

other option is to book a seat with Eday Minibus Tours (May to mid-Sept Mon, Wed & Fri or by appointment; £14; ☎ 01857 622206), who will collect you from the ferry. Eday has a Ranger service, too, who offer weekly guided walks – book ahead on ☎ 07964 149155 or check Eday Scarfs' Facebook page.

ACCOMMODATION AND EATING

Blett ☎ 01857 622248. A crofthouse with two rooms, near Carrick House, overlooking the bay. They'll provide packed lunches, and excellent, locally sourced evening meals are available on request. **£70**

Eday SYHA Hostel ☎ 01857 622283, ⓦ syha.org.uk. An SYHA-affiliated, community-run hostel, situated in an exposed spot just north of the airport – phone ahead as

there's no resident warden. Washing machine and dryer, bike hire and internet access, and you can camp there, too. Dorms **£15**

Roadside Pub ☎ 01857 622303. Eday's one and only pub is in a pleasant old building overlooking the ferry terminal, and offers B&B in two en-suite rooms and evening meals on request (mains under £10). **£60**

Stronsay

A low-lying, three-legged island, **Stronsay** is strongly agricultural, its interior an almost uninterrupted collage of green pastures. The island features few real sights, but the coastline has enormous appeal: a beguiling combination of sandstone cliffs, home to several sea-bird colonies, interspersed with wide white sands and (in fine weather) clear turquoise bays. The most dramatic section of coastline, featuring great, layered slices of sandstone, lies in the southeast corner of the island. Stronsay has a population of around 350 and has seen two economic booms in the last 300 years. The first took place in the eighteenth century, employing as many as 3000 people; it was built on collecting vast quantities of seaweed and exporting the **kelp** for use in the chemical industry, particularly in making iodine, soap and glass. In the following century, **fishing** came to dominate life here, as Whitehall harbour became one of the main Scottish centres for curing the herring caught by French, Dutch and Scottish boats. By the 1840s, up to 400 boats were working out of the port, attracting hundreds of female herring-gutters. By the 1930s, however, the herring stocks had been severely depleted and the industry began a long decline.

7

Whitehall

WHITEHALL, in the north of the island, is the only real village on Stronsay, made up of rows of stone-built fishermen's cottages set between two large piers. Wandering along the tranquil, rather forlorn harbour-front today, you'll find it hard to believe that the village once supported 5000 people in the fishing industry during the summer season, as well as a small army of coopers, coal merchants, butchers, bakers, several Italian ice-cream parlours and a cinema. It was said that, on a Sunday, you could walk across the decks of the boats all the way to **Papa Stronsay**, the tiny island that shelters Whitehall from the north. The old Fish Mart by the pier houses a small **museum**, with a few photos and artefacts from the herring days – ask at the adjacent café for access.

Papa Stronsay

Ferry The island's monks will take visitors across to (and around) the island by boat, by prior arrangement • ☎ 01857 616210, Ⓦ papastronsay.com

Clearly visible from the harbour-front at Whitehall is the tiny island of **Papa Stronsay**, which features in the *Orkneyinga Saga* (see p.419) as the place where Earl Rognvald Brusason was murdered by Earl Thorfinn Sigurdarson. Later, during the herring boom, it was home to five fish-curing stations. The island is thought originally to have been a **monastic retreat**, a theory given extra weight by the discovery of an eighth-century chapel during recent excavations. In 2000, Papa Stronsay was bought by Transalpine Redemptorist monks, who had broken with the Vatican over their refusal to stop celebrating Mass in Latin. They have subsequently built themselves the multi-million-pound Golgotha Monastery, with a creamery for making their Monastery Cheese. Since 2008, they have been accepted into the Roman Catholic Church and renamed the Sons of the Most Holy Redeemer.

Vat of Kirbuster to Lamb Head

Signposts show the way to Orkney's biggest and most dramatic natural arch, the **Vat of Kirbuster**. Before you reach it there's a seaweedy, shallow pool in a natural sandstone amphitheatre, where the water is warmed by the sun, and kids and adults can safely wallow: close by is a rocky inlet for those who prefer colder, more adventurous swimming. You'll find nesting seabirds, including a few puffins, as you approach **Burgh Head**. Meanwhile, at the promontory of **Lamb Head**, there are usually loads of seals, a large colony of arctic terns, and good views out to the lighthouse on the outlying island of **Auskerry**.

ARRIVAL AND GETTING AROUND

By plane Flights from Kirkwall (Mon–Fri 2 daily, 1 on Sat; 25min) and from Sanday (Mon–Sat 1 daily; 6min).

By ferry Stronsay is served by a regular car ferry service

STRONSAY

from Kirkwall to Whitehall (2–3 daily; 1hr 40min–2hr).

By taxi/car There's no bus service, but D.S. Peace (☎01857 616335) operates taxis and offers car rental.

ACCOMMODATION AND EATING

Storehouse ☎01857 616263, ✉annemaree.carter @byinternet.com. A good alternative to the *Stronsay Hotel* is this welcoming little B&B in Whitehall, with en-suite rooms, a guest lounge and full board on request. £65

Stronsay Fish Mart ☎01857 616339, ⓦstronsay.org. The old fish market, by the ferry terminal, now serves as a hostel, and should be newly refurbished by the time you

read this. A cheap and cheerful café is also run from the same building – check Facebook for the latest opening hours. Dorms £16

Stronsay Hotel ☎01857 616213, ⓦstronsayhotel orkney.co.uk. Stronsay's only hotel, right by the ferry terminal, has modern en-suite rooms, while the hotel bar does good pub food – try the seafood taster. £80

7

Sanday

Despite being the largest of the northern isles, and the most populous after Westray, **Sanday** is the least substantial, a great low-lying, drifting dune strung out between several rocky points. The island's sweeping aquamarine bays and vast stretches of clean white sand are the finest in Orkney, and in good weather it's a superb place to spend a day or two. The sandy soil is very fertile, and the island remains predominantly agricultural even today, holding its own agricultural show each year at the beginning of August. The shoreline supports a healthy seal, otter and wading bird population, and behind the sandy beaches are stretches of beautiful open machair and grassland, thick with wild flowers during spring and summer. The entire coastline offers superb walks, with particularly spectacular sand dunes to the south of the vast, shallow, tidal bay of **Cata Sand**.

Start Point Lighthouse

Accessible only during low tide • Tours ☎01857 600341

The island has a long history as a shipping hazard, with many wrecks smashed against its shores, although the construction of the **Start Point Lighthouse** in 1802 on the island's exposed eastern tip reduced the risk for seafarers. Shipwrecks were, in fact, not an unwelcome sight on Sanday, as the island has no peat, and driftwood was the only source of fuel other than cow dung – it's even said that the locals used to pray for shipwrecks in church. The present 82ft-high Stevenson lighthouse, dating from 1870, now sports very natty, unusual, vertical black-and-white stripes. It actually stands on a tidal island, so ask locally for the tide times before setting out (it takes an hour to walk there and back). Better still, phone and arrange a tour, which allows you to climb to the top of the lighthouse.

Quoyness Chambered Cairn

Sanday is rich in archeology, with hundreds of mostly unexcavated sites including brochs, burnt mounds and cairns, the most impressive of which is **Quoyness Chambered Cairn**, on the fertile farmland of Els Ness peninsula. The tomb, which dates from before 2000 BC, has been partially reconstructed, and rises to a height of around 13ft. The imposing, narrow entrance, flanked by high dry-stone walls, would originally have been roofed for the whole of the way into the 13ft-long main chamber, where skeletal remains were discovered in the six small side-cells.

Orkney Angora

Mon–Fri 9am–5pm • ☎ 01857 600421, ⓦ orkneyangora.co.uk

In Upper Breckan in the parish of Burness, you can visit Sanday's **Orkney Angora** craft shop. The owner will usually let you stroke one of the comically long-haired albino rabbits that supply the wool. Close by is the stone tower of an old windmill, which belonged to the neighbouring farmstead, where you can still see the chimney from the old steam-powered meal mill.

ARRIVAL AND DEPARTURE SANDAY

By plane The airfield is in the centre of the island and there are regular flights to Kirkwall (Mon–Fri 2 daily, 1 on Sat; 10min) and a daily connection to Sanday (Mon–Fri 1 daily; 6min).

By ferry Ferries from Kirkwall to Sanday (2 daily; 1hr 25min) arrive at Loth Pier, at the southern tip of the island. **By bus** All sailings are met by the Sanday Bus (☎ 01857 600438), which will take you to most points on Sanday.

INFORMATION AND TOURS

7

Tourist information ⓦ sanday.co.uk, ⓦ sandayorkney .co.uk.
Tours The Sanday Ranger (☎ 01857 600341, ⓦ sanday

orkney.co.uk) organizes activities and guided walks throughout the summer, as well as regular Sanday bus tours (May–Sept Wed; £25).

ACCOMMODATION AND EATING

Ayre's Rock ☎ 01857 600410, ⓦ ayres-rock-hostel -orkney.com. If you're on a budget, this is a great place to stay: a well-equipped eight-bed hostel, a caravan, and a small campsite (with several camping huts for hire) over-looking the bay, with washing and laundry facilities, a chip shop (every Sat) and bike rental. Dorms £15; camping £5/pitch
Backaskaill Farmhouse ☎ 01857 600305, ⓦ bedand breakfastsandayorkney.com. Lovely old farmhouse idyllically positioned overlooking a glorious sandy bay. Evening meals offered (bring your own bottle), and packed lunches if required. £70
Braeswick ☎ 01857 600708, ⓦ braeswick.co.uk. Despite the dour exterior, this B&B is a good choice. Just a couple of

miles from the ferry terminal, it has very pleasantly decorated rooms with free wi-fi and a resident dog – the breakfast room has lovely views over the bay. £70
Newquoy Guest House & Writers Retreat ☎ 01857 600284, ⓦ newquoy.com. The old school in Burness, in the north of the island, is now a B&B run by an enterprising couple who put on writing courses and storytelling evenings. £70
Retreat Tea & Coffee Shop ☎ 01857 600284, ⓦ newquoy.com. The owners of *Newquoy* also run a really nice café serving soups, toasties and delicious home-baked cakes all served on vintage crockery. May & Sept Tues & Thurs noon–4pm; June–Aug Tues, Thurs & Sat noon–4pm.

North Ronaldsay

North Ronaldsay – or "North Ron" as it's fondly known – is Orkney's most northerly island. Separated from Sanday by treacherous waters, it has an outpost atmosphere, brought about by its extreme isolation. Measuring just three miles by one, and rising only 66ft above sea level, the only features to interrupt the flat horizon are **Holland House** – built by the Traill family, who bought the island in 1727 – and the two lighthouses at **Dennis Head**. The rest of the island is almost overwhelmed by the magnitude of the sky, the strength of wind and the ferocity of the sea so that its very existence seems an act of tenacious defiance. Despite this, North Ronaldsay has been inhabited for centuries, and continues to be heavily farmed, from old-style crofts whose roofs are made from huge local flagstones. With no natural harbours and precious little farmland, the islanders have been forced to make the most of what they have, and **seaweed** has played an important role in the local economy. During the eighteenth century, kelp was gathered here, burnt in pits and sent south for use in the chemicals industry.

NORTH RONALDSAY SHEEP

The island's **sheep** are a unique, tough, goat-like breed, who feed mostly on seaweed, giving their flesh a dark tone and a rich, gamey taste, and making their thick wool highly prized. A high **dry-stone dyke**, completed in the mid-nineteenth century and running the thirteen miles around the edge of the island, keeps them off the farmland, except during lambing season, when the ewes are allowed onto the pastureland. North Ronaldsay sheep are also unusual in that they can't be rounded up by sheepdogs like ordinary sheep, but scatter far and wide at some considerable speed. Instead, once a year the islanders herd the sheep communally into a series of **dry-stone "punds"** near Dennis Head, for clipping and dipping, in what is one of the last acts of communal farming practised in Orkney.

Bird Observatory

The most frequent visitors to the island are ornithologists, who come in considerable numbers to clock the rare migrants who land here briefly on their spring and autumn migrations. The peak times of year for migrants are from late March to early June, and from mid-August to early November. However, many breeding species spend the spring and summer here, including gulls, terns, waders, black guillemots, cormorants and even the odd corncrake. The permanent **Bird Observatory** (see below), in the southwest corner of the island, can give advice on recent sightings.

The Lighthouses and the Wool Mill

Exhibitions May–Aug daily 10am–5pm · Free · **Guided tours** May–Sept Sun noon–5.30pm; at other times by appointment · £5 or £7 with the Mill · ☎ 01857 633297, ⓦ northronaldsay.co.uk

The attractive, stone-built **Old Beacon** was first lit in 1789, but the lantern was replaced by the huge bauble of masonry you now see as long ago as 1809. The **New Lighthouse**, designed by Alan Stevenson in 1854 half a mile to the north, is the tallest land-based lighthouse in Britain, rising to a height of over 100ft. There's an exhibition on the lighthouse in one of the keepers' cottages, as well as an exhibition on the history of life on the island and a café (see below). You can also climb to the top of the lighthouse, don white gloves (to protect the brass) and admire the view – on a clear day you can see Fair Isle, and even Sumburgh and Fitful Head on Shetland. Finally, you can combine this with a tour of the island's **Wool Mill** where they turn the North Ron fleeces into yarn and felt.

ARRIVAL AND INFORMATION — NORTH RONALDSAY

By plane Your best bet is to catch a flight from Kirkwall (Mon–Sat 3 daily, 2 on Sun; 15min): if you stay the night on the island, you're eligible for a bargain £21 return fare.

By ferry The ferry from Kirkwall to North Ronaldsay runs just once a week (usually Fri; 2hr 40min), though there are also summer sailings via Papa Westray (usually Tues; 3hr 10min), and day-trips are possible on occasional Sundays between late May and early September (☎ 01856 872044 for details).

Tourist information ⓦ northronaldsaytrust.co.uk.

GETTING AROUND

By bus A minibus usually meets the ferries and planes (☎ 01857 633244) and will take you to the lighthouse.

Bike rental Contact Mark (☎ 01857 633297, ⓦ north ronaldsay.co.uk).

ACCOMMODATION AND EATING

Bird Observatory ☎ 01857 633200, ⓦ nrbo.co.uk. You can stay (or camp) at the ecofriendly bird observatory, either in an en-suite guest room or in a hostel bunkbed. The *Obscafé* serves decent evening meals (£14 for two courses) – obviously try the mutton, washed down with Dark Island beer. Food served daily noon–2pm & evenings by arrangement. Doubles **£72**; dorms **£16.50**; camping **£5**/pitch

The Lighthouse ☎ 01857 633297, ⓦ northronaldsay .co.uk. Great little café in the old lighthouse keepers' cottages serving snacks and evening meals (by arrangement) – make sure you sample one of their famous North Ronaldsay mutton pies. May–Aug daily 10am–5pm; Sept–April phone ahead.

Shetland

FAIR ISLE

Shetland

Shetland is surprisingly different from neighbouring Orkney. While Orkney lies within sight of the Scottish mainland, Shetland lies beyond the horizon, closer to Bergen in Norway than Edinburgh, and to the Arctic Circle than Manchester. With little fertile ground, Shetlanders have traditionally been crofters, often looking to the sea for an uncertain living in fishing and whaling or the naval and merchant services. The 23,000 islanders tend to refer to themselves as Shetlanders first, and, with the Shetland flag widely displayed, they regard Scotland as a separate entity. As in Orkney, the Mainland is the one in their own archipelago, not the Scottish mainland.

Most folk come here for the unique **wildlife** and **landscape**. Smoothed by the last glaciation, the coastline's crust of cliffs with caves, blowholes and stacks, testifies to the continuing battle with the weather. Inland (a relative term, since you're never more than three miles from the sea), the treeless terrain is a barren mix of moorland, studded with peaty lochs.

The islands' capital, **Lerwick**, is a busy port and the only town of any size, with many parts of Shetland easily reached on a day-trip. **South Mainland**, a narrow finger of land that runs 25 miles from Lerwick to **Sumburgh Head**, is an area rich in archeological remains, including the Iron Age **Mousa Broch** and the ancient settlement of **Jarlshof**. A further 25 miles south of Sumburgh Head is the remote but thriving **Fair Isle**, synonymous with knitwear and exceptional birdlife. The **Westside** of Mainland is bleaker and more sparsely inhabited, as is **North Mainland**. A mile off the west coast, **Papa Stour** boasts some spectacular caves and stacks; much further out are the distinctive peaks and precipitous cliffs of the remote island of **Foula**. Shetland's three **North Isles** bring Britain to a dramatic, windswept end: **Yell** has the largest population of otters in Shetland; **Fetlar** is home to the rare red-necked phalarope; north of **Unst**, there's nothing until you reach the North Pole.

Weather has a serious influence in these parts. In winter, gales are routine and Shetlanders take even the occasional hurricane in their stride. Even in the summer months it will often be windy and rainy. The wind-chill factor is not to be taken lightly, and there is often a dampness in the air, even when it's not actually raining. While there are some good spells of dry, sunny weather (which often brings in sea mist) from May to September, it's the **simmer dim**, the twilight which lingers through the small hours at this latitude, which makes Shetland summers so memorable.

Brief history

Since people first began to explore the North Atlantic, Shetland has been a stepping stone on routes between Britain, Ireland and Scandinavia; people have lived here since **prehistoric times**, certainly from about 3500 BC. The **Norse settlers** began to arrive from about 800 AD, and established Shetland first as part of the Orkney earldom, ruling it directly from Norway after 1195. The Vikings left the islands with a unique cultural character, most evident today in the place names and in the **dialect**, which contains

Highlights

❶ **Traditional music** Catch some local music at the weekly Simmer'n Sessions in Lerwick, or the annual Shetland Folk Festival. **See p.378**

❷ **Isle of Noss** Guaranteed seals, puffins and dive-bombing "bonxies". **See p.379**

❸ **Mousa** Remote islet with a 2000-year-old broch and nesting storm petrels. **See p.382**

❹ **Jarlshof** Site mingling Iron Age, Bronze Age, Pictish, Viking and medieval settlements. **See p.384**

❺ **Fair Isle** Magical little island halfway between Shetland and Orkney, with a lighthouse at each end and a world-famous bird observatory in the middle. **See p.386**

❻ **Lunna House** Superb B&B in an old laird's house, used as the headquarters of the Norwegian Resistance in World War II. **See p.394**

❼ **Hermaness** More puffins, gannets and "bonxies", and spectacular views out to Muckle Flugga and Britain's most northerly point. **See p.403**

HIGHLIGHTS ARE MARKED ON THE MAP ON P.372

many words from **Norn**, the language spoken here until the nineteenth century (for more on Norn, see p.424). Shetland was never part of the Gaelic-speaking culture of Highland Scotland, and the later Scottish influence is essentially a Lowland one.

Scottish takeover

In 1469, Shetland followed Orkney in being **mortgaged to Scotland**, Christian I of Norway being unable to raise the dowry for the marriage of his daughter, Margaret,

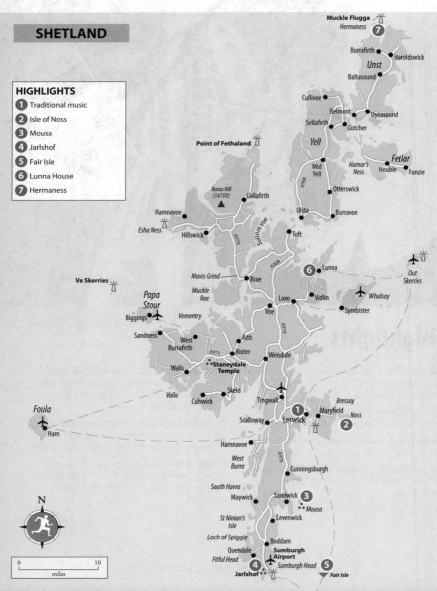

SHETLAND

HIGHLIGHTS

1. Traditional music
2. Isle of Noss
3. Mousa
4. Jarlshof
5. Fair Isle
6. Lunna House
7. Hermaness

SHETLAND PONIES, SHEEP AND SHEEPDOGS

Shetland is famous for its diminutive **ponies**, but it is still a surprise to find so many of them on the islands. A local ninth-century carving shows a hooded priest riding a very small pony, but traditionally they were used as pack animals, and their tails were essential for making fishing nets. During the Industrial Revolution, Shetland ponies were exported to work in the mines in England, being the only animals small enough to cope with the low galleries. Shetlands then became the playthings of the English upper classes (the Queen Mother was patron of the Shetland Pony Stud Book Society) and they still enjoy the limelight at the Horse of the Year show. You can see them in action at the annual **Shetland Pony Show** in August, or visit Trondra & Gott Shetland pony stud near Tingwall airport (☎01595 840330, ⓦtrondraandgottponies.co.uk).

Shetland sheep are also less substantial than their mainland counterparts, and are thought to be descended from those brought by the Vikings. Shetland wool comes in a wide range of colours, is very fine and is used to make the famous "Fair Isle" patterns and shawls so gossamer-thin that they can be passed through a wedding ring. To round up Shetland's small sheep, an even smaller **sheepdog** was bred, crossed with rough-coated collies. These dogs are now recognized as a separate breed, called "shelties", known for their gentleness and devotion as well as their agility and obedience. Their coat is distinctive, being long, straight and rough over a dense, furry undercoat – perfect for Shetland weather.

to James III, who annexed Shetland in 1472: the mortgage was never redeemed. Though Shetland retained links with other North Sea communities, religious and administrative practice gradually became Scottish, and **mainland lairds** set about grabbing what land and power they could. The economy soon fell into the hands of **merchant lairds**; they controlled the fish trade and the tenants who supplied it through a system of truck, or forced barter. It wasn't until the 1886 Crofters' Act and the simultaneous rise of **herring fishing** that ordinary Shetlanders gained some security. However, the boom and the prosperity it brought were short-lived and the economy soon slipped into depression.

The world wars and the oil boom

During the two world wars, thousands of naval, army and air force personnel were drafted in and some notable relics, such as huge coastal guns, remain. **World War II** also cemented the old links with Norway, Shetland playing a remarkable role in supporting the Norwegian Resistance (see box, p.380). Since the 1970s, the **oil industry** has provided a substantial income, which the Shetland Islands Council (SIC) have wisely reinvested in the community, building roads, improving housing and keeping the price of ferry tickets down. In Shetland, at least, the oil boom seems set to continue for some time, with **tourism** playing only a minor role in the economy. Comparatively few travellers make it out here, and those who do are as likely to be Faroese or Norwegian as British.

ARRIVAL AND DEPARTURE   SHETLAND

By plane ⓦhial.co.uk. Flybe (☎0871 700 2000, ⓦflybe .com) operate direct flights to Sumburgh airport, 25 miles south of Lerwick, from Inverness, Aberdeen, Edinburgh, Glasgow and Kirkwall in Orkney, plus summer flights from Bergen in Norway. Regular buses take you to Lerwick; a taxi will cost around £25.

By ferry Northlink (☎0845 600 0449, ⓦnorthlinkferries .co.uk) run overnight car ferries from Aberdeen to Lerwick, sometimes calling in at Kirkwall in Orkney on the way.

GETTING AROUND AND TOURS

By plane Directflight (☎01595 840306, ⓦdirectflight .co.uk/shetland) runs flights from Tingwall airport (☎01595 745745), 5 miles west of Lerwick, to the more remote islands. To reach Tingwall airport, there's a dial-a-ride taxi service (£1.70), which must be booked a day in advance.

By ferry The council-run interisland ferries (☎01595 743970, ⓦshetland.gov.uk/ferries) are excellent and fares are very low.

BÖDS

With only one SYHA hostel in Shetland, it's worth knowing about the islands' unique network of **camping böds** (March–Oct). Traditionally, a böd was a small building beside the shore, where fishermen stored their gear and occasionally slept; the word was also applied to trading posts established by Hanseatic merchants. Today, the tourist board uses the term pretty loosely: the places they run range from stone-built cottages to weatherboarded sail lofts. To stay at a böd, you must **book in advance** with the Shetland Amenity Trust (☎01595 694688, ⓦcamping-bods.co.uk), as there are no live-in wardens. The more basic böds have no cooking facilities or electricity, but all have a solid-fuel stove, cold water, toilets and bunk beds with mattresses – those with electricity have a meter, for which you need £1 coins. If you're camping, they're a great way to escape the wind and rain.

By bus The bus network (☎01595 744868, ⓦzettrans.org.uk) is pretty good in Shetland, with buses from Lerwick to every corner of Mainland, and even via ferries across to Yell and Unst.

Car rental It's worth considering car rental once on the islands. Bolts Car Hire (☎01595 693636, ⓦboltscarhire.co.uk) and Star Rent-a-Car (☎01595 692075, ⓦstarrentacar.co.uk) have vehicles at Sumburgh airport and Lerwick.

Tours There's a range of escorted tours and boat trips around the Mainland, great for those without a vehicle. Specific tours are mentioned throughout the text, but Shetland Wildlife (☎01950 422483, ⓦshetlandwildlife.co.uk) offer a variety of tours and boat trips, while the more adventurous might consider Sea Kayak Shetland (☎01595 840272, ⓦseakayakshetland.co.uk).

8

Lerwick

The focus of Shetland's commercial life, **LERWICK** is home to about 7500 people, a third of the islands' population. Its sheltered **harbour** at the heart of the town is busy with ferries, fishing boats, and oil-rig supply vessels. In summer, the quayside comes alive with visiting yachts, cruise liners, historic vessels such as the *Swan* and the occasional tall ship. Behind the old harbour is the compact town centre, made up of one long main street, Commercial Street; from here, narrow lanes, known as "**closses**", rise westwards to the late-Victorian new town.

Established in the seventeenth century as *Leir Vik* ("Muddy Bay") to cater for the **Dutch** herring fleet, the town was burnt down in 1614 and 1625 by the jealous folk of Scalloway, and again in 1702 by the French fleet. During the nineteenth century, with the presence of ever-larger Scottish, English and Scandinavian boats, it became a major **fishing** centre, and whalers called to pick up crews on their way to the northern hunting grounds. Business was from the jetties of buildings known as **lodberries**, several of which survive beyond the *Queen's Hotel*. **Smuggling** was part of the daily routine, and secret tunnels – some of which still exist – connected the lodberries to illicit stores. Lerwick expanded in the Victorian era, and the large houses and grand public buildings established then still dominate, notably the **Town Hall**. Another period of rapid growth began during the oil boom of the 1970s, with the farmland to the southwest disappearing under a suburban sprawl, the town's northern approaches becoming an industrial estate.

Commercial Street

Lerwick's attractive main street is the narrow, winding, flagstone-clad **Commercial Street**, whose buildings exhibit a mixed bag of architectural styles, from the powerful neo-Baroque of the Bank of Scotland at no. 117 to the plainer houses and old lodberries at the south end, beyond the *Queen's Hotel*. Here, you'll find **Bain's Beach**, a small, hidden stretch of golden sand that's one of the prettiest spots in Lewick.

The closses

Although the narrow lanes, or **closses**, that connect the Street to Hillhead are now desirable, it's not so long ago that they were regarded as slum-like dens of iniquity, from which the better-off escaped to the Victorian new town laid out to the west on a grid plan. The steep stone-flagged lanes are fun to explore, each one lined by tall houses with trees, fuchsias, flowering currants and honeysuckle pouring over the garden walls. If you look at the street signs, you can see that all the closses have two names: their former ones and their current titles, chosen in 1845 by the Police Commissioners – Reform, Fox and Pitt, reflecting the liberal political culture of the period – or derived from the writings of Sir Walter Scott.

Fort Charlotte

Commercial St • Daily: June–Sept 9am–10pm; Oct–May 9am–4pm • Free • ☎ 01856 841815

Commercial Street's northern end is marked by the towering walls of **Fort Charlotte**, which once stood directly above the beach. Begun for Charles II in 1665, the fort was attacked and burnt down by the Dutch in August 1673. In the 1780s it was repaired and named in honour of George III's queen. Since then, it's served as a prison and a Royal Navy training centre; it's now open to the public, except when used by the Territorial Army.

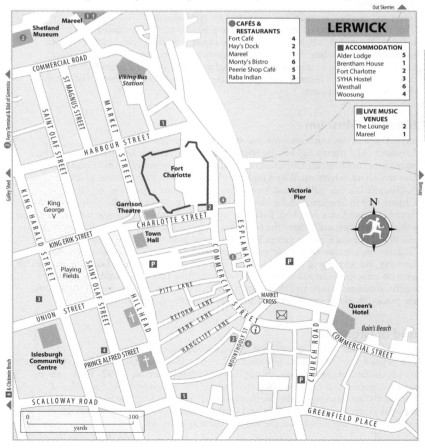

8

UP HELLY-AA

On the last Tuesday in January, Lerwick plays host to **Up Helly-Aa** (ⓦuphellyaa.org), the largest of the fire festivals held in Shetland (Jan–March). Around nine hundred torchbearing participants, all male and all in extraordinary costumes, march in procession. The annually appointed Guizer Jarl and his "squad" appear as Vikings brandishing shields and silver axes; the other squads are dressed randomly as giant insects, space invaders, ballet dancers and the like. They all congregate at the King George V Playing Field where, after due ceremony, the torches are thrown into the longship. A firework display follows, then the squads to do the rounds of a dozen "halls" (including the Town Hall) from around 8.30pm until the early house, giving comic performances at each.

Up Helly-Aa dates from Victorian times, when it was introduced to replace the banned Christmas tradition of rolling burning tar-barrels through the streets. Although this is essentially a community event with entry by invitation only, visitors are welcome at the Town Hall – contact the tourist office in advance. To find out more, head over to the Galley Shed (May to mid-Aug Tues 2–4 & 7–9pm, Fri 7–9pm, Sat 2–4pm; £3), on St Sunniva St, where you can view this year's longship and the costumes, shields and photographs.

Town Hall

HIllhead • Mon–Thurs 9am–5pm, Fri 9am–4pm • Free • ☎ 01595 693535, ⓦ shetland.gov.uk

The Victorian new town, on the hill above the harbour, is dominated by the splendid **Town Hall**, a Scottish Baronial monument to civic pride, built by public subscription. Providing there are no functions going on, you are free to wander round the building to admire the stained-glass windows in the main hall, which celebrate Shetland's history, and to climb the castellated central tower that occupies the town's highest point.

Shetland Museum

Hay's Dock • Mon–Sat 10am–5pm, Sun noon–5pm • Free • ☎ 01595 695057, ⓦ shetland-museum.org.uk

Lerwick's chief tourist sight is the **Shetland Museum**, housed in a stylishly modern waterfront building, off Commercial Road. The permanent exhibition begins in the Lower Gallery, where you'll find replicas of the hoard of Pictish silver found at St Ninian's Isle (see p.383); the Monks Stone, thought to show the arrival of Christianity in Shetland; and a block of butter, tax payment for the King of Norway, found preserved in a peat bog. Kids can try grinding flour with a quern stone, and visit a dark "trowie knowe" where the trows live. Among the boats artistically suspended in the Boat Hall is a sixareen (see p.395), once used as a mailboat to Foula. The Upper Gallery concentrates on the last two centuries of the islands' social history, from knitting and whaling to the oil industry. The museum also houses Da Gadderie, which puts on temporary art exhibitions, runs the excellent *Hay's Dock* **café** and puts on events, demonstrations and shows archive films. Meanwhile, out on the waterfront, the wacky Shetland Receivers emit snippets of Shetland conversation.

Böd of Gremista

May–Sept Tues–Sat noon–4pm • £2 • ☎ 01595 694386, ⓦ shetlandtextilemuseum.wordpress.com

Just beyond Lerwick's main ferry terminal, a mile and a half north of the town centre, stands the **Böd of Gremista**, the birthplace of **Arthur Anderson** (1792–1868), naval seaman, businessman, philanthropist, Shetland's first native MP and founder of Shetland's first newspaper, the *Shetland Journal*. The building has been completely restored and now houses the **Shetland Textile Museum**, which puts on special exhibitions on the heritage of the islands' knitting culture.

Clickimin Broch

A mile southwest of Lerwick town centre on the road leading to Sumburgh, the much-restored **Clickimin Broch** stands on what was once a small island in Loch Clickimin. The settlement here began as a small farmstead around 700 BC and was later enclosed by a defensive wall. The main tower served as a castle and probably rose to around 40ft, as at Mousa (see p.382), though the remains are now around 10ft high. There are two small entrances, one at ground level and the other on the first floor, carefully protected by outer defences and smaller walls. With the modern housing in the middle distance, it's pretty hard to imagine the original setting.

ARRIVAL AND DEPARTURE   LERWICK

By plane Flights from outside Shetland land at Sumburgh Airport, 25 miles to the south. Flights within Shetland depart from Tingwall Airport (see p.382).

Destinations within Shetland Fair Isle (Mon, Wed & Fri 2 daily, 1 on Sat; 25min); Foula (Mon & Tues 1 daily, Wed & Fri 2 daily; 15min); Out Skerries, calling at Whalsay on request (Mon & Wed 1 daily, Thurs 2 daily; 20min); Papa Stour (Tues 2 daily; 10min).

By ferry ☎ 0845 600 0449, ⓦ northlinkferries.co.uk. Ferries from Aberdeen (daily; 12hr) and Orkney (3–4 weekly; 6hr) arrive at Lerwick's ferry terminal, about a mile north of the town centre. Ferries to other islands within Shetland leave from the town harbour.

Destinations Bressay (every 30min–1hr; 7min); Fair Isle (alternate Thurs; 5hr); Skerries (Tues & Thurs; 2hr 30min).

By bus Buses stop on the Esplanade, close to the old harbour, or at the Viking Bus Station on Commercial Rd, north of the town centre.

Destinations Brae (Mon–Fri 5 daily, 3 on Sat; 45min); Hamnavoe (2–3 daily; 30min); Hillswick (Mon–Sat 1–2 daily; 1hr 40min); Laxo (Mon–Sat 1 daily; 40min); Levenwick (Mon–Sat 6–8 daily, 4 on Sun; 30min); Sandwick (Mon–Fri 8–10 daily, 6 on Sat, 4 on Sun; 25min); Scalloway (Mon–Sat hourly, 2 on Sun; 25min); Skeld (Mon–Sat 2 daily; 1hr); Sumburgh Airport (Mon–Sat 5–6 daily, 4 on Sun; 45min); Tingwall (Mon–Fri 7 daily, Sat 3 daily; 10min); Toft (Mon–Sat 3–4 daily; 45–55min); Vidlin (Mon–Sat 2 daily; 45min); Voe (Mon–Fri 5 daily, 3 on Sat; 35min); Walls (Mon–Sat 4 daily; 45min).

INFORMATION

Tourist office Market Cross, Commercial St (April–Oct Mon–Fri 9am–5pm, Sat & Sun 10am–4pm; Nov–March Mon–Fri 9am–5pm; ☎ 01595 693434, ⓦ visitshetland.com).
Radio station/newspaper For what's on, listen to

BBC Radio Shetland, 92.7 FM (Mon–Fri 5.30pm), visit ⓦ shetland-music.com, or buy the *Shetland Times* on Fridays (ⓦ shetlandtoday.co.uk) from any newsagent or the excellent Shetland Times bookshop on Commercial St.

TOURS AND ACTIVITIES

Another Shetland passion is **boating** and **yachting**, and regattas take place most summer weekends, throughout the islands. The sport of yoal racing has a big following, too, and teams from different districts compete in sixareens, large six-oared boats which replaced yoals as the backbone of Shetland's fishing fleet.

BOAT TOURS

Dim Riv ☎ 07901 588168, ⓦ dimriv.co.uk. The replica Viking longship, *Dim Riv*, takes passengers on regular trips around Bressay Sound.

Swan ☎ 01595 695193, ⓦ swantrust.com. If you plan ahead, you could take a trip on the *Swan*, a restored wooden sailing ship, which undertakes trips lasting from one to nine days.

ACCOMMODATION

Alder Lodge 6 Clairmont Place ☎ 01595 695705, ⓦ alderlodgeguesthouse.com. A solid, dependable choice, with eleven rooms, all en suite except the single. Breakfasts are good, with local smoked haddock an option and free wi-fi throughout the building. £70
Brentham House 7 Harbour St ☎ 01950 460201, ⓦ brenthamhouse.com. Spacious, newly furnished rooms in a Victorian, bay-fronted terrace; no reception, and no proper breakfast – you pick the keys up from *Baroc*, the bar

a couple of doors down. £75
Fort Charlotte Guest House 1 Charlotte St ☎ 01595 692140, ⓦ fortcharlotte.co.uk. Small guesthouse with a great central location (on the south side of the fort), spacious rooms and a friendly proprietor. £65
SYHA hostel Islesburgh House, King Harald St ☎ 01595 692114. Spacious Victorian building offering unusually comfortable surroundings, family rooms, a café, internet and laundry facilities. April–Sept. Dorms £17.50

8

★ **Westhall** Lower Sound ☎01595 694247, ⓦbedand breakfastlerwick.co.uk. A splendid Victorian mansion, known as the "Sheriff's Hoose", set in its own grounds a mile southwest of town with fabulous views over to Bressay. Rooms are spacious, the breakfasts are immense and there's free wi-fi. **£110**

Woosung 43 St Olaf St ☎01595 693687, ⓦvisit .shetland.org/woosung. Family-run B&B, up on the hill above the harbour, run by a genuinely friendly local landlady. The whole place is kept spotlessly clean, but not all rooms are en suite. Free wi-fi. **£60**

EATING AND DRINKING

Fort Café 2 Commercial St ☎01595 693125. Lerwick's best fish-and-chip shop, situated below Fort Charlotte: takeaway or eat inside in the small café (closes 8pm). Mon–Fri 11am–10pm, Sat 11am–9pm, Sun 4–10pm.

★ **Hay's Dock** Shetland Museum, Hay's Dock ☎01595 741569, ⓦhaysdock.co.uk. Bright, modern, licensed café-restaurant in the museum, with a great view over the north bay. Sandwiches, bagels and simple lunch dishes, from chowder to burgers are all under £10; the more adventurous evening menu features local salmon and lamb dishes (mains £13–20). Mon–Thurs 10.30am–4.30pm, Fri & Sat 10.30am–4.30pm & 6.30–9pm, Sun noon–4.30pm.

Mareel North Ness ☎01595 745555, ⓦmareel.org. If you've missed breakfast at your B&B, come to the café-bar in Lerwick's new cultural complex. Sandwiches or baked tatties are available until 4pm and hummus or mackerel ciabatta and nachos after that. Mon–Wed & Sun

9am–11pm, Thurs–Sat 9am–1am.

Monty's Bistro 5 Mounthooly St ☎01595 696555, ⓦmontys-shetland.co.uk. Unpretentious place serving sandwiches, pasta and spicy curry dishes, and snacks at lunchtimes (under £10); and the likes of pot-roasted local lamb and reestit mutton in the evening (mains £14–22). Tues–Sat noon–2pm & 5–9pm.

Peerie Shop Café Esplanade ☎01595 692816, ⓦpeerieshopcafe.com. Designer shop/gallery/café in an old lodberry, with a good range of cakes, soup and sandwiches, and what is probably Britain's northernmost latte. Mon–Sat 9am–6pm.

Raba Indian Restaurant 26 Commercial Rd ☎01595 690805. Reliably good curry house, with cheerful, efficient service and reasonable prices – try the *jalfreezi* and mop it up with some garlic naan (mains under £10), or go for the all-day Sunday buffet (£10 per person). Mon–Sat noon–2pm & 5–11pm, Sun 1–10pm.

NIGHTLIFE AND ENTERTAINMENT

The Lounge 4 Mounthooly St ☎01595 692231. Lerwick's friendliest pub is the upstairs bar where local musicians often gather for a session – Thursday night is quiz night. Daily 11am–1am.

Mareel North Ness ☎01595 745555, ⓦmareel.org. Lerwick's new cultural hub is primarily the local cinema, but also puts on regular gigs. Mon–Wed & Sun 9am–11pm, Thurs–Sat 9am–1am.

Bressay and Noss

Shielding Lerwick from the full force of the North Sea is the island of **Bressay**, dominated at its southern end by the conical Ward Hill (744ft) – "da Wart" – and accessible on an hourly car and passenger ferry from Lerwick (takes 5min). The chief reason for visiting Bressay is the tiny but spectacular island of **Noss**, off the east coast, whose high cliffs support a huge seabird colony in breeding season.

Bressay Heritage Centre

May–Sept Tues, Wed, Fri & Sat 10am–4pm, Sun 11am–5pm • Free

If you've time to kill before the ferry, pop into the **Bressay Heritage Centre**, by the ferry terminal in Maryfield, where there are temporary exhibitions. A Bronze Age **burnt mound** – essentially a pile of discarded rocks and charcoal used in fires – has been reconstructed next to the centre. Visible to the north is **Gardie House**, built in 1724 and, in its Neoclassical detail, one of the finest of Shetland's laird houses, where the likes of Sir Walter Scott and minor royalty once stayed, and now home to the Lord Lieutenant of Shetland.

Noss

Appropriately enough for an island that slopes gently into the sea at its western end, and plunges vertically 500ft at its eastern end, **Noss** has the dramatic and distinctive outline of a half-sunk ocean liner, while its name means "a point of rock". Inhabited until World War II, it's now a nature reserve and sheep farm, managed by Scottish Natural Heritage, who operate an RIB **ferry** from Bressay.

On the island, the old farmhouse contains a small visitor centre, where the warden will give you a quick briefing and a free map. Nearby is a sandy beach, while behind the haa (laird's house) is a **Pony Pund**, a square stone enclosure built for the breeding of Shetland ponies. The most memorable feature of Noss is its eastern **sea cliffs**, rising to a peak at the massive Noup (500ft), from which can be seen vast colonies of cliff-nesting gannets, puffins, guillemots, shags, razorbills and fulmars: a wonderful sight and one of the highlights of Shetland. As Noss is only a mile or so wide, it's easy enough to walk to the sea cliffs and back (allow 4hr), but make sure you keep close to the coast, since otherwise the great skuas (locally known as "bonxies") will dive-bomb you.

ARRIVAL AND GETTING AROUND

BRESSAY AND NOSS

By ferry The car ferry to Bressay departs from the town harbour in Lerwick (every 30min–1hr; 7min; ☎ 01595 743974) and arrives in Maryfield on the west coast. The RIB ferry to Noss (May–Aug Mon & Thurs 11am–5pm; £3 return; before setting out phone ☎ 0800 107 7818, ⓦ nature-shetland.co.uk) leaves from the east coast, 3 miles from Maryfield – an easy walk or short journey on a bike, bus or car.

By bus A bus will meet the 9am Bressay ferry (Mon, Wed & Fri) and take you to Noss, but for the return journey book the Dial-a-Ride service (☎ 01595 745745) the day before.

By boat Seabirds and Seals run a 3hr sightseeing boat from Lerwick (mid-April to mid-Sept daily 10am & 2pm; £45; ☎ 07595 540224, ⓦ seabirds-and-seals.com), allowing you a sea view of the vast bird colonies.

Central Mainland

The districts of Tingwall and Weisdale, plus the old capital of **Scalloway**, make up the **Central Mainland**, an area of minor interest in the grand scheme of things, but very easy to reach from Lerwick. In fine weather, it's a captivating mix of farms, moors and lochs, and includes Shetland's only significant woodland. The area also holds strong historical associations, with the Norse parliament at **Law Ting Holm**, unhappy memories of Earl Patrick Stewart's harsh rule at Scalloway and nineteenth-century Clearances at Weisdale.

Scalloway

Approaching **SCALLOWAY** from the east, there's a dramatic view over the town and the islands beyond. Once the capital of Shetland, Scalloway's importance waned through the eighteenth century as Lerwick, just six miles to the east, grew in trading success and status. Nowadays, Scalloway is fairly sleepy, though its harbour remains busy enough, with a small fishing fleet and the North Atlantic Fisheries College on the far side.

Scalloway Castle

If door is locked, get key from Scalloway Museum or *Scalloway Hotel* • Free; HS

In spite of modern developments nearby, Scalloway is dominated by the imposing shell of **Scalloway Castle**, a classic fortified tower-house built with forced labour in 1600 by the infamous Earl Patrick Stewart, and thus seen as a powerful symbol of oppression. Stewart, who'd succeeded to the Earldom of Orkney and Lordship of Shetland in 1592, held court here, reputedly increasing his power and wealth by using harsh justice to confiscate assets. He was eventually arrested and imprisoned in 1609 for his aggression toward his fellow landowners; his son, Robert, attempted an insurrection and both were executed in Edinburgh in 1615. The castle was used for a time by Cromwell's army, but had fallen into disrepair by 1700; what remains is well preserved and fun to explore.

Scalloway Museum

Castle St • May–Sept Mon–Sat 11am–4pm, Sun 2–4pm • £3 • ☎ 01595 880734, ⓦ scallowaymuseum.org

The **Scalloway Museum**, in an old knitwear outlet, has a café overlooking the adjacent castle. The displays range from Neolithic finds to the impact of modern aquaculture, and there's a replica wheelhouse and a longship for the kids to play with, but the most interesting section tells the story of the **Shetland Bus** (see box below). There are models of some of the fishing boats that made the trip across the North Sea, a replica of the Lewis guns that were hidden in oil drums aboard the ships and a miniature radio receiver supplied to the Norwegian Resistance.

8

ARRIVAL AND DEPARTURE SCALLOWAY

By bus There are regular buses to Scalloway from Lerwick (Mon–Sat hourly, 2 on Sun; 25min) and a less frequent service from Scalloway to Trondra and Burra (Mon–Sat 2 daily; 20min).

ACCOMMODATION AND EATING

Scalloway Hotel ☎ 01595 880444, ⓦ scallowayhotel .com. Well-established hotel on the harbour front, with plain, slightly cramped rooms and a bar that doubles as the local pub. The menu features lots of local fish and seafood – try the platter for around £15. Food served daily noon–3pm & 5–8.30pm. **£70**

Windward B&B Port Arthur ☎ 01595 880769, ⓦ accommodation-shetland.co.uk. Very comfortable, modern, wood-clad two-room B&B at the far western end of the bay, close to the North Atlantic Fisheries College. Great views from the conservatory and free wi-fi. **£80**

THE SHETLAND BUS

The story of the **Shetland Bus** – the link between Shetland and Norway that helped to sustain the Norwegian Resistance through the years of Nazi occupation – is quite extraordinary. Under threat of attack by enemy aircraft or naval action, small Norwegian fishing boats set out from Shetland to run arms and resistance workers into lonely fjords. The trip took at least 24 hours and on the return journey boats brought back Norwegians in danger of arrest by the Gestapo, or those who wanted to join Norwegian forces fighting with the Allies. For three years, through careful planning, the operation was remarkably successful: instructions to boats were passed in cryptic messages in BBC radio broadcasts. Local people knew what was going on, but the secret was generally well kept. In total, 350 refugees were evacuated, and more than 400 tonnes of arms, large amounts of explosives and 60 radio transmitters were landed in Norway.

Originally established at **Lunna** in the northeast of the Mainland, the service moved to **Scalloway** in 1942, partly because the village offered good marine-engineering facilities at Moore's Shipyard on Main Street, where a plaque records the morale-boosting visit of the Norwegian Crown Prince Olav. Explosives and weapons were stored in the castle and **Kergord House** in Weisdale was used as a safe house and training centre for intelligence personnel and saboteurs. The hazards, tragedies and elations of the exercise are brilliantly described in David Howarth's book, *The Shetland Bus*; their legacy today is a heartfelt closeness between Shetland and Norway.

Trondra

Southwest of Scalloway – and connected to the Mainland by a bridge since 1971 – is the island of **Trondra**, where you can visit a working crofthouse. Pick up a leaflet and a bucket of feed for the hens from the barn, and head off along the **Croft Trail**, which takes you to see the ducks, down to the shore (a good picnic spot), over to a restored watermill and then through a field of orchids and other wild flowers.

Burra

Burra Bridge connects Trondra with the twin islands of East and West **Burra**, which have some beautiful beaches and some fairly gentle coastal walks.

West Burra

West Burra has the largest settlement in the area, **HAMNAVOE**, unique in having been planned by the local landlord as a fishing port. Just south of Hamnavoe, a small path leads down from the road to the white sandy beach at **Meal**. At the southern end of West Burra, at **Banna Minn**, is another fine beach, with excellent walking nearby on the cliffs of Kettla Ness, linked to the rest of West Burra only by a sliver of tombolo.

East Burra

East Burra, joined to West Burra at the middle like a Siamese twin, ends at the hamlet of **HOUSS**, distinguished by the tall, ruined laird's house or haa. From the turning place outside the cattle-grid, continue walking southwards, following the track to the left, down the hill and across the beach, and after about a mile you'll reach the deserted settlement of **Symbister**, inhabited until the 1940s. You can now see ancient field boundaries and, just south of the ruins, a **burnt mound**. Half a mile further south, the island ends in cliffs, caves and wheeling fulmars.

Tingwall and around

TINGWALL, the name for the loch-studded, fertile valley north of Scalloway, takes its name from the **Lawting** or Althing (from *thing*, the Old Norse for "parliament"), in existence from the eleventh to the sixteenth century, where local people and officials gathered to make or amend laws and discuss evidence. The Lawting was situated at **Law Ting Holm**, the small peninsula at the northern end of the Loch of Tingwall that was once an island linked to the shore by a causeway. Structures on the holm have long since vanished, but an information board helps in visualizing the scene. At the southwest corner of the loch, a 7ft **standing stone** by the roadside is said to mark the spot where, after a dispute at the Lawting in 1389, Earl Henry Sinclair killed his cousin and rival, Marise Sperra, together with seven of his followers.

Tingwall Kirk

Just north of the Loch of Tingwall is **Tingwall Kirk**, unexceptional from the outside, but preserving its simple late eighteenth-century interior. In the burial ground, a dank, turf-covered **burial aisle** survives from the medieval church demolished in 1788. Inside are several very old gravestones, including one to a local official called a *Foud* – a representative of the king – who died in 1603.

Weisdale Mill

Tues–Sat 10.30am–4.30pm, Sun noon–4.30pm • Free • ☎ 01595 745750, ⓦ shetlandarts.org

The parish of **WEISDALE**, five miles northwest of Tingwall, is notable primarily for **Weisdale Mill**, situated up the B9075 from the head of Weisdale Voe. Built for milling grain in 1855, this is now an attractively converted arts centre, housing the small,

8

beautifully designed **Bonhoga Gallery**, in which touring and local exhibitions of painting, sculpture and other media are shown.

| ARRIVAL AND DEPARTURE | TINGWALL AND AROUND |

By plane Tingwall Airport (☎01595 840306), about a mile north of the Loch of Tingwall, is the main airport for flights to other islands within Shetland (see p.377 for details).
By bus There are buses from Lerwick's Viking Bus Station to

Tingwall (Mon–Fri 7 daily, Sat 4 daily; 10min) and to Weisdale (Mon–Sat 2–5 daily; 20min). There's no direct service to Tingwall Airport – you can either walk the half mile from the crossroads, or pre-order a Dial-a-Ride taxi (☎01595 745745).

EATING AND DRINKING

Herrislea House Hotel Veensgarth ☎01595 840208, ⓦherrisleahouse.co.uk. North of the loch and a stone's throw from the airport, this large hotel has a great bar for a drink or two and some pub food (under £12). Food served 6.30–8.45pm.

Weisdale Mill ☎01595 745750, ⓦshetlandarts.org. Weisdale Mill has a very pleasant café, serving soup, scones and snacks in the south-facing conservatory overlooking the stream. Tues–Sat 10.30am–4.30pm, Sun noon–4.30pm.

South Mainland

Shetland's **South Mainland** is a long, thin finger of land, only three or four miles wide but 25 miles long, ending in the cliffs of **Sumburgh Head** and **Fitful Head**. It's a beautiful area with wild undulating landscapes, lots of good green farmland, fabulous views out to sea and the mother of all brochs on the island of **Mousa**, just off the east coast in **Sandwick**. The most concentrated points of interest are in **Dunrossness**, at the southern end of the peninsula, with its seabird colonies, crofting museum, and **Jarlshof**, Shetland's most impressive archeological site.

Sandwick

SANDWICK is a township made up of a number of close, but distinct settlements, about halfway down the east coast of South Mainland. Most visitors come here to take a boat from Leebotton to the island of **Mousa**, under a mile off the coast, which boasts the most amazingly well-preserved broch in the whole of Scotland.

Mousa

Day-trip April to mid-Sept Mon, Tues & Thurs–Sat 1 & 4.15pm, Wed 10am & 1pm, Sun 1.30 & 4.30pm; takes 25min • £16 return • **Storm petrel trip** Mid-May to July Wed & Sat 11pm–12.30am • £20 • ☎01950 431367, ⓦmousa.co.uk

If the weather's fine, you could easily spend the whole day on **Mousa**, watching the seals sun themselves on the rocks in the southeastern corner of the island, and looking out for black guillemots (or "tysties" as they're known locally) and arctic terns, which breed here.

Mousa Broch

Mousa's main attraction is **Mousa Broch**, which features in both *Egil's Saga* and the *Orkneyinga Saga*, contemporary chronicles of Norse exploration and settlement. In the former, a couple eloping from Norway to Iceland around 900 AD take refuge in it after being shipwrecked, while in the latter the broch is besieged by an Earl Harald Maddadarson when his mother is abducted and brought here from Orkney by Erlend the Young, who wanted to marry her. Rising to more than 40ft, and looking rather like a Stone-Age cooling tower, Mousa Broch has a remarkable presence, its low entrance-passage passing through two concentric walls to a central courtyard, divided into separate beehive chambers. Between the walls, a rough (very dark) staircase leads to the top parapet; a torch is provided for visitors.

Thousands of **storm petrels** breed around the broch, fishing out at sea during the day and only returning to the nests after dark. The ferry runs special late-night trips, setting off in the "simmer dim" twilight around 11pm. Even if you've no interest in the storm petrels, which appear like bats as they flit about in the half-light, the chance to explore the broch at midnight is worth it alone.

Sandsayre Interpretive Centre

May–Sept daily 10am–5pm • Free

Beside the Stevenson-built Sandsayre Pier, from which you catch the boat to Mousa, is an **interpretive centre**. It's really just a glorified waiting room (handy in bad weather) with some local history displays, but there's also an old boatshed with a restored flitboat, originally used to transport sheep to Mousa for grazing, and a good account of the remarkable story of Betty Mouat who survived nine days lost at sea, at the age of 60.

Hoswick Visitor Centre

May–Sept Mon–Sat 10am–5pm, Sun 11am–5pm • Free • ☎ 01950 431406, ⓦ shetlandheritageassociation.com

In Hoswick, a mile or so southwest of Leebotton, **Hoswick Visitor Centre** has a fantastic collection of vintage radios, and a permanent exhibition on crofting, haaf fishing, whaling, and the copper and iron mines beyond Sand Lodge. The Betty Mouat story (see above) is also told here and a café serves cakes, tea and coffee.

Dunrossness

Shetland's southernmost parish is known as **DUNROSSNESS** or "The Ness", a rolling agricultural landscape (often likened to that of Orkney), dominated in the southwest by the great brooding mass of Fitful Head (929ft). The main road leads eventually to **Sumburgh**, whose **airport** is busy with helicopters and aircraft shuttling to and from the North Sea oilfields, as well as passenger services, and **Grutness**, the minuscule **ferry terminal** for Fair Isle. It's worth venturing this far to see the Neolithic and Viking remains at **Jarlshof** and the lighthouse and the seabirds (including puffin) at **Sumburgh Head**.

8

St Ninian's Isle

On the west coast of South Mainland, a signposted track leads down from the village of **BIGTON** to a spectacular sandy causeway, or **tombolo**, which connects the Mainland to **St Ninian's Isle**. The tombolo – a concave strip of shell sand with Atlantic breakers crashing on either side – is usually exposed; you can walk over to the island, where there are the ruins of a church probably dating from the twelfth century and built on the site of an earlier, Pictish, one. Excavated in the 1950s, a hoard of 28 objects of Pictish silver was found beneath a slab in the floor of the earlier building. It included bowls, a spoon and brooches, thought to date from around 800 AD. Replicas are in the Shetland Museum and the originals in the Museum of Scotland in Edinburgh.

Loch of Spiggie

South of Bigton, the coast is attractive: cliffs alternate with beaches and the vivid greens and yellows of the farmland contrast with black rocks and a sea which may be grey, deep blue or turquoise. The **Loch of Spiggie**, which used to be a sea inlet, attracts large autumn flocks of some two hundred whooper swans. A track leads from the east side of the loch to a long, reasonably sheltered sandy beach known as the **Scousburgh Sands** or Spiggie Beach.

Crofthouse Museum

Mid-April to Sept daily 10am–1pm & 2–5pm • Free • ☎ 01950 460557, ⓦ shetlandheritageassociation.com

On the east coast, a back road winds to the **Crofthouse Museum** in Southvoe. Housed in a fairly well-to-do thatched croft built around 1870, the museum re-creates the feel of late nineteenth-century crofting life, with a peat fire, traditional box beds and so forth. Adjacent to the living quarters are the byre for the cows and tatties, and the kiln for drying the grain. Crofting was mostly done by women in Shetland, while the men went out haaf fishing for the laird. Down by the burn, there's also a restored, thatched horizontal mill.

Quendale Mill

Mid-April to mid-Oct daily 10am–5pm • £3 • ☎ 01950 460969, Ⓦ shetlandheritageassociation.com

A few miles south of the Loch of Spiggie lies the beautifully restored full-size **Quendale Mill**, in the village of the same name, overlooking a sandy south-facing bay. It was built in the 1860s but not in operation since the early 1970s; you can explore the interior and watch a short video of the mill working, and there's a tearoom attached.

Old Scatness Broch and Iron Age Village

☎ 01595 694688, Ⓦ shetlandamenity.org

Extending the airport revealed a vast Iron-Age archeological site known as **Old Scatness Broch and Iron Age Village**. At the centre of the site are the remains of an Iron Age broch, surrounded by a settlement of interlocking wheelhouses – so called because of their circular ground plan. Two of the wheelhouses have been either partially or wholly reconstructed, but visits currently need to be arranged in advance with Shetland Amenity Trust.

Jarlshof

Daily: April–Sept 9.30am–5.30pm; Oct–March 9.30am to dusk • £5.50; HS

Of all the archeological sites in Shetland, **Jarlshof** is the largest and most impressive. What makes Jarlshof so amazing is the fact that you can walk right into a house built 1600 years ago, which is still intact to above head height. The site is big and confusing, scattered with the ruins of buildings dating from the Bronze Age to the early seventeenth century. The name, which is misleading as it is not primarily a Viking site, was coined by Sir Walter Scott, who used the ruins of the Old House in his novel *The Pirate*. However, it was only at the end of the nineteenth century that the Bronze Age, Iron Age and Viking settlements were discovered, after a violent storm ripped off the top layer of turf.

The Bronze Age smithy and Iron Age dwellings nearest the entrance, dating from the second and first millennia BC, are nothing compared with the cells which cluster around the **broch**, close to the sea. Only half of the original broch survives, and its courtyard is now an Iron-Age aisled roundhouse, with stone piers. It's difficult to distinguish the broch from the later Pictish **wheelhouses** that now surround it, but it's all great fun to explore, as you're free to roam around the cells, checking out the in-built stone shelving, water tanks, beds and so on. Inland lies the maze of grass-topped foundations marking out the **Viking longhouses**, from the ninth century AD. Towering over the whole complex are the ruins of the laird's house, built by Robert Stewart, Earl of Orkney and Lord of Shetland, in the late sixteenth century, and the **Old House of Sumburgh**, built by his son, Earl Patrick.

Sumburgh Head

The Mainland comes to a dramatic end at **Sumburgh Head** (262ft), which rises sharply out of the land only to drop vertically into the sea. The clifftop **lighthouse** was built by Robert Stevenson in 1821, and the road up to it is the perfect site for watching nesting seabirds such as kittiwakes, fulmars, shags, razorbills and guillemots, as well as gannets diving for fish. This is also the easiest place in Shetland to get close to **puffins**: during the nesting season (May to early Aug), you simply need to look over the western wall, just before you enter the lighthouse complex, to see them arriving at their burrows a few yards below with beakfuls of sand eels or giving flying lessons to their offspring.

FROM TOP JARLSHOF (P.384); UP HELLY-AA (P.376) >

ARRIVAL AND DEPARTURE

By plane Sumburgh Airport, at the southernmost tip of South Mainland, is Shetland's main airport. There's a regular bus service to Lerwick (Mon–Sat 5–6 daily, 4 on Sun; 45min) and a taxi ride to Lerwick will cost around £25.

By bus There are regular buses from Lerwick to Levenwick (Mon–Sat 6–8 daily, 4 on Sun; 30min); Sandwick (Mon–Fri 8–10 daily, 6 on Sat, 4 on Sun; 25min); Sumburgh (Mon–Sat 5–6 daily, 4 on Sun; 45min).

SOUTH MAINLAND

ACCOMMODATION AND EATING

Betty Mouat's Cottage Scatness ☎ 01595 694688, ⓦ camping-bods.com. Next to an excavated broch and not far from the airport, this stone-built cottage is a camping böd with two bedrooms and a solid-fuel stove. April–Oct. **£10**/person

Levenwick Campsite ☎ 01950 422320, ⓦ levenwick .shetland.co.uk. Small, terraced campsite run by the local community with hot showers, a tennis court and a superb view over the east coast. May–Sept. **£6**/pitch

★ **Mucklehus** ☎ 01950 422370, ⓦ mucklehus.co.uk. A lovely B&B in a former Master Mariner's house built in 1890 near the beach in Levenwick, 18 miles south of Lerwick; the rooms are small, but stylish, and there's free wi-fi. **£80**

Setterbrae ☎ 01950 460468, ⓦ setterbrae.co.uk. A stone's throw from Spiggie Loch, this comfortable modern B&B has a residents' lounge and conservatory, lots of books on Shetland and free wi-fi. **£70**

Spiggie Hotel ☎ 01950 460409, ⓦ thespiggiehotel .co.uk. The *Spiggie* has a popular bar serving real ales and a restaurant with great views over the nearby loch and out to Foula and, if you're lucky, incredible sunsets. Fish and chips and the like in the bar are priced around £10, or you can have well-presented dishes such as lobster or whatever the local catch is, à la carte in the restaurant (mains £12–18). Food served Mon & Tues 6–10pm, Wed–Sun noon–2.30pm & 6–10pm. **£110**

8 | Fair Isle

Fair Isle – just three miles by one and a half – is marooned in the sea halfway between Shetland and Orkney and very different from both. The weather reflects its isolated position: you can almost guarantee that it'll be windy, though if you're lucky your visit might coincide with fine weather – what the islanders call "a given day". At one time Fair Isle's population was not far short of four hundred, but Clearances forced emigration from the middle of the nineteenth century. By the 1950s, the population had shrunk to 44, and evacuation of the island was seriously considered. **George Waterston**, who'd bought the island and set up a bird observatory in 1948, passed it into the care of the NTS in 1954 and rejuvenation began. Today Fair Isle supports a community of around seventy.

The north end of the island rises like a wall, while the Sheep Rock, a sculpted stack of rock and grass on the east side, is another dramatic feature. The croft land and the island's scattered white houses are concentrated in the south. Fair Isle has two **lighthouses**, one at either end of the island, both designed by the Stevenson family and erected in 1892. Earlier, the Vikings used to light beacons to signal an enemy fleet advancing, and in the nineteenth century a semaphore consisting of a tall wooden pole was used; it can still be seen on the hill above South Lighthouse. The North Lighthouse was considered to be on such an exposed spot that the foghorn was operated from within. The South Lighthouse has the distinction of having a short, very challenging, six-hole golf course.

Fair Isle Bird Observatory

April–Oct • Free • ☎ 01595 760258, ⓦ fairislebirdobs.co.uk

The most significant building on Fair Isle is the **Fair Isle Bird Observatory** (FIBO), a large building just above the sandy bay of North Haven, where the ferry from Shetland Mainland arrives, with an exhibition on the island past and present. As well as providing accommodation and food to visitors, it's one of the major European centres for ornithology, and its work in watching, trapping, recording and ringing birds goes on all year. Fair Isle is a landfall for a huge number and range of migrant birds during

the spring and autumn passages. Migration routes converge here and more than
345 species, including many rarities, have been noted. As a result, Fair Isle is a haven
for twitchers, who descend on the island in planes and boats whenever a major rarity is
spotted; for more casual birders, however, there's also plenty of summer resident birdlife
to enjoy. The high-pitched screeching that fills the sky above the airstrip comes from
hundreds of **arctic terns**, and arctic skuas can also be seen here. Those in search of
puffins should head for the cliffs around Furse, while to find **gannets** aim for the
spectacular Stacks of Scroo.

George Waterston Museum

Mon 2–4pm, Wed 10.30am–noon, Fri 2–3.30pm • Free • ☎ 01595 760244

Fair Isle is, of course, better known for its knitting patterns, still produced with great
skill by the local knitwear cooperative. There are samples on display at the island's
George Waterson Museum, next to the Methodist chapel. Particularly memorable are
stories of shipwrecks; in 1868 the islanders undertook a heroic rescue of all 465
German emigrants aboard the *Lessing*. More famously, *El Gran Grifón*, part of the
retreating Spanish Armada, was lost here in 1588 and three hundred Spanish seamen
were washed up on the island. Food was in such short supply that fifty died of
starvation before help could be summoned from Shetland.

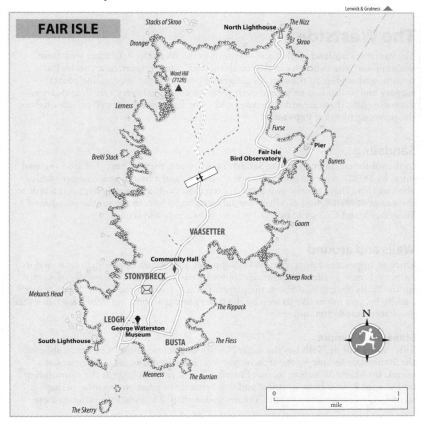

8

By plane Directflight (☎01595 840246, ⓦdirectflight .co.uk) runs a service from Tingwall to Fair Isle (Mon–Sat 1–3 daily) and from Sumburgh (Sat only).

By ferry The passenger ferry connects Fair Isle with either Lerwick (alternate Thurs; 4–5hr) or Grutness in Sumburgh

(Tues, alternate Thurs & Sat; 3hr); since the boat only takes a limited number of passengers, it's advisable to book in advance (☎01595 760363). The crossing can be very rough at times, so if you're at all susceptible to seasickness it might be worth considering catching a flight.

ACCOMMODATION AND EATING

Be sure to book accommodation in advance as demand is high in the summer; note that camping is not permitted. Although casual visitors can get something to eat at the observatory, all accommodation is booked on a full-board basis. There is a shop/post office, Stackhoull Stores, in the south of the island (closed Tues & Sat afternoon, and all day Thurs & Sun).

Fair Isle Bird Observatory Lodge ☎01595 760258, ⓦfairislebirdobs.co.uk. Full-board accommodation is available at the modern observatory in en-suite doubles/ twins and singles. FIBO is the island's social hub and offers self-service tea and coffee, and a tuck shop with honesty box; meals by arrangement. April–Oct. **£120**

South Light House ☎01595 760355, ⓦsouthlight

fairisle.co.uk. B&B memorably situated at the southern-most tip of the island, not literally in the lighthouse, but in the adjacent keepers' cottages. **£100**

Upper Leogh ☎01595 760248, ⓦkathycoull.com. You'll be well looked after in this whitewashed crofthouse B&B by spinning, knitting and weaving expert, Kathy Coull, who also runs textile courses. **£100**

8 The Westside

The western Mainland of Shetland – known as the **Westside** – stretches west from Weisdale and Voe to Sandness. Although there are some important archeological remains and wildlife in the area, its greatest appeal lies in its outstanding **coastal scenery** and walks. Cut by several deep voes, the coastline is very varied; aside from dramatic cliffs, there are intimate coves and some fine beaches, as well as, just offshore, the stunning island of **Papa Stour**.

Sandsting

In the south, on the picturesque **Sandsting** peninsula, there's a very sheltered voe (sed inlet) by **SKELD**, with a working harbour, a marina and a brand-new creamery which you can visit. There are also two beautiful terracotta-coloured **sandy bays** just a mile to the east at **REAWICK**, and excellent **coastal walks** to be had, to the southwest, around Westerwick and Culswick, past red-granite cliffs, caves and stacks.

Walls and around

Once an important fishing port, **WALLS** (pronounced *waas*), appealingly set round its harbour, is now a quiet village which comes alive once a year in the middle of August for the Walls Agricultural Show, the biggest farming bash on the island. If you're just passing by, you might like to stop by the **bakery and tearoom**, but Walls also has several good **accommodation** options.

Staneydale Temple

Three miles east of Walls lies the finest Neolithic structure in the Westside, dubbed the **Staneydale Temple** by the archeologist who excavated it because it resembled a temple on Malta. Whatever its true function, it was twice as large as the surrounding oval-shaped houses (now in ruins) and was certainly of great importance, perhaps as some kind of community centre. The horseshoe-shaped foundations measure more than 40ft by 20ft internally, with immensely thick walls, still around 4ft high, whose roof would have been supported by spruce posts (two postholes can still be clearly seen). To reach the temple, take the path marked out by black-and-white poles across the moorland for half a mile from the road.

Vaila

A short distance across the sea south of Walls lies the island of **Vaila**, from where in 1837 Lerwick philanthropist Arthur Anderson operated a fishing station in an unsuccessful attempt to break down the system of fishing tenures under which tenants were forced to fish for the landlords under pain of eviction. The ruins of Anderson's fishing station still stand on the shore, but the most conspicuous monument is **Vaila Hall**, the largest laird's house on Shetland, originally built in 1696, but massively enlarged by a wealthy Yorkshire mill-owner, Herbert Anderton, who bought the island in 1893. Anderton also restored the island's ancient watchtower of Mucklaberry Castle, built a Buddhist temple (now sadly in ruins), and had a cannon fired whenever he arrived on the island. The island is currently owned by Dorota Rychlik, an equally eccentric Polish émigré and her husband, Richard Rowland. They welcome visitors who should make a point of popping into the Whalehouse at Cloudin, where they'll find the 42ft skeleton of a young male **sperm whale** – nicknamed "Bony Dick" – who washed up on the island in 2000. Enquire at *Burrastow House* about transport.

Sandness

8

At the end of a long winding road across an undulating, uninhabited, boulder-strewn landscape, you eventually reach the fertile scattered crofting settlement of **SANDNESS** (pronounced "saaness"), which you can also reach by walking along the coast from Walls past the dramatic Deepdale and across Sandness Hill. It's an oasis of green meadows in the peat moorland, with a nice beach, too.

Jamieson's Spinning Mill

Mon–Fri 8am–1pm & 2–5pm • Free • ☎ 01595 870285, ⓦ jamiesonsofshetland.co.uk

The family-run **Jamieson's Spinning Mill** at Sandness is the only one on Shetland producing pure Shetland wool; the modern factory welcomes visitors, and you can watch how workers take the fleece and then wash, card and spin the exceptionally fine Shetland wool into yarn.

ARRIVAL AND DEPARTURE | THE WESTSIDE

By bus There's an infrequent bus service between Lerwick and Skeld (Mon–Sat 2 daily; 1hr), and between Lerwick and Walls (Mon–Sat 4 daily; 45min), with a feeder service from Sandness (Mon–Sat 2–3 daily; 45min).

ACCOMMODATION AND EATING

SKELD

Skeld böd ☎ 01595 694688, ⓦ camping-bods.com. A lovely old whitewashed building overlooking the campsite and the harbour; there's electricity, a solid-fuel stove and a small shop and café (with free wi-fi) in the local creamery. March–Oct. **£10**/person

Skeld campsite ☎ 01595 860287. A flat patch of grass (with hard standing and electric points), right by the pier and marina in the sheltered port of Skeld. The campsite's little, white, weatherboarded amenity block (with kitchen), is positively picturesque. **£8**/pitch

WALLS AND AROUND

Baker's Rest ☎ 01595 809308, ⓦ wallsbakery.co.uk. Places to get a cup of tea or coffee, filled bannocks and sandwiches, are few and far between in the Westside, so this simple little tearoom above the bakery in Walls is useful to know about. Mon–Sat 9am–5pm.

★ **Burrastow House** ☎ 01595 809307, ⓦ burrastow house.co.uk. Beautifully situated about 3 miles southwest of Walls, parts of the house date back to 1759 and have real character; others are more modern. With fresh Shetland ingredients and a French chef, the cooking is superb. **£110**

Skeoverick ☎ 01595 809349, ✉ skeoverick@btinternet.com. Bargain rates at this lovely modern crofthouse B&B which lies a mile or so north of Walls. Residents' lounge and free wi-fi. **£50**

Voe House ☎ 01595 694688, ⓦ camping-bods.com. This five-bedroom camping böd is the largest on Shetland, with its own peat fire. Note that *Voe House* is confusingly not in Voe but in Walls. April–Oct. **£10**/person

Papa Stour

A mile offshore from Sandness is the rocky island of **Papa Stour**, formed of volcanic lava and ash and subsequently eroded into some of the most impressive coastal scenery in Shetland. In good weather, it makes for a perfect day-trip, but in foul weather or a sea mist it can certainly appear pretty bleak. Its name, meaning "big island of the priests", derives from its early Celtic Christian connections, and the island was home, in the eighteenth century, to people who were mistakenly believed to have been lepers (it seems more likely they were suffering from vitamin deficiency).

The land is fertile, and in the nineteenth century Papa Stour supported a community of three hundred, but by the early 1970s there was a population crisis. With just sixteen inhabitants, and no children, the islanders made appeals for new blood to revive the fragile economy and staged a dramatic recovery, releasing croft land to young incomers. Papa Stour was briefly dubbed "the hippie isle". A new harbour and roll-on-roll-off ferry in 2005 gave the island some hope, but the school is currently closed, there is no accommodation apart from wild camping and internal feuding has brought the population down to single figures.

Papa Stour's main settlement, **BIGGINGS**, lies in the east near the pier, and it was here that excavation in the early 1980s revealed the remains of a thirteenth-century Norse house or "**stofa**", thought to have belonged to the future King Haakon V of Norway. In 2008, the house was partially reconstructed; an explanatory panel explains its significance.

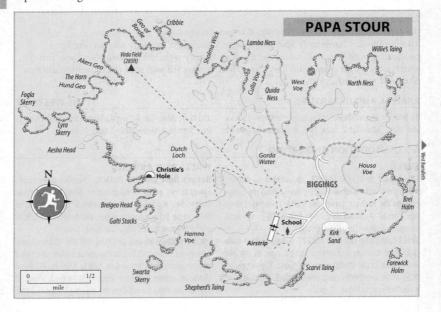

WALKING ON PAPA STOUR
Ordnance Survey Explorer map 467

The chief attraction of Papa Stour is **walking**; to reach the best of the coastal scenery, head for the far west of the island. From **Virda Field** (285ft), the highest point, in the far northwest, you can see the treacherous rocks of **Ve Skerries**, where a lighthouse was erected as recently as 1979. The couple of miles of coastline from here southeast to **Hamna Voe** has some of the island's best stacks, blowholes and natural arches. The most spectacular is **Kirstan's Hole**, a gloup or partly roofed cleft, extending far inland, where shags nest on precipitous ledges. Other points of interest include a couple of defunct horizontal click-mills, below **Dutch Loch**, and the remains of a "meal road", so called because the workmen were paid in oatmeal or flour. In addition, several pairs of red-throated divers regularly breed on inland lochs such as **Gorda Water**.

ARRIVAL AND DEPARTURE   PAPA STOUR

By plane Directflight (☎01595 840246, ⌨directflight .co.uk) flies from Tingwall twice every Tuesday, so a day-trip is feasible; tickets cost around £60 return.
By ferry The ferry runs from West Burrafirth, 5 miles or so

north of Walls on the Westside, to the east coast of Papa Stour (Mon & Sun 1 daily, Wed, Fri & Sat 2 daily; 45min; ☎01955 745804) – book in advance, and reconfirm the day before departure.

Foula

Separated from the nearest point on Shetland's Mainland by about fourteen miles of often turbulent ocean, **Foula** is without a doubt the most isolated inhabited island in

8

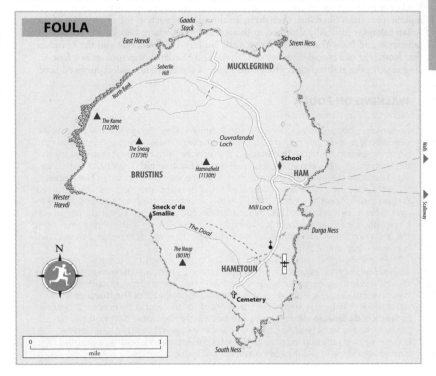

the British Isles. Seen from the Mainland, its distinctive mountainous form changes subtly, depending upon the vantage point, but the outline is unforgettable. Its western **cliffs**, the second highest in Britain after those of St Kilda, rise at **The Kame** to some 1220ft above sea level; a clear day at The Kame offers a magnificent panorama stretching from Unst to Fair Isle. On a bad day, the isolation and exposure are complete and the cliffs generate turbulent blasts of wind known as "flans", which rip through the hills with tremendous force.

Arriving on Foula, you can't help but be amazed by the sheer size of the island's immense, bare mountains, whose summits are often hidden in cloud, known on the Mainland as "Foula's hat". The gentler eastern slopes provide good crofting land, and plentiful peat, and it is along this "green belt" that the island's population is scattered. The only road runs along the eastern side of the island, and is used by Foula's remarkable fleet of clapped-out vehicles.

Foula's name is derived from the Old Norse for "bird island" and it's home to a quarter of a million **birds**. Arctic terns wheel overhead at the airstrip, red-throated divers can usually be seen on the island's smaller lochs, while fulmars, guillemots, razorbills, puffins and gannets cling to the rock ledges. However, it's the island's colony of **great skuas** or "bonxies" that you can't fail to notice with an estimated 3000 pairs on Foula, making it the largest colony in the world. During the nesting season (May–Aug), they attack anyone who comes near. Although their dive-bombing antics are primarily meant as a threat, they can make walking across the moorland fairly stressful: the best advice is to hold a stick above your head or stick to the road and the coast.

Brief history

Foula has been inhabited since prehistoric times, and the people here take pride in their separateness from Shetland, cherishing local traditions such as the observance of the **Julian calendar** (officially dropped in Britain in 1752), where Old Yule is celebrated on January 6 and New Year doesn't arrive until January 13. Foula was also the last place that **Norn**, the old Norse language of Orkney and Shetland, was spoken as a first language, in the eighteenth century, and more of the Shetland dialect survived here

---

WALKING ON FOULA

Ordnance Survey Explorer map 467

Many people come to Foula to view the island's famous cliffs – though in actual fact they are very difficult to appreciate except from the air or the sea. If the weather's fine, though, it's worth climbing to the top of **The Sneug** (1373ft), for the views stretching from Unst to Fair Isle. From the airstrip, climb up the southeast ridge of **Hamnafield** (1130ft), and then continue along the ridge of Brustins to The Sneug itself. From The Sneug, drop down to **The Kame** (1220ft), Foula's sheer cliff, the best view of which is from Nebbiefield, to the south. Return via Da Nort Bank to Soberlie Hill, from where you can pick up the island's road. In total it's only a walk of five or six miles, but it'll take three to four hours. If you're coming from the ferry at Ham, it's probably best to do the circuit in reverse, which is no bad thing, as the climb from Soberlie Hill up Da Nort Bank is one of the most exhilarating on the island, as the edge of the hill is an ever-increasing vertical drop.

There are other, more gentle walks on Foula. The coastal scenery to the north of the island, beyond Mucklegrind, features several stacks and natural arches, with the waves crashing over skerries, and seals sunning themselves. One of the easiest places to spot seabirds is from beyond the graveyard in Biggings, past Hametoun. The nearby hill of **The Noup** (803ft) is a relatively easy climb, compared to The Sneug, and, if you descend to the northwest, brings you to **Sneck o' da Smallie**, where there's a narrow slit in the cliffs, some 200ft high. You can return to the airstrip by heading back down the valley known as The Daal, although the bonxies are pretty thick on the ground. All Foula's cliffs are potentially lethal, especially in wet weather, and all the usual safety precautions should be taken (see p.42).

than elsewhere. Foula's population peaked at two hundred at the end of the nineteenth century, and today numbers around forty.

ARRIVAL AND DEPARTURE   FOULA

By plane Directflight (☎ 01595 840246, ⓦ directflight.co .uk) flies from Tingwall (Mon 1 daily, Tues, Wed & Fri 2 daily, 15min); tickets cost around £70 return.
By ferry Be sure to book and reconfirm your journey by ferry

(Tues, Thurs & Sat; 2hr; ☎ 01595 5840208, ⓦ bkmarine.org), which departs from Walls (Tues, Sat & alternate Thurs; 2hr) or Scalloway (alternate Thurs; 3hr 30min). The ferry arrives at Ham, in the middle of Foula's east coast.

INFORMATION AND TOURS

Tourist information Foula has its own resident part-time ranger, who usually greets new arrivals and offers local advice (mid-April–Oct). It's also possible to arrange for guided walks with the ranger (Wed & Fri; ☎ 01595 753236, ⓦ foulaheritage.org.uk), or you can download

self-guided walk leaflets from the website. There's no shop on the island, so bring your own supplies.
Boat trips Day-trips are not possible on the regular ferry, but Cycharters (☎ 01595 696598, ⓦ cycharters.co.uk) do boat trips on Wednesdays from Scalloway.

ACCOMMODATION

Leraback ☎ 01595 753226, ⓦ originart.eu/leraback /leraback.html. The only accommodation on Foula is at this

B&B near Ham. Fortunately, it's a great place to stay; full board only, and they'll collect you from the airstrip or pier. **£80**

North Mainland

8

The **North Mainland**, stretching more than thirty miles north from the central belt around Lerwick, is wilder than much of Shetland, with almost relentlessly bleak moorland and some rugged and dramatic coastal scenery. It is all but split in two by the isthmus of **Mavis Grind**: to the south is **Sullom Voe**, Shetland's oil terminal, and **Brae**, the area's largest town; to the north is the remote region of **Northmavine**, which boasts some of the most scenic cliffs in Shetland.

Voe

If you're travelling north, you're bound to pass by **VOE**, but if you stay on the A970 it's easy to miss the picturesque old village, a tight huddle of homes and workshops down below the road around the pier (signposted "Lower Voe"). Set at the head of a deep, sheltered, sea loch, Voe has a Scandinavian appearance, helped by the presence of the **Sail Loft**, painted in a rich, deep red. The building was originally used by fishermen and whalers for storing their gear; later, it became a knitwear workshop, and it was here that woollen jumpers were knitted for Edmund Hillary's 1953 Mount Everest expedition. Today, the building has been converted into a large **camping böd**.

ACCOMMODATION AND EATING   VOE

Pierhead Restaurant & Bar ☎ 01806 588332. The former butcher's in Voe is now a cosy wood-panelled pub with a real fire, occasional live music and a good bar menu, a longer version of which is on offer in the upstairs restaurant, featuring local scallops and the odd catch from the fishing boats (mains £12–18). Mon–Thurs & Sun

11am–10pm, Fri & Sat 11am–1am.
Sail Loft ☎ 01595 694688, ⓦ camping-bods.com. Originally a giant storeroom, this enormous böd is situated right by the loch and has hot showers, a kitchen and a solid fuel fire in the smaller of the rooms. April–Oct. **£10**/person

Lunnasting

Lunnasting is the area to the northeast of Voe, on the east coast. The main town is **VIDLIN**, departure point for the Out Skerries (see p.397), three miles east of Laxo, the ferry terminal for Whalsay (see p.396).

The Cabin Museum

April–Sept Tues, Thurs, Sat & Sun 1–5pm • Free • ☎ 01806 577232

Halfway between Laxo and Vidlin, the B9071 passes **The Cabin Museum**, a modern barn packed to the rafters with wartime memorabilia collected by the late Andy Robertson. You can try on some of the uniforms and caps or pore over the many personal accounts of the war written by locals.

Lunna

The long, thin peninsula of Lunna Ness, to the northeast of Vidlin, is pinched in the middle at the tiny remote settlement of **LUNNA**. It was here, at **Lunna House**, that the Shetland Bus made its headquarters during World War II (see p.380); originally built in 1660 and set above a sheltered harbour a couple of miles northeast of Vidlin, it's now a great place to stay (see below). Down the hill from Lunna House lies the little whitewashed **Lunna Kirk**, built in 1753, with a simple, tiny interior including a carved hexagonal pulpit. On the outside wall is a "lepers' squint", through which those believed to have the disease (then believed to be highly contagious) could participate in the service without risk of infecting the congregation; there was, however, no leprosy here, the outcasts in fact suffering from a hereditary, noninfectious skin condition brought on by malnutrition. In the graveyard, several unidentified Norwegian sailors, torpedoed by the Nazis, are buried.

ACCOMMODATION   **LUNNA**

⭐ **Lunna House** ☎ 01806 577311, ⓦ www.lunna house.co.uk. *Lunna House* is a wonderful, remote place to stay. The bedrooms, though not en suite, have lovely views and you get a top-class breakfast. **£60**

Brae

BRAE, a sprawling settlement that still has the feel of a frontier town, was expanded hastily in the 1970s to accommodate the workforce for the **Sullom Voe Oil Terminal**, the largest of its kind in Europe, situated just to the northeast of the town. During World War II Sullom Voe was home to the Norwegian Air Force and a base for RAF seaplanes.

ACCOMMODATION AND EATING   **BRAE**

⭐ **Busta House** ☎ 01806 522506, ⓦ bustahouse .com. Brae may not appear somewhere to spend the night, but does boast this fine hotel, a laird's house with stepped gables that sits across the bay of Busta Voe from the modern sprawl of Brae. Even if you're not staying the night here, it's worth coming for afternoon tea in the Long Room, for a stroll around the lovely wooded grounds, or for a drink and a bar meal in the hotel's pub-like bar. Free wi-fi. **£115**

Frankie's ☎ 01806 522700, ⓦ frankiesfishandchips .com. Brae's best food option, aside from *Busta House*, is the very popular fish and chip café with great views over Busta Voe. As well as the usuals, you can get smoked haddock and mussels. Mon–Sat 9.30am–8pm, Sun noon–8pm.

Westayre ☎ 01806 522368, ⓦ westayre.shetland.co .uk. A modern crofthouse B&B overlooking a red sandy bay at the very end of the road on the peaceful island of Muckle Roe, linked to the mainland by a bridge. **£70**

Northmavine

Northmavine, the northwest peninsula of North Mainland, is unquestionably one of the most picturesque areas of Shetland, with its often rugged scenery, magnificent coastline and wide-open spaces. The peninsula begins a mile west of Brae at **Mavis Grind**, a narrow isthmus at which it's said you can throw a stone from the Atlantic to the North Sea, or at least to Sullom Voe. Just by the roadside, here, there's a great little display on the area's incredible **geodiversity**, thanks to its violent, volcanic past.

Hillswick

HILLSWICK, the main settlement in the area, is situated on another narrow isthmus, and was once a centre for deep-sea or haaf fishing, and later a herring station. In 1900, the North of Scotland, Orkney & Shetland Steam Navigation Company built the **St Magnus Hotel** to house their customers, importing it in the form of a timber kit from Norway. Despite various alterations over the years, it still stands overlooking St Magnus Bay, rather magnificently clad in black timber-framing and white weatherboarding.

Down by the ancient harbour, **Da Böd** was founded by a Hanseatic merchant in 1684, later became Shetland's oldest pub and is now a seal and wildlife sanctuary and occasional weekend café. The stony beach by the harbour is very sheltered, but the nicest, sandiest **beach** is on the west side of the Hillswick isthmus, overlooking Dore Holm, a short walk across the fields from the hotel.

Esha Ness

Just outside Hillswick, a side road leads west to the exposed headland of **Esha Ness**, celebrated for its splendid coastline views. Spectacular red-granite **cliffs**, shaped into fantastic forms by the elements, spread out before you as the road climbs away from Hillswick: to the south, out at sea, are the stacks known as **The Drongs** off the Ness of Hillswick, while in the distance the Westside and Papa Stour are visible. After about three miles, you reach *Braewick* café and campsite, where there's a great view over the wide bay of Brae Wick, from which several small dead-end roads lead off to the coast.

Tangwick Haa Museum

Easter–Sept daily 11am–5pm • Free • ☎ 01806 503389, ⓦ tangwickhaa.org.uk

One small dead-end road, off the main road, leads south to the **Tangwick Haa Museum**, housed in a seventeenth-century building, which, through photographs, old documents and fishing gear, tells the often moving story of this remote corner of Shetland and its role in the dangerous trade of deep-sea fishing and whaling. All ages will also enjoy the shells and the Shetland wool and sand samples.

Stenness fishing station

West of Braewick, the road divides, with the southern branch leading to the remains of **Stenness fishing station**, once one of the most important haaf-fishing stations in Shetland. A few ruined böds used by the fishermen are still visible along the sloping pebbly beach where they would dry their catch. In the early nineteenth century, as many as eighteen trips a year were made in up to seventy open, six-oared boats, known as "sixareens", to the fishing grounds thirty or forty miles to the west. A Shetland folk song, *Rowin' Foula Doon*, recalls how the crews rowed so far west that the island of Foula began to sink below the eastern horizon.

Esha Ness Lighthouse

West of Braewick, where the road divides, the northernmost branch ends at **Esha Ness Lighthouse**, a great place to view the red-sandstone cliffs, stacks and blowholes of this stretch of coast. An information board at the lighthouse details some of the dramatic geological features here and, if the weather's a bit rough, you should be treated to some spectacular crashing waves. One of the features to beware of here are the blowholes, some of which are hidden far inland. The best example is the **Holes of Scraada**, a partly roofed cleft, half a mile north of the lighthouse, where the sea suddenly appears 300yd inland from the cliff line. The incredible power of the sea can be seen in the various giant boulder fields above the cliffs: these **storm beaches** are formed by rocks torn from the cliffs in storms and deposited inland.

8

HILLSWICK AND AROUND

Almara Urafirth ☎01806 503261, ⓦalmara.shetland
.co.uk. This is without a doubt the best B&B in Northmavine, serving up a friendly family welcome, good food,
free wi-fi and excellent views. **£70**

Da Böd ☎01806 503348, ⓦshetlandwildlifesanctuary
.com. This eccentric, weekend-only café occupies a rambling,
ancient building and the proceeds go to the nearby wildlife
sanctuary. April–Sept Sat & Sun 11am–5pm.

ESHA NESS

Braewick café and campsite ☎01806 503345,
ⓦeshaness.moonfruit.com. Café with great views of the

Drongs, serving soup, sandwiches and toasties, plus home-
made cakes and scones; phone to check opening times.
The campsite is pretty exposed but you can always book
one of the four wooden wigwams if the wind gets too
much. Food served Mon–Thurs & Sun 10am–5pm, Fri &
Sat 10am–8pm. Wigwams **£40**; camping **£5**/pitch

Johnnie Notions Böd ☎01595 694688, ⓦcamping
-bods.com. One of the few places to stay in Esha Ness,
this tiny böd – the birthplace of a pioneer in smallpox
inoculation – is in a remote hamlet of Hamnavoe, north
of Braewick. There's no electricity, but there is a solid-fuel
stove. April–Oct. **£8**/person

Whalsay

The island of **Whalsay**, known in Shetland as the "Bonnie Isle", is in a world of its own,
with a friendly community of over a thousand, devoted almost entirely to fishing, and
a dialect even other Shetlanders struggle to fathom. The islands' fishing crews operate a
very successful pelagic fleet of immense super-trawlers which can fish far afield in all
weathers catching a wide range of species. The island is also extremely fertile, but
crofting takes second place to fishing here; there are also plentiful supplies of peat,
which can be seen in spring and summer, stacked neatly to dry out above huge peat
banks, ready to be bagged for the winter.

Although the majority of folk live in or around Symbister, the rest of Whalsay
– which measures roughly two miles by eight – is quite evenly and fairly densely
populated. Of the prehistoric remains, the most notable are the two **Bronze Age houses**
on the northeastern coast of the island, half a mile south of Skaw, known respectively
as the "Benie Hoose" and "Yoxie Biggins". The latter is also known as the "Standing
Stones of Yoxie", due to the use of megaliths to form large sections of the walls, many
of which still stand.

Symbister

Ferries from the Mainland arrive at **SYMBISTER** in the southwest, whose harbour is
usually dominated by the presence of several of the island's sophisticated, multi-
million-pound purse-netters, some over 180ft long; you'll also see smaller fishing boats
and probably a few "fourareens", which the locals race regularly in the summer months.

Pier House

Mon–Sat 9am–1pm & 2–5pm, Sun 2–4pm • Free

Across the busy harbour from the ferry berth stands the tiny grey-granite **Pier House**,
the key for which resides in the shop opposite. This picturesque little building, with a
hoist built into one side, is thought to have been a Hanseatic merchants' store, and
contains a good display on how the Germans traded salt, tobacco, spirits and cloth for
Whalsay's salted, dried fish from medieval times until the eighteenth century; close by
is the Harbour View house, thought to have been a Hanseatic storehouse or booth.

Symbister House

Heritage Centre May–Sept Wed & Fri–Sun 2–5pm; Oct–May Wed 7–9pm • Free • ☎01806 566397, ⓦwhalsayheritage.co.uk

On a hill overlooking the town is the imposing Georgian mansion of **Symbister House**,
built in grey granite and boasting a Neoclassical portico. It was built in the 1830s at

great expense by the laird Robert Bruce, reputedly not because he wanted to live on Whalsay but because he wanted to deprive his heirs of his fortune. Since 1960, it has served as the local school, though you can still see the old doocot behind the house, and various outbuildings in the Midden Court, one of which houses a **heritage centre** on the history of the island.

Grieve House

About half a mile east of Symbister at the hamlet of **SODOM** – an anglicized version of Sudheim, meaning "South House" – is **Grieve House** (now a camping böd; see below), the modest former home of celebrated Scots poet, writer and Communist **Hugh MacDiarmid** (1892–1978), born Christopher Grieve in the Borders town of Langholm. He stayed here from 1933 until 1942, writing about half of his output, including much of his best work: lonely, contemplative poems honouring fishing and fishermen, with whom he sometimes went out to sea. At first, he seems to have fallen in love with the islands, but poor physical and mental health, exacerbated by chronic poverty, dogged him. Eventually, unwillingly conscripted to work in a Glasgow munitions factory, he left with his new wife and young son, never to return.

ARRIVAL AND DEPARTURE   WHALSAY

By plane There are also request-only flights from Tingwall (Mon, Wed & Thurs; ☎01595 840246, ⓦdirectflight.co .uk); day-trips are only possible on Thursdays.

By ferry Car ferries run regularly to Whalsay from Laxo on the Mainland (☎01806 566259; 30min) – book ahead to take a car. In bad weather, especially southeasterly gales, the service operates from Vidlin instead. Laxo–Symbister (every 45min; 30min).

ACCOMMODATION AND EATING

Grieve House ☎01595 694688, ⓦcamping-bods.com. The only accommodation on Whalsay is this camping böd in Sodom, on the edge of Symbister. The house has lovely views overlooking Linga Sound, but is hidden from the road to the Loch of Huxter, so ask for directions. No electricity, but a solid fuel stove. April–Oct. __£8__/person

Oot Ower Lounge & Campsite ☎01595 566658. A family-run pub overlooking the Loch of Huxter – this is pretty much the only place to eat and drink on the island (phone ahead to check they're open and serving food), with fish and chips for £10, and somewhere you're welcome to camp. __£5__/person

SHOPPING

Shoard (no phone or website). The country's remotest charity shop is in Brough, halfway between Symbister and the golf course; it has limited opening hours, but is a must if you're in the area. Shetland's take on Aladdin's Cave. Wed, Thurs & Sat 2–4pm.

Out Skerries

Four miles out to sea, off the northeast tip of Whalsay, the **Out Skerries** ("Oot Skerries" or plain "Skerries" as the locals call them), consist of three tiny low-lying rocky islands, Housay, Bruray and Grunay, the first two linked by a bridge, with a population of around seventy. That people live here at all is remarkable, and that it is one of Shetland's most dynamic communities is astonishing, its affluence based on fishing from a superb, small natural harbour and on salmon farming in a nearby inlet. There are good, if short, walks, with a few prehistoric remains, but the majority of visitors are divers exploring the wreck-strewn coastline, and ornithologists who come here when the wind is in the east, hoping to catch a glimpse of rare migrants.

The Skerries' jetty and airstrip are both on the middle island of **Bruray**, which also boasts the Skerries' highest point, Bruray Wart (173ft), an easy climb, and one which brings you up close to the islands' ingenious spiral-channel collection system for rainwater, which can become scarce in summer. The largest of the Skerries' trio,

Housay, has the most indented and intriguing coastline, to which you should head if the weather's fine.

ARRIVAL AND DEPARTURE OUT SKERRIES

By plane There are regular flights from Tingwall (Mon, Wed & Thurs), with day-trips possible on Thursdays.

By ferry Ferries to and from Skerries leave from Vidlin on the Mainland (Mon & Fri–Sun; 1hr 30min) and Lerwick (Tues & Thurs; 2hr 30min), but day-trips are only possible

from Vidlin (Fri–Sun). Make sure you book your journey by 5pm the previous evening (☎01806 515226), or the ferry might not run. You can take your car over, but, with less than a mile of road to drive along, it's not worth it.

ACCOMMODATION

Wild Camping is allowed, with permission. There is a shop, and a shower/toilet block by the pier.

Rocklea ☎01806 515228, ⓦ rockleaok.co.uk. The only B&B on the islands is a modern crofthouse on Bruray run

by the very welcoming Johnsons, who offer optional full board. <u>£64</u>

The North Isles

Many visitors never make it out to Shetland's trio of remote **North Isles**, which is a shame, as the ferry links are frequent and inexpensive, and the roads fast. Certainly, there is no dramatic shift in scenery: much of what awaits you is the familiar Shetland landscape of undulating peat moorland, dramatic coastal cliffs and silent glacial voes. However, with Lerwick that much further away, the spirit of independence and self-sufficiency in the North Isles is much more keenly felt. **Yell**, the largest of the three, is best known for its vast otter population, but is otherwise often overlooked. **Fetlar**, the smallest of the trio, is home to the rare red-necked phalarope, but **Unst** has probably the widest appeal, partly as the most northerly landmass in the British Isles, but also for its nesting seabird population. Note that **public transport** on all three islands is very limited, and that often it's necessary to book your journey the day before to ensure that the service runs.

Yell

Historically, **Yell** hasn't had good write-ups. The writer Eric Linklater described it as "dull and dark", while the Scottish historian Buchanan claimed it was "so uncouth a place that no creature can live therein, except such as are born there". If you keep to the fast main road, which links the island's two ferry terminals of **Ulsta** and **Gutcher**, you'll pass a lot of uninspiring peat moorland, but the landscape is relieved by several voes, which cut deeply into it, providing superb natural harbours used as hiding places by German submarines during World War II. Yell's coastline, too, is gentler and greener than the interior and provides an ideal habitat for a large population of **otters**.

Burravoe and around

At **BURRAVOE**, in the southeastern corner of Yell, there's a lovely whitewashed laird's house dating from 1672, with crow-stepped gables, that now houses the **Old Haa Museum** (April–Sept Tues–Thurs & Sat 10am–4pm, Sun 2–5pm; free; ☎01957 702431), which is stuffed with artefacts, and has lots of material on the history of the local herring and whaling industry; there's a very pleasant wood-panelled café on the ground floor, too. Back at the crossroads stands **St Colman's Kirk**, completed in 1900, featuring an apsed chancel and several winsome Gothic windows, and is surmounted by a tiny little spire. From May to August, you'll find thousands of **seabirds** (including puffin) nesting in the cliffs above Ladies Hole, less than a mile to the northeast of the village.

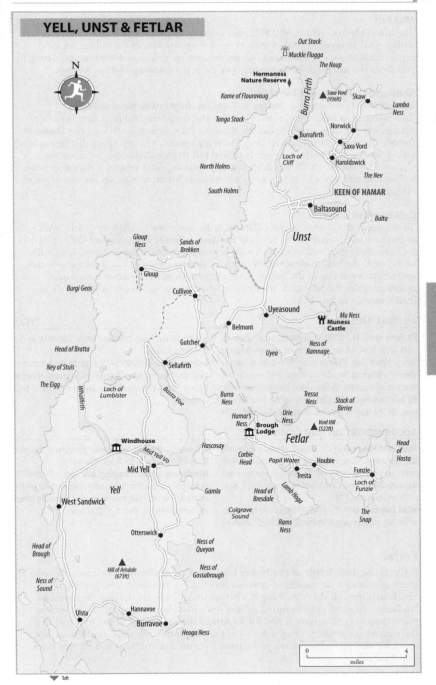

YELL, UNST & FETLAR

N

Out Stack
Muckle Flugga
The Noup
**Hermaness
Nature Reserve**
Kame of Flouravoug
Burra Firth
*Saxa Vord
(936ft)*
Skaw
*Lamba
Ness*
Tonga Stack
Norwick
Burrafirth
Saxa Vord
Loch of
Cliff
Haroldswick
North Holms
The Nev
South Holms
KEEN OF HAMAR
Baltasound
Balta
Unst
Gloup
Ness
Sands of
Brekken
Burgi Geos
Gloup
Cullivoe
Uyeasound
Mu Ness
**Muness
Castle**
Belmont
Head of Bratta
Gutcher
*Ness of
Ramnage*
Ney of Stuis
Uyea
The Eigg
Sellafirth
Whalfirth
Bosta Voe
*Burra
Ness*
*Tressa
Ness*
*Stack of
Birrier*
Loch of
Lumbister
*Urie
Ness*
*Vord Hill
(522ft)*
*Hamar's
Ness*
**Brough
Lodge**
Windhouse
Fetlar
*Head
of
Hosta*
Mid Yell Vo
Hascosay
*Corbie
Head*
Papil Water
Houbie
Mid Yell
Funzie
Yell
Tresta
Loch of
Funzie
West Sandwick
Gamla
*Head of
Bresdale*
Lamb Hoga
*The
Snap*
Otterswick
*Colgrave
Sound*
*Rams
Ness*
*Head of
Brough*
*Hill of Arisdale
(673ft)*
*Ness of
Queyon*
*Ness of
Gossabrough*
*Ness of
Sound*
Ulsta
Hannavoe
Burravoe
Heoga Ness

0   4
miles

8

Toft

Mid Yell

The island's largest village, **MID YELL**, has a couple of shops, a pub and a leisure centre with a good swimming pool. A mile or so to the northwest of the village, on an exposed hill above the main road, stands the spooky, abandoned **Windhouse**, dating in part from the early eighteenth century (its lodge is a camping böd; see below).

Shetland Gallery and Global Yell

Shetland Gallery · Easter–Sept Tues–Sat 11am–5pm, Sun 2–5pm · Free · ☎ 01957 744386, ⓦ shetlandgallery.com

Two miles or so before you reach Gutcher, the ferry terminal for Unst, the main road passes the diminutive Sellafirth Business Park, where you'll find the **Shetland Gallery**, Britain's northernmost art gallery, a pleasant, modern space displaying local artists' works. Across the car park is **Global Yell** (ⓦ globalyell.org), a Centre for Creative Industries in Shetland, specifically weaving (and singing); they're extremely welcoming and you can have a go at a miniature loom, or sign up for one of their longer courses.

Cullivoe and around

To the north of Gutcher, around **CULLIVOE** the landscape is relatively gentle, with attractive coastal scenery. The **Sands of Brekken** are made from crushed shells, and are beautifully sheltered in a cove a mile or two north of Cullivoe. A couple of miles to the west, the road ends at **GLOUP**, with its secretive, narrow voe. In the nineteenth century, this was one of the largest haaf-fishing stations in Shetland; a memorial commemorates the 58 men who were lost when a great storm overwhelmed six of their sixareens in July 1881.

ARRIVAL AND TOURS   YELL

By ferry ☎ 01595 745804, ⓦ shetland.gov.uk. Ferries to Ulsta (Yell) from Toft on the Mainland are very frequent (every 30min–1hr; 20min), as are ferries from Gutcher across the Bluemull Sound to Belmont (Unst) and Hamar's Ness (Fetlar) – and there's free wi-fi at both ferry terminals. **By bus** An integrated bus and ferry service from Lerwick goes all the way to Gutcher (Mon–Sat 1–2 daily; 2hr

10min). On Yell, buses from Ulsta run to Gutcher (Mon–Sat 2–4 daily; 30min).

Guided tours ☎ 01806 577358, ⓦ shetlandotters.com. Local otter-spotter John Campbell takes groups of two or three in search of otters (£125 a day for a couple) – book in advance.

ACCOMMODATION AND EATING

Pinewood House ☎ 01957 702092, ⓦ pinewoodhouse shetland.co.uk. Great option on the east coast of Yell: rooms are plain but comfy, and the guest lounge has a real fire, views over to Fetlar and lots of books on the local area. Full board available. **£70**

Wind Dog Café ☎ 01957 744321. Quirky café in a prefab at Gutcher, offering soup, baked tatties and filled bannocks,

and hosting the odd local event throughout the year. Mon–Fri 9am–5pm, Sat & Sun 10am–5pm.

Windhouse Lodge camping böd ☎ 01595 694688, ⓦ camping-bods.com. The *Windhouse* gatehouse, on the main road near Mid Yell, has a wood- and peat-fired heater and hot showers. April–Oct. **£10**/person

Fetlar

Fetlar is the most fertile of the North Isles, much of it grassy moorland and lush green meadows with masses of summer flowers. It's known as "the garden of Shetland", though that's pushing it a bit, as it's still a fairly unforgiving, treeless landscape. Around nine hundred people once lived here and there might well be more than sixty now were it not for **Sir Arthur Nicolson** who, in the first half of the nineteenth century, cleared many of the people at forty days' notice to make room for sheep. Today Fetlar's population lives on the southern and eastern sides of the island.

Brough Lodge

Sir Arthur Nicolson's architectural tastes were rather more eccentric than some other local tyrants; his rotting but still astonishing **Brough Lodge**, a rambling castellated composition built in stone and brick in the 1820s, can be seen about a mile south of the ferry terminal, and owes something – perhaps an apology – to Gothic, Classical and maybe even Tudor styles. Nicolson is also responsible for the nearby round-tower folly, which was built with stone from the abandoned crofthouses.

Vord Hill

Much of the northern half of the island around Fetlar's highest point, **Vord Hill** (522ft), is now an RSPB Reserve. As well as harbouring important colonies of arctic skua and whimbrel, Fetlar is perhaps best known for having harboured Britain's only breeding pair of **snowy owls**, which bred on Stackaberg, to the southwest of Vord Hill, from 1967 to 1975.

Houbie and around

At the tiny, main settlement, **HOUBIE**, in the centre of the island on the south coast, there's a rather less adventurously styled laird's house called Leagarth, with an impressive conservatory, built by Fetlar's most famous son, Sir William Watson Cheyne (1852–1932), who, with Lord Lister, pioneered antiseptic surgery. You can learn more about Cheyne's colourful life from the nearby **Fetlar Interpretive Centre** (May–Sept Mon–Sat 11am–3pm, Sun 1–4pm; £2; ☏01957 733206, ⓦfetlar.com), a welcoming museum with information on Fetlar's outstanding birdlife.

The **Sand of Tresta** is less than a mile to the west of Houbie, with a beautiful, sheltered beach of golden sand, and the freshwater loch of Papil Water immediately behind it. Fetlar also shelters Britain's most northerly religious community, the **Society of Our Lady of the Isles**, a small Anglican religious order for women based in the modern lodge on the edge of the cliffs at Aith Ness, to the east of Houbie. There are two chapels at the nunnery, both open to visitors: the Byre Chapel, a converted barn with a resident goat, and a modern chapel where the daily office takes place.

Loch of Funzie

Fetlar is also one of very few places in Britain where you'll see the graceful **red-necked phalarope** (late May–early Aug): the birds are unusual in that the female does the courting and then leaves the male in charge of incubation. There is a hide overlooking the marshes (or mires) to the east of the **Loch of Funzie** (pronounced "Finny").

ARRIVAL AND GETTING AROUND

FETLAR

By ferry Ferries to Fetlar (Mon–Sat 7–9 daily; 25–40min) depart regularly from both Gutcher (Yell) and Belmont (Unst), and dock at Hamar's Ness, 3 miles northwest of Houbie.

By bus There's a Funzie to Fetlar ferry service (Mon–Sat 3 daily), and a dial-a-ride electric minibus service – to use it you must book your journey the day before (☏01595 745745).

By car Bear in mind that there's no petrol station on Fetlar, so fill up before you come across.

ACCOMMODATION AND EATING

Aithbank Böd ☏01595 694688, ⓦcamping-bods .com. A cosy wood-panelled cottage, a mile east of Houbie, with two rooms, sleeping a total of seven. Hot water, kitchen, solid-fuel stove. March–Oct. **£10**/person

Fetlar Café ☏01957 733227. The island's only café lives inside the island shop/post office in Houbie. Cooked breakfasts (Fridays only), soup and a few light snacks is all you can hope for. Mon–Sat 11am–4pm.

Garths Campsite ☏01957 733227. A simple camping field just to the west of Houbie and a stone's throw from the Sand of Tresta, with toilets, showers and drying facilities. May–Sept. **£7**/pitch

Gord ☏01957 733227, ✉nicboxall@btinternet.com. The modern house attached to the island shop in Houbie is also a B&B with great sea views from all the rooms. Full board only; meals for non-residents by arrangement. **£100**

Unst

Much of **Unst** is rolling grassland – a blessed relief for some after the peaty moorland of Yell – but the coast is more dramatic: a fringe of cliffs relieved by some beautiful sandy beaches. As Britain's most northerly inhabited island, there is a surfeit of "most northerly" sights, and many visitors only come here in order to head straight for Hermaness, to see the seabirds and look out over Muckle Flugga and the northernmost tip of Britain, to the North Pole beyond. The island's population recently plummeted following the closure of the local RAF radar base at Saxa Vord, which used to employ a third of the population.

Uyeasound and around

On the south coast, not far from the ferry terminal, is **UYEASOUND**, with Greenwell's Booth, an old Hanseatic merchants' warehouse by the pier, sadly now roofless. Further east lie the ruins of **Muness Castle**, a diminutive defensive structure, with matching bulging bastions and corbelled turrets at opposite corners. It was built in 1598 by the Scots incomer, Laurence Bruce, stepbrother and chief bullyboy of the infamous Earl Robert Stewart, and probably designed by Andrew Crawford, who shortly afterwards built Scalloway Castle for Robert's son, Patrick. The inscription above the entrance asks visitors "not to hurt this vark aluayis", but the castle was sacked by Danish pirates in 1627 and never really re-roofed. A little to the north is a vast sandy beach, backed by the deserted crofting settlement of Sandwick.

Baltasound and around

8

Unst's main settlement is **BALTASOUND**, five miles north of Uyeasound; its herring industry used to boost the local population of around five hundred to as much as ten thousand during the fishing season. As you leave Baltasound, heading to Haroldswick, be sure to take a look at **Bobby's bus shelter** (ⓦunstbusshelter.shetland.co.uk), an eccentric, fully furnished, award-winning Shetland bus shelter on the edge of town.

The **Keen of Hamar**, east of Baltasound, and clearly signposted from the main road, is one of the largest expanses of serpentine debris in Europe, and is home to an extraordinary array of plantlife. It's worth taking a walk on this barren, exposed, almost lunar landscape that's thought to resemble what most of northern Europe looked like at the end of the last Ice Age. With the help of one of the SNH leaflets (kept in a box by the stile), you can try to identify some of the area's numerous rare and minuscule plants, including Norwegian sandwort, frog orchid, moonwort and the mouse-eared Edmondston's chickweed, which flowers in June and July and is found nowhere else in the world.

From the Keen of Hamar to Haroldswick, the main road crosses a giant boulder field of **serpentine**, a greyish-green, occasionally turquoise rock found widely on Unst, and which weathers to a rusty orange.

Haroldswick

Beyond the Keen of Hamar, the road drops down into **HAROLDSWICK**, where near the shore you'll find the **Unst Boat Haven** (May–Sept daily 11am–5pm; ☏01957 711809; £3), displaying a beautifully presented collection of historic boats with many tools of the trade and information on fishing. If you want to learn about other aspects of Unst's history, head for the nearby **Unst Heritage Centre** (May–Sept daily 11am–5pm; £3; ☏01957 711528), housed in the old school building by the main crossroads, where they also put on have-a-go activities such as spinning, knitting and potting.

Saxa Vord

Less than a mile north of Haroldswick is **SAXA VORD** (also, confusingly, the name of the nearby hill), home to the eyesore former **RAF base**, now containing a restaurant, bar and hostel, but also a **chocolate factory** (Mon–Sat 11.30am–5pm, Sun 1–4pm;

free; ⓦfoordschocolates.co.uk), where there's also an **exhibition** on the history of the RAF on Unst. The former base is also now home to Britain's most northerly brewery, the **Valhalla Brewery**, source of the Shetland Ales you see around the islands, which welcomes visits by appointment (☎01957 711658, ⓦvalhallabrewery.co.uk).

Hermaness Nature Reserve
To the west of Burra Firth lies the bleak headland of **Hermaness**, now a National Nature Reserve and home to more than 100,000 nesting seabirds. There's an excellent **visitor centre** in the former lighthouse-keepers' shore station, where you can pick up a leaflet showing the marked routes across the heather, which allow you access into the reserve. Whatever you do, stick to the path so as to avoid annoying the vast numbers of nesting great skuas.

From Hermaness Hill, you can look down over the jagged rocks of the wonderfully named Vesta Skerry, Rumblings, Tipta Skerry and **Muckle Flugga**, the latter providing the dramatic setting for a lighthouse. Few sites could ever have presented as great a challenge to the builders, who erected it in 1858. Beyond Muckle Flugga is **Out Stack**, the most northerly bit of Britain, where Lady Franklin landed in 1849 in order to pray (in vain, as it turned out) for the safe return of her husband from his expedition to discover the Northwest Passage, undertaken four years previously. The views from here are inevitably marvellous, as is the birdlife; there's a huge gannetry on one of the stacks, and puffins burrow all along the clifftops. The walk down the west side of Unst towards Westing is one of the finest in Shetland: if the wind's blowing hard, the seascape is memorably dramatic.

8

ARRIVAL AND DEPARTURE   UNST

By ferry ☎01595 745804. Ferries shuttle regularly across Bluemull Sound from Gutcher on Yell over to Belmont on Unst (every 30–1hr; 10min).
By bus An integrated bus and ferry service goes all the way from Lerwick to Baltasound on Unst (Mon–Sat 1–2

daily; 2hr 40min). From Belmont, the ferry terminal on Unst, buses run to Uyeasound (Mon–Sat 2–4 daily; 5min), continuing to Baltasound (Mon–Sat 2–3 daily; 15min) and even Haroldswick (Mon–Sat 1–2 daily; 30min).

TOURS

Boat trips If your sea legs are better than your walking boots, you can opt to see the great seabird colonies of Hermaness with Muckle Flugga Charters (☎01806 522447,

ⓦmuckleflugga.co.uk), which operate out of Baltasound or Burrafirth.

ACCOMMODATION

Gardiesfauld Uyeasound ☎01957 755279, ⓦgardies fauld.shetland.co.uk. A clean and modern hostel near Uyeasound pier which allows camping, and offers bike rental. April–Sept. Dorms **£15**; camping **£6**/person

Prestagaard Uyeasound ☎01957 755234, ⓔpreste gaard@postmaster.co.uk. This attractive, whitewashed Victorian B&B, with just three rooms, is situated in Uyeasound and has great sea views. **£60**

EATING AND DRINKING

Baltasound Hotel Baltasound ☎01957 711334, ⓦbaltasoundhotel.co.uk. Wherever you stay, it's a good idea to book yourself in for dinner or self-cater – the only other option is the bar food at the *Baltasound Hotel* (mains £10–18). Food served daily 5–8pm.
Northern Lights Bistro Haroldswick ☎01957 711557. Spacious, modern café, serving soup, sandwiches and

toasties, with views across the bay, near the Unst Boat Haven in Haroldswick. April–Sept daily 10am–6pm.
Skibhoul Café & Stores Baltasound. The island's main shop is attached to the local bakery, has the odd chip supper night and will fill your flask – there's also a self-service café and reading corner in the store. Mon–Sat 9.30am–5.30pm.

Contexts

History

It's hard to look at a landscape in the Scottish Highlands and Islands and not have a sense of the stories from history swirling around, from the ancient Stone Age settlers whose dwellings and stone circles are still so well preserved around the Northern and Western Isles, to the empty villages and lonely glens depopulated during the Clearances. Unusually for Europe, the history of the region is dominated more by the wildness of the sea and harshness of the landscape than the politics of London or Paris, and even Edinburgh has often felt distant, another landscape, another language and another difficult journey away.

Prehistoric Scotland

Scotland's first inhabitants were Mesolithic **hunter-gatherers**, who arrived as the last Ice Age retreated around 8000 BC. They lived initially in the area south of Oban, where heaps of animal bones and shells have been excavated in the caves on the Mull of Kintyre and on the plains north of Crinan. From here there is evidence of their moving onto the islands of Arran, Jura, Rùm, Skye and Lewis, where the damp and relatively warm coastal climate would have been preferable to the harsher inland hills and glens. Around 4500 BC, **Neolithic farming peoples** from the European mainland began moving into Scotland. To provide themselves with land for their cereal crops and grazing for their livestock, they cleared large areas of upland forest, usually by fire, and in the process created the characteristic moorland landscapes of much of modern Scotland. These early farmers established permanent settlements, some of which, like the well-preserved village of **Skara Brae** on Orkney, were near the sea, enabling them to supplement their diet by fishing and to develop their skills as boatbuilders. The Neolithic settlements were not as isolated as was once imagined: geological evidence has, for instance, revealed that the stone used to make axe heads found in the Hebrides was quarried in Northern Ireland.

Settlement spurred the development of more complex forms of religious belief. The Neolithic peoples built large chambered burial mounds or **cairns**, such as Maes Howe in Orkney (see p.337) and the Clava Cairns near Inverness. This reverence for human remains suggests a belief in some form of afterlife, a concept that the next wave of settlers, the **Beaker people**, certainly believed in. They built the mysterious **stone circles**, thirty of which have been discovered in Scotland. Such monuments were a massive commitment in terms of time and energy, with many of the stones carried from miles away, just as they were at Stonehenge in England. The best-known Scottish circle is that of **Callanish** (Calanais) on the Isle of Lewis (see p.307), where a dramatic series of monoliths form avenues leading towards a circle made up of thirteen standing stones. The exact function of the circles is still unknown, but many of the stones are aligned with the position of the sun at certain points in its annual cycle, suggesting that the monuments are related to the changing of the seasons.

4500 BC	3000 BC	2000 BC	100 BC–100 AD
Neolithic people move into Scotland	Neolithic township of Skara Brae built	Callanish standing stones erected on Lewis in the Western Isles	Fortified Iron Age brochs built across Scotland

The Beaker people also brought the **Bronze Age** to Scotland. New materials led directly to the development of more effective weapons, and the sword and the shield made their first appearance around 1000 BC. Agricultural needs plus new weaponry added up to a state of endemic warfare as villagers raided their neighbours to steal livestock and grain. The Bronze Age peoples responded to the danger by developing a range of defences, among them the spectacular **hillforts**, great earthwork defences, many of which are thought to have been occupied from around 1000 BC and remained in use throughout the Iron Age, sometimes far longer. Less spectacular but equally practical were the **crannogs**, smaller settlements built on artificial islands constructed of logs, earth, stones and brush, such as those found on Loch Tay (see p.143).

The Celts and the Picts

Conflict in Scotland intensified in the first millennium BC as successive waves of **Celtic** settlers, arriving from the south, increased competition for land. Around 400 BC, the Celts brought the technology of **iron** with them. These fractious times witnessed the construction of hundreds of **brochs** or fortified towers. Concentrated along the Atlantic coast and in the Northern and Western Isles, the brochs were dry-stone fortifications (built without mortar or cement) often over 40ft in height. Some historians claim they provided protection for small coastal settlements from the attentions of Roman slave-traders. Much the best-preserved broch is on the Shetland island of **Mousa** (see p.382); its double walls rise to about 40ft, only a little short of their original height. The Celts continued to migrate north almost up until Julius Caesar's first incursion into Britain in 55 BC.

At the end of the prehistoric period, immediately prior to the arrival of the Romans, Scotland was divided among a number of warring Iron Age tribes, who, apart from the raiding, were preoccupied with wresting a living from the land, growing barley and oats, rearing sheep, hunting deer and fishing for salmon. The Romans were to write these people into history under the collective name Picti, or **Picts**, meaning "painted people", after their body tattoos.

The Romans

The **Roman conquest** of Britain began in 43 AD, almost a century after Caesar's first invasion. By 80 AD the Roman governor Agricola felt secure enough in the south of Britain to begin an invasion of the north, building a string of forts along the southern edge of the Highlands and defeating a large force of Scottish tribes at Mons Graupius. Precisely where this is remains a puzzle for historians, though most place it somewhere in the northeast, possibly on the slopes of Bennachie, near Inverurie in Aberdeenshire. The long-term effect of his campaign, however, was slight. Work on a major fort – to be the base for 5000 soldiers – at Inchtuthill, north of Perth on the Tay, was abandoned before it was finished, and the legions withdrew south. In 123 AD **Emperor Hadrian** decided to seal the frontier against the northern tribes and built **Hadrian's Wall**, which stretched from the Solway Firth to the Tyne and was the first formal division of the mainland of Britain. Twenty years later, the Romans again ventured north and built the **Antonine Wall** between the Clyde and the Forth rivers, a clear statement of the hostility they perceived to the north. This was occupied for about forty years, but thereafter the

43 AD	**83**	**142**	**162**
Britain is invaded by the Romans	British tribes defeated by the Romans at the Battle of Mons Graupius in northeast Scotland	The Romans build the Antonine Wall between the Firth of Forth and the Firth of Clyde	The Roman army retreat behind Hadrian's Wall

Romans, frustrated by the inhospitable terrain of the Highlands, largely gave up their attempt to subjugate the north, and instead adopted a policy of containment.

The Dark Ages

In the years following the departure of the Romans in 410 AD, the population of Scotland changed considerably. By 500 AD there were four groups of people, or nations, dominant in different parts of the country. The **Picts** occupied the Northern Isles, the north and the east as far south as Fife. Today their settlements can be generally identified by place names with a "Pit" prefix, such as Pitlochry, and by the existence of carved symbol stones, like those found at Aberlemno in Angus. To the southwest, between Dumbarton and Carlisle, was a population of **Britons**. Many of the Briton leaders had Roman names, which suggests that they were a Romanized Celtic people, possibly a combination of tribes maintained by the Romans as a buffer between the Wall and the northern tribes, and peoples pushed west by the Anglo-Saxon invaders landing on the east coast. Both the Britons and the Picts spoke variations of P-Celtic, from which Welsh, Cornish and Breton developed.

On the west coast, to the north and west of the Britons (in what is now Argyll), lived the **Scotti**, Irish-Celtic invaders who would eventually give their name to the whole country. The first Scotti arrived in the Western Isles from Ireland in the fourth century AD, and about a century later their great king, Fergus Mor, moved his base from Antrim to Dunadd, near Lochgilphead, where he founded the Kingdom of Dalriada. The Scotti spoke Q-Celtic, the precursor of modern Scottish Gaelic. On the east coast, the Germanic **Angles** had sailed north along the coast to carve out an enclave around Dunbar in East Lothian.

Within three centuries, another non-Celtic invader was making significant incursions. From around 795 AD, **Norse** raids began on the Scottish coast and Hebrides, soon followed by the arrival of settlers, mainly in the Northern Isles and along the Caithness and Sutherland coastline. In 872 AD, the king of Norway set up an earldom in **Orkney**, from which **Shetland** was also governed, and for the next six centuries the Northern Isles took a path distinct from the rest of Scotland, becoming a base for raiding and colonizing much of the rest of Britain and Ireland – and a link in the chain that connected the Faroes, Iceland, Greenland and, more tenuously, North America.

The next few centuries saw almost constant warfare among the different groups. The main issue was land, but this was frequently complicated by the need of the warrior castes, who dominated all of these cultures, to exhibit martial prowess. Military conquests did play their part in bringing the peoples of Scotland together, but the most persuasive force was **Christianity**. Many of the Britons had been Christians since Roman times and it had been a Briton, St Ninian, who conducted the first missionary work among the Picts at the end of the fourth century. Attempts to convert the Picts were resumed in the sixth century by St Columba, who, as a Gaelic-speaking Scot, demonstrated that Christianity could provide a bridge between the different tribes.

Columba's establishment of the island of **Iona** (see p.82) as a centre of Christian culture opened the way for many peaceable contacts between the Picts and the Scotti. Intermarriage became commonplace, so much so that the king of the Scotti, Kenneth MacAlpine, who united Dalriada and Pictland in 843, was the son of a Pictish princess – the Picts traced succession through the female line. Similarly, MacAlpine's creation of

410	563	795	843
The Romans withdraw from Britain	St Columba founds a monastery on Iona and begins to convert the Picts	Viking raids on the Scottish coast and islands begin	Kenneth MacAlpine becomes the first King of the Scots and the Picts

the united kingdom of **Alba**, later known as **Scotia**, was part of a process of integration rather than outright conquest, though it was the Scots' religion, Columba's Christianity and their language (Gaelic) that were to dominate the merger, allowing many aspects of Pictish life, including their language, to fall forgotten and untraceable into the depths of history. Kenneth and his successors gradually extended the frontiers of their kingdom by marriage and force of arms until, by 1034, almost all of what we now call Scotland – on the mainland, at least – was under their rule.

The Middle Ages

By the time of his death in 1034, **Malcolm II** was recognized as the king of Scotia. He was not, though, a national king in the sense that we understand the term, as under the Gaelic system kings were elected from the *derbfine*, a group made up of those whose great-grandfathers had been kings. The chosen successor, supposedly the fittest to rule, was known as the tanist (*tànaiste*). By the eleventh century, however, Scottish kings had become familiar with the principle of heredity, and were often tempted to bend the rules of tanistry. Thus, Malcolm secured the succession of his grandson **Duncan** by murdering a potential rival tanist. Duncan, in turn, was killed by **Macbeth** near Elgin in 1040. Macbeth was not, therefore, the villain of Shakespeare's imagination, but simply an ambitious Scot of royal blood acting in a relatively conventional way.

The Canmores

The victory of **Malcolm III**, known as Canmore (Bighead), over Macbeth in 1057 marked the beginning of a period of fundamental change in Scottish society. Having avenged his father Duncan, Malcolm III, who had spent the previous seventeen years at the English court, sought to apply to Scotland a range of ideas he had brought back with him. He and his heirs established a secure dynasty based on succession through the male line and introduced **feudalism** into Scotland, a system that was diametrically opposed to the Gaelic system, which rested on blood ties: the followers of a Gaelic king were his kindred, whereas the followers of a feudal king were vassals bought with land. The Canmores successfully feudalized much of southern and eastern Scotland by making grants to their Norman, Breton and Flemish followers; they preferred to make their capital in Edinburgh, and in these regions, Scots – a northern version of Anglo-Saxon – pushed out Gaelic as the lingua franca. They also began to reform the **Church**, a development started with the efforts of Margaret, Malcolm III's second wife, who, though English, had been brought up in Hungary, and brought Scottish religious practices into line with those of the rest of Europe, for which she was eventually canonized.

The policies of the Canmores laid the basis for a **cultural rift** in Scotland between the Highland and Lowland communities. Factionalism between various chiefs tended to distract the Highland tribes from their widening differences with the rulers to the south, while the ever-present Viking threat also served to keep many of the clans looking to the west and north rather than the south.

Norwegian rule over the islands

In 1098, a **treaty** between Edgar, King of Scots, and Magnus Bareleg, King of Norway, ceded sovereignty of all the islands to the Norwegians – Magnus even

872	1040	1156	1266
Orkney and Shetland come under Viking rule	Macbeth crowned King of Scotland	Somerled seizes the Kingdom of the Isles	The Treaty of Perth hands the Hebrides back to Scotland from the Norwegians

managed to include Kintyre in his swag by being hauled across the isthmus at Tarbet sitting in a boat, thus proving it an "island", as it could be circumnavigated. In practice, however, power in this Viking kingdom of *Súðreyjar* (Southern Islands) was in the control of local chiefs, lieutenants of a king on the Isle of Man who was himself subordinate to the king of Norway. By marrying the daughter of one of the Manx kings and skilful raiding of neighbouring islands, **Somerled**, King of Argyll, established himself and his successors as Lords of the Isles. Their natural ally was to the Scottish rather than the Norwegian king, and when **Alexander III** (1249–86), Scotland's strongest king in two centuries, sought to buy back the Hebrides from King Håkon of Norway in 1263, the offended Norwegian king sent a fleet of 120 ships to teach the Scots a lesson and drag the islands back into line. Initially the bullying tactics worked, but the fleet lingered too long, was battered by a series of autumnal storms, and retreated back to Orkney in disarray following a skirmish with Alexander's army at the **Battle of Largs** on the Clyde coast. While in Orkney, King Håkon died, and three years later the **Treaty of Perth** of 1266 returned the Isle of Man and the Hebrides to Scotland in exchange for an annual rent.

The Wars of Scottish Independence

In 1286 **Alexander III** died, and a hotly disputed succession gave Edward I, King of England, an opportunity to subjugate Scotland. In 1291 Edward presided over a conference where the rival claimants to the Scottish throne presented their cases. Edward chose **John Balliol** in preference to Robert the Bruce, his main rival, and obliged John to pay him homage, thus turning Scotland into a vassal kingdom. Bruce refused to accept the decision, thereby continuing the conflict, and in 1295 Balliol renounced his allegiance to Edward and formed an alliance with France – the beginning of what is known as the "**Auld Alliance**". In the conflict that followed, the Bruce family sided with the English, Balliol was defeated and imprisoned, and Edward seized control of almost all of Scotland.

Edward had shown little mercy during his conquest of Scotland – he had, for example, had most of the population of Berwick massacred – and his cruelty seems to have provoked a truly national resistance. This focused on **William Wallace**, a man of relatively lowly origins from southwest Scotland who forged an army of peasants, lesser knights and townsmen that was fundamentally different to the armies raised by the nobility. Figures like Balliol, holding lands in England, France and Scotland, were part of an international aristocracy for whom warfare was merely the means by which they struggled for power. Wallace, by contrast, led proto-nationalist forces drawn from both Lowlands and Highlands determined to expel the English from their country. Probably for that very reason Wallace never received the support of the nobility and, after a bitter ten-year campaign, he was betrayed and executed in London in 1305.

With Wallace out of the way, feudal intrigue resumed. In 1306 **Robert the Bruce**, the erstwhile ally of the English, defied Edward and had himself crowned king of Scotland. Edward died the following year, but the unrest dragged on until 1314, when Bruce decisively defeated a huge English army under Edward II at the **Battle of Bannockburn**. At last Bruce was firmly in control of his kingdom, and in 1320 the Scots asserted their right to independence in a successful petition to the pope, now known as the **Declaration of Arbroath**.

1286	1314	1320
Death of Alexander III sparks the Wars of Scottish Independence	Under Robert the Bruce, the Scots defeat the English at the Battle of Bannockburn	The Declaration of Arbroath, asserting Scottish independence, is sent to the pope

THE HIGHLAND CLANS

The term "**clan**", as it is commonly used to refer to the quasi-tribal associations found in the Highlands of Scotland, only appears in its modern usage in the sixteenth century. In theory, the clan bound together blood relatives who shared a common ancestor, a concept clearly derived from the ancient Gaelic notion of kinship. But in practice many of the clans were of non-Gaelic origin – such as the Frasers, Sinclairs and Stewarts, all of Anglo-Norman descent – and it was the mythology of a common ancestor, rather than the actuality, that cemented the clans together. Furthermore, clans were often made up of people with a variety of surnames, and there are documented cases of individuals changing their names when they swapped allegiances. At the upper end of Highland society was the clan chief (who might have been a minor figure, like MacDonald of Glencoe, or a great lord, like the Duke of Argyll, head of the Campbells), who provided protection for his followers: they would, in turn, fight for him when called upon to do so. Below the clan chief were the chieftains of the septs, or subunits of the clan, and then came the tacksmen, major tenants of the chief to whom they were frequently related. The tacksmen sublet their land to tenants, who were at the bottom of the social scale. The Highlanders wore a simple belted plaid wrapped around the body – rather than the kilt – and not until the late seventeenth century were certain tartans roughly associated with particular clans. The detailed codification of the tartan was produced by the Victorians, whose romantic vision of Highland life originated with George IV's visit to Scotland in 1822, when he appeared in an elaborate version of Highland dress, complete with flesh-coloured tights (see box, p.203).

The Stewarts

In the years following Bruce's death in 1329, the Scottish monarchy gradually declined in influence. The last of the Bruce dynasty died in 1371, to be succeeded by the "Stewards", hence **Stewarts**. The reign of **James IV** (1488–1513), the most talented of the early Stewarts, ended in a terrible defeat for the Scots – and his own death – at the **Battle of Flodden Field**.

Meanwhile, the shape of modern-day Scotland was completed when the Northern Isles were gradually wrested from Norway. In 1469, a marriage was arranged between Margaret, daughter of the Danish king, Christian I, and the future **King James III** (1460–88) of Scotland. Short of cash for her dowry, Christian mortgaged Orkney to Scotland in 1468, followed by Shetland in 1469; neither pledge was ever successfully redeemed. The laws, religion and administration of the Northern Isles became Scottish, though their Norse heritage is still very evident in place names, dialect and culture. Meanwhile, the MacDonald Lords of the Isles had become too unruly for the more unified vision of James IV, and in 1493 the title reverted to the Crown. It still remains there: the current Lord of the Isles is Prince Charles.

The religious wars

In many respects the **Reformation** in Scotland was driven as much by the political intrigue of the reign of **Mary**, **Queen of Scots** (1542–67), as it was by religious conviction. Although in later years the hard-line Presbyterianism of the Highlands and Hebrides would triumph over political expediency, the revolutionary thinking of **John Knox** and his Protestant die-hards initially made little impact in the north.

1371	1468	1488
Robert II becomes the first of the Stewart (Stuart) kings to rule Scotland	James III marries Margaret of Denmark and receives Orkney and Shetland as part of her dowry	The Western Isles come under the rule of the Scottish Crown

If some of the Lowland lords were still inclined to see religious affiliation as a negotiable tool in the quest for power and influence, the loyalty – if not, perhaps, the piety – of many of the Highland chiefs to both their monarch and the Catholic faith was much more solid.

James VI (1567–1625), who in 1603 also became James I of England, disliked Presbyterianism because its quasi-democratic structure – particularly the lack of royally appointed bishops – appeared to threaten his authority. In 1610 he restored the Scottish bishops, leaving a legacy that his son, **Charles I** (1625–49), who was raised in Episcopalian England, could not handle. He provoked the **National Covenant**, a religious pledge that committed the signatories to "labour by all means lawful to recover the purity and liberty of the Gospel as it was established and professed".

Charles declared all the "**Covenanters**" to be rebels, a proclamation endorsed by his Scottish bishops. The Covenanters, well financed by the Kirk, assembled a proficient army under Alexander Leslie. In desperation, Charles summoned the English Parliament, the first for eleven years, hoping it would pay for an army. But the decision was a disaster and Parliament was much keener to criticize his policies than to raise taxes. In response Charles declared war on Parliament in 1642.

The Civil War

The major conflicts of the ensuing **Civil War** were mostly confined to England. In Scotland, the English Parliamentarians made an uneasy alliance with the Covenanters, who ruled over Scotland until 1650. During this period, the power of the Presbyterian Kirk grew considerably: laws were passed establishing schools in every parish and, less usefully, banning trade with Catholic countries. The only effective opposition to the theocratic state came from the **Marquis of Montrose**, who had initially supported the Covenant but lined up with the king when war broke out. Montrose was a gifted campaigner whose army was drawn from the Highlands and Islands, where the Kirk's influence was still weak, and included a frightening rabble of islanders and Irishmen under the inspiration of Colonsay chief Alasdair MacDonald, or **Colkitto**, whose appetite for the fray was fed by Montrose's willingness to send them charging into battle at the precise moment they could inflict most damage. For a golden year Montrose's army roamed the Highlands undefeated, scoring a number of brilliant tactical victories over the Covenanters, but the reluctance of his troops to stay south of the Highland Line made it impossible for him to capitalize on his successes and, as the clansmen dispersed with the spoils of victory back to their lands, Montrose was left weak and exposed. Unfailingly loyal to a king who was unwilling to take the same risks for his most gifted general, Montrose was eventually captured and executed in 1650.

Many English Parliamentarians suspected the Scots of hankering for the return of the monarchy, a suspicion confirmed when, at the invitation of the earl of Argyll, the future **Charles II** came back to Scotland in 1650. To regain his Scottish kingdom, Charles was obliged to renounce his father and sign the Covenant, two bitter pills taken to impress the population. In the event, the "Presbyterian restoration" was short-lived. Cromwell invaded, defeated the Scots at Dunbar and forced Charles into exile. Until the Restoration of 1660, Scotland was united with England and governed by seven commissioners.

1513	**1560**	**1567**
The Scots are defeated by the English at the Battle of Flodden Field	The Scottish Church breaks with the Roman Catholic Church	Abdication of Mary, Queen of Scots, and accession of James VI (aged 1)

The Restoration

The Restoration brought bishops back to the Kirk, integrated into an essentially Presbyterian structure of Kirk sessions and presbyteries. Over three hundred clergymen, a third of the Scottish ministry, refused to accept the reinstatement of the bishops and were edged out of the Church and forced to hold open-air services, called **Conventicles**, which Charles did his best to suppress.

When **James VII** (James II of England), whose ardent Catholicism caused a Protestant backlash in England, was forced into exile in France in 1689, the throne passed to **Mary**, his Protestant daughter, and her Dutch husband, **William of Orange**. In Scotland there was a brief flurry of opposition to William when **Graham of Claverhouse**, known as "Bonnie Dundee", united the Jacobite clans against the government army at the **Battle of Killiekrankie**, just north of Pitlochry. However, the inspirational Claverhouse was killed on the point of claiming a famous victory, and again the clans, leaderless and unwilling to press south, dissipated and the threat passed.

William and Mary quickly consolidated their position, restoring the full Presbyterian structure in Scotland and abolishing the bishops, though they chose not to restore the political and legal functions of the Kirk, which remained subject to parliamentary control. It was sufficient, however, to bring the religious wars to a close, essentially completing the Reformation in Scotland and establishing a platform on which political union would be built.

The Union

Highland loyalty to the Stewart line lingered on into the eighteenth century, something both William and the political pragmatists saw as a significant threat. In 1691, William offered pardons to those Highland chiefs who had opposed his accession, on condition that they took an oath of allegiance by New Year's Day 1692. Alastair Maclain, one of the MacDonalds of Glencoe had turned up at the last minute, but his efforts to take the oath were frustrated by the king's officials, who were determined to see his clan, well known for their support of the Stewarts, destroyed. In February 1692, Captain Robert Campbell of Glenlyon quartered his men with the MacDonalds of Glencoe and, two weeks later, in the middle of the night, his troops acted on their secret orders, turned on their hosts and carried out the infamous **Massacre of Glencoe**. Thirty-eight MacDonalds died, and the slaughter caused a national scandal, especially among the clans, where "murder under trust" – killing those offering you shelter – was considered a particularly heinous crime.

The situation in Scotland was further complicated by the question of the succession. Mary died without leaving an heir and, on William's death in 1702, the crown passed to her sister **Anne**, James VII's second daughter, who was also childless. In response, the English Parliament secured the Protestant succession by passing the **Act of Settlement**, which named the Electress Sophia of Hanover, a granddaughter of James VI (I), as the next in line to the throne. The Act did not, however, apply in Scotland, and the English feared that the Scots would invite James Edward Stewart, the son of James VII (II) by his second wife, back from France to be their king. Consequently, Parliament appointed commissioners charged with the consideration of "proper methods towards attaining a union with Scotland". The project seemed doomed to failure when the Scottish

1587	1603	1638
Mary, Queen of Scots, is executed on the orders of Queen Elizabeth I	James VI of Scotland becomes James I of England	National Covenant proclaimed by Scottish Presbyterians

Parliament passed the **Act of Security**, in 1703, stating that Scotland would not accept a Hanoverian monarch unless they had first received guarantees protecting their religion and their trade.

The Act of Union

Despite the strength of anti-English feeling, the Scottish Parliament passed the **Act of Union** by 110 votes to 69 in 1707. Some historians have explained the vote in terms of bribery and corruption, but there were other factors. Scottish politicians were divided between the Cavaliers – Jacobites (supporters of the Stewarts) and Episcopalians – and the Country party, whose Presbyterian members dreaded the return of the Stewarts more than they disliked the Hanoverians. To the Highlands and Islands, however, the shift of government four hundred miles further south from Edinburgh, itself distant enough for many, was to make relatively little difference to their lives for the best part of the rest of the century.

The country that was united with England in 1707 contained three distinct cultures: in south and east Scotland, they spoke Scots; in Shetland, Orkney and the far northeast, the local dialect, though Scots-based, contained elements of Norn (Old Norse); in the rest of north and west Scotland, including the Hebrides, Gaelic was spoken. These linguistic differences were paralleled by different forms of social organization and customs. The people of north and west Scotland were mostly pastoralists, moving their sheep and cattle to Highland pastures in the summer, and returning to the glens in the winter. They lived in single-room dwellings, heated by a central peat fire and sometimes shared with livestock, and in hard times they would subsist on cakes made from the blood of their live cattle mixed with oatmeal. Highlanders supplemented their meagre income by raiding their clan neighbours and the prosperous Lowlands, whose inhabitants regarded their northern compatriots with a mixture of fear and contempt. This was the background for the exploits of Scotland's very own Robin Hood character, **Rob Roy** (see box, p.136).

The Jacobite uprisings

When James VII (II) was deposed, he had fled to France, where he planned the reconquest of his kingdom with the support of the French king. When James died in 1701, the hopes of the Stewarts passed to his only son, James Edward Stewart, the "Old Pretender" ("Pretender" in the sense of having pretensions to the throne; "Old" to distinguish him from his son Charles, the "Young Pretender"). James's followers became known as **Jacobites**, derived from Jacobus, the Latin equivalent of James.

The Fifteen

After the accession to the British throne of the Hanoverian George I, son of Sophia, Electress of Hanover, it sparked the **Jacobite uprising of 1715** (also known as The Fifteen): its timing appeared perfect. Scottish opinion was moving against the Union, which had failed to bring Scotland any tangible economic benefits. The English had also been accused of bad faith when, contrary to their pledges, they attempted to impose their legal practices on the Scots. Neither were Jacobite sentiments confined

1650	1689	1692	1698
The Scots Royalist army are defeated at the Battle of Dunbar by the English under Oliver Cromwell	Unsuccessful Jacobite uprising against William of Orange	Glencoe massacre: 38 members of the MacDonald clan murdered by anti-Jacobite Campbells	1200 Scots leave to establish a colony in Panama

BONNIE PRINCE CHARLIE

Prince Charles Edward Stuart – better known as **Bonnie Prince Charlie** or "The Young Pretender" – was born in 1720 in Rome, where his father, "The Old Pretender", claimant to the British throne (as the son of James VII), was living in exile with his Polish wife. At the age of 25, with no knowledge of Gaelic, an imperfect grasp of English and a strong attachment to the Catholic faith, the prince set out for Scotland with two French ships, disguised as a seminarist from the Scots College in Paris. He arrived on the Hebridean island of **Eriskay** (see p.323) on July 23, 1745, with just seven companions, and was immediately implored to return to France by the clan chiefs, who were singularly unimpressed by his lack of army. Charles was unmoved and went on to raise the royal standard at **Glenfinnan** (see p.221), thus signalling the beginning of the **Jacobite uprising**. He only attracted less than half of the potential 20,000 clansmen who could have marched with him, and promises of support from the French and English Jacobites failed to materialize. Nevertheless, after a decisive victory over government forces at the **Battle of Prestonpans**, near Edinburgh, Charles made a spectacular advance into England, getting as far as Derby. London was in a state of panic: its shops were closed and the Bank of England, fearing a run on sterling, slowed withdrawals by paying out in sixpences. But Derby was as far as Charles got. On December 6, threatened by superior forces, the Jacobites decided to retreat to Scotland against Charles's wishes. Pursued back to Scotland by the Duke of Cumberland, he won one last victory, at Falkirk, before the final disaster at **Culloden** (see p.208) in April 1746.

The prince spent the following five months in hiding, with a price of £30,000 on his head, and literally thousands of government troops searching for him. He certainly endured his fair share of cold and hunger while on the run, but the real price was paid by the Highlanders themselves, who risked their lives (and often paid for it with them) by aiding and abetting the prince. The most famous of these was, of course, 23-year-old **Flora MacDonald**, whom Charles first met on South Uist in June 1746. Flora was persuaded – either by his looks or her relatives, depending on which account you believe – to convey Charles "over the sea to Skye", disguised as an Irish servant girl by the name of Betty Burke. She was arrested just seven days after parting with the prince in Portree, and held in the Tower of London until July 1747. She went on to marry a local man, had seven children, and in 1774 emigrated to America where her husband was taken prisoner during the American War of Independence. Flora returned to Scotland and was reunited with her husband on his release; they resettled in Skye and she died at the age of 68.

Charles eventually boarded a ship back to France in September 1746, but, despite his promises – "For all that has happened, Madam, I hope we shall meet in St James's yet" – never returned to Scotland, nor did he ever see Flora again. After mistreating a string of mistresses, he eventually got married at the age of 52 to the 19-year-old **Princess Louise of Stolberg-Gedern** in an effort to produce a Stuart heir. They had no children, and she eventually fled from his violent drunkenness; in 1788, a none-too-"bonnie" Prince Charles died in the arms of his illegitimate daughter in Rome. Bonnie Prince Charlie became a legend in his own lifetime, but it was the Victorians who really milked the myth for all its sentimentality, conveniently overlooking the fact that the real consequence of 1745 was the virtual annihilation of the Highland way of life.

to Scotland. There were many in England who toasted the "King across the water" and showed no enthusiasm for the new German ruler. In September 1715, the fiercely Jacobite John Erskine, Earl of Mar, raised the Stewart standard at Braemar Castle. Just eight days later, he captured Perth, where he gathered an army of over

1707	1715	1746	1762
The Act of Union unites the kingdoms of Scotland and England	Jacobite uprising against the accession of Hanoverian King George I	Bonnie Prince Charlie's Jacobite army is defeated at the Battle of Culloden	Beginning of the Highland Clearances

10,000 men, drawn mostly from the Episcopalians of northeast Scotland and from the Highlands. Mar's rebellion took the government by surprise. They had only 4000 soldiers in Scotland, under the Duke of Argyll, but Mar dithered until he lost the military advantage. The **Battle of Sheriffmuir** in November was indecisive, but by the time the Old Pretender arrived the following month, 6000 veteran Dutch troops had reinforced Argyll. The rebellion disintegrated rapidly and James slunk back to exile in France in February 1716.

The Forty-Five

Led by James's dashing son, Charles Edward Stewart (Bonnie Prince Charlie), the **Jacobite uprising of 1745** (known as The Forty-Five), though better known, had even less chance of success than the 1715 rising. In the intervening thirty years, the Hanoverians had consolidated their hold on the English throne, Lowland society had become uniformly loyalist and access into the Highlands for both trade and internal peacekeeping had been vastly improved by the military roads built by General Wade. Even among the clans, regiments such as the Black Watch were recruited, which drew on the Highlanders' military tradition, but formed part of the government's standing army. Despite a promising start to his campaign, Charles met his match at the **Battle of Culloden**, near Inverness, in April 1746, the last set-piece battle on British soil, and the last time a claymore-wielding Highland charge would be set against organized ranks of musket-bearing troops, and the last time a Stewart would take up arms in pursuit of the throne. As with so many of the other critical points in the campaign, the Jacobite leadership at Culloden was divided and ill-prepared. When it came to the fight, the Highlanders were in the wrong place, exhausted after a forced overnight march, and seriously outnumbered and outgunned. They were swept from the field, with over 1500 men killed or wounded compared to Cumberland's 300 or so. After the battle, many of the wounded Jacobites were slaughtered, an atrocity that earned Cumberland the nickname "Butcher".

In the aftermath of the uprising, the wearing of tartan, the bearing of arms and the playing of bagpipes were all banned. Rebel chiefs lost their land and the Highlands were placed under military occupation. Most significantly, the government prohibited the private armies of the chiefs, thereby effectively destroying the clan system. Within a few years, more Highland regiments were recruited for the British army, and by the end of the century thousands of Scots were fighting and dying for their Hanoverian king against Napoleon.

The Highland Clearances

Once the clan chief was forbidden his own army, he had no need of the large tenantry that had previously been a vital military asset. Conversely, the second half of the eighteenth century saw the Highland **population increase** dramatically after the introduction of the easy-to-grow and nutritious potato. Between 1745 and 1811, the population of the Outer Hebrides, for example, rose from 13,000 to 24,500. The clan chiefs adopted different policies to deal with the new situation. Some encouraged emigration, and as many as 6000 Highlanders left for the Americas between 1800 and 1803 alone. Other landowners saw the economic advantages of developing alternative

1843	1846	1886	1914–18
The Great Disruption: a third of the Church of Scotland leave to form the Free Church of Scotland	Highland potato famine: 1.7 million Scots emigrate	Crofters' Holdings Act grants security of tenure in the Highlands and Islands	100,000 Scots lose their lives in World War I

forms of employment for their tenantry, mainly fishing and kelping. **Kelp** (brown seaweed) was gathered and burnt to produce soda ash, which was used in the manufacture of soap, glass and explosives. There was a rising market for soda ash until the 1810s, with the price increasing from £2 a tonne in 1760 to £20 in 1808, making a fortune for some landowners and providing thousands of Highlanders with temporary employment. Fishing for **herring** – the "silver darlings" – was also encouraged, and new harbours and coastal settlements were built all around the Highland coastline. Other landowners developed **sheep runs** on the Highland pastures, introducing hardy breeds like the black-faced Linton and the Cheviot. But extensive sheep-farming proved incompatible with a high peasant population, and many landowners decided to clear their estates of tenants, some of whom were forcibly moved to tiny plots of marginal land, where they were to farm as **crofters**.

The pace of the **Highland Clearances** accelerated after the end of the Napoleonic Wars in 1815, when the market price for kelp, fish and cattle declined, leaving sheep as the only profitable Highland product. The most notorious Clearances took place on the estates of the Countess of Sutherland, who owned a million acres in northern Scotland. Between 1807 and 1821, around 15,000 people were thrown off her land, evictions carried out with considerable brutality. A potato famine followed in 1846, forcing large-scale emigration to America and Canada and leaving the huge uninhabited areas found in the region today.

The crofters fight back

The crofters eked out a precarious existence, but they hung on throughout the nineteenth century, often by taking seasonal employment away from home. In the 1880s, however, a sharp downturn in agricultural prices made it difficult for many crofters to pay their rent. This time, inspired by the example of the Irish Land League, they resisted eviction, forming the **Highland Land League** or **Crofters' Party**, and taking part in direct action protests, in particular land occupations, or **land raids**, as they became known. In 1886, in response to the social unrest, Gladstone's Liberal government passed the **Crofters' Holdings Act**, which conceded three of the crofters' demands: security of tenure, fair rents to be decided independently, and the right to pass on crofts by inheritance. But Gladstone did not attempt to increase the amount of land available for crofting, and shortage of land remained a major problem until the **Land Settlement Act** of 1919 made provision for the creation of new crofts. Nevertheless, the population of the Highlands continued to fall into the twentieth century, with many of the region's young people finding city life more appealing.

The world wars

Depopulation of an all-too-familiar kind was present in the early decades of the twentieth century, with Highland regiments at the vanguard of the British Army's infantry offensives in both the Anglo-Boer wars at the start of the century and **World War I**. The months after hostilities ended also saw one of the most remarkable spectacles in Orkney's long seafaring history, when 74 vessels from the German naval fleet, lying at anchor in **Scapa Flow** having surrendered to the British at the armistice, were scuttled by the skeleton German crews that remained aboard (see p.345).

1928	1939	1939–45	1961
The National Party of Scotland is formed	The population of Scotland reaches five million	34,000 Scottish soldiers lose their lives in World War II; 6000 civilians die in air raids	The US deploy Polaris nuclear missiles in Holy Loch

The same harbour was immediately involved in **World War II**, when a German U-boat breached the defences around Orkney in October 1939 and torpedoed HMS *Royal Oak*, with the loss of 833 men (see p.345). Many more ships and lives were lost in the waters off the Hebrides during the hard-fought Battle of the Atlantic, when convoys carrying supplies and troops were constantly harried by German U-boats. Various bases were established in the Highlands and Islands, including a flying-boat squadron at Kerrera, by Oban, with Air Force bases on Islay, Benbecula, Tiree and Lewis, and a Royal Naval anchorage at Tobermory; on the mainland, commandos were trained in survival skills and offensive landings in the area around lochs Lochy and Arkaig, near Fort William. Though men of fighting age again left the Highlands to serve in the forces, the war years were not altogether bleak, as the influx of servicemen ensured a certain prosperity to the places where they were based, and the need for the country to remain self-sufficient meant that farms and crofts – often worked by the women and children left behind – were encouraged to keep production levels high.

Even before the war, efforts had been made to recognize the greater social and economic needs of the Highlands and Islands with the establishment of the **Highlands and Islands Medical Service**, a precursor to the National Health Service introduced by the first postwar Labour government. Other agencies were set up in the 1940s, including the **North of Scotland Hydro Electric Board** and the **Forestry Commission**, both of which were tasked to improve the local infrastructure and create state-sponsored employment.

The Highlands and Islands today

After Britain joined the EEC in 1972, the Highlands and Islands were identified as an area in need of special assistance and, in harness with the **Highlands and Islands Development Board**, significant investment was made in the area's infrastructure, including roads, schools, medical facilities and harbours. European funding was also used to support the increased use and teaching of **Gaelic**, and the encouragement of Gaelic broadcasting, publishing and education. At the same time there was renaissance of Gaelic culture across Scotland as a whole, from the annual National Mod (see p.37) to the nationwide success of folk-rock bands such as Runrig and Capercaillie, with the result that the indigenous language and culture of the Highlands and Islands, while still vulnerable, is as healthy now as it has been for a century.

Employment in the Highlands and Islands

The strength of cultural identity – even in its more clichéd forms – has always been a vital aspect of the Highlands and Islands' attraction as a tourist destination. **Tourism** remains the dominant industry in the region, despite the furrowed brows of, on the one hand, businesses vulnerable to dips in numbers and spending, and on the other, conservationists concerned by the impact of increased numbers. The main traditional industries, **farming** and **fishing**, continue with European support to struggle against European competition, while others, such as **whisky** and **tweed making**, remain prominent in certain pockets although they have never, in fact, been large-scale employers. Few of the region's new industries have quite fulfilled the initial hopes

1979	1996	1999	2009
Scottish referendum for devolution fails to gain the required forty percent	The Stone of Scone is returned to Scotland	Labour win the most seats in Scotland's first-ever general election	Carol Ann Duffy becomes the first Scottish Poet Laureate

raised of them, but most remain to contribute to the economic diversity of the region. **Forestry**, for example, has seen large tracts of the Highlands planted, more sensitively now than in the past; North Sea **oil** has brought serious economic benefits not just to the northeast coast but also to Orkney and Shetland; **salmon farming** has become widespread, tainting many otherwise idyllic west-coast scenes, but long accepted as a vital part of numerous coastal communities. The new growth industry is **alternative energy**, most controversially large "wind farms", but also schemes to harness tidal and wave energy. More unequivocally positive is the emergence of "**cyber-crofting**" – essentially the operation of internet-based businesses or services from remoter areas. The possibilities thrown up by the communications revolution have also led to the establishment of the **University of the Highlands**, with various colleges linked to each other and to outlying students by networked computers.

Immigration and land ownership

As remote living is made more viable, however, it is not just the indigenous population who benefit, and **immigration** into the Highlands now matches the long-term trend of emigration, with Inverness ranking as one of the fastest-growing urban areas in Britain and most islands enjoying a steady increase in population (the 2011 Census revealed a rise of four percent). The incomers – invariably called "white settlers" – are now an established aspect of Highland life, often providing economic impetus in the form of enthusiastically run small businesses, though their presence can still rankle in the intimate lives of small communities. Any prejudicial control from outside the region is looked on suspiciously, not least in the question of **land ownership**, which remains one of the keys to Highland development – some would say the most important of all. Some of the largest Highland estates continue to be owned and managed from afar, with little regard to local needs or priorities; two-thirds of the private land in Scotland is owned by a mere 1250 people, many of them aristocrats or foreign nationals. However, the success of groups of crofters in buying estates in Assynt and Knoydart, as well as the purchase of the islands of Eigg and Gigha by their inhabitants, hints at a gradual broadening of land ownership.

Devolution and independence

With so many unique issues to tackle, it is perhaps not surprising that the Highlands and Islands have always maintained an independent and generally restrained voice in Scottish **politics**. Despite the unshakable Scottishness of the region, it has remained largely ambivalent to the surges of nationalism seen in other parts of the country. **Devolution** was regarded with scepticism by Highlanders and Islanders for the likelihood of any Scottish Parliament being dominated by the politics of the Central Belt. With the establishment of the **Scottish Parliament** in Edinburgh in 1999, the demands for a more sensitive and understanding handling of the issues that matter to the Highlands and Islands have justifiably grown. After centuries of what has often seemed like ostracism from the rest of Scotland, the Highlands and Islands have good reason to believe that they are now partners in the dance. The region has not been immune to the rise of the Scottish National Party, though whether a majority will vote for independence in the **2014 referendum**, or remain characteristically aloof from the nationalist debate, remains to be seen.

2011	**2013**	**2014**
The Scottish National Party win a majority in the Scottish Parliament	Andy Murray becomes the first Scot to win Wimbledon men's singles title since 1896	Scotland votes in a referendum on independence

Books

We've highlighted a selection of books below that will give you a flavour of the Scottish Highlands and Islands, past and present; books marked with ★ are particularly recommended.

HISTORY, POLITICS AND CULTURE

★ **Neal Ascherson** *Stones Voices*. Intelligent, thought-provoking ponderings on the nature of Scotland and the road to devolution from Scots-born *Observer* journalist, interspersed with personal anecdotes.

Joni Buchanan *The Lewis Land Struggle*. A history of crucial encounters between the crofters of Lewis and their various landlords, written from the crofters' point of view using contemporary sources.

Tom Devine *The Scottish Nation 1700–2000*. Best post-Union history from the last Scottish Parliament to the new one.

★ **David Howarth** *The Shetland Bus*. Wonderfully detailed story of the espionage and resistance operations carried out

from Shetland by British and Norwegian servicemen, written by someone who was directly involved.

Fitzroy Maclean *Bonnie Prince Charlie*. Very readable and more or less definitive biography of Scotland's most romantic historical figure written by the "real" James Bond.

John Prebble *Glencoe, Culloden* and *The Highland Clearances*. Emotive and subjective accounts of key events in Highland history, which are very readable.

★ **Author unknown** *Orkneyinga Saga*. Probably written about 1200 AD, this is a Norse saga which sheds light on the connection between Norway and the Northern Isles, still felt strongly today; contains history of the early earls of Orkney, and is, incidentally, a stirring, bloodthirsty thriller.

GUIDES AND PICTURE BOOKS

George Mackay Brown *Portrait of Orkney*. A personal account by the famous Orcadian poet of the island, its history and way of life, illustrated with photographs and drawings.

Derek Cooper *Skye*. A gazetteer and guide, and an indispensable mine of information; although first written in 1970, it has been revised where necessary.

Sheila Gear *Foula, Island West of the Sun*. An attempt to convey what it is like to live far out in the sea on an island of savage beauty.

★ **Hamish Haswell-Smith** *The Scottish Islands*. An

exhaustive and impressive gazetteer with maps and absorbing information on all the Scottish islands. Filled with attractive sketches and paintings, the book is breathtaking in its thoroughness and lovingly gathered detail.

Charles Maclean *St Kilda*. Traces the social history of the island, from its earliest beginnings to the seemingly inevitable end of the community, with moving compassion.

Magnus Magnusson *Rùm: Nature's Island*. A detailed history of Rùm from earliest times up to its current position as a National Nature Reserve.

MEMOIRS AND TRAVELOGUES

Jim Crumley *The Great Wood*. The history, wildlife and folk-lore of the 5000-year-old Caledonian forest, is the latest work from this prolific author who writes with a poetic intensity. Also *Among Islands, The Isle of Skye* and *Gulfs of Blue Air*.

David Duff (ed.) *Queen Victoria's Highland Journals*. The daily diary of the Scottish adventures of "Mrs Brown" – Victoria's writing is detailed and interesting without being twee, and she lovingly conveys her affection for Deeside and the Highlands.

★ **Rowena Farre** *Seal Morning*. An absorbing account of a young girl growing up on a remote croft in the Highlands towards the beginning of the last century and the wildlife she adopted. Eight-year-olds and upwards will love it and so will adults.

★ **Elizabeth Grant of Rothiemurchus** *Memoirs of a Highland Lady*. Hugely readable recollections, written with wit and perception at the beginning of the eighteenth century, charting the social changes in Edinburgh, London

and particularly Speyside.

Peter Hill *Stargazing*. Engaging account of being a tyro lighthouse-keeper on three of Scotland's most famous lighthouses: Pladda, Ailsa Craig and Hyskeir.

★ **Samuel Johnson & James Boswell** *A Journey to the Western Isles of Scotland* and *The Journal of a Tour to the Hebrides*. Lively accounts of a famous journey around the islands taken by the noted lexicographer Dr Samuel Johnson, and his biographer and friend.

Alasdair Maclean *Night Falls on Ardnamurchan*. First published in 1984 but frequently reprinted, this is a classic and moving story of the life and death of the Highland community in which the author grew up.

Gavin Maxwell *Ring of Bright Water*. Heart-warming true tale of a man's relationship with three otters. Suitable for 7-year-olds upwards.

★ **Iain Mitchell** *Isles of the West; Isle of the North*. In the first book, Mitchell sails round the Inner Hebrides, talking to locals and incomers, siding with the former, caricaturing the latter, and, with a fair bit of justification, laying into the likes of the RSPB and SNH. *Isles of the North* gives Orkney and Shetland the same treatment, before heading off to Norway to find out how it can be done differently.

Edwin Muir *Scottish Journey*. A classic travelogue written

in 1935 by the troubled Orcadian writer on his return to Scotland from London.

Sir Walter Scott *The Voyage of the Pharos*. In 1814 Scott accompanied Stevenson senior on a tour of the northern lighthouses, visiting Shetland, Orkney, the Hebrides and even nipping across to Ireland; he wrote a lively diary of their adventures, which included dodging American privateers.

FICTION

George Mackay Brown *Beside the Ocean of Time*. A child's journey through the history of an Orkney island, and an adult's effort to make sense of the place's secrets in the late twentieth century. *Magnus* is his retelling of the death of St Magnus, with parallels for modern times.

★ **Lewis Grassic Gibbon** *Sunset Song, Cloud Howe* and *Grey Granite*. This trilogy, known as *A Scots Quair* and set in northeast Scotland, has become a classic, telling the story of the conflict in one man's life between Scottish and English culture.

★ **Neil M. Gunn** *The Silver Darlings*. Probably Gunn's most representative and best-known book, evocatively set on the northeast coast and telling the story of the herring fishermen during the great years of the industry. Other examples of his romantic, symbolic works include *The Lost Glen*, *The Silver Bough* and *Wild Geese Overhead*.

Eric Linklater *The Dark of Summer*. Set on the Faroes, Shetland, Orkney (where the author was born), and in theatres of war, this novel exhibits the best of Linklater's

compelling narrative style, although his comic *Private Angelo* is better known.

Compton MacKenzie *Whisky Galore*. Comic novel based on a true story of the wartime wreck of a cargo of whisky off Eriskay. Full of predictable stereotypes, but still funny.

Peter May *The Blackhouse*, *The Lewis Man* and *The Chessmen*. A trilogy of dark detective stories set on the Isle of Lewis featuring a policeman from Edinburgh who grew up on the island. Good on atmosphere.

Sir Walter Scott *The Pirate*. Inspired by stories of Viking raids and set in Orkney and Shetland, this novel was very popular in Victorian times.

★ **Iain Crichton Smith** *Consider the Lilies*. Poetic lament about the Highland Clearances by Scotland's finest bilingual (English and Gaelic) writer.

Robert Louis Stevenson *Kidnapped*. A thrilling historical adventure set in the eighteenth century, every bit as exciting as the better-known *Treasure Island*.

POETRY

★ **George Mackay Brown** *Selected Poems 1954–1992*. Brown's work is as haunting, beautiful and gritty as the Orkney islands which inspire it. *Travellers* – compiled after his death – features work either previously unpublished or appearing only in newspapers and periodicals.

Robert Burns *Selected Poems*. Scotland's most famous bard. Immensely popular all over the world, his best-known works are his earlier ones, including *Auld Lang Syne* and *My Love is Like a Red, Red Rose*.

★ **Norman MacCaig** *Selected Poems*. This selection includes some of the best work from this important Scottish poet, whose deep love of nature and of the Highland landscape is always evident. *Norman MacCaig: A Celebration*, an anthology written for his 85th birthday, includes work by more than ninety writers, including Ted Hughes and Seamus Heaney.

★ **Sorley Maclean (Somhairle Macgill-Eain)** *From Wood to Ridge: Collected Poems*. Written in Gaelic, his

poems have been translated into bilingual editions all over the world, dealing as they do with the sorrows of poverty, war and love.

Edwin Morgan *New Selected Poems*. A love of words and their sounds is evident in Morgan's poems, which are refreshingly varied and often experimental. He comments on the Scottish scene with shrewdness and humour.

Edwin Muir *Collected Poems*. Muir's childhood on Orkney at the turn of the twentieth century remained with him as a dream of paradise from which he was banished to Glasgow. His poems are passionately concerned with Scotland.

Iain Crichton Smith *Collected Poems*. Born on the Isle of Lewis, Iain Crichton Smith wrote with feeling, and sometimes bitterness, in both Gaelic and English, of the life of the rural communities, the iniquities of the Free Church, the need to revive Gaelic culture and the glory of the Scottish landscape.

Language

Language is a thorny, complex and often highly political issue in Scotland. If you're not from Scotland yourself, you're most likely to be addressed in a variety of English, spoken in a Scottish accent. Even then, you're likely to hear phrases and words that are part of what is known as Lowland Scottish or Scots, which is now officially recognized as a distinct language in its own right. To a lesser extent, Gaelic, too, remains a living language, particularly in the *Gàidhealtachd* or Gaelic-speaking areas of the northwest Highlands, the Western Isles, parts of Skye and a few scattered Hebridean islands. In Orkney and Shetland, the local dialect of Scots contains many words carried over from Norn, the Old Norse language spoken in the Northern Isles from the time of the Vikings until the eighteenth century.

Scots

Scots began life as a northern branch of Anglo-Saxon, emerging as a distinct language in the Middle Ages. From the 1370s until the Union in 1707, it was the country's main literary and documentary language. Since the eighteenth century, however, it has been systematically suppressed to give preference to English.

Robbie Burns is the most obvious literary exponent of the Scots language, which he referred to as "Lallans", as did Robert Louis Stevenson, but there was a revival in the last century led by poets such as Hugh MacDiarmid. Only recently has Scots enjoyed something of a renaissance, getting itself on the Scottish school curriculum in 1996, and achieving official recognition as a distinct language in 1998. Despite these enormous political achievements, many people (rightly or wrongly) still regard Scots as a dialect of English. For more on the Scots language, visit ⓦsco.wikipedia.org.

Gaelic

Scottish **Gaelic** (*Gàidhlig*, pronounced like "garlic") is one of only four Celtic languages to survive into the modern age (Welsh, Breton and Irish are the other three). Manx, the old language of the Isle of Man, died out early last century, while Cornish was finished as a community language way back in the eighteenth century. Scottish Gaelic is most closely related to Irish and Manx – hardly surprising, since Gaelic was introduced to Scotland from Ireland around the third century BC. Some folk still argue that Scottish Gaelic is merely a dialect of its parent language, Irish, and indeed the two languages remain more or less mutually intelligible. From the fifth to the twelfth centuries, Gaelic enjoyed an expansionist phase, gradually becoming the national language, thanks partly to the backing of the Celtic Church in Iona.

Since then Gaelic has been in steady decline. Even before Union with England, power, religious ideology and wealth gradually passed into non-Gaelic hands. The royal court was transferred to Edinburgh and an Anglo-Norman legal system was put in place. The Celtic Church was Romanized by the introduction of foreign clergy and, most importantly of all, English and Flemish merchants colonized the new trading towns of the east coast. In addition, the pro-English attitudes held by the Covenanters led to strong anti-Gaelic feeling within the Church of Scotland from its inception.

The two abortive Jacobite rebellions of 1715 and 1745 furthered the language's decline, as did the Clearances that took place in the Gaelic-speaking Highlands from the 1770s to the 1850s, which forced thousands to migrate to central Scotland's new industrial belt or emigrate to North America. Although efforts were made to halt the decline in the first half of the nineteenth century, the 1872 Education Act gave no official recognition to Gaelic, and children were severely punished if they were caught speaking the language in school.

The 2001 census put the number of Gaelic speakers at under 60,000 (just over one percent of the population), the majority of whom live in the *Gàidhealtachd*, though there is thought to be an extended Gaelic community of perhaps 250,000 who have some understanding of the language. Since the 1980s, great efforts have been made to try to save the language, including the introduction of bilingual primary and nursery schools, a huge increase in the amount of broadcasting time given to Gaelic-language and Gaelic-music programmes, and the establishment of highly successful Gaelic colleges such as Sabhal Mòr Ostaig (Ⓦ www.smo.uhi.ac.uk).

Gaelic grammar and pronunciation

Gaelic is a highly complex tongue, with a fiendish, antiquated **grammar** and, with only eighteen letters, an intimidating system of spelling. **Pronunciation** is easier than it appears at first glance – one general rule to remember is that the **stress** always falls on the first syllable of a word. The general rule of syntax is that the verb starts the sentence whether it's a question or not, followed by the subject and then the object; adjectives generally follow the word they are describing.

SHORT AND LONG VOWELS

Gaelic has both short and long vowels, the latter being denoted by an acute or grave accent.

a as in cat; before nn and ll, as in cow	**o** as in pot
à as in bar	**ò** like enthral
e as in pet	**ó** like cow
é like rain	**u** like scoot
i as in sight	**ù** like loo
í like free	

VOWEL COMBINATIONS

Gaelic is littered with diphthongs, which, rather like in English, can be pronounced in several different ways depending on the individual word.

ai like cat, or pet; before dh or gh, like street	**èa** as in hear
ao like the sound in the middle of colonel	**eu** like train, or fear
ei like mate	**ia** like fear
ea like pet, or cat, and sometimes like mate; before ll or nn, like in cow	**io** like fear, or shorter than street
	ua like wooer

CONSONANTS

The consonants listed below are those that differ substantially from the English.

b at the beginning of a word like the **b** in big; in the middle/end of a word like the **p** in pair

bh at the beginning of a word like the **v** in van; elsewhere it is silent

c as in cat; after a vowel it has aspiration before it

ch always as in loch, never as in church

cn like the **cr** in crowd

d like the **d** in dog, but with the tongue pressed against the back of the upper teeth; at the beginning of a word or before e or i, like the **j** in jam; in the middle or at the end of a word like the **t** in cat; after i like the **ch** in church

dh before and after a, o or u is an aspirated **g**, rather like a gargle; before e or i like the **y** in yes; elsewhere silent

fh usually silent; sometimes like the **h** in house

g at the beginning of a word as in **g**et; before e like the **y** in yes; in the middle or end of a word like the **ck** in sock; after i like the **ch** in loch

gh at the beginning of a word as in get; before or after a, o or u rather like a gargle; after i sometimes like the **y** in gay, but often silent

l after i and sometimes before e like the **l** in lot; elsewhere a peculiarly Gaelic sound produced by flattening the front of the tongue against the palate

mh like the **v** in van

p at the beginning of a word as in pet; elsewhere it has aspiration before it

rt pronounced as **sht**

s before e or i like the **sh** in ship; otherwise as in English

sh before a, o or u like the **h** in house; before e like the **ch** in loch

t before e or i like the **ch** in church; in the middle or at the end of a word it has aspiration before it; otherwise as in English

th at the beginning of a word, like the **h** in house; elsewhere, and in the word *thu* (you) silent

GAELIC PHRASES, VOCABULARY AND COURSES

One of the best introductory **teach-yourself Gaelic** courses is *Speaking Our Language* by Richard Cox, based on the TV series, much of which you can watch on YouTube. If you just want to get better at pronouncing Gaelic words, try *Blas na Gàidhlig* by Michael Bauer, or for a phrasebook, your best bet is *Everyday Gaelic* by Morag MacNeill. You can also do some self-learning on the Gaelic section of the BBC website ⓦ bbc.co.uk.

BASIC WORDS AND GREETINGS

yes	tha
no	chan eil
hello	hallo
how are you?	ciamar a tha thu?
fine	tha gu math
thank you	tapadh leat
welcome	fàilte
come in	thig a-staigh
good day	latha math
goodbye	mar sin leat
good night	oidhche mhath
who?	cò?
where is...?	càit a bheil...?
when?	cuine?
what is it?	dé tha ann?
morning	madainn
evening	feasgar
day	là
night	oidhche
tomorrow	a-màireach
tonight	a-nochd
cheers	slàinte
yesterday	an-dé
today	an-diugh
tomorrow	maireach
now	a-nise
food	lòn
bread	aran
water	uisge
milk	bainne
beer	leann
wine	fìon
whisky	uisge beatha
Edinburgh	Dun Eideann
Glasgow	Glaschu
America	Ameireaga
Ireland	Eire
England	Sasainn
London	Lunnain

SOME USEFUL PHRASES

How much is that?	Dè tha e 'cosg?
What's your name?	Dè 'n t-ainm a th'ort?
Excuse me	Gabh mo leisgeul
I'd like a double room	'Se rùm dùbailte tha mi'giarraigh
Do you speak Gaelic?	A bheil Gàidhlig agad?
What is the Gaelic for ...?	Dé a' Ghàidhlig a tha ... air?
I don't understand	Chan eil mi 'tuigsinn
I don't know	Chan eil fhios agam
It doesn't matter	'S coma
I'm sorry	Tha mi duilich

NUMBERS AND DAYS

1	aon
2	dà/dhà
3	trì
4	ceithir
5	còig
6	sia
7	seachd
8	ochd
9	naoi
10	deich
11	aon deug
20	fichead
21	aon ar fhichead
30	deug ar fhichead
40	dà fhichead
50	lethcheud
60	trì fichead
100	ceud
1000	mìle

Monday	Diluain	**Friday**	Dihaoine
Tuesday	Dimàirt	**Saturday**	Disathurna
Wednesday	Diciadain	**Sunday**	Didòmhnaich/La na Sàbaid
Thursday	Diardaoin		

GAELIC GEOGRAPHICAL AND PLACE-NAME TERMS

The purpose of the list below is to help with place-name derivations from Gaelic and with more detailed map-reading.

abhainn	river	fin, from fionn	white
ach or auch, from achadh	field	gair or gare, from geàrr	short
ail, aileach	rock	garv, from garbh	rough
Alba	Scotland	geodha	cove
aonach	ridge	glen, from gleann	valley
ard, ardan or arden, from àird	a point of land or height	gower or gour, from gabhar	goat
aros	dwelling	inch, from innis	meadow or island
ault, from allt	stream	inver, from inbhir	river mouth
bad	brake or clump of trees	ken or kin, from ceann	head
bagh	bay	knock, from cnoc	hill
bal or bally, from baile	town, village	kyle, from caolas	narrow strait
balloch, from bealach	mountain pass	lag	hollow
ban	white, fair	larach	site of an old ruin
bàrr	summit	liath	grey
beg, from beag	small	loch	lake
ben, from beinn	mountain	meall	round hill
blair, from blàr	field or battlefield	mon, from monadh	hill
cairn, from càrn	pile of stones	more, from mór	large, great
camas	bay, harbour	rannoch, from raineach	bracken
cnoc	hill	ross, from ros	promontory
coll or colly, from coille	wood or forest	rubha	promontory
corran	a spit or point jutting into the sea	sgeir	sea rock
		sgurr	sharp point
corrie, from coire	round hollow in mountainside, whirlpool	sron	nose, prow or promontory
		strath, from srath	broad valley
craig, from creag	rock, crag	tarbet, from tairbeart	isthmus
cruach	bold hill	tigh	house
drum, from druim	ridge	tir or tyre, from tìr	land
dubh	black	torr	hill, castle
dun or dum, from dùn	for	tràigh	shore
eilean	island	uig	shelter
ess, from eas	waterfall	uisge	water

Norn (Orkney and Shetland)

Between the tenth and seventeenth centuries, the chief language of Orkney and Shetland was **Norn**, a Scandinavian tongue close to modern Faroese and Icelandic. After the end of Norse rule, and with the transformation of the church, the law, commerce and education, Norn gradually lost out to Scots and English, eventually petering out completely in the eighteenth century. Today, Orkney and Shetland have their own dialects, and individual islands and communities within each group have local variations. The **dialects** have a Scots base, with some Old Norse words; however, they don't sound strongly Scottish, with the Orkney accent – which has been likened to the Welsh one – especially distinctive. Listed below are some of the words you're most likely to hear, including some birds' names and common elements in place names.

NORN PHRASES AND VOCABULARY

aak	guillemot
alan	storm petrel
ayre	beach
bister	farm
böd	fisherman's store
bonxie	great skua
bruck	rubbish
burra	heath rush
crö	sheepfold
eela	rod-fishing from small boats
ferrylouper	incomer (Orkney)
fourareen	four-oared boat
foy	party or festival
geo	coastal inlet
gloup	blowhole, behind a cliff face, where spray is blasted out from the cave below (from Old Norse glup, a throat)
haa	laird's house
haaf	deep-sea fishing. Lit. "heave" (Shetland)
hap	hand-knitted shawl
howe	mound
kame	ridge of hills
kishie	basket
maa	seagull
mool	headland

moorit	brown
mootie	tiny
muckle	large
noost	hollow place where a boat is drawn up
norie (or tammie-norie)	puffin
noup	steep headland
peerie/peedie	small
plantiecrub (or plantiecrö)	small dry-stone enclosure for growing cabbages
quoy	enclosed, cultivated common land
roost	tide race
scattald	common grazing land
scord	gap or pass in a ridge of hills
setter	farm
shaela	dark grey
simmer dim	summer twilight
sixern/sixareen	six-oared boat
solan	gannet
soothmoother	incomer (Shetland)
udal	Norse law designating land as a freehold without any charter or feudal-type arrangement
voe	sea inlet
yoal	rowing boat used for fishing (Shetland)

Glossary

Auld Old

Bairn Baby

Bannock Unleavened bread made from oats or barley

Ben Hill or mountain

Blackhouse Thick-walled traditional dwelling

Bonnie Pretty

Bothy Primitive cottage, hut or mountain shelter

Brae Slope or hill

Brig Bridge

Broch Circular prehistoric stone fort

Burn Small stream or brook

Byre Shelter for cattle; cottage

Cairn Mound of stones

CalMac Caledonian MacBrayne ferry company

Ceilidh (pronounced "kay-lee"). Social gathering involving dancing, drinking, singing and storytelling

Central belt Central Scotland between the Forth and Clyde including Edinburgh and Glasgow

Clan Extended family

Clearances Evictions from the Highlands (see p.415)

Corbett A mountain between 2500ft and 3000ft high

Covenanters Supporters of the Presbyterian Church in the seventeenth century

Crannog Celtic lake or bog dwelling

Croft Small plot of farmland with house, common in the Highlands

Dirk A long dagger

Dolmen Grave chamber

Doocot Dovecot

Dram Literally, one-eighth of a fluid ounce. Usually refers to any small measure of whisky

Dun Fortified mound

Episcopalian A church which has bishops in its organizational structure

Firth A wide sea inlet or estuary

Gillie Personal guide used on hunting or fishing trips

Glen Deep, narrow mountain valley

Harling Limestone and gravel mix used to cover buildings

Henge Circular ditch with a bank

Hogmanay New Year's Eve

Howe Valley

Howff Meeting place; pub

HS Historic Scotland, a government-funded heritage organization

Kilt Knee-length tartan skirt worn by Highland men

Kirk Church

Laird Landowner; aristocrat

Law Rounded hill

Links Grassy coastal land; coastal golf-course

Loch Lake

Lochan Little loch

Mac/Mc These prefixes in Scottish surnames derive from the Gaelic, meaning "son of". In Scots "Mac" is used for both sexes. In Gaelic "Nic" is used for women: Donnchadh Mac Aodh is Duncan MacKay, Iseabail Nic Aodh is Isabel MacKay

Machair Sandy, grassy, lime-rich coastal land, generally used for grazing

Manse Official home of a Presbyterian minister

Munro A mountain over 3000ft high

Munro-bagging The sport of trying to climb as many Munros as possible

Neuk Corner

NTS The National Trust for Scotland, a heritage organization

Pend Archway or vaulted passage

Presbyterian The form of church government used in the official (Protestant) Church of Scotland, established by John Knox during the Reformation

RIB Rigid Inflatable Boat

Runrig A common form of farming in which separate ridges are cultivated by different occupiers under joint agreement

Sassenach Derives from the Gaelic *Sasunnach*, meaning literally "Saxon"; used by Scots to describe the English Scottish Baronial style of architecture favoured by the Scottish landowning class, featuring crow-stepped gables and round turrets

Sheila na gig Female fertility symbol, usually a naked woman displaying her vulva

Shieling Simple huts or shelters used by shepherds during summer grazing

Shinty Stick-and-ball game played in the Highlands, with similarities to hockey

Smiddy Smithy

SNH Scottish Natural Heritage, a government-funded conservation body

SNP Scottish National Party

Sporran Leather purse worn in front of, or at the side of, a kilt

Tartan Check-patterned woollen cloth, particular patterns being associated with particular clans

Thane A landowner of high rank; the chief of a clan

Tombolo A spit of sand connecting an island to the mainland

Trews Tartan trousers

Wee Small

Wee Frees Followers of the Free Presbyterian or Free Church of Scotland

Wynd Narrow lane

Yett Gate or door

Small print and index

A ROUGH GUIDE TO ROUGH GUIDES

Published in 1982, the first Rough Guide – to Greece – was a student scheme that became a publishing phenomenon. Mark Ellingham, a recent graduate in English from Bristol University, had been travelling in Greece the previous summer and couldn't find the right guidebook. With a small group of friends he wrote his own guide, combining a highly contemporary, journalistic style with a thoroughly practical approach to travellers' needs.

The immediate success of the book spawned a series that rapidly covered dozens of destinations. And, in addition to impecunious backpackers, Rough Guides soon acquired a much broader readership that relished the guides' wit and inquisitiveness as much as their enthusiastic, critical approach and value-for-money ethos.

These days, Rough Guides include recommendations from budget to luxury and cover more than 120 destinations around the globe, as well as producing an ever-growing range of eBooks.

Visit **roughguides.com** to find all our latest books, read articles, get inspired and share travel tips with the Rough Guides community.

Rough Guide credits

Editors: Alison Roberts, Melissa Graham, Tim Locke, Natasha Foges, Alice Park, Olivia Rawes
Layout: Nikhil Agarwal
Cartography: Reetu Pandey, Ashutosh Bharti
Picture editor: Marta Bescos
Proofreader: Diane Margolis
Managing editor: Mani Ramaswamy

Assistant editor: Dipika Dasgupta
Production: Charlotte Cade
Cover design: Alice Earle, Nikhil Agarwal, Wilf Matos, Nicole Newman
Senior pre-press designer: Dan May
Programme manager: Helen Blount
Publisher: Joanna Kirby

Publishing information

This seventh edition published May 2014 by
Rough Guides Ltd,
80 Strand, London WC2R 0RL
11, Community Centre, Panchsheel Park, New Delhi 110017, India
Distributed by Penguin Random House
Penguin Books Ltd,
80 Strand, London WC2R 0RL
Penguin Group (USA)
345 Hudson Street, NY 10014, USA
Penguin Group (Australia)
250 Camberwell Road, Camberwell, Victoria 3124, Australia
Penguin Group (NZ)
67 Apollo Drive, Mairangi Bay, Auckland 1310, New Zealand
Penguin Group (South Africa)
Block D, Rosebank Office Park, 181 Jan Smuts Avenue, Parktown North, Gauteng, South Africa 2193
Rough Guides is represented in Canada by Tourmaline Editions Inc. 662 King Street West, Suite 304, Toronto, Ontario M5V 1M7
Printed in Malaysia by Vivar Printing Sdn.Bhd.
© Rough Guides 2014

Maps © Rough Guides
Contains Ordnance Survey data © Crown copyright and database rights 2014
No part of this book may be reproduced in any form without permission from the publisher except for the quotation of brief passages in reviews.
440pp includes index
A catalogue record for this book is available from the British Library
ISBN: 978-1-40933-986-1
The publishers and authors have done their best to ensure the accuracy and currency of all the information in **The Rough Guide to Scottish Highlands & Islands**, however, they can accept no responsibility for any loss, injury, or inconvenience sustained by any traveller as a result of information or advice contained in the guide.
3 5 7 9 8 6 4

Help us update

We've gone to a lot of effort to ensure that the seventh edition of **The Rough Guide to Scottish Highlands & Islands** is accurate and up-to-date. However, things change – places get "discovered", opening hours are notoriously fickle, restaurants and rooms raise prices or lower standards. If you feel we've got it wrong or left something out, we'd like to know, and if you can remember the address, the price, the hours, the phone number, so much the better.

Please send your comments with the subject line "**Rough Guide Scottish Highlands & Islands Update**" to ⊜ mail@uk.roughguides.com. We'll credit all contributions and send a copy of the next edition (or any other Rough Guide if you prefer) for the very best emails.

Find more travel information, connect with fellow travellers and plan your trip on ⊛ roughguides.com

Acknowledgements

Norm Longley: Norm would like to thank Alison for her patient and skilful editing during the course of this book. Very special thanks are due to Carron Tobin at Rural Dimensions for her fantastic assistance throughout; Roisin, Connie and the team at Mount Stuart; and Karen Moreland at CalMac. Thanks are also due to Sheila and Lynn from VisitArran, Angela and Robbie in Brodick, David and Jo in Tobermory, Oly Hemmings and Darren Dobson in Cairnbaan, Calum Ross in Loch Melfort, Alistair Wilkey in Tarbert, Marion Spears in Port Askaig, Linda Battison in Oban and Erin Hickey at VisitScotland. Thanks,

too, to Stuart Ellis for a terrific round of golf (and not a single ball lost!). Last and by no means least, to Christian, Luka, Patrick and Anna.
Helena Smith: Thanks to my parents Angela and Grahame for a lovely stay and an especially wonderful concert in Stirling Castle, to Helen Reid for her suggestions and to Claire Reid for a night out in our home town of Stirling.
Steve Vickers: Would like to thank Mandy Wood, Billy Gatt, Celia and Derek Kitchingman, and staff at *The Tufted Duck Hotel*. Finally, special thanks to Karin Ingesten.

Readers' updates

Thanks to all the readers who have taken the time to write in with comments and suggestions (and apologies if we've inadvertently omitted or misspelt anyone's name):

Andy Bennetts, Colleen Foggo, Mike Foster, Murray Grant, John Kemp, Adrian Moorman, Kenneth Nichol, Claire Shirlaw.

ABOUT THE AUTHORS

Rob Humphreys has spent some part of every year in Scotland since he was nowt but a lad in rural Yorkshire. One day he hopes to sail round the islands, but in the meantime, he can be found steering a Norfolk reed cutter up and down the Thames.

Norm Longley Having spent most of his life writing Rough Guides to countries in Eastern Europe and the Balkans, Norm has now turned his hand to the UK, having researched guides to Wales and Scotland, which, this time, led him to explore the splendour of Argyll. He lives in Bath and can occasionally be seen erecting marquees on the Rec.

Helena Smith was lucky to grow up in the Trossachs region of central Scotland and under the Zomba Plateau in Malawi. She is a travel writer and photographer, and blogs about food and community at ⊕eathackney.com.

James Stewart researched the north and northwest Highlands and Skye chapters of this book by campervan, bivvy bag and surfboard. A freelance travel journalist specializing in wilderness and activities, he writes for international newspapers and magazines such as *The Guardian*, *The Sunday Times*, *The Independent* and *Wanderlust*. He is the author of around fifteen guidebooks; ⊕jamesstewart.biz, @itsjamesstewart.

Steve Vickers splits a large chunk of his time between England and Sweden, and is no stranger to the cold, wind and rain. Needless to say, the parts of Scotland he covered for this book felt just like home. When he's not roaming Northern Europe, you'll find Steve in Asia, where he's worked on Rough Guides to Thailand, Laos and Southeast Asia.

Photo credits

Index

Maps are marked in grey

Map symbols

The symbols below are used on maps throughout the book

✈ International airport	⚐ Campsite	Rocks	Abbey
✈ Domestic airport	ⓘ Tourist office	Waterfall	Monastery
🅿 Parking	✉ Post office	Cave	Chapel
◆ Point of interest	Whisky distillery	Cairn(s)	Building
@ Internet access	Skiing	Standing stones	Church
∴ Ruins/archeological site	Golf course	Stone circle	Cemetery
🏛 Stately home	Swimming Pool	Cup- and ring-marked rocks	Park
♜ Castle	Bridge	Hill shading	Forest
♟ Museum	▲ Peak	Wall	Beach
⊤ Gardens	Viewpoint	Cable car	Pedestrianized area
✂ Battlefield	Lighthouse	Ferry route	

Listings key

■ Accommodation
● Café/restaurant/pub
■ Bar/club/music venue
● Shop